CRACKING *the* CODING INTERVIEW

6TH EDITION

Also by Gayle Laakmann McDowell

Cracking the PM Interview

How to Land a Product Manager Job in Technology

Cracking the Tech Career

Insider Advice on Landing a Job at Google, Microsoft, Apple, or Any Top Tech Company

CRACKING
the
CODING INTERVIEW

6th Edition

189 Programming Questions and Solutions

GAYLE LAAKMANN MCDOWELL

Founder and CEO, CareerCup.com

CareerCup, LLC
Palo Alto, CA

CRACKING THE CODING INTERVIEW, SIXTH EDITION

Published by CareerCup, LLC, Palo Alto, CA. Compiled Jun 14, 2016.

For more information, contact support@careercup.com.

978-0-9847828-5-7 (ISBN 13)

For Davis and Tobin,
and all the things that bring us joy in life.

Introduction

Introduction . . . 2

I. **The Interview Process** . . . 4

Why? . . . 4

How Questions are Selected . . . 6

It's All Relative . . . 7

Frequently Asked Questions . . . 7

II. **Behind the Scenes** . . . 8

The Microsoft Interview . . . 9

The Amazon Interview . . . 10

The Google Interview . . . 10

The Apple Interview . . . 11

The Facebook Interview . . . 12

The Palantir Interview . . . 13

III. **Special Situations** . . . 15

Experienced Candidates . . . 15

Testers and SDETs . . . 15

Product (and Program) Management . . . 16

Dev Lead and Managers . . . 17

Startups . . . 18

Acquisitions and Acquihires . . . 19

For Interviewers . . . 21

IV. **Before the Interview** . . . 26

Getting the Right Experience . . . 26

Writing a Great Resume . . . 27

Preparation Map . . . 30

V. **Behavioral Questions** . . . 32

Interview Preparation Grid . . . 32

Know Your Technical Projects . . . 33

Responding to Behavioral Questions . . . 34

So, tell me about yourself... . . . 36

VI. **Big O** . . . 38

An Analogy . . . 38

Time Complexity . . . 38

Space Complexity . . . 40

Drop the Constants . . . 41

Drop the Non-Dominant Terms . . . 42

Multi-Part Algorithms: Add vs. Multiply 42

Amortized Time 43

Log N Runtimes 44

Recursive Runtimes 44

Examples and Exercises 45

VII. Technical Questions 60

How to Prepare 60

What You Need To Know 60

Walking Through a Problem 62

Optimize & Solve Technique #1: Look for BUD 67

Optimize & Solve Technique #2: DIY (Do It Yourself) 69

Optimize & Solve Technique #3: Simplify and Generalize 71

Optimize & Solve Technique #4: Base Case and Build 71

Optimize & Solve Technique #5: Data Structure Brainstorm 72

Best Conceivable Runtime (BCR) 72

Handling Incorrect Answers 76

When You've Heard a Question Before 76

The "Perfect" Language for Interviews 76

What Good Coding Looks Like 77

Don't Give Up! 81

VIII. The Offer and Beyond 82

Handling Offers and Rejection 82

Evaluating the Offer 83

Negotiation 84

On the Job 85

IX. Interview Questions 87

Data Structures 88

Chapter 1 | Arrays and Strings 88

Hash Tables 88

ArrayList & Resizable Arrays 89

StringBuilder 89

Chapter 2 | Linked Lists 92

Creating a Linked List 92

Deleting a Node from a Singly Linked List 93

The "Runner" Technique 93

Recursive Problems 93

Chapter 3 | Stacks and Queues . . . 96

Implementing a Stack . . . 96

Implementing a Queue . . . 97

Chapter 4 | Trees and Graphs . . . 100

Types of Trees . . . 100

Binary Tree Traversal . . . 103

Binary Heaps (Min-Heaps and Max-Heaps) . . . 103

Tries (Prefix Trees) . . . 105

Graphs . . . 105

Graph Search . . . 107

Concepts and Algorithms . . . 112

Chapter 5 | Bit Manipulation . . . 112

Bit Manipulation By Hand . . . 112

Bit Facts and Tricks . . . 112

Two's Complement and Negative Numbers . . . 113

Arithmetic vs. Logical Right Shift . . . 113

Common Bit Tasks: Getting and Setting . . . 114

Chapter 6 | Math and Logic Puzzles . . . 117

Prime Numbers . . . 117

Probability . . . 119

Start Talking . . . 121

Develop Rules and Patterns . . . 121

Worst Case Shifting . . . 122

Algorithm Approaches . . . 122

Chapter 7 | Object-Oriented Design . . . 125

How to Approach . . . 125

Design Patterns . . . 126

Chapter 8 | Recursion and Dynamic Programming . . . 130

How to Approach . . . 130

Recursive vs. Iterative Solutions . . . 131

Dynamic Programming & Memoization . . . 131

Chapter 9 | System Design and Scalability . . . 137

Handling the Questions . . . 137

Design: Step-By-Step . . . 138

Algorithms that Scale: Step-By-Step . . . 139

Key Concepts . . . 140

Considerations 142

There is no "perfect" system.. 143

Example Problem 143

Chapter 10 | Sorting and Searching 146

Common Sorting Algorithms 146

Searching Algorithms 149

Chapter 11 | Testing 152

What the Interviewer Is Looking For 152

Testing a Real World Object 153

Testing a Piece of Software 154

Testing a Function 155

Troubleshooting Questions 156

Knowledge Based 158

Chapter 12 | C and C++ 158

Classes and Inheritance. 158

Constructors and Destructors. 159

Virtual Functions 159

Virtual Destructor 160

Default Values 161

Operator Overloading. 161

Pointers and References 162

Templates 163

Chapter 13 | Java. 165

How to Approach 165

Overloading vs. Overriding 165

Collection Framework 166

Chapter 14 | Databases. 169

SQL Syntax and Variations. 169

Denormalized vs. Normalized Databases 169

SQL Statements 169

Small Database Design 171

Large Database Design 172

Chapter 15 | Threads and Locks 174

Threads in Java 174

Synchronization and Locks 176

Deadlocks and Deadlock Prevention 179

Additional Review Problems **181**

Chapter 16 | Moderate 181

Chapter 17 | Hard 186

X. Solutions **191**

Data Structures 192

Concepts and Algorithms 276

Knowledge Based 422

Additional Review Problems 462

XI. Advanced Topics **628**

Useful Math 629

Topological Sort 632

Dijkstra's Algorithm 633

Hash Table Collision Resolution 636

Rabin-Karp Substring Search 636

AVL Trees 637

Red-Black Trees 639

MapReduce 642

Additional Studying 644

XII. Code Library **645**

HashMapList<T, E> 646

TreeNode (Binary Search Tree) 647

LinkedListNode (Linked List) 649

Trie & TrieNode 649

XIII. Hints **652**

Hints for Data Structures. 653

Hints for Concepts and Algorithms 662

Hints for Knowledge-Based Questions. 676

Hints for Additional Review Problems 679

XIV. About the Author **696**

*Join us at **www.CrackingTheCodingInterview.com** to download the complete solutions, contribute or view solutions in other programming languages, discuss problems from this book with other readers, ask questions, report issues, view this book's errata, and seek additional advice.*

Dear Reader,

Let's get the introductions out of the way.

I am not a recruiter. I am a software engineer. And as such, I know what it's like to be asked to whip up brilliant algorithms on the spot and then write flawless code on a whiteboard. I know because I've been asked to do the same thing—in interviews at Google, Microsoft, Apple, and Amazon, among other companies.

I also know because I've been on the other side of the table, asking candidates to do this. I've combed through stacks of resumes to find the engineers who I thought might be able to actually pass these interviews. I've evaluated them as they solved—or tried to solve—challenging questions. And I've debated in Google's Hiring Committee whether a candidate did well enough to merit an offer. I understand the full hiring circle because I've been through it all, repeatedly.

And you, reader, are probably preparing for an interview, perhaps tomorrow, next week, or next year. I am here to help you solidify your understanding of computer science fundamentals and then learn how to apply those fundamentals to crack the coding interview.

The 6th edition of *Cracking the Coding Interview* updates the 5th edition with 70% more content: additional questions, revised solutions, new chapter introductions, more algorithm strategies, hints for all problems, and other content. Be sure to check out our website, CrackingTheCodingInterview.com, to connect with other candidates and discover new resources.

I'm excited for you and for the skills you are going to develop. Thorough preparation will give you a wide range of technical and communication skills. It will be well worth it, no matter where the effort takes you!

I encourage you to read these introductory chapters carefully. They contain important insight that just might make the difference between a "hire" and a "no hire."

And remember—interviews are hard! In my years of interviewing at Google, I saw some interviewers ask "easy" questions while others ask harder questions. But you know what? Getting the easy questions doesn't make it any easier to get the offer. Receiving an offer is not about solving questions flawlessly (very few candidates do!). Rather, it is about answering questions *better than other candidates*. So don't stress out when you get a tricky question—everyone else probably thought it was hard too. It's okay to not be flawless.

Study hard, practice—and good luck!

Gayle L. McDowell

Founder/CEO, CareerCup.com
Author of *Cracking the PM Interview* and *Cracking the Tech Career*

Introduction

Something's Wrong

We walked out of the hiring meeting frustrated—again. Of the ten candidates we reviewed that day, none would receive offers. Were we being too harsh, we wondered?

I, in particular, was disappointed. We had rejected one of *my* candidates. A former student. One I had referred. He had a 3.73 GPA from the University of Washington, one of the best computer science schools in the world, and had done extensive work on open-source projects. He was energetic. He was creative. He was sharp. He worked hard. He was a true geek in all the best ways.

But I had to agree with the rest of the committee: the data wasn't there. Even if my emphatic recommendation could sway them to reconsider, he would surely get rejected in the later stages of the hiring process. There were just too many red flags.

Although he was quite intelligent, he struggled to solve the interview problems. Most successful candidates could fly through the first question, which was a twist on a well-known problem, but he had trouble developing an algorithm. When he came up with one, he failed to consider solutions that optimized for other scenarios. Finally, when he began coding, he flew through the code with an initial solution, but it was riddled with mistakes that he failed to catch. Though he wasn't the worst candidate we'd seen by any measure, he was far from meeting the "bar." Rejected.

When he asked for feedback over the phone a couple of weeks later, I struggled with what to tell him. Be smarter? No, I knew he was brilliant. Be a better coder? No, his skills were on par with some of the best I'd seen.

Like many motivated candidates, he had prepared extensively. He had read K&R's classic C book, and he'd reviewed CLRS' famous algorithms textbook. He could describe in detail the myriad of ways of balancing a tree, and he could do things in C that no sane programmer should ever want to do.

I had to tell him the unfortunate truth: those books aren't enough. Academic books prepare you for fancy research, and they will probably make you a better software engineer, but they're not sufficient for interviews. Why? I'll give you a hint: Your interviewers haven't seen red-black trees since *they* were in school either.

To crack the coding interview, you need to prepare with *real* interview questions. You must practice on *real* problems and learn their patterns. It's about developing a fresh algorithm, not memorizing existing problems.

Cracking the Coding Interview is the result of my first-hand experience interviewing at top companies and later coaching candidates through these interviews. It is the result of hundreds of conversations with candidates. It is the result of the thousands of questions contributed by candidates and interviewers. And it's the result of seeing so many interview questions from so many firms. Enclosed in this book are 189 of the best interview questions, selected from thousands of potential problems.

My Approach

The focus of ***Cracking the Coding Interview*** is algorithm, coding, and design questions. Why? Because while you can and will be asked behavioral questions, the answers will be as varied as your resume. Likewise, while many firms will ask so-called "trivia" questions (e.g., "What is a virtual function?"), the skills developed through practicing these questions are limited to very specific bits of knowledge. The book will briefly touch on some of these questions to show you what they're like, but I have chosen to allocate space to areas where there's more to learn.

My Passion

Teaching is my passion. I love helping people understand new concepts and giving them tools to help them excel in their passions.

My first official experience teaching was in college at the University of Pennsylvania, when I became a teaching assistant for an undergraduate computer science course during my second year. I went on to TA for several other courses, and I eventually launched my own computer science course there, focused on hands-on skills.

As an engineer at Google, training and mentoring new engineers were some of the things I enjoyed most. I even used my "20% time" to teach two computer science courses at the University of Washington.

Now, years later, I continue to teach computer science concepts, but this time with the goal of preparing engineers at startups for their acquisition interviews. I've seen their mistakes and struggles, and I've developed techniques and strategies to help them combat those very issues.

Cracking the Coding Interview, ***Cracking the PM Interview***, ***Cracking the Tech Career***, and **CareerCup** reflect my passion for teaching. Even now, you can often find me "hanging out" at CareerCup.com, helping users who stop by for assistance.

Join us.

Gayle L. McDowell

I

The Interview Process

At most of the top tech companies (and many other companies), algorithm and coding problems form the largest component of the interview process. Think of these as problem-solving questions. The interviewer is looking to evaluate your ability to solve algorithmic problems you haven't seen before.

Very often, you might get through only one question in an interview. Forty-five minutes is not a long time, and it's difficult to get through several different questions in that time frame.

You should do your best to talk out loud throughout the problem and explain your thought process. Your interviewer might jump in sometimes to help you; let them. It's normal and doesn't really mean that you're doing poorly. (That said, of course not needing hints is even better.)

At the end of the interview, the interviewer will walk away with a gut feel for how you did. A numeric score might be assigned to your performance, but it's not actually a quantitative assessment. There's no chart that says how many points you get for different things. It just doesn't work like that.

Rather, your interviewer will make an assessment of your performance, usually based on the following:

- Analytical skills: Did you need much help solving the problem? How optimal was your solution? How long did it take you to arrive at a solution? If you had to design/architect a new solution, did you structure the problem well and think through the tradeoffs of different decisions?
- Coding skills: Were you able to successfully translate your algorithm to reasonable code? Was it clean and well-organized? Did you think about potential errors? Did you use good style?
- Technical knowledge / Computer Science fundamentals: Do you have a strong foundation in computer science and the relevant technologies?
- Experience: Have you made good technical decisions in the past? Have you built interesting, challenging projects? Have you shown drive, initiative, and other important factors?
- Culture fit / Communication skills: Do your personality and values fit with the company and team? Did you communicate well with your interviewer?

The weighting of these areas will vary based on the question, interviewer, role, team, and company. In a standard algorithm question, it might be almost entirely the first three of those.

▸ Why?

This is one of the most common questions candidates have as they get started with this process. Why do things this way? After all,

1. Lots of great candidates don't do well in these sorts of interviews.

2. You could look up the answer if it did ever come up.
3. You rarely have to use data structures such as binary search trees in the real world. If you did need to, you could surely learn it.
4. Whiteboard coding is an artificial environment. You would never code on the whiteboard in the real world, obviously.

These complaints aren't without merit. In fact, I agree with all of them, at least in part.

At the same time, there is reason to do things this way for some—not all—positions. It's not important that you agree with this logic, but it is a good idea to understand why these questions are being asked. It helps offer a little insight into the interviewer's mindset.

False negatives are acceptable.

This is sad (and frustrating for candidates), but true.

From the company's perspective, it's actually acceptable that some good candidates are rejected. The company is out to build a great set of employees. They can accept that they miss out on some good people. They'd prefer not to, of course, as it raises their recruiting costs. It is an acceptable tradeoff, though, provided they can still hire enough good people.

They're far more concerned with false positives: people who do well in an interview but are not in fact very good.

Problem-solving skills are valuable.

If you're able to work through several hard problems (with some help, perhaps), you're probably pretty good at developing optimal algorithms. You're smart.

Smart people tend to do good things, and that's valuable at a company. It's not the only thing that matters, of course, but it is a really good thing.

Basic data structure and algorithm knowledge is useful.

Many interviewers would argue that basic computer science knowledge is, in fact, useful. Understanding trees, graphs, lists, sorting, and other knowledge does come up periodically. When it does, it's really valuable.

Could you learn it as needed? Sure. But it's very difficult to know that you should use a binary search tree if you don't know of its existence. And if you do know of its existence, then you pretty much know the basics.

Other interviewers justify the reliance on data structures and algorithms by arguing that it's a good "proxy." Even if the skills wouldn't be that hard to learn on their own, they say it's reasonably well-correlated with being a good developer. It means that you've either gone through a computer science program (in which case you've learned and retained a reasonably broad set of technical knowledge) or learned this stuff on your own. Either way, it's a good sign.

There's another reason why data structure and algorithm knowledge comes up: because it's hard to ask problem-solving questions that *don't* involve them. It turns out that the vast majority of problem-solving questions involve some of these basics. When enough candidates know these basics, it's easy to get into a pattern of asking questions with them.

Whiteboards let you focus on what matters.

It's absolutely true that you'd struggle with writing perfect code on a whiteboard. Fortunately, your interviewer doesn't expect that. Virtually everyone has some bugs or minor syntactical errors.

The nice thing about a whiteboard is that, in some ways, you can focus on the big picture. You don't have a compiler, so you don't need to make your code compile. You don't need to write the entire class definition and boilerplate code. You get to focus on the interesting, "meaty" parts of the code: the function that the question is really all about.

That's not to say that you should just write pseudocode or that correctness doesn't matter. Most interviewers aren't okay with pseudocode, and fewer errors are better.

Whiteboards also tend to encourage candidates to speak more and explain their thought process. When a candidate is given a computer, their communication drops substantially.

But it's not for everyone or every company or every situation.

The above sections are intended to help you understand the thought process of the company.

My personal thoughts? For the right situation, when done well, it's a reasonable judge of someone's problem-solving skills, in that people who do well tend to be fairly smart.

However, it's often not done very well. You have bad interviewers or people who just ask bad questions.

It's also not appropriate for all companies. Some companies should value someone's prior experience more or need skills with particular technologies. These sorts of questions don't put much weight on that.

It also won't measure someone's work ethic or ability to focus. Then again, almost no interview process can really evaluate this.

This is not a perfect process by any means, but what is? All interview processes have their downsides.

I'll leave you with this: it is what it is, so let's do the best we can with it.

▸ How Questions are Selected

Candidates frequently ask what the "recent" interview questions are at a specific company. Just asking this question reveals a fundamental misunderstanding of where questions come from.

At the vast majority of companies, there are no lists of what interviewers should ask. Rather, each interviewer selects their own questions.

Since it's somewhat of a "free for all" as far as questions, there's nothing that makes a question a "recent Google interview question" other than the fact that some interviewer who happens to work at Google just so happened to ask that question recently.

The questions asked this year at Google do not really differ from those asked three years ago. In fact, the questions asked at Google generally don't differ from those asked at similar companies (Amazon, Facebook, etc.).

There are some broad differences across companies. Some companies focus on algorithms (often with some system design worked in), and others really like knowledge-based questions. But within a given category of question, there is little that makes it "belong" to one company instead of another. A Google algorithm question is essentially the same as a Facebook algorithm question.

▸ It's All Relative

If there's no grading system, how are you evaluated? How does an interviewer know what to expect of you?

Good question. The answer actually makes a lot of sense once you understand it.

Interviewers assess you relative to other candidates on that same question by the same interviewer. It's a relative comparison.

For example, suppose you came up with some cool new brainteaser or math problem. You ask your friend Alex the question, and it takes him 30 minutes to solve it. You ask Bella and she takes 50 minutes. Chris is never able to solve it. Dexter takes 15 minutes, but you had to give him some major hints and he probably would have taken far longer without them. Ellie takes 10—and comes up with an alternate approach you weren't even aware of. Fred takes 35 minutes.

You'll walk away saying, "Wow, Ellie did really well. I'll bet she's pretty good at math." (Of course, she could have just gotten lucky. And maybe Chris got unlucky. You might ask a few more questions just to really make sure that it wasn't good or bad luck.)

Interview questions are much the same way. Your interviewer develops a feel for your performance by comparing you to other people. It's not about the candidates she's interviewing *that* week. It's about all the candidates that she's *ever* asked this question to.

For this reason, getting a hard question isn't a bad thing. When it's harder for you, it's harder for everyone. It doesn't make it any less likely that you'll do well.

▸ Frequently Asked Questions

I didn't hear back immediately after my interview. Am I rejected?

No. There are a number of reasons why a company's decision might be delayed. A very simple explanation is that one of your interviewers hasn't provided their feedback yet. Very, very few companies have a policy of not responding to candidates they reject.

If you haven't heard back from a company within 3 - 5 business days after your interview, check in (politely) with your recruiter.

Can I re-apply to a company after getting rejected?

Almost always, but you typically have to wait a bit (6 months to a 1 year). Your first bad interview usually won't affect you too much when you re-interview. Lots of people get rejected from Google or Microsoft and later get offers from them.

Behind the Scenes

Most companies conduct their interviews in very similar ways. We will offer an overview of how companies interview and what they're looking for. This information should guide your interview preparation and your reactions during and after the interview.

Once you are selected for an interview, you usually go through a screening interview. This is typically conducted over the phone. College candidates who attend top schools may have these interviews in-person.

Don't let the name fool you; the "screening" interview often involves coding and algorithms questions, and the bar can be just as high as it is for in-person interviews. If you're unsure whether or not the interview will be technical, ask your recruiting coordinator what position your interviewer holds (or what the interview might cover). An engineer will usually perform a technical interview.

Many companies have taken advantage of online synchronized document editors, but others will expect you to write code on paper and read it back over the phone. Some interviewers may even give you "homework" to solve after you hang up the phone or just ask you to email them the code you wrote.

You typically do one or two screening interviewers before being brought on-site.

In an on-site interview round, you usually have 3 to 6 in-person interviews. One of these is often over lunch. The lunch interview is usually not technical, and the interviewer may not even submit feedback. This is a good person to discuss your interests with and to ask about the company culture. Your other interviews will be mostly technical and will involve a combination of coding, algorithm, design/architecture, and behavioral/experience questions.

The distribution of questions between the above topics varies between companies and even teams due to company priorities, size, and just pure randomness. Interviewers are often given a good deal of freedom in their interview questions.

After your interview, your interviewers will provide feedback in some form. In some companies, your interviewers meet together to discuss your performance and come to a decision. In other companies, interviewers submit a recommendation to a hiring manager or hiring committee to make a final decision. In some companies, interviewers don't even make the decision; their feedback goes to a hiring committee to make a decision.

Most companies get back after about a week with next steps (offer, rejection, further interviews, or just an update on the process). Some companies respond much sooner (sometimes same day!) and others take much longer.

If you have waited more than a week, you should follow up with your recruiter. If your recruiter does not respond, this does *not* mean that you are rejected (at least not at any major tech company, and almost any other company). Let me repeat that again: not responding indicates nothing about your status. The intention is that all recruiters should tell candidates once a final decision is made.

Delays can and do happen. Follow up with your recruiter if you expect a delay, but be respectful when you do. Recruiters are just like you. They get busy and forgetful too.

▸ The Microsoft Interview

Microsoft wants smart people. Geeks. People who are passionate about technology. You probably won't be tested on the ins and outs of C++ APIs, but you will be expected to write code on the board.

In a typical interview, you'll show up at Microsoft at some time in the morning and fill out initial paper work. You'll have a short interview with a recruiter who will give you a sample question. Your recruiter is usually there to prep you, not to grill you on technical questions. If you get asked some basic technical questions, it may be because your recruiter wants to ease you into the interview so that you're less nervous when the "real" interview starts.

Be nice to your recruiter. Your recruiter can be your biggest advocate, even pushing to re-interview you if you stumbled on your first interview. They can fight for you to be hired–or not!

During the day, you'll do four or five interviews, often with two different teams. Unlike many companies, where you meet your interviewers in a conference room, you'll meet with your Microsoft interviewers in their office. This is a great time to look around and get a feel for the team culture.

Depending on the team, interviewers may or may not share their feedback on you with the rest of the interview loop.

When you complete your interviews with a team, you might speak with a hiring manager (often called the "as app", short for "as appropriate"). If so, that's a great sign! It likely means that you passed the interviews with a particular team. It's now down to the hiring manager's decision.

You might get a decision that day, or it might be a week. After one week of no word from HR, send a friendly email asking for a status update.

If your recruiter isn't very responsive, it's because she's busy, not because you're being silently rejected.

Definitely Prepare:

"Why do you want to work for Microsoft?"

In this question, Microsoft wants to see that you're passionate about technology. A great answer might be, "I've been using Microsoft software as long as I can remember, and I'm really impressed at how Microsoft manages to create a product that is universally excellent. For example, I've been using Visual Studio recently to learn game programming, and its APIs are excellent." Note how this shows a passion for technology!

What's Unique:

You'll only reach the hiring manager if you've done well, so if you do, that's a great sign!

Additionally, Microsoft tends to give teams more individual control, and the product set is diverse. Experiences can vary substantially across Microsoft since different teams look for different things.

▸ The Amazon Interview

Amazon's recruiting process typically begins with a phone screen in which a candidate interviews with a specific team. A small portion of the time, a candidate may have two or more interviews, which can indicate either that one of their interviewers wasn't convinced or that they are being considered for a different team or profile. In more unusual cases, such as when a candidate is local or has recently interviewed for a different position, a candidate may only do one phone screen.

The engineer who interviews you will usually ask you to write simple code via a shared document editor. They will also often ask a broad set of questions to explore what areas of technology you're familiar with.

Next, you fly to Seattle (or whichever office you're interviewing for) for four or five interviews with one or two teams that have selected you based on your resume and phone interviews. You will have to code on a whiteboard, and some interviewers will stress other skills. Interviewers are each assigned a specific area to probe and may seem very different from each other. They cannot see the other feedback until they have submitted their own, and they are discouraged from discussing it until the hiring meeting.

The "bar raiser" interviewer is charged with keeping the interview bar high. They attend special training and will interview candidates outside their group in order to balance out the group itself. If one interview seems significantly harder and different, that's most likely the bar raiser. This person has both significant experience with interviews and veto power in the hiring decision. Remember, though: just because you seem to be struggling more in this interview doesn't mean you're actually doing worse. Your performance is judged relative to other candidates; it's not evaluated on a simple "percent correct" basis.

Once your interviewers have entered their feedback, they will meet to discuss it. They will be the people making the hiring decision.

While Amazon's recruiters are usually excellent at following up with candidates, occasionally there are delays. If you haven't heard from Amazon within a week, we recommend a friendly email.

Definitely Prepare:

Amazon cares a lot about scale. Make sure you prepare for scalability questions. You don't need a background in distributed systems to answer these questions. See our recommendations in the System Design and Scalability chapter.

Additionally, Amazon tends to ask a lot of questions about object-oriented design. Check out the Object-Oriented Design chapter for sample questions and suggestions.

What's Unique:

The Bar Raiser is brought in from a different team to keep the bar high. You need to impress both this person and the hiring manager.

Amazon tends to experiment more with its hiring process than other companies do. The process described here is the typical experience, but due to Amazon's experimentation, it's not necessarily universal.

▸ The Google Interview

There are many scary rumors floating around about Google interviews, but they're mostly just that: rumors. The interview is not terribly different from Microsoft's or Amazon's.

A Google engineer performs the first phone screen, so expect tough technical questions. These questions may involve coding, sometimes via a shared document. Candidates are typically held to the same standard and are asked similar questions on phone screens as in on-site interviews.

On your on-site interview, you'll interview with four to six people, one of whom will be a lunch interviewer. Interviewer feedback is kept confidential from the other interviewers, so you can be assured that you enter each interview with blank slate. Your lunch interviewer doesn't submit feedback, so this is a great opportunity to ask honest questions.

Interviewers are typically not given specific focuses, and there is no "structure" or "system" as to what you're asked when. Each interviewer can conduct the interview however she would like.

Written feedback is submitted to a hiring committee (HC) of engineers and managers to make a hire / no-hire recommendation. Feedback is typically broken down into four categories (Analytical Ability, Coding, Experience, and Communication) and you are given an overall score from 1.0 to 4.0. The HC usually does not include any of your interviewers. If it does, it was purely by random chance.

To extend an offer, the HC wants to see at least one interviewer who is an "enthusiastic endorser." In other words, a packet with scores of 3.6, 3.1, 3.1 and 2.6 is better than all 3.1s.

You do not necessarily need to excel in every interview, and your phone screen performance is usually not a strong factor in the final decision.

If the hiring committee recommends an offer, your packet will go to a compensation committee and then to the executive management committee. Returning a decision can take several weeks because there are so many stages and committees.

Definitely Prepare:

As a web-based company, Google cares about how to design a scalable system. So, make sure you prepare for questions from System Design and Scalability.

Google puts a strong focus on analytical (algorithm) skills, regardless of experience. You should be very well prepared for these questions, even if you think your prior experience should count for more.

What's Different:

Your interviewers do not make the hiring decision. Rather, they enter feedback which is passed to a hiring committee. The hiring committee recommends a decision which can be—though rarely is—rejected by Google executives.

▸ The Apple Interview

Much like the company itself, Apple's interview process has minimal bureaucracy. The interviewers will be looking for excellent technical skills, but a passion for the position and the company is also very important. While it's not a prerequisite to be a Mac user, you should at least be familiar with the system.

The interview process usually begins with a recruiter phone screen to get a basic sense of your skills, followed up by a series of technical phone screens with team members.

Once you're invited on campus, you'll typically be greeted by the recruiter who provides an overview of the process. You will then have 6-8 interviews with members of the team with which you're interviewing, as well as key people with whom your team works.

You can expect a mix of one-on-one and two-on-one interviews. Be ready to code on a whiteboard and make sure all of your thoughts are clearly communicated. Lunch is with your potential future manager and appears more casual, but it is still an interview. Each interviewer usually focuses on a different area and is discouraged from sharing feedback with other interviewers unless there's something they want subsequent interviewers to drill into.

Towards the end of the day, your interviewers will compare notes. If everyone still feels you're a viable candidate, you will have an interview with the director and the VP of the organization to which you're applying. While this decision is rather informal, it's a very good sign if you make it. This decision also happens behind the scenes, and if you don't pass, you'll simply be escorted out of the building without ever having been the wiser (until now).

If you made it to the director and VP interviews, all of your interviewers will gather in a conference room to give an official thumbs up or thumbs down. The VP typically won't be present but can still veto the hire if they weren't impressed. Your recruiter will usually follow up a few days later, but feel free to ping him or her for updates.

Definitely Prepare:

If you know what team you're interviewing with, make sure you read up on that product. What do you like about it? What would you improve? Offering specific recommendations can show your passion for the job.

What's Unique:

Apple does two-on-one interviews often, but don't get stressed out about them–it's the same as a one-on-one interview!

Also, Apple employees are huge Apple fans. You should show this same passion in your interview.

▸ The Facebook Interview

Once selected for an interview, candidates will generally do one or two phone screens. Phone screens will be technical and will involve coding, usually an online document editor.

After the phone interview(s), you might be asked to do a homework assignment that will include a mix of coding and algorithms. Pay attention to your coding style here. If you've never worked in an environment which had thorough code reviews, it may be a good idea to get someone who has to review your code.

During your on-site interview, you will interview primarily with other software engineers, but hiring managers are also involved whenever they are available. All interviewers have gone through comprehensive interview training, and who you interview with has no bearing on your odds of getting an offer.

Each interviewer is given a "role" during the on-site interviews, which helps ensure that there are no repetitive questions and that they get a holistic picture of a candidate. These roles are:

- Behavioral ("Jedi"): This interview assesses your ability to be successful in Facebook's environment. Would you fit well with the culture and values? What are you excited about? How do you tackle challenges? Be prepared to talk about your interest in Facebook as well. Facebook wants passionate people. You might also be asked some coding questions in this interview.
- Coding and Algorithms ("Ninja"): These are your standard coding and algorithms questions, much like what you'll find in this book. These questions are designed to be challenging. You can use any programming language you want.

- Design/Architecture ("Pirate"): For a backend software engineer, you might be asked system design questions. Front-end or other specialties will be asked design questions related to that discipline. You should openly discuss different solutions and their tradeoffs.

You can typically expect two "ninja" interviews and one "jedi" interview. Experienced candidates will also usually get a "pirate" interview.

After your interview, interviewers submit written feedback, prior to discussing your performance with each other. This ensures that your performance in one interview will not bias another interviewer's feedback.

Once everyone's feedback is submitted, your interviewing team and a hiring manager get together to collaborate on a final decision. They come to a consensus decision and submit a final hire recommendation to the hiring committee.

Definitely Prepare:

The youngest of the "elite" tech companies, Facebook wants developers with an entrepreneurial spirit. In your interviews, you should show that you love to build stuff fast.

They want to know you can hack together an elegant and scalable solution using any language of choice. Knowing PHP is not especially important, particularly given that Facebook also does a lot of backend work in C++, Python, Erlang, and other languages.

What's Unique:

Facebook interviews developers for the company "in general," not for a specific team. If you are hired, you will go through a six-week "bootcamp" which will help ramp you up in the massive code base. You'll get mentorship from senior devs, learn best practices, and, ultimately, get a greater flexibility in choosing a project than if you were assigned to a project in your interview.

▸ The Palantir Interview

Unlike some companies which do "pooled" interviews (where you interview with the company as a whole, not with a specific team), Palantir interviews for a specific team. Occasionally, your application might be re-routed to another team where there is a better fit.

The Palantir interview process typically starts with two phone interviews. These interviews are about 30 to 45 minutes and will be primarily technical. Expect to cover a bit about your prior experience, with a heavy focus on algorithm questions.

You might also be sent a HackerRank coding assessment, which will evaluate your ability to write optimal algorithms and correct code. Less experienced candidates, such as those in college, are particularly likely to get such a test.

After this, successful candidates are invited to campus and will interview with up to five people. Onsite interviews cover your prior experience, relevant domain knowledge, data structures and algorithms, and design.

You may also likely get a demo of Palantir's products. Ask good questions and demonstrate your passion for the company.

After the interview, the interviewers meet to discuss your feedback with the hiring manager.

Definitely Prepare:

Palantir values hiring brilliant engineers. Many candidates report that Palantir's questions were harder than those they saw at Google and other top companies. This doesn't necessarily mean it's harder to get an offer (although it certainly can); it just means interviewers prefer more challenging questions. If you're interviewing with Palantir, you should learn your core data structures and algorithms inside and out. Then, focus on preparing with the hardest algorithm questions.

Brush up on system design too if you're interviewing for a backend role. This is an important part of the process.

What's Unique:

A coding challenge is a common part of Palantir's process. Although you'll be at your computer and can look up material as needed, don't walk into this unprepared. The questions can be extremely challenging and the efficiency of your algorithm will be evaluated. Thorough interview preparation will help you here. You can also practice coding challenges online at HackerRank.com.

Special Situations

There are many paths that lead someone to this book. Perhaps you have more experience but have never done this sort of interview. Perhaps you're a tester or a PM. Or perhaps you're actually using this book to teach yourself how to interview better. Here's a little something for all these "special situations."

▸ Experienced Candidates

Some people assume that the algorithm-style questions you see in this book are only for recent grads. That's not entirely true.

More experienced engineers might see slightly less focus on algorithm questions—but only slightly

If a company asks algorithm questions to inexperienced candidates, they tend to ask them to experienced candidates too. Rightly or wrongly, they feel that the skills demonstrated in these questions are important for all developers.

Some interviewers might hold experience candidates to a somewhat lower standard. After all, it's been years since these candidates took an algorithms class. They're out of practice.

Others though hold experienced candidates to a higher standard, reasoning that the more years of experience allow a candidate to have seen many more types of problems.

On average, it balances out.

The exception to this rule is system design and architecture questions, as well as questions about your resume. Typically, students don't study much system architecture, so experience with such challenges would only come professionally. Your performance in such interview questions would be evaluated with respect to your experience level. However, students and recent graduates are still asked these questions and should be prepared to solve them as well as they can.

Additionally, experienced candidates will be expected to give a more in-depth, impressive response to questions like, "What was the hardest bug you've faced?" You have more experience, and your response to these questions should show it.

▸ Testers and SDETs

SDETs (software design engineers in test) write code, but to test features instead of build features. As such, they have to be great coders and great testers. Double the prep work!

If you're applying for an SDET role, take the following approach:

- *Prepare the Core Testing Problems:* For example, how would you test a light bulb? A pen? A cash register? Microsoft Word? The Testing chapter will give you more background on these problems.
- *Practice the Coding Questions:* The number one thing that SDETs get rejected for is coding skills. Although coding standards are typically lower for an SDET than for a traditional developer, SDETs are still expected to be very strong in coding and algorithms. Make sure that you practice solving all the same coding and algorithm questions that a regular developer would get.
- *Practice Testing the Coding Questions:* A very popular format for SDET questions is "Write code to do X," followed up by, "Okay, now test it." Even when the question doesn't specifically require this, you should ask yourself, "How would I test this?" Remember: any problem can be an SDET problem!

Strong communication skills can also be very important for testers, since your job requires you to work with so many different people. Do not neglect the Behavioral Questions section.

Career Advice

Finally, a word of career advice: If, like many candidates, you are hoping to apply to an SDET position as the "easy" way into a company, be aware that many candidates find it very difficult to move from an SDET position to a dev position. Make sure to keep your coding and algorithms skills very sharp if you hope to make this move, and try to switch within one to two years. Otherwise, you might find it very difficult to be taken seriously in a dev interview.

Never let your coding skills atrophy.

▸ Product (and Program) Management

These "PM" roles vary wildly across companies and even within a company. At Microsoft, for instance, some PMs may be essentially customer evangelists, working in a customer-facing role that borders on marketing. Across campus though, other PMs may spend much of their day coding. The latter type of PMs would likely be tested on coding, since this is an important part of their job function.

Generally speaking, interviewers for PM positions are looking for candidates to demonstrate skills in the following areas:

- *Handling Ambiguity:* This is typically not the most critical area for an interview, but you should be aware that interviewers do look for skill here. Interviewers want to see that, when faced with an ambiguous situation, you don't get overwhelmed and stall. They want to see you tackle the problem head on: seeking new information, prioritizing the most important parts, and solving the problem in a structured way. This typically will not be tested directly (though it can be), but it may be one of many things the interviewer is looking for in a problem.
- *Customer Focus (Attitude):* Interviewers want to see that your attitude is customer-focused. Do you assume that everyone will use the product just like you do? Or are you the type of person who puts himself in the customer's shoes and tries to understand how they want to use the product? Questions like "Design an alarm clock for the blind" are ripe for examining this aspect. When you hear a question like this, be sure to ask a lot of questions to understand *who* the customer is and *how* they are using the product. The skills covered in the Testing section are closely related to this.
- *Customer Focus (Technical Skills):* Some teams with more complex products need to ensure that their PMs walk in with a strong understanding of the product, as it would be difficult to acquire this knowledge on the job. Deep technical knowledge of mobile phones is probably not necessary to work on the Android or Windows Phone teams (although it might still be nice to have), whereas an understanding of security might be necessary to work on Windows Security. Hopefully, you wouldn't interview with a team that

required specific technical skills unless you at least claim to possess the requisite skills.

- *Multi-Level Communication:* PMs need to be able to communicate with people at all levels in the company, across many positions and ranges of technical skills. Your interviewer will want to see that you possess this flexibility in your communication. This is often examined directly, through a question such as, "Explain TCP/IP to your grandmother." Your communication skills may also be assessed by how you discuss your prior projects.
- *Passion for Technology:* Happy employees are productive employees, so a company wants to make sure that you'll enjoy the job and be excited about your work. A passion for technology—and, ideally, the company or team—should come across in your answers. You may be asked a question directly like, "Why are you interested in Microsoft?" Additionally, your interviewers will look for enthusiasm in how you discuss your prior experience and how you discuss the team's challenges. They want to see that you will be eager to face the job's challenges.
- *Teamwork / Leadership:* This may be the most important aspect of the interview, and—not surprisingly—the job itself. All interviewers will be looking for your ability to work well with other people. Most commonly, this is assessed with questions like, "Tell me about a time when a teammate wasn't pulling his / her own weight." Your interviewer is looking to see that you handle conflicts well, that you take initiative, that you understand people, and that people like working with you. Your work preparing for behavioral questions will be extremely important here.

All of the above areas are important skills for PMs to master and are therefore key focus areas of the interview. The weighting of each of these areas will roughly match the importance that the area holds in the actual job.

▸ Dev Lead and Managers

Strong coding skills are almost always required for dev lead positions and often for management positions as well. If you'll be coding on the job, make sure to be very strong with coding and algorithms—just like a dev would be. Google, in particular, holds managers to high standards when it comes to coding.

In addition, prepare to be examined for skills in the following areas:

- *Teamwork / Leadership:* Anyone in a management-like role needs to be able to both lead and work with people. You will be examined implicitly and explicitly in these areas. Explicit evaluation will come in the form of asking you how you handled prior situations, such as when you disagreed with a manager. The implicit evaluation comes in the form of your interviewers watching how you interact with them. If you come off as too arrogant or too passive, your interviewer may feel you aren't great as a manager.
- *Prioritization:* Managers are often faced with tricky issues, such as how to make sure a team meets a tough deadline. Your interviewers will want to see that you can prioritize a project appropriately, cutting the less important aspects. Prioritization means asking the right questions to understand what is critical and what you can reasonably expect to accomplish.
- *Communication:* Managers need to communicate with people both above and below them, and potentially with customers and other much less technical people. Interviewers will look to see that you can communicate at many levels and that you can do so in a way that is friendly and engaging. This is, in some ways, an evaluation of your personality.
- *"Getting Things Done":* Perhaps the most important thing that a manager can do is be a person who "gets things done." This means striking the right balance between preparing for a project and actually implementing it. You need to understand how to structure a project and how to motivate people so you can accomplish the team's goals.

Ultimately, most of these areas come back to your prior experience and your personality. Be sure to prepare very, very thoroughly using the interview preparation grid.

▸ Startups

The application and interview process for startups is highly variable. We can't go through every startup, but we can offer some general pointers. Understand, however, that the process at a specific startup might deviate from this.

The Application Process

Many startups might post job listings, but for the hottest startups, often the best way in is through a personal referral. This reference doesn't necessarily need to be a close friend or a coworker. Often just by reaching out and expressing your interest, you can get someone to pick up your resume to see if you're a good fit.

Visas and Work Authorization

Unfortunately, many smaller startups in the U.S. are not able to sponsor work visas. They hate the system as much you do, but you won't be able to convince them to hire you anyway. If you require a visa and wish to work at a startup, your best bet is to reach out to a professional recruiter who works with many startups (and may have a better idea of which startups will work with visa issues), or to focus your search on bigger startups.

Resume Selection Factors

Startups tend to want engineers who are not only smart and who can code, but also people who would work well in an entrepreneurial environment. Your resume should ideally show initiative. What sort of projects have you started?

Being able to "hit the ground running" is also very important; they want people who already know the language of the company.

The Interview Process

In contrast to big companies, which tend to look mostly at your general aptitude with respect to software development, startups often look closely at your personality fit, skill set, and prior experience.

- *Personality Fit:* Personality fit is typically assessed by how you interact with your interviewer. Establishing a friendly, engaging conversation with your interviewers is your ticket to many job offers.
- *Skill Set:* Because startups need people who can hit the ground running, they are likely to assess your skills with specific programming languages. If you know a language that the startup works with, make sure to brush up on the details.
- *Experience:* Startups are likely to ask you a lot of questions about your experience. Pay special attention to the Behavioral Questions section.

In addition to the above areas, the coding and algorithms questions that you see in this book are also very common.

Acquisitions and Acquihires

During the technical due diligence process for many acquisitions, the acquirer will often interview most or all of a startup's employees. Google, Yahoo, Facebook, and many other companies have this as a standard part of many acquisitions.

Which startups go through this? And why?

Part of the reasoning for this is that their employees had to go through this process to get hired. They don't want acquisitions to be an "easy way" into the company. And, since the team is a core motivator for the acquisition, they figure it makes sense to assess the skills of the team.

Not all acquisitions are like this, of course. The famous multi-billion dollar acquisitions generally did not have to go through this process. Those acquisitions, after all, are usually about the user base and community, less so about the employees or even the technology. Assessing the team's skills is less essential.

However, it is not as simple as "acquihires get interviewed, traditional acquisitions do not." There is a big gray area between acquihires (i.e., talent acquisitions) and product acquisitions. Many startups are acquired for the team and ideas behind the technology. The acquirer might discontinue the product, but have the team work on something very similar.

If your startup is going through this process, you can typically expect your team to have interviews very similar to what a normal candidate would experience (and, therefore, very similar to what you'll see in this book).

How important are these interviews?

These interviews can carry enormous importance. They have three different roles:

- They can make or break acquisitions. They are often the reason a company does not get acquired.
- They determine which employees receive offers to join the acquirer.
- They can affect the acquisition price (in part as a consequence of the number of employees who join).

These interviews are much more than a mere "screen."

Which employees go through the interviews?

For tech startups, usually all of the engineers go through the interview process, as they are one of the core motivators for the acquisition.

In addition, sales, customer support, product managers, and essentially any other role might have to go through it.

The CEO is often slotted into a product manager interview or a dev manager interview, as this is often the closest match for the CEO's current responsibilities. This is not an absolute rule, though. It depends on what the CEO's role presently is and what the CEO is interested in. With some of my clients, the CEO has even opted to not interview and to leave the company upon the acquisition.

What happens to employees who don't perform well in the interview?

Employees who underperform will often not receive offers to join the acquirer. (If many employees don't perform well, then the acquisition will likely not go through.)

In some cases, employees who performed poorly in interviews will get contract positions for the purpose of "knowledge transfer." These are temporary positions with the expectation that the employee leaves at the termination of the contract (often six months), although sometimes the employee ends up being retained.

In other cases, the poor performance was a result of the employee being mis-slotted. This occurs in two common situations:

- Sometimes a startup labels someone who is not a "traditional" software engineer as a software engineer. This often happens with data scientists or database engineers. These people may underperform during the software engineer interviews, as their actual role involves other skills.
- In other cases, a CEO "sells" a junior software engineer as more senior than he actually is. He underperforms for the senior bar because he's being held to an unfairly high standard.

In either case, sometimes the employee will be re-interviewed for a more appropriate position. (Other times though, the employee is just out of luck.)

In rare cases, a CEO is able to override the decision for a particularly strong employee whose interview performance didn't reflect this.

Your "best" (and worst) employees might surprise you.

The problem-solving/algorithm interviews conducted at the top tech companies evaluate particular skills, which might not perfectly match what their manager evaluates in their employees.

I've worked with many companies that are surprised at who their strongest and weakest performers are in interviews. That junior engineer who still has a lot to learn about professional development might turn out to be a great problem-solver in these interviews.

Don't count anyone out—or in—until you've evaluated them the same way their interviewers will.

Are employees held to the same standards as typical candidates?

Essentially yes, although there is a bit more leeway.

The big companies tend to take a risk-averse approach to hiring. If someone is on the fence, they often lean towards a no-hire.

In the case of an acquisition, the "on the fence" employees can be pulled through by strong performance from the rest of the team.

How do employees tend to react to the news of an acquisition/acquihire?

This is a big concern for many startup CEOs and founders. Will the employees be upset about this process? Or, what if we get their hopes up but it doesn't happen?

What I've seen with my clients is that the leadership is worried about this more than is necessary.

Certainly, some employees are upset about the process. They might not be excited about joining one of the big companies for any number of reasons.

Most employees, though, are cautiously optimistic about the process. They hope it goes through, but they know that the existence of these interviews means that it might not.

What happens to the team after an acquisition?

Every situation is different. However, most of my clients have been kept together as a team, or possibly integrated into an existing team.

How should you prepare your team for acquisition interviews?

Interview prep for acquisition interviews is fairly similar to typical interviews at the acquirer. The difference is that your company is doing this as a team and that each employee wasn't individually selected for the interview on their own merits.

You're all in this together.

Some startups I've worked with put their "real" work on hold and have their teams spend the next two or three weeks on interview prep.

Obviously, that's not a choice all companies can make, but—from the perspective of wanting the acquisition to go through—that does increase your results substantially.

Your team should study individually, in teams of two or three, or by doing mock interviews with each other. If possible, use all three of these approaches.

Some people may be less prepared than others.

Many developers at startups might have only vaguely heard of big O time, binary search tree, breadth-first search, and other important concepts. They'll need some extra time to prepare.

People without computer science degrees (or who earned their degrees a long time ago) should focus first on learning the core concepts discussed in this book, especially big O time (which is one of the most important). A good first exercise is to implement all the core data structures and algorithms from scratch.

If the acquisition is important to your company, give these people the time they need to prepare. They'll need it.

Don't wait until the last minute.

As a startup, you might be used to taking things as they come without a ton of planning. Startups that do this with acquisition interviews tend not to fare well.

Acquisition interviews often come up very suddenly. A company's CEO is chatting with an acquirer (or several acquirers) and conversations get increasingly serious. The acquirer mentions the possibility of interviews at some point in the future. Then, all of a sudden, there's a "come in at the end of this week" message.

If you wait until there's a firm date set for the interviews, you probably won't get much more than a couple of days to prepare. That might not be enough time for your engineers to learn core computer science concepts and practice interview questions.

▸ For Interviewers

Since writing the last edition, I've learned that a lot of interviewers are using *Cracking the Coding Interview* to learn how to interview. That wasn't really the book's intention, but I might as well offer some guidance for interviews.

Don't actually ask the exact questions in here.

First, these questions were selected because they're good for interview preparation. Some questions that are good for interview preparation are not always good for interviewing. For example, there are some brainteasers in this book because sometimes interviewers ask these sorts of questions. It's worthwhile for candidates to practice those if they're interviewing at a company that likes them, even though I personally find them to be bad questions.

Second, your candidates are reading this book, too. You don't want to ask questions that your candidates have already solved.

You can ask questions *similar* to these, but don't just pluck questions out of here. Your goal is to test their problem-solving skills, not their memorization skills.

Ask Medium and Hard Problems

The goal of these questions is to evaluate someone's problem-solving skills. When you ask questions that are too easy, performance gets clustered together. Minor issues can substantially drop someone's performance. It's not a reliable indicator.

Look for questions with multiple hurdles.

Some questions have "Aha!" moments. They rest on a particular insight. If the candidate doesn't get that one bit, then they do poorly. If they get it, then suddenly they've outperformed many candidates.

Even if that insight is an indicator of skills, it's still only one indicator. Ideally, you want a question that has a series of hurdles, insights, or optimizations. Multiple data points beat a single data point.

Here's a test: if you can give a hint or piece of guidance that makes a substantial difference in a candidate's performance, then it's probably not a good interview question.

Use hard questions, not hard knowledge.

Some interviewers, in an attempt to make a question hard, inadvertently make the *knowledge* hard. Sure enough, fewer candidates do well so the statistics look right, but it's not for reasons that indicate much about the candidates' skills.

The knowledge you are expecting candidates to have should be fairly straightforward data structure and algorithm knowledge. It's reasonable to expect a computer science graduate to understand the basics of big O and trees. Most won't remember Dijkstra's algorithm or the specifics of how AVL trees works.

If your interview question expects obscure knowledge, ask yourself: is this truly an important skill? Is it so important that I would like to either reduce the number of candidates I hire or reduce the amount to which I focus on problem-solving or other skills?

Every new skill or attribute you evaluate shrinks the number of offers extended, unless you counter-balance this by relaxing the requirements for a different skill. Sure, all else being equal, you might prefer someone who could recite the finer points of a two-inch thick algorithms textbook. But all else isn't equal.

Avoid "scary" questions.

Some questions intimidate candidates because it seems like they involve some specialized knowledge, even if they really don't. This often includes questions that involve:

- Math or probability.

- Low-level knowledge (memory allocation, etc.).
- System design or scalability.
- Proprietary systems (Google Maps, etc.).

For example, one question I sometimes ask is to find all positive integer solutions under 1,000 to $a^3 + b^3 = c^3 + d^3$ (page 68).

Many candidates will at first think they have to do some sort of fancy factorization of this or semi-advanced math. They don't. They need to understand the concept of exponents, sums, and equality, and that's it.

When I ask this question, I explicitly say, "I know this sounds like a math problem. Don't worry. It's not. It's an algorithm question." If they start going down the path of factorization, I stop them and remind them that it's not a math question.

Other questions might involve a bit of probability. It might be stuff that a candidate would surely know (e.g., to pick between five options, pick a random number between 1 and 5). But simply the fact that it involves probability will intimidate candidates.

Be careful asking questions that sound intimidating. Remember that this is already a really intimidating situation for candidates. Adding on a "scary" question might just fluster a candidate and cause him to underperform.

If you're going to ask a question that sounds "scary," make sure you really reassure candidates that it doesn't require the knowledge that they think it does.

Offer positive reinforcement.

Some interviewers put so much focus on the "right" question that they forget to think about their own behavior.

Many candidates are intimidated by interviewing and try to read into the interviewer's every word. They can cling to each thing that might possibly sound positive or negative. They interpret that little comment of "good luck" to mean something, even though you say it to everyone regardless of performance.

You want candidates to feel good about the experience, about you, and about their performance. You want them to feel comfortable. A candidate who is nervous will perform poorly, and it doesn't mean that they aren't good. Moreover, a good candidate who has a negative reaction to you or to the company is less likely to accept an offer—and they might dissuade their friends from interviewing/accepting as well.

Try to be warm and friendly to candidates. This is easier for some people than others, but do your best.

Even if being warm and friendly doesn't come naturally to you, you can still make a concerted effort to sprinkle in positive remarks throughout the interview:

- "Right, exactly."
- "Great point."
- "Good work."
- "Okay, that's a really interesting approach."
- "Perfect."

No matter how poorly a candidate is doing, there is always something they got right. Find a way to infuse some positivity into the interview.

Probe deeper on behavioral questions.

Many candidates are poor at articulating their specific accomplishments.

You ask them a question about a challenging situation, and they tell you about a difficult situation their team faced. As far as you can tell, the candidate didn't really do much.

Not so fast, though. A candidate might not focus on themselves because they've been trained to celebrate their team's accomplishments and not boast about themselves. This is especially common for people in leadership roles and female candidates.

Don't assume that a candidate didn't do much in a situation just because you have trouble understanding what they did. Call out the situation (nicely!). Ask them specifically if they can tell you what their role was.

If it didn't really sound like resolving the situation was difficult, then, again, probe deeper. Ask them to go into more details about how they thought about the issue and the different steps they took. Ask them why they took certain actions. Not describing the details of the actions they took makes them a flawed *candidate*, but not necessarily a flawed employee.

Being a good interview candidate is its own skill (after all, that's part of why this book exists), and it's probably not one you want to evaluate.

Coach your candidates.

Read through the sections on how candidates can develop good algorithms. Many of these tips are ones you can offer to candidates who are struggling. You're not "teaching to the test" when you do this; you're separating interview skills from job skills.

- Many candidates don't use an example to solve an interview question (or they don't use a *good* example). This makes it substantially more difficult to develop a solution, but it doesn't necessarily mean that they're not very good problem solvers. If candidates don't write an example themselves, or if they inadvertently write a special case, guide them.
- Some candidates take a long time to find the bug because they use an enormous example. This doesn't make them a bad tester or developer. It just means that they didn't realize that it would be more efficient to analyze their code conceptually first, or that a small example would work nearly as well. Guide them.
- If they dive into code before they have an optimal solution, pull them back and focus them on the algorithm (if that's what you want to see). It's unfair to say that a candidate never found or implemented the optimal solution if they didn't really have the time to do so.
- If they get nervous and stuck and aren't sure where to go, suggest to them that they walk through the brute force solution and look for areas to optimize.
- If they haven't said anything and there is a fairly obvious brute force, remind them that they can start off with a brute force. Their first solution doesn't have to be perfect.

Even if you think that a candidate's ability in one of these areas is an important factor, it's not the only factor. You can always mark someone down for "failing" this hurdle while helping to guide them past it.

While this book is here to coach candidates through interviews, one of your goals as an interviewer is to remove the effect of not preparing. After all, some candidates have studied for interviews and some candidates haven't, and this probably doesn't reveal much about their skills as an engineer.

Guide candidates using the tips in this book (within reason, of course—you don't want to coach candidates through the problems so much that you're not evaluating their problem-solving skills anymore).

Be careful here, though. If you're someone who comes off as intimidating to candidates, this coaching could make things worse. It can come off as your telling candidates that they're constantly messing up by creating bad examples, not prioritizing testing the right way, and so on.

If they want silence, give them silence.

One of the most common questions that candidates ask me is how to deal with an interviewer who insists on talking when they just need a moment to think in silence.

If your candidate needs this, give your candidate this time to think. Learn to distinguish between "I'm stuck and have no idea what to do," and "I'm thinking in silence."

It might help you to guide your candidate, and it might help many candidates, but it doesn't necessarily help *all* candidates. Some need a moment to think. Give them that time, and take into account when you're evaluating them that they got a bit less guidance than others.

Know your mode: sanity check, quality, specialist, and proxy.

At a very, very high level, there are four modes of questions:

- **Sanity Check:** These are often easy problem-solving or design questions. They assess a minimum degree of competence in problem-solving. They won't tell distinguish between "okay" versus "great", so don't evaluate them as such. You can use them early in the process (to filter out the worst candidates), or when you only need a minimum degree of competency.
- **Quality Check:** These are the more challenging questions, often in problem-solving or design. They are designed to be rigorous and really make a candidate think. Use these when algorithmic/problem-solving skills are of high importance. The biggest mistake people make here is asking questions that are, in fact, bad problem-solving questions.
- **Specialist Questions:** These questions test knowledge of specific topics, such as Java or machine learning. They should be used when for skills a good engineer couldn't quickly learn on the job. These questions need to be appropriate for true specialists. Unfortunately, I've seen situations where a company asks a candidate who just completed a 10-week coding bootcamp detailed questions about Java. What does this show? If she has this knowledge, then she only learned it recently and, therefore, it's likely to be easily acquirable. If it's easily acquirable, then there's no reason to hire for it.
- **Proxy Knowledge:** This is knowledge that is not quite at the specialist level (in fact, you might not even need it), but that you would expect a candidate at their level to know. For example, it might not be very important to you if a candidate knows CSS or HTML. But if a candidate has worked in depth with these technologies and can't talk about why tables are or aren't good, that suggests an issue. They're not absorbing information core to their job.

When companies get into trouble is when they mix and match these:

- They ask specialist questions to people who aren't specialists.
- They hire for specialist roles when they don't need specialists.
- They need specialists but are only assessing pretty basic skills.
- They are asking sanity check (easy) questions, but think they're asking quality check questions. They therefore interpret a strong difference between "okay" and "great" performance, even though a very minor detail might have separated these.

In fact, having worked with a number of small and large tech companies on their hiring process, I have found that most companies are doing one of these things wrong.

Before the Interview

Acing an interview starts well before the interview itself—years before, in fact. The following timeline outlines what you should be thinking about when.

If you're starting late into this process, don't worry. Do as much "catching up" as you can, and then focus on preparation. Good luck!

▸ Getting the Right Experience

Without a great resume, there's no interview. And without great experience, there's no great resume. Therefore, the first step in landing an interview is getting great experience. The further in advance you can think about this the better.

For current students, this may mean the following:

- *Take the Big Project Classes:* Seek out the classes with big coding projects. This is a great way to get somewhat practical experience before you have any formal work experience. The more relevant the project is to the real world, the better.
- *Get an Internship:* Do everything you can to land an internship early in school. It will pave the way for even better internships before you graduate. Many of the top tech companies have internship programs designed especially for freshman and sophomores. You can also look at startups, which might be more flexible.
- *Start Something:* Build a project on your own time, participate in hackathons, or contribute to an open source project. It doesn't matter too much what it is. The important thing is that you're coding. Not only will this develop your technical skills and practical experience, your initiative will impress companies.

Professionals, on the other hand, may already have the right experience to switch to their dream company. For instance, a Google dev probably already has sufficient experience to switch to Facebook. However, if you're trying to move from a lesser-known company to one of the "biggies," or from testing/IT into a dev role, the following advice will be useful:

- *Shift Work Responsibilities More Towards Coding:* Without revealing to your manager that you are thinking of leaving, you can discuss your eagerness to take on bigger coding challenges. As much as possible, try to ensure that these projects are "meaty," use relevant technologies, and lend themselves well to a resume bullet or two. It is these coding projects that will, ideally, form the bulk of your resume.
- *Use Your Nights and Weekends:* If you have some free time, use it to build a mobile app, a web app, or a piece of desktop software. Doing such projects is also a great way to get experience with new technologies, making you more relevant to today's companies. This project work should definitely be listed on your resume; few things are as impressive to an interviewer as a candidate who built something "just

for fun."

All of these boil down to the two big things that companies want to see: that you're smart and that you can code. If you can prove that, you can land your interview.

In addition, you should think in advance about where you want your career to go. If you want to move into management down the road, even though you're currently looking for a dev position, you should find ways now of developing leadership experience.

▸ Writing a Great Resume

Resume screeners look for the same things that interviewers do. They want to know that you're smart and that you can code.

That means you should prepare your resume to highlight those two things. Your love of tennis, traveling, or magic cards won't do much to show that. Think twice before cutting more technical lines in order to allow space for your non-technical hobbies.

Appropriate Resume Length

In the US, it is strongly advised to keep a resume to one page if you have less than ten years of experience. More experienced candidates can often justify 1.5 - 2 pages otherwise.

Think twice about a long resume. Shorter resumes are often more impressive.

- Recruiters only spend a fixed amount of time (about 10 seconds) looking at your resume. If you limit the content to the most impressive items, the recruiter is sure to see them. Adding additional items just distracts the recruiter from what you'd really like them to see.
- Some people just flat-out refuse to read long resumes. Do you really want to risk having your resume tossed for this reason?

If you are thinking right now that you have too much experience and can't fit it all on one or two pages, trust me, *you can*. Long resumes are not a reflection of having tons of experience; they're a reflection of not understanding how to prioritize content.

Employment History

Your resume does not—and should not—include a full history of every role you've ever had. Include only the relevant positions—the ones that make you a more impressive candidate.

Writing Strong Bullets

For each role, try to discuss your accomplishments with the following approach: "Accomplished X by implementing Y which led to Z." Here's an example:

- "Reduced object rendering time by 75% by implementing distributed caching, leading to a 10% reduction in log-in time."

Here's another example with an alternate wording:

- "Increased average match accuracy from 1.2 to 1.5 by implementing a new comparison algorithm based on windiff."

Not everything you did will fit into this approach, but the principle is the same: show what you did, how you did it, and what the results were. Ideally, you should try to make the results "measurable" somehow.

Projects

Developing the projects section on your resume is often the best way to present yourself as more experienced. This is especially true for college students or recent grads.

The projects should include your 2 - 4 most significant projects. State what the project was and which languages or technologies it employed. You may also want to consider including details such as whether the project was an individual or a team project, and whether it was completed for a course or independently. These details are not required, so only include them if they make you look better. Independent projects are generally preferred over course projects, as it shows initiative.

Do not add too many projects. Many candidates make the mistake of adding all 13 of their prior projects, cluttering their resume with small, non-impressive projects.

So what should you build? Honestly, it doesn't matter that much. Some employers really like open source projects (it offers experience contributing to a large code base), while others prefer independent projects (it's easier to understand your personal contributions). You could build a mobile app, a web app, or almost anything. The most important thing is that you're building something.

Programming Languages and Software

Software

Be conservative about what software you list, and understand what's appropriate for the company. Software like Microsoft Office can almost always be cut. Technical software like Visual Studio and Eclipse is somewhat more relevant, but many of the top tech companies won't even care about that. After all, is it really that hard to learn Visual Studio?

Of course, it won't hurt you to list all this software. It just takes up valuable space. You need to evaluate the trade-off of that.

Languages

Should you list everything you've ever worked with, or shorten the list to just the ones that you're most comfortable with?

Listing everything you've ever worked with is dangerous. Many interviewers consider anything on your resume to be "fair game" as far as the interview.

One alternative is to list most of the languages you've used, but add your experience level. This approach is shown below:

- Languages: Java (expert), C++ (proficient), JavaScript (prior experience).

Use whatever wording ("expert", "fluent", etc.) effectively communicates your skillset.

Some people list the number of years of experience they have with a particular language, but this can be really confusing. If you first learned Java 10 years ago, and have used it occasionally throughout that time, how many years of experience is this?

For this reason, the number of years of experience is a poor metric for resumes. It's better to just describe what you mean in plain English.

Advice for Non-Native English Speakers and Internationals

Some companies will throw out your resume just because of a typo. Please get at least one native English speaker to proofread your resume.

Additionally, for US positions, do *not* include age, marital status, or nationality. This sort of personal information is not appreciated by companies, as it creates a legal liability for them.

Beware of (Potential) Stigma

Certain languages have stigmas associated with them. Sometimes this is because of the language themselves, but often it's because of the places where this language is used. I'm not defending the stigma; I'm just letting you know of it.

A few stigmas you should be aware of:

- **Enterprise Languages:** Certain languages have a stigma associated with them, and those are often the ones that are used for enterprise development. Visual Basic is a good example of this. If you show yourself to be an expert with VB, it can cause people to assume that you're less skilled. Many of these same people will admit that, yes, VB.NET is actually perfectly capable of building sophisticated applications. But still, the kinds of applications that people tend to build with it are not very sophisticated. You would be unlikely to see a big name Silicon Valley company using VB.

  In fact, the same argument (although less strong) applies to the whole .NET platform. If your primary focus is .NET and you're not applying for .NET roles, you'll have to do more to show that you're strong technically than if you were coming in with a different background.

- **Being Too Language Focused:** When recruiters at some of the top tech companies see resumes that list every flavor of Java on their resume, they make negative assumptions about the caliber of candidate. There is a belief in many circles that the best software engineers don't define themselves around a particular language. Thus, when they see a candidate seems to flaunt which specific versions of a language they know, recruiters will often bucket the candidate as "not our kind of person."

  Note that this does not mean that you should necessarily take this "language flaunting" off your resume. You need to understand what that company values. Some companies do value this.

- **Certifications:** Certifications for software engineers can be anything from a positive, to a neutral, to a negative. This goes hand-in-hand with being too language focused; the companies that are biased against candidates with a very lengthy list of technologies tend to also be biased against certifications. This means that in some cases, you should actually remove this sort of experience from your resume.

- **Knowing Only One or Two Languages:** The more time you've spent coding, the more things you've built, the more languages you will have tended to work with. The assumption then, when they see a resume with only one language, is that you haven't experienced very many problems. They also often worry that candidates with only one or two languages will have trouble learning new technologies (why hasn't the candidate learned more things?) or will just feel too tied with a specific technology (potentially not using the best language for the task).

This advice is here not just to help you work on your resume, but also to help you develop the right experience. If your expertise is in C#.NET, try developing some projects in Python and JavaScript. If you only know one or two languages, build some applications in a different language.

Where possible, try to truly diversify. The languages in the cluster of {Python, Ruby, and JavaScript} are somewhat similar to each other. It's better if you can learn languages that are more different, like Python, C++, and Java.

▸ Preparation Map

The following map should give you an idea of how to tackle the interview preparation process. One of the key takeaways here is that it's not just about interview questions. Do projects and write code, too!

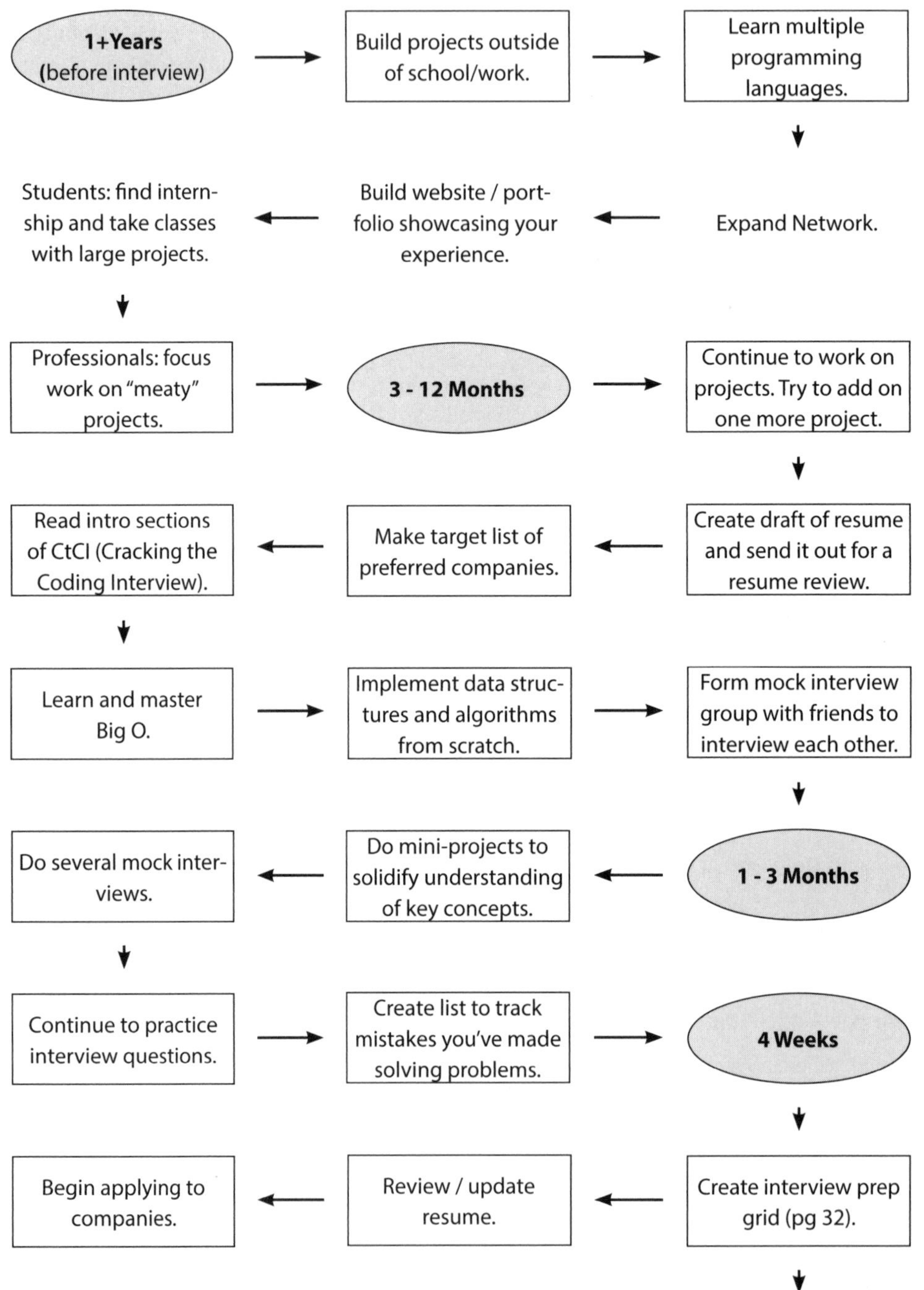

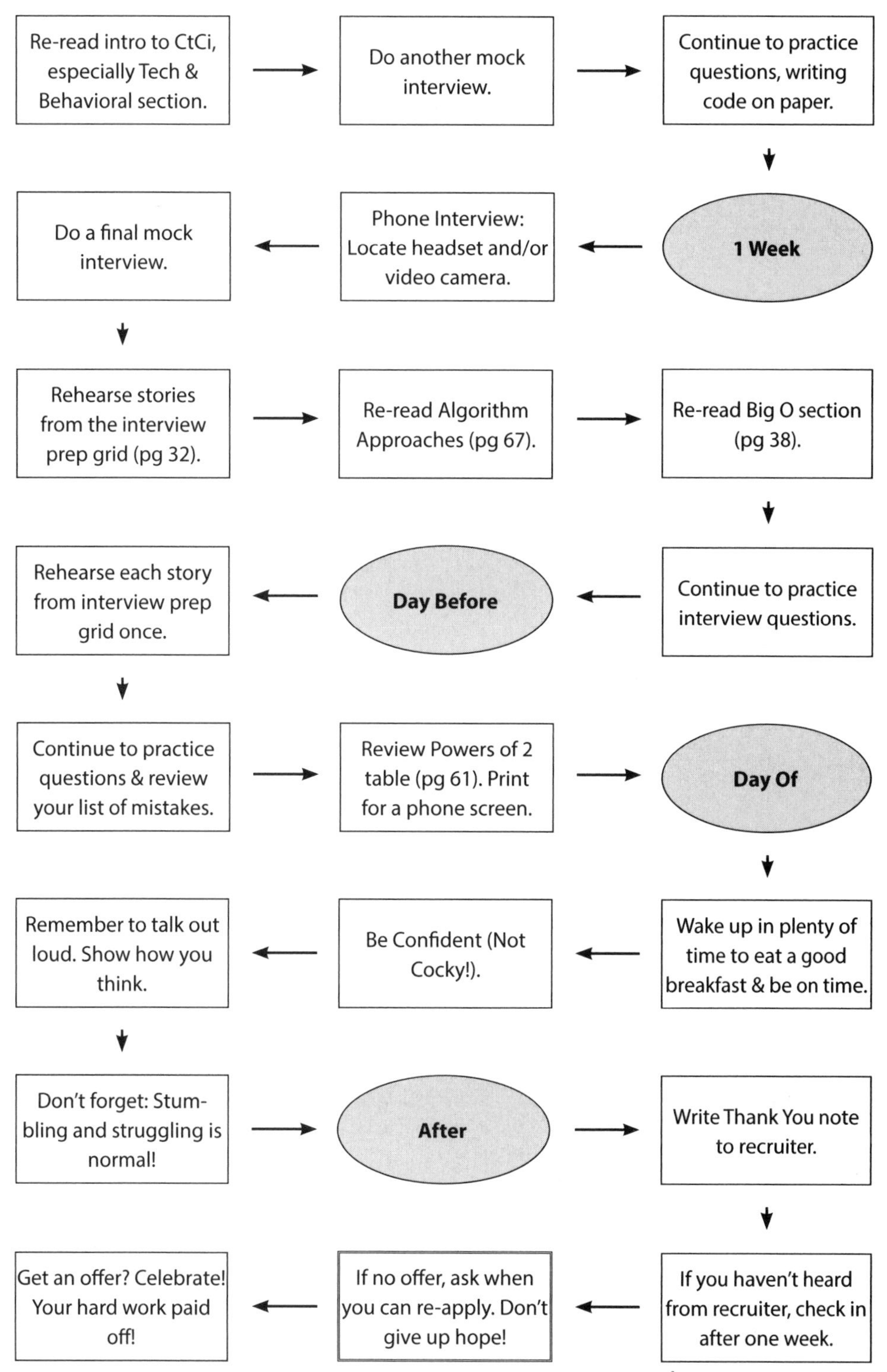
Re-read intro to CtCi, especially Tech & Behavioral section.
Do another mock interview.
Continue to practice questions, writing code on paper.
1 Week
Phone Interview: Locate headset and/or video camera.
Do a final mock interview.
Rehearse stories from the interview prep grid (pg 32).
Re-read Algorithm Approaches (pg 67).
Re-read Big O section (pg 38).
Continue to practice interview questions.
Day Before
Rehearse each story from interview prep grid once.
Continue to practice questions & review your list of mistakes.
Review Powers of 2 table (pg 61). Print for a phone screen.
Day Of
Wake up in plenty of time to eat a good breakfast & be on time.
Be Confident (Not Cocky!).
Remember to talk out loud. Show how you think.
Don't forget: Stumbling and struggling is normal!
After
Write Thank You note to recruiter.
If you haven't heard from recruiter, check in after one week.
If no offer, ask when you can re-apply. Don't give up hope!
Get an offer? Celebrate! Your hard work paid off!

Behavioral Questions

Behavioral questions are asked to get to know your personality, to understand your resume more deeply, and just to ease you into an interview. They are important questions and can be prepared for.

▸ Interview Preparation Grid

Go through each of the projects or components of your resume and ensure that you can talk about them in detail. Filling out a grid like this may help:

Common Questions	**Project 1**	**Project 2**	**Project 3**
Challenges			
Mistakes/Failures			
Enjoyed			
Leadership			
Conflicts			
What You'd Do Differently			

Along the top, as columns, you should list all the major aspects of your resume, including each project, job, or activity. Along the side, as rows, you should list the common behavioral questions.

Study this grid before your interview. Reducing each story to just a couple of keywords may make the grid easier to study and recall. You can also more easily have this grid in front of you during an interview without it being a distraction.

In addition, ensure that you have one to three projects that you can talk about in detail. You should be able to discuss the technical components in depth. These should be projects where you played a central role.

What are your weaknesses?

When asked about your weaknesses, give a real weakness! Answers like "My greatest weakness is that I work too hard" tell your interviewer that you're arrogant and/or won't admit to your faults. A good answer conveys a real, legitimate weakness but emphasizes how you work to overcome it.

For example:

> "Sometimes, I don't have a very good attention to detail. While that's good because it lets me execute quickly, it also means that I sometimes make careless mistakes. Because of that, I make sure to always have someone else double check my work."

What questions should you ask the interviewer?

Most interviewers will give you a chance to ask them questions. The quality of your questions will be a factor, whether subconsciously or consciously, in their decisions. Walk into the interview with some questions in mind.

You can think about three general types of questions.

Genuine Questions

These are the questions you actually want to know the answers to. Here are a few ideas of questions that are valuable to many candidates:

1. "What is the ratio of testers to developers to program managers? What is the interaction like? How does project planning happen on the team?"
2. "What brought you to this company? What has been most challenging for you?"

These questions will give you a good feel for what the day-to-day life is like at the company.

Insightful Questions

These questions demonstrate your knowledge or understanding of technology.

1. "I noticed that you use technology X. How do you handle problem Y?"
2. "Why did the product choose to use the X protocol over the Y protocol? I know it has benefits like A, B, C, but many companies choose not to use it because of issue D."

Asking such questions will typically require advance research about the company.

Passion Questions

These questions are designed to demonstrate your passion for technology. They show that you're interested in learning and will be a strong contributor to the company.

1. "I'm very interested in scalability, and I'd love to learn more about it. What opportunities are there at this company to learn about this?"
2. "I'm not familiar with technology X, but it sounds like a very interesting solution. Could you tell me a bit more about how it works?"

▸ Know Your Technical Projects

As part of your preparation, you should focus on two or three technical projects that you should deeply master. Select projects that ideally fit the following criteria:

- The project had challenging components (beyond just "learning a lot").
- You played a central role (ideally on the challenging components).
- You can talk at technical depth.

For those projects, and all your projects, be able to talk about the challenges, mistakes, technical decisions, choices of technologies (and tradeoffs of these), and the things you would do differently.

You can also think about follow-up questions, like how you would scale the application.

Responding to Behavioral Questions

Behavioral questions allow your interviewer to get to know you and your prior experience better. Remember the following advice when responding to questions.

Be Specific, Not Arrogant

Arrogance is a red flag, but you still want to make yourself sound impressive. So how do you make yourself sound good without being arrogant? By being specific!

Specificity means giving just the facts and letting the interviewer derive an interpretation. For example, rather than saying that you "did all the hard parts," you can instead describe the specific bits you did that were challenging.

Limit Details

When a candidate blabbers on about a problem, it's hard for an interviewer who isn't well versed in the subject or project to understand it.

Stay light on details and just state the key points. When possible, try to translate it or at least explain the impact. You can always offer the interviewer the opportunity to drill in further.

> "By examining the most common user behavior and applying the Rabin-Karp algorithm, I designed a new algorithm to reduce search from `O(n)` to `O(log n)` in 90% of cases. I can go into more details if you'd like."

This demonstrates the key points while letting your interviewer ask for more details if he wants to.

Focus on Yourself, Not Your Team

Interviews are fundamentally an individual assessment. Unfortunately, when you listen to many candidates (especially those in leadership roles), their answers are about "we", "us", and "the team." The interviewer walks away having little idea what the candidate's actual impact was and might conclude that the candidate did little.

Pay attention to your answers. Listen for how much you say "we" versus "I." Assume that every question is about your role, and speak to that.

Give Structured Answers

There are two common ways to think about structuring responses to a behavioral question: nugget first and S.A.R. These techniques can be used separately or together.

Nugget First

Nugget First means starting your response with a "nugget" that succinctly describes what your response will be about.

For example:

- Interviewer: "Tell me about a time you had to persuade a group of people to make a big change."
- Candidate: "Sure, let me tell you about the time when I convinced my school to let undergraduates teach their own courses. Initially, my school had a rule where..."

This technique grabs your interviewer's attention and makes it very clear what your story will be about. It also helps you be more focused in your communication, since you've made it very clear to yourself what the gist of your response is.

S.A.R. (Situation, Action, Result)

The S.A.R. approach means that you start off outlining the situation, then explaining the actions you took, and lastly, describing the result.

Example: "Tell me about a challenging interaction with a teammate."

- **Situation:** On my operating systems project, I was assigned to work with three other people. While two were great, the third team member didn't contribute much. He stayed quiet during meetings, rarely chipped in during email discussions, and struggled to complete his components. This was an issue not only because it shifted more work onto us, but also because we didn't know if we could count on him.
- **Action:** I didn't want to write him off completely yet, so I tried to resolve the situation. I did three things.

  First, I wanted to understand why he was acting like this. Was it laziness? Was he busy with something else? I struck up a conversation with him and then asked him open-ended questions about how he felt it was going. Interestingly, basically out of nowhere, he said that he wanted to take on the writeup, which is one of the most time intensive parts. This showed me that it wasn't laziness; it was that he didn't feel like he was good enough to write code.

  Second, now that I understand the cause, I tried to make it clear that he shouldn't fear messing up. I told him about some of the bigger mistakes that I made and admitted that I wasn't clear about a lot of parts of the project either.

  Third and finally, I asked him to help me with breaking out some of the components of the project. We sat down together and designed a thorough spec for one of the big component, in much more detail than we had before. Once he could see all the pieces, it helped show him that the project wasn't as scary as he'd assumed.
- **Result:** With his confidence raised, he now offered to take on a bunch of the smaller coding work, and then eventually some of the biggest parts. He finished all his work on time, and he contributed more in discussions. We were happy to work with him on a future project.

The situation and the result should be succinct. Your interviewer generally does not need many details to understand what happened and, in fact, may be confused by them.

By using the S.A.R. model with clear situations, actions and results, the interviewer will be able to easily identify how you made an impact and why it mattered.

Consider putting your stories into the following grid:

	Nugget	Situation	Action(s)	Result	What It Says
Story 1			1. ... 2. ... 3. ...		
Story 2					

Explore the Action

In almost all cases, the "action" is the most important part of the story. Unfortunately, far too many people talk on and on about the situation, but then just breeze through the action.

Instead, dive into the action. Where possible, break down the action into multiple parts. For example: "I did three things. First, I..." This will encourage sufficient depth.

Think About What It Says

Re-read the story on page 35. What personality attributes has the candidate demonstrated?

- **Initiative/Leadership:** The candidate tried to resolve the situation by addressing it head-on.
- **Empathy:** The candidate tried to understand what was happening to the person. The candidate also showed empathy in knowing what would resolve the teammate's insecurity.
- **Compassion:** Although the teammate was harming the team, the candidate wasn't angry at the teammate. His empathy led him to compassion.
- **Humility:** The candidate was able to admit to his own flaws (not only to the teammate, but also to the interviewer).
- **Teamwork/Helpfulness:** The candidate worked with the teammate to break down the project into manageable chunks.

You should think about your stories from this perspective. Analyze the actions you took and how you reacted. What personality attributes does your reaction demonstrate?

In many cases, the answer is "none." That usually means you need to rework how you communicate the story to make the attribute clearer. You don't want to explicitly say, "I did X because I have empathy," but you can go one step away from that. For example:

- **Less Clear Attribute:** "I called up the client and told him what happened."
- **More Clear Attribute (Empathy and Courage):** "I made sure to call the client myself, because I knew that he would appreciate hearing it directly from me."

If you still can't make the personality attributes clear, then you might need to come up with a new story entirely.

▸ So, tell me about yourself...

Many interviewers kick off the session by asking you to tell them a bit about yourself, or asking you to walk through your resume. This is essentially a "pitch". It's your interviewer's first impression of you, so you want to be sure to nail this.

Structure

A typical structure that works well for many people is essentially chronological, with the opening sentence describing their current job and the conclusion discussing their relevant and interesting hobbies outside of work (if any).

1. **Current Role [Headline Only]:** "I'm a software engineer at Microworks, where I've been leading the Android team for the last five years."
2. **College:** My background is in computer science. I did my undergrad at Berkeley and spent a few summers working at startups, including one where I attempted to launch my own business.
3. **Post College & Onwards:** After college, I wanted to get some exposure to larger corporations so I joined Amazon as a developer. It was a great experience. I learned a ton about large system design and I got to really drive the launch of a key part of AWS. That actually showed me that I really wanted to be in a more

entrepreneurial environment.

4. **Current Role [Details]:** One of my old managers from Amazon recruited me out to join her startup, which was what brought me to Microworks. Here, I did the initial system architecture, which has scaled pretty well with our rapid growth. I then took an opportunity to lead the Android team. I do manage a team of three, but my role is primarily with technical leadership: architecture, coding, etc.
5. **Outside of Work:** Outside of work, I've been participating in some hackathons—mostly doing iOS development there as a way to learn it more deeply. I'm also active as a moderator on online forums around Android development.
6. **Wrap Up:** I'm looking now for something new, and your company caught my eye. I've always loved the connection with the user, and I really want to get back to a smaller environment too.

This structure works well for about 95% of candidates. For candidate with more experience, you might condense part of it. Ten years from now, the candidate's initial statements might become just: "After my CS degree from Berkeley, I spent a few years at Amazon and then joined a startup where I led the Android team."

Hobbies

Think carefully about your hobbies. You may or may not want to discuss them.

Often they're just fluff. If your hobby is just generic activities like skiing or playing with your dog, you can probably skip it.

Sometimes though, hobbies can be useful. This often happens when:

- The hobby is extremely unique (e.g., fire breathing). It may strike up a bit of a conversation and kick off the interview on a more amiable note.
- The hobby is technical. This not only boosts your actual skillset, but it also shows passion for technology.
- The hobby demonstrates a positive personality attribute. A hobby like "remodeling your house yourself" shows a drive to learn new things, take some risks, and get your hands dirty (literally and figuratively).

It would rarely hurt to mention hobbies, so when in doubt, you might as well.

Think about how to best frame your hobby though. Do you have any successes or specific work to show from it (e.g., landing a part in a play)? Is there a personality attribute this hobby demonstrates?

Sprinkle in Shows of Successes

In the above pitch, the candidate has casually dropped in some highlights of his background.

- He specifically mentioned that he was recruited out of Microworks by his old manager, which shows that he was successful at Amazon.
- He also mentions wanting to be in a smaller environment, which shows some element of culture fit (assuming this is a startup he's applying for).
- He mentions some successes he's had, such as launching a key part of AWS and architecting a scalable system.
- He mentions his hobbies, both of which show a drive to learn.

When you think about your pitch, think about what different aspects of your background say about you. Can you can drop in shows of successes (awards, promotions, being recruited out by someone you worked with, launches, etc.)? What do you want to communicate about yourself?

VI

Big O

This is such an important concept that we are dedicating an entire (long!) chapter to it.

Big O time is the language and metric we use to describe the efficiency of algorithms. Not understanding it thoroughly can really hurt you in developing an algorithm. Not only might you be judged harshly for not really understanding big O, but you will also struggle to judge when your algorithm is getting faster or slower.

Master this concept.

▸ An Analogy

Imagine the following scenario: You've got a file on a hard drive and you need to send it to your friend who lives across the country. You need to get the file to your friend as fast as possible. How should you send it?

Most people's first thought would be email, FTP, or some other means of electronic transfer. That thought is reasonable, but only half correct.

If it's a small file, you're certainly right. It would take 5 - 10 hours to get to an airport, hop on a flight, and then deliver it to your friend.

But what if the file were really, really large? Is it possible that it's faster to physically deliver it via plane?

Yes, actually it is. A one-terabyte (1 TB) file could take more than a day to transfer electronically. It would be much faster to just fly it across the country. If your file is that urgent (and cost isn't an issue), you might just want to do that.

What if there were no flights, and instead you had to drive across the country? Even then, for a really huge file, it would be faster to drive.

▸ Time Complexity

This is what the concept of asymptotic runtime, or big O time, means. We could describe the data transfer "algorithm" runtime as:

- Electronic Transfer: `O(s)`, where `s` is the size of the file. This means that the time to transfer the file increases linearly with the size of the file. (Yes, this is a bit of a simplification, but that's okay for these purposes.)
- Airplane Transfer: `O(1)` with respect to the size of the file. As the size of the file increases, it won't take any longer to get the file to your friend. The time is constant.

No matter how big the constant is and how slow the linear increase is, linear will at some point surpass constant.

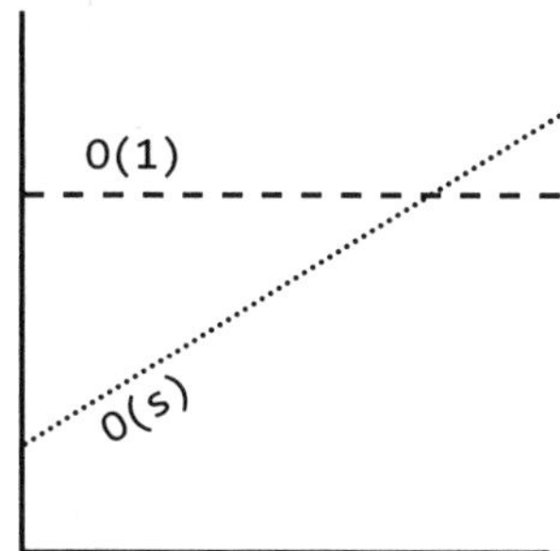

There are many more runtimes than this. Some of the most common ones are `O(log N)`, `O(N log N)`, `O(N)`, `O(N²)` and `O(2^N)`. There's no fixed list of possible runtimes, though.

You can also have multiple variables in your runtime. For example, the time to paint a fence that's w meters wide and h meters high could be described as `O(wh)`. If you needed p layers of paint, then you could say that the time is `O(whp)`.

Big O, Big Theta, and Big Omega

If you've never covered big O in an academic setting, you can probably skip this subsection. It might confuse you more than it helps. This "FYI" is mostly here to clear up ambiguity in wording for people who have learned big O before, so that they don't say, "But I thought big O meant..."

Academics use big O, big Θ (theta), and big Ω (omega) to describe runtimes.

- **O (big O):** In academia, big O describes an upper bound on the time. An algorithm that prints all the values in an array could be described as $O(N)$, but it could also be described as $O(N^2)$, $O(N^3)$, or $O(2^N)$ (or many other big O times). The algorithm is at least as fast as each of these; therefore they are upper bounds on the runtime. This is similar to a less-than-or-equal-to relationship. If Bob is X years old (I'll assume no one lives past age 130), then you could say $X \leq 130$. It would also be correct to say that $X \leq 1,000$ or $X \leq 1,000,000$. It's technically true (although not terribly useful). Likewise, a simple algorithm to print the values in an array is $O(N)$ as well as $O(N^3)$ or any runtime bigger than $O(N)$.
- **Ω (big omega):** In academia, Ω is the equivalent concept but for lower bound. Printing the values in an array is $\Omega(N)$ as well as $\Omega(\log N)$ and $\Omega(1)$. After all, you know that it won't be *faster* than those runtimes.
- **Θ (big theta):** In academia, Θ means both O and Ω. That is, an algorithm is $\Theta(N)$ if it is both $O(N)$ and $\Omega(N)$. Θ gives a tight bound on runtime.

In industry (and therefore in interviews), people seem to have merged Θ and O together. Industry's meaning of big O is closer to what academics mean by Θ, in that it would be seen as incorrect to describe printing an array as $O(N^2)$. Industry would just say this is $O(N)$.

For this book, we will use big O in the way that industry tends to use it: By always trying to offer the tightest description of the runtime.

Best Case, Worst Case, and Expected Case

We can actually describe our runtime for an algorithm in three different ways.

Let's look at this from the perspective of quick sort. Quick sort picks a random element as a "pivot" and then swaps values in the array such that the elements less than pivot appear before elements greater than pivot. This gives a "partial sort." Then it recursively sorts the left and right sides using a similar process.

- **Best Case:** If all elements are equal, then quick sort will, on average, just traverse through the array once. This is `O(N)`. (This actually depends slightly on the implementation of quick sort. There are implementations, though, that will run very quickly on a sorted array.)
- **Worst Case:** What if we get really unlucky and the pivot is repeatedly the biggest element in the array? (Actually, this can easily happen. If the pivot is chosen to be the first element in the subarray and the array is sorted in reverse order, we'll have this situation.) In this case, our recursion doesn't divide the array in half and recurse on each half. It just shrinks the subarray by one element. This will degenerate to an $O(N^2)$ runtime.
- **Expected Case:** Usually, though, these wonderful or terrible situations won't happen. Sure, sometimes the pivot will be very low or very high, but it won't happen over and over again. We can expect a runtime of `O(N log N)`.

We rarely ever discuss best case time complexity, because it's not a very useful concept. After all, we could take essentially any algorithm, special case some input, and then get an `O(1)` time in the best case.

For many—probably most—algorithms, the worst case and the expected case are the same. Sometimes they're different, though, and we need to describe both of the runtimes.

What is the relationship between best/worst/expected case and big O/theta/omega?

It's easy for candidates to muddle these concepts (probably because both have some concepts of "higher", "lower" and "exactly right"), but there is no particular relationship between the concepts.

Best, worst, and expected cases describe the big O (or big theta) time for particular inputs or scenarios.

Big O, big omega, and big theta describe the upper, lower, and tight bounds for the runtime.

Space Complexity

Time is not the only thing that matters in an algorithm. We might also care about the amount of memory—or space—required by an algorithm.

Space complexity is a parallel concept to time complexity. If we need to create an array of size n, this will require `O(n)` space. If we need a two-dimensional array of size nxn, this will require $O(n^2)$ space.

Stack space in recursive calls counts, too. For example, code like this would take `O(n)` time and `O(n)` space.

```
int sum(int n) { /* Ex 1.*/
   if (n <= 0) {
      return 0;
   }
   return n + sum(n-1);
}
```

Each call adds a level to the stack.

```
sum(4)
   -> sum(3)
      -> sum(2)
         -> sum(1)
            -> sum(0)
```

Each of these calls is added to the call stack and takes up actual memory.

However, just because you have n calls total doesn't mean it takes O(n) space. Consider the below function, which adds adjacent elements between 0 and n:

```
int pairSumSequence(int n) { /* Ex 2.*/
   int sum = 0;
   for (int i = 0; i < n; i++) {
      sum += pairSum(i, i + 1);
   }
   return sum;
}

int pairSum(int a, int b) {
   return a + b;
}
```

There will be roughly O(n) calls to `pairSum`. However, those calls do not exist simultaneously on the call stack, so you only need O(1) space.

▸ Drop the Constants

It is very possible for O(N) code to run faster than O(1) code for specific inputs. Big O just describes the rate of increase.

For this reason, we drop the constants in runtime. An algorithm that one might have described as O(2N) is actually O(N).

Many people resist doing this. They will see code that has two (non-nested) for loops and continue this O(2N). They think they're being more "precise." They're not.

Consider the below code:

Min and Max 1

```
int min = Integer.MAX_VALUE;
int max = Integer.MIN_VALUE;
for (int x : array) {
   if (x < min) min = x;
   if (x > max) max = x;
}
```

Min and Max 2

```
int min = Integer.MAX_VALUE;
int max = Integer.MIN_VALUE;
for (int x : array) {
   if (x < min) min = x;
}
for (int x : array) {
   if (x > max) max = x;
}
```

Which one is faster? The first one does one for loop and the other one does two for loops. But then, the first solution has two lines of code per for loop rather than one.

If you're going to count the number of instructions, then you'd have to go to the assembly level and take into account that multiplication requires more instructions than addition, how the compiler would optimize something, and all sorts of other details.

This would be horrendously complicated, so don't even start going down this road. Big O allows us to express how the runtime scales. We just need to accept that it doesn't mean that O(N) is always better than $O(N^2)$.

Drop the Non-Dominant Terms

What do you do about an expression such as $O(N^2 + N)$? That second N isn't exactly a constant. But it's not especially important.

We already said that we drop constants. Therefore, $O(N^2 + N^2)$ would be $O(N^2)$. If we don't care about that latter N^2 term, why would we care about N? We don't.

You should drop the non-dominant terms.

- $O(N^2 + N)$ becomes $O(N^2)$.
- $O(N + \log N)$ becomes $O(N)$.
- $O(5*2^N + 1000N^{100})$ becomes $O(2^N)$.

We might still have a sum in a runtime. For example, the expression $O(B^2 + A)$ cannot be reduced (without some special knowledge of A and B).

The following graph depicts the rate of increase for some of the common big O times.

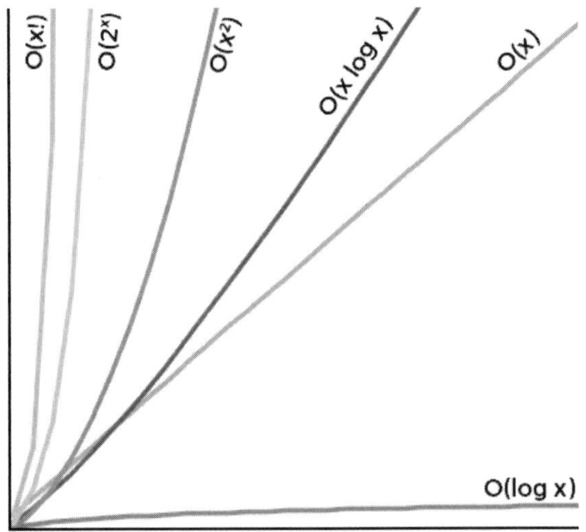

As you can see, $O(x^2)$ is much worse than $O(x)$, but it's not nearly as bad as $O(2^x)$ or $O(x!)$. There are lots of runtimes worse than $O(x!)$ too, such as $O(x^x)$ or $O(2^x * x!)$.

Multi-Part Algorithms: Add vs. Multiply

Suppose you have an algorithm that has two steps. When do you multiply the runtimes and when do you add them?

This is a common source of confusion for candidates.

Add the Runtimes: O(A + B)

```
for (int a : arrA) {
  print(a);
}

for (int b : arrB) {
  print(b);
}
```

Multiply the Runtimes: O(A*B)

```
for (int a : arrA) {
  for (int b : arrB) {
    print(a + "," + b);
  }
}
```

In the example on the left, we do A chunks of work then B chunks of work. Therefore, the total amount of work is O(A + B).

In the example on the right, we do B chunks of work for each element in A. Therefore, the total amount of work is O(A * B).

In other words:

- If your algorithm is in the form "do this, then, when you're all done, do that" then you add the runtimes.
- If your algorithm is in the form "do this for each time you do that" then you multiply the runtimes.

It's very easy to mess this up in an interview, so be careful.

Amortized Time

An ArrayList, or a dynamically resizing array, allows you to have the benefits of an array while offering flexibility in size. You won't run out of space in the ArrayList since its capacity will grow as you insert elements.

An ArrayList is implemented with an array. When the array hits capacity, the ArrayList class will create a new array with double the capacity and copy all the elements over to the new array.

How do you describe the runtime of insertion? This is a tricky question.

The array could be full. If the array contains N elements, then inserting a new element will take O(N) time. You will have to create a new array of size 2N and then copy N elements over. This insertion will take O(N) time.

However, we also know that this doesn't happen very often. The vast majority of the time insertion will be in O(1) time.

We need a concept that takes both into account. This is what amortized time does. It allows us to describe that, yes, this worst case happens every once in a while. But once it happens, it won't happen again for so long that the cost is "amortized."

In this case, what is the amortized time?

As we insert elements, we double the capacity when the size of the array is a power of 2. So after X elements, we double the capacity at array sizes 1, 2, 4, 8, 16, ..., X. That doubling takes, respectively, 1, 2, 4, 8, 16, 32, 64, ..., X copies.

What is the sum of 1 + 2 + 4 + 8 + 16 + ... + X? If you read this sum left to right, it starts with 1 and doubles until it gets to X. If you read right to left, it starts with X and halves until it gets to 1.

What then is the sum of $X + \frac{X}{2} + \frac{X}{4} + \frac{X}{8} + ... + 1$? This is roughly 2X.

Therefore, X insertions take O(2X) time. The amortized time for each insertion is O(1).

Log N Runtimes

We commonly see `O(log N)` in runtimes. Where does this come from?

Let's look at binary search as an example. In binary search, we are looking for an example x in an N-element sorted array. We first compare x to the midpoint of the array. If `x == middle`, then we return. If `x < middle`, then we search on the left side of the array. If `x > middle`, then we search on the right side of the array.

```
search 9 within {1, 5, 8, 9, 11, 13, 15, 19, 21}
    compare 9 to 11 -> smaller.
    search 9 within {1, 5, 8, 9}
        compare 9 to 8 -> bigger
        search 9 within {9}
            compare 9 to 9
            return
```

We start off with an N-element array to search. Then, after a single step, we're down to $N/2$ elements. One more step, and we're down to $N/4$ elements. We stop when we either find the value or we're down to just one element.

The total runtime is then a matter of how many steps (dividing N by 2 each time) we can take until N becomes 1.

```
N = 16
N = 8       /* divide by 2 */
N = 4       /* divide by 2 */
N = 2       /* divide by 2 */
N = 1       /* divide by 2 */
```

We could look at this in reverse (going from 1 to 16 instead of 16 to 1). How many times we can multiply 1 by 2 until we get N?

```
N = 1
N = 2       /* multiply by 2 */
N = 4       /* multiply by 2 */
N = 8       /* multiply by 2 */
N = 16      /* multiply by 2 */
```

What is k in the expression $2^k = N$? This is exactly what `log` expresses.

$$2^4 = 16 \rightarrow \log_2 16 = 4$$
$$\log_2 N = k \rightarrow 2^k = N$$

This is a good takeaway for you to have. When you see a problem where the number of elements in the problem space gets halved each time, that will likely be a `O(log N)` runtime.

This is the same reason why finding an element in a balanced binary search tree is `O(log N)`. With each comparison, we go either left or right. Half the nodes are on each side, so we cut the problem space in half each time.

> What's the base of the log? That's an excellent question! The short answer is that it doesn't matter for the purposes of big O. The longer explanation can be found at "Bases of Logs" on page 630.

Recursive Runtimes

Here's a tricky one. What's the runtime of this code?

```
int f(int n) {
```

```
    if (n <= 1) {
        return 1;
    }
    return f(n - 1) + f(n - 1);
}
```

A lot of people will, for some reason, see the two calls to `f` and jump to $O(N^2)$. This is completely incorrect.

Rather than making assumptions, let's derive the runtime by walking through the code. Suppose we call `f(4)`. This calls `f(3)` twice. Each of those calls to `f(3)` calls `f(2)`, until we get down to `f(1)`.

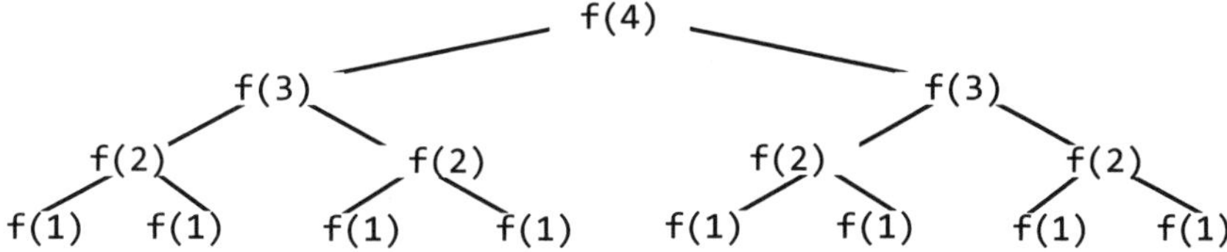

How many calls are in this tree? (Don't count!)

The tree will have depth N. Each node (i.e., function call) has two children. Therefore, each level will have twice as many calls as the one above it. The number of nodes on each level is:

Level	# Nodes	Also expressed as...	Or...
0	1		2^0
1	2	2 * previous level = 2	2^1
2	4	2 * previous level = $2 * 2^1 = 2^2$	2^2
3	8	2 * previous level = $2 * 2^2 = 2^3$	2^3
4	16	2 * previous level = $2 * 2^3 = 2^4$	2^4

Therefore, there will be $2^0 + 2^1 + 2^2 + 2^3 + 2^4 + \ldots + 2^N$ (which is $2^{N+1} - 1$) nodes. (See "Sum of Powers of 2" on page 630.)

Try to remember this pattern. When you have a recursive function that makes multiple calls, the runtime will often (but not always) look like $O(\text{branches}^{\text{depth}})$, where branches is the number of times each recursive call branches. In this case, this gives us $O(2^N)$.

> As you may recall, the base of a log doesn't matter for big O since logs of different bases are only different by a constant factor. However, this does not apply to exponents. The base of an exponent does matter. Compare 2^n and 8^n. If you expand 8^n, you get $(2^3)^n$, which equals 2^{3n}, which equals $2^{2n} * 2^n$. As you can see, 8^n and 2^n are different by a factor of 2^{2n}. That is very much not a constant factor!

The space complexity of this algorithm will be $O(N)$. Although we have $O(2^N)$ nodes in the tree total, only $O(N)$ exist at any given time. Therefore, we would only need to have $O(N)$ memory available.

▸ Examples and Exercises

Big O time is a difficult concept at first. However, once it "clicks," it gets fairly easy. The same patterns come up again and again, and the rest you can derive.

We'll start off easy and get progressively more difficult.

Example 1

What is the runtime of the below code?

```
void foo(int[] array) {
   int sum = 0;
   int product = 1;
   for (int i = 0; i < array.length; i++) {
      sum += array[i];
   }
   for (int i = 0; i < array.length; i++) {
      product *= array[i];
   }
   System.out.println(sum + ", " + product);
}
```

This will take O(N) time. The fact that we iterate through the array twice doesn't matter.

Example 2

What is the runtime of the below code?

```
void printPairs(int[] array) {
   for (int i = 0; i < array.length; i++) {
      for (int j = 0; j < array.length; j++) {
         System.out.println(array[i] + "," + array[j]);
      }
   }
}
```

The inner for loop has O(N) iterations and it is called N times. Therefore, the runtime is $O(N^2)$.

Another way we can see this is by inspecting what the "meaning" of the code is. It is printing all pairs (two-element sequences). There are $O(N^2)$ pairs; therefore, the runtime is $O(N^2)$.

Example 3

This is very similar code to the above example, but now the inner for loop starts at `i + 1`.

```
void printUnorderedPairs(int[] array) {
   for (int i = 0; i < array.length; i++) {
      for (int j = i + 1; j < array.length; j++) {
         System.out.println(array[i] + "," + array[j]);
      }
   }
}
```

We can derive the runtime several ways.

> This pattern of for loop is very common. It's important that you know the runtime and that you deeply understand it. You can't rely on just memorizing common runtimes. Deep comprehension is important.

Counting the Iterations

The first time through `j` runs for `N-1` steps. The second time, it's `N-2` steps. Then `N-3` steps. And so on.

Therefore, the number of steps total is:

```
(N-1) + (N-2) + (N-3) + ... + 2 + 1
```

```
= 1 + 2 + 3 + ... + N-1
= sum of 1 through N-1
```

The sum of 1 through `N-1` is $\frac{N(N-1)}{2}$ (see "Sum of Integers 1 through N" on page 630), so the runtime will be $O(N^2)$.

What It Means

Alternatively, we can figure out the runtime by thinking about what the code "means." It iterates through each pair of values for `(i, j)` where `j` is bigger than `i`.

There are N^2 total pairs. Roughly half of those will have `i < j` and the remaining half will have `i > j`. This code goes through roughly $N^2/2$ pairs so it does $O(N^2)$ work.

Visualizing What It Does

The code iterates through the following `(i, j)` pairs when `N = 8`:

```
(0, 1) (0, 2) (0, 3) (0, 4) (0, 5) (0, 6) (0, 7)
       (1, 2) (1, 3) (1, 4) (1, 5) (1, 6) (1, 7)
              (2, 3) (2, 4) (2, 5) (2, 6) (2, 7)
                     (3, 4) (3, 5) (3, 6) (3, 7)
                            (4, 5) (4, 6) (4, 7)
                                   (5, 6) (5, 7)
                                          (6, 7)
```

This looks like half of an NxN matrix, which has size (roughly) $N^2/2$. Therefore, it takes $O(N^2)$ time.

Average Work

We know that the outer loop runs N times. How much work does the inner loop do? It varies across iterations, but we can think about the average iteration.

What is the average value of `1, 2, 3, 4, 5, 6, 7, 8, 9, 10`? The average value will be in the middle, so it will be *roughly* 5. (We could give a more precise answer, of course, but we don't need to for big O.)

What about for `1, 2, 3, ..., N`? The average value in this sequence is `N/2`.

Therefore, since the inner loop does $N/2$ work on average and it is run N times, the total work is $N^2/2$ which is $O(N^2)$.

Example 4

This is similar to the above, but now we have two different arrays.

```
void printUnorderedPairs(int[] arrayA, int[] arrayB) {
  for (int i = 0; i < arrayA.length; i++) {
    for (int j = 0; j < arrayB.length; j++) {
      if (arrayA[i] < arrayB[j]) {
        System.out.println(arrayA[i] + "," + arrayB[j]);
      }
    }
  }
}
```

We can break up this analysis. The if-statement within `j`'s for loop is `O(1)` time since it's just a sequence of constant-time statements.

We now have this:

```
void printUnorderedPairs(int[] arrayA, int[] arrayB) {
```

```
    for (int i = 0; i < arrayA.length; i++) {
        for (int j = 0; j < arrayB.length; j++) {
            /* O(1) work */
        }
    }
}
```

For each element of arrayA, the inner for loop goes through b iterations, where b = arrayB.length. If a = arrayA.length, then the runtime is O(ab).

If you said $O(N^2)$, then remember your mistake for the future. It's not $O(N^2)$ because there are two different inputs. Both matter. This is an extremely common mistake.

Example 5

What about this strange bit of code?

```
void printUnorderedPairs(int[] arrayA, int[] arrayB) {
    for (int i = 0; i < arrayA.length; i++) {
        for (int j = 0; j < arrayB.length; j++) {
            for (int k = 0; k < 100000; k++) {
                System.out.println(arrayA[i] + "," + arrayB[j]);
            }
        }
    }
}
```

Nothing has really changed here. 100,000 units of work is still constant, so the runtime is O(ab).

Example 6

The following code reverses an array. What is its runtime?

```
void reverse(int[] array) {
    for (int i = 0; i < array.length / 2; i++) {
        int other = array.length - i - 1;
        int temp = array[i];
        array[i] = array[other];
        array[other] = temp;
    }
}
```

This algorithm runs in O(N) time. The fact that it only goes through half of the array (in terms of iterations) does not impact the big O time.

Example 7

Which of the following are equivalent to O(N)? Why?

- O(N + P), where $P < \frac{N}{2}$
- O(2N)
- O(N + log N)
- O(N + M)

Let's go through these.

- If $P < \frac{N}{2}$, then we know that N is the dominant term so we can drop the O(P).
- O(2N) is O(N) since we drop constants.

- O(N) dominates O(log N), so we can drop the O(log N).
- There is no established relationship between N and M, so we have to keep both variables in there.

Therefore, all but the last one are equivalent to O(N).

Example 8

Suppose we had an algorithm that took in an array of strings, sorted each string, and then sorted the full array. What would the runtime be?

Many candidates will reason the following: sorting each string is O(N log N) and we have to do this for each string, so that's O(N*N log N). We also have to sort this array, so that's an additional O(N log N) work. Therefore, the total runtime is $O(N^2 \log N + N \log N)$, which is just $O(N^2 \log N)$.

This is completely incorrect. Did you catch the error?

The problem is that we used N in two different ways. In one case, it's the length of the string (which string?). And in another case, it's the length of the array.

In your interviews, you can prevent this error by either not using the variable "N" at all, or by only using it when there is no ambiguity as to what N could represent.

In fact, I wouldn't even use a and b here, or m and n. It's too easy to forget which is which and mix them up. An $O(a^2)$ runtime is completely different from an O(a*b) runtime.

Let's define new terms—and use names that are logical.

- Let s be the length of the longest string.
- Let a be the length of the array.

Now we can work through this in parts:

- Sorting each string is O(s log s).
- We have to do this for every string (and there are a strings), so that's O(a*s log s).
- Now we have to sort all the strings. There are a strings, so you may be inclined to say that this takes O(a log a) time. This is what most candidates would say. You should also take into account that you need to compare the strings. Each string comparison takes O(s) time. There are O(a log a) comparisons, therefore this will take O(a*s log a) time.

If you add up these two parts, you get O(a*s(log a + log s)).

This is it. There is no way to reduce it further.

Example 9

The following simple code sums the values of all the nodes in a balanced binary search tree. What is its runtime?

```
int sum(Node node) {
   if (node == null) {
      return 0;
   }
   return sum(node.left) + node.value + sum(node.right);
}
```

Just because it's a binary search tree doesn't mean that there is a log in it!

We can look at this two ways.

What It Means

The most straightforward way is to think about what this means. This code touches each node in the tree once and does a constant time amount of work with each "touch" (excluding the recursive calls).

Therefore, the runtime will be linear in terms of the number of nodes. If there are N nodes, then the runtime is O(N).

Recursive Pattern

On page 44, we discussed a pattern for the runtime of recursive functions that have multiple branches. Let's try that approach here.

We said that the runtime of a recursive function with multiple branches is typically $O(branches^{depth})$. There are two branches at each call, so we're looking at $O(2^{depth})$.

At this point many people might assume that something went wrong since we have an exponential algorithm—that something in our logic is flawed or that we've inadvertently created an exponential time algorithm (yikes!).

The second statement is correct. We do have an exponential time algorithm, but it's not as bad as one might think. Consider what variable it's exponential with respect to.

What is `depth`? The tree is a balanced binary search tree. Therefore, if there are N total nodes, then `depth` is roughly `log N`.

By the equation above, we get $O(2^{\log N})$.

Recall what $\log_2$ means:

$$2^P = Q \rightarrow \log_2 Q = P$$

What is $2^{\log N}$? There is a relationship between 2 and log, so we should be able to simplify this.

Let $P = 2^{\log N}$. By the definition of $\log_2$, we can write this as $\log_2 P = \log_2 N$. This means that $P = N$.

$$\begin{aligned} &\text{Let } P = 2^{\log N} \\ &\quad \rightarrow \log_2 P = \log_2 N \\ &\quad \rightarrow P = N \\ &\quad \rightarrow 2^{\log N} = N \end{aligned}$$

Therefore, the runtime of this code is O(N), where N is the number of nodes.

Example 10

The following method checks if a number is prime by checking for divisibility on numbers less than it. It only needs to go up to the square root of n because if n is divisible by a number greater than its square root then it's divisible by something smaller than it.

For example, while 33 is divisible by 11 (which is greater than the square root of 33), the "counterpart" to 11 is 3 (3 * 11 = 33). 33 will have already been eliminated as a prime number by 3.

What is the time complexity of this function?

```
boolean isPrime(int n) {
   for (int x = 2; x * x <= n; x++) {
      if (n % x == 0) {
         return false;
      }
   }
   return true;
```

```
}
```

Many people get this question wrong. If you're careful about your logic, it's fairly easy.

The work inside the for loop is constant. Therefore, we just need to know how many iterations the for loop goes through in the worst case.

The for loop will start when x = 2 and end when x*x = n. Or, in other words, it stops when x = √n (when x equals the square root of n).

This for loop is really something like this:

```
boolean isPrime(int n) {
   for (int x = 2; x <= sqrt(n); x++) {
      if (n % x == 0) {
         return false;
      }
   }
   return true;
}
```

This runs in O(√n) time.

Example 11

The following code computes n! (n factorial). What is its time complexity?

```
int factorial(int n) {
   if (n < 0) {
      return -1;
   } else if (n == 0) {
      return 1;
   } else {
      return n * factorial(n - 1);
   }
}
```

This is just a straight recursion from n to n-1 to n-2 down to 1. It will take O(n) time.

Example 12

This code counts all permutations of a string.

```
void permutation(String str) {
   permutation(str, “”);
}

void permutation(String str, String prefix) {
   if (str.length() == 0) {
      System.out.println(prefix);
   } else {
      for (int i = 0; i < str.length(); i++) {
         String rem = str.substring(0, i) + str.substring(i + 1);
         permutation(rem, prefix + str.charAt(i));
      }
   }
}
```

This is a (very!) tricky one. We can think about this by looking at how many times `permutation` gets called and how long each call takes. We'll aim for getting as tight of an upper bound as possible.

How many times does permutation get called in its base case?

If we were to generate a permutation, then we would need to pick characters for each "slot." Suppose we had 7 characters in the string. In the first slot, we have 7 choices. Once we pick the letter there, we have 6 choices for the next slot. (Note that this is 6 choices *for each* of the 7 choices earlier.) Then 5 choices for the next slot, and so on.

Therefore, the total number of options is 7 * 6 * 5 * 4 * 3 * 2 * 1, which is also expressed as 7! (7 factorial).

This tells us that there are n! permutations. Therefore, `permutation` is called `n!` times in its base case (when `prefix` is the full permutation).

How many times does permutation get called before its base case?

But, of course, we also need to consider how many times lines 9 through 12 are hit. Picture a large call tree representing all the calls. There are `n!` leaves, as shown above. Each leaf is attached to a path of length n. Therefore, we know there will be no more than `n * n!` nodes (function calls) in this tree.

How long does each function call take?

Executing line 7 takes `O(n)` time since each character needs to be printed.

Line 10 and line 11 will also take `O(n)` time combined, due to the string concatenation. Observe that the sum of the lengths of `rem`, `prefix`, and `str.charAt(i)` will always be n.

Each node in our call tree therefore corresponds to `O(n)` work.

What is the total runtime?

Since we are calling `permutation` `O(n * n!)` times (as an upper bound), and each one takes `O(n)` time, the total runtime will not exceed $O(n^2 * n!)$.

Through more complex mathematics, we can derive a tighter runtime equation (though not necessarily a nice closed-form expression). This would almost certainly be beyond the scope of any normal interview.

Example 13

The following code computes the Nth Fibonacci number.

```
int fib(int n) {
  if (n <= 0) return 0;
  else if (n == 1) return 1;
  return fib(n - 1) + fib(n - 2);
}
```

We can use the earlier pattern we'd established for recursive calls: $O(branches^{depth})$.

There are 2 branches per call, and we go as deep as N, therefore the runtime is $O(2^N)$.

> Through some very complicated math, we can actually get a tighter runtime. The time is indeed exponential, but it's actually closer to $O(1.6^N)$. The reason that it's not exactly $O(2^N)$ is that, at the bottom of the call stack, there is sometimes only one call. It turns out that a lot of the nodes are at the bottom (as is true in most trees), so this single versus double call actually makes a big difference. Saying $O(2^N)$ would suffice for the scope of an interview, though (and is still technically correct, if you read the note about big theta on page 39). You might get "bonus points" if you can recognize that it'll actually be less than that.

Generally speaking, when you see an algorithm with multiple recursive calls, you're looking at exponential runtime.

Example 14

The following code prints all Fibonacci numbers from 0 to n. What is its time complexity?

```
void allFib(int n) {
  for (int i = 0; i < n; i++) {
    System.out.println(i + “: ” + fib(i));
  }
}

int fib(int n) {
  if (n <= 0) return 0;
  else if (n == 1) return 1;
  return fib(n - 1) + fib(n - 2);
}
```

Many people will rush to concluding that since fib(n) takes $O(2^n)$ time and it's called n times, then it's $O(n2^n)$.

Not so fast. Can you find the error in the logic?

The error is that the n is changing. Yes, fib(n) takes $O(2^n)$ time, but it matters what that value of n is.

Instead, let's walk through each call.

fib(1) -> 2^1 steps
fib(2) -> 2^2 steps
fib(3) -> 2^3 steps
fib(4) -> 2^4 steps
...
fib(n) -> 2^n steps

Therefore, the total amount of work is:

$$2^1 + 2^2 + 2^3 + 2^4 + \ldots + 2^n$$

As we showed on page 44, this is 2^{n+1}. Therefore, the runtime to compute the first n Fibonacci numbers (using this terrible algorithm) is still $O(2^n)$.

Example 15

The following code prints all Fibonacci numbers from 0 to n. However, this time, it stores (i.e., caches) previously computed values in an integer array. If it has already been computed, it just returns the cache. What is its runtime?

```
void allFib(int n) {
  int[] memo = new int[n + 1];
  for (int i = 0; i < n; i++) {
    System.out.println(i + “: ” + fib(i, memo));
  }
}

int fib(int n, int[] memo) {
  if (n <= 0) return 0;
  else if (n == 1) return 1;
  else if (memo[n] > 0) return memo[n];

  memo[n] = fib(n - 1, memo) + fib(n - 2, memo);
```

```
    return memo[n];
}
```

Let's walk through what this algorithm does.

```
fib(0) -> return 0
fib(1) -> return 1
fib(2)
    fib(1) -> return 1
    fib(0) -> return 0
    store 1 at memo[2]
fib(3)
    fib(2) -> lookup memo[2] -> return 1
    fib(1) -> return 1
    store 2 at memo[3]
fib(4)
    fib(3) -> lookup memo[3] -> return 2
    fib(2) -> lookup memo[2] -> return 1
    store 3 at memo[4]
fib(5)
    fib(4) -> lookup memo[4] -> return 3
    fib(3) -> lookup memo[3] -> return 2
    store 5 at memo[5]
...
```

At each call to `fib(i)`, we have already computed and stored the values for `fib(i-1)` and `fib(i-2)`. We just look up those values, sum them, store the new result, and return. This takes a constant amount of time.

We're doing a constant amount of work N times, so this is `O(n)` time.

This technique, called memoization, is a very common one to optimize exponential time recursive algorithms.

Example 16

The following function prints the powers of 2 from 1 through n (inclusive). For example, if n is 4, it would print 1, 2, and 4. What is its runtime?

```
int powersOf2(int n) {
   if (n < 1) {
      return 0;
   } else if (n == 1) {
      System.out.println(1);
      return 1;
   } else {
      int prev = powersOf2(n / 2);
      int curr = prev * 2;
      System.out.println(curr);
      return curr;
   }
}
```

There are several ways we could compute this runtime.

What It Does

Let's walk through a call like `powersOf2(50)`.

```
powersOf2(50)
```

```
-> powersOf2(25)
    -> powersOf2(12)
        -> powersOf2(6)
            -> powersOf2(3)
                -> powersOf2(1)
                    -> print & return 1
                print & return 2
            print & return 4
        print & return 8
    print & return 16
print & return 32
```

The runtime, then, is the number of times we can divide 50 (or n) by 2 until we get down to the base case (1). As we discussed on page 44, the number of times we can halve n until we get 1 is `O(log n)`.

What It Means

We can also approach the runtime by thinking about what the code is supposed to be doing. It's supposed to be computing the powers of 2 from 1 through n.

Each call to `powersOf2` results in exactly one number being printed and returned (excluding what happens in the recursive calls). So if the algorithm prints `13` values at the end, then `powersOf2` was called 13 times.

In this case, we are told that it prints all the powers of 2 between 1 and n. Therefore, the number of times the function is called (which will be its runtime) must equal the number of powers of 2 between 1 and n.

There are `log N` powers of 2 between 1 and n. Therefore, the runtime is `O(log n)`.

Rate of Increase

A final way to approach the runtime is to think about how the runtime changes as n gets bigger. After all, this is exactly what big O time means.

If `N` goes from `P` to `P+1`, the number of calls to `powersOfTwo` might not change at all. When will the number of calls to `powersOfTwo` increase? It will increase by 1 each time n doubles in size.

So, each time n doubles, the number of calls to `powersOfTwo` increases by `1`. Therefore, the number of calls to `powersOfTwo` is the number of times you can double `1` until you get n. It is x in the equation $2^x = n$.

What is x? The value of x is `log n`. This is exactly what meant by `x = log n`.

Therefore, the runtime is `O(log n)`.

Additional Problems

VI.1 The following code computes the product of a **and** b. **What is its runtime?**

```
int product(int a, int b) {
    int sum = 0;
    for (int i = 0; i < b; i++) {
        sum += a;
    }
    return sum;
}
```

VI.2 The following code computes a^b. **What is its runtime?**

```
int power(int a, int b) {
```

```
        if (b < 0) {
            return 0; // error
        } else if (b == 0) {
            return 1;
        } else {
            return a * power(a, b - 1);
        }
    }
```

VI.3 The following code computes a % b**. What is its runtime?**

```
int mod(int a, int b) {
    if (b <= 0) {
        return -1;
    }
    int div = a / b;
    return a - div * b;
}
```

VI.4 The following code performs integer division. What is its runtime (assume a and b are both positive)?

```
int div(int a, int b) {
    int count = 0;
    int sum = b;
    while (sum <= a) {
        sum += b;
        count++;
    }
    return count;
}
```

VI.5 The following code computes the [integer] square root of a number. If the number is not a perfect square (there is no integer square root), then it returns -1. It does this by successive guessing. If n is 100, it first guesses 50. Too high? Try something lower – halfway between 1 and 50. What is its runtime?

```
int sqrt(int n) {
    return sqrt_helper(n, 1, n);
}

int sqrt_helper(int n, int min, int max) {
    if (max < min) return -1; // no square root

    int guess = (min + max) / 2;
    if (guess * guess == n) { // found it!
        return guess;
    } else if (guess * guess < n) { // too low
        return sqrt_helper(n, guess + 1, max); // try higher
    } else { // too high
        return sqrt_helper(n, min, guess - 1); // try lower
    }
}
```

VI.6 The following code computes the [integer] square root of a number. If the number is not a perfect square (there is no integer square root), then it returns -1. It does this by trying increasingly large numbers until it finds the right value (or is too high). What is its runtime?

```
int sqrt(int n) {
    for (int guess = 1; guess * guess <= n; guess++) {
        if (guess * guess == n) {
```

```
                return guess;
            }
        }
        return -1;
    }
```

VI.7 **If a binary search tree is not balanced, how long might it take (worst case) to find an element in it?**

VI.8 **You are looking for a specific value in a binary tree, but the tree is not a binary search tree. What is the time complexity of this?**

VI.9 **The appendToNew method appends a value to an array by creating a new, longer array and returning this longer array. You've used the appendToNew method to create a copyArray function that repeatedly calls appendToNew. How long does copying an array take?**

```
int[] copyArray(int[] array) {
    int[] copy = new int[0];
    for (int value : array) {
        copy = appendToNew(copy, value);
    }
    return copy;
}

int[] appendToNew(int[] array, int value) {
    // copy all elements over to new array
    int[] bigger = new int[array.length + 1];
    for (int i = 0; i < array.length; i++) {
        bigger[i] = array[i];
    }

    // add new element
    bigger[bigger.length - 1] = value;
    return bigger;
}
```

VI.10 **The following code sums the digits in a number. What is its big O time?**

```
int sumDigits(int n) {
    int sum = 0;
    while (n > 0) {
        sum += n % 10;
        n /= 10;
    }
    return sum;
}
```

VI.11 **The following code prints all strings of length k where the characters are in sorted order. It does this by generating all strings of length k and then checking if each is sorted. What is its runtime?**

```
int numChars = 26;

void printSortedStrings(int remaining) {
    printSortedStrings(remaining, "");
}

void printSortedStrings(int remaining, String prefix) {
    if (remaining == 0) {
        if (isInOrder(prefix)) {
            System.out.println(prefix);
```

```
            }
        } else {
            for (int i = 0; i < numChars; i++) {
                char c = ithLetter(i);
                printSortedStrings(remaining - 1, prefix + c);
            }
        }
    }

    boolean isInOrder(String s) {
        for (int i = 1; i < s.length(); i++) {
            int prev = ithLetter(s.charAt(i - 1));
            int curr = ithLetter(s.charAt(i));
            if (prev > curr) {
                return false;
            }
        }
        return true;
    }

    char ithLetter(int i) {
        return (char) (((int) 'a') + i);
    }
```

VI.12 The following code computes the intersection (the number of elements in common) of two arrays. It assumes that neither array has duplicates. It computes the intersection by sorting one array (array b) and then iterating through array a checking (via binary search) if each value is in b. What is its runtime?

```
    int intersection(int[] a, int[] b) {
        mergesort(b);
        int intersect = 0;

        for (int x : a) {
            if (binarySearch(b, x) >= 0) {
                intersect++;
            }
        }

        return intersect;
    }
```

Solutions

1. `O(b)`. The for loop just iterates through b.
2. `O(b)`. The recursive code iterates through b calls, since it subtracts one at each level.
3. `O(1)`. It does a constant amount of work.
4. O(a/b). The variable `count` will eventually equal a/b. The while loop iterates count times. Therefore, it iterates a/b times.
5. `O(log n)`. This algorithm is essentially doing a binary search to find the square root. Therefore, the runtime is `O(log n)`.
6. `O(sqrt(n))`. This is just a straightforward loop that stops when `guess*guess > n` (or, in other words, when `guess > sqrt(n)`).

7. O(n), where n is the number of nodes in the tree. The max time to find an element is the depth tree. The tree could be a straight list downwards and have depth n.

8. O(n). Without any ordering property on the nodes, we might have to search through all the nodes.

9. $O(n^2)$, where n is the number of elements in the array. The first call to appendToNew takes 1 copy. The second call takes 2 copies. The third call takes 3 copies. And so on. The total time will be the sum of 1 through n, which is $O(n^2)$.

10. O(log n). The runtime will be the number of digits in the number. A number with d digits can have a value up to 10^d. If $n = 10^d$, then d = log n. Therefore, the runtime is O(log n).

11. $O(kc^k)$, where k is the length of the string and c is the number of characters in the alphabet. It takes $O(c^k)$ time to generate each string. Then, we need to check that each of these is sorted, which takes O(k) time.

12. O(b log b + a log b). First, we have to sort array b, which takes O(b log b) time. Then, for each element in a, we do binary search in O(log b) time. The second part takes O(a log b) time.

Technical Questions

Technical questions form the basis for how many of the top tech companies interview. Many candidates are intimidated by the difficulty of these questions, but there are logical ways to approach them.

▸ How to Prepare

Many candidates just read through problems and solutions. That's like trying to learn calculus by reading a problem and its answer. You need to practice solving problems. Memorizing solutions won't help you much.

For each problem in this book (and any other problem you might encounter), do the following:

1. *Try to solve the problem on your own.* Hints are provided at the back of this book, but push yourself to develop a solution with as little help as possible. Many questions are designed to be tough—that's okay! When you're solving a problem, make sure to think about the space and time efficiency.
2. *Write the code on paper.* Coding on a computer offers luxuries such as syntax highlighting, code completion, and quick debugging. Coding on paper does not. Get used to this—and to how slow it is to write and edit code—by coding on paper.
3. *Test your code—on paper.* This means testing the general cases, base cases, error cases, and so on. You'll need to do this during your interview, so it's best to practice this in advance.
4. *Type your paper code as-is into a computer.* You will probably make a bunch of mistakes. Start a list of all the errors you make so that you can keep these in mind during the actual interview.

In addition, try to do as many mock interviews as possible. You and a friend can take turns giving each other mock interviews. Though your friend may not be an expert interviewer, he or she may still be able to walk you through a coding or algorithm problem. You'll also learn a lot by experiencing what it's like to be an interviewer.

▸ What You Need To Know

The sorts of data structure and algorithm questions that many companies focus on are not knowledge tests. However, they do assume a baseline of knowledge.

Core Data Structures, Algorithms, and Concepts

Most interviewers won't ask about specific algorithms for binary tree balancing or other complex algorithms. Frankly, being several years out of school, they probably don't remember these algorithms either.

You're usually only expected to know the basics. Here's a list of the absolute, must-have knowledge:

Data Structures	Algorithms	Concepts
Linked Lists	Breadth-First Search	Bit Manipulation
Trees, Tries, & Graphs	Depth-First Search	Memory (Stack vs. Heap)
Stacks & Queues	Binary Search	Recursion
Heaps	Merge Sort	Dynamic Programming
Vectors / ArrayLists	Quick Sort	Big O Time & Space
Hash Tables		

For each of these topics, make sure you understand how to use and implement them and, where applicable, the space and time complexity.

Practicing implementing the data structures and algorithm (on paper, and then on a computer) is also a great exercise. It will help you learn how the internals of the data structures work, which is important for many interviews.

> Did you miss that paragraph above? It's important. If you don't feel very, very comfortable with each of the data structures and algorithms listed, practice implementing them from scratch.

In particular, hash tables are an extremely important topic. Make sure you are very comfortable with this data structure.

Powers of 2 Table

The table below is useful for many questions involving scalability or any sort of memory limitation. Memorizing this table isn't strictly required, but it can be useful. You should at least be comfortable deriving it.

Power of 2	Exact Value (X)	Approx. Value	X Bytes into MB, GB, etc.
7	128		
8	256		
10	1024	1 thousand	1 KB
16	65,536		64 KB
20	1,048,576	1 million	1 MB
30	1,073,741,824	1 billion	1 GB
32	4,294,967,296		4 GB
40	1,099,511,627,776	1 trillion	1 TB

For example, you could use this table to quickly compute that a bit vector mapping every 32-bit integer to a boolean value could fit in memory on a typical machine. There are 2^{32} such integers. Because each integer takes one bit in this bit vector, we need 2^{32} bits (or 2^{29} bytes) to store this mapping. That's about half a gigabyte of memory, which can be easily held in memory on a typical machine.

If you are doing a phone screen with a web-based company, it may be useful to have this table in front of you.

Walking Through a Problem

The below map/flowchart walks you through how to solve a problem. Use this in your practice. You can download this handout and more at CrackingTheCodingInterview.com.

A Problem-Solving Flowchart

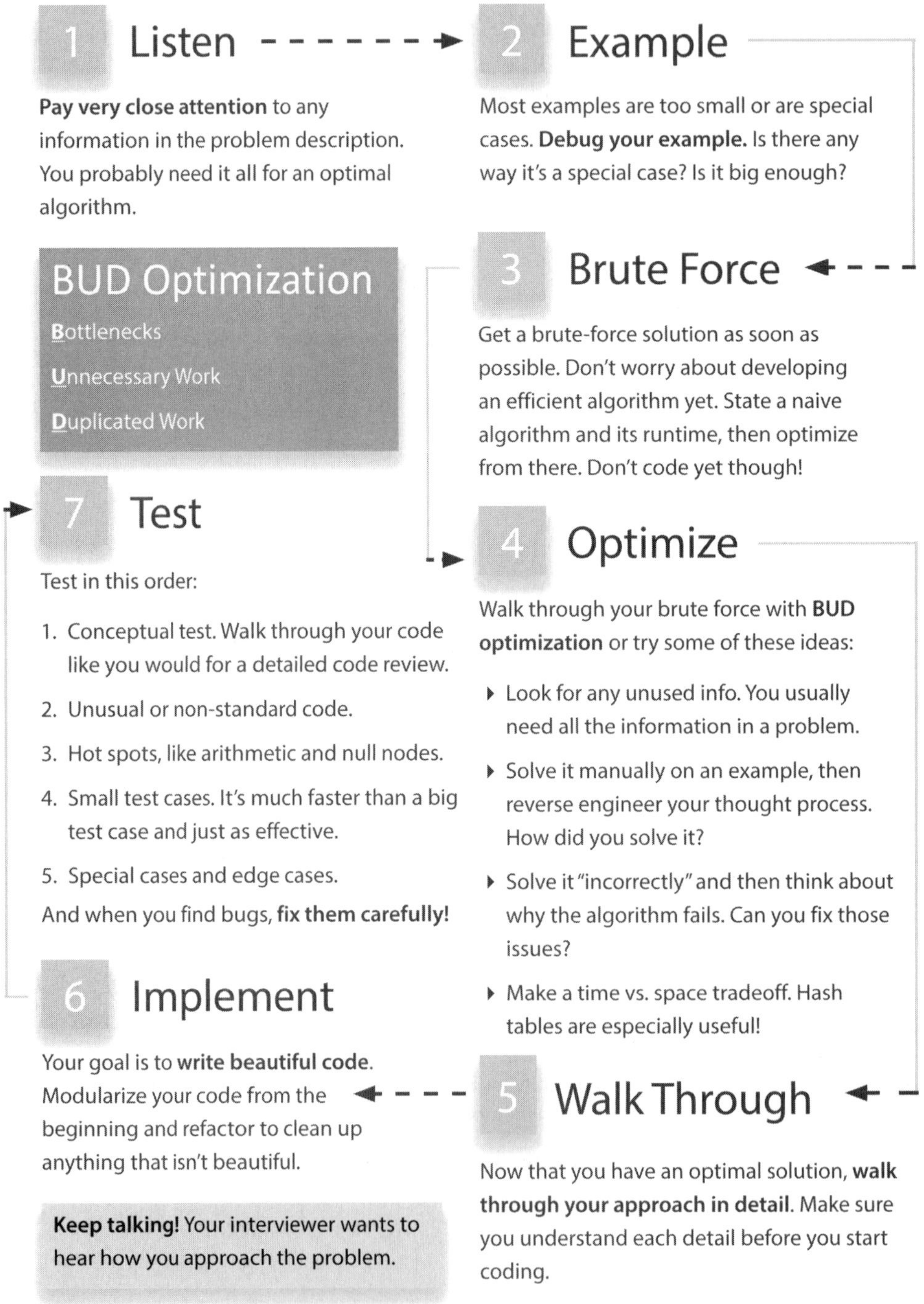

1 Listen

Pay very close attention to any information in the problem description. You probably need it all for an optimal algorithm.

2 Example

Most examples are too small or are special cases. **Debug your example.** Is there any way it's a special case? Is it big enough?

3 Brute Force

Get a brute-force solution as soon as possible. Don't worry about developing an efficient algorithm yet. State a naive algorithm and its runtime, then optimize from there. Don't code yet though!

BUD Optimization

Bottlenecks

Unnecessary Work

Duplicated Work

4 Optimize

Walk through your brute force with **BUD optimization** or try some of these ideas:

- Look for any unused info. You usually need all the information in a problem.
- Solve it manually on an example, then reverse engineer your thought process. How did you solve it?
- Solve it "incorrectly" and then think about why the algorithm fails. Can you fix those issues?
- Make a time vs. space tradeoff. Hash tables are especially useful!

5 Walk Through

Now that you have an optimal solution, **walk through your approach in detail**. Make sure you understand each detail before you start coding.

6 Implement

Your goal is to **write beautiful code**. Modularize your code from the beginning and refactor to clean up anything that isn't beautiful.

Keep talking! Your interviewer wants to hear how you approach the problem.

7 Test

Test in this order:

1. Conceptual test. Walk through your code like you would for a detailed code review.
2. Unusual or non-standard code.
3. Hot spots, like arithmetic and null nodes.
4. Small test cases. It's much faster than a big test case and just as effective.
5. Special cases and edge cases.

And when you find bugs, **fix them carefully!**

We'll go through this flowchart in more detail.

What to Expect

Interviews are supposed to be difficult. If you don't get every—or any—answer immediately, that's okay! That's the normal experience, and it's not bad.

Listen for guidance from the interviewer. The interviewer might take a more active or less active role in your problem solving. The level of interviewer participation depends on your performance, the difficulty of the question, what the interviewer is looking for, and the interviewer's own personality.

When you're given a problem (or when you're practicing), work your way through it using the approach below.

1. Listen Carefully

You've likely heard this advice before, but I'm saying something a bit more than the standard "make sure you hear the problem correctly" advice.

Yes, you do want to listen to the problem and make sure you heard it correctly. You do want to ask questions about anything you're unsure about.

But I'm saying something more than that.

Listen carefully to the problem, and be sure that you've mentally recorded any *unique* information in the problem.

For example, suppose a question starts with one of the following lines. It's reasonable to assume that the information is there for a reason.

- "Given two arrays that are sorted, find ..."

  You probably need to know that the data is sorted. The optimal algorithm for the sorted situation is probably different than the optimal algorithm for the unsorted situation.
- "Design an algorithm to be run repeatedly on a server that ..."

  The server/to-be-run-repeatedly situation is different from the run-once situation. Perhaps this means that you cache data? Or perhaps it justifies some reasonable precomputation on the initial dataset?

It's unlikely (although not impossible) that your interviewer would give you this information if it didn't affect the algorithm.

Many candidates will hear the problem correctly. But ten minutes into developing an algorithm, some of the key details of the problem have been forgotten. Now they are in a situation where they actually can't solve the problem optimally.

Your first algorithm doesn't need to use the information. But if you find yourself stuck, or you're still working to develop something more optimal, ask yourself if you've used all the information in the problem.

You might even find it useful to write the pertinent information on the whiteboard.

2. Draw an Example

An example can dramatically improve your ability to solve an interview question, and yet so many candidates just try to solve the question in their heads.

When you hear a question, get out of your chair, go to the whiteboard, and draw an example.

There's an art to drawing an example though. You want a good example.

Very typically, a candidate might draw something like this for an example of a binary search tree:

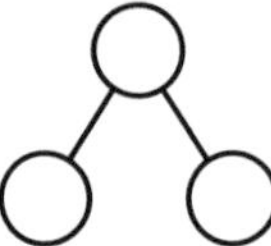

This is a bad example for several reasons. First, it's too small. You will have trouble finding a pattern in such a small example. Second, it's not specific. A binary search tree has values. What if the numbers tell you something about how to approach the problem? Third, it's actually a special case. It's not just a balanced tree, but it's also a beautiful, perfect tree where every node other than the leaves has two children. Special cases can be very deceiving.

Instead, you want to create an example that is:

- Specific. It should use real numbers or strings (if applicable to the problem).
- Sufficiently large. Most examples are too small, by about 50%.
- Not a special case. Be careful. It's very easy to inadvertently draw a special case. If there's any way your example is a special case (even if you think it probably won't be a big deal), you should fix it.

Try to make the best example you can. If it later turns out your example isn't quite right, you can and should fix it.

3. State a Brute Force

Once you have an example done (actually, you can switch the order of steps 2 and 3 in some problems), state a brute force. It's okay and expected that your initial algorithm won't be very optimal.

Some candidates don't state the brute force because they think it's both obvious and terrible. But here's the thing: Even if it's obvious for you, it's not necessarily obvious for all candidates. You don't want your interviewer to think that you're struggling to see even the easy solution.

It's okay that this initial solution is terrible. Explain what the space and time complexity is, and then dive into improvements.

Despite being possibly slow, a brute force algorithm is valuable to discuss. It's a starting point for optimizations, and it helps you wrap your head around the problem.

4. Optimize

Once you have a brute force algorithm, you should work on optimizing it. A few techniques that work well are:

1. Look for any unused information. Did your interviewer tell you that the array was sorted? How can you leverage that information?
2. Use a fresh example. Sometimes, just seeing a different example will unclog your mind or help you see a pattern in the problem.
3. Solve it "incorrectly." Just like having an inefficient solution can help you find an efficient solution, having an incorrect solution might help you find a correct solution. For example, if you're asked to generate a

random value from a set such that all values are equally likely, an incorrect solution might be one that returns a semi-random value: Any value could be returned, but some are more likely than others. You can then think about why that solution isn't perfectly random. Can you rebalance the probabilities?

4. Make time vs. space tradeoff. Sometimes storing extra state about the problem can help you optimize the runtime.
5. Precompute information. Is there a way that you can reorganize the data (sorting, etc.) or compute some values upfront that will help save time in the long run?
6. Use a hash table. Hash tables are widely used in interview questions and should be at the top of your mind.
7. Think about the best conceivable runtime (discussed on page 72).

Walk through the brute force with these ideas in mind and look for BUD (page 67).

5. Walk Through

After you've nailed down an optimal algorithm, don't just dive into coding. Take a moment to solidify your understanding of the algorithm.

Whiteboard coding is slow—very slow. So is testing your code and fixing it. As a result, you need to make sure that you get it as close to "perfect" in the beginning as possible.

Walk through your algorithm and get a feel for the structure of the code. Know what the variables are and when they change.

> What about pseudocode? You can write pseudocode if you'd like. Be careful about what you write. Basic steps ("(1) Search array. (2) Find biggest. (3) Insert in heap.") or brief logic ("if `p < q`, move p. else move q") can be valuable. But when your pseudocode starts having for loops that are written in plain English, then you're essentially just writing sloppy code. It'd probably be faster to just write the code.

If you don't understand exactly what you're about to write, you'll struggle to code it. It will take you longer to finish the code, and you're more likely to make major errors.

6. Implement

Now that you have an optimal algorithm and you know exactly what you're going to write, go ahead and implement it.

Start coding in the far top left corner of the whiteboard (you'll need the space). Avoid "line creep" (where each line of code is written an awkward slant). It makes your code look messy and can be very confusing when working in a whitespace-sensitive language, like Python.

Remember that you only have a short amount of code to demonstrate that you're a great developer. Everything counts. Write beautiful code.

Beautiful code means:

- Modularized code. This shows good coding style. It also makes things easier for you. If your algorithm uses a matrix initialized to `{{1, 2, 3}, {4, 5, 6}, ...}`, don't waste your time writing this initialization code. Just pretend you have a function `initIncrementalMatrix(int size)`. Fill in the details later if you need to.

- Error checks. Some interviewers care a lot about this, while others don't. A good compromise here is to add a `todo` and then just explain out loud what you'd like to test.
- Use other classes/structs where appropriate. If you need to return a list of start and end points from a function, you could do this as a two-dimensional array. It's better though to do this as a list of `StartEndPair` (or possibly Range) objects. You don't necessarily have to fill in the details for the class. Just pretend it exists and deal with the details later if you have time.
- Good variable names. Code that uses single-letter variables everywhere is difficult to read. That's not to say that there's anything wrong with using `i` and `j`, where appropriate (such as in a basic for-loop iterating through an array). However, be careful about where you do this. If you write something like `int i = startOfChild(array)`, there might be a better name for this variable, such as `startChild`.

  Long variable names can also be slow to write though. A good compromise that most interviewers will be okay with is to abbreviate it after the first usage. You can use `startChild` the first time, and then explain to your interviewer that you will abbreviate this as `sc` after this.

The specifics of what makes good code vary between interviewers and candidates, and the problem itself. Focus on writing beautiful code, whatever that means to you.

If you see something you can refactor later on, then explain this to your interviewer and decide whether or not it's worth the time to do so. Usually it is, but not always.

If you get confused (which is common), go back to your example and walk through it again.

7. Test

You wouldn't check in code in the real world without testing it, and you shouldn't "submit" code in an interview without testing it either.

There are smart and not-so-smart ways to test your code though.

What many candidates do is take their earlier example and test it against their code. That might discover bugs, but it'll take a really long time to do so. Hand testing is very slow. If you really did use a nice, big example to develop your algorithm, then it'll take you a very long time to find that little off-by-one error at the end of your code.

Instead, try this approach:

1. Start with a "conceptual" test. A conceptual test means just reading and analyzing what each line of code does. Think about it like you're explaining the lines of code for a code reviewer. Does the code do what you think it should do?
2. Weird looking code. Double check that line of code that says `x = length - 2`. Investigate that for loop that starts at `i = 1`. While you undoubtedly did this for a reason, it's really easy to get it just slightly wrong.
3. Hot spots. You've coded long enough to know what things are likely to cause problems. Base cases in recursive code. Integer division. Null nodes in binary trees. The start and end of iteration through a linked list. Double check that stuff.
4. Small test cases. This is the first time we use an actual, specific test case to test the code. Don't use that nice, big 8-element array from the algorithm part. Instead, use a 3 or 4 element array. It'll likely discover the same bugs, but it will be much faster to do so.
5. Special cases. Test your code against null or single element values, the extreme cases, and other special cases.

When you find bugs (and you probably will), you should of course fix them. But don't just make the first correction you think of. Instead, carefully analyze why the bug occurred and ensure that your fix is the best one.

▸ Optimize & Solve Technique #1: Look for BUD

This is perhaps the most useful approach I've found for optimizing problems. "BUD" is a silly acronym for:

- Bottlenecks
- Unnecessary work
- Duplicated work

These are three of the most common things that an algorithm can "waste" time doing. You can walk through your brute force looking for these things. When you find one of them, you can then focus on getting rid of it.

If it's still not optimal, you can repeat this approach on your current best algorithm.

Bottlenecks

A bottleneck is a part of your algorithm that slows down the overall runtime. There are two common ways this occurs:

- You have one-time work that slows down your algorithm. For example, suppose you have a two-step algorithm where you first sort the array and then you find elements with a particular property. The first step is `O(N log N)` and the second step is `O(N)`. Perhaps you could reduce the second step to `O(log N)` or `O(1)`, but would it matter? Not too much. It's certainly not a priority, as the `O(N log N)` is the bottleneck. Until you optimize the first step, your overall algorithm will be `O(N log N)`.
- You have a chunk of work that's done repeatedly, like searching. Perhaps you can reduce that from `O(N)` to `O(log N)` or even `O(1)`. That will greatly speed up your overall runtime.

Optimizing a bottleneck can make a big difference in your overall runtime.

> Example: Given an array of distinct integer values, count the number of pairs of integers that have difference k. For example, given the array `{1, 7, 5, 9, 2, 12, 3}` and the difference `k = 2`, there are four pairs with difference 2: `(1, 3), (3, 5), (5, 7), (7, 9)`.

A brute force algorithm is to go through the array, starting from the first element, and then search through the remaining elements (which will form the other side of the pair). For each pair, compute the difference. If the difference equals k, increment a counter of the difference.

The bottleneck here is the repeated search for the "other side" of the pair. It's therefore the main thing to focus on optimizing.

How can we more quickly find the right "other side"? Well, we actually know the other side of `(x, ?)`. It's `x + k` or `x - k`. If we sorted the array, we could find the other side for each of the N elements in `O(log N)` time by doing a binary search.

We now have a two-step algorithm, where both steps take `O(N log N)` time. Now, sorting is the new bottleneck. Optimizing the second step won't help because the first step is slowing us down anyway.

We just have to get rid of the first step entirely and operate on an unsorted array. How can we find things quickly in an unsorted array? With a hash table.

Throw everything in the array into the hash table. Then, to look up if `x + k` or `x - k` exist in the array, we just look it up in the hash table. We can do this in `O(N)` time.

Unnecessary Work

> Example: Print all positive integer solutions to the equation $a^3 + b^3 = c^3 + d^3$ where a, b, c, and d are integers between 1 and 1000.

A brute force solution will just have four nested for loops. Something like:

```
n = 1000
for a from 1 to n
   for b from 1 to n
      for c from 1 to n
         for d from 1 to n
            if a^3 + b^3 == c^3 + d^3
               print a, b, c, d
```

This algorithm iterates through all possible values of a, b, c, and d and checks if that combination happens to work.

It's unnecessary to continue checking for other possible values of d. Only one could work. We should at least break after we find a valid solution.

```
n = 1000
for a from 1 to n
   for b from 1 to n
      for c from 1 to n
         for d from 1 to n
            if a^3 + b^3 == c^3 + d^3
               print a, b, c, d
               break // break out of d's loop
```

This won't make a meaningful change to the runtime—our algorithm is still $O(N^4)$—but it's still a good, quick fix to make.

Is there anything else that is unnecessary? Yes. If there's only one valid d value for each (a, b, c), then we can just compute it. This is just simple math: $d = \sqrt[3]{a^3 + b^3 - c^3}$.

```
1  n = 1000
2  for a from 1 to n
3     for b from 1 to n
4        for c from 1 to n
5           d = pow(a^3 + b^3 - c^3, 1/3) // Will round to int
6           if a^3 + b^3 == c^3 + d^3 && 0 <= d && d <= n // Validate that the value works
7              print a, b, c, d
```

The `if` statement on line 6 is important. Line 5 will always find a value for d, but we need to check that it's the right integer value.

This will reduce our runtime from $O(N^4)$ to $O(N^3)$.

Duplicated Work

Using the same problem and brute force algorithm as above, let's look for duplicated work this time.

The algorithm operates by essentially iterating through all `(a, b)` pairs and then searching all `(c, d)` pairs to find if there are any matches to that `(a, b)` pair.

Why do we keep on computing all (c, d) pairs for each (a, b) pair? We should just create the list of (c, d) pairs once. Then, when we have an (a, b) pair, find the matches within the (c, d) list. We can quickly locate the matches by inserting each (c, d) pair into a hash table that maps from the sum to the pair (or, rather, the list of pairs that have that sum).

```
n = 1000
for c from 1 to n
   for d from 1 to n
      result = c^3 + d^3
      append (c, d) to list at value map[result]
for a from 1 to n
   for b from 1 to n
      result = a^3 + b^3
      list = map.get(result)
      for each pair in list
         print a, b, pair
```

Actually, once we have the map of all the (c, d) pairs, we can just use that directly. We don't need to generate the (a, b) pairs. Each (a, b) will already be in the map.

```
n = 1000
for c from 1 to n
   for d from 1 to n
      result = c^3 + d^3
      append (c, d) to list at value map[result]

for each result, list in map
   for each pair1 in list
      for each pair2 in list
         print pair1, pair2
```

This will take our runtime to $O(N^2)$.

▸ Optimize & Solve Technique #2: DIY (Do It Yourself)

The first time you heard about how to find an element in a sorted array (before being taught binary search), you probably didn't jump to, "Ah ha! We'll compare the target element to the midpoint and then recurse on the appropriate half."

And yet, you could give someone who has no knowledge of computer science an alphabetized pile of student papers and they'll likely implement something like binary search to locate a student's paper. They'll probably say, "Gosh, Peter Smith? He'll be somewhere in the bottom of the stack." They'll pick a random paper in the middle(ish), compare the name to "Peter Smith", and then continue this process on the remainder of the papers. Although they have no knowledge of binary search, they intuitively "get it."

Our brains are funny like this. Throw the phrase "Design an algorithm" in there and people often get all jumbled up. But give people an actual example—whether just of the data (e.g., an array) or of the real-life parallel (e.g., a pile of papers)—and their intuition gives them a very nice algorithm.

I've seen this come up countless times with candidates. Their computer algorithm is extraordinarily slow, but when asked to solve the same problem manually, they immediately do something quite fast. (And it's not too surprising, in some sense. Things that are slow for a computer are often slow by hand. Why would you put yourself through extra work?)

Therefore, when you get a question, try just working it through intuitively on a real example. Often a bigger example will be easier.

> Example: Given a smaller string s and a bigger string b, design an algorithm to find all permutations of the shorter string within the longer one. Print the location of each permutation.

Think for a moment about how you'd solve this problem. Note permutations are rearrangements of the string, so the characters in s can appear in any order in b. They must be contiguous though (not split by other characters).

If you're like most candidates, you probably thought of something like: Generate all permutations of s and then look for each in b. Since there are S! permutations, this will take `O(S! * B)` time, where S is the length of s and B is the length of b.

This works, but it's an extraordinarily slow algorithm. It's actually *worse* than an exponential algorithm. If s has 14 characters, that's over 87 billion permutations. Add one more character into s and we have 15 times more permutations. Ouch!

Approached a different way, you could develop a decent algorithm fairly easily. Give yourself a big example, like this one:

```
s: abbc
b: cbabadcbbabbcbabaabccbabc
```

Where are the permutations of s within b? Don't worry about how you're doing it. Just find them. Even a 12 year old could do this!

(No, really, go find them. I'll wait!)

I've underlined below each permutation.

```
s: abbc
b: cbabadcbbabbcbabaabccbabc
   ----     ----       ----
         ---- ----      ----
               ----
```

Did you find these? How?

Few people—even those who earlier came up with the `O(S! * B)` algorithm—actually generate all the permutations of abbc to locate those permutations in b. Almost everyone takes one of two (very similar) approaches:

1. Walk through b and look at sliding windows of 4 characters (since s has length 4). Check if each window is a permutation of s.
2. Walk through b. Every time you see a character in s, check if the next four (the length of s) characters are a permutation of s.

Depending on the exact implementation of the "is this a permutation" part, you'll probably get a runtime of either `O(B * S)`, `O(B * S log S)`, or `O(B * S²)`. None of these are the most optimal algorithm (there is an `O(B)` algorithm), but it's a lot better than what we had before.

Try this approach when you're solving questions. Use a nice, big example and intuitively—manually, that is—solve it for the specific example. Then, afterwards, think hard about how you solved it. Reverse engineer your own approach.

Be particularly aware of any "optimizations" you intuitively or automatically made. For example, when you were doing this problem, you might have just skipped right over the sliding window with "d" in it, since "d" isn't in abbc. That's an optimization your brain made, and it's something you should at least be aware of in your algorithm.

▸ Optimize & Solve Technique #3: Simplify and Generalize

With Simplify and Generalize, we implement a multi-step approach. First, we simplify or tweak some constraint, such as the data type. Then, we solve this new simplified version of the problem. Finally, once we have an algorithm for the simplified problem, we try to adapt it for the more complex version.

> Example: A ransom note can be formed by cutting words out of a magazine to form a new sentence. How would you figure out if a ransom note (represented as a string) can be formed from a given magazine (string)?

To simplify the problem, we can modify it so that we are cutting *characters* out of a magazine instead of whole words.

We can solve the simplified ransom note problem with characters by simply creating an array and counting the characters. Each spot in the array corresponds to one letter. First, we count the number of times each character in the ransom note appears, and then we go through the magazine to see if we have all of those characters.

When we generalize the algorithm, we do a very similar thing. This time, rather than creating an array with character counts, we create a hash table that maps from a word to its frequency.

▸ Optimize & Solve Technique #4: Base Case and Build

With Base Case and Build, we solve the problem first for a base case (e.g., n = 1) and then try to build up from there. When we get to more complex/interesting cases (often n = 3 or n = 4), we try to build those using the prior solutions.

> Example: Design an algorithm to print all permutations of a string. For simplicity, assume all characters are unique.

Consider a test string `abcdefg`.

```
Case "a" --> {"a"}
Case "ab" --> {"ab", "ba"}
Case "abc" --> ?
```

This is the first "interesting" case. If we had the answer to `P("ab")`, how could we generate `P("abc")`? Well, the additional letter is "c," so we can just stick c in at every possible point. That is:

```
P("abc") = insert "c" into all locations of all strings in P("ab")
P("abc") = insert "c" into all locations of all strings in {"ab","ba"}
P("abc") = merge({"cab", "acb", "abc"}, {"cba", "bca", bac"})
P("abc") = {"cab", "acb", "abc", "cba", "bca", bac"}
```

Now that we understand the pattern, we can develop a general recursive algorithm. We generate all permutations of a string $s_1 \ldots s_n$ by "chopping off" the last character and generating all permutations of $s_1 \ldots s_{n-1}$. Once we have the list of all permutations of $s_1 \ldots s_{n-1}$, we iterate through this list. For each string in it, we insert s_n into every location of the string.

Base Case and Build algorithms often lead to natural recursive algorithms.

▸ Optimize & Solve Technique #5: Data Structure Brainstorm

This approach is certainly hacky, but it often works. We can simply run through a list of data structures and try to apply each one. This approach is useful because solving a problem may be trivial once it occurs to us to use, say, a tree.

> Example: Numbers are randomly generated and stored into an (expanding) array. How would you keep track of the median?

Our data structure brainstorm might look like the following:

- Linked list? Probably not. Linked lists tend not to do very well with accessing and sorting numbers.
- Array? Maybe, but you already have an array. Could you somehow keep the elements sorted? That's probably expensive. Let's hold off on this and return to it if it's needed.
- Binary tree? This is possible, since binary trees do fairly well with ordering. In fact, if the binary search tree is perfectly balanced, the top might be the median. But, be careful—if there's an even number of elements, the median is actually the average of the middle two elements. The middle two elements can't both be at the top. This is probably a workable algorithm, but let's come back to it.
- Heap? A heap is really good at basic ordering and keeping track of max and mins. This is actually interesting—if you had two heaps, you could keep track of the bigger half and the smaller half of the elements. The bigger half is kept in a min heap, such that the smallest element in the bigger half is at the root. The smaller half is kept in a max heap, such that the biggest element of the smaller half is at the root. Now, with these data structures, you have the potential median elements at the roots. If the heaps are no longer the same size, you can quickly "rebalance" the heaps by popping an element off the one heap and pushing it onto the other.

Note that the more problems you do, the more developed your instinct on which data structure to apply will be. You will also develop a more finely tuned instinct as to which of these approaches is the most useful.

▸ Best Conceivable Runtime (BCR)

Considering the best conceivable runtime can offer a useful hint for some problem.

The best conceivable runtime is, literally, the *best* runtime you could *conceive* of a solution to a problem having. You can easily prove that there is no way you could beat the BCR.

For example, suppose you want to compute the number of elements that two arrays (of length A and B) have in common. You immediately know that you can't do that in better than `O(A + B)` time because you have to "touch" each element in each array. `O(A + B)` is the BCR.

Or, suppose you want to print all pairs of values within an array. You know you can't do that in better than $O(N^2)$ time because there are N^2 pairs to print.

Be careful though! Suppose your interviewer asks you to find all pairs with sum k within an array (assuming all distinct elements). Some candidates who have not fully mastered the concept of BCR will say that the BCR is $O(N^2)$ because you have to look at N^2 pairs.

That's not true. Just because you want all pairs with a particular sum doesn't mean you have to look at *all* pairs. In fact, you don't.

> What's the relationship between the Best Conceivable Runtime and Best Case Runtime? Nothing at all! The Best Conceivable Runtime is for a *problem* and is largely a function of the inputs and outputs. It has no particular connection to a specific algorithm. In fact, if you compute the Best Conceivable Runtime by thinking about what *your* algorithm does, you're probably doing something wrong. The Best Case Runtime is for a specific algorithm (and is a mostly useless value).

Note that the best conceivable runtime is not necessarily achievable. It says only that you can't do *better* than it.

An Example of How to Use BCR

Question: Given two sorted arrays, find the number of elements in common. The arrays are the same length and each has all distinct elements.

Let's start with a good example. We'll underline the elements in common.

```
A: 13  27  35  40  49  55  59
B: 17  35  39  40  55  58  60
```

A brute force algorithm for this problem is to start with each element in A and search for it in B. This takes $O(N^2)$ time since for each of N elements in A, we need to do an $O(N)$ search in B.

The BCR is $O(N)$, because we know we will have to look at each element at least once and there are **2N** total elements. (If we skipped an element, then the value of that element could change the result. For example, if we never looked at the last value in B, then that 60 could be a 59.)

Let's think about where we are right now. We have an $O(N^2)$ algorithm and we want to do better than that—potentially, but not necessarily, as fast as $O(N)$.

```
Brute Force:         O(N²)
Optimal Algorithm:   ?
BCR:                 O(N)
```

What is between $O(N^2)$ and $O(N)$? Lots of things. Infinite things actually. We could theoretically have an algorithm that's $O(N \log(\log(\log(\log(N)))))$. However, both in interviews and in real life, that runtime doesn't come up a whole lot.

> Try to remember this for your interview because it throws a lot of people off. Runtime is not a multiple choice question. Yes, it's very common to have a runtime that's $O(\log N)$, $O(N)$, $O(N \log N)$, $O(N^2)$ or $O(2^N)$. But you shouldn't assume that something has a particular runtime by sheer process of elimination. In fact, those times when you're confused about the runtime and so you want to take a guess—those are the times when you're most likely to have a non-obvious and less common runtime. Maybe the runtime is $O(N^2K)$, where N is the size of the array and K is the number of pairs. Derive, don't guess.

Most likely, we're driving towards an $O(N)$ algorithm or an $O(N \log N)$ algorithm. What does that tell us?

If we imagine our current algorithm's runtime as $O(N \times N)$, then getting to $O(N)$ or $O(N \times \log N)$ might mean reducing that second $O(N)$ in the equation to $O(1)$ or $O(\log N)$.

> This is one way that BCR can be useful. We can use the runtimes to get a "hint" for what we need to reduce.

That second O(N) comes from searching. The array is sorted. Can we search in a sorted array in faster than O(N) time?

Why, yes. We can use binary search to find an element in a sorted array in O(log N) time.

We now have an improved algorithm: O(N log N).

```
Brute Force:        O(N²)
Improved Algorithm: O(N log N)
Optimal Algorithm:  ?
BCR:                O(N)
```

Can we do even better? Doing better likely means reducing that O(log N) to O(1).

In general, we cannot search an array—even a sorted array—in better than O(log N) time. This is *not* the general case though. We're doing this search over and over again.

The BCR is telling us that we will never, ever have an algorithm that's faster than O(N). Therefore, any work we do in O(N) time is a "freebie"—it won't impact our runtime.

Re-read the list of optimization tips on page 64. Is there anything that can help us?

One of the tips there suggests precomputing or doing upfront work. Any upfront work we do in O(N) time is a freebie. It won't impact our runtime.

> This is another place where BCR can be useful. Any work you do that's less than or equal to the BCR is "free," in the sense that it won't impact your runtime. You might want to eliminate it eventually, but it's not a top priority just yet.

Our focus is still on reducing search from O(log N) to O(1). Any precomputation that's O(N) or less is "free."

In this case, we can just throw everything in B into a hash table. This will take O(N) time. Then, we just go through A and look up each element in the hash table. This look up (or search) is O(1), so our runtime is O(N).

Suppose our interviewer hits us with a question that makes us cringe: Can we do better?

No, not in terms of runtime. We have achieved the fastest possible runtime, therefore we cannot optimize the big O time. We could potentially optimize the space complexity.

> This is another place where BCR is useful. It tells us that we're "done" in terms of optimizing the runtime, and we should therefore turn our efforts to the space complexity.

In fact, even without the interviewer prompting us, we should have a question mark with respect to our algorithm. We would have achieved the exact same runtime if the data wasn't sorted. So why did the interviewer give us sorted arrays? That's not unheard of, but it is a bit strange.

Let's turn back to our example.

```
A: 13  27  35  40  49  55  59
B: 17  35  39  40  55  58  60
```

We're now looking for an algorithm that:

- Operates in O(1) space (probably). We already have an O(N) space algorithm with optimal runtime. If we want to use less additional space, that probably means no additional space. Therefore, we need to drop the hash table.

- Operates in `O(N)` time (probably). We'll probably want to at least match the current best runtime, and we know we can't beat it.
- Uses the fact that the arrays are sorted.

Our best algorithm that doesn't use extra space was the binary search one. Let's think about optimizing that. We can try walking through the algorithm.

1. Do a binary search in B for `A[0] = 13`. Not found.
2. Do a binary search in B for `A[1] = 27`. Not found.
3. Do a binary search in B for `A[2] = 35`. Found at `B[1]`.
4. Do a binary search in B for `A[3] = 40`. Found at `B[5]`.
5. Do a binary search in B for `A[4] = 49`. Not found.
6. `...`

Think about BUD. The bottleneck is the searching. Is there anything unnecessary or duplicated?

It's unnecessary that `A[3] = 40` searched over all of B. We know that we just found 35 at `B[1]`, so 40 certainly won't be before 35.

Each binary search should start where the last one left off.

In fact, we don't need to do a binary search at all now. We can just do a linear search. As long as the linear search in B is just picking up where the last one left off, we know that we're going to be operating in linear time.

1. Do a linear search in B for `A[0] = 13`. Start at `B[0] = 17`. Stop at `B[0] = 17`. Not found.
2. Do a linear search in B for `A[1] = 27`. Start at `B[0] = 17`. Stop at `B[1] = 35`. Not found.
3. Do a linear search in B for `A[2] = 35`. Start at `B[1] = 35`. Stop at `B[1] = 35`. Found.
4. Do a linear search in B for `A[3] = 40`. Start at `B[2] = 39`. Stop at `B[3] = 40`. Found.
5. Do a linear search in B for `A[4] = 49`. Start at `B[3] = 40`. Stop at `B[4] = 55`. Not found.
6. ...

This algorithm is very similar to merging two sorted arrays. It operates in `O(N)` time and `O(1)` space.

We have now reached the BCR and have minimal space. We know that we cannot do better.

> This is another way we can use BCR. If you ever reach the BCR and have `O(1)` additional space, then you know that you can't optimize the big O time or space.

Best Conceivable Runtime is not a "real" algorithm concept, in that you won't find it in algorithm textbooks. But I have found it personally very useful, when solving problems myself, as well as while coaching people through problems.

If you're struggling to grasp it, make sure you understand big O time first (page 38). You need to master it. Once you do, figuring out the BCR of a problem should take literally seconds.

Handling Incorrect Answers

One of the most pervasive—and dangerous—rumors is that candidates need to get every question right. That's not quite true.

First, responses to interview questions shouldn't be thought of as "correct" or "incorrect." When I evaluate how someone performed in an interview, I never think, "How many questions did they get right?" It's not a binary evaluation. Rather, it's about how optimal their final solution was, how long it took them to get there, how much help they needed, and how clean was their code. There is a range of factors.

Second, your performance is evaluated *in comparison to other candidates*. For example, if you solve a question optimally in 15 minutes, and someone else solves an easier question in five minutes, did that person do better than you? Maybe, but maybe not. If you are asked really easy questions, then you might be expected to get optimal solutions really quickly. But if the questions are hard, then a number of mistakes are expected.

Third, many—possibly most—questions are too difficult to expect even a strong candidate to immediately spit out the optimal algorithm. The questions I tend to ask would take strong candidates typically 20 to 30 minutes to solve.

In evaluating thousands of hiring packets at Google, I have only once seen a candidate have a "flawless" set of interviews. Everyone else, including the hundreds who got offers, made mistakes.

When You've Heard a Question Before

If you've heard a question before, admit this to your interviewer. Your interviewer is asking you these questions in order to evaluate your problem-solving skills. If you already know the question, then you aren't giving them the opportunity to evaluate you.

Additionally, your interviewer may find it highly dishonest if you don't reveal that you know the question. (And, conversely, you'll get big honesty points if you do reveal this.)

The "Perfect" Language for Interviews

At many of the top companies, interviewers aren't picky about languages. They're more interested in how well you solve the problems than whether you know a specific language.

Other companies though are more tied to a language and are interested in seeing how well you can code in a particular language.

If you're given a choice of languages, then you should probably pick whatever language you're most comfortable with.

That said, if you have several good languages, you should keep in mind the following.

Prevalence

It's not required, but it is ideal for your interviewer to know the language you're coding in. A more widely known language can be better for this reason.

Language Readability

Even if your interviewer doesn't know your programming language, they should hopefully be able to basically understand it. Some languages are more naturally readable than others, due to their similarity to other languages.

For example, Java is fairly easy for people to understand, even if they haven't worked in it. Most people have worked in something with Java-like syntax, such as C and C++.

However, languages such as Scala or Objective C have fairly different syntax.

Potential Problems

Some languages just open you up to potential issues. For example, using C++ means that, in addition to all the usual bugs you can have in your code, you can have memory management and pointer issues.

Verbosity

Some languages are more verbose than others. Java for example is a fairly verbose language as compared with Python. Just compare the following code snippets.

Python:

```
dict = {"left": 1, "right": 2, "top": 3, "bottom": 4};
```

Java:

```
HashMap<String, Integer> dict = new HashMap<String, Integer>().
dict.put("left", 1);
dict.put("right", 2);
dict.put("top", 3);
dict.put("bottom", 4);
```

However, some of the verbosity of Java can be reduced by abbreviating code. I could imagine a candidate on a whiteboard writing something like this:

```
HM<S, I> dict = new HM<S, I>().
dict.put("left", 1);
...       "right", 2
...       "top", 3
...       "bottom", 4
```

The candidate would need to explain the abbreviations, but most interviewers wouldn't mind.

Ease of Use

Some operations are easier in some languages than others. For example, in Python, you can very easily return multiple values from a function. In Java, the same action would require a new class. This can be handy for certain problems.

Similar to the above though, this can be mitigated by just abbreviating code or presuming methods that you don't actually have. For example, if one language provides a function to transpose a matrix and another language doesn't, this doesn't necessarily make the first language much better to code in (for a problem that needs such a function). You could just assume that the other language has a similar method.

▸ What Good Coding Looks Like

You probably know by now that employers want to see that you write "good, clean" code. But what does this really mean, and how is this demonstrated in an interview?

Broadly speaking, good code has the following properties:

- **Correct:** The code should operate correctly on all expected and unexpected inputs.
- **Efficient:** The code should operate as efficiently as possible in terms of both time and space. This "efficiency" includes both the asymptotic (big O) efficiency and the practical, real-life efficiency. That is, a

constant factor might get dropped when you compute the big O time, but in real life, it can very much matter.

- **Simple:** If you can do something in 10 lines instead of 100, you should. Code should be as quick as possible for a developer to write.
- **Readable:** A different developer should be able to read your code and understand what it does and how it does it. Readable code has comments where necessary, but it implements things in an easily understandable way. That means that your fancy code that does a bunch of complex bit shifting is not necessarily *good* code.
- **Maintainable:** Code should be reasonably adaptable to changes during the life cycle of a product and should be easy to maintain by other developers, as well as the initial developer.

Striving for these aspects requires a balancing act. For example, it's often advisable to sacrifice some degree of efficiency to make code more maintainable, and vice versa.

You should think about these elements as you code during an interview. The following aspects of code are more specific ways to demonstrate the earlier list.

Use Data Structures Generously

Suppose you were asked to write a function to add two simple mathematical expressions which are of the form $Ax^a + Bx^b + \dots$ (where the coefficients and exponents can be any positive or negative real number). That is, the expression is a sequence of terms, where each term is simply a constant times an exponent. The interviewer also adds that she doesn't want you to have to do string parsing, so you can use whatever data structure you'd like to hold the expressions.

There are a number of different ways you can implement this.

Bad Implementation

A bad implementation would be to store the expression as a single array of doubles, where the kth element corresponds to the coefficient of the x^k term in the expression. This structure is problematic because it could not support expressions with negative or non-integer exponents. It would also require an array of 1000 elements to store just the expression x^{1000}.

```
int[] sum(double[] expr1, double[] expr2) {
  ...
}
```

Less Bad Implementation

A slightly less bad implementation would be to store the expression as a set of two arrays, `coefficients` and `exponents`. Under this approach, the terms of the expression are stored in any order, but "matched" such that the ith term of the expression is represented by `coefficients[i] *` $x^{exponents[i]}$.

Under this implementation, if `coefficients[p] = k` and `exponents[p] = m`, then the pth term is kx^m. Although this doesn't have the same limitations as the earlier solution, it's still very messy. You need to keep track of two arrays for just one expression. Expressions could have "undefined" values if the arrays were of different lengths. And returning an expression is annoying because you need to return two arrays.

```
??? sum(double[] coeffs1, double[] expon1, double[] coeffs2, double[] expon2) {
  ...
}
```

Good Implementation

A good implementation for this problem is to design your own data structure for the expression.

```
class ExprTerm {
  double coefficient;
  double exponent;
}

ExprTerm[] sum(ExprTerm[] expr1, ExprTerm[] expr2) {
  ...
}
```

Some might (and have) argued that this is "over-optimizing." Perhaps so, perhaps not. Regardless of whether you think it's over-optimizing, the above code demonstrates that you think about how to design your code and don't just slop something together in the fastest way possible.

Appropriate Code Reuse

Suppose you were asked to write a function to check if the value of a binary number (passed as a string) equals the hexadecimal representation of a string.

An elegant implementation of this problem leverages code reuse.

```
boolean compareBinToHex(String binary, String hex) {
  int n1 = convertFromBase(binary, 2);
  int n2 = convertFromBase(hex, 16);
  if (n1 < 0 || n2 < 0) {
    return false;
  }
  return n1 == n2;
}

int convertFromBase(String number, int base) {
  if (base < 2 || (base > 10 && base != 16)) return -1;
  int value = 0;
  for (int i = number.length() - 1; i >= 0; i--) {
    int digit = digitToValue(number.charAt(i));
    if (digit < 0 || digit >= base) {
      return -1;
    }
    int exp = number.length() - 1 - i;
    value += digit * Math.pow(base, exp);
  }
  return value;
}

int digitToValue(char c) { ... }
```

We could have implemented separate code to convert a binary number and a hexadecimal code, but this just makes our code harder to write and harder to maintain. Instead, we reuse code by writing one `convertFromBase` method and one `digitToValue` method.

Modular

Writing modular code means separating isolated chunks of code out into their own methods. This helps keep the code more maintainable, readable, and testable.

Imagine you are writing code to swap the minimum and maximum element in an integer array. You could implement it all in one method like this:

```
void swapMinMax(int[] array) {
   int minIndex = 0;
   for (int i = 1; i < array.length; i++) {
      if (array[i] < array[minIndex]) {
         minIndex = i;
      }
   }

   int maxIndex = 0;
   for (int i = 1; i < array.length; i++) {
      if (array[i] > array[maxIndex]) {
         maxIndex = i;
      }
   }

   int temp = array[minIndex];
   array[minIndex] = array[maxIndex];
   array[maxIndex] = temp;
}
```

Or, you could implement in a more modular way by separating the relatively isolated chunks of code into their own methods.

```
void swapMinMaxBetter(int[] array) {
   int minIndex = getMinIndex(array);
   int maxIndex = getMaxIndex(array);
   swap(array, minIndex, maxIndex);
}

int getMinIndex(int[] array) { ... }
int getMaxIndex(int[] array) { ... }
void swap(int[] array, int m, int n) { ... }
```

While the non-modular code isn't particularly awful, the nice thing about the modular code is that it's easily testable because each component can be verified separately. As code gets more complex, it becomes increasingly important to write it in a modular way. This will make it easier to read and maintain. Your interviewer wants to see you demonstrate these skills in your interview.

Flexible and Robust

Just because your interviewer only asks you to write code to check if a normal tic-tac-toe board has a winner, doesn't mean you *must* assume that it's a 3x3 board. Why not write the code in a more general way that implements it for an NxN board?

Writing flexible, general-purpose code may also mean using variables instead of hard-coded values or using templates / generics to solve a problem. If we can write our code to solve a more general problem, we should.

Of course, there is a limit. If the solution is much more complex for the general case, and it seems unnecessary at this point in time, it may be better just to implement the simple, expected case.

Error Checking

One sign of a careful coder is that she doesn't make assumptions about the input. Instead, she validates that the input is what it should be, either through ASSERT statements or if-statements.

For example, recall the earlier code to convert a number from its base `i` (e.g., base 2 or base 16) representation to an `int`.

```
1  int convertFromBase(String number, int base) {
2     if (base < 2 || (base > 10 && base != 16)) return -1;
3     int value = 0;
4     for (int i = number.length() - 1; i >= 0; i--) {
5        int digit = digitToValue(number.charAt(i));
6        if (digit < 0 || digit >= base) {
7           return -1;
8        }
9        int exp = number.length() - 1 - i;
10       value += digit * Math.pow(base, exp);
11    }
12    return value;
13 }
```

In line 2, we check to see that `base` is valid (we assume that bases greater than 10, other than base 16, have no standard representation in string form). In line 6, we do another error check: making sure that each digit falls within the allowable range.

Checks like these are critical in production code and, therefore, in interview code as well.

Of course, writing these error checks can be tedious and can waste precious time in an interview. The important thing is to point out that you *would* write the checks. If the error checks are much more than a quick if-statement, it may be best to leave some space where the error checks would go and indicate to your interviewer that you'll fill them in when you're finished with the rest of the code.

▸ Don't Give Up!

I know interview questions can be overwhelming, but that's part of what the interviewer is testing. Do you rise to a challenge, or do you shrink back in fear? It's important that you step up and eagerly meet a tricky problem head-on. After all, remember that interviews are supposed to be hard. It shouldn't be a surprise when you get a really tough problem.

For extra "points," show excitement about solving hard problems.

The Offer and Beyond

Just when you thought you could sit back and relax after your interviews, now you're faced with the post-interview stress: Should you accept the offer? Is it the right one? How do you decline an offer? What about deadlines? We'll handle a few of these issues here and go into more details about how to evaluate an offer, and how to negotiate it.

▸ Handling Offers and Rejection

Whether you're accepting an offer, declining an offer, or responding to a rejection, it matters what you do.

Offer Deadlines and Extensions

When companies extend an offer, there's almost always a deadline attached to it. Usually these deadlines are one to four weeks out. If you're still waiting to hear back from other companies, you can ask for an extension. Companies will usually try to accommodate this, if possible.

Declining an Offer

Even if you aren't interested in working for this company right now, you might be interested in working for it in a few years. (Or, your contacts might one day move to a more exciting company.) It's in your best interest to decline the offer on good terms and keep a line of communication open.

When you decline an offer, provide a reason that is non-offensive and inarguable. For example, if you were declining a big company for a startup, you could explain that you feel a startup is the right choice for you at this time. The big company can't suddenly "become" a startup, so they can't argue about your reasoning.

Handling Rejection

Getting rejected is unfortunate, but it doesn't mean that you're not a great engineer. Lots of great engineers do poorly, either because they don't "test well" on these sort of interviewers, or they just had an "off" day.

Fortunately, most companies understand that these interviews aren't perfect and many good engineers get rejected. For this reason, companies are often eager to re-interview previously rejected candidate. Some companies will even reach out to old candidates or expedite their application *because* of their prior performance.

When you do get the unfortunate call, use this as an opportunity to build a bridge to re-apply. Thank your recruiter for his time, explain that you're disappointed but that you understand their position, and ask when you can reapply to the company.

You can also ask for feedback from the recruiter. In most cases, the big tech companies won't offer feedback, but there are some companies that will. It doesn't hurt to ask a question like, "Is there anything you'd suggest I work on for next time?"

▸ Evaluating the Offer

Congratulations! You got an offer! And—if you're lucky—you may have even gotten multiple offers. Your recruiter's job is now to do everything he can to encourage you to accept it. How do you know if the company is the right fit for you? We'll go through a few things you should consider in evaluating an offer.

The Financial Package

Perhaps the biggest mistake that candidates make in evaluating an offer is looking too much at their salary. Candidates often look so much at this one number that they wind up accepting the offer that is *worse* financially. Salary is just one part of your financial compensation. You should also look at:

- *Signing Bonus, Relocation, and Other One Time Perks:* Many companies offer a signing bonus and/or relocation. When comparing offers, it's wise to amortize this cash over three years (or however long you expect to stay).
- *Cost of Living Difference:* Taxes and other cost of living differences can make a big difference in your take-home pay. Silicon Valley, for example, is 30+% more expensive than Seattle.
- *Annual Bonus:* Annual bonuses at tech companies can range from anywhere from 3% to 30%. Your recruiter might reveal the average annual bonus, but if not, check with friends at the company.
- *Stock Options and Grants:* Equity compensation can form another big part of your annual compensation. Like signing bonuses, stock compensation between companies can be compared by amortizing it over three years and then lumping that value into salary.

Remember, though, that what you learn and how a company advances your career often makes far more of a difference to your long term finances than the salary. Think very carefully about how much emphasis you really want to put on money right now.

Career Development

As thrilled as you may be to receive this offer, odds are, in a few years, you'll start thinking about interviewing again. Therefore, it's important that you think right now about how this offer would impact your career path. This means considering the following questions:

- How good does the company's name look on my resume?
- How much will I learn? Will I learn relevant things?
- What is the promotion plan? How do the careers of developers progress?
- If I want to move into management, does this company offer a realistic plan?
- Is the company or team growing?
- If I do want to leave the company, is it situated near other companies I'm interested in, or will I need to move?

The final point is extremely important and usually overlooked. If you only have a few other companies to pick from in your city, your career options will be more restricted. Fewer options means that you're less likely to discover really great opportunities.

Company Stability

All else being equal, of course stability is a good thing. No one wants to be fired or laid off.

However, all else isn't actually equal. The more stable companies are also often growing more slowly.

How much emphasis you should put on company stability really depends on you and your values. For some candidates, stability should not be a large factor. Can you fairly quickly find a new job? If so, it might be better to take the rapidly growing company, even if it's unstable? If you have work visa restrictions or just aren't confident in your ability to find something new, stability might be more important.

The Happiness Factor

Last but not least, you should of course consider how happy you will be. Any of the following factors may impact that:

- *The Product:* Many people look heavily at what product they are building, and of course this matters a bit. However, for most engineers, there are more important factor, such as who you work with.
- *Manager and Teammates:* When people say that they love, or hate, their job, it's often because of their teammates and their manager. Have you met them? Did you enjoy talking with them?
- *Company Culture:* Culture is tied to everything from how decisions get made, to the social atmosphere, to how the company is organized. Ask your future teammates how they would describe the culture.
- *Hours:* Ask future teammates about how long they typically work, and figure out if that meshes with your lifestyle. Remember, though, that hours before major deadlines are typically much longer.

Additionally, note that if you are given the opportunity to switch teams easily (like you are at Google and Facebook), you'll have an opportunity to find a team and product that matches you well.

▸ Negotiation

Years ago, I signed up for a negotiations class. On the first day, the instructor asked us to imagine a scenario where we wanted to buy a car. Dealership A sells the car for a fixed \$20,000—no negotiating. Dealership B allows us to negotiate. How much would the car have to be (after negotiating) for us to go to Dealership B? (Quick! Answer this for yourself!)

On average, the class said that the car would have to be \$750 cheaper. In other words, students were willing to pay \$750 just to avoid having to negotiate for an hour or so. Not surprisingly, in a class poll, most of these students also said they didn't negotiate their job offer. They just accepted whatever the company gave them.

Many of us can probably sympathize with this position. Negotiation isn't fun for most of us. But still, the financial benefits of negotiation are usually worth it.

Do yourself a favor. Negotiate. Here are some tips to get you started.

1. *Just Do It.* Yes, I know it's scary; (almost) no one likes negotiating. But it's so, so worth it. Recruiters will not revoke an offer because you negotiated, so you have little to lose. This is especially true if the offer is from a larger company. You probably won't be negotiating with your future teammates.
2. *Have a Viable Alternative.* Fundamentally, recruiters negotiate with you because they're concerned you may not join the company otherwise. If you have alternative options, that will make their concern much more real.
3. *Have a Specific "Ask":* It's more effective to ask for an additional \$7000 in salary than to just ask for "more."

After all, if you just ask for more, the recruiter could throw in another $1000 and technically have satisfied your wishes.

4. *Overshoot:* In negotiations, people usually don't agree to whatever you demand. It's a back and forth conversation. Ask for a bit more than you're really hoping to get, since the company will probably meet you in the middle.
5. *Think Beyond Salary:* Companies are often more willing to negotiate on non-salary components, since boosting your salary too much could mean that they're paying you more than your peers. Consider asking for more equity or a bigger signing bonus. Alternatively, you may be able to ask for your relocation benefits in cash, instead of having the company pay directly for the moving fees. This is a great avenue for many college students, whose actual moving expenses are fairly cheap.
6. *Use Your Best Medium:* Many people will advise you to only negotiate over the phone. To a certain extent, they're right; it is better to negotiate over the phone. However, if you don't feel comfortable on a phone negotiation, do it via email. It's more important that you attempt to negotiate than that you do it via a specific medium.

Additionally, if you're negotiating with a big company, you should know that they often have "levels" for employees, where all employees at a particular level are paid around the same amount. Microsoft has a particularly well-defined system for this. You can negotiate within the salary range for your level, but going beyond that requires bumping up a level. If you're looking for a big bump, you'll need to convince the recruiter and your future team that your experience matches this higher level—a difficult, but feasible, thing to do.

On the Job

Navigating your career path doesn't end at the interview. In fact, it's just getting started. Once you actually join a company, you need to start thinking about your career path. Where will you go from here, and how will you get there?

Set a Timeline

It's a common story: you join a company, and you're psyched. Everything is great. Five years later, you're still there. And it's then that you realize that these last three years didn't add much to your skill set or to your resume. Why didn't you just leave after two years?

When you're enjoying your job, it's very easy to get wrapped up in it and not realize that your career is not advancing. This is why you should outline your career path before starting a new job. Where do you want to be in ten years? And what are the steps necessary to get there? In addition, each year, think about what the next year of experience will bring you and how your career or your skill set advanced in the last year.

By outlining your path in advance and checking in on it regularly, you can avoid falling into this complacency trap.

Build Strong Relationships

When you want to move on to something new, your network will be critical. After all, applying online is tricky; a personal referral is much better, and your ability to do so hinges on your network.

At work, establish strong relationships with your manager and teammates. When employees leave, keep in touch with them. Just a friendly note a few weeks after their departure will help to bridge that connection from a work acquaintance to a personal acquaintance.

This same approach applies to your personal life. Your friends, and your friends of friends, are valuable connections. Be open to helping others, and they'll be more likely to help you.

Ask for What You Want

While some managers may really try to grow your career, others will take a more hands-off approach. It's up to you to pursue the challenges that are right for your career.

Be (reasonably) frank about your goals with your manager. If you want to take on more back-end coding projects, say so. If you'd like to explore more leadership opportunities, discuss how you might be able to do so.

You need to be your best advocate, so that you can achieve goals according to your timeline.

Keep Interviewing

Set a goal of interviewing at least once a year, even if you aren't actively looking for a new job. This will keep your interview skills fresh, and also keep you in tune with what sorts of opportunities (and salaries) are out there.

If you get an offer, you don't have to take it. It will still build a connection with that company in case you want to join at a later date.

IX Interview Questions

Join us at ***www.CrackingTheCodingInterview.com*** *to download the complete solutions, contribute or view solutions in other programming languages, discuss problems from this book with other readers, ask questions, report issues, view this book's errata, and seek additional advice.*

1

Arrays and Strings

Hopefully, all readers of this book are familiar with arrays and strings, so we won't bore you with such details. Instead, we'll focus on some of the more common techniques and issues with these data structures.

Please note that array questions and string questions are often interchangeable. That is, a question that this book states using an array may be asked instead as a string question, and vice versa.

Hash Tables

A hash table is a data structure that maps keys to values for highly efficient lookup. There are a number of ways of implementing this. Here, we will describe a simple but common implementation.

In this simple implementation, we use an array of linked lists and a hash code function. To insert a key (which might be a string or essentially any other data type) and value, we do the following:

1. First, compute the key's hash code, which will usually be an `int` or `long`. Note that two different keys could have the same hash code, as there may be an infinite number of keys and a finite number of ints.
2. Then, map the hash code to an index in the array. This could be done with something like `hash(key) % array_length`. Two different hash codes could, of course, map to the same index.
3. At this index, there is a linked list of keys and values. Store the key and value in this index. We must use a linked list because of collisions: you could have two different keys with the same hash code, or two different hash codes that map to the same index.

To retrieve the value pair by its key, you repeat this process. Compute the hash code from the key, and then compute the index from the hash code. Then, search through the linked list for the value with this key.

If the number of collisions is very high, the worst case runtime is `O(N)`, where `N` is the number of keys. However, we generally assume a good implementation that keeps collisions to a minimum, in which case the lookup time is `O(1)`.

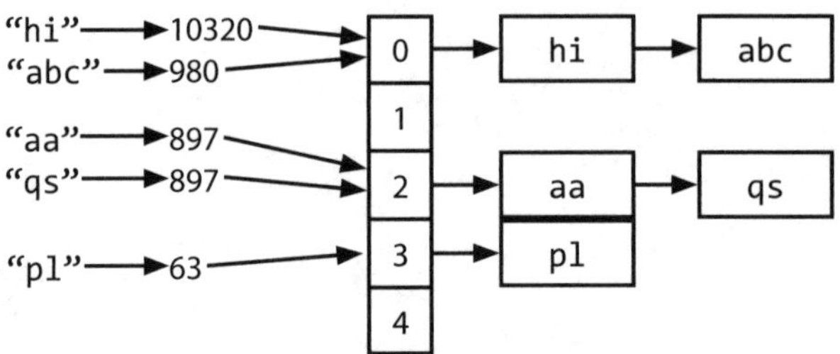

Alternatively, we can implement the hash table with a balanced binary search tree. This gives us an `O(log N)` lookup time. The advantage of this is potentially using less space, since we no longer allocate a large array. We can also iterate through the keys in order, which can be useful sometimes.

▸ ArrayList & Resizable Arrays

In some languages, arrays (often called lists in this case) are automatically resizable. The array or list will grow as you append items. In other languages, like Java, arrays are fixed length. The size is defined when you create the array.

When you need an array-like data structure that offers dynamic resizing, you would usually use an ArrayList. An ArrayList is an array that resizes itself as needed while still providing `O(1)` access. A typical implementation is that when the array is full, the array doubles in size. Each doubling takes `O(n)` time, but happens so rarely that its amortized insertion time is still `O(1)`.

```
ArrayList<String> merge(String[] words, String[] more) {
  ArrayList<String> sentence = new ArrayList<String>();
  for (String w : words) sentence.add(w);
  for (String w : more) sentence.add(w);
  return sentence;
}
```

This is an essential data structure for interviews. Be sure you are comfortable with dynamically resizable arrays/lists in whatever language you will be working with. Note that the name of the data structure as well as the "resizing factor" (which is 2 in Java) can vary.

Why is the amortized insertion runtime O(1)?

Suppose you have an array of size N. We can work backwards to compute how many elements we copied at each capacity increase. Observe that when we increase the array to K elements, the array was previously half that size. Therefore, we needed to copy $\frac{K}{2}$ elements.

```
final capacity increase   : n/2 elements to copy
previous capacity increase: n/4 elements to copy
previous capacity increase: n/8 elements to copy
previous capacity increase: n/16 elements to copy
...
second capacity increase  : 2 elements to copy
first capacity increase   : 1 element to copy
```

Therefore, the total number of copies to insert N elements is roughly $\frac{N}{2} + \frac{N}{4} + \frac{N}{8} + \ldots + 2 + 1$, which is just less than N.

> If the sum of this series isn't obvious to you, imagine this: Suppose you have a kilometer-long walk to the store. You walk 0.5 kilometers, and then 0.25 kilometers, and then 0.125 kilometers, and so on. You will never exceed one kilometer (although you'll get very close to it).

Therefore, inserting N elements takes `O(N)` work total. Each insertion is `O(1)` on average, even though some insertions take `O(N)` time in the worst case.

▸ StringBuilder

Imagine you were concatenating a list of strings, as shown below. What would the running time of this code be? For simplicity, assume that the strings are all the same length (call this x) and that there are n strings.

```
String joinWords(String[] words) {
   String sentence = "";
   for (String w : words) {
      sentence = sentence + w;
   }
   return sentence;
}
```

On each concatenation, a new copy of the string is created, and the two strings are copied over, character by character. The first iteration requires us to copy x characters. The second iteration requires copying 2x characters. The third iteration requires 3x, and so on. The total time therefore is $O(x + 2x + ... + nx)$. This reduces to $O(xn^2)$.

> Why is it $O(xn^2)$? Because $1 + 2 + ... + n$ equals $n(n+1)/2$, or $O(n^2)$.

`StringBuilder` can help you avoid this problem. `StringBuilder` simply creates a resizable array of all the strings, copying them back to a string only when necessary.

```
String joinWords(String[] words) {
   StringBuilder sentence = new StringBuilder();
   for (String w : words) {
      sentence.append(w);
   }
   return sentence.toString();
}
```

A good exercise to practice strings, arrays, and general data structures is to implement your own version of `StringBuilder`, `HashTable` and `ArrayList`.

Additional Reading: Hash Table Collision Resolution (pg 636), Rabin-Karp Substring Search (pg 636).

Interview Questions

1.1 **Is Unique:** Implement an algorithm to determine if a string has all unique characters. What if you cannot use additional data structures?

Hints: #44, #117, #132

pg 192

1.2 **Check Permutation:** Given two strings, write a method to decide if one is a permutation of the other.

Hints: #1, #84, #122, #131

pg 193

1.3 **URLify:** Write a method to replace all spaces in a string with '%20'. You may assume that the string has sufficient space at the end to hold the additional characters, and that you are given the "true" length of the string. (Note: If implementing in Java, please use a character array so that you can perform this operation in place.)

EXAMPLE

Input: `"Mr John Smith    ", 13`

Output: `"Mr%20John%20Smith"`

Hints: #53, #118

pg 194

1.4 **Palindrome Permutation:** Given a string, write a function to check if it is a permutation of a palindrome. A palindrome is a word or phrase that is the same forwards and backwards. A permutation is a rearrangement of letters. The palindrome does not need to be limited to just dictionary words.

EXAMPLE

Input: `Tact Coa`

Output: `True (permutations: "taco cat", "atco cta", etc.)`

Hints: #106, #121, #134, #136

pg 195

1.5 **One Away:** There are three types of edits that can be performed on strings: insert a character, remove a character, or replace a character. Given two strings, write a function to check if they are one edit (or zero edits) away.

EXAMPLE

```
pale,  ple  -> true
pales, pale -> true
pale,  bale -> true
pale,  bake -> false
```

Hints: #23, #97, #130

pg 199

1.6 **String Compression:** Implement a method to perform basic string compression using the counts of repeated characters. For example, the string `aabcccccaaa` would become `a2b1c5a3`. If the "compressed" string would not become smaller than the original string, your method should return the original string. You can assume the string has only uppercase and lowercase letters (a - z).

Hints: #92, #110

pg 201

1.7 **Rotate Matrix:** Given an image represented by an `NxN` matrix, where each pixel in the image is 4 bytes, write a method to rotate the image by 90 degrees. Can you do this in place?

Hints: #51, #100

pg 203

1.8 **Zero Matrix:** Write an algorithm such that if an element in an `MxN` matrix is 0, its entire row and column are set to 0.

Hints: #17, #74, #102

pg 204

1.9 **String Rotation:** Assume you have a method `isSubstring` which checks if one word is a substring of another. Given two strings, `s1` and `s2`, write code to check if `s2` is a rotation of `s1` using only one call to `isSubstring` (e.g., "`waterbottle`" is a rotation of "`erbottlewat`").

Hints: #34, #88, #104

pg 206

Additional Questions: Object-Oriented Design (#7.12), Recursion (#8.3), Sorting and Searching (#10.9), C++ (#12.11), Moderate Problems (#16.8, #16.17, #16.22), Hard Problems (#17.4, #17.7, #17.13, #17.22, #17.26).

Hints start on page 653.

2

Linked Lists

A linked list is a data structure that represents a sequence of nodes. In a singly linked list, each node points to the next node in the linked list. A doubly linked list gives each node pointers to both the next node and the previous node.

The following diagram depicts a doubly linked list:

Unlike an array, a linked list does not provide constant time access to a particular "index" within the list. This means that if you'd like to find the Kth element in the list, you will need to iterate through K elements.

The benefit of a linked list is that you can add and remove items from the beginning of the list in constant time. For specific applications, this can be useful.

▸ Creating a Linked List

The code below implements a very basic singly linked list.

```
class Node {
   Node next = null;
   int data;

   public Node(int d) {
      data = d;
   }

   void appendToTail(int d) {
      Node end = new Node(d);
      Node n = this;
      while (n.next != null) {
         n = n.next;
      }
      n.next = end;
   }
}
```

In this implementation, we don't have a `LinkedList` data structure. We access the linked list through a reference to the head Node of the linked list. When you implement the linked list this way, you need to be a bit careful. What if multiple objects need a reference to the linked list, and then the head of the linked list changes? Some objects might still be pointing to the old head.

We could, if we chose, implement a `LinkedList` class that wraps the Node class. This would essentially just have a single member variable: the head Node. This would largely resolve the earlier issue.

Remember that when you're discussing a linked list in an interview, you must understand whether it is a singly linked list or a doubly linked list.

▸ Deleting a Node from a Singly Linked List

Deleting a node from a linked list is fairly straightforward. Given a node n, we find the previous node `prev` and set `prev.next` equal to `n.next`. If the list is doubly linked, we must also update `n.next` to set `n.next.prev` equal to `n.prev`. The important things to remember are (1) to check for the null pointer and (2) to update the head or tail pointer as necessary.

Additionally, if you implement this code in C, C++ or another language that requires the developer to do memory management, you should consider if the removed node should be deallocated.

```
Node deleteNode(Node head, int d) {
   Node n = head;

   if (n.data == d) {
      return head.next; /* moved head */
   }

   while (n.next != null) {
      if (n.next.data == d) {
         n.next = n.next.next;
         return head; /* head didn't change */
      }
      n = n.next;
   }
   return head;
}
```

▸ The "Runner" Technique

The "runner" (or second pointer) technique is used in many linked list problems. The runner technique means that you iterate through the linked list with two pointers simultaneously, with one ahead of the other. The "fast" node might be ahead by a fixed amount, or it might be hopping multiple nodes for each one node that the "slow" node iterates through.

For example, suppose you had a linked list a_1->a_2->...->a_n->b_1->b_2->...->b_n and you wanted to rearrange it into a_1->b_1->a_2->b_2->...->a_n->b_n. You do not know the length of the linked list (but you do know that the length is an even number).

You could have one pointer `p1` (the fast pointer) move every two elements for every one move that p2 makes. When p1 hits the end of the linked list, p2 will be at the midpoint. Then, move p1 back to the front and begin "weaving" the elements. On each iteration, p2 selects an element and inserts it after p1.

▸ Recursive Problems

A number of linked list problems rely on recursion. If you're having trouble solving a linked list problem, you should explore if a recursive approach will work. We won't go into depth on recursion here, since a later chapter is devoted to it.

However, you should remember that recursive algorithms take at least `O(n)` space, where `n` is the depth of the recursive call. All recursive algorithms *can* be implemented iteratively, although they may be much more complex.

Interview Questions

2.1 **Remove Dups:** Write code to remove duplicates from an unsorted linked list.

FOLLOW UP

How would you solve this problem if a temporary buffer is not allowed?

Hints: #9, #40

pg 208

2.2 **Return Kth to Last:** Implement an algorithm to find the kth to last element of a singly linked list.

Hints: #8, #25, #41, #67, #126

pg 209

2.3 **Delete Middle Node:** Implement an algorithm to delete a node in the middle (i.e., any node but the first and last node, not necessarily the exact middle) of a singly linked list, given only access to that node.

EXAMPLE

Input: the node c from the linked list `a->b->c->d->e->f`

Result: nothing is returned, but the new linked list looks like `a->b->d->e->f`

Hints: #72

pg 211

2.4 **Partition:** Write code to partition a linked list around a value x, such that all nodes less than x come before all nodes greater than or equal to x. If x is contained within the list, the values of x only need to be after the elements less than x (see below). The partition element x can appear anywhere in the "right partition"; it does not need to appear between the left and right partitions.

EXAMPLE

Input: `3 -> 5 -> 8 -> 5 -> 10 -> 2 -> 1` [partition = 5]

Output: `3 -> 1 -> 2 -> 10 -> 5 -> 5 -> 8`

Hints: #3, #24

pg 212

2.5 **Sum Lists:** You have two numbers represented by a linked list, where each node contains a single digit. The digits are stored in *reverse* order, such that the 1's digit is at the head of the list. Write a function that adds the two numbers and returns the sum as a linked list.

EXAMPLE

Input: `(7-> 1 -> 6) + (5 -> 9 -> 2)`. That is, `617 + 295`.

Output: `2 -> 1 -> 9`. That is, `912`.

FOLLOW UP

Suppose the digits are stored in forward order. Repeat the above problem.

EXAMPLE

Input: `(6 -> 1 -> 7) + (2 -> 9 -> 5)`. That is, `617 + 295`.

Output: `9 -> 1 -> 2`. That is, `912`.

Hints: #7, #30, #71, #95, #109

pg 214

2.6 **Palindrome:** Implement a function to check if a linked list is a palindrome.

Hints: #5, #13, #29, #61, #101

pg 216

2.7 **Intersection**: Given two (singly) linked lists, determine if the two lists intersect. Return the intersecting node. Note that the intersection is defined based on reference, not value. That is, if the `kth` node of the first linked list is the exact same node (by reference) as the `jth` node of the second linked list, then they are intersecting.

Hints: #20, #45, #55, #65, #76, #93, #111, #120, #129

pg 221

2.8 **Loop Detection:** Given a circular linked list, implement an algorithm that returns the node at the beginning of the loop.

DEFINITION

Circular linked list: A (corrupt) linked list in which a node's next pointer points to an earlier node, so as to make a loop in the linked list.

EXAMPLE

Input: `A -> B -> C -> D -> E -> C` [the same C as earlier]

Output: `C`

Hints: #50, #69, #83, #90

pg 223

Additional Questions: Trees and Graphs (#4.3), Object-Oriented Design (#7.12), System Design and Scalability (#9.5), Moderate Problems (#16.25), Hard Problems (#17.12).

Hints start on page 653.

3

Stacks and Queues

Questions on stacks and queues will be much easier to handle if you are comfortable with the ins and outs of the data structure. The problems can be quite tricky, though. While some problems may be slight modifications on the original data structure, others have much more complex challenges.

▸ Implementing a Stack

The stack data structure is precisely what it sounds like: a stack of data. In certain types of problems, it can be favorable to store data in a stack rather than in an array.

A stack uses LIFO (last-in first-out) ordering. That is, as in a stack of dinner plates, the most recent item added to the stack is the first item to be removed.

It uses the following operations:

- `pop()`: Remove the top item from the stack.
- `push(item)`: Add an item to the top of the stack.
- `peek()`: Return the top of the stack.
- `isEmpty()`: Return true if and only if the stack is empty.

Unlike an array, a stack does not offer constant-time access to the `i`th item. However, it does allow constant-time adds and removes, as it doesn't require shifting elements around.

We have provided simple sample code to implement a stack. Note that a stack can also be implemented using a linked list, if items were added and removed from the same side.

```
public class MyStack<T> {
  private static class StackNode<T> {
    private T data;
    private StackNode<T> next;

    public StackNode(T data) {
      this.data = data;
    }
  }

  private StackNode<T> top;

  public T pop() {
    if (top == null) throw new EmptyStackException();
    T item = top.data;
```

```
        top = top.next;
        return item;
    }

    public void push(T item) {
        StackNode<T> t = new StackNode<T>(item);
        t.next = top;
        top = t;
    }

    public T peek() {
        if (top == null) throw new EmptyStackException();
        return top.data;
    }

    public boolean isEmpty() {
        return top == null;
    }
}
```

One case where stacks are often useful is in certain recursive algorithms. Sometimes you need to push temporary data onto a stack as you recurse, but then remove them as you backtrack (for example, because the recursive check failed). A stack offers an intuitive way to do this.

A stack can also be used to implement a recursive algorithm iteratively. (This is a good exercise! Take a simple recursive algorithm and implement it iteratively.)

▸ Implementing a Queue

A queue implements FIFO (first-in first-out) ordering. As in a line or queue at a ticket stand, items are removed from the data structure in the same order that they are added.

It uses the operations:

- `add(item)`: Add an item to the end of the list.
- `remove()`: Remove the first item in the list.
- `peek()`: Return the top of the queue.
- `isEmpty()`: Return true if and only if the queue is empty.

A queue can also be implemented with a linked list. In fact, they are essentially the same thing, as long as items are added and removed from opposite sides.

```
public class MyQueue<T> {
   private static class QueueNode<T> {
      private T data;
      private QueueNode<T> next;

      public QueueNode(T data) {
         this.data = data;
      }
   }

   private QueueNode<T> first;
   private QueueNode<T> last;

   public void add(T item) {
```

```
        QueueNode<T> t = new QueueNode<T>(item);
        if (last != null) {
            last.next = t;
        }
        last = t;
        if (first == null) {
            first = last;
        }
    }

    public T remove() {
        if (first == null) throw new NoSuchElementException();
        T data = first.data;
        first = first.next;
        if (first == null) {
            last = null;
        }
        return data;
    }

    public T peek() {
        if (first == null) throw new NoSuchElementException();
        return first.data;
    }

    public boolean isEmpty() {
        return first == null;
    }
}
```

It is especially easy to mess up the updating of the first and last nodes in a queue. Be sure to double check this.

One place where queues are often used is in breadth-first search or in implementing a cache.

In breadth-first search, for example, we used a queue to store a list of the nodes that we need to process. Each time we process a node, we add its adjacent nodes to the back of the queue. This allows us to process nodes in the order in which they are viewed.

Interview Questions

3.1 **Three in One:** Describe how you could use a single array to implement three stacks.

Hints: #2, #12, #38, #58

pg 227

3.2 **Stack Min:** How would you design a stack which, in addition to `push` and `pop`, has a function `min` which returns the minimum element? `Push`, `pop` and `min` should all operate in `O(1)` time.

Hints: #27, #59, #78

pg 232

3.3 **Stack of Plates:** Imagine a (literal) stack of plates. If the stack gets too high, it might topple. Therefore, in real life, we would likely start a new stack when the previous stack exceeds some threshold. Implement a data structure `SetOfStacks` that mimics this. `SetOfStacks` should be composed of several stacks and should create a new stack once the previous one exceeds capacity. `SetOfStacks.push()` and `SetOfStacks.pop()` should behave identically to a single stack (that is, `pop()` should return the same values as it would if there were just a single stack).

FOLLOW UP

Implement a function `popAt(int index)` which performs a pop operation on a specific sub-stack.

Hints: #64, #81

pg 233

3.4 **Queue via Stacks:** Implement a `MyQueue` class which implements a queue using two stacks.

Hints: #98, #114

pg 236

3.5 **Sort Stack:** Write a program to sort a stack such that the smallest items are on the top. You can use an additional temporary stack, but you may not copy the elements into any other data structure (such as an array). The stack supports the following operations: `push`, `pop`, `peek`, and `isEmpty`.

Hints: #15, #32, #43

pg 237

3.6 **Animal Shelter:** An animal shelter, which holds only dogs and cats, operates on a strictly "first in, first out" basis. People must adopt either the "oldest" (based on arrival time) of all animals at the shelter, or they can select whether they would prefer a dog or a cat (and will receive the oldest animal of that type). They cannot select which specific animal they would like. Create the data structures to maintain this system and implement operations such as `enqueue`, `dequeueAny`, `dequeueDog`, and `dequeueCat`. You may use the built-in `LinkedList` data structure.

Hints: #22, #56, #63

pg 239

Additional Questions: Linked Lists (#2.6), Moderate Problems (#16.26), Hard Problems (#17.9).

Hints start on page 653.

Trees and Graphs

Many interviewees find tree and graph problems to be some of the trickiest. Searching a tree is more complicated than searching in a linearly organized data structure such as an array or linked list. Additionally, the worst case and average case time may vary wildly, and we must evaluate both aspects of any algorithm. Fluency in implementing a tree or graph from scratch will prove essential.

Because most people are more familiar with trees than graphs (and they're a bit simpler), we'll discuss trees first. This is a bit out of order though, as a tree is actually a type of graph.

> Note: Some of the terms in this chapter can vary slightly across different textbooks and other sources. If you're used to a different definition, that's fine. Make sure to clear up any ambiguity with your interviewer.

▸ Types of Trees

A nice way to understand a tree is with a recursive explanation. A tree is a data structure composed of nodes.

- Each tree has a root node. (Actually, this isn't strictly necessary in graph theory, but it's usually how we use trees in programming, and especially programming interviews.)
- The root node has zero or more child nodes.
- Each child node has zero or more child nodes, and so on.

The tree cannot contain cycles. The nodes may or may not be in a particular order, they could have any data type as values, and they may or may not have links back to their parent nodes.

A very simple class definition for `Node` is:

```
class Node {
  public String name;
  public Node[] children;
}
```

You might also have a `Tree` class to wrap this node. For the purposes of interview questions, we typically do not use a `Tree` class. You can if you feel it makes your code simpler or better, but it rarely does.

```
class Tree {
  public Node root;
}
```

Tree and graph questions are rife with ambiguous details and incorrect assumptions. Be sure to watch out for the following issues and seek clarification when necessary.

Trees vs. Binary Trees

A binary tree is a tree in which each node has up to two children. Not all trees are binary trees. For example, this tree is not a binary tree. You could call it a ternary tree.

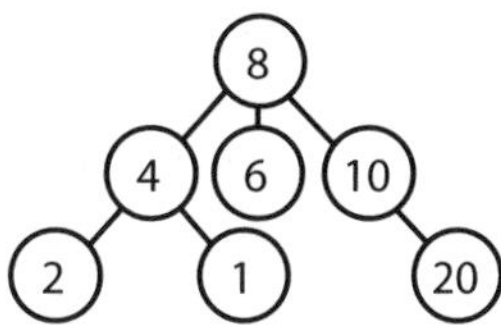

There are occasions when you might have a tree that is not a binary tree. For example, suppose you were using a tree to represent a bunch of phone numbers. In this case, you might use a 10-ary tree, with each node having up to 10 children (one for each digit).

A node is called a "leaf" node if it has no children.

Binary Tree vs. Binary Search Tree

A binary search tree is a binary tree in which every node fits a specific ordering property: `all left descendents <= n < all right descendents`. This must be true for each node n.

> The definition of a binary search tree can vary slightly with respect to equality. Under some definitions, the tree cannot have duplicate values. In others, the duplicate values will be on the right or can be on either side. All are valid definitions, but you should clarify this with your interviewer.

Note that this inequality must be true for all of a node's descendents, not just its immediate children. The following tree on the left below is a binary search tree. The tree on the right is not, since 12 is to the left of 8.

A binary search tree.

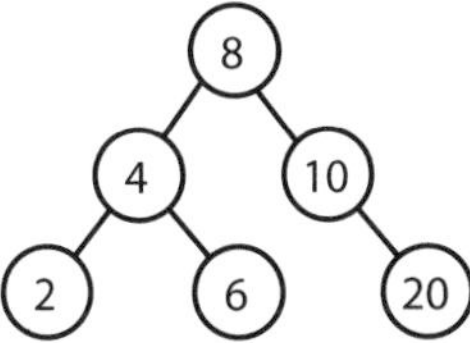

Not a binary search tree.

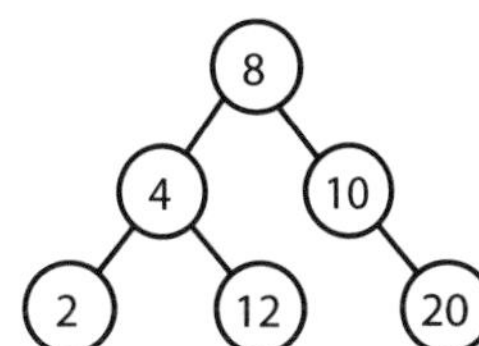

When given a tree question, many candidates assume the interviewer means a binary *search* tree. Be sure to ask. A binary search tree imposes the condition that, for each node, its left descendents are less than or equal to the current node, which is less than the right descendents.

Balanced vs. Unbalanced

While many trees are balanced, not all are. Ask your interviewer for clarification here. Note that balancing a tree does not mean the left and right subtrees are exactly the same size (like you see under "perfect binary trees" in the following diagram).

One way to think about it is that a "balanced" tree really means something more like "not terribly imbalanced." It's balanced enough to ensure `O(log n)` times for `insert` and `find`, but it's not necessarily as balanced as it could be.

Two common types of balanced trees are red-black trees (pg 639) and AVL trees (pg 637). These are discussed in more detail in the Advanced Topics section.

Complete Binary Trees

A complete binary tree is a binary tree in which every level of the tree is fully filled, except for perhaps the last level. To the extent that the last level is filled, it is filled left to right.

not a complete binary tree

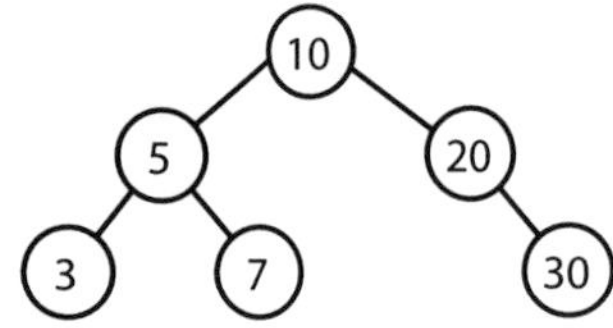

a complete binary tree

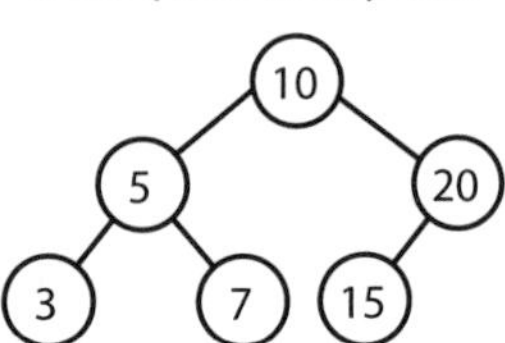

Full Binary Trees

A full binary tree is a binary tree in which every node has either zero or two children. That is, no nodes have only one child.

not a full binary tree

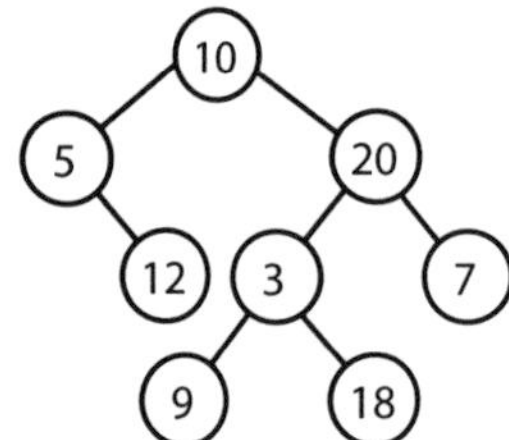

a full binary tree

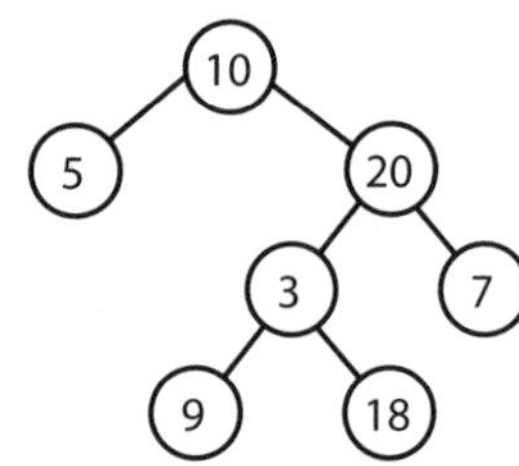

Perfect Binary Trees

A perfect binary tree is one that is both full and complete. All leaf nodes will be at the same level, and this level has the maximum number of nodes.

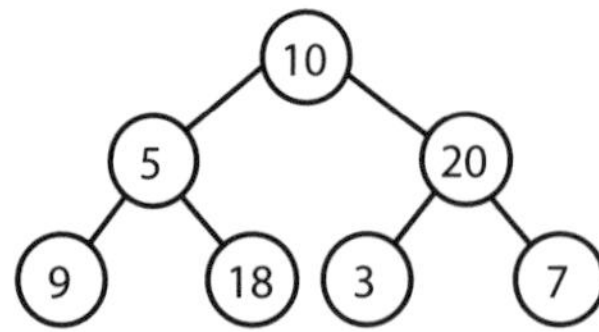

Note that perfect trees are rare in interviews and in real life, as a perfect tree must have exactly $2^k - 1$ nodes (where k is the number of levels). In an interview, do not assume a binary tree is perfect.

Binary Tree Traversal

Prior to your interview, you should be comfortable implementing in-order, post-order, and pre-order traversal. The most common of these is in-order traversal.

In-Order Traversal

In-order traversal means to "visit" (often, print) the left branch, then the current node, and finally, the right branch.

```
void inOrderTraversal(TreeNode node) {
   if (node != null) {
      inOrderTraversal(node.left);
      visit(node);
      inOrderTraversal(node.right);
   }
}
```

When performed on a binary search tree, it visits the nodes in ascending order (hence the name "in-order").

Pre-Order Traversal

Pre-order traversal visits the current node before its child nodes (hence the name "pre-order").

```
void preOrderTraversal(TreeNode node) {
   if (node != null) {
      visit(node);
      preOrderTraversal(node.left);
      preOrderTraversal(node.right);
   }
}
```

In a pre-order traversal, the root is always the first node visited.

Post-Order Traversal

Post-order traversal visits the current node after its child nodes (hence the name "post-order").

```
void postOrderTraversal(TreeNode node) {
   if (node != null) {
      postOrderTraversal(node.left);
      postOrderTraversal(node.right);
      visit(node);
   }
}
```

In a post-order traversal, the root is always the last node visited.

Binary Heaps (Min-Heaps and Max-Heaps)

We'll just discuss min-heaps here. Max-heaps are essentially equivalent, but the elements are in descending order rather than ascending order.

A min-heap is a *complete* binary tree (that is, totally filled other than the rightmost elements on the last level) where each node is smaller than its children. The root, therefore, is the minimum element in the tree.

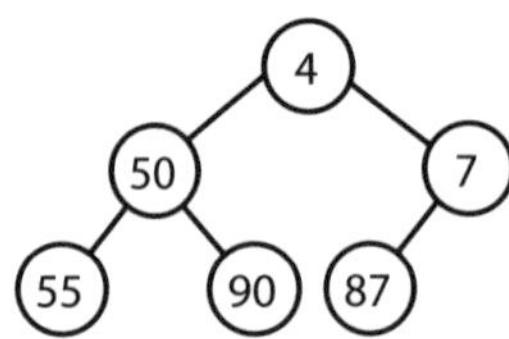

We have two key operations on a min-heap: `insert` and `extract_min`.

Insert

When we insert into a min-heap, we always start by inserting the element at the bottom. We insert at the rightmost spot so as to maintain the complete tree property.

Then, we "fix" the tree by swapping the new element with its parent, until we find an appropriate spot for the element. We essentially bubble up the minimum element.

Step 1: Insert 2 Step 2: Swap 2 and 7 Step 3: Swap 2 and 4

This takes `O(log n)` time, where n is the number of nodes in the heap.

Extract Minimum Element

Finding the minimum element of a min-heap is easy: it's always at the top. The trickier part is how to remove it. (In fact, this isn't that tricky.)

First, we remove the minimum element and swap it with the last element in the heap (the bottommost, rightmost element). Then, we bubble down this element, swapping it with one of its children until the min-heap property is restored.

Do we swap it with the left child or the right child? That depends on their values. There's no inherent ordering between the left and right element, but you'll need to take the smaller one in order to maintain the min-heap ordering.

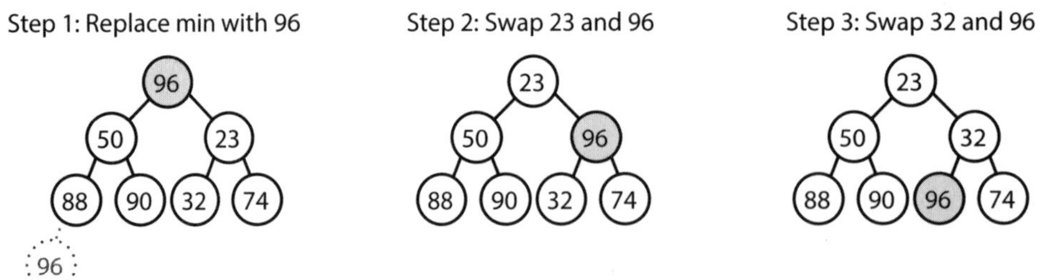

This algorithm will also take `O(log n)` time.

▸ Tries (Prefix Trees)

A trie (sometimes called a prefix tree) is a funny data structure. It comes up a lot in interview questions, but algorithm textbooks don't spend much time on this data structure.

A trie is a variant of an n-ary tree in which characters are stored at each node. Each path down the tree may represent a word.

The * nodes (sometimes called "null nodes") are often used to indicate complete words. For example, the fact that there is a * node under MANY indicates that MANY is a complete word. The existence of the MA path indicates there are words that start with MA.

The actual implementation of these * nodes might be a special type of child (such as a `TerminatingTrieNode`, which inherits from `TrieNode`). Or, we could use just a boolean flag `terminates` within the "parent" node.

A node in a trie could have anywhere from 1 through `ALPHABET_SIZE + 1` children (or, 0 through `ALPHABET_SIZE` if a boolean flag is used instead of a * node).

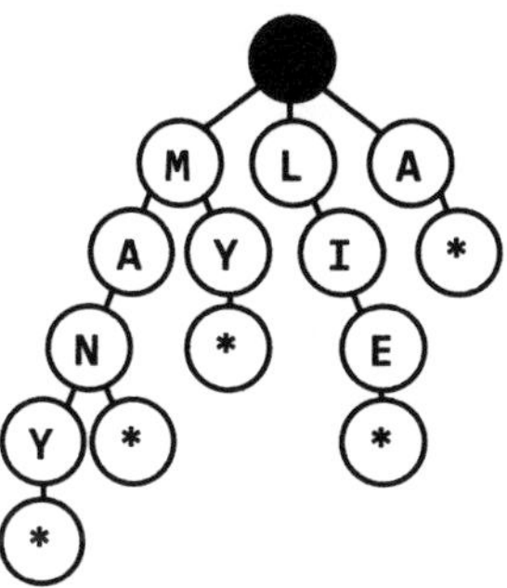

Very commonly, a trie is used to store the entire (English) language for quick prefix lookups. While a hash table can quickly look up whether a string is a valid word, it cannot tell us if a string is a prefix of any valid words. A trie can do this very quickly.

> How quickly? A trie can check if a string is a valid prefix in `O(K)` time, where K is the length of the string. This is actually the same runtime as a hash table will take. Although we often refer to hash table lookups as being `O(1)` time, this isn't entirely true. A hash table must read through all the characters in the input, which takes `O(K)` time in the case of a word lookup.

Many problems involving lists of valid words leverage a trie as an optimization. In situations when we search through the tree on related prefixes repeatedly (e.g., looking up M, then MA, then MAN, then MANY), we might pass around a reference to the current node in the tree. This will allow us to just check if Y is a child of MAN, rather than starting from the root each time.

▸ Graphs

A tree is actually a type of graph, but not all graphs are trees. Simply put, a tree is a connected graph without cycles.

A graph is simply a collection of nodes with edges between (some of) them.

- Graphs can be either directed (like the following graph) or undirected. While directed edges are like a one-way street, undirected edges are like a two-way street.

- The graph might consist of multiple isolated subgraphs. If there is a path between every pair of vertices, it is called a "connected graph."
- The graph can also have cycles (or not). An "acyclic graph" is one without cycles.

Visually, you could draw a graph like this:

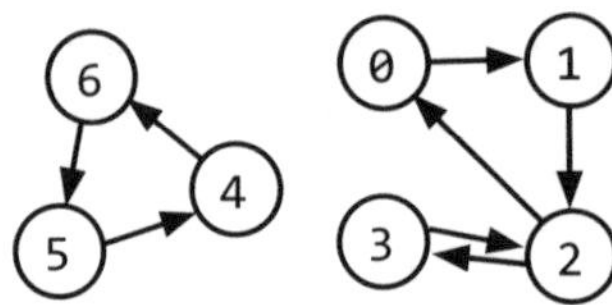

In terms of programming, there are two common ways to represent a graph.

Adjacency List

This is the most common way to represent a graph. Every vertex (or node) stores a list of adjacent vertices. In an undirected graph, an edge like `(a, b)` would be stored twice: once in a's adjacent vertices and once in b's adjacent vertices.

A simple class definition for a graph node could look essentially the same as a tree node.

```
class Graph {
  public Node[] nodes;
}

class Node {
   public String name;
   public Node[] children;
}
```

The Graph class is used because, unlike in a tree, you can't necessarily reach all the nodes from a single node.

You don't necessarily need any additional classes to represent a graph. An array (or a hash table) of lists (arrays, arraylists, linked lists, etc.) can store the adjacency list. The graph above could be represented as:

```
0: 1
1: 2
2: 0, 3
3: 2
4: 6
5: 4
6: 5
```

This is a bit more compact, but it isn't quite as clean. We tend to use node classes unless there's a compelling reason not to.

Adjacency Matrices

An adjacency matrix is an NxN boolean matrix (where N is the number of nodes), where a `true` value at `matrix[i][j]` indicates an edge from node `i` to node `j`. (You can also use an integer matrix with 0s and 1s.)

In an undirected graph, an adjacency matrix will be symmetric. In a directed graph, it will not (necessarily) be.

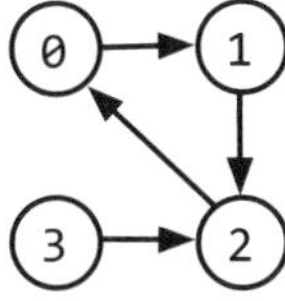

	0	1	2	3
0	0	1	0	0
1	0	0	1	0
2	1	0	0	0
3	0	0	1	0

The same graph algorithms that are used on adjacency lists (breadth-first search, etc.) can be performed with adjacency matrices, but they may be somewhat less efficient. In the adjacency list representation, you can easily iterate through the neighbors of a node. In the adjacency matrix representation, you will need to iterate through all the nodes to identify a node's neighbors.

Graph Search

The two most common ways to search a graph are depth-first search and breadth-first search.

In depth-first search (DFS), we start at the root (or another arbitrarily selected node) and explore each branch completely before moving on to the next branch. That is, we go deep first (hence the name *depth-first search*) before we go wide.

In breadth-first search (BFS), we start at the root (or another arbitrarily selected node) and explore each neighbor before going on to any of their children. That is, we go wide (hence *breadth*-first search) before we go deep.

See the below depiction of a graph and its depth-first and breadth-first search (assuming neighbors are iterated in numerical order).

Graph

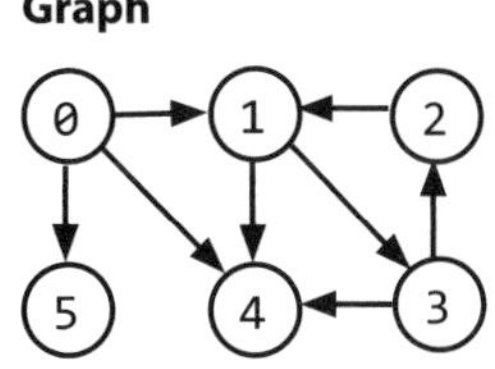

Depth-First Search

```
Node 0
 Node 1
  Node 3
   Node 2
   Node 4
Node 5
```

Breadth-First Search

```
Node 0
Node 1
Node 4
Node 5
Node 3
Node 2
```

Breadth-first search and depth-first search tend to be used in different scenarios. DFS is often preferred if we want to visit every node in the graph. Both will work just fine, but depth-first search is a bit simpler.

However, if we want to find the shortest path (or just any path) between two nodes, BFS is generally better. Consider representing all the friendships in the entire world in a graph and trying to find a path of friendships between `Ash` and `Vanessa`.

In depth-first search, we could take a path like `Ash -> Brian -> Carleton -> Davis -> Eric -> Farah -> Gayle -> Harry -> Isabella -> John -> Kari`... and then find ourselves very far away. We could go through most of the world without realizing that, in fact, `Vanessa` is `Ash`'s friend. We will still eventually find the path, but it may take a long time. It also won't find us the shortest path.

In breadth-first search, we would stay close to `Ash` for as long as possible. We might iterate through many of `Ash`'s friends, but we wouldn't go to his more distant connections until absolutely necessary. If `Vanessa` is `Ash`'s friend, or his friend-of-a-friend, we'll find this out relatively quickly.

Depth-First Search (DFS)

In DFS, we visit a node a and then iterate through each of a's neighbors. When visiting a node b that is a neighbor of a, we visit all of b's neighbors before going on to a's other neighbors. That is, a exhaustively searches b's branch before any of its other neighbors.

Note that pre-order and other forms of tree traversal are a form of DFS. The key difference is that when implementing this algorithm for a graph, we must check if the node has been visited. If we don't, we risk getting stuck in an infinite loop.

The pseudocode below implements DFS.

```
void search(Node root) {
   if (root == null) return;
   visit(root);
   root.visited = true;
   for each (Node n in root.adjacent) {
      if (n.visited == false) {
         search(n);
      }
   }
}
```

Breadth-First Search (BFS)

BFS is a bit less intuitive, and many interviewees struggle with the implementation unless they are already familiar with it. The main tripping point is the (false) assumption that BFS is recursive. It's not. Instead, it uses a queue.

In BFS, node a visits each of a's neighbors before visiting any of *their* neighbors. You can think of this as searching level by level out from a. An iterative solution involving a queue usually works best.

```
void search(Node root) {
   Queue queue = new Queue();
   root.marked = true;
   queue.enqueue(root); // Add to the end of queue

   while (!queue.isEmpty()) {
      Node r = queue.dequeue(); // Remove from the front of the queue
      visit(r);
      foreach (Node n in r.adjacent) {
         if (n.marked == false) {
            n.marked = true;
            queue.enqueue(n);
         }
      }
   }
}
```

If you are asked to implement BFS, the key thing to remember is the use of the queue. The rest of the algorithm flows from this fact.

Bidirectional Search

Bidirectional search is used to find the shortest path between a source and destination node. It operates by essentially running two simultaneous breadth-first searches, one from each node. When their searches collide, we have found a path.

Breadth-First Search
Single search from s to t that collides after four levels.

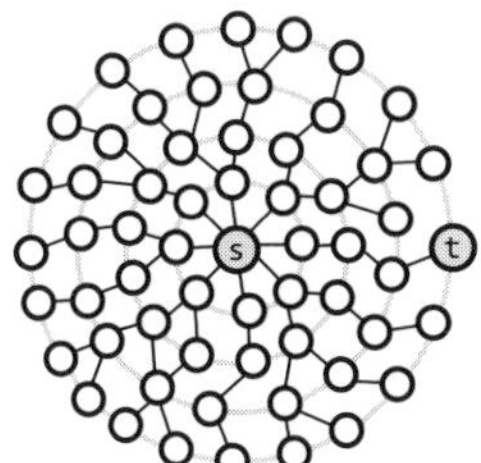

Bidirectional Search
Two searches (one from s and one from t) that collide after four levels total (two levels each).

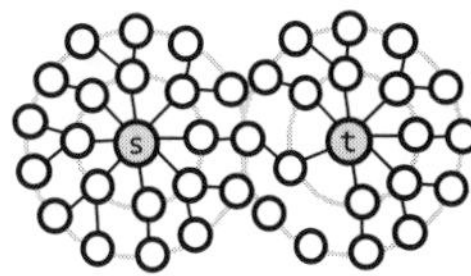

To see why this is faster, consider a graph where every node has at most k adjacent nodes and the shortest path from node s to node t has length d.

- In traditional breadth-first search, we would search up to k nodes in the first "level" of the search. In the second level, we would search up to k nodes for each of those first k nodes, so k^2 nodes total (thus far). We would do this d times, so that's $O(k^d)$ nodes.
- In bidirectional search, we have two searches that collide after approximately $d/2$ levels (the midpoint of the path). The search from s visits approximately $k^{d/2}$, as does the search from t. That's approximately $2\ k^{d/2}$, or $O(k^{d/2})$, nodes total.

This might seem like a minor difference, but it's not. It's huge. Recall that $(k^{d/2})*(k^{d/2}) = k^d$. The bidirectional search is actually faster by a factor of $k^{d/2}$.

Put another way: if our system could only support searching "friend of friend" paths in breadth-first search, it could now likely support "friend of friend of friend of friend" paths. We can support paths that are twice as long.

Additional Reading: Topological Sort (pg 632), Dijkstra's Algorithm (pg 633), AVL Trees (pg 637), Red-Black Trees (pg 639).

Interview Questions

4.1 **Route Between Nodes:** Given a directed graph, design an algorithm to find out whether there is a route between two nodes.

Hints: #127

pg 241

4.2 **Minimal Tree:** Given a sorted (increasing order) array with unique integer elements, write an algorithm to create a binary search tree with minimal height.

Hints: #19, #73, #116

pg 242

4.3 **List of Depths:** Given a binary tree, design an algorithm which creates a linked list of all the nodes at each depth (e.g., if you have a tree with depth D, you'll have D linked lists).

Hints: #107, #123, #135

pg 243

4.4 **Check Balanced:** Implement a function to check if a binary tree is balanced. For the purposes of this question, a balanced tree is defined to be a tree such that the heights of the two subtrees of any node never differ by more than one.

Hints: #21, #33, #49, #105, #124

pg 244

4.5 **Validate BST:** Implement a function to check if a binary tree is a binary search tree.

Hints: #35, #57, #86, #113, #128

pg 245

4.6 **Successor:** Write an algorithm to find the "next" node (i.e., in-order successor) of a given node in a binary search tree. You may assume that each node has a link to its parent.

Hints: #79, #91

pg 248

4.7 **Build Order:** You are given a list of projects and a list of dependencies (which is a list of pairs of projects, where the second project is dependent on the first project). All of a project's dependencies must be built before the project is. Find a build order that will allow the projects to be built. If there is no valid build order, return an error.

EXAMPLE

Input:

```
projects: a, b, c, d, e, f
dependencies: (a, d), (f, b), (b, d), (f, a), (d, c)
```

Output: `f, e, a, b, d, c`

Hints: #26, #47, #60, #85, #125, #133

pg 250

4.8 **First Common Ancestor:** Design an algorithm and write code to find the first common ancestor of two nodes in a binary tree. Avoid storing additional nodes in a data structure. NOTE: This is not necessarily a binary search tree.

Hints: #10, #16, #28, #36, #46, #70, #80, #96

pg 257

4.9 **BST Sequences:** A binary search tree was created by traversing through an array from left to right and inserting each element. Given a binary search tree with distinct elements, print all possible arrays that could have led to this tree.

EXAMPLE

Input:

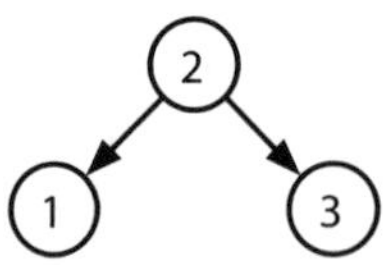

Output: `{2, 1, 3}, {2, 3, 1}`

Hints: #39, #48, #66, #82

pg 262

4.10 **Check Subtree:** T1 and T2 are two very large binary trees, with T1 much bigger than T2. Create an algorithm to determine if T2 is a subtree of T1.

A tree T2 is a subtree of T1 if there exists a node n in T1 such that the subtree of n is identical to T2. That is, if you cut off the tree at node n, the two trees would be identical.

Hints: #4, #11, #18, #31, #37

pg 265

4.11 **Random Node:** You are implementing a binary tree class from scratch which, in addition to `insert`, `find`, and `delete`, has a method `getRandomNode()` which returns a random node from the tree. All nodes should be equally likely to be chosen. Design and implement an algorithm for `getRandomNode`, and explain how you would implement the rest of the methods.

Hints: #42, #54, #62, #75, #89, #99, #112, #119

pg 268

4.12 **Paths with Sum:** You are given a binary tree in which each node contains an integer value (which might be positive or negative). Design an algorithm to count the number of paths that sum to a given value. The path does not need to start or end at the root or a leaf, but it must go downwards (traveling only from parent nodes to child nodes).

Hints: #6, #14, #52, #68, #77, #87, #94, #103, #108, #115

pg 272

Additional Questions: Recursion (#8.10), System Design and Scalability (#9.2, #9.3), Sorting and Searching (#10.10), Hard Problems (#17.7, #17.12, #17.13, #17.14, #17.17, #17.20, #17.22, #17.25).

Hints start on page 653.

5

Bit Manipulation

Bit manipulation is used in a variety of problems. Sometimes, the question explicitly calls for bit manipulation. Other times, it's simply a useful technique to optimize your code. You should be comfortable doing bit manipulation by hand, as well as with code. Be careful; it's easy to make little mistakes.

▸ Bit Manipulation By Hand

If you're rusty on bit manipulation, try the following exercises by hand. The items in the third column can be solved manually or with "tricks" (described below). For simplicity, assume that these are four-bit numbers.

If you get confused, work them through as a base 10 number. You can then apply the same process to a binary number. Remember that ^ indicates an XOR, and ~ is a NOT (negation).

`0110 + 0010`	`0011 * 0101`	`0110 + 0110`
`0011 + 0010`	`0011 * 0011`	`0100 * 0011`
`0110 - 0011`	`1101 >> 2`	`1101 ^ (~1101)`
`1000 - 0110`	`1101 ^ 0101`	`1011 & (~0 << 2)`

Solutions: line 1 (1000, 1111, 1100); line 2 (0101, 1001, 1100); line 3 (0011, 0011, 1111); line 4 (0010, 1000, 1000).

The tricks in Column 3 are as follows:

1. `0110 + 0110` is equivalent to `0110 * 2`, which is equivalent to shifting `0110` left by 1.
2. `0100` equals 4, and multiplying by 4 is just left shifting by 2. So we shift `0011` left by 2 to get `1100`.
3. Think about this operation bit by bit. If you XOR a bit with its own negated value, you will always get 1. Therefore, the solution to `a^(~a)` will be a sequence of 1s.
4. `~0` is a sequence of 1s, so `~0 << 2` is 1s followed by two 0s. ANDing that with another value will clear the last two bits of the value.

If you didn't see these tricks immediately, think about them logically.

▸ Bit Facts and Tricks

The following expressions are useful in bit manipulation. Don't just memorize them, though; think deeply about why each of these is true. We use "1s" and "0s" to indicate a sequence of 1s or 0s, respectively.

```
x ^ 0s = x        x & 0s = 0        x | 0s = x
x ^ 1s = ~x       x & 1s = x        x | 1s = 1s
x ^ x = 0         x & x = x         x | x = x
```

To understand these expressions, recall that these operations occur bit-by-bit, with what's happening on one bit never impacting the other bits. This means that if one of the above statements is true for a single bit, then it's true for a sequence of bits.

▸ Two's Complement and Negative Numbers

Computers typically store integers in two's complement representation. A positive number is represented as itself while a negative number is represented as the two's complement of its absolute value (with a 1 in its sign bit to indicate that a negative value). The two's complement of an N-bit number (where N is the number of bits used for the number, *excluding* the sign bit) is the complement of the number with respect to 2^N.

Let's look at the 4-bit integer -3 as an example. If it's a 4-bit number, we have one bit for the sign and three bits for the value. We want the complement with respect to 2^3, which is 8. The complement of 3 (the absolute value of -3) with respect to 8 is 5. 5 in binary is `101`. Therefore, -3 in binary as a 4-bit number is 1101, with the first bit being the sign bit.

In other words, the binary representation of -K (negative K) as a N-bit number is `concat(1, 2^(N-1) - K)`.

Another way to look at this is that we invert the bits in the positive representation and then add 1. 3 is `011` in binary. Flip the bits to get `100`, add `1` to get `101`, then prepend the sign bit (1) to get `1101`.

In a four-bit integer, this would look like the following.

Positive Values		Negative Values	
7	0 111	-1	1 111
6	0 110	-2	1 110
5	0 101	-3	1 101
4	0 100	-4	1 100
3	0 011	-5	1 011
2	0 010	-6	1 010
1	0 001	-7	1 001
0	0 000		

Observe that the absolute values of the integers on the left and right always sum to 2^3, and that the binary values on the left and right sides are identical, other than the sign bit. Why is that?

▸ Arithmetic vs. Logical Right Shift

There are two types of right shift operators. The arithmetic right shift essentially divides by two. The logical right shift does what we would visually see as shifting the bits. This is best seen on a negative number.

In a logical right shift, we shift the bits and put a `0` in the most significant bit. It is indicated with a >>> operator. On an 8-bit integer (where the sign bit is the most significant bit), this would look like the image below. The sign bit is indicated with a gray background.

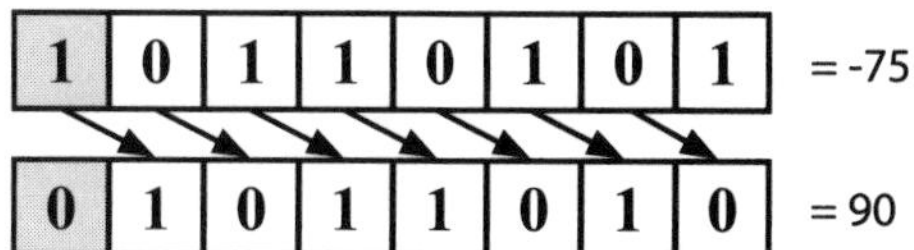

In an arithmetic right shift, we shift values to the right but fill in the new bits with the value of the sign bit. This has the effect of (roughly) dividing by two. It is indicated by a >> operator.

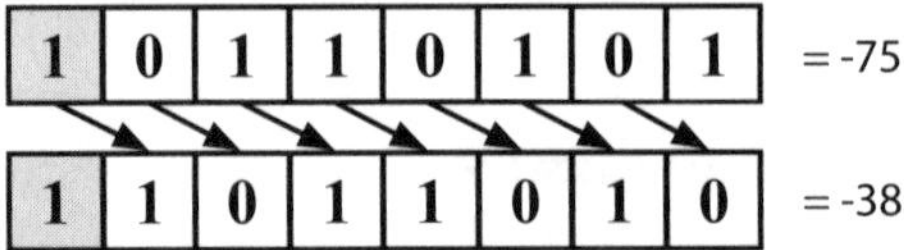

What do you think these functions would do on parameters `x = -93242` and `count = 40`?

```
int repeatedArithmeticShift(int x, int count) {
  for (int i = 0; i < count; i++) {
    x >>= 1; // Arithmetic shift by 1
  }
  return x;
}

int repeatedLogicalShift(int x, int count) {
  for (int i = 0; i < count; i++) {
    x >>>= 1; // Logical shift by 1
  }
  return x;
}
```

With the logical shift, we would get `0` because we are shifting a zero into the most significant bit repeatedly.

With the arithmetic shift, we would get `-1` because we are shifting a one into the most significant bit repeatedly. A sequence of all `1`s in a (signed) integer represents `-1`.

▸ Common Bit Tasks: Getting and Setting

The following operations are very important to know, but do not simply memorize them. Memorizing leads to mistakes that are impossible to recover from. Rather, understand *how* to implement these methods, so that you can implement these, and other, bit problems.

Get Bit

This method shifts `1` over by `i` bits, creating a value that looks like `00010000`. By performing an AND with `num`, we clear all bits other than the bit at bit `i`. Finally, we compare that to `0`. If that new value is not zero, then bit `i` must have a `1`. Otherwise, bit `i` is a 0.

```
boolean getBit(int num, int i) {
  return ((num & (1 << i)) != 0);
}
```

Set Bit

`SetBit` shifts `1` over by `i` bits, creating a value like `00010000`. By performing an OR with `num`, only the value at bit `i` will change. All other bits of the mask are zero and will not affect `num`.

```
int setBit(int num, int i) {
  return num | (1 << i);
}
```

Clear Bit

This method operates in almost the reverse of `setBit`. First, we create a number like **11101111** by creating the reverse of it (`00010000`) and negating it. Then, we perform an AND with `num`. This will clear the `i`th bit and leave the remainder unchanged.

```
int clearBit(int num, int i) {
  int mask = ~(1 << i);
  return num & mask;
}
```

To clear all bits from the most significant bit through `i` (inclusive), we create a mask with a `1` at the `i`th bit (`1 << i`). Then, we subtract `1` from it, giving us a sequence of `0`s followed by `i` `1`s. We then AND our number with this mask to leave just the last `i` bits.

```
int clearBitsMSBthroughI(int num, int i) {
  int mask = (1 << i) - 1;
  return num & mask;
}
```

To clear all bits from `i` through `0` (inclusive), we take a sequence of all `1`s (which is `-1`) and shift it left by `i + 1` bits. This gives us a sequence of 1s (in the most significant bits) followed by `i` `0` bits.

```
int clearBitsIthrough0(int num, int i) {
  int mask = (-1 << (i + 1));
  return num & mask;
}
```

Update Bit

To set the `i`th bit to a value `v`, we first clear the bit at position `i` by using a mask that looks like **11101111**. Then, we shift the intended value, `v`, left by `i` bits. This will create a number with bit `i` equal to `v` and all other bits equal to `0`. Finally, we OR these two numbers, updating the `i`th bit if `v` is `1` and leaving it as `0` otherwise.

```
int updateBit(int num, int i, boolean bitIs1) {
  int value = bitIs1 ? 1 : 0;
  int mask = ~(1 << i);
  return (num & mask) | (value << i);
}
```

Interview Questions

5.1 **Insertion:** You are given two 32-bit numbers, `N` and `M`, and two bit positions, `i` and `j`. Write a method to insert `M` into `N` such that `M` starts at bit `j` and ends at bit `i`. You can assume that the bits `j` through `i` have enough space to fit all of `M`. That is, if `M` = **10011**, you can assume that there are at least 5 bits between `j` and `i`. You would not, for example, have `j` = 3 and `i` = 2, because `M` could not fully fit between bit 3 and bit 2.

EXAMPLE

Input: `N = 10000000000, M = 10011, i = 2, j = 6`

Output: `N = 10001001100`

Hints: #137, #169, #215

pg 276

5.2 **Binary to String:** Given a real number between 0 and 1 (e.g., 0.72) that is passed in as a double, print the binary representation. If the number cannot be represented accurately in binary with at most 32 characters, print "ERROR."

Hints: #143, #167, #173, #269, #297

pg 277

5.3 **Flip Bit to Win:** You have an integer and you can flip exactly one bit from a `0` to a `1`. Write code to find the length of the longest sequence of `1`s you could create.

EXAMPLE

Input: `1775 (or: 11011101111)`

Output: `8`

Hints: #159, #226, #314, #352

pg 278

5.4 **Next Number:** Given a positive integer, print the next smallest and the next largest number that have the same number of 1 bits in their binary representation.

Hints: #147, #175, #242, #312, #339, #358, #375, #390

pg 280

5.5 **Debugger:** Explain what the following code does: `((n & (n-1)) == 0)`.

Hints: #151, #202, #261, #302, #346, #372, #383, #398

pg 285

5.6 **Conversion:** Write a function to determine the number of bits you would need to flip to convert integer A to integer B.

EXAMPLE

Input: `29 (or: 11101), 15 (or: 01111)`

Output: `2`

Hints: #336, #369

pg 286

5.7 **Pairwise Swap:** Write a program to swap odd and even bits in an integer with as few instructions as possible (e.g., bit `0` and bit `1` are swapped, bit 2 and bit 3 are swapped, and so on).

Hints: #145, #248, #328, #355

pg 286

5.8 **Draw Line:** A monochrome screen is stored as a single array of bytes, allowing eight consecutive pixels to be stored in one byte. The screen has width `w`, where `w` is divisible by 8 (that is, no byte will be split across rows). The height of the screen, of course, can be derived from the length of the array and the width. Implement a function that draws a horizontal line from `(x1, y)` to `(x2, y)`.

The method signature should look something like:

```
drawLine(byte[] screen, int width, int x1, int x2, int y)
```

Hints: #366, #381, #384, #391

pg 287

Additional Questions: Arrays and Strings (#1.1, #1.4, #1.8), Math and Logic Puzzles (#6.10), Recursion (#8.4, #8.14), Sorting and Searching (#10.7, #10.8), C++ (#12.10), Moderate Problems (#16.1, #16.7), Hard Problems (#17.1).

Hints start on page 662.

6

Math and Logic Puzzles

So-called "puzzles" (or brain teasers) are some of the most hotly debated questions, and many companies have policies banning them. Unfortunately, even when these questions are banned, you still may find yourself being asked one of them. Why? Because no one can agree on a definition of what a brainteaser is.

The good news is that if you are asked a puzzle or brainteaser, it's likely to be a reasonably fair one. It probably won't rely on a trick of wording, and it can almost always be logically deduced. Many have their foundations in mathematics or computer science, and almost all have solutions that can be logically deduced.

We'll go through some common approaches for tackling these questions, as well as some of the essential knowledge.

▸ Prime Numbers

As you probably know, every positive integer can be decomposed into a product of primes. For example:

$$84 = 2^2 * 3^1 * 5^0 * 7^1 * 11^0 * 13^0 * 17^0 * \ldots$$

Note that many of these primes have an exponent of zero.

Divisibility

The prime number law stated above means that, in order for a number x to divide a number y (written x\y, or `mod(y, x) = 0`), all primes in x's prime factorization must be in y's prime factorization. Or, more specifically:

Let $x = 2^{j0} * 3^{j1} * 5^{j2} * 7^{j3} * 11^{j4} * \ldots$

Let $y = 2^{k0} * 3^{k1} * 5^{k2} * 7^{k3} * 11^{k4} * \ldots$

If x\y, then for all i, `ji <= ki`.

In fact, the greatest common divisor of x and y will be:

$$gcd(x, y) = 2^{min(j0, k0)} * 3^{min(j1, k1)} * 5^{min(j2, k2)} * \ldots$$

The least common multiple of x and y will be:

$$lcm(x, y) = 2^{max(j0, k0)} * 3^{max(j1, k1)} * 5^{max(j2, k2)} * \ldots$$

As a fun exercise, stop for a moment and think what would happen if you did `gcd * lcm`:

$$\begin{aligned} gcd * lcm &= 2^{min(j0, k0)} * 2^{max(j0, k0)} * 3^{min(j1, k1)} * 3^{max(j1, k1)} * \ldots \\ &= 2^{min(j0, k0) + max(j0, k0)} * 3^{min(j1, k1) + max(j1, k1)} * \ldots \\ &= 2^{j0 + k0} * 3^{j1 + k1} * \ldots \\ &= 2^{j0} * 2^{k0} * 3^{j1} * 3^{k1} * \ldots \end{aligned}$$

```
= xy
```

Checking for Primality

This question is so common that we feel the need to specifically cover it. The naive way is to simply iterate from 2 through n-1, checking for divisibility on each iteration.

```
boolean primeNaive(int n) {
   if (n < 2) {
      return false;
   }
   for (int i = 2; i < n; i++) {
      if (n % i == 0) {
         return false;
      }
   }
   return true;
}
```

A small but important improvement is to iterate only up through the square root of n.

```
boolean primeSlightlyBetter(int n) {
   if (n < 2) {
      return false;
   }
   int sqrt = (int) Math.sqrt(n);
   for (int i = 2; i <= sqrt; i++) {
      if (n % i == 0) return false;
   }
   return true;
}
```

The $\sqrt{n}$ is sufficient because, for every number a which divides n evenly, there is a complement b, where a * b = n. If a > $\sqrt{n}$, then b < $\sqrt{n}$ (since $(\sqrt{n})^2 = n$). We therefore don't need a to check n's primality, since we would have already checked with b.

Of course, in reality, all we *really* need to do is to check if n is divisible by a prime number. This is where the Sieve of Eratosthenes comes in.

Generating a List of Primes: The Sieve of Eratosthenes

The Sieve of Eratosthenes is a highly efficient way to generate a list of primes. It works by recognizing that all non-prime numbers are divisible by a prime number.

We start with a list of all the numbers up through some value max. First, we cross off all numbers divisible by 2. Then, we look for the next prime (the next non-crossed off number) and cross off all numbers divisible by it. By crossing off all numbers divisible by 2, 3, 5, 7, 11, and so on, we wind up with a list of prime numbers from 2 through max.

The code below implements the Sieve of Eratosthenes.

```
boolean[] sieveOfEratosthenes(int max) {
   boolean[] flags = new boolean[max + 1];
   int count = 0;

   init(flags); // Set all flags to true other than 0 and 1
   int prime = 2;

   while (prime <= Math.sqrt(max)) {
```

```
        /* Cross off remaining multiples of prime */
        crossOff(flags, prime);

        /* Find next value which is true */
        prime = getNextPrime(flags, prime);
    }

    return flags;
}

void crossOff(boolean[] flags, int prime) {
    /* Cross off remaining multiples of prime. We can start with (prime*prime),
     * because if we have a k * prime, where k < prime, this value would have
     * already been crossed off in a prior iteration. */
    for (int i = prime * prime; i < flags.length; i += prime) {
        flags[i] = false;
    }
}

int getNextPrime(boolean[] flags, int prime) {
    int next = prime + 1;
    while (next < flags.length && !flags[next]) {
        next++;
    }
    return next;
}
```

Of course, there are a number of optimizations that can be made to this. One simple one is to only use odd numbers in the array, which would allow us to reduce our space usage by half.

▸ Probability

Probability can be a complex topic, but it's based in a few basic laws that can be logically derived.

Let's look at a Venn diagram to visualize two events A and B. The areas of the two circles represent their relative probability, and the overlapping area is the event `{A and B}`.

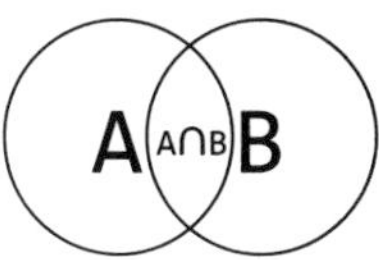

Probability of A and B

Imagine you were throwing a dart at this Venn diagram. What is the probability that you would land in the intersection between A and B? If you knew the odds of landing in A, and you also knew the percent of A that's also in B (that is, the odds of being in B given that you were in A), then you could express the probability as:

```
P(A and B) = P(B given A) P(A)
```

For example, imagine we were picking a number between 1 and 10 (inclusive). What's the probability of picking a number that is both even and between 1 and 5? The odds of picking a number between 1 and 5 is 50%, and the odds of a number between 1 and 5 being even is 40%. So, the odds of doing both are:

```
P(x is even and x <= 5)
```

```
    = P(x is even given x <= 5) P(x <= 5)
    = (2/5) * (1/2)
    = 1/5
```

Observe that since `P(A and B) = P(B given A) P(A) = P(A given B) P(B)`, you can express the probability of A given B in terms of the reverse:

```
P(A given B) = P(B given A) P(A) / P(B)
```

The above equation is called Bayes' Theorem.

Probability of A or B

Now, imagine you wanted to know what the probability of landing in A or B is. If you knew the odds of landing in each individually, and you also knew the odds of landing in their intersection, then you could express the probability as:

```
P(A or B) = P(A) + P(B) - P(A and B)
```

Logically, this makes sense. If we simply added their sizes, we would have double-counted their intersection. We need to subtract this out. We can again visualize this through a Venn diagram:

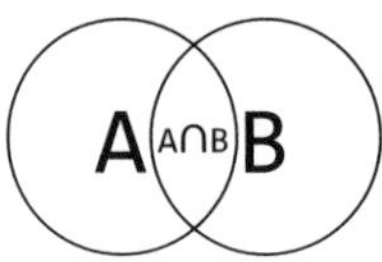

For example, imagine we were picking a number between 1 and 10 (inclusive). What's the probability of picking an even number *or* a number between 1 and 5? We have a 50% probability of picking an even number and a 50% probability of picking a number between 1 and 5. The odds of doing both are 20%. So the odds are:

```
P(x is even or x <=5)
    = P(x is even) + P(x <= 5) - P(x is even and x <= 5)
```

$= \frac{1}{2} + \frac{1}{2} - \frac{1}{5}$

$= \frac{4}{5}$

From here, getting the special case rules for independent events and for mutually exclusive events is easy.

Independence

If A and B are independent (that is, one happening tells you nothing about the other happening), then `P(A and B) = P(A) P(B)`. This rule simply comes from recognizing that `P(B given A) = P(B)`, since A indicates nothing about B.

Mutual Exclusivity

If A and B are mutually exclusive (that is, if one happens, then the other cannot happen), then `P(A or B) = P(A) + P(B)`. This is because `P(A and B) = 0`, so this term is removed from the earlier `P(A or B)` equation.

Many people, strangely, mix up the concepts of independence and mutual exclusivity. They are *entirely* different. In fact, two events cannot be both independent and mutually exclusive (provided both have probabilities greater than 0). Why? Because mutual exclusivity means that if one happens then the other cannot. Independence, however, says that one event happening means absolutely *nothing* about the other event. Thus, as long as two events have non-zero probabilities, they will never be both mutually exclusive and independent.

If one or both events have a probability of zero (that is, it is impossible), then the events are both independent and mutually exclusive. This is provable through a simple application of the definitions (that is, the formulas) of independence and mutual exclusivity.

▸ Start Talking

Don't panic when you get a brainteaser. Like algorithm questions, interviewers want to see how you tackle a problem; they don't expect you to immediately know the answer. Start talking, and show the interviewer how you approach a problem.

▸ Develop Rules and Patterns

In many cases, you will find it useful to write down "rules" or patterns that you discover while solving the problem. And yes, you really should write these down—it will help you remember them as you solve the problem. Let's demonstrate this approach with an example.

You have two ropes, and each takes exactly one hour to burn. How would you use them to time exactly 15 minutes? Note that the ropes are of uneven densities, so half the rope length-wise does not necessarily take half an hour to burn.

> *Tip: Stop here and spend some time trying to solve this problem on your own. If you absolutely must, read through this section for hints—but do so slowly. Every paragraph will get you a bit closer to the solution.*

From the statement of the problem, we immediately know that we can time one hour. We can also time two hours, by lighting one rope, waiting until it is burnt, and then lighting the second. We can generalize this into a rule.

Rule 1: Given a rope that takes x minutes to burn and another that takes y minutes, we can time x+y minutes.

What else can we do with the rope? We can probably assume that lighting a rope in the middle (or anywhere other than the ends) won't do us much good. The flames would expand in both directions, and we have no idea how long it would take to burn.

However, we can light a rope at both ends. The two flames would meet after 30 minutes.

Rule 2: Given a rope that takes x minutes to burn, we can time $x/2$ minutes.

We now know that we can time 30 minutes using a single rope. This also means that we can remove 30 minutes of burning time from the second rope, by lighting rope 1 on both ends and rope 2 on just one end.

Rule 3: If rope 1 takes x minutes to burn and rope 2 takes y minutes, we can turn rope 2 into a rope that takes (y-x) minutes or ($y-x/2$) minutes.

Now, let's piece all of these together. We can turn rope 2 into a rope with 30 minutes of burn time. If we then light rope 2 on the other end (see rule 2), rope 2 will be done after 15 minutes.

From start to end, our approach is as follows:

1. Light rope 1 at both ends and rope 2 at one end.
2. When the two flames on Rope 1 meet, 30 minutes will have passed. Rope 2 has 30 minutes left of burn-time.

3. At that point, light Rope 2 at the other end.
4. In exactly fifteen minutes, Rope 2 will be completely burnt.

Note how solving this problem is made easier by listing out what you've learned and what "rules" you've discovered.

▸ Worst Case Shifting

Many brainteasers are worst-case minimization problems, worded either in terms of *minimizing* an action or in doing something at most a specific number of times. A useful technique is to try to "balance" the worst case. That is, if an early decision results in a skewing of the worst case, we can sometimes change the decision to balance out the worst case. This will be clearest when explained with an example.

The "nine balls" question is a classic interview question. You have nine balls. Eight are of the same weight, and one is heavier. You are given a balance which tells you only whether the left side or the right side is heavier. Find the heavy ball in just two uses of the scale.

A first approach is to divide the balls in sets of four, with the ninth ball sitting off to the side. The heavy ball is in the heavier set. If they are the same weight, then we know that the ninth ball is the heavy one. Replicating this approach for the remaining sets would result in a worst case of three weighings—one too many!

This is an imbalance in the worst case: the ninth ball takes just one weighing to discover if it's heavy, whereas others take three. If we *penalize* the ninth ball by putting more balls off to the side, we can lighten the load on the others. This is an example of "worst case balancing."

If we divide the balls into sets of three items each, we will know after just one weighing which set has the heavy one. We can even formalize this into a *rule*: given N balls, where N is divisible by 3, one use of the scale will point us to a set of $^{N}/_{3}$ balls with the heavy ball.

For the final set of three balls, we simply repeat this: put one ball off to the side and weigh two. Pick the heavier of the two. Or, if the balls are the same weight, pick the third one.

▸ Algorithm Approaches

If you're stuck, consider applying one of the approaches for solving algorithm questions (starting on page 67). Brainteasers are often nothing more than algorithm questions with the technical aspects removed. Base Case and Build and Do It Yourself (DIY) can be especially useful.

Additional Reading: Useful Math (pg 629).

Interview Questions

6.1 **The Heavy Pill:** You have 20 bottles of pills. 19 bottles have 1.0 gram pills, but one has pills of weight 1.1 grams. Given a scale that provides an exact measurement, how would you find the heavy bottle? You can only use the scale once.

Hints: #186, #252, #319, #387

pg 289

6.2 **Basketball:** You have a basketball hoop and someone says that you can play one of two games.

Game 1: You get one shot to make the hoop.

Game 2: You get three shots and you have to make two of three shots.

If p is the probability of making a particular shot, for which values of p should you pick one game or the other?

Hints: #181, #239, #284, #323

pg 290

6.3 **Dominos:** There is an 8x8 chessboard in which two diagonally opposite corners have been cut off. You are given 31 dominos, and a single domino can cover exactly two squares. Can you use the 31 dominos to cover the entire board? Prove your answer (by providing an example or showing why it's impossible).

Hints: #367, #397

pg 291

6.4 **Ants on a Triangle:** There are three ants on different vertices of a triangle. What is the probability of collision (between any two or all of them) if they start walking on the sides of the triangle? Assume that each ant randomly picks a direction, with either direction being equally likely to be chosen, and that they walk at the same speed.

Similarly, find the probability of collision with n ants on an n-vertex polygon.

Hints: #157, #195, #296

pg 291

6.5 **Jugs of Water:** You have a five-quart jug, a three-quart jug, and an unlimited supply of water (but no measuring cups). How would you come up with exactly four quarts of water? Note that the jugs are oddly shaped, such that filling up exactly "half" of the jug would be impossible.

Hints: #149, #379, #400

pg 292

6.6 **Blue-Eyed Island:** A bunch of people are living on an island, when a visitor comes with a strange order: all blue-eyed people must leave the island as soon as possible. There will be a flight out at 8:00 pm every evening. Each person can see everyone else's eye color, but they do not know their own (nor is anyone allowed to tell them). Additionally, they do not know how many people have blue eyes, although they do know that at least one person does. How many days will it take the blue-eyed people to leave?

Hints: #218, #282, #341, #370

pg 293

6.7 **The Apocalypse**: In the new post-apocalyptic world, the world queen is desperately concerned about the birth rate. Therefore, she decrees that all families should ensure that they have one girl or else they face massive fines. If all families abide by this policy—that is, they have continue to have children until they have one girl, at which point they immediately stop—what will the gender ratio of the new generation be? (Assume that the odds of someone having a boy or a girl on any given pregnancy is equal.) Solve this out logically and then write a computer simulation of it.

Hints: #154, #160, #171, #188, #201

pg 293

6.8 **The Egg Drop Problem:** There is a building of 100 floors. If an egg drops from the Nth floor or above, it will break. If it's dropped from any floor below, it will not break. You're given two eggs. Find N, while minimizing the number of drops for the worst case.

Hints: #156, #233, #294, #333, #357, #374, #395

pg 296

6.9 **100 Lockers:** There are 100 closed lockers in a hallway. A man begins by opening all 100 lockers. Next, he closes every second locker. Then, on his third pass, he toggles every third locker (closes it if it is open or opens it if it is closed). This process continues for 100 passes, such that on each pass `i`, the man toggles every `i`th locker. After his 100th pass in the hallway, in which he toggles only locker #100, how many lockers are open?

Hints: #139, #172, #264, #306

pg 297

6.10 **Poison**: You have 1000 bottles of soda, and exactly one is poisoned. You have 10 test strips which can be used to detect poison. A single drop of poison will turn the test strip positive permanently. You can put any number of drops on a test strip at once and you can reuse a test strip as many times as you'd like (as long as the results are negative). However, you can only run tests once per day and it takes seven days to return a result. How would you figure out the poisoned bottle in as few days as possible?

FOLLOW UP

Write code to simulate your approach.

HInts: #146, #163, #183, #191, #205, #221, #230, #241, #249

pg 298

Additional Problems: Moderate Problems (#16.5), Hard Problems (#17.19)

Hints start on page 662.

7

Object-Oriented Design

Object-oriented design questions require a candidate to sketch out the classes and methods to implement technical problems or real-life objects. These problems give—or at least are believed to give—an interviewer insight into your coding style.

These questions are not so much about regurgitating design patterns as they are about demonstrating that you understand how to create elegant, maintainable object-oriented code. Poor performance on this type of question may raise serious red flags.

▸ How to Approach

Regardless of whether the object is a physical item or a technical task, object-oriented design questions can be tackled in similar ways. The following approach will work well for many problems.

Step 1: Handle Ambiguity

Object-oriented design (OOD) questions are often intentionally vague in order to test whether you'll make assumptions or if you'll ask clarifying questions. After all, a developer who just codes something without understanding what she is expected to create wastes the company's time and money, and may create much more serious issues.

When being asked an object-oriented design question, you should inquire *who* is going to use it and *how* they are going to use it. Depending on the question, you may even want to go through the "six Ws": who, what, where, when, how, why.

For example, suppose you were asked to describe the object-oriented design for a coffee maker. This seems straightforward enough, right? Not quite.

Your coffee maker might be an industrial machine designed to be used in a massive restaurant servicing hundreds of customers per hour and making ten different kinds of coffee products. Or it might be a very simple machine, designed to be used by the elderly for just simple black coffee. These use cases will significantly impact your design.

Step 2: Define the Core Objects

Now that we understand what we're designing, we should consider what the "core objects" in a system are. For example, suppose we are asked to do the object-oriented design for a restaurant. Our core objects might be things like `Table`, `Guest`, `Party`, `Order`, `Meal`, `Employee`, `Server`, and `Host`.

Step 3: Analyze Relationships

Having more or less decided on our core objects, we now want to analyze the relationships between the objects. Which objects are members of which other objects? Do any objects inherit from any others? Are relationships many-to-many or one-to-many?

For example, in the restaurant question, we may come up with the following design:

- `Party` should have an array of `Guests`.
- `Server` and `Host` inherit from `Employee`.
- Each `Table` has one `Party`, but each `Party` may have multiple `Tables`.
- There is one `Host` for the `Restaurant`.

Be very careful here—you can often make incorrect assumptions. For example, a single `Table` may have multiple `Parties` (as is common in the trendy "communal tables" at some restaurants). You should talk to your interviewer about how general purpose your design should be.

Step 4: Investigate Actions

At this point, you should have the basic outline of your object-oriented design. What remains is to consider the key actions that the objects will take and how they relate to each other. You may find that you have forgotten some objects, and you will need to update your design.

For example, a `Party` walks into the `Restaurant`, and a `Guest` requests a `Table` from the `Host`. The `Host` looks up the `Reservation` and, if it exists, assigns the `Party` to a `Table`. Otherwise, the `Party` is added to the end of the list. When a `Party` leaves, the `Table` is freed and assigned to a new `Party` in the list.

▸ Design Patterns

Because interviewers are trying to test your capabilities and not your knowledge, design patterns are mostly beyond the scope of an interview. However, the Singleton and Factory Method design patterns are widely used in interviews, so we will cover them here.

There are far more design patterns than this book could possibly discuss. A great way to improve your software engineering skills is to pick up a book that focuses on this area specifically.

Be careful you don't fall into a trap of constantly trying to find the "right" design pattern for a particular problem. You should create the design that works for that problem. In some cases it might be an established pattern, but in many other cases it is not.

Singleton Class

The Singleton pattern ensures that a class has only one instance and ensures access to the instance through the application. It can be useful in cases where you have a "global" object with exactly one instance. For example, we may want to implement `Restaurant` such that it has exactly one instance of `Restaurant`.

```
public class Restaurant {
   private static Restaurant _instance = null;
   protected Restaurant() { ... }
   public static Restaurant getInstance() {
      if (_instance == null) {
         _instance = new Restaurant();
      }
```

```
        return _instance;
    }
}
```

It should be noted that many people dislike the Singleton design pattern, even calling it an "anti-pattern." One reason for this is that it can interfere with unit testing.

Factory Method

The Factory Method offers an interface for creating an instance of a class, with its subclasses deciding which class to instantiate. You might want to implement this with the creator class being abstract and not providing an implementation for the Factory method. Or, you could have the Creator class be a concrete class that provides an implementation for the Factory method. In this case, the Factory method would take a parameter representing which class to instantiate.

```
public class CardGame {
   public static CardGame createCardGame(GameType type) {
      if (type == GameType.Poker) {
         return new PokerGame();
      } else if (type == GameType.BlackJack) {
         return new BlackJackGame();
      }
      return null;
   }
}
```

Interview Questions

7.1 **Deck of Cards:** Design the data structures for a generic deck of cards. Explain how you would subclass the data structures to implement blackjack.

Hints: #153, #275

pg 305

7.2 **Call Center:** Imagine you have a call center with three levels of employees: respondent, manager, and director. An incoming telephone call must be first allocated to a respondent who is free. If the respondent can't handle the call, he or she must escalate the call to a manager. If the manager is not free or not able to handle it, then the call should be escalated to a director. Design the classes and data structures for this problem. Implement a method `dispatchCall()` which assigns a call to the first available employee.

Hints: #363

pg 307

7.3 **Jukebox:** Design a musical jukebox using object-oriented principles.

Hints: #198

pg 310

7.4 **Parking Lot:** Design a parking lot using object-oriented principles.

Hints: #258

pg 312

7.5 **Online Book Reader:** Design the data structures for an online book reader system.

Hints: #344

pg 318

7.6 **Jigsaw:** Implement an NxN jigsaw puzzle. Design the data structures and explain an algorithm to solve the puzzle. You can assume that you have a `fitsWith` method which, when passed two puzzle edges, returns true if the two edges belong together.

Hints: #192, #238, #283

pg 318

7.7 **Chat Server:** Explain how you would design a chat server. In particular, provide details about the various backend components, classes, and methods. What would be the hardest problems to solve?

Hints: #213, #245, #271

pg 326

7.8 **Othello:** Othello is played as follows: Each Othello piece is white on one side and black on the other. When a piece is surrounded by its opponents on both the left and right sides, or both the top and bottom, it is said to be captured and its color is flipped. On your turn, you must capture at least one of your opponent's pieces. The game ends when either user has no more valid moves. The win is assigned to the person with the most pieces. Implement the object-oriented design for Othello.

Hints: #179, #228

pg 326

7.9 **Circular Array:** Implement a `CircularArray` class that supports an array-like data structure which can be efficiently rotated. If possible, the class should use a generic type (also called a template), and should support iteration via the standard `for (Obj o : circularArray)` notation.

Hints: #389

pg 329

7.10 **Minesweeper:** Design and implement a text-based Minesweeper game. Minesweeper is the classic single-player computer game where an NxN grid has B mines (or bombs) hidden across the grid. The remaining cells are either blank or have a number behind them. The numbers reflect the number of bombs in the surrounding eight cells. The user then uncovers a cell. If it is a bomb, the player loses. If it is a number, the number is exposed. If it is a blank cell, this cell and all adjacent blank cells (up to and including the surrounding numeric cells) are exposed. The player wins when all non-bomb cells are exposed. The player can also flag certain places as potential bombs. This doesn't affect game play, other than to block the user from accidentally clicking a cell that is thought to have a bomb. (Tip for the reader: if you're not familiar with this game, please play a few rounds online first.)

This is a fully exposed board with 3 bombs. This is not shown to the user.

	1	1	1			
	1	*	1			
	2	2	2			
	1	*	1			
	1	1	1			
			1	1	1	
			1	*	1	

The player initially sees a board with nothing exposed.

?	?	?	?	?	?	?
?	?	?	?	?	?	?
?	?	?	?	?	?	?
?	?	?	?	?	?	?
?	?	?	?	?	?	?
?	?	?	?	?	?	?
?	?	?	?	?	?	?

Clicking on cell (row = 1, col = 0) would expose this:

	1	?	?	?	?	?
	1	?	?	?	?	?
	2	?	?	?	?	?
	1	?	?	?	?	?
	1	1	1	?	?	?
			1	?	?	?
			1	?	?	?

The user wins when everything other than bombs has been exposed.

	1	1	1			
	1	?	1			
	2	2	2			
	1	?	1			
	1	1	1			
			1	1	1	
			1	?	1	

Hints: #351, #361, #377, #386, #399

pg 332

7.11 **File System:** Explain the data structures and algorithms that you would use to design an in-memory file system. Illustrate with an example in code where possible.

Hints: #141, #216

pg 337

7.12 **Hash Table:** Design and implement a hash table which uses chaining (linked lists) to handle collisions.

Hints: #287, #307

pg 339

Additional Questions: Threads and Locks (#15.3)

Hints start on page 662.

Recursion and Dynamic Programming

While there are a large number of recursive problems, many follow similar patterns. A good hint that a problem is recursive is that it can be built off of subproblems.

When you hear a problem beginning with the following statements, it's often (though not always) a good candidate for recursion: "Design an algorithm to compute the nth ...", "Write code to list the first n...", "Implement a method to compute all...", and so on.

> Tip: In my experience coaching candidates, people typically have about 50% accuracy in their "this sounds like a recursive problem" instinct. Use that instinct, since that 50% is valuable. But don't be afraid to look at the problem in a different way, even if you initially thought it seemed recursive. There's also a 50% chance that you were wrong.

Practice makes perfect! The more problems you do, the easier it will be to recognize recursive problems.

How to Approach

Recursive solutions, by definition, are built off of solutions to subproblems. Many times, this will mean simply to compute `f(n)` by adding something, removing something, or otherwise changing the solution for `f(n-1)`. In other cases, you might solve the problem for the first half of the data set, then the second half, and then merge those results.

There are many ways you might divide a problem into subproblems. Three of the most common approaches to develop an algorithm are bottom-up, top-down, and half-and-half.

Bottom-Up Approach

The bottom-up approach is often the most intuitive. We start with knowing how to solve the problem for a simple case, like a list with only one element. Then we figure out how to solve the problem for two elements, then for three elements, and so on. The key here is to think about how you can *build* the solution for one case off of the previous case (or multiple previous cases).

Top-Down Approach

The top-down approach can be more complex since it's less concrete. But sometimes, it's the best way to think about the problem.

In these problems, we think about how we can divide the problem for case **N** into subproblems.

Be careful of overlap between the cases.

Half-and-Half Approach

In addition to top-down and bottom-up approaches, it's often effective to divide the data set in half.

For example, binary search works with a "half-and-half" approach. When we look for an element in a sorted array, we first figure out which half of the array contains the value. Then we recurse and search for it in that half.

Merge sort is also a "half-and-half" approach. We sort each half of the array and then merge together the sorted halves.

Recursive vs. Iterative Solutions

Recursive algorithms can be very space inefficient. Each recursive call adds a new layer to the stack, which means that if your algorithm recurses to a depth of n, it uses at least O(n) memory.

For this reason, it's often better to implement a recursive algorithm iteratively. *All* recursive algorithms can be implemented iteratively, although sometimes the code to do so is much more complex. Before diving into recursive code, ask yourself how hard it would be to implement it iteratively, and discuss the tradeoffs with your interviewer.

Dynamic Programming & Memoization

Although people make a big deal about how scary dynamic programming problems are, there's really no need to be afraid of them. In fact, once you get the hang of them, these can actually be very easy problems.

Dynamic programming is mostly just a matter of taking a recursive algorithm and finding the overlapping subproblems (that is, the repeated calls). You then cache those results for future recursive calls.

Alternatively, you can study the pattern of the recursive calls and implement something iterative. You still "cache" previous work.

> A note on terminology: Some people call top-down dynamic programming "memoization" and only use "dynamic programming" to refer to bottom-up work. We do not make such a distinction here. We call both dynamic programming.

One of the simplest examples of dynamic programming is computing the nth Fibonacci number. A good way to approach such a problem is often to implement it as a normal recursive solution, and then add the caching part.

Fibonacci Numbers

Let's walk through an approach to compute the nth Fibonacci number.

Recursive

We will start with a recursive implementation. Sounds simple, right?

```
int fibonacci(int i) {
   if (i == 0) return 0;
   if (i == 1) return 1;
   return fibonacci(i - 1) + fibonacci(i - 2);
}
```

What is the runtime of this function? Think for a second before you answer.

If you said O(n) or $O(n^2)$ (as many people do), think again. Study the code path that the code takes. Drawing the code paths as a tree (that is, the recursion tree) is useful on this and many recursive problems.

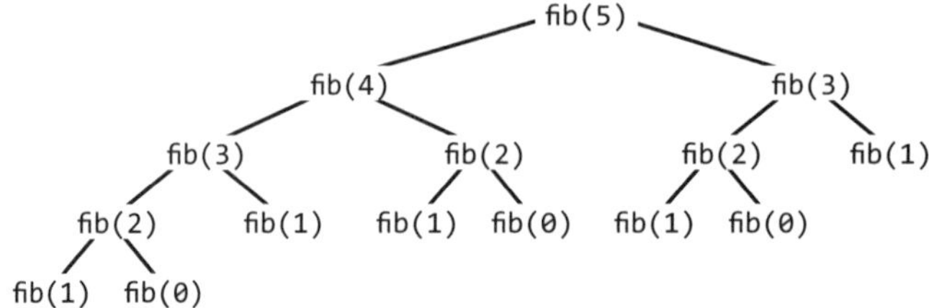

Observe that the leaves on the tree are all `fib(1)` and `fib(0)`. Those signify the base cases.

The total number of nodes in the tree will represent the runtime, since each call only does O(1) work outside of its recursive calls. Therefore, the number of calls is the runtime.

> Tip: Remember this for future problems. Drawing the recursive calls as a tree is a great way to figure out the runtime of a recursive algorithm.

How many nodes are in the tree? Until we get down to the base cases (leaves), each node has two children. Each node branches out twice.

The root node has two children. Each of those children has two children (so four children total in the "grandchildren" level). Each of those grandchildren has two children, and so on. If we do this n times, we'll have roughly $O(2^n)$ nodes. This gives us a runtime of roughly $O(2^n)$.

> Actually, it's slightly better than $O(2^n)$. If you look at the subtree, you might notice that (excluding the leaf nodes and those immediately above it) the right subtree of any node is always smaller than the left subtree. If they were the same size, we'd have an $O(2^n)$ runtime. But since the right and left subtrees are not the same size, the true runtime is closer to $O(1.6^n)$. Saying $O(2^n)$ is still technically correct though as it describes an upper bound on the runtime (see "Big O, Big Theta, and Big Omega" on page 39). Either way, we still have an exponential runtime.

Indeed, if we implemented this on a computer, we'd see the number of seconds increase exponentially.

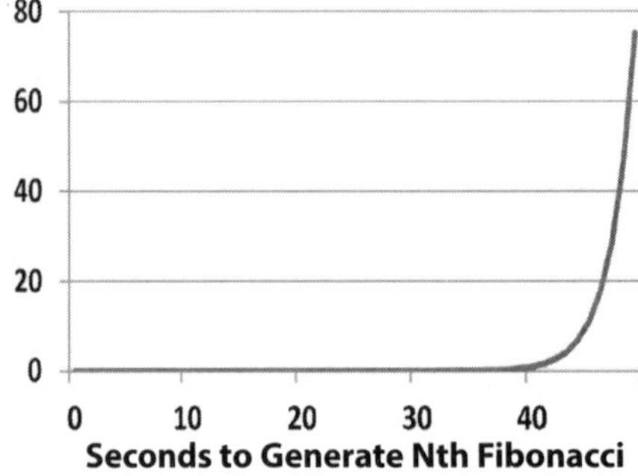

We should look for a way to optimize this.

Top-Down Dynamic Programming (or Memoization)

Study the recursion tree. Where do you see identical nodes?

There are lots of identical nodes. For example, `fib(3)` appears twice and fib(2) appears three times. Why should we recompute these from scratch each time?

In fact, when we call `fib(n)`, we shouldn't have to do much more than `O(n)` calls, since there's only `O(n)` possible values we can throw at `fib`. Each time we compute `fib(i)`, we should just cache this result and use it later.

This is exactly what memoization is.

With just a small modification, we can tweak this function to run in `O(n)` time. We simply cache the results of `fibonacci(i)` between calls.

```
int fibonacci(int n) {
  return fibonacci(n, new int[n + 1]);
}

int fibonacci(int i, int[] memo) {
  if (i == 0 || i == 1) return i;

  if (memo[i] == 0) {
    memo[i] = fibonacci(i - 1, memo) + fibonacci(i - 2, memo);
  }
  return memo[i];
}
```

While the first recursive function may take over a minute to generate the 50th Fibonacci number on a typical computer, the dynamic programming method can generate the 10,000th Fibonacci number in just fractions of a millisecond. (Of course, with this exact code, the `int` would have overflowed very early on.)

Now, if we draw the recursion tree, it looks something like this (the black boxes represent cached calls that returned immediately):

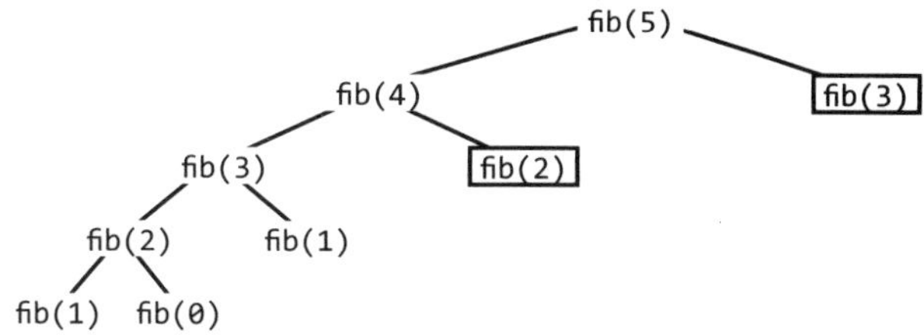

How many nodes are in this tree now? We might notice that the tree now just shoots straight down, to a depth of roughly n. Each node of those nodes has one other child, resulting in roughly 2n children in the tree. This gives us a runtime of `O(n)`.

Often it can be useful to picture the recursion tree as something like this:

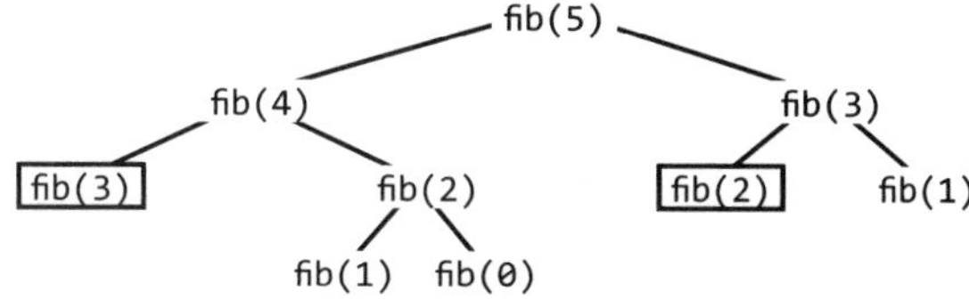

This is *not* actually how the recursion occurred. However, by expanding the further up nodes rather than the lower nodes, you have a tree that grows wide before it grows deep. (It's like doing this breadth-first rather than depth-first.) Sometimes this makes it easier to compute the number of nodes in the tree. All you're really doing is changing which nodes you expand and which ones return cached values. Try this if you're stuck on computing the runtime of a dynamic programming problem.

Bottom-Up Dynamic Programming

We can also take this approach and implement it with bottom-up dynamic programming. Think about doing the same things as the recursive memoized approach, but in reverse.

First, we compute `fib(1)` and `fib(0)`, which are already known from the base cases. Then we use those to compute `fib(2)`. Then we use the prior answers to compute `fib(3)`, then `fib(4)`, and so on.

```
int fibonacci(int n) {
   if (n == 0) return 0;
   else if (n == 1) return 1;

   int[] memo = new int[n];
   memo[0] = 0;
   memo[1] = 1;
   for (int i = 2; i < n; i++) {
      memo[i] = memo[i - 1] + memo[i - 2];
   }
   return memo[n - 1] + memo[n - 2];
}
```

If you really think about how this works, you only use `memo[i]` for `memo[i+1]` and `memo[i+2]`. You don't need it after that. Therefore, we can get rid of the memo table and just store a few variables.

```
int fibonacci(int n) {
   if (n == 0) return 0;
   int a = 0;
   int b = 1;
   for (int i = 2; i < n; i++) {
      int c = a + b;
      a = b;
      b = c;
   }
   return a + b;
}
```

This is basically storing the results from the last two Fibonacci values into a and b. At each iteration, we compute the next value (`c = a + b`) and then move (`b, c = a + b`) into (`a, b`).

This explanation might seem like overkill for such a simple problem, but truly understanding this process will make more difficult problems much easier. Going through the problems in this chapter, many of which use dynamic programming, will help solidify your understanding.

Additional Reading: Proof by Induction (pg 631).

Interview Questions

8.1 **Triple Step:** A child is running up a staircase with n steps and can hop either 1 step, 2 steps, or 3 steps at a time. Implement a method to count how many possible ways the child can run up the stairs.

Hints: #152, #178, #217, #237, #262, #359

pg 342

8.2 **Robot in a Grid:** Imagine a robot sitting on the upper left corner of grid with `r` rows and `c` columns. The robot can only move in two directions, right and down, but certain cells are "off limits" such that the robot cannot step on them. Design an algorithm to find a path for the robot from the top left to the bottom right.

Hints: #331, #360, #388

pg 344

8.3 **Magic Index:** A magic index in an array `A[0...n-1]` is defined to be an index such that `A[i] = i`. Given a sorted array of distinct integers, write a method to find a magic index, if one exists, in array A.

FOLLOW UP

What if the values are not distinct?

Hints: #170, #204, #240, #286, #340

pg 346

8.4 **Power Set:** Write a method to return all subsets of a set.

Hints: #273, #290, #338, #354, #373

pg 348

8.5 **Recursive Multiply:** Write a recursive function to multiply two positive integers without using the * operator. You can use addition, subtraction, and bit shifting, but you should minimize the number of those operations.

Hints: #166, #203, #227, #234, #246, #280

pg 350

8.6 **Towers of Hanoi:** In the classic problem of the Towers of Hanoi, you have 3 towers and N disks of different sizes which can slide onto any tower. The puzzle starts with disks sorted in ascending order of size from top to bottom (i.e., each disk sits on top of an even larger one). You have the following constraints:

(1) Only one disk can be moved at a time.

(2) A disk is slid off the top of one tower onto another tower.

(3) A disk cannot be placed on top of a smaller disk.

Write a program to move the disks from the first tower to the last using stacks.

Hints: #144, #224, #250, #272, #318

pg 353

8.7 **Permutations without Dups:** Write a method to compute all permutations of a string of unique characters.

Hints: #150, #185, #200, #267, #278, #309, #335, #356

pg 355

8.8 **Permutations with Dups:** Write a method to compute all permutations of a string whose characters are not necessarily unique. The list of permutations should not have duplicates.

Hints: #161, #190, #222, #255

pg 357

8.9 **Parens:** Implement an algorithm to print all valid (e.g., properly opened and closed) combinations of n pairs of parentheses.

EXAMPLE

Input: 3

Output: `((()))`, `(()())`, `(())()`, `()(())`, `()()()`

Hints: #138, #174, #187, #209, #243, #265, #295

pg 359

8.10 **Paint Fill:** Implement the "paint fill" function that one might see on many image editing programs. That is, given a screen (represented by a two-dimensional array of colors), a point, and a new color, fill in the surrounding area until the color changes from the original color.

Hints: #364, #382

pg 361

8.11 **Coins:** Given an infinite number of quarters (25 cents), dimes (10 cents), nickels (5 cents), and pennies (1 cent), write code to calculate the number of ways of representing n cents.

Hints: #300, #324, #343, #380, #394

pg 362

8.12 **Eight Queens:** Write an algorithm to print all ways of arranging eight queens on an 8x8 chess board so that none of them share the same row, column, or diagonal. In this case, "diagonal" means all diagonals, not just the two that bisect the board.

Hints: #308, #350, #371

pg 364

8.13 **Stack of Boxes:** You have a stack of n boxes, with widths w_i, heights h_i, and depths d_i. The boxes cannot be rotated and can only be stacked on top of one another if each box in the stack is strictly larger than the box above it in width, height, and depth. Implement a method to compute the height of the tallest possible stack. The height of a stack is the sum of the heights of each box.

Hints: #155, #194, #214, #260, #322, #368, #378

pg 366

8.14 **Boolean Evaluation:** Given a boolean expression consisting of the symbols `0` (false), `1` (true), `&` (AND), `|` (OR), and `^` (XOR), and a desired boolean result value `result`, implement a function to count the number of ways of parenthesizing the expression such that it evaluates to `result`. The expression should be fully parenthesized (e.g., `(0)^(1)`) but not extraneously (e.g., `(((0))^(1))`).

EXAMPLE

```
countEval("1^0|0|1", false) -> 2
countEval("0&0&0&1^1|0", true) -> 10
```

Hints: #148, #168, #197, #305, #327

pg 368

Additional Questions: Linked Lists (#2.2, #2.5, #2.6), Stacks and Queues (#3.3), Trees and Graphs (#4.2, #4.3, #4.4, #4.5, #4.8, #4.10, #4.11, #4.12), Math and Logic Puzzles (#6.6), Sorting and Searching (#10.5, #10.9, #10.10), C++ (#12.8), Moderate Problems (#16.11), Hard Problems (#17.4, #17.6, #17.8, #17.12, #17.13, #17.15, #17.16, #17.24, #17.25).

Hints start on page 662.

9

System Design and Scalability

Despite how intimidating they seem, scalability questions can be among the easiest questions. There are no "gotchas," no tricks, and no fancy algorithms—at least not usually. What trips up many people is that they believe there's something "magic" to these problems—some hidden bit of knowledge.

It's not like that. These questions are simply designed to see how you would perform in the real world. If you were asked by your manager to design some system, what would you do?

That's why you should approach it just like this. Tackle the problem by doing it just like you would at work. Ask questions. Engage the interviewer. Discuss the tradeoffs.

We will touch on some key concepts in this chapter, but recognize it's not really about memorizing these concepts. Yes, understanding some big components of system design can be useful, but it's much more about the process you take. There are good solutions and bad solutions. There is no perfect solution.

▸ Handling the Questions

- **Communicate**: A key goal of system design questions is to evaluate your ability to communicate. Stay engaged with the interviewer. Ask them questions. Be open about the issues of your system.
- **Go broad first**: Don't dive straight into the algorithm part or get excessively focused on one part.
- **Use the whiteboard**: Using a whiteboard helps your interviewer follow your proposed design. Get up to the whiteboard in the very beginning and use it to draw a picture of what you're proposing.
- **Acknowledge interviewer concerns**: Your interviewer will likely jump in with concerns. Don't brush them off; validate them. Acknowledge the issues your interviewer points out and make changes accordingly.
- **Be careful about assumptions**: An incorrect assumption can dramatically change the problem. For example, if your system produces analytics / statistics for a dataset, it matters whether those analytics must be totally up to date.
- **State your assumptions explicitly**: When you do make assumptions, state them. This allows your interviewer to correct you if you're mistaken, and shows that you at least know what assumptions you're making.
- **Estimate when necessary**: In many cases, you might not have the data you need. For example, if you're designing a web crawler, you might need to estimate how much space it will take to store all the URLs. You can estimate this with other data you know.
- **Drive**: As the candidate, you should stay in the driver's seat. This doesn't mean you don't talk to your interviewer; in fact, you *must* talk to your interviewer. However, you should be driving through the ques-

tion. Ask questions. Be open about tradeoffs. Continue to go deeper. Continue to make improvements.

These questions are largely about the process rather than the ultimate design.

▸ Design: Step-By-Step

If your manager asked you to design a system such as TinyURL, you probably wouldn't just say, "Okay", then lock yourself in your office to design it by yourself. You would probably have a lot more questions before you do it. This is the way you should handle it in an interview.

Step 1: Scope the Problem

You can't design a system if you don't know what you're designing. Scoping the problem is important because you want to ensure that you're building what the interviewer wants and because this might be something that interviewer is specifically evaluating.

If you're asked something such as "Design TinyURL", you'll want to understand what exactly you need to implement. Will people be able to specify their own short URLs? Or will it all be auto-generated? Will you need to keep track of any stats on the clicks? Should the URLs stay alive forever, or do they have a timeout?

These are questions that must be answered before going further.

Make a list here as well of the major features or use cases. For example, for TinyURL, it might be:

- Shortening a URL to a TinyURL.
- Analytics for a URL.
- Retrieving the URL associated with a TinyURL.
- User accounts and link management.

Step 2: Make Reasonable Assumptions

It's okay to make some assumptions (when necessary), but they should be reasonable. For example, it would not be reasonable to assume that your system only needs to process 100 users per day, or to assume that you have infinite memory available.

However, it might be reasonable to design for a max of one million new URLs per day. Making this assumption can help you calculate how much data your system might need to store.

Some assumptions might take some "product sense" (which is not a bad thing). For example, is it okay for the data to be stale by a max of ten minutes? That all depends. If it takes 10 minutes for a just-entered URL to work, that's a deal-breaking issue. People usually want these URLs to be active immediately. However, if the statistics are ten minutes out of date, that might be okay. Talk to your interviewer about these sorts of assumptions.

Step 3: Draw the Major Components

Get up out of that chair and go to the whiteboard. Draw a diagram of the major components. You might have something like a frontend server (or set of servers) that pull data from the backend's data store. You might have another set of servers that crawl the internet for some data, and another set that process analytics. Draw a picture of what this system might look like.

Walk through your system from end-to-end to provide a flow. A user enters a new URL. Then what?

It may help here to ignore major scalability challenges and just pretend that the simple, obvious approaches will be okay. You'll handle the big issues in Step 4.

Step 4: Identify the Key Issues

Once you have a basic design in mind, focus on the key issues. What will be the bottlenecks or major challenges in the system?

For example, if you were designing TinyURL, one situation you might consider is that while some URLs will be infrequently accessed, others can suddenly peak. This might happen if a URL is posted on Reddit or another popular forum. You don't necessarily want to constantly hit the database.

Your interviewer might provide some guidance here. If so, take this guidance and use it.

Step 5: Redesign for the Key Issues

Once you have identified the key issues, it's time to adjust your design for it. You might find that it involves a major redesign or just some minor tweaking (like using a cache).

Stay up at the whiteboard here and update your diagram as your design changes.

Be open about any limitations in your design. Your interviewer will likely be aware of them, so it's important to communicate that you're aware of them, too.

▸ Algorithms that Scale: Step-By-Step

In some cases, you're not being asked to design an entire system. You're just being asked to design a single feature or algorithm, but you have to do it in a scalable way. Or, there might be one algorithm part that is the "real" focus of a broader design question.

In these cases, try the following approach.

Step 1: Ask Questions

As in the earlier approach, ask questions to make sure you really understand the question. There might be details the interviewer left out (intentionally or unintentionally). You can't solve a problem if you don't understand exactly what the problem is.

Step 2: Make Believe

Pretend that the data can all fit on one machine and there are no memory limitations. How would you solve the problem? The answer to this question will provide the general outline for your solution.

Step 3: Get Real

Now go back to the original problem. How much data can you fit on one machine, and what problems will occur when you split up the data? Common problems include figuring out how to logically divide the data up, and how one machine would identify where to look up a different piece of data.

Step 4: Solve Problems

Finally, think about how to solve the issues you identified in Step 3. Remember that the solution for each issue might be to actually remove the issue entirely, or it might be to simply mitigate the issue. Usually, you can continue using (with modifications) the approach you outlined in Step 2, but occasionally you will need to fundamentally alter the approach.

Note that an iterative approach is typically useful. That is, once you have solved the problems from Step 3, new problems may have emerged, and you must tackle those as well.

Your goal is not to re-architect a complex system that companies have spent millions of dollars building, but rather to demonstrate that you can analyze and solve problems. Poking holes in your own solution is a fantastic way to demonstrate this.

▸ Key Concepts

While system design questions aren't really tests of what you know, certain concepts can make things a lot easier. We will give a brief overview here. All of these are deep, complex topics, so we encourage you to use online resources for more research.

Horizontal vs. Vertical Scaling

A system can be scaled one of two ways.

- Vertical scaling means increasing the resources of a specific node. For example, you might add additional memory to a server to improve its ability to handle load changes.
- Horizontal scaling means increasing the number of nodes. For example, you might add additional servers, thus decreasing the load on any one server.

Vertical scaling is generally easier than horizontal scaling, but it's limited. You can only add so much memory or disk space.

Load Balancer

Typically, some frontend parts of a scalable website will be thrown behind a load balancer. This allows a system to distribute the load evenly so that one server doesn't crash and take down the whole system. To do so, of course, you have to build out a network of cloned servers that all have essentially the same code and access to the same data.

Database Denormalization and NoSQL

Joins in a relational database such as SQL can get very slow as the system grows bigger. For this reason, you would generally avoid them.

Denormalization is one part of this. Denormalization means adding redundant information into a database to speed up reads. For example, imagine a database describing projects and tasks (where a project can have multiple tasks). You might need to get the project name and the task information. Rather than doing a join across these tables, you can store the project name within the task table (in addition to the project table).

Or, you can go with a NoSQL database. A NoSQL database does not support joins and might structure data in a different way. It is designed to scale better.

Database Partitioning (Sharding)

Sharding means splitting the data across multiple machines while ensuring you have a way of figuring out which data is on which machine.

A few common ways of partitioning include:

- **Vertical Partitioning**: This is basically partitioning by feature. For example, if you were building a social network, you might have one partition for tables relating to profiles, another one for messages, and so on. One drawback of this is that if one of these tables gets very large, you might need to repartition that database (possibly using a different partitioning scheme).
- **Key-Based (or Hash-Based) Partitioning**: This uses some part of the data (for example an ID) to partition it. A very simple way to do this is to allocate N servers and put the data on `mod(key, n)`. One issue with this is that the number of servers you have is effectively fixed. Adding additional servers means reallocating all the data—a very expensive task.
- **Directory-Based Partitioning**: In this scheme, you maintain a lookup table for where the data can be found. This makes it relatively easy to add additional servers, but it comes with two major drawbacks. First, the lookup table can be a single point of failure. Second, constantly accessing this table impacts performance.

Many architectures actually end up using multiple partitioning schemes.

Caching

An in-memory cache can deliver very rapid results. It is a simple key-value pairing and typically sits between your application layer and your data store.

When an application requests a piece of information, it first tries the cache. If the cache does not contain the key, it will then look up the data in the data store. (At this point, the data might—or might not—be stored in the data store.)

When you cache, you might cache a query and its results directly. Or, alternatively, you can cache the specific object (for example, a rendered version of a part of the website, or a list of the most recent blog posts).

Asynchronous Processing & Queues

Slow operations should ideally be done asynchronously. Otherwise, a user might get stuck waiting and waiting for a process to complete.

In some cases, we can do this in advance (i.e., we can pre-process). For example, we might have a queue of jobs to be done that update some part of the website. If we were running a forum, one of these jobs might be to re-render a page that lists the most popular posts and the number of comments. That list might end up being slightly out of date, but that's perhaps okay. It's better than a user stuck waiting on the website to load simply because someone added a new comment and invalidated the cached version of this page.

In other cases, we might tell the user to wait and notify them when the process is done. You've probably seen this on websites before. Perhaps you enabled some new part of a website and it says it needs a few minutes to import your data, but you'll get a notification when it's done.

Networking Metrics

Some of the most important metrics around networking include:

- **Bandwidth**: This is the maximum amount of data that can be transferred in a unit of time. It is typically expressed in bits per second (or some similar ways, such as gigabytes per second).
- **Throughput**: Whereas bandwidth is the maximum data that can be transferred in a unit of time, throughput is the actual amount of data that is transferred.
- **Latency**: This is how long it takes data to go from one end to the other. That is, it is the delay between the sender sending information (even a very small chunk of data) and the receiver receiving it.

Imagine you have a conveyor belt that transfers items across a factory. Latency is the time it takes an item to go from one side to another. Throughput is the number of items that roll off the conveyor belt per second.

- Building a fatter conveyor belt will not change latency. It will, however, change throughput and bandwidth. You can get more items on the belt, thus transferring more in a given unit of time.
- Shortening the belt will decrease latency, since items spend less time in transit. It won't change the throughput or bandwidth. The same number of items will roll off the belt per unit of time.
- Making a faster conveyor belt will change all three. The time it takes an item to travel across the factory decreases. More items will also roll off the conveyor belt per unit of time.
- Bandwidth is the number of items that can be transferred per unit of time, in the best possible conditions. Throughput is the time it really takes, when the machines perhaps aren't operating smoothly.

Latency can be easy to disregard, but it can be very important in particular situations. For example, if you're playing certain online games, latency can be a very big deal. How can you play a typical online sports game (like a two-player football game) if you aren't notified very quickly of your opponent's movement? Additionally, unlike throughput where at least you have the option of speeding things up through data compression, there is often little you can do about latency.

MapReduce

MapReduce is often associated with Google, but it's used much more broadly than that. A MapReduce program is typically used to process large amounts of data.

As its name suggests, a MapReduce program requires you to write a Map step and a Reduce step. The rest is handled by the system.

- `Map` takes in some data and emits a `<key, value>` pair.
- `Reduce` takes a key and a set of associated values and "reduces" them in some way, emitting a new key and value. The results of this might be fed back into the `Reduce` program for more reducing.

MapReduce allows us to do a lot of processing in parallel, which makes processing huge amounts of data more scalable.

For more information, see "MapReduce" on page 642.

▸ Considerations

In addition to the earlier concepts to learn, you should consider the following issues when designing a system.

- **Failures**: Essentially any part of a system can fail. You'll need to plan for many or all of these failures.
- **Availability and Reliability**: Availability is a function of the percentage of time the system is operational. Reliability is a function of the probability that the system is operational for a certain unit of time.
- **Read-heavy vs. Write-heavy**: Whether an application will do a lot of reads or a lot of writes impacts the design. If it's write-heavy, you could consider queuing up the writes (but think about potential failure here!). If it's read-heavy, you might want to cache. Other design decisions could change as well.
- **Security**: Security threats can, of course, be devastating for a system. Think about the types of issues a system might face and design around those.

This is just to get you started with the potential issues for a system. Remember to be open in your interview about the tradeoffs.

▸ There is no "perfect" system.

There is no single design for TinyURL or Google Maps or any other system that works perfectly (although there are a great number that would work terribly). There are always tradeoffs. Two people could have substantially different designs for a system, with both being excellent given different assumptions.

Your goal in these problems is to be able to understand use cases, scope a problem, make reasonable assumptions, create a solid design based on those assumptions, and be open about the weaknesses of your design. Do not expect something perfect.

▸ Example Problem

Given a list of millions of documents, how would you find all documents that contain a list of words? The words can appear in any order, but they must be complete words. That is, "book" does not match "bookkeeper."

Before we start solving the problem, we need to understand whether this is a one time only operation, or if this `findWords` procedure will be called repeatedly. Let's assume that we will be calling `findWords` many times for the same set of documents, and, therefore, we can accept the burden of pre-processing.

Step 1

The first step is to pretend we just have a few dozen documents. How would we implement `findWords` in this case? (Tip: stop here and try to solve this yourself before reading on.)

One way to do this is to pre-process each document and create a hash table index. This hash table would map from a word to a list of the documents that contain that word.

```
"books" -> {doc2, doc3, doc6, doc8}
"many"  -> {doc1, doc3, doc7, doc8, doc9}
```

To search for "`many books`," we would simply do an intersection on the values for "`books`" and "`many`", and return `{doc3, doc8}` as the result.

Step 2

Now go back to the original problem. What problems are introduced with millions of documents? For starters, we probably need to divide up the documents across many machines. Also, depending on a variety of factors, such as the number of possible words and the repetition of words in a document, we may not be able to fit the full hash table on one machine. Let's assume that this is the case.

This division introduces the following key concerns:

1. How will we divide up our hash table? We could divide it up by keyword, such that a given machine contains the full document list for a given word. Or, we could divide by document, such that a machine contains the keyword mapping for only a subset of the documents.
2. Once we decide how to divide up the data, we may need to process a document on one machine and push the results off to other machines. What does this process look like? (Note: if we divide the hash table by document, this step may not be necessary.)
3. We will need a way of knowing which machine holds a piece of data. What does this lookup table look like, and where is it stored?

These are just three concerns. There may be many others.

Step 3

In Step 3, we find solutions to each of these issues. One solution is to divide up the words alphabetically by keyword, such that each machine controls a range of words (e.g., "after" through "apple").

We can implement a simple algorithm in which we iterate through the keywords alphabetically, storing as much data as possible on one machine. When that machine is full, we can move to the next machine.

The advantage of this approach is that the lookup table is small and simple (since it must only specify a range of values), and each machine can store a copy of the lookup table. However, the disadvantage is that if new documents or words are added, we may need to perform an expensive shift of keywords.

To find all the documents that match a list of strings, we would first sort the list and then send each machine a lookup request for the strings that the machine owns. For example, if our string is `"after builds boat amaze banana"`, machine 1 would get a lookup request for `{"after", "amaze"}`.

Machine 1 looks up the documents containing "after" and "amaze," and performs an intersection on these document lists. Machine 3 does the same for `{"banana", "boat", "builds"}`, and intersects their lists.

In the final step, the initial machine would do an intersection on the results from Machine 1 and Machine 3.

The following diagram explains this process.

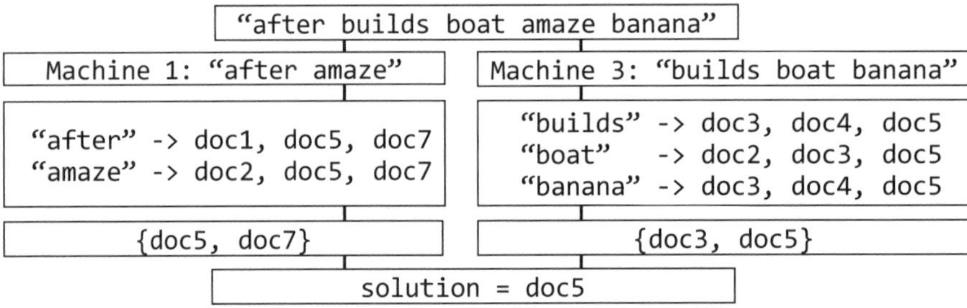

Interview Questions

These questions are designed to mirror a real interview, so they will not always be well defined. Think about what questions you would ask your interviewer and then make reasonable assumptions. You may make different assumptions than us, and that will lead you to a very different design. That's okay!

9.1 **Stock Data:** Imagine you are building some sort of service that will be called by up to 1,000 client applications to get simple end-of-day stock price information (open, close, high, low). You may assume that you already have the data, and you can store it in any format you wish. How would you design the client-facing service that provides the information to client applications? You are responsible for the development, rollout, and ongoing monitoring and maintenance of the feed. Describe the different methods you considered and why you would recommend your approach. Your service can use any technologies you wish, and can distribute the information to the client applications in any mechanism you choose.

Hints: #385, #396

pg 372

9.2 **Social Network:** How would you design the data structures for a very large social network like Facebook or LinkedIn? Describe how you would design an algorithm to show the shortest path between two people (e.g., Me -> Bob -> Susan -> Jason -> You).

Hints: #270, #285, #304, #321

pg 374

9.3 **Web Crawler:** If you were designing a web crawler, how would you avoid getting into infinite loops?

Hints: #334, #353, #365

pg 378

9.4 **Duplicate URLs:** You have 10 billion URLs. How do you detect the duplicate documents? In this case, assume "duplicate" means that the URLs are identical.

Hints: #326, #347

pg 380

9.5 **Cache:** Imagine a web server for a simplified search engine. This system has 100 machines to respond to search queries, which may then call out using `processSearch(string query)` to another cluster of machines to actually get the result. The machine which responds to a given query is chosen at random, so you cannot guarantee that the same machine will always respond to the same request. The method `processSearch` is very expensive. Design a caching mechanism for the most recent queries. Be sure to explain how you would update the cache when data changes.

Hints: #259, #274, #293, #311

pg 381

9.6 **Sales Rank**: A large eCommerce company wishes to list the best-selling products, overall and by category. For example, one product might be the #1056th best-selling product overall but the #13th best-selling product under "Sports Equipment" and the #24th best-selling product under "Safety." Describe how you would design this system.

Hints: #142, #158, #176, #189, #208, #223, #236, #244

pg 385

9.7 **Personal Financial Manager**: Explain how you would design a personal financial manager (like Mint.com). This system would connect to your bank accounts, analyze your spending habits, and make recommendations.

Hints: #162, #180, #199, #212, #247, #276

pg 388

9.8 **Pastebin**: Design a system like Pastebin, where a user can enter a piece of text and get a randomly generated URL to access it.

Hints: #165, #184, #206, #232

pg 392

Additional Questions: Object-Oriented Design (#7.7)

Hints start on page 662.

10

Sorting and Searching

Understanding the common sorting and searching algorithms is incredibly valuable, as many sorting and searching problems are tweaks of the well-known algorithms. A good approach is therefore to run through the different sorting algorithms and see if one applies particularly well.

For example, suppose you are asked the following question: Given a very large array of `Person` objects, sort the people in increasing order of age.

We're given two interesting bits of knowledge here:

1. It's a large array, so efficiency is very important.
2. We are sorting based on ages, so we know the values are in a small range.

By scanning through the various sorting algorithms, we might notice that bucket sort (or radix sort) would be a perfect candidate for this algorithm. In fact, we can make the buckets small (just 1 year each) and get $O(n)$ running time.

▸ Common Sorting Algorithms

Learning (or re-learning) the common sorting algorithms is a great way to boost your performance. Of the five algorithms explained below, Merge Sort, Quick Sort and Bucket Sort are the most commonly used in interviews.

Bubble Sort | Runtime: $O(n^2)$ **average and worst case. Memory:** $O(1)$.

In bubble sort, we start at the beginning of the array and swap the first two elements if the first is greater than the second. Then, we go to the next pair, and so on, continuously making sweeps of the array until it is sorted. In doing so, the smaller items slowly "bubble" up to the beginning of the list.

Selection Sort | Runtime: $O(n^2)$ **average and worst case. Memory:** $O(1)$.

Selection sort is the child's algorithm: simple, but inefficient. Find the smallest element using a linear scan and move it to the front (swapping it with the front element). Then, find the second smallest and move it, again doing a linear scan. Continue doing this until all the elements are in place.

Merge Sort | Runtime: $O(n \log(n))$ **average and worst case. Memory:** Depends.

Merge sort divides the array in half, sorts each of those halves, and then merges them back together. Each of those halves has the same sorting algorithm applied to it. Eventually, you are merging just two single-element arrays. It is the "merge" part that does all the heavy lifting.

The merge method operates by copying all the elements from the target array segment into a helper array, keeping track of where the start of the left and right halves should be (`helperLeft` and `helperRight`). We then iterate through `helper`, copying the smaller element from each half into the array. At the end, we copy any remaining elements into the target array.

```
void mergesort(int[] array) {
  int[] helper = new int[array.length];
  mergesort(array, helper, 0, array.length - 1);
}

void mergesort(int[] array, int[] helper, int low, int high) {
  if (low < high) {
    int middle = (low + high) / 2;
    mergesort(array, helper, low, middle); // Sort left half
    mergesort(array, helper, middle+1, high); // Sort right half
    merge(array, helper, low, middle, high); // Merge them
  }
}

void merge(int[] array, int[] helper, int low, int middle, int high) {
  /* Copy both halves into a helper array */
  for (int i = low; i <= high; i++) {
    helper[i] = array[i];
  }

  int helperLeft = low;
  int helperRight = middle + 1;
  int current = low;

  /* Iterate through helper array. Compare the left and right half, copying back
   * the smaller element from the two halves into the original array. */
  while (helperLeft <= middle && helperRight <= high) {
    if (helper[helperLeft] <= helper[helperRight]) {
      array[current] = helper[helperLeft];
      helperLeft++;
    } else { // If right element is smaller than left element
      array[current] = helper[helperRight];
      helperRight++;
    }
    current++;
  }

  /* Copy the rest of the left side of the array into the target array */
  int remaining = middle - helperLeft;
  for (int i = 0; i <= remaining; i++) {
    array[current + i] = helper[helperLeft + i];
  }
}
```

You may notice that only the remaining elements from the left half of the helper array are copied into the target array. Why not the right half? The right half doesn't need to be copied because it's *already* there.

Consider, for example, an array like `[1, 4, 5 || 2, 8, 9]` (the "||" indicates the partition point). Prior to merging the two halves, both the helper array and the target array segment will end with `[8, 9]`. Once we copy over four elements (`1, 4, 5`, and 2) into the target array, the `[8, 9]` will still be in place in both arrays. There's no need to copy them over.

The space complexity of merge sort is $O(n)$ due to the auxiliary space used to merge parts of the array.

Quick Sort | Runtime: $O(n \log(n))$ **average,** $O(n^2)$ **worst case. Memory:** $O(\log(n))$.

In quick sort, we pick a random element and partition the array, such that all numbers that are less than the partitioning element come before all elements that are greater than it. The partitioning can be performed efficiently through a series of swaps (see below).

If we repeatedly partition the array (and its sub-arrays) around an element, the array will eventually become sorted. However, as the partitioned element is not guaranteed to be the median (or anywhere near the median), our sorting could be very slow. This is the reason for the $O(n^2)$ worst case runtime.

```
void quickSort(int[] arr, int left, int right) {
   int index = partition(arr, left, right);
   if (left < index - 1) { // Sort left half
      quickSort(arr, left, index - 1);
   }
   if (index < right) { // Sort right half
      quickSort(arr, index, right);
   }
}

int partition(int[] arr, int left, int right) {
   int pivot = arr[(left + right) / 2]; // Pick pivot point
   while (left <= right) {
      // Find element on left that should be on right
      while (arr[left] < pivot) left++;

      // Find element on right that should be on left
      while (arr[right] > pivot) right--;

      // Swap elements, and move left and right indices
      if (left <= right) {
         swap(arr, left, right); // swaps elements
         left++;
         right--;
      }
   }
   return left;
}
```

Radix Sort | Runtime: $O(kn)$ **(see below)**

Radix sort is a sorting algorithm for integers (and some other data types) that takes advantage of the fact that integers have a finite number of bits. In radix sort, we iterate through each digit of the number, grouping numbers by each digit. For example, if we have an array of integers, we might first sort by the first digit, so that the 0s are grouped together. Then, we sort each of these groupings by the next digit. We repeat this process sorting by each subsequent digit, until finally the whole array is sorted.

Unlike comparison sorting algorithms, which cannot perform better than $O(n \log(n))$ in the average case, radix sort has a runtime of $O(kn)$, where n is the number of elements and k is the number of passes of the sorting algorithm.

▸ Searching Algorithms

When we think of searching algorithms, we generally think of binary search. Indeed, this is a very useful algorithm to study.

In binary search, we look for an element x in a sorted array by first comparing x to the midpoint of the array. If x is less than the midpoint, then we search the left half of the array. If x is greater than the midpoint, then we search the right half of the array. We then repeat this process, treating the left and right halves as subarrays. Again, we compare x to the midpoint of this subarray and then search either its left or right side. We repeat this process until we either find x or the subarray has size 0.

Note that although the concept is fairly simple, getting all the details right is far more difficult than you might think. As you study the code below, pay attention to the plus ones and minus ones.

```
int binarySearch(int[] a, int x) {
  int low = 0;
  int high = a.length - 1;
  int mid;

  while (low <= high) {
    mid = (low + high) / 2;
    if (a[mid] < x) {
      low = mid + 1;
    } else if (a[mid] > x) {
      high = mid - 1;
    } else {
      return mid;
    }
  }
  return -1; // Error
}

int binarySearchRecursive(int[] a, int x, int low, int high) {
  if (low > high) return -1; // Error

  int mid = (low + high) / 2;
  if (a[mid] < x) {
    return binarySearchRecursive(a, x, mid + 1, high);
  } else if (a[mid] > x) {
    return binarySearchRecursive(a, x, low, mid - 1);
  } else {
    return mid;
  }
}
```

Potential ways to search a data structure extend beyond binary search, and you would do best not to limit yourself to just this option. You might, for example, search for a node by leveraging a binary tree, or by using a hash table. Think beyond binary search!

Interview Questions

10.1 **Sorted Merge:** You are given two sorted arrays, A and B, where A has a large enough buffer at the end to hold B. Write a method to merge B into A in sorted order.

Hints: #332

pg 396

10.2 Group Anagrams: Write a method to sort an array of strings so that all the anagrams are next to each other.

Hints: #177, #182, #263, #342

pg 397

10.3 Search in Rotated Array: Given a sorted array of n integers that has been rotated an unknown number of times, write code to find an element in the array. You may assume that the array was originally sorted in increasing order.

EXAMPLE

Input: find 5 in `{15, 16, 19, 20, 25, 1, 3, 4, 5, 7, 10, 14}`

Output: 8 (the index of 5 in the array)

Hints: #298, #310

pg 398

10.4 Sorted Search, No Size: You are given an array-like data structure `Listy` which lacks a size method. It does, however, have an `elementAt(i)` method that returns the element at index `i` in `O(1)` time. If `i` is beyond the bounds of the data structure, it returns `-1`. (For this reason, the data structure only supports positive integers.) Given a `Listy` which contains sorted, positive integers, find the index at which an element x occurs. If x occurs multiple times, you may return any index.

Hints: #320, #337, #348

pg 400

10.5 Sparse Search: Given a sorted array of strings that is interspersed with empty strings, write a method to find the location of a given string.

EXAMPLE

Input: `ball, {"at", "", "", "", "ball", "", "", "car", "", "", "dad", "", ""}`

Output: 4

Hints: #256

pg 401

10.6 Sort Big File: Imagine you have a 20 GB file with one string per line. Explain how you would sort the file.

Hints: #207

pg 402

10.7 Missing Int: Given an input file with four billion non-negative integers, provide an algorithm to generate an integer that is not contained in the file. Assume you have 1 GB of memory available for this task.

FOLLOW UP

What if you have only 10 MB of memory? Assume that all the values are distinct and we now have no more than one billion non-negative integers.

Hints: #235, #254, #281

pg 403

10.8 Find Duplicates: You have an array with all the numbers from 1 to N, where N is at most 32,000. The array may have duplicate entries and you do not know what N is. With only 4 kilobytes of memory available, how would you print all duplicate elements in the array?

Hints: #289, #315

pg 406

10.9 Sorted Matrix Search: Given an `M x N` matrix in which each row and each column is sorted in ascending order, write a method to find an element.

Hints: #193, #211, #229, #251, #266, #279, #288, #291, #303, #317, #330

pg 407

10.10 Rank from Stream: Imagine you are reading in a stream of integers. Periodically, you wish to be able to look up the rank of a number x (the number of values less than or equal to x). Implement the data structures and algorithms to support these operations. That is, implement the method `track(int x)`, which is called when each number is generated, and the method `getRankOfNumber(int x)`, which returns the number of values less than or equal to `x` (not including `x` itself).

EXAMPLE

Stream (in order of appearance): `5, 1, 4, 4, 5, 9, 7, 13, 3`

```
getRankOfNumber(1) = 0
getRankOfNumber(3) = 1
getRankOfNumber(4) = 3
```

Hints: #301, #376, #392

pg 412

10.11 Peaks and Valleys: In an array of integers, a "peak" is an element which is greater than or equal to the adjacent integers and a "valley" is an element which is less than or equal to the adjacent integers. For example, in the array {5, 8, 6, 2, 3, 4, 6}, {8, 6} are peaks and {5, 2} are valleys. Given an array of integers, sort the array into an alternating sequence of peaks and valleys.

EXAMPLE

Input: {5, 3, 1, 2, 3}

Output: {5, 1, 3, 2, 3}

Hints: #196, #219, #231, #253, #277, #292, #316

pg 414

Additional Questions: Arrays and Strings (#1.2), Recursion (#8.3), Moderate (#16.10, #16.16, #16.21, #16.24), Hard (#17.11, #17.26).

Hints start on page 662.

11

Testing

Before you flip past this chapter saying, "but I'm not a tester," stop and think. Testing is an important task for a software engineer, and for this reason, testing questions may come up during your interview. Of course, if you are applying for Testing roles (or Software Engineer in Test), then that's all the more reason why you need to pay attention.

Testing problems usually fall under one of four categories: (1) Test a real world object (like a pen); (2) Test a piece of software; (3) Write test code for a function; (4) Troubleshoot an existing issue. We'll cover approaches for each of these four types.

Remember that all four types require you to not make an assumption that the input or the user will play nice. Expect abuse and plan for it.

▸ What the Interviewer Is Looking For

At their surface, testing questions seem like they're just about coming up with an extensive list of test cases. And to some extent, that's right. You do need to come up with a reasonable list of test cases.

But in addition, interviewers want to test the following:

- *Big Picture Understanding:* Are you a person who understands what the software is really about? Can you prioritize test cases properly? For example, suppose you're asked to test an e-commerce system like Amazon. It's great to make sure that the product images appear in the right place, but it's even more important that payments work reliably, products are added to the shipment queue, and customers are never double charged.
- *Knowing How the Pieces Fit Together:* Do you understand how software works, and how it might fit into a greater ecosystem? Suppose you're asked to test Google Spreadsheets. It's important that you test opening, saving, and editing documents. But, Google Spreadsheets is part of a larger ecosystem. You need to test integration with Gmail, with plug-ins, and with other components.
- *Organization:* Do you approach the problem in a structured manner, or do you just spout off anything that comes to your head? Some candidates, when asked to come up with test cases for a camera, will just state anything and everything that comes to their head. A good candidate will break down the parts into categories like Taking Photos, Image Management, Settings, and so on. This structured approach will also help you to do a more thorough job creating the test cases.
- *Practicality:* Can you actually create reasonable testing plans? For example, if a user reports that the software crashes when they open a specific image, and you just tell them to reinstall the software, that's typically not very practical. Your testing plans need to be feasible and realistic for a company to implement.

Demonstrating these aspects will show that you will be a valuable member of the testing team.

▸ Testing a Real World Object

Some candidates are surprised to be asked questions like how to test a pen. After all, you should be testing software, right? Maybe, but these "real world" questions are still very common. Let's walk through this with an example.

Question: How would you test a paperclip?

Step 1: Who will use it? And why?

You need to discuss with your interviewer who is using the product and for what purpose. The answer may not be what you think. The answer could be "by teachers, to hold papers together," or it could be "by artists, to bend into the shape of animal." Or, it could be both. The answer to this question will shape how you handle the remaining questions.

Step 2: What are the use cases?

It will be useful for you to make a list of the use cases. In this case, the use case might be simply fastening paper together in a non-damaging (to the paper) way.

For other questions, there might be multiple use cases. It might be, for example, that the product needs to be able to send and receive content, or write and erase, and so on.

Step 3: What are the bounds of use?

The bounds of use might mean holding up to thirty sheets of paper in a single usage without permanent damage (e.g., bending), and thirty to fifty sheets with minimal permanent bending.

The bounds also extend to environmental factors as well. For example, should the paperclip work during very warm temperatures (90 - 110 degrees Fahrenheit)? What about extreme cold?

Step 4: What are the stress / failure conditions?

No product is fail-proof, so analyzing failure conditions needs to be part of your testing. A good discussion to have with your interviewer is about when it's acceptable (or even necessary) for the product to fail, and what failure should mean.

For example, if you were testing a laundry machine, you might decide that the machine should be able to handle at least 30 shirts or pants. Loading 30 - 45 pieces of clothing may result in minor failure, such as the clothing being inadequately cleaned. At more than 45 pieces of clothing, extreme failure might be acceptable. However, extreme failure in this case should probably mean the machine never turning on the water. It should certainly *not* mean a flood or a fire.

Step 5: How would you perform the testing?

In some cases, it might also be relevant to discuss the details of performing the testing. For example, if you need to make sure a chair can withstand normal usage for five years, you probably can't actually place it in a home and wait five years. Instead, you'd need to define what "normal" usage is (How many "sits" per year on the seat? What about the armrest?). Then, in addition to doing some manual testing, you would likely want a machine to automate some of the usage.

▸ Testing a Piece of Software

Testing a piece of software is actually very similar to testing a real world object. The major difference is that software testing generally places a greater emphasis on the details of performing testing.

Note that software testing has two core aspects to it:

- *Manual vs. Automated Testing:* In an ideal world, we might love to automate everything, but that's rarely feasible. Some things are simply much better with manual testing because some features are too qualitative for a computer to effectively examine (such as if content represents pornography). Additionally, whereas a computer can generally recognize only issues that it's been told to look for, human observation may reveal new issues that haven't been specifically examined. Both humans and computers form an essential part of the testing process.
- *Black Box Testing vs. White Box Testing:* This distinction refers to the degree of access we have into the software. In black box testing, we're just given the software as-is and need to test it. With white box testing, we have additional programmatic access to test individual functions. We can also automate some black box testing, although it's certainly much harder.

Let's walk through an approach from start to end.

Step 1: Are we doing Black Box Testing or White Box Testing?

Though this question can often be delayed to a later step, I like to get it out of the way early on. Check with your interviewer as to whether you're doing black box testing or white box testing—or both.

Step 2: Who will use it? And why?

Software typically has one or more target users, and the features are designed with this in mind. For example, if you're asked to test software for parental controls on a web browser, your target users include both parents (who are implementing the blocking) and children (who are the recipients of blocking). You may also have "guests" (people who should neither be implementing nor receiving blocking).

Step 3: What are the use cases?

In the software blocking scenario, the use cases of the parents include installing the software, updating controls, removing controls, and of course their own personal internet usage. For the children, the use cases include accessing legal content as well as "illegal" content.

Remember that it's not up to you to just magically decide the use cases. This is a conversation to have with your interviewer.

Step 4: What are the bounds of use?

Now that we have the vague use cases defined, we need to figure out what exactly this means. What does it mean for a website to be blocked? Should just the "illegal" page be blocked, or the entire website? Is the application supposed to "learn" what is bad content, or is it based on a white list or black list? If it's supposed to learn what inappropriate content is, what degree of false positives or false negatives is acceptable?

Step 5: What are the stress conditions / failure conditions?

When the software fails—which it inevitably will—what should the failure look like? Clearly, the software failure shouldn't crash the computer. Instead, it's likely that the software should just permit a blocked site, or ban an allowable site. In the latter case, you might want to discuss the possibility of a selective override with a password from the parents.

Step 6: What are the test cases? How would you perform the testing?

Here is where the distinctions between manual and automated testing, and between black box and white box testing, really come into play.

Steps 3 and 4 should have roughly defined the use cases. In step 6, we further define them and discuss how to perform the testing. What exact situations are you testing? Which of these steps can be automated? Which require human intervention?

Remember that while automation allows you to do some very powerful testing, it also has some significant drawbacks. Manual testing should usually be part of your test procedures.

When you go through this list, don't just rattle off every scenario you can think of. It's disorganized, and you're sure to miss major categories. Instead, approach this in a structured manner. Break down your testing into the main components, and go from there. Not only will you give a more complete list of test cases, but you'll also show that you're a structured, methodical person.

▸ Testing a Function

In many ways, testing a function is the easiest type of testing. The conversation is typically briefer and less vague, as the testing is usually limited to validating input and output.

However, don't overlook the value of some conversation with your interviewer. You should discuss any assumptions with your interviewer, particularly with respect to how to handle specific situations.

Suppose you were asked to write code to test `sort(int[] array)`, which sorts an array of integers. You might proceed as follows.

Step 1: Define the test cases

In general, you should think about the following types of test cases:

- *The normal case:* Does it generate the correct output for typical inputs? Remember to think about potential issues here. For example, because sorting often requires some sort of partitioning, it's reasonable to think that the algorithm might fail on arrays with an odd number of elements, since they can't be evenly partitioned. Your test case should list both examples.
- *The extremes:* What happens when you pass in an empty array? Or a very small (one element) array? What if you pass in a very large one?
- *Nulls and "illegal" input:* It is worthwhile to think about how the code should behave when given illegal input. For example, if you're testing a function to generate the nth Fibonacci number, your test cases should probably include the situation where n is negative.
- *Strange input:* A fourth kind of input sometimes comes up: strange input. What happens when you pass in an already sorted array? Or an array that's sorted in reverse order?

Generating these tests does require knowledge of the function you are writing. If you are unclear as to the constraints, you will need to ask your interviewer about this first.

Step 2: Define the expected result

Often, the expected result is obvious: the right output. However, in some cases, you might want to validate additional aspects. For instance, if the `sort` method returns a new sorted copy of the array, you should probably validate that the original array has not been touched.

Step 3: Write test code

Once you have the test cases and results defined, writing the code to implement the test cases should be fairly straightforward. Your code might look something like:

```
void testAddThreeSorted() {
  MyList list = new MyList();
  list.addThreeSorted(3, 1, 2); // Adds 3 items in sorted order
  assertEquals(list.getElement(0), 1);
  assertEquals(list.getElement(1), 2);
  assertEquals(list.getElement(2), 3);
}
```

▸ Troubleshooting Questions

A final type of question is explaining how you would debug or troubleshoot an existing issue. Many candidates balk at a question like this, giving unrealistic answers like "reinstall the software." You can approach these questions in a structured manner, like anything else.

Let's walk through this problem with an example: You're working on the Google Chrome team when you receive a bug report: Chrome crashes on launch. What would you do?

Reinstalling the browser might solve this user's problem, but it wouldn't help the other users who might be experiencing the same issue. Your goal is to understand what's *really* happening, so that the developers can fix it.

Step 1: Understand the Scenario

The first thing you should do is ask questions to understand as much about the situation as possible.

- How long has the user been experiencing this issue?
- What version of the browser is it? What operating system?
- Does the issue happen consistently, or how often does it happen? When does it happen?
- Is there an error report that launches?

Step 2: Break Down the Problem

Now that you understand the details of the scenario, you want to break down the problem into testable units. In this case, you can imagine the flow of the situation as follows:

1. Go to Windows Start menu.
2. Click on Chrome icon.
3. Browser instance starts.
4. Browser loads settings.
5. Browser issues HTTP request for homepage.

6. Browser gets HTTP response.
7. Browser parses webpage.
8. Browser displays content.

At some point in this process, something fails and it causes the browser to crash. A strong tester would iterate through the elements of this scenario to diagnose the problem.

Step 3: Create Specific, Manageable Tests

Each of the above components should have realistic instructions—things that you can ask the user to do, or things that you can do yourself (such as replicating steps on your own machine). In the real world, you will be dealing with customers, and you can't give them instructions that they can't or won't do.

Interview Questions

11.1 **Mistake:** Find the mistake(s) in the following code:

```
unsigned int i;
for (i = 100; i >= 0; --i)
  printf("%d\n", i);
```

Hints: #257, #299, #362

pg 417

11.2 **Random Crashes:** You are given the source to an application which crashes when it is run. After running it ten times in a debugger, you find it never crashes in the same place. The application is single threaded, and uses only the C standard library. What programming errors could be causing this crash? How would you test each one?

Hints: #325

pg 417

11.3 **Chess Test:** We have the following method used in a chess game: `boolean canMoveTo(int x, int y)`. This method is part of the `Piece` class and returns whether or not the piece can move to position `(x, y)`. Explain how you would test this method.

Hints: #329, #401

pg 418

11.4 **No Test Tools:** How would you load test a webpage without using any test tools?

Hints: #313, #345

pg 419

11.5 **Test a Pen:** How would you test a pen?

Hints: #140, #164, #220

pg 420

11.6 **Test an ATM:** How would you test an ATM in a distributed banking system?

Hints: #210, #225, #268, #349, #393

pg 421

Hints start on page 662.

12

C and C++

A good interviewer won't demand that you code in a language you don't profess to know. Hopefully, if you're asked to code in C++, it's listed on your resume. If you don't remember all the APIs, don't worry—most interviewers (though not all) don't care that much. We do recommend, however, studying up on basic C++ syntax so that you can approach these questions with ease.

▸ Classes and Inheritance

Though C++ classes have similar characteristics to those of other languages, we'll review some of the syntax below.

The code below demonstrates the implementation of a basic class with inheritance.

```
#include <iostream>
using namespace std;

#define NAME_SIZE 50 // Defines a macro

class Person {
   int id; // all members are private by default
   char name[NAME_SIZE];

 public:
   void aboutMe() {
      cout << "I am a person.";
   }
};

class Student : public Person {
 public:
   void aboutMe() {
      cout << "I am a student.";
   }
};

int main() {
   Student * p = new Student();
   p->aboutMe(); // prints "I am a student."
   delete p; // Important! Make sure to delete allocated memory.
   return 0;
}
```

All data members and methods are private by default in C++. One can modify this by introducing the keyword `public`.

▸ Constructors and Destructors

The constructor of a class is automatically called upon an object's creation. If no constructor is defined, the compiler automatically generates one called the Default Constructor. Alternatively, we can define our own constructor.

If you just need to initialize primitive types, a simple way to do it is this:

```
Person(int a) {
   id = a;
}
```

This works for primitive types, but you might instead want to do this:

```
Person(int a) : id(a) {
   ...
}
```

The data member `id` is assigned before the actual object is created and before the remainder of the constructor code is called. This approach is necessary when the fields are constant or class types.

The destructor cleans up upon object deletion and is automatically called when an object is destroyed. It cannot take an argument as we don't explicitly call a destructor.

```
~Person() {
   delete obj; // free any memory allocated within class
}
```

▸ Virtual Functions

In an earlier example, we defined p to be of type `Student`:

```
Student * p = new Student();
p->aboutMe();
```

What would happen if we defined p to be a `Person*`, like so?

```
Person * p = new Student();
p->aboutMe();
```

In this case, "`I am a person`" would be printed instead. This is because the function `aboutMe` is resolved at compile-time, in a mechanism known as *static binding*.

If we want to ensure that the `Student`'s implementation of `aboutMe` is called, we can define `aboutMe` in the `Person` class to be `virtual`.

```
class Person {
   ...
   virtual void aboutMe() {
      cout << "I am a person.";
   }
};

class Student : public Person {
 public:
   void aboutMe() {
      cout << "I am a student.";
   }
```

```
};
```

Another usage for virtual functions is when we can't (or don't want to) implement a method for the parent class. Imagine, for example, that we want `Student` and `Teacher` to inherit from `Person` so that we can implement a common method such as `addCourse(string s)`. Calling `addCourse` on `Person`, however, wouldn't make much sense since the implementation depends on whether the object is actually a `Student` or `Teacher`.

In this case, we might want `addCourse` to be a virtual function defined within `Person`, with the implementation being left to the subclass.

```
class Person {
  int id; // all members are private by default
  char name[NAME_SIZE];
  public:
  virtual void aboutMe() {
    cout << "I am a person." << endl;
  }
  virtual bool addCourse(string s) = 0;
};

class Student : public Person {
  public:
  void aboutMe() {
    cout << "I am a student." << endl;
  }

  bool addCourse(string s) {
    cout << "Added course " << s << " to student." << endl;
    return true;
  }
};

int main() {
  Person * p = new Student();
  p->aboutMe(); // prints "I am a student."
  p->addCourse("History");
  delete p;
}
```

Note that by defining `addCourse` to be a "pure virtual function," `Person` is now an abstract class and we cannot instantiate it.

Virtual Destructor

The virtual function naturally introduces the concept of a "virtual destructor." Suppose we wanted to implement a destructor method for `Person` and `Student`. A naive solution might look like this:

```
class Person {
 public:
  ~Person() {
    cout << "Deleting a person." << endl;
  }
};

class Student : public Person {
 public:
```

```
   ~Student() {
      cout << "Deleting a student." << endl;
   }
};

int main() {
   Person * p = new Student();
   delete p; // prints "Deleting a person."
}
```

As in the earlier example, since p is a `Person`, the destructor for the `Person` class is called. This is problematic because the memory for `Student` may not be cleaned up.

To fix this, we simply define the destructor for `Person` to be virtual.

```
class Person {
 public:
   virtual ~Person() {
      cout << "Deleting a person." << endl;
   }
};

class Student : public Person {
 public:
   ~Student() {
      cout << "Deleting a student." << endl;
   }
};

int main() {
   Person * p = new Student();
   delete p;
}
```

This will output the following:

```
Deleting a student.
Deleting a person.
```

Default Values

Functions can specify default values, as shown below. Note that all default parameters must be on the right side of the function declaration, as there would be no other way to specify how the parameters line up.

```
int func(int a, int b = 3) {
   x = a;
   y = b;
   return a + b;
}

w = func(4);
z = func(4, 5);
```

Operator Overloading

Operator overloading enables us to apply operators like + to objects that would otherwise not support these operations. For example, if we wanted to merge two `BookShelves` into one, we could overload the + operator as follows.

```
BookShelf BookShelf::operator+(BookShelf &other) { ... }
```

Pointers and References

A pointer holds the address of a variable and can be used to perform any operation that could be directly done on the variable, such as accessing and modifying it.

Two pointers can equal each other, such that changing one's value also changes the other's value (since they, in fact, point to the same address).

```
int * p = new int;
*p = 7;
int * q = p;
*p = 8;
cout << *q; // prints 8
```

Note that the size of a pointer varies depending on the architecture: 32 bits on a 32-bit machine and 64 bits on a 64-bit machine. Pay attention to this difference, as it's common for interviewers to ask exactly how much space a data structure takes up.

References

A reference is another name (an alias) for a pre-existing object and it does not have memory of its own. For example:

```
1   int a = 5;
2   int & b = a;
3   b = 7;
4   cout << a; // prints 7
```

In line 2 above, b is a reference to a; modifying b will also modify a.

You cannot create a reference without specifying where in memory it refers to. However, you can create a free-standing reference as shown below:

```
/* allocates memory to store 12 and makes b a reference to this
 * piece of memory. */
const int & b = 12;
```

Unlike pointers, references cannot be null and cannot be reassigned to another piece of memory.

Pointer Arithmetic

One will often see programmers perform addition on a pointer, such as what you see below:

```
int * p = new int[2];
p[0] = 0;
p[1] = 1;
p++;
cout << *p; // Outputs 1
```

Performing p++ will skip ahead by `sizeof(int)` bytes, such that the code outputs 1. Had p been of different type, it would skip ahead as many bytes as the size of the data structure.

Templates

Templates are a way of reusing code to apply the same class to different data types. For example, we might have a list-like data structure which we would like to use for lists of various types. The code below implements this with the `ShiftedList` class.

```
template <class T>class ShiftedList {
  T* array;
  int offset, size;
 public:
  ShiftedList(int sz) : offset(0), size(sz) {
    array = new T[size];
  }

  ~ShiftedList() {
    delete [] array;
  }

  void shiftBy(int n) {
    offset = (offset + n) % size;
  }

  T getAt(int i) {
    return array[convertIndex(i)];
  }

  void setAt(T item, int i) {
    array[convertIndex(i)] = item;
  }

private:
  int convertIndex(int i) {
    int index = (i - offset) % size;
    while (index < 0) index += size;
    return index;
  }
};
```

Interview Questions

12.1 Last K Lines: Write a method to print the last K lines of an input file using C++.

Hints: #449, #459

pg 422

12.2 Reverse String: Implement a function `void reverse(char* str)` in C or C++ which reverses a null-terminated string.

Hints: #410, #452

pg 423

12.3 Hash Table vs. STL Map: Compare and contrast a hash table and an STL map. How is a hash table implemented? If the number of inputs is small, which data structure options can be used instead of a hash table?

Hints: #423

pg 423

12.4 Virtual Functions: How do virtual functions work in C++?

Hints: #463

pg 424

12.5 Shallow vs. Deep Copy: What is the difference between deep copy and shallow copy? Explain how you would use each.

Hints: #445

pg 425

12.6 Volatile: What is the significance of the keyword "volatile" in C?

Hints: #456

pg 426

12.7 Virtual Base Class: Why does a destructor in base class need to be declared `virtual`?

Hints: #421, #460

pg 427

12.8 Copy Node: Write a method that takes a pointer to a `Node` structure as a parameter and returns a complete copy of the passed in data structure. The `Node` data structure contains two pointers to other `Nodes`.

Hints: #427, #462

pg 427

12.9 Smart Pointer: Write a smart pointer class. A smart pointer is a data type, usually implemented with templates, that simulates a pointer while also providing automatic garbage collection. It automatically counts the number of references to a `SmartPointer<T*>` object and frees the object of type T when the reference count hits zero.

Hints: #402, #438, #453

pg 428

12.10 Malloc: Write an aligned malloc and free function that supports allocating memory such that the memory address returned is divisible by a specific power of two.

EXAMPLE

`align_malloc(1000,128)` will return a memory address that is a multiple of 128 and that points to memory of size 1000 bytes.

`aligned_free()` will free memory allocated by `align_malloc`.

Hints: #413, #432, #440

pg 430

12.11 2D Alloc: Write a function in C called `my2DAlloc` which allocates a two-dimensional array. Minimize the number of calls to `malloc` and make sure that the memory is accessible by the notation `arr[i][j]`.

Hints: #406, #418, #426

pg 431

Additional Questions: Linked Lists (#2.6), Testing (#11.1), Java (#13.4), Threads and Locks (#15.3).

Hints start on page 676.

13

Java

While Java-related questions are found throughout this book, this chapter deals with questions about the language and syntax. Such questions are more unusual at bigger companies, which believe more in testing a candidate's aptitude than a candidate's knowledge (and which have the time and resources to train a candidate in a particular language). However, at other companies, these pesky questions can be quite common.

▸ How to Approach

As these questions focus so much on knowledge, it may seem silly to talk about an approach to these problems. After all, isn't it just about knowing the right answer?

Yes and no. Of course, the best thing you can do to master these questions is to learn Java inside and out. But, if you do get stumped, you can try to tackle it with the following approach:

1. Create an example of the scenario, and ask yourself how things should play out.
2. Ask yourself how other languages would handle this scenario.
3. Consider how you would design this situation if you were the language designer. What would the implications of each choice be?

Your interviewer may be equally—or more—impressed if you can derive the answer than if you automatically knew it. Don't try to bluff though. Tell the interviewer, "I'm not sure I can recall the answer, but let me see if I can figure it out. Suppose we have this code..."

▸ Overloading vs. Overriding

Overloading is a term used to describe when two methods have the same name but differ in the type or number of arguments.

```
public double computeArea(Circle c) { ... }
public double computeArea(Square s) { ... }
```

Overriding, however, occurs when a method shares the same name and function signature as another method in its super class.

```
public abstract class Shape {
  public void printMe() {
    System.out.println("I am a shape.");
  }
  public abstract double computeArea();
}
```

```

public class Circle extends Shape {
  private double rad = 5;
  public void printMe() {
    System.out.println("I am a circle.");
  }

  public double computeArea() {
    return rad * rad * 3.15;
  }
}

public class Ambiguous extends Shape {
  private double area = 10;
  public double computeArea() {
    return area;
  }
}

public class IntroductionOverriding {
  public static void main(String[] args) {
    Shape[] shapes = new Shape[2];
    Circle circle = new Circle();
    Ambiguous ambiguous = new Ambiguous();

    shapes[0] = circle;
    shapes[1] = ambiguous;

    for (Shape s : shapes) {
      s.printMe();
      System.out.println(s.computeArea());
    }
  }
}
```

The above code will print:

```
I am a circle.
78.75
I am a shape.
10.0
```

Observe that `Circle` overrode `printMe()`, whereas `Ambiguous` just left this method as-is.

▸ Collection Framework

Java's collection framework is incredibly useful, and you will see it used throughout this book. Here are some of the most useful items:

`ArrayList`: An `ArrayList` is a dynamically resizing array, which grows as you insert elements.

```
ArrayList<String> myArr = new ArrayList<String>();
myArr.add("one");
myArr.add("two");
System.out.println(myArr.get(0)); /* prints <one> */
```

`Vector`: A `vector` is very similar to an `ArrayList`, except that it is synchronized. Its syntax is almost identical as well.

```
Vector<String> myVect = new Vector<String>();
myVect.add("one");
myVect.add("two");
System.out.println(myVect.get(0));
```

`LinkedList`: `LinkedList` is, of course, Java's built-in `LinkedList` class. Though it rarely comes up in an interview, it's useful to study because it demonstrates some of the syntax for an iterator.

```
LinkedList<String> myLinkedList = new LinkedList<String>();
myLinkedList.add("two");
myLinkedList.addFirst("one");
Iterator<String> iter = myLinkedList.iterator();
while (iter.hasNext()) {
  System.out.println(iter.next());
}
```

`HashMap`: The `HashMap` collection is widely used, both in interviews and in the real world. We've provided a snippet of the syntax below.

```
HashMap<String, String> map = new HashMap<String, String>();
map.put("one", "uno");
map.put("two", "dos");
System.out.println(map.get("one"));
```

Before your interview, make sure you're very comfortable with the above syntax. You'll need it.

Interview Questions

Please note that because virtually all the solutions in this book are implemented with Java, we have selected only a small number of questions for this chapter. Moreover, most of these questions deal with the "trivia" of the languages, since the rest of the book is filled with Java programming questions.

13.1 **Private Constructor:** In terms of inheritance, what is the effect of keeping a constructor private?

Hints: #404

pg 433

13.2 **Return from Finally:** In Java, does the `finally` block get executed if we insert a `return` statement inside the try block of a `try-catch-finally`?

Hints: #409

pg 433

13.3 **Final, etc.:** What is the difference between `final`, `finally`, and `finalize`?

Hints: #412

pg 433

13.4 **Generics vs. Templates:** Explain the difference between templates in C++ and generics in Java.

Hints: #416, #425

pg 435

13.5 **TreeMap, HashMap, LinkedHashMap:** Explain the differences between `TreeMap`, `HashMap`, and `LinkedHashMap`. Provide an example of when each one would be best.

Hints: #420, #424, #430, #454

pg 436

13.6 Object Reflection: Explain what object reflection is in Java and why it is useful.

Hints: #435

pg 437

13.7 Lambda Expressions: There is a class `Country` that has methods `getContinent()` and `getPopulation()`. Write a function `int getPopulation(List<Country> countries, String continent)` that computes the total population of a given continent, given a list of all countries and the name of a continent.

Hints: #448, #461, #464

pg 438

13.8 Lambda Random: Using Lambda expressions, write a function `List<Integer> getRandomSubset(List<Integer> list)` that returns a random subset of arbitrary size. All subsets (including the empty set) should be equally likely to be chosen.

Hints: #443, #450, #457

pg 439

Additional Questions: Arrays and Strings (#1.3), Object-Oriented Design (#7.12), Threads and Locks (#15.3)

Hints start on page 676.

14

Databases

If you profess knowledge of databases, you might be asked some questions on it. We'll review some of the key concepts and offer an overview of how to approach these problems. As you read these queries, don't be surprised by minor variations in syntax. There are a variety of flavors of SQL, and you might have worked with a slightly different one. The examples in this book have been tested against Microsoft SQL Server.

▸ SQL Syntax and Variations

Implicit and explicit joins are shown below. These two statements are equivalent, and it's a matter of personal preference which one you choose. For consistency, we will stick to the explicit join.

Explicit Join

```
SELECT CourseName, TeacherName
FROM Courses INNER JOIN Teachers
ON Courses.TeacherID = Teachers.TeacherID
```

Implicit Join

```
SELECT CourseName, TeacherName
FROM   Courses, Teachers
WHERE  Courses.TeacherID =
       Teachers.TeacherID
```

▸ Denormalized vs. Normalized Databases

Normalized databases are designed to minimize redundancy, while denormalized databases are designed to optimize read time.

In a traditional normalized database with data like `Courses` and `Teachers`, `Courses` might contain a column called `TeacherID`, which is a foreign key to `Teacher`. One benefit of this is that information about the teacher (name, address, etc.) is only stored once in the database. The drawback is that many common queries will require expensive joins.

Instead, we can denormalize the database by storing redundant data. For example, if we knew that we would have to repeat this query often, we might store the teacher's name in the `Courses` table. Denormalization is commonly used to create highly scalable systems.

▸ SQL Statements

Let's walk through a review of basic SQL syntax, using as an example the database that was mentioned earlier. This database has the following simple structure (* indicates a primary key):

```
Courses: CourseID*, CourseName, TeacherID
Teachers: TeacherID*, TeacherName
Students: StudentID*, StudentName
```

```
StudentCourses: CourseID*, StudentID*
```

Using the above table, implement the following queries.

Query 1: Student Enrollment

Implement a query to get a list of all students and how many courses each student is enrolled in.

At first, we might try something like this:

```
/* Incorrect Code */
SELECT Students.StudentName, count(*)
FROM Students INNER JOIN StudentCourses
ON Students.StudentID = StudentCourses.StudentID
GROUP BY Students.StudentID
```

This has three problems:

1. We have excluded students who are not enrolled in any courses, since `StudentCourses` only includes enrolled students. We need to change this to a `LEFT JOIN`.
2. Even if we changed it to a `LEFT JOIN`, the query is still not quite right. Doing `count(*)` would return how many items there are in a given group of `StudentID`s. Students enrolled in zero courses would still have one item in their group. We need to change this to count the number of `CourseID`s in each group: `count(StudentCourses.CourseID)`.
3. We've grouped by `Students.StudentID`, but there are still multiple `StudentName`s in each group. How will the database know which `StudentName` to return? Sure, they may all have the same value, but the database doesn't understand that. We need to apply an *aggregate* function to this, such as `first(Students.StudentName)`.

Fixing these issues gets us to this query:

```
1   /* Solution 1: Wrap with another query */
2   SELECT StudentName, Students.StudentID, Cnt
3   FROM (
4     SELECT  Students.StudentID, count(StudentCourses.CourseID) as [Cnt]
5     FROM Students LEFT JOIN StudentCourses
6     ON Students.StudentID = StudentCourses.StudentID
7     GROUP BY Students.StudentID
8   ) T INNER JOIN Students on T.studentID = Students.StudentID
```

Looking at this code, one might ask why we don't just select the student name on line 3 to avoid having to wrap lines 3 through 6 with another query. This (incorrect) solution is shown below.

```
/* Incorrect Code */
SELECT StudentName, Students.StudentID, count(StudentCourses.CourseID) as [Cnt]
FROM Students LEFT JOIN StudentCourses
ON Students.StudentID = StudentCourses.StudentID
GROUP BY Students.StudentID
```

The answer is that we *can't* do that - at least not exactly as shown. We can only select values that are in an aggregate function or in the GROUP BY clause.

Alternatively, we could resolve the above issues with either of the following statements:

```
/* Solution 2: Add StudentName to GROUP BY clause. */
SELECT StudentName, Students.StudentID, count(StudentCourses.CourseID) as [Cnt]
FROM Students LEFT JOIN StudentCourses
ON Students.StudentID = StudentCourses.StudentID
GROUP BY Students.StudentID, Students.StudentName
```

OR

```
/* Solution 3: Wrap with aggregate function. */
SELECT  max(StudentName) as [StudentName], Students.StudentID,
        count(StudentCourses.CourseID) as [Count]
FROM Students LEFT JOIN StudentCourses
ON Students.StudentID = StudentCourses.StudentID
GROUP BY Students.StudentID
```

Query 2: Teacher Class Size

Implement a query to get a list of all teachers and how many students they each teach. If a teacher teaches the same student in two courses, you should double count the student. Sort the list in descending order of the number of students a teacher teaches.

We can construct this query step by step. First, let's get a list of `TeacherID`s and how many students are associated with each `TeacherID`. This is very similar to the earlier query.

```
SELECT TeacherID, count(StudentCourses.CourseID) AS [Number]
FROM Courses INNER JOIN StudentCourses
ON Courses.CourseID = StudentCourses.CourseID
GROUP BY Courses.TeacherID
```

Note that this `INNER JOIN` will not select teachers who aren't teaching classes. We'll handle that in the below query when we join it with the list of all teachers.

```
SELECT TeacherName, isnull(StudentSize.Number, 0)
FROM Teachers LEFT JOIN
     (SELECT TeacherID, count(StudentCourses.CourseID) AS [Number]
      FROM Courses INNER JOIN StudentCourses
      ON Courses.CourseID = StudentCourses.CourseID
      GROUP BY Courses.TeacherID) StudentSize
ON Teachers.TeacherID = StudentSize.TeacherID
ORDER BY StudentSize.Number DESC
```

Note how we handled the `NULL` values in the `SELECT` statement to convert the `NULL` values to zeros.

▸ Small Database Design

Additionally, you might be asked to design your own database. We'll walk you through an approach for this. You might notice the similarities between this approach and the approach for object-oriented design.

Step 1: Handle Ambiguity

Database questions often have some ambiguity, intentionally or unintentionally. Before you proceed with your design, you must understand exactly what you need to design.

Imagine you are asked to design a system to represent an apartment rental agency. You will need to know whether this agency has multiple locations or just one. You should also discuss with your interviewer how general you should be. For example, it would be extremely rare for a person to rent two apartments in the same building. But does that mean you shouldn't be able to handle that? Maybe, maybe not. Some very rare conditions might be best handled through a work around (like duplicating the person's contact information in the database).

Step 2: Define the Core Objects

Next, we should look at the core objects of our system. Each of these core objects typically translates into a table. In this case, our core objects might be `Property`, `Building`, `Apartment`, `Tenant` and `Manager`.

Step 3: Analyze Relationships

Outlining the core objects should give us a good sense of what the tables should be. How do these tables relate to each other? Are they many-to-many? One-to-many?

If `Buildings` has a one-to-many relationship with `Apartments` (one `Building` has many `Apartments`), then we might represent this as follows:

Apartments	
ApartmentID	int
ApartmentAddress	varchar(100)
BuildingID	int

Buildings	
BuildingID	int
BuildingName	varchar(100)
BuildingAddress	varchar(500)

Note that the `Apartments` table links back to `Buildings` with a `BuildingID` column.

If we want to allow for the possibility that one person rents more than one apartment, we might want to implement a many-to-many relationship as follows:

TenantApartments	
TenantID	int
ApartmentID	int

Apartments	
ApartmentID	int
ApartmentAddress	varchar(500)
BuildingID	int

Tenants	
TenantID	int
TenantName	varchar(100)
TenantAddress	varchar(500)

The `TenantApartments` table stores a relationship between `Tenants` and `Apartments`.

Step 4: Investigate Actions

Finally, we fill in the details. Walk through the common actions that will be taken and understand how to store and retrieve the relevant data. We'll need to handle lease terms, moving out, rent payments, etc. Each of these actions requires new tables and columns.

▸ Large Database Design

When designing a large, scalable database, joins (which are required in the above examples) are generally very slow. Thus, you must *denormalize* your data. Think carefully about how data will be used—you'll probably need to duplicate the data in multiple tables.

Interview Questions

Questions 1 through 3 refer to the database schema at the end of the chapter. Each apartment can have multiple tenants, and each tenant can have multiple apartments. Each apartment belongs to one building, and each building belongs to one complex.

14.1 Multiple Apartments: Write a SQL query to get a list of tenants who are renting more than one apartment.

Hints: #408

pg 441

14.2 **Open Requests:** Write a SQL query to get a list of all buildings and the number of open requests (`Requests` in which `status` equals `'Open'`).

Hints: #411

pg 442

14.3 **Close All Requests:** Building #11 is undergoing a major renovation. Implement a query to close all requests from apartments in this building.

Hints: #431

pg 442

14.4 **Joins:** What are the different types of joins? Please explain how they differ and why certain types are better in certain situations.

Hints: #451

pg 442

14.5 **Denormalization:** What is denormalization? Explain the pros and cons.

Hints: #444, #455

pg 443

14.6 **Entity-Relationship Diagram:** Draw an entity-relationship diagram for a database with companies, people, and professionals (people who work for companies).

Hints: #436

pg 444

14.7 **Design Grade Database:** Imagine a simple database storing information for students' grades. Design what this database might look like and provide a SQL query to return a list of the honor roll students (top 10%), sorted by their grade point average.

Hints: #428, #442

pg 445

Additional Questions: Object-Oriented Design (#7.7), System Design and Scalability (#9.6)

Hints start on page 676.

Apartments	
AptID	int
UnitNumber	varchar(10)
BuildingID	int

Buildings	
BuildingID	int
ComplexID	int
BuildingName	varchar(100)
Address	varchar(500)

Requests	
RequestID	int
Status	varchar(100)
AptID	int
Description	varchar(500)

Complexes	
ComplexID	int
ComplexName	varchar(100)

AptTenants	
TenantID	int
AptID	int

Tenants	
TenantID	int
TenantName	varchar(100)

15

Threads and Locks

In a Microsoft, Google or Amazon interview, it's not terribly common to be asked to implement an algorithm with threads (unless you're working in a team for which this is a particularly important skill). It is, however, relatively common for interviewers at any company to assess your general understanding of threads, particularly your understanding of deadlocks.

This chapter will provide an introduction to this topic.

▸ Threads in Java

Every thread in Java is created and controlled by a unique object of the `java.lang.Thread` class. When a standalone application is run, a user thread is automatically created to execute the `main()` method. This thread is called the main thread.

In Java, we can implement threads in one of two ways:

- By implementing the `java.lang.Runnable` interface
- By extending the `java.lang.Thread` class

We will cover both of these below.

Implementing the Runnable Interface

The `Runnable` interface has the following very simple structure.

```
public interface Runnable {
  void run();
}
```

To create and use a thread using this interface, we do the following:

1. Create a class which implements the `Runnable` interface. An object of this class is a `Runnable` object.
2. Create an object of type `Thread` by passing a `Runnable` object as argument to the `Thread` constructor. The `Thread` object now has a `Runnable` object that implements the `run()` method.
3. The `start()` method is invoked on the `Thread` object created in the previous step.

For example:

```
public class RunnableThreadExample implements Runnable {
  public int count = 0;

  public void run() {
    System.out.println("RunnableThread starting.");
```

```
6         try {
7            while (count < 5) {
8               Thread.sleep(500);
9               count++;
10           }
11        } catch (InterruptedException exc) {
12           System.out.println(“RunnableThread interrupted.”);
13        }
14        System.out.println(“RunnableThread terminating.”);
15     }
16  }
17
18  public static void main(String[] args) {
19     RunnableThreadExample instance = new RunnableThreadExample();
20     Thread thread = new Thread(instance);
21     thread.start();
22
23     /* waits until above thread counts to 5 (slowly) */
24     while (instance.count != 5) {
25        try {
26           Thread.sleep(250);
27        } catch (InterruptedException exc) {
28           exc.printStackTrace();
29        }
30     }
31  }
```

In the above code, observe that all we really needed to do is have our class implement the `run()` method (line 4). Another method can then pass an instance of the class to `new Thread(obj)` (lines 19 - 20) and call `start()` on the thread (line 21).

Extending the Thread Class

Alternatively, we can create a thread by extending the `Thread` class. This will almost always mean that we override the `run()` method, and the subclass may also call the thread constructor explicitly in its constructor.

The below code provides an example of this.

```
public class ThreadExample extends Thread {
   int count = 0;

   public void run() {
      System.out.println(“Thread starting.”);
      try {
         while (count < 5) {
            Thread.sleep(500);
            System.out.println(“In Thread, count is ” + count);
            count++;
         }
      } catch (InterruptedException exc) {
         System.out.println(“Thread interrupted.”);
      }
      System.out.println(“Thread terminating.”);
   }
}

```

```
public class ExampleB {
   public static void main(String args[]) {
      ThreadExample instance = new ThreadExample();
      instance.start();

      while (instance.count != 5) {
         try {
            Thread.sleep(250);
         } catch (InterruptedException exc) {
            exc.printStackTrace();
         }
      }
   }
}
```

This code is very similar to the first approach. The difference is that since we are extending the `Thread` class, rather than just implementing an interface, we can call `start()` on the instance of the class itself.

Extending the Thread Class vs. Implementing the Runnable Interface

When creating threads, there are two reasons why implementing the `Runnable` interface may be preferable to extending the `Thread` class:

- Java does not support multiple inheritance. Therefore, extending the `Thread` class means that the subclass cannot extend any other class. A class implementing the `Runnable` interface will be able to extend another class.
- A class might only be interested in being runnable, and therefore, inheriting the full overhead of the `Thread` class would be excessive.

Synchronization and Locks

Threads within a given process share the same memory space, which is both a positive and a negative. It enables threads to share data, which can be valuable. However, it also creates the opportunity for issues when two threads modify a resource at the same time. Java provides synchronization in order to control access to shared resources.

The keyword `synchronized` and the `lock` form the basis for implementing synchronized execution of code.

Synchronized Methods

Most commonly, we restrict access to shared resources through the use of the `synchronized` keyword. It can be applied to methods and code blocks, and restricts multiple threads from executing the code simultaneously *on the same object*.

To clarify the last point, consider the following code:

```
public class MyClass extends Thread  {
   private String name;
   private MyObject myObj;

   public MyClass(MyObject obj, String n) {
      name = n;
      myObj = obj;
   }
```

```

  public void run() {
    myObj.foo(name);
  }
}

public class MyObject {
  public synchronized void foo(String name) {
    try {
      System.out.println("Thread " + name + ".foo(): starting");
      Thread.sleep(3000);
      System.out.println("Thread " + name + ".foo(): ending");
    } catch (InterruptedException exc) {
      System.out.println("Thread " + name + ": interrupted.");
    }
  }
}
```

Can two instances of `MyClass` call `foo` at the same time? It depends. If they have the same instance of `MyObject`, then no. But, if they hold different references, then the answer is yes.

```
/* Difference references - both threads can call MyObject.foo() */
MyObject obj1 = new MyObject();
MyObject obj2 = new MyObject();
MyClass thread1 = new MyClass(obj1, "1");
MyClass thread2 = new MyClass(obj2, "2");
thread1.start();
thread2.start()

/* Same reference to obj. Only one will be allowed to call foo,
 * and the other will be forced to wait. */
MyObject obj = new MyObject();
MyClass thread1 = new MyClass(obj, "1");
MyClass thread2 = new MyClass(obj, "2");
thread1.start()
thread2.start()
```

Static methods synchronize on the *class lock*. The two threads above could not simultaneously execute synchronized static methods on the same class, even if one is calling `foo` and the other is calling `bar`.

```
public class MyClass extends Thread  {
  ...
  public void run() {
    if (name.equals("1")) MyObject.foo(name);
    else if (name.equals("2")) MyObject.bar(name);
  }
}

public class MyObject {
  public static synchronized void foo(String name) { /* same as before */ }
  public static synchronized void bar(String name) { /* same as foo */ }
}
```

If you run this code, you will see the following printed:

```
Thread 1.foo(): starting
Thread 1.foo(): ending
Thread 2.bar(): starting
Thread 2.bar(): ending
```

Synchronized Blocks

Similarly, a block of code can be synchronized. This operates very similarly to synchronizing a method.

```
public class MyClass extends Thread  {
   ...
   public void run() {
      myObj.foo(name);
   }
}
public class MyObject {
   public void foo(String name) {
      synchronized(this) {
         ...
      }
   }
}
```

Like synchronizing a method, only one thread per instance of `MyObject` can execute the code within the `synchronized` block. That means that, if `thread1` and `thread2` have the same instance of `MyObject`, only one will be allowed to execute the code block at a time.

Locks

For more granular control, we can utilize a lock. A lock (or monitor) is used to synchronize access to a shared resource by associating the resource with the lock. A thread gets access to a shared resource by first acquiring the lock associated with the resource. At any given time, at most one thread can hold the lock and, therefore, only one thread can access the shared resource.

A common use case for locks is when a resource is accessed from multiple places, but should be only accessed by one thread *at a time*. This case is demonstrated in the code below.

```
public class LockedATM {
   private Lock lock;
   private int balance = 100;

   public LockedATM() {
      lock = new ReentrantLock();
   }

   public int withdraw(int value) {
      lock.lock();
      int temp = balance;
      try {
         Thread.sleep(100);
         temp = temp - value;
         Thread.sleep(100);
         balance = temp;
      } catch (InterruptedException e) {      }
      lock.unlock();
      return temp;
   }

   public int deposit(int value) {
      lock.lock();
      int temp = balance;
      try {
         Thread.sleep(100);
```

```
            temp = temp + value;
            Thread.sleep(300);
            balance = temp;
        } catch (InterruptedException e) {      }
        lock.unlock();
        return temp;
    }
}
```

Of course, we've added code to intentionally slow down the execution of `withdraw` and `deposit`, as it helps to illustrate the potential problems that can occur. You may not write code exactly like this, but the situation it mirrors is very, very real. Using a lock will help protect a shared resource from being modified in unexpected ways.

▸ Deadlocks and Deadlock Prevention

A deadlock is a situation where a thread is waiting for an object lock that another thread holds, and this second thread is waiting for an object lock that the first thread holds (or an equivalent situation with several threads). Since each thread is waiting for the other thread to relinquish a lock, they both remain waiting forever. The threads are said to be deadlocked.

In order for a deadlock to occur, you must have all four of the following conditions met:

1. *Mutual Exclusion:* Only one process can access a resource at a given time. (Or, more accurately, there is limited access to a resource. A deadlock could also occur if a resource has limited quantity.)
2. *Hold and Wait:* Processes already holding a resource can request additional resources, without relinquishing their current resources.
3. *No Preemption:* One process cannot forcibly remove another process' resource.
4. *Circular Wait:* Two or more processes form a circular chain where each process is waiting on another resource in the chain.

Deadlock prevention entails removing any of the above conditions, but it gets tricky because many of these conditions are difficult to satisfy. For instance, removing #1 is difficult because many resources can only be used by one process at a time (e.g., printers). Most deadlock prevention algorithms focus on avoiding condition #4: circular wait.

Interview Questions

15.1 **Thread vs. Process:** What's the difference between a thread and a process?

Hints: #405

pg 447

15.2 **Context Switch:** How would you measure the time spent in a context switch?

Hints: #403, #407, #415, #441

pg 447

15.3 Dining Philosophers: In the famous dining philosophers problem, a bunch of philosophers are sitting around a circular table with one chopstick between each of them. A philosopher needs both chopsticks to eat, and always picks up the left chopstick before the right one. A deadlock could potentially occur if all the philosophers reached for the left chopstick at the same time. Using threads and locks, implement a simulation of the dining philosophers problem that prevents deadlocks.

Hints: #419, #437

pg 449

15.4 Deadlock-Free Class: Design a class which provides a lock only if there are no possible deadlocks.

Hints: #422, #434

pg 452

15.5 Call In Order: Suppose we have the following code:

```
public class Foo {
   public Foo() { ... }
   public void first() { ... }
   public void second() { ... }
   public void third() { ... }
}
```

The same instance of `Foo` will be passed to three different threads. `ThreadA` will call `first`, `threadB` will call `second`, and `threadC` will call `third`. Design a mechanism to ensure that `first` is called before `second` and `second` is called before `third`.

Hints: #417, #433, #446

pg 456

15.6 Synchronized Methods: You are given a class with synchronized method A and a normal method B. If you have two threads in one instance of a program, can they both execute A at the same time? Can they execute A and B at the same time?

Hints: #429

pg 458

15.7 FizzBuzz: In the classic problem FizzBuzz, you are told to print the numbers from 1 to n. However, when the number is divisible by 3, print "Fizz". When it is divisible by 5, print "Buzz". When it is divisible by 3 and 5, print "FizzBuzz". In this problem, you are asked to do this in a multithreaded way. Implement a multithreaded version of FizzBuzz with four threads. One thread checks for divisibility of 3 and prints "Fizz". Another thread is responsible for divisibility of 5 and prints "Buzz". A third thread is responsible for divisibility of 3 and 5 and prints "FizzBuzz". A fourth thread does the numbers.

Hints: #414, #439, #447, #458

pg 458

Hints start on page 676.

16

Moderate

16.1 **Number Swapper:** Write a function to swap a number in place (that is, without temporary variables).

Hints: #491, #715, #736

pg 462

16.2 **Word Frequencies:** Design a method to find the frequency of occurrences of any given word in a book. What if we were running this algorithm multiple times?

Hints: #488, #535

pg 463

16.3 **Intersection:** Given two straight line segments (represented as a start point and an end point), compute the point of intersection, if any.

Hints: #471, #496, #516, #526

pg 464

16.4 **Tic Tac Win:** Design an algorithm to figure out if someone has won a game of tic-tac-toe.

Hints: #709, #731

pg 466

16.5 **Factorial Zeros:** Write an algorithm which computes the number of trailing zeros in n factorial.

Hints: #584, #710, #728, #732, #744

pg 473

16.6 **Smallest Difference:** Given two arrays of integers, compute the pair of values (one value in each array) with the smallest (non-negative) difference. Return the difference.

EXAMPLE

Input: {1, 3, 15, 11, 2}, {23, 127, 235, 19, 8}

Output: 3. That is, the pair (11, 8).

Hints: #631, #669, #678

pg 474

16.7 **Number Max:** Write a method that finds the maximum of two numbers. You should not use if-else or any other comparison operator.

Hints: #472, #512, #706, #727

pg 475

16.8 English Int: Given any integer, print an English phrase that describes the integer (e.g., "One Thousand, Two Hundred Thirty Four").

Hints: #501, #587, #687

pg 477

16.9 Operations: Write methods to implement the multiply, subtract, and divide operations for integers. The results of all of these are integers. Use only the add operator.

Hints: #571, #599, #612, #647

pg 478

16.10 Living People: Given a list of people with their birth and death years, implement a method to compute the year with the most number of people alive. You may assume that all people were born between 1900 and 2000 (inclusive). If a person was alive during any portion of that year, they should be included in that year's count. For example, Person (birth = 1908, death = 1909) is included in the counts for both 1908 and 1909.

Hints: #475, #489, #506, #513, #522, #531, #540, #548, #575

pg 482

16.11 Diving Board: You are building a diving board by placing a bunch of planks of wood end-to-end. There are two types of planks, one of length `shorter` and one of length `longer`. You must use exactly K planks of wood. Write a method to generate all possible lengths for the diving board.

Hints: #689, #699, #714, #721, #739, #746

pg 486

16.12 XML Encoding: Since XML is very verbose, you are given a way of encoding it where each tag gets mapped to a pre-defined integer value. The language/grammar is as follows:

```
Element   --> Tag Attributes END Children END
Attribute --> Tag Value
END       --> 0
Tag       --> some predefined mapping to int
Value     --> string value
```

For example, the following XML might be converted into the compressed string below (assuming a mapping of `family -> 1, person ->2, firstName -> 3, lastName -> 4, state -> 5`).

```
<family lastName="McDowell" state="CA">
  <person firstName="Gayle">Some Message</person>
</family>
```

Becomes:

```
1 4 McDowell 5 CA 0 2 3 Gayle 0 Some Message 0 0
```

Write code to print the encoded version of an XML element (passed in `Element` and `Attribute` objects).

Hints: #465

pg 489

16.13 Bisect Squares: Given two squares on a two-dimensional plane, find a line that would cut these two squares in half. Assume that the top and the bottom sides of the square run parallel to the x-axis.

Hints: #467, #478, #527, #559

pg 490

16.14 Best Line: Given a two-dimensional graph with points on it, find a line which passes the most number of points.

Hints: #490, #519, #528, #562

pg 492

16.15 Master Mind: The Game of Master Mind is played as follows:

The computer has four slots, and each slot will contain a ball that is red (R), yellow (Y), green (G) or blue (B). For example, the computer might have RGGB (Slot #1 is red, Slots #2 and #3 are green, Slot #4 is blue).

You, the user, are trying to guess the solution. You might, for example, guess YRGB.

When you guess the correct color for the correct slot, you get a "hit." If you guess a color that exists but is in the wrong slot, you get a "pseudo-hit." Note that a slot that is a hit can never count as a pseudo-hit.

For example, if the actual solution is RGBY and you guess GGRR, you have one hit and one pseudo-hit.

Write a method that, given a guess and a solution, returns the number of hits and pseudo-hits.

Hints: #638, #729

pg 494

16.16 Sub Sort: Given an array of integers, write a method to find indices `m` and `n` such that if you sorted elements `m` through `n`, the entire array would be sorted. Minimize `n - m` (that is, find the smallest such sequence).

EXAMPLE

Input: `1, 2, 4, 7, 10, 11, 7, 12, 6, 7, 16, 18, 19`

Output: `(3, 9)`

Hints: #481, #552, #666, #707, #734, #745

pg 496

16.17 Contiguous Sequence: You are given an array of integers (both positive and negative). Find the contiguous sequence with the largest sum. Return the sum.

EXAMPLE

Input: `2, -8, 3, -2, 4, -10`

Output: `5 (i.e., {3, -2, 4})`

Hints: #530, #550, #566, #593, #613

pg 498

16.18 Pattern Matching: You are given two strings, `pattern` and `value`. The `pattern` string consists of just the letters a and b, describing a pattern within a string. For example, the string `catcatgocatgo` matches the pattern `aabab` (where `cat` is a and `go` is b). It also matches patterns like a, ab, and b. Write a method to determine if `value` matches `pattern`.

Hints: #630, #642, #652, #662, #684, #717, #726

pg 499

16.19 Pond Sizes: You have an integer matrix representing a plot of land, where the value at that location represents the height above sea level. A value of zero indicates water. A pond is a region of water connected vertically, horizontally, or diagonally. The size of the pond is the total number of connected water cells. Write a method to compute the sizes of all ponds in the matrix.

EXAMPLE

Input:

```
0 2 1 0
0 1 0 1
1 1 0 1
0 1 0 1
```

Output: 2, 4, 1 (in any order)

Hints: #673, #686, #705, #722

pg 503

16.20 T9: On old cell phones, users typed on a numeric keypad and the phone would provide a list of words that matched these numbers. Each digit mapped to a set of 0 - 4 letters. Implement an algorithm to return a list of matching words, given a sequence of digits. You are provided a list of valid words (provided in whatever data structure you'd like). The mapping is shown in the diagram below:

1	**2** abc	**3** def
4 ghi	**5** jkl	**6** mno
7 pqrs	**8** tuv	**9** wxyz
	0	

EXAMPLE

Input: `8733`

Output: `tree, used`

Hints: #470, #486, #653, #702, #725, #743

pg 505

16.21 Sum Swap: Given two arrays of integers, find a pair of values (one value from each array) that you can swap to give the two arrays the same sum.

EXAMPLE

Input: {4, 1, 2, 1, 1, 2} and {3, 6, 3, 3}

Output: {1, 3}

Hints: #544, #556, #563, #570, #582, #591, #601, #605, #634

pg 509

16.22 Langton's Ant: An ant is sitting on an infinite grid of white and black squares. Initially, the grid is all white and the ant faces right. At each step, it does the following:

(1) At a white square, flip the color of the square, turn 90 degrees right (clockwise), and move forward one unit.

(2) At a black square, flip the color of the square, turn 90 degrees left (counter-clockwise), and move forward one unit.

Write a program to simulate the first K moves that the ant makes and print the final board as a grid. Note that you are not provided with the data structure to represent the grid. This is something you must design yourself. The only input to your method is K. You should print the final grid and return nothing. The method signature might be something like `void printKMoves(int K)`.

Hints: #473, #480, #532, #539, #558, #569, #598, #615, #626

pg 512

16.23 Rand7 from Rand5: Implement a method `rand7()` given `rand5()`. That is, given a method that generates a random integer between 0 and 4 (inclusive), write a method that generates a random integer between 0 and 6 (inclusive).

Hints: #504, #573, #636, #667, #696, #719

pg 518

16.24 Pairs with Sum: Design an algorithm to find all pairs of integers within an array which sum to a specified value.

Hints: #547, #596, #643, #672

pg 520

16.25 LRU Cache: Design and build a "least recently used" cache, which evicts the least recently used item. The cache should map from keys to values (allowing you to insert and retrieve a value associated with a particular key) and be initialized with a max size. When it is full, it should evict the least recently used item.

Hints: #523, #629, #693

pg 521

16.26 Calculator: Given an arithmetic equation consisting of positive integers, +, -, * and / (no parentheses), compute the result.

EXAMPLE

Input: `2*3+5/6*3+15`

Output: `23.5`

Hints: #520, #623, #664, #697

pg 524

17

Hard

17.1 **Add Without Plus:** Write a function that adds two numbers. You should not use + or any arithmetic operators.

Hints: #466, #543, #600, #627, #641, #663, #691, #711, #723

pg 530

17.2 **Shuffle:** Write a method to shuffle a deck of cards. It must be a perfect shuffle—in other words, each of the 52! permutations of the deck has to be equally likely. Assume that you are given a random number generator which is perfect.

Hints: #482, #578, #633

pg 531

17.3 **Random Set:** Write a method to randomly generate a set of `m` integers from an array of size n. Each element must have equal probability of being chosen.

Hints: #493, #595

pg 532

17.4 **Missing Number:** An array A contains all the integers from 0 to n, except for one number which is missing. In this problem, we cannot access an entire integer in A with a single operation. The elements of A are represented in binary, and the only operation we can use to access them is "fetch the `j`th bit of `A[i]`," which takes constant time. Write code to find the missing integer. Can you do it in `O(n)` time?

Hints: #609, #658, #682

pg 533

17.5 **Letters and Numbers:** Given an array filled with letters and numbers, find the longest subarray with an equal number of letters and numbers.

Hints: #484, #514, #618, #670, #712

pg 536

17.6 **Count of 2s:** Write a method to count the number of 2s that appear in all the numbers between 0 and n (inclusive).

EXAMPLE

Input: 25

Output: 9 (2, 12, 20, 21, 22, 23, 24 and 25. Note that 22 counts for two 2s.)

Hints: #572, #611, #640

pg 538

17.7 **Baby Names:** Each year, the government releases a list of the 10000 most common baby names and their frequencies (the number of babies with that name). The only problem with this is that some names have multiple spellings. For example, "John" and "Jon" are essentially the same name but would be listed separately in the list. Given two lists, one of names/frequencies and the other of pairs of equivalent names, write an algorithm to print a new list of the true frequency of each name. Note that if John and Jon are synonyms, and Jon and Johnny are synonyms, then John and Johnny are synonyms. (It is both transitive and symmetric.) In the final list, any name can be used as the "real" name.

EXAMPLE

Input:

Names: John (15), Jon (12), Chris (13), Kris (4), Christopher (19)

Synonyms: (Jon, John), (John, Johnny), (Chris, Kris), (Chris, Christopher)

Output: John (27), Kris (36)

Hints: #477, #492, #511, #536, #585, #604, #654, #674, #703

pg 541

17.8 **Circus Tower:** A circus is designing a tower routine consisting of people standing atop one another's shoulders. For practical and aesthetic reasons, each person must be both shorter and lighter than the person below him or her. Given the heights and weights of each person in the circus, write a method to compute the largest possible number of people in such a tower.

EXAMPLE

Input (ht, wt): `(65, 100) (70, 150) (56, 90) (75, 190) (60, 95) (68, 110)`

Output: The longest tower is length 6 and includes from top to bottom:

`(56, 90) (60,95) (65,100) (68,110) (70,150) (75,190)`

Hints: #637, #656, #665, #681, #698

pg 546

17.9 **Kth Multiple:** Design an algorithm to find the kth number such that the only prime factors are 3, 5, and 7. Note that 3, 5, and 7 do not have to be factors, but it should not have any other prime factors. For example, the first several multiples would be (in order) 1, 3, 5, 7, 9, 15, 21.

Hints: #487, #507, #549, #590, #621, #659, #685

pg 549

17.10 **Majority Element:** A majority element is an element that makes up more than half of the items in an array. Given a positive integers array, find the majority element. If there is no majority element, return -1. Do this in `O(N)` time and `O(1)` space.

EXAMPLE

Input: `1 2 5 9 5 9 5 5 5`

Output: 5

Hints: #521, #565, #603, #619, #649

pg 553

17.11 **Word Distance:** You have a large text file containing words. Given any two words, find the shortest distance (in terms of number of words) between them in the file. If the operation will be repeated many times for the same file (but different pairs of words), can you optimize your solution?

Hints: #485, #500, #537, #557, #632

pg 557

17.12 BiNode: Consider a simple data structure called BiNode, which has pointers to two other nodes.

```
public class BiNode {
   public BiNode node1, node2;
   public int data;
}
```

The data structure BiNode could be used to represent both a binary tree (where node1 is the left node and node2 is the right node) or a doubly linked list (where node1 is the previous node and node2 is the next node). Implement a method to convert a binary search tree (implemented with BiNode) into a doubly linked list. The values should be kept in order and the operation should be performed in place (that is, on the original data structure).

Hints: #508, #607, #645, #679, #700, #718

pg 559

17.13 Re-Space: Oh, no! You have accidentally removed all spaces, punctuation, and capitalization in a lengthy document. A sentence like "I reset the computer. It still didn't boot!" became "iresetthecomputeritstilldidntboot". You'll deal with the punctuation and capitalization later; right now you need to re-insert the spaces. Most of the words are in a dictionary but a few are not. Given a dictionary (a list of strings) and the document (a string), design an algorithm to unconcatenate the document in a way that minimizes the number of unrecognized characters.

EXAMPLE:

Input: jesslookedjustliketimherbrother

Output: jess looked just like tim her brother (7 unrecognized characters)

Hints: #495, #622, #655, #676, #738, #748

pg 563

17.14 Smallest K: Design an algorithm to find the smallest K numbers in an array.

Hints: #469, #529, #551, #592, #624, #646, #660, #677

pg 566

17.15 Longest Word: Given a list of words, write a program to find the longest word made of other words in the list.

EXAMPLE

Input: cat, banana, dog, nana, walk, walker, dogwalker

Output: dogwalker

Hints: #474, #498, #542, #588

pg 572

17.16 The Masseuse: A popular masseuse receives a sequence of back-to-back appointment requests and is debating which ones to accept. She needs a 15-minute break between appointments and therefore she cannot accept any adjacent requests. Given a sequence of back-to-back appointment requests (all multiples of 15 minutes, none overlap, and none can be moved), find the optimal (highest total booked minutes) set the masseuse can honor. Return the number of minutes.

EXAMPLE

Input: {30, 15, 60, 75, 45, 15, 15, 45}

Output: 180 minutes ({30, 60, 45, 45}).

Hints: #494, #503, #515, #525, #541, #553, #561, #567, #577, #586, #606

pg 573

17.17 **Multi Search:** Given a string b and an array of smaller strings T, design a method to search b for each small string in T.

Hints: #479, #581, #616, #742

pg 577

17.18 **Shortest Supersequence:** You are given two arrays, one shorter (with all distinct elements) and one longer. Find the shortest subarray in the longer array that contains all the elements in the shorter array. The items can appear in any order.

EXAMPLE

Input: `{1, 5, 9}` | `{7, 5, 9, 0, 2, 1, 3, 5, 7, 9, 1, 1, 5, 8, 8, 9, 7}`

Output: `[7, 10]` (the underlined portion above)

Hints: #644, #651, #668, #680, #690, #724, #730, #740

pg 583

17.19 **Missing Two:** You are given an array with all the numbers from 1 to N appearing exactly once, except for one number that is missing. How can you find the missing number in `O(N)` time and `O(1)` space? What if there were two numbers missing?

Hints: #502, #589, #608, #625, #648, #671, #688, #695, #701, #716

pg 590

17.20 **Continuous Median:** Numbers are randomly generated and passed to a method. Write a program to find and maintain the median value as new values are generated.

Hints: #518, #545, #574, #708

pg 594

17.21 **Volume of Histogram:** Imagine a histogram (bar graph). Design an algorithm to compute the volume of water it could hold if someone poured water across the top. You can assume that each histogram bar has width 1.

EXAMPLE (Black bars are the histogram. Gray is water.)

Input: `{0, 0, 4, 0, 0, 6, 0, 0, 3, 0, 5, 0, 1, 0, 0, 0}`

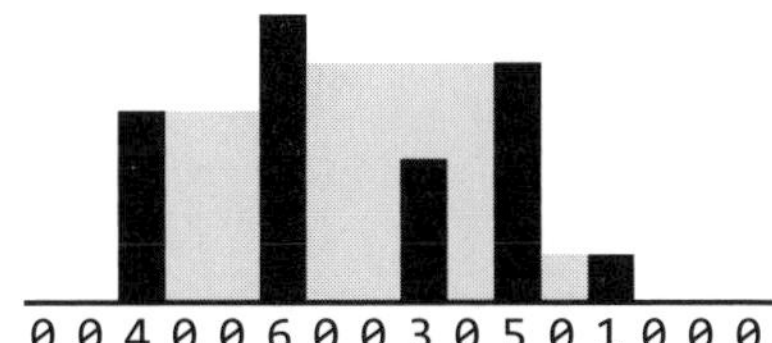

Output: 26

Hints: #628, #639, #650, #657, #661, #675, #692, #733, #741

pg 595

17.22 **Word Transformer:** Given two words of equal length that are in a dictionary, write a method to transform one word into another word by changing only one letter at a time. The new word you get in each step must be in the dictionary.

EXAMPLE

Input: DAMP, LIKE

Output: DAMP -> LAMP -> LIMP -> LIME -> LIKE

Hints: #505, #534, #555, #579, #597, #617, #737

pg 601

17.23 Max Black Square: Imagine you have a square matrix, where each cell (pixel) is either black or white Design an algorithm to find the maximum subsquare such that all four borders are filled with black pixels.

Hints: #683, #694, #704, #713, #720, #735

pg 607

17.24 Max Submatrix: Given an NxN matrix of positive and negative integers, write code to find the submatrix with the largest possible sum.

Hints: #468, #510, #524, #538, #564, #580, #594, #614, #620

pg 610

17.25 Word Rectangle: Given a list of millions of words, design an algorithm to create the largest possible rectangle of letters such that every row forms a word (reading left to right) and every column forms a word (reading top to bottom). The words need not be chosen consecutively from the list, but all rows must be the same length and all columns must be the same height.

Hints: #476, #499, #747

pg 615

17.26 Sparse Similarity: The similarity of two documents (each with distinct words) is defined to be the size of the intersection divided by the size of the union. For example, if the documents consist of integers, the similarity of `{1, 5, 3}` and `{1, 7, 2, 3}` is `0.4`, because the intersection has size 2 and the union has size 5.

We have a long list of documents (with distinct values and each with an associated ID) where the similarity is believed to be "sparse." That is, any two arbitrarily selected documents are very likely to have similarity 0. Design an algorithm that returns a list of pairs of document IDs and the associated similarity.

Print only the pairs with similarity greater than 0. Empty documents should not be printed at all. For simplicity, you may assume each document is represented as an array of distinct integers.

EXAMPLE

Input:

```
13: {14, 15, 100, 9, 3}
16: {32, 1, 9, 3, 5}
19: {15, 29, 2, 6, 8, 7}
24: {7, 10}
```

Output:

```
ID1, ID2 : SIMILARITY
13, 19   : 0.1
13, 16   : 0.25
19, 24   : 0.14285714285714285
```

Hints: #483, #497, #509, #517, #533, #546, #554, #560, #568, #576, #583, #602, #610, #635

pg 619

X Solutions

*Join us at **www.CrackingTheCodingInterview.com** to download the complete solutions, contribute or view solutions in other programming languages, discuss problems from this book with other readers, ask questions, report issues, view this book's errata, and seek additional advice.*

1

Solutions to Arrays and Strings

1.1 Is Unique: Implement an algorithm to determine if a string has all unique characters. What if you cannot use additional data structures?

pg 90

SOLUTION

You should first ask your interviewer if the string is an ASCII string or a Unicode string. Asking this question will show an eye for detail and a solid foundation in computer science. We'll assume for simplicity the character set is ASCII. If this assumption is not valid, we would need to increase the storage size.

One solution is to create an array of boolean values, where the flag at index `i` indicates whether character `i` in the alphabet is contained in the string. The second time you see this character you can immediately return `false`.

We can also immediately return `false` if the string length exceeds the number of unique characters in the alphabet. After all, you can't form a string of 280 unique characters out of a 128-character alphabet.

> It's also okay to assume 256 characters. This would be the case in extended ASCII. You should clarify your assumptions with your interviewer.

The code below implements this algorithm.

```
boolean isUniqueChars(String str) {
  if (str.length() > 128) return false;

  boolean[] char_set = new boolean[128];
  for (int i = 0; i < str.length(); i++) {
    int val = str.charAt(i);
    if (char_set[val]) { // Already found this char in string
      return false;
    }
    char_set[val] = true;
  }
  return true;
}
```

The time complexity for this code is `O(n)`, where `n` is the length of the string. The space complexity is `O(1)`. (You could also argue the time complexity is `O(1)`, since the for loop will never iterate through more than 128 characters.) If you didn't want to assume the character set is fixed, you could express the complexity as `O(c)` space and `O(min(c, n))` or `O(c)` time, where `c` is the size of the character set.

We can reduce our space usage by a factor of eight by using a bit vector. We will assume, in the below code, that the string only uses the lowercase letters a through z. This will allow us to use just a single `int`.

```
boolean isUniqueChars(String str) {
   int checker = 0;
   for (int i = 0; i < str.length(); i++) {
      int val = str.charAt(i) - 'a';
      if ((checker & (1 << val)) > 0) {
         return false;
      }
      checker |= (1 << val);
   }
   return true;
}
```

If we can't use additional data structures, we can do the following:

1. Compare every character of the string to every other character of the string. This will take $O(n^2)$ time and $O(1)$ space.
2. If we are allowed to modify the input string, we could sort the string in $O(n \log(n))$ time and then linearly check the string for neighboring characters that are identical. Careful, though: many sorting algorithms take up extra space.

These solutions are not as optimal in some respects, but might be better depending on the constraints of the problem.

1.2 **Check Permutation:** Given two strings, write a method to decide if one is a permutation of the other.

pg 90

SOLUTION

Like in many questions, we should confirm some details with our interviewer. We should understand if the permutation comparison is case sensitive. That is: is God a permutation of dog? Additionally, we should ask if whitespace is significant. We will assume for this problem that the comparison is case sensitive and whitespace is significant. So, "god   " is different from "dog".

Observe first that strings of different lengths cannot be permutations of each other. There are two easy ways to solve this problem, both of which use this optimization.

Solution #1: Sort the strings.

If two strings are permutations, then we know they have the same characters, but in different orders. Therefore, sorting the strings will put the characters from two permutations in the same order. We just need to compare the sorted versions of the strings.

```
String sort(String s) {
   char[] content = s.toCharArray();
   java.util.Arrays.sort(content);
   return new String(content);
}

boolean permutation(String s, String t) {
   if (s.length() != t.length()) {
      return false;
   }
```

```
    return sort(s).equals(sort(t));
}
```

Though this algorithm is not as optimal in some senses, it may be preferable in one sense: It's clean, simple and easy to understand. In a practical sense, this may very well be a superior way to implement the problem.

However, if efficiency is very important, we can implement it a different way.

Solution #2: Check if the two strings have identical character counts.

We can also use the definition of a permutation—two words with the same character counts—to implement this algorithm. We create an array (lines 4 - 7) that operates somewhat like a hash table, mapping each character to its frequency. We increment through the first string, then decrement through the second string. If the strings are permutations, then the array will be all zeroes at the end.

We can terminate early if a value ever turns negative (once negative, the value will stay negative and therefore non-zero). If we don't terminate early, then the array must be all zeros. This is because the strings are the same lengths and we incremented the same number of times we decremented. The array cannot have any positive values if it doesn't have any negative values.

```
1  boolean permutation(String s, String t) {
2     if (s.length() != t.length()) return false; // Permutations must be same length
3  
4     int[] letters = new int[128]; // Assumption: ASCII
5     for (int i = 0; i < s.length(); i++) {
6        letters[s.charAt(i)]++;
7     }
8  
9     for (int i = 0; i < t.length(); i++) {
10       letters[t.charAt(i)]--;
11       if (letters[t.charAt(i)] < 0) {
12          return false;
13       }
14    }
15    return true; // letters has no neg values, and therefore no pos values either
16 }
```

Note the assumption on line 4. In your interview, you should always check with your interviewer about the size of the character set. We assumed that the character set was ASCII.

1.3 **URLify:** Write a method to replace all spaces in a string with '%20'. You may assume that the string has sufficient space at the end to hold the additional characters, and that you are given the "true" length of the string. (Note: if implementing in Java, please use a character array so that you can perform this operation in place.)

EXAMPLE

Input: "Mr John Smith   ", 13

Output: "Mr%20John%20Smith"

pg 90

SOLUTION

A common approach in string manipulation problems is to edit the string starting from the end and working backwards. This is useful because we have an extra buffer at the end, which allows us to change characters without worrying about what we're overwriting.

We will use this approach in this problem. The algorithm employs a two-scan approach. In the first scan, we count the number of spaces. By tripling this number, we can compute how many extra characters we will have in the final string. In the second pass, which is done in reverse order, we actually edit the string. When we see a space, we replace it with %20. If there is no space, then we copy the original character.

The code below implements this algorithm.

```
void replaceSpaces(char[] str, int trueLength) {
   int spaceCount = 0, index, i = 0;
   for (i = 0; i < trueLength; i++) {
      if (str[i] == ' ') {
         spaceCount++;
      }
   }
   index = trueLength + spaceCount * 2;
   if (trueLength < str.length) str[trueLength] = '\0'; // End array
   for (i = trueLength - 1; i >= 0; i--) {
      if (str[i] == ' ') {
         str[index - 1] = '0';
         str[index - 2] = '2';
         str[index - 3] = '%';
         index = index - 3;
      } else {
         str[index - 1] = str[i];
         index--;
      }
   }
}
```

We have implemented this problem using character arrays, because Java strings are immutable. If we used strings directly, the function would have to return a new copy of the string, but it would allow us to implement this in just one pass.

1.4 Palindrome Permutation: Given a string, write a function to check if it is a permutation of a palindrome. A palindrome is a word or phrase that is the same forwards and backwards. A permutation is a rearrangement of letters. The palindrome does not need to be limited to just dictionary words.

EXAMPLE

Input: `Tact Coa`

Output: `True` (permutations: "`taco cat`", "`atco cta`", etc.)

pg 91

SOLUTION

This is a question where it helps to figure out what it means for a string to be a permutation of a palindrome. This is like asking what the "defining features" of such a string would be.

A palindrome is a string that is the same forwards and backwards. Therefore, to decide if a string is a permutation of a palindrome, we need to know if it can be written such that it's the same forwards and backwards.

What does it take to be able to write a set of characters the same way forwards and backwards? We need to have an even number of almost all characters, so that half can be on one side and half can be on the other side. At most one character (the middle character) can have an odd count.

For example, we know `tactcoapapa` is a permutation of a palindrome because it has two Ts, four As, two

Cs, two Ps, and one O. That O would be the center of all possible palindromes.

> To be more precise, strings with even length (after removing all non-letter characters) must have all even counts of characters. Strings of an odd length must have exactly one character with an odd count. Of course, an "even" string can't have an odd number of exactly one character, otherwise it wouldn't be an even-length string (an odd number + many even numbers = an odd number). Likewise, a string with odd length can't have all characters with even counts (sum of evens is even). It's therefore sufficient to say that, to be a permutation of a palindrome, a string can have no more than one character that is odd. This will cover both the odd and the even cases.

This leads us to our first algorithm.

Solution #1

Implementing this algorithm is fairly straightforward. We use a hash table to count how many times each character appears. Then, we iterate through the hash table and ensure that no more than one character has an odd count.

```
boolean isPermutationOfPalindrome(String phrase) {
  int[] table = buildCharFrequencyTable(phrase);
  return checkMaxOneOdd(table);
}

/* Check that no more than one character has an odd count. */
boolean checkMaxOneOdd(int[] table) {
  boolean foundOdd = false;
  for (int count : table) {
    if (count % 2 == 1) {
      if (foundOdd) {
        return false;
      }
      foundOdd = true;
    }
  }
  return true;
}

/* Map each character to a number. a -> 0, b -> 1, c -> 2, etc.
 * This is case insensitive. Non-letter characters map to -1. */
int getCharNumber(Character c) {
  int a = Character.getNumericValue('a');
  int z = Character.getNumericValue('z');
  int val = Character.getNumericValue(c);
  if (a <= val && val <= z) {
    return val - a;
  }
  return -1;
}

/* Count how many times each character appears. */
int[] buildCharFrequencyTable(String phrase) {
  int[] table = new int[Character.getNumericValue(‘z’) -
                        Character.getNumericValue(‘a’) + 1];
  for (char c : phrase.toCharArray()) {
    int x = getCharNumber(c);
```

```
      if (x != -1) {
         table[x]++;
      }
   }
   return table;
}
```

This algorithm takes O(N) time, where N is the length of the string.

Solution #2

We can't optimize the big O time here since any algorithm will always have to look through the entire string. However, we can make some smaller incremental improvements. Because this is a relatively simple problem, it can be worthwhile to discuss some small optimizations or at least some tweaks.

Instead of checking the number of odd counts at the end, we can check as we go along. Then, as soon as we get to the end, we have our answer.

```
boolean isPermutationOfPalindrome(String phrase) {
   int countOdd = 0;
   int[] table = new int[Character.getNumericValue('z') -
                         Character.getNumericValue('a') + 1];
   for (char c : phrase.toCharArray()) {
      int x = getCharNumber(c);
      if (x != -1) {
         table[x]++;
         if (table[x] % 2 == 1) {
            countOdd++;
         } else {
            countOdd--;
         }
      }
   }
   return countOdd <= 1;
}
```

It's important to be very clear here that this is not necessarily more optimal. It has the same big O time and might even be slightly slower. We have eliminated a final iteration through the hash table, but now we have to run a few extra lines of code for each character in the string.

You should discuss this with your interviewer as an alternate, but not necessarily more optimal, solution.

Solution #3

If you think more deeply about this problem, you might notice that we don't actually need to know the counts. We just need to know if the count is even or odd. Think about flipping a light on/off (that is initially off). If the light winds up in the `off` state, we don't know how many times we flipped it, but we do know it was an even count.

Given this, we can use a single integer (as a bit vector). When we see a letter, we map it to an integer between 0 and 26 (assuming an English alphabet). Then we toggle the bit at that value. At the end of the iteration, we check that at most one bit in the integer is set to 1.

We can easily check that no bits in the integer are 1: just compare the integer to 0. There is actually a very elegant way to check that an integer has exactly one bit set to 1.

Picture an integer like `00010000`. We could of course shift the integer repeatedly to check that there's only a single 1. Alternatively, if we subtract 1 from the number, we'll get `00001111`. What's notable about this is that there is no overlap between the numbers (as opposed to say 00101000, which, when we subtract 1 from, we get 00100111.) So, we can check to see that a number has exactly one 1 because if we subtract 1 from it and then AND it with the new number, we should get 0.

```
00010000 - 1 = 00001111
00010000 & 00001111 = 0
```

This leads us to our final implementation.

```
boolean isPermutationOfPalindrome(String phrase) {
  int bitVector = createBitVector(phrase);
  return bitVector == 0 || checkExactlyOneBitSet(bitVector);
}

/* Create a bit vector for the string. For each letter with value i, toggle the
 * ith bit. */
int createBitVector(String phrase) {
  int bitVector = 0;
  for (char c : phrase.toCharArray()) {
    int x = getCharNumber(c);
    bitVector = toggle(bitVector, x);
  }
  return bitVector;
}

/* Toggle the ith bit in the integer. */
int toggle(int bitVector, int index) {
  if (index < 0) return bitVector;

  int mask = 1 << index;
  if ((bitVector & mask) == 0) {
    bitVector |= mask;
  } else {
    bitVector &= ~mask;
  }
  return bitVector;
}

/* Check that exactly one bit is set by subtracting one from the integer and
 * ANDing it with the original integer. */
boolean checkExactlyOneBitSet(int bitVector) {
  return (bitVector & (bitVector - 1)) == 0;
}
```

Like the other solutions, this is O(N).

It's interesting to note a solution that we did not explore. We avoided solutions along the lines of "create all possible permutations and check if they are palindromes." While such a solution would work, it's entirely infeasible in the real world. Generating all permutations requires factorial time (which is actually worse than exponential time), and it is essentially infeasible to perform on strings longer than about 10–15 characters.

I mention this (impractical) solution because a lot of candidates hear a problem like this and say, "In order to check if A is in group B, I must know everything that is in B and then check if one of the items equals A." That's not always the case, and this problem is a simple demonstration of it. You don't need to generate all permutations in order to check if one is a palindrome.

1.5 **One Away:** There are three types of edits that can be performed on strings: insert a character, remove a character, or replace a character. Given two strings, write a function to check if they are one edit (or zero edits) away.

EXAMPLE

```
pale,  ple  -> true
pales, pale -> true
pale,  bale -> true
pale,  bae -> false
```

pg 91

SOLUTION

There is a "brute force" algorithm to do this. We could check all possible strings that are one edit away by testing the removal of each character (and comparing), testing the replacement of each character (and comparing), and then testing the insertion of each possible character (and comparing).

That would be too slow, so let's not bother with implementing it.

This is one of those problems where it's helpful to think about the "meaning" of each of these operations. What does it mean for two strings to be one insertion, replacement, or removal away from each other?

- **Replacement:** Consider two strings, such as `bale` and `pale`, that are one replacement away. Yes, that does mean that you could replace a character in `bale` to make `pale`. But more precisely, it means that they are different only in one place.
- **Insertion:** The strings `apple` and `aple` are one insertion away. This means that if you compared the strings, they would be identical—except for a shift at some point in the strings.
- **Removal:** The strings `apple` and `aple` are also one removal away, since removal is just the inverse of insertion.

We can go ahead and implement this algorithm now. We'll merge the insertion and removal check into one step, and check the replacement step separately.

Observe that you don't need to check the strings for insertion, removal, and replacement edits. The lengths of the strings will indicate which of these you need to check.

```
boolean oneEditAway(String first, String second) {
  if (first.length() == second.length()) {
    return oneEditReplace(first, second);
  } else if (first.length() + 1 == second.length()) {
    return oneEditInsert(first, second);
  } else if (first.length() - 1 == second.length()) {
    return oneEditInsert(second, first);
  }
  return false;
}

boolean oneEditReplace(String s1, String s2) {
  boolean foundDifference = false;
  for (int i = 0; i < s1.length(); i++) {
    if (s1.charAt(i) != s2.charAt(i)) {
      if (foundDifference) {
        return false;
      }

```

```
            foundDifference = true;
        }
    }
    return true;
}

/* Check if you can insert a character into s1 to make s2. */
boolean oneEditInsert(String s1, String s2) {
    int index1 = 0;
    int index2 = 0;
    while (index2 < s2.length() && index1 < s1.length()) {
        if (s1.charAt(index1) != s2.charAt(index2)) {
            if (index1 != index2) {
                return false;
            }
            index2++;
        } else {
            index1++;
            index2++;
        }
    }
    return true;
}
```

This algorithm (and almost any reasonable algorithm) takes `O(n)` time, where n is the length of the shorter string.

> Why is the runtime dictated by the shorter string instead of the longer string? If the strings are the same length (plus or minus one character), then it doesn't matter whether we use the longer string or the shorter string to define the runtime. If the strings are very different lengths, then the algorithm will terminate in `O(1)` time. One really, really long string therefore won't significantly extend the runtime. It increases the runtime only if both strings are long.

We might notice that the code for `oneEditReplace` is very similar to that for `oneEditInsert`. We can merge them into one method.

To do this, observe that both methods follow similar logic: compare each character and ensure that the strings are only different by one. The methods vary in how they handle that difference. The method `oneEditReplace` does nothing other than flag the difference, whereas `oneEditInsert` increments the pointer to the longer string. We can handle both of these in the same method.

```
boolean oneEditAway(String first, String second) {
    /* Length checks. */
    if (Math.abs(first.length() - second.length()) > 1) {
        return false;
    }

    /* Get shorter and longer string.*/
    String s1 = first.length() < second.length() ? first : second;
    String s2 = first.length() < second.length() ? second : first;

    int index1 = 0;
    int index2 = 0;
    boolean foundDifference = false;
    while (index2 < s2.length() && index1 < s1.length()) {
        if (s1.charAt(index1) != s2.charAt(index2)) {
```

```
        /* Ensure that this is the first difference found.*/
        if (foundDifference) return false;
        foundDifference = true;

        if (s1.length() == s2.length()) { // On replace, move shorter pointer
          index1++;
        }
      } else {
        index1++; // If matching, move shorter pointer
      }
      index2++; // Always move pointer for longer string
    }
    return true;
}
```

Some people might argue the first approach is better, as it is clearer and easier to follow. Others, however, will argue that the second approach is better, since it's more compact and doesn't duplicate code (which can facilitate maintainability).

You don't necessarily need to "pick a side." You can discuss the tradeoffs with your interviewer.

1.6 **String Compression:** Implement a method to perform basic string compression using the counts of repeated characters. For example, the string `aabcccccaaa` would become `a2b1c5a3`. If the "compressed" string would not become smaller than the original string, your method should return the original string. You can assume the string has only uppercase and lowercase letters (a - z).

pg 91

SOLUTION

At first glance, implementing this method seems fairly straightforward, but perhaps a bit tedious. We iterate through the string, copying characters to a new string and counting the repeats. At each iteration, check if the current character is the same as the next character. If not, add its compressed version to the result.

How hard could it be?

```
String compressBad(String str) {
  String compressedString = "";
  int countConsecutive = 0;
  for (int i = 0; i < str.length(); i++) {
    countConsecutive++;

    /* If next character is different than current, append this char to result.*/
    if (i + 1 >= str.length() || str.charAt(i) != str.charAt(i + 1)) {
      compressedString += "" + str.charAt(i) + countConsecutive;
      countConsecutive = 0;
    }
  }
  return compressedString.length() < str.length() ? compressedString : str;
}
```

This works. Is it efficient, though? Take a look at the runtime of this code.

The runtime is $O(p + k^2)$, where p is the size of the original string and k is the number of character sequences. For example, if the string is `aabccdeeaa`, then there are six character sequences. It's slow because string concatenation operates in $O(n^2)$ time (see `StringBuilder` on pg 89).

We can fix this by using a `StringBuilder`.

```
String compress(String str) {
   StringBuilder compressed = new StringBuilder();
   int countConsecutive = 0;
   for (int i = 0; i < str.length(); i++) {
      countConsecutive++;

      /* If next character is different than current, append this char to result.*/
      if (i + 1 >= str.length() || str.charAt(i) != str.charAt(i + 1)) {
         compressed.append(str.charAt(i));
         compressed.append(countConsecutive);
         countConsecutive = 0;
      }
   }
   return compressed.length() < str.length() ? compressed.toString() : str;
}
```

Both of these solutions create the compressed string first and then return the shorter of the input string and the compressed string.

Instead, we can check in advance. This will be more optimal in cases where we don't have a large number of repeating characters. It will avoid us having to create a string that we never use. The downside of this is that it causes a second loop through the characters and also adds nearly duplicated code.

```
String compress(String str) {
   /* Check final length and return input string if it would be longer. */
   int finalLength = countCompression(str);
   if (finalLength >= str.length()) return str;

   StringBuilder compressed = new StringBuilder(finalLength); // initial capacity
   int countConsecutive = 0;
   for (int i = 0; i < str.length(); i++) {
      countConsecutive++;

      /* If next character is different than current, append this char to result.*/
      if (i + 1 >= str.length() || str.charAt(i) != str.charAt(i + 1)) {
         compressed.append(str.charAt(i));
         compressed.append(countConsecutive);
         countConsecutive = 0;
      }
   }
   return compressed.toString();
}

int countCompression(String str) {
   int compressedLength = 0;
   int countConsecutive = 0;
   for (int i = 0; i < str.length(); i++) {
      countConsecutive++;

      /* If next character is different than current, increase the length.*/
      if (i + 1 >= str.length() || str.charAt(i) != str.charAt(i + 1)) {
         compressedLength += 1 + String.valueOf(countConsecutive).length();
         countConsecutive = 0;
      }
   }
   return compressedLength;
}
```

One other benefit of this approach is that we can initialize `StringBuilder` to its necessary capacity up-front. Without this, `StringBuilder` will (behind the scenes) need to double its capacity every time it hits capacity. The capacity could be double what we ultimately need.

1.7 Rotate Matrix: Given an image represented by an NxN matrix, where each pixel in the image is 4 bytes, write a method to rotate the image by 90 degrees. Can you do this in place?

pg 91

SOLUTION

Because we're rotating the matrix by 90 degrees, the easiest way to do this is to implement the rotation in layers. We perform a circular rotation on each layer, moving the top edge to the right edge, the right edge to the bottom edge, the bottom edge to the left edge, and the left edge to the top edge.

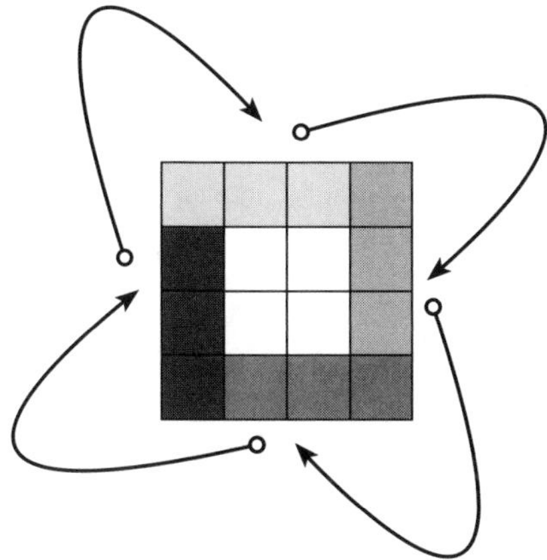

How do we perform this four-way edge swap? One option is to copy the top edge to an array, and then move the left to the top, the bottom to the left, and so on. This requires `O(N)` memory, which is actually unnecessary.

A better way to do this is to implement the swap index by index. In this case, we do the following:

```
for i = 0 to n
  temp = top[i];
  top[i] = left[i]
  left[i] = bottom[i]
  bottom[i] = right[i]
  right[i] = temp
```

We perform such a swap on each layer, starting from the outermost layer and working our way inwards. (Alternatively, we could start from the inner layer and work outwards.)

The code for this algorithm is below.

```
boolean rotate(int[][] matrix) {
  if (matrix.length == 0 || matrix.length != matrix[0].length) return false;
  int n = matrix.length;
  for (int layer = 0; layer < n / 2; layer++) {
    int first = layer;
    int last = n - 1 - layer;
    for(int i = first; i < last; i++) {
      int offset = i - first;
```

```
         int top = matrix[first][i]; // save top

         // left -> top
         matrix[first][i] = matrix[last-offset][first];

         // bottom -> left
         matrix[last-offset][first] = matrix[last][last - offset];

         // right -> bottom
         matrix[last][last - offset] = matrix[i][last];

         // top -> right
         matrix[i][last] = top; // right <- saved top
      }
   }
   return true;
}
```

This algorithm is $O(N^2)$, which is the best we can do since any algorithm must touch all N^2 elements.

1.8 Zero Matrix: Write an algorithm such that if an element in an MxN matrix is 0, its entire row and column are set to 0.

pg 91

SOLUTION

At first glance, this problem seems easy: just iterate through the matrix and every time we see a cell with value zero, set its row and column to 0. There's one problem with that solution though: when we come across other cells in that row or column, we'll see the zeros and change their row and column to zero. Pretty soon, our entire matrix will be set to zeros.

One way around this is to keep a second matrix which flags the zero locations. We would then do a second pass through the matrix to set the zeros. This would take O(MN) space.

Do we really need O(MN) space? No. Since we're going to set the entire row and column to zero, we don't need to track that it was exactly `cell[2][4]` (row 2, column 4). We only need to know that row 2 has a zero somewhere, and column 4 has a zero somewhere. We'll set the entire row and column to zero anyway, so why would we care to keep track of the exact location of the zero?

The code below implements this algorithm. We use two arrays to keep track of all the rows with zeros and all the columns with zeros. We then nullify rows and columns based on the values in these arrays.

```
void setZeros(int[][] matrix) {
   boolean[] row = new boolean[matrix.length];
   boolean[] column = new boolean[matrix[0].length];

   // Store the row and column index with value 0
   for (int i = 0; i < matrix.length; i++) {
      for (int j = 0; j < matrix[0].length;j++) {
         if (matrix[i][j] == 0) {
            row[i] = true;
            column[j] = true;
         }
      }
   }

```

```
    // Nullify rows
    for (int i = 0; i < row.length; i++) {
      if (row[i]) nullifyRow(matrix, i);
    }

    // Nullify columns
    for (int j = 0; j < column.length; j++) {
      if (column[j]) nullifyColumn(matrix, j);
    }
  }

  void nullifyRow(int[][] matrix, int row) {
    for (int j = 0; j < matrix[0].length; j++) {
      matrix[row][j] = 0;
    }
  }

  void nullifyColumn(int[][] matrix, int col) {
    for (int i = 0; i < matrix.length; i++) {
      matrix[i][col] = 0;
    }
  }
```

To make this somewhat more space efficient, we could use a bit vector instead of a boolean array. It would still be O(N) space.

We can reduce the space to O(1) by using the first row as a replacement for the `row` array and the first column as a replacement for the `column` array. This works as follows:

1. Check if the first row and first column have any zeros, and set variables `rowHasZero` and `columnHasZero`. (We'll nullify the first row and first column later, if necessary.)
2. Iterate through the rest of the matrix, setting `matrix[i][0]` and `matrix[0][j]` to zero whenever there's a zero in `matrix[i][j]`.
3. Iterate through rest of matrix, nullifying row `i` if there's a zero in `matrix[i][0]`.
4. Iterate through rest of matrix, nullifying column `j` if there's a zero in `matrix[0][j]`.
5. Nullify the first row and first column, if necessary (based on values from Step 1).

This code is below:

```
void setZeros(int[][] matrix) {
  boolean rowHasZero = false;
  boolean colHasZero = false;

  // Check if first row has a zero
  for (int j = 0; j < matrix[0].length; j++) {
    if (matrix[0][j] == 0) {
      rowHasZero = true;
      break;
    }
  }

  // Check if first column has a zero
  for (int i = 0; i < matrix.length; i++) {
    if (matrix[i][0] == 0) {
      colHasZero = true;
      break;
```

```
      }
   }

   // Check for zeros in the rest of the array
   for (int i = 1; i < matrix.length; i++) {
      for (int j = 1; j < matrix[0].length;j++) {
         if (matrix[i][j] == 0) {
            matrix[i][0] = 0;
            matrix[0][j] = 0;
         }
      }
   }

   // Nullify rows based on values in first column
   for (int i = 1; i < matrix.length; i++) {
      if (matrix[i][0] == 0) {
         nullifyRow(matrix, i);
      }
   }

   // Nullify columns based on values in first row
   for (int j = 1; j < matrix[0].length; j++) {
      if (matrix[0][j] == 0) {
         nullifyColumn(matrix, j);
      }
   }

   // Nullify first row
   if (rowHasZero) {
      nullifyRow(matrix, 0);
   }

   // Nullify first column
   if (colHasZero) {
      nullifyColumn(matrix, 0);
   }
}
```

This code has a lot of "do this for the rows, then the equivalent action for the column." In an interview, you could abbreviate this code by adding comments and TODOs that explain that the next chunk of code looks the same as the earlier code, but using rows. This would allow you to focus on the most important parts of the algorithm.

1.9 **String Rotation:** Assume you have a method `isSubstring` which checks if one word is a substring of another. Given two strings, `s1` and `s2`, write code to check if `s2` is a rotation of `s1` using only one call to `isSubstring` (e.g., "`waterbottle`" is a rotation of "`erbottlewat`").

pg 91

SOLUTION

If we imagine that `s2` is a rotation of `s1`, then we can ask what the rotation point is. For example, if you rotate `waterbottle` after `wat`, you get `erbottlewat`. In a rotation, we cut `s1` into two parts, `x` and `y`, and rearrange them to get `s2`.

```
s1 = xy = waterbottle
x = wat
```

```
y = erbottle
s2 = yx = erbottlewat
```

So, we need to check if there's a way to split `s1` into x and y such that xy = `s1` and yx = `s2`. Regardless of where the division between x and y is, we can see that yx will always be a substring of `xyxy`. That is, `s2` will always be a substring of `s1s1`.

And this is precisely how we solve the problem: simply do `isSubstring(s1s1, s2)`.

The code below implements this algorithm.

```
boolean isRotation(String s1, String s2) {
  int len = s1.length();
  /* Check that s1 and s2 are equal length and not empty */
  if (len == s2.length() && len > 0) {
    /* Concatenate s1 and s1 within new buffer */
    String s1s1 = s1 + s1;
    return isSubstring(s1s1, s2);
  }
  return false;
}
```

The runtime of this varies based on the runtime of `isSubstring`. But if you assume that `isSubstring` runs in `O(A+B)` time (on strings of length A and B), then the runtime of `isRotation` is `O(N)`.

2

Solutions to Linked Lists

2.1 **Remove Dups:** Write code to remove duplicates from an unsorted linked list.

FOLLOW UP

How would you solve this problem if a temporary buffer is not allowed?

pg 94

SOLUTION

In order to remove duplicates from a linked list, we need to be able to track duplicates. A simple hash table will work well here.

In the below solution, we simply iterate through the linked list, adding each element to a hash table. When we discover a duplicate element, we remove the element and continue iterating. We can do this all in one pass since we are using a linked list.

```
void deleteDups(LinkedListNode n) {
   HashSet<Integer> set = new HashSet<Integer>();
   LinkedListNode previous = null;
   while (n != null) {
      if (set.contains(n.data)) {
         previous.next = n.next;
      } else {
         set.add(n.data);
         previous = n;
      }
      n = n.next;
   }
}
```

The above solution takes O(N) time, where N is the number of elements in the linked list.

Follow Up: No Buffer Allowed

If we don't have a buffer, we can iterate with two pointers: `current` which iterates through the linked list, and `runner` which checks all subsequent nodes for duplicates.

```
void deleteDups(LinkedListNode head) {
   LinkedListNode current = head;
   while (current != null) {
      /* Remove all future nodes that have the same value */
      LinkedListNode runner = current;
      while (runner.next != null) {
         if (runner.next.data == current.data) {
```

```
            runner.next = runner.next.next;
         } else {
            runner = runner.next;
         }
      }
      current = current.next;
   }
}
```

This code runs in O(1) space, but O(N^2) time.

2.2 Return Kth to Last: Implement an algorithm to find the kth to last element of a singly linked list.

pg 223

SOLUTION

We will approach this problem both recursively and non-recursively. Remember that recursive solutions are often cleaner but less optimal. For example, in this problem, the recursive implementation is about half the length of the iterative solution but also takes O(n) space, where n is the number of elements in the linked list.

Note that for this solution, we have defined k such that passing in k = 1 would return the last element, k = 2 would return to the second to last element, and so on. It is equally acceptable to define k such that k = 0 would return the last element.

Solution #1: If linked list size is known

If the size of the linked list is known, then the kth to last element is the (length - k)th element. We can just iterate through the linked list to find this element. Because this solution is so trivial, we can almost be sure that this is not what the interviewer intended.

Solution #2: Recursive

This algorithm recurses through the linked list. When it hits the end, the method passes back a counter set to 0. Each parent call adds 1 to this counter. When the counter equals k, we know we have reached the kth to last element of the linked list.

Implementing this is short and sweet—provided we have a way of "passing back" an integer value through the stack. Unfortunately, we can't pass back a node and a counter using normal return statements. So how do we handle this?

Approach A: Don't Return the Element.

One way to do this is to change the problem to simply printing the kth to last element. Then, we can pass back the value of the counter simply through return values.

```
int printKthToLast(LinkedListNode head, int k) {
   if (head == null) {
      return 0;
   }
   int index = printKthToLast(head.next, k) + 1;
   if (index == k) {
      System.out.println(k + "th to last node is " + head.data);
   }
   return index;
}
```

Of course, this is only a valid solution if the interviewer says it is valid.

Approach B: Use C++.

A second way to solve this is to use C++ and to pass values by reference. This allows us to return the node value, but also update the counter by passing a pointer to it.

```
node* nthToLast(node* head, int k, int& i) {
   if (head == NULL) {
      return NULL;
   }
   node* nd = nthToLast(head->next, k, i);
   i = i + 1;
   if (i == k) {
      return head;
   }
   return nd;
}

node* nthToLast(node* head, int k) {
   int i = 0;
   return nthToLast(head, k, i);
}
```

Approach C: Create a Wrapper Class.

We described earlier that the issue was that we couldn't simultaneously return a counter and an index. If we wrap the `counter` value with simple class (or even a single element array), we can mimic passing by reference.

```
class Index {
   public int value = 0;
}

LinkedListNode kthToLast(LinkedListNode head, int k) {
   Index idx = new Index();
   return kthToLast(head, k, idx);
}

LinkedListNode kthToLast(LinkedListNode head, int k, Index idx) {
   if (head == null) {
      return null;
   }
   LinkedListNode node = kthToLast(head.next, k, idx);
   idx.value = idx.value + 1;
   if (idx.value == k) {
      return head;
   }
   return node;
}
```

Each of these recursive solutions takes `O(n)` space due to the recursive calls.

There are a number of other solutions that we haven't addressed. We could store the counter in a static variable. Or, we could create a class that stores both the node and the counter, and return an instance of that class. Regardless of which solution we pick, we need a way to update both the node and the counter in a way that all levels of the recursive stack will see.

Solution #3: Iterative

A more optimal, but less straightforward, solution is to implement this iteratively. We can use two pointers, p1 and p2. We place them k nodes apart in the linked list by putting p2 at the beginning and moving p1 k nodes into the list. Then, when we move them at the same pace, p1 will hit the end of the linked list after LENGTH - k steps. At that point, p2 will be LENGTH - k nodes into the list, or k nodes from the end.

The code below implements this algorithm.

```
LinkedListNode nthToLast(LinkedListNode head, int k) {
  LinkedListNode p1 = head;
  LinkedListNode p2 = head;

  /* Move p1 k nodes into the list.*/
  for (int i = 0; i < k; i++) {
    if (p1 == null) return null; // Out of bounds
    p1 = p1.next;
  }

  /* Move them at the same pace. When p1 hits the end, p2 will be at the right
   * element. */
  while (p1 != null) {
    p1 = p1.next;
    p2 = p2.next;
  }
  return p2;
}
```

This algorithm takes O(n) time and O(1) space.

2.3 Delete Middle Node: Implement an algorithm to delete a node in the middle (i.e., any node but the first and last node, not necessarily the exact middle) of a singly linked list, given only access to that node.

EXAMPLE

Input: the node c from the linked list a->b->c->d->e->f

Result: nothing is returned, but the new linked list looks like a->b->d->e->f

pg 94

SOLUTION

In this problem, you are not given access to the head of the linked list. You only have access to that node. The solution is simply to copy the data from the next node over to the current node, and then to delete the next node.

The code below implements this algorithm.

```
boolean deleteNode(LinkedListNode n) {
  if (n == null || n.next == null) {
    return false; // Failure
  }
  LinkedListNode next = n.next;
  n.data = next.data;
  n.next = next.next;
  return true;
}
```

Note that this problem cannot be solved if the node to be deleted is the last node in the linked list. That's okay—your interviewer wants you to point that out, and to discuss how to handle this case. You could, for example, consider marking the node as dummy.

2.4 **Partition:** Write code to partition a linked list around a value x, such that all nodes less than x come before all nodes greater than or equal to x. If x is contained within the list, the values of x only need to be after the elements less than x (see below). The partition element x can appear anywhere in the "right partition"; it does not need to appear between the left and right partitions.

EXAMPLE

Input: `3 -> 5 -> 8 -> 5 -> 10 -> 2 -> 1` [partition = 5]

Output: `3 -> 1 -> 2 -> 10 -> 5 -> 5 -> 8`

pg 94

SOLUTION

If this were an array, we would need to be careful about how we shifted elements. Array shifts are very expensive.

However, in a linked list, the situation is much easier. Rather than shifting and swapping elements, we can actually create two different linked lists: one for elements less than x, and one for elements greater than or equal to x.

We iterate through the linked list, inserting elements into our `before` list or our `after` list. Once we reach the end of the linked list and have completed this splitting, we merge the two lists.

This approach is mostly "stable" in that elements stay in their original order, other than the necessary movement around the partition. The code below implements this approach.

```
/* Pass in the head of the linked list and the value to partition around */
LinkedListNode partition(LinkedListNode node, int x) {
   LinkedListNode beforeStart = null;
   LinkedListNode beforeEnd = null;
   LinkedListNode afterStart = null;
   LinkedListNode afterEnd = null;

   /* Partition list */
   while (node != null) {
      LinkedListNode next = node.next;
      node.next = null;
      if (node.data < x) {
         /* Insert node into end of before list */
         if (beforeStart == null) {
            beforeStart = node;
            beforeEnd = beforeStart;
         } else {
            beforeEnd.next = node;
            beforeEnd = node;
         }
      } else {
         /* Insert node into end of after list */
         if (afterStart == null) {
            afterStart = node;
            afterEnd = afterStart;
         } else {
```

```
          afterEnd.next = node;
          afterEnd = node;
        }
      }
      node = next;
    }

    if (beforeStart == null) {
      return afterStart;
    }

    /* Merge before list and after list */
    beforeEnd.next = afterStart;
    return beforeStart;
}
```

If it bugs you to keep around four different variables for tracking two linked lists, you're not alone. We can make this code a bit shorter.

If we don't care about making the elements of the list "stable" (which there's no obligation to, since the interviewer hasn't specified that), then we can instead rearrange the elements by growing the list at the head and tail.

In this approach, we start a "new" list (using the existing nodes). Elements bigger than the pivot element are put at the tail and elements smaller are put at the head. Each time we insert an element, we update either the head or tail.

```
LinkedListNode partition(LinkedListNode node, int x) {
  LinkedListNode head = node;
  LinkedListNode tail = node;

  while (node != null) {
    LinkedListNode next = node.next;
    if (node.data < x) {
      /* Insert node at head. */
      node.next = head;
      head = node;
    } else {
      /* Insert node at tail. */
      tail.next = node;
      tail = node;
    }
    node = next;
  }
  tail.next = null;

  // The head has changed, so we need to return it to the user.
  return head;
}
```

There are many equally optimal solutions to this problem. If you came up with a different one, that's okay!

2.5 **Sum Lists:** You have two numbers represented by a linked list, where each node contains a single digit. The digits are stored in reverse order, such that the 1's digit is at the head of the list. Write a function that adds the two numbers and returns the sum as a linked list.

EXAMPLE

Input: `(7-> 1 -> 6) + (5 -> 9 -> 2)`. That is, `617 + 295`.

Output: `2 -> 1 -> 9`. That is, 912.

FOLLOW UP

Suppose the digits are stored in forward order. Repeat the above problem.

Input: `(6 -> 1 -> 7) + (2 -> 9 -> 5)`. That is, `617 + 295`.

Output: `9 -> 1 -> 2`. That is, 912.

pg 95

SOLUTION

It's useful to remember in this problem how exactly addition works. Imagine the problem:

```
   6 1 7
 + 2 9 5
```

First, we add 7 and 5 to get 12. The digit 2 becomes the last digit of the number, and 1 gets carried over to the next step. Second, we add 1, 1, and 9 to get 11. The 1 becomes the second digit, and the other 1 gets carried over the final step. Third and finally, we add 1, 6 and 2 to get 9. So, our value becomes 912.

We can mimic this process recursively by adding node by node, carrying over any "excess" data to the next node. Let's walk through this for the below linked list:

```
    7 -> 1 -> 6
 +  5 -> 9 -> 2
```

We do the following:

1. We add 7 and 5 first, getting a result of 12. 2 becomes the first node in our linked list, and we "carry" the 1 to the next sum.

   `List: 2 -> ?`

2. We then add 1 and 9, as well as the "carry," getting a result of 11. 1 becomes the second element of our linked list, and we carry the 1 to the next sum.

   `List: 2 -> 1 -> ?`

3. Finally, we add 6, 2 and our "carry," to get 9. This becomes the final element of our linked list.

   `List: 2 -> 1 -> 9.`

The code below implements this algorithm.

```
LinkedListNode addLists(LinkedListNode l1, LinkedListNode l2, int carry) {
   if (l1 == null && l2 == null && carry == 0) {
      return null;
   }

   LinkedListNode result = new LinkedListNode();
   int value = carry;
   if (l1 != null) {
      value += l1.data;
   }
   if (l2 != null) {
```

```
      value += l2.data;
    }

    result.data = value % 10; /* Second digit of number */

    /* Recurse */
    if (l1 != null || l2 != null) {
      LinkedListNode more = addLists(l1 == null ? null : l1.next,
                                     l2 == null ? null : l2.next,
                                     value >= 10 ? 1 : 0);
      result.setNext(more);
    }
    return result;
  }
```

In implementing this code, we must be careful to handle the condition when one linked list is shorter than another. We don't want to get a null pointer exception.

Follow Up

Part B is conceptually the same (recurse, carry the excess), but has some additional complications when it comes to implementation:

1. One list may be shorter than the other, and we cannot handle this "on the fly." For example, suppose we were adding (1 -> 2 -> 3 -> 4) and (5 -> 6 -> 7). We need to know that the 5 should be "matched" with the 2, not the 1. We can accomplish this by comparing the lengths of the lists in the beginning and padding the shorter list with zeros.
2. In the first part, successive results were added to the tail (i.e., passed forward). This meant that the recursive call would be *passed* the carry, and would return the result (which is then appended to the tail). In this case, however, results are added to the head (i.e., passed backward). The recursive call must return the result, as before, as well as the carry. This is not terribly challenging to implement, but it is more cumbersome. We can solve this issue by creating a wrapper class called Partial Sum.

The code below implements this algorithm.

```
class PartialSum {
  public LinkedListNode sum = null;
  public int carry = 0;
}

LinkedListNode addLists(LinkedListNode l1, LinkedListNode l2) {
  int len1 = length(l1);
  int len2 = length(l2);

  /* Pad the shorter list with zeros - see note (1) */
  if (len1 < len2) {
    l1 = padList(l1, len2 - len1);
  } else {
    l2 = padList(l2, len1 - len2);
  }

  /* Add lists */
  PartialSum sum = addListsHelper(l1, l2);

  /* If there was a carry value left over, insert this at the front of the list.
   * Otherwise, just return the linked list. */
  if (sum.carry == 0) {
```

```
        return sum.sum;
     } else {
        LinkedListNode result = insertBefore(sum.sum, sum.carry);
        return result;
     }
  }

  PartialSum addListsHelper(LinkedListNode l1, LinkedListNode l2) {
     if (l1 == null && l2 == null) {
        PartialSum sum = new PartialSum();
        return sum;
     }
     /* Add smaller digits recursively */
     PartialSum sum = addListsHelper(l1.next, l2.next);

     /* Add carry to current data */
     int val = sum.carry + l1.data + l2.data;

     /* Insert sum of current digits */
     LinkedListNode full_result = insertBefore(sum.sum, val % 10);

     /* Return sum so far, and the carry value */
     sum.sum = full_result;
     sum.carry = val / 10;
     return sum;
  }

  /* Pad the list with zeros */
  LinkedListNode padList(LinkedListNode l, int padding) {
     LinkedListNode head = l;
     for (int i = 0; i < padding; i++) {
        head = insertBefore(head, 0);
     }
     return head;
  }

  /* Helper function to insert node in the front of a linked list */
  LinkedListNode insertBefore(LinkedListNode list, int data) {
     LinkedListNode node = new LinkedListNode(data);
     if (list != null) {
        node.next = list;
     }
     return node;
  }
```

Note how we have pulled `insertBefore()`, `padList()`, and `length()` (not listed) into their own methods. This makes the code cleaner and easier to read—a wise thing to do in your interviews!

2.6 Palindrome: Implement a function to check if a linked list is a palindrome.

pg 95

SOLUTION

To approach this problem, we can picture a palindrome like `0 -> 1 -> 2 -> 1 -> 0`. We know that, since it's a palindrome, the list must be the same backwards and forwards. This leads us to our first solution.

Solution #1: Reverse and Compare

Our first solution is to reverse the linked list and compare the reversed list to the original list. If they're the same, the lists are identical.

Note that when we compare the linked list to the reversed list, we only actually need to compare the first half of the list. If the first half of the normal list matches the first half of the reversed list, then the second half of the normal list must match the second half of the reversed list.

```
boolean isPalindrome(LinkedListNode head) {
  LinkedListNode reversed = reverseAndClone(head);
  return isEqual(head, reversed);
}

LinkedListNode reverseAndClone(LinkedListNode node) {
  LinkedListNode head = null;
  while (node != null) {
    LinkedListNode n = new LinkedListNode(node.data); // Clone
    n.next = head;
    head = n;
    node = node.next;
  }
  return head;
}

boolean isEqual(LinkedListNode one, LinkedListNode two) {
  while (one != null && two != null) {
    if (one.data != two.data) {
      return false;
    }
    one = one.next;
    two = two.next;
  }
  return one == null && two == null;
}
```

Observe that we've modularized this code into `reverse` and `isEqual` functions.

Solution #2: Iterative Approach

We want to detect linked lists where the front half of the list is the reverse of the second half. How would we do that? By reversing the front half of the list. A stack can accomplish this.

We need to push the first half of the elements onto a stack. We can do this in two different ways, depending on whether or not we know the size of the linked list.

If we know the size of the linked list, we can iterate through the first half of the elements in a standard for loop, pushing each element onto a stack. We must be careful, of course, to handle the case where the length of the linked list is odd.

If we don't know the size of the linked list, we can iterate through the linked list, using the fast runner / slow runner technique described in the beginning of the chapter. At each step in the loop, we push the data from the slow runner onto a stack. When the fast runner hits the end of the list, the slow runner will have reached the middle of the linked list. By this point, the stack will have all the elements from the front of the linked list, but in reverse order.

Now, we simply iterate through the rest of the linked list. At each iteration, we compare the node to the top of the stack. If we complete the iteration without finding a difference, then the linked list is a palindrome.

```
boolean isPalindrome(LinkedListNode head) {
   LinkedListNode fast = head;
   LinkedListNode slow = head;

   Stack<Integer> stack = new Stack<Integer>();

   /* Push elements from first half of linked list onto stack. When fast runner
    * (which is moving at 2x speed) reaches the end of the linked list, then we
    * know we're at the middle */
   while (fast != null && fast.next != null) {
      stack.push(slow.data);
      slow = slow.next;
      fast = fast.next.next;
   }

   /* Has odd number of elements, so skip the middle element */
   if (fast != null) {
      slow = slow.next;
   }

   while (slow != null) {
      int top = stack.pop().intValue();

      /* If values are different, then it's not a palindrome */
      if (top != slow.data) {
         return false;
      }
      slow = slow.next;
   }
   return true;
}
```

Solution #3: Recursive Approach

First, a word on notation: in this solution, when we use the notation node Kx, the variable K indicates the value of the node data, and x (which is either f or b) indicates whether we are referring to the front node with that value or the back node. For example, in the below linked list, node 2b would refer to the second (back) node with value 2.

Now, like many linked list problems, you can approach this problem recursively. We may have some intuitive idea that we want to compare element 0 and element n - 1, element 1 and element n-2, element 2 and element n-3, and so on, until the middle element(s). For example:

```
0 ( 1 ( 2 ( 3 ) 2 ) 1 ) 0
```

In order to apply this approach, we first need to know when we've reached the middle element, as this will form our base case. We can do this by passing in length - 2 for the length each time. When the length equals 0 or 1, we're at the center of the linked list. This is because the length is reduced by 2 each time. Once we've recursed $N/2$ times, length will be down to 0.

```
recurse(Node n, int length) {
   if (length == 0 || length == 1) {
      return [something]; // At middle
   }
   recurse(n.next, length - 2);
   ...
}
```

This method will form the outline of the `isPalindrome` method. The "meat" of the algorithm though is comparing node `i` to node `n - i` to check if the linked list is a palindrome. How do we do that?

Let's examine what the call stack looks like:

```
1  v1 = isPalindrome: list = 0 ( 1 ( 2 ( 3 ) 2 ) 1 ) 0. length = 7
2    v2 = isPalindrome: list = 1 ( 2 ( 3 ) 2 ) 1 ) 0. length = 5
3      v3 = isPalindrome: list = 2 ( 3 ) 2 ) 1 ) 0. length = 3
4        v4 = isPalindrome: list = 3 ) 2 ) 1 ) 0. length = 1
5        returns v3
6      returns v2
7    returns v1
8  returns ?
```

In the above call stack, each call wants to check if the list is a palindrome by comparing its head node with the corresponding node from the back of the list. That is:

- Line 1 needs to compare node `0f` with node `0b`
- Line 2 needs to compare node `1f` with node `1b`
- Line 3 needs to compare node `2f` with node `2b`
- Line 4 needs to compare node `3f` with node `3b`.

If we rewind the stack, passing nodes back as described below, we can do just that:

- Line 4 sees that it is the middle node (since `length = 1`), and passes back `head.next`. The value `head` equals `node 3`, so `head.next` is `node 2b`.
- Line 3 compares its head, `node 2f`, to `returned_node` (the value from the previous recursive call), which is `node 2b`. If the values match, it passes a reference to `node 1b` (`returned_node.next`) up to line 2.
- Line 2 compares its head (`node 1f`) to `returned_node` (`node 1b`). If the values match, it passes a reference to `node 0b` (or, `returned_node.next`) up to line 1.
- Line 1 compares its head, `node 0f`, to `returned_node`, which is `node 0b`. If the values match, it returns true.

To generalize, each call compares its head to `returned_node`, and then passes `returned_node.next` up the stack. In this way, every node `i` gets compared to node `n - i`. If at any point the values do not match, we return `false`, and every call up the stack checks for that value.

But wait, you might ask, sometimes we said we'll return a `boolean` value, and sometimes we're returning a `node`. Which is it?

It's both. We create a simple class with two members, a `boolean` and a `node`, and return an instance of that class.

```
class Result {
  public LinkedListNode node;
  public boolean result;
}
```

The example below illustrates the parameters and return values from this sample list.

```
isPalindrome: list = 0 ( 1 ( 2 ( 3 ( 4 ) 3 ) 2 ) 1 ) 0. len = 9
  isPalindrome: list = 1 ( 2 ( 3 ( 4 ) 3 ) 2 ) 1 ) 0. len = 7
    isPalindrome: list = 2 ( 3 ( 4 ) 3 ) 2 ) 1 ) 0. len = 5
      isPalindrome: list = 3 ( 4 ) 3 ) 2 ) 1 ) 0. len = 3
        isPalindrome: list = 4 ) 3 ) 2 ) 1 ) 0. len = 1
```

```
          returns node 3b, true
        returns node 2b, true
      returns node 1b, true
    returns node 0b, true
returns null, true
```

Implementing this code is now just a matter of filling in the details.

```
boolean isPalindrome(LinkedListNode head) {
  int length = lengthOfList(head);
  Result p = isPalindromeRecurse(head, length);
  return p.result;
}

Result isPalindromeRecurse(LinkedListNode head, int length) {
  if (head == null || length <= 0) { // Even number of nodes
    return new Result(head, true);
  } else if (length == 1) { // Odd number of nodes
    return new Result(head.next, true);
  }

  /* Recurse on sublist. */
  Result res = isPalindromeRecurse(head.next, length - 2);

  /* If child calls are not a palindrome, pass back up
   * a failure. */
  if (!res.result || res.node == null) {
    return res;
  }

  /* Check if matches corresponding node on other side. */
  res.result = (head.data == res.node.data);

  /* Return corresponding node. */
  res.node = res.node.next;

  return res;
}

int lengthOfList(LinkedListNode n) {
  int size = 0;
  while (n != null) {
    size++;
    n = n.next;
  }
  return size;
}
```

Some of you might be wondering why we went through all this effort to create a special `Result` class. Isn't there a better way? Not really—at least not in Java.

However, if we were implementing this in C or C++, we could have passed in a double pointer.

```
bool isPalindromeRecurse(Node head, int length, Node** next) {
  ...
}
```

It's ugly, but it works.

2.7 **Intersection**: Given two (singly) linked lists, determine if the two lists intersect. Return the intersecting node. Note that the intersection is defined based on reference, not value. That is, if the kth node of the first linked list is the exact same node (by reference) as the `j`th node of the second linked list, then they are intersecting.

pg 95

SOLUTION

Let's draw a picture of intersecting linked lists to get a better feel for what is going on.

Here is a picture of intersecting linked lists:

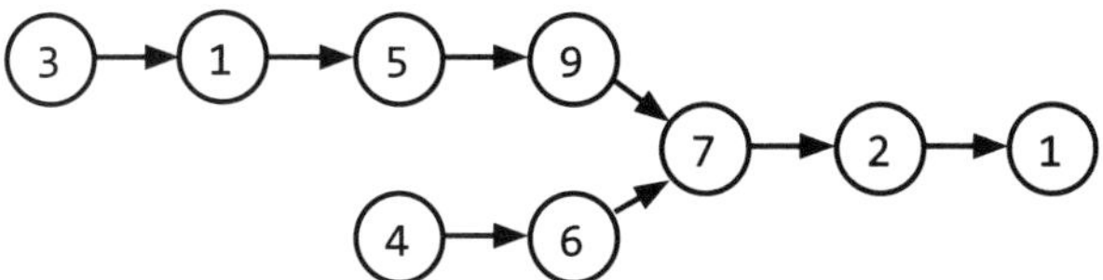

And here is a picture of non-intersecting linked lists:

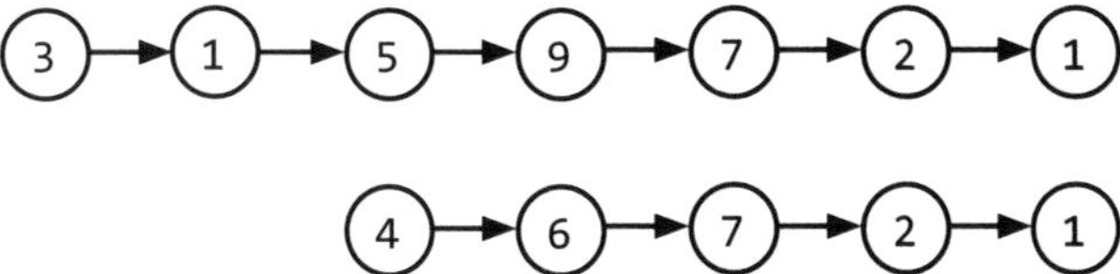

We should be careful here to not inadvertently draw a special case by making the linked lists the same length.

Let's first ask how we would determine if two linked lists intersect.

Determining if there's an intersection.

How would we detect if two linked lists intersect? One approach would be to use a hash table and just throw all the linked lists nodes into there. We would need to be careful to reference the linked lists by their memory location, not by their value.

There's an easier way though. Observe that two intersecting linked lists will always have the same last node. Therefore, we can just traverse to the end of each linked list and compare the last nodes.

How do we find where the intersection is, though?

Finding the intersecting node.

One thought is that we could traverse backwards through each linked list. When the linked lists "split", that's the intersection. Of course, you can't really traverse backwards through a singly linked list.

If the linked lists were the same length, you could just traverse through them at the same time. When they collide, that's your intersection.

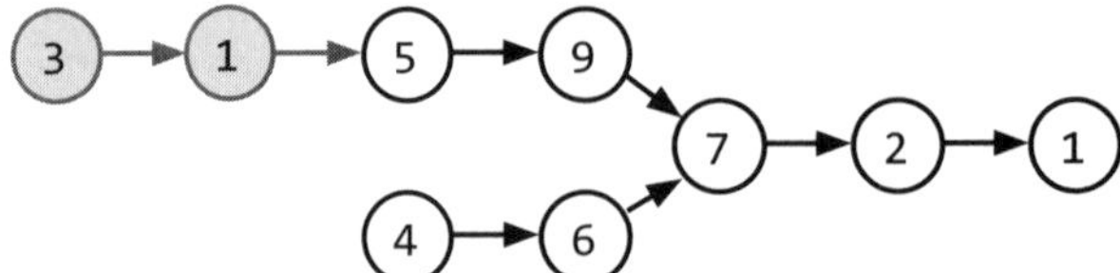

When they're not the same length, we'd like to just "chop off"—or ignore—those excess (gray) nodes.

How can we do this? Well, if we know the lengths of the two linked lists, then the difference between those two linked lists will tell us how much to chop off.

We can get the lengths at the same time as we get the tails of the linked lists (which we used in the first step to determine if there's an intersection).

Putting it all together.

We now have a multistep process.

1. Run through each linked list to get the lengths and the tails.
2. Compare the tails. If they are different (by reference, not by value), return immediately. There is no intersection.
3. Set two pointers to the start of each linked list.
4. On the longer linked list, advance its pointer by the difference in lengths.
5. Now, traverse on each linked list until the pointers are the same.

The implementation for this is below.

```
LinkedListNode findIntersection(LinkedListNode list1, LinkedListNode list2) {
  if (list1 == null || list2 == null) return null;

  /* Get tail and sizes. */
  Result result1 = getTailAndSize(list1);
  Result result2 = getTailAndSize(list2);

  /* If different tail nodes, then there's no intersection. */
  if (result1.tail != result2.tail) {
    return null;
  }

  /* Set pointers to the start of each linked list. */
  LinkedListNode shorter = result1.size < result2.size ? list1 : list2;
  LinkedListNode longer = result1.size < result2.size ? list2 : list1;

  /* Advance the pointer for the longer linked list by difference in lengths. */
  longer = getKthNode(longer, Math.abs(result1.size - result2.size));

  /* Move both pointers until you have a collision. */
  while (shorter != longer) {
    shorter = shorter.next;
    longer = longer.next;
  }

  /* Return either one. */
  return longer;
}

```

```
class Result {
  public LinkedListNode tail;
  public int size;
  public Result(LinkedListNode tail, int size) {
    this.tail = tail;
    this.size = size;
  }
}

Result getTailAndSize(LinkedListNode list) {
  if (list == null) return null;

  int size = 1;
  LinkedListNode current = list;
  while (current.next != null) {
    size++;
    current = current.next;
  }
  return new Result(current, size);
}

LinkedListNode getKthNode(LinkedListNode head, int k) {
  LinkedListNode current = head;
  while (k > 0 && current != null) {
    current = current.next;
    k--;
  }
  return current;
}
```

This algorithm takes `O(A + B)` time, where A and B are the lengths of the two linked lists. It takes `O(1)` additional space.

2.8 **Loop Detection:** Given a circular linked list, implement an algorithm that returns the node at the beginning of the loop.

DEFINITION

Circular linked list: A (corrupt) linked list in which a node's next pointer points to an earlier node, so as to make a loop in the linked list.

EXAMPLE

Input: `A -> B -> C -> D -> E -> C` [the same C as earlier]

Output: `C`

pg 95

SOLUTION

This is a modification of a classic interview problem: detect if a linked list has a loop. Let's apply the Pattern Matching approach.

Part 1: Detect If Linked List Has A Loop

An easy way to detect if a linked list has a loop is through the `FastRunner` / `SlowRunner` approach. `FastRunner` moves two steps at a time, while `SlowRunner` moves one step. Much like two cars racing around a track at different steps, they must eventually meet.

An astute reader may wonder if `FastRunner` might "hop over" `SlowRunner` completely, without ever colliding. That's not possible. Suppose that `FastRunner` *did* hop over `SlowRunner`, such that `SlowRunner` is at spot `i` and `FastRunner` is at spot `i + 1`. In the previous step, `SlowRunner` would be at spot `i - 1` and `FastRunner` would at spot `((i + 1) - 2)`, or spot `i - 1`. That is, they would have collided.

Part 2: When Do They Collide?

Let's assume that the linked list has a "non-looped" part of size k.

If we apply our algorithm from part 1, when will `FastRunner` and `SlowRunner` collide?

We know that for every p steps that `SlowRunner` takes, `FastRunner` has taken 2p steps. Therefore, when `SlowRunner` enters the looped portion after k steps, `FastRunner` has taken 2k steps total and must be `2k - k` steps, or k steps, into the looped portion. Since k might be much larger than the loop length, we should actually write this as `mod(k, LOOP_SIZE)` steps, which we will denote as K.

At each subsequent step, `FastRunner` and `SlowRunner` get either one step farther away or one step closer, depending on your perspective. That is, because we are in a circle, when A moves q steps away from B, it is also moving q steps closer to B.

So now we know the following facts:

1. `SlowRunner` is 0 steps into the loop.
2. `FastRunner` is K steps into the loop.
3. `SlowRunner` is K steps behind `FastRunner`.
4. `FastRunner` is `LOOP_SIZE - K` steps behind `SlowRunner`.
5. `FastRunner` catches up to `SlowRunner` at a rate of 1 step per unit of time.

So, when do they meet? Well, if `FastRunner` is `LOOP_SIZE - K` steps behind `SlowRunner`, and `FastRunner` catches up at a rate of 1 step per unit of time, then they meet after `LOOP_SIZE - K` steps. At this point, they will be K steps before the head of the loop. Let's call this point `CollisionSpot`.

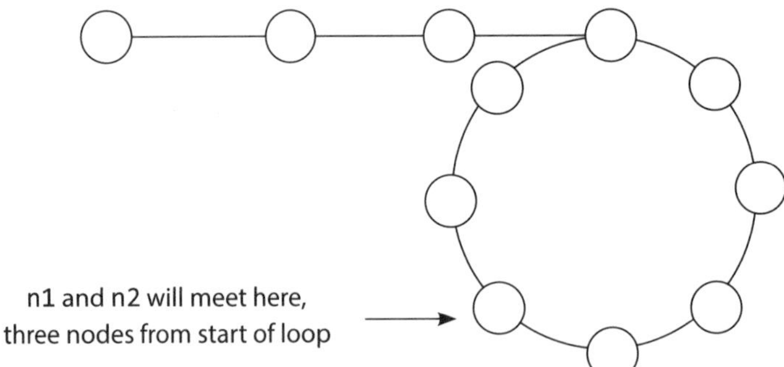
n1 and n2 will meet here,
three nodes from start of loop

Part 3: How Do You Find The Start of the Loop?

We now know that `CollisionSpot` is K nodes before the start of the loop. Because `K = mod(k, LOOP_SIZE)` (or, in other words, `k = K + M * LOOP_SIZE`, for any integer M), it is also correct to say that it is k nodes from the loop start. For example, if node N is 2 nodes into a 5 node loop, it is also correct to say that it is 7, 12, or even 397 nodes into the loop.

Therefore, both `CollisionSpot` and `LinkedListHead` are k nodes from the start of the loop.

Now, if we keep one pointer at `CollisionSpot` and move the other one to `LinkedListHead`, they will each be k nodes from `LoopStart`. Moving the two pointers at the same speed will cause them to collide again—this time after k steps, at which point they will both be at `LoopStart`. All we have to do is return this node.

Part 4: Putting It All Together

To summarize, we move `FastPointer` twice as fast as `SlowPointer`. When `SlowPointer` enters the loop, after k nodes, `FastPointer` is k nodes into the loop. This means that `FastPointer` and `SlowPointer` are `LOOP_SIZE - k` nodes away from each other.

Next, if `FastPointer` moves two nodes for each node that `SlowPointer` moves, they move one node closer to each other on each turn. Therefore, they will meet after `LOOP_SIZE - k` turns. Both will be k nodes from the front of the loop.

The head of the linked list is also k nodes from the front of the loop. So, if we keep one pointer where it is, and move the other pointer to the head of the linked list, then they will meet at the front of the loop.

Our algorithm is derived directly from parts 1, 2 and 3.

1. Create two pointers, `FastPointer` and `SlowPointer`.
2. Move `FastPointer` at a rate of 2 steps and `SlowPointer` at a rate of 1 step.
3. When they collide, move `SlowPointer` to `LinkedListHead`. Keep `FastPointer` where it is.
4. Move `SlowPointer` and `FastPointer` at a rate of one step. Return the new collision point.

The code below implements this algorithm.

```
LinkedListNode FindBeginning(LinkedListNode head) {
   LinkedListNode slow = head;
   LinkedListNode fast = head;

   /* Find meeting point. This will be LOOP_SIZE - k steps into the linked list. */
   while (fast != null && fast.next != null) {
      slow = slow.next;
      fast = fast.next.next;
      if (slow == fast) { // Collision
         break;
      }
   }

   /* Error check - no meeting point, and therefore no loop */
   if (fast == null || fast.next == null) {
      return null;
   }

   /* Move slow to Head. Keep fast at Meeting Point. Each are k steps from the
    * Loop Start. If they move at the same pace, they must meet at Loop Start. */
   slow = head;
   while (slow != fast) {
      slow = slow.next;
      fast = fast.next;
   }

   /* Both now point to the start of the loop. */
   return fast;
}
```

3

Solutions to Stacks and Queues

3.1 Three in One: Describe how you could use a single array to implement three stacks.

pg 98

SOLUTION

Like many problems, this one somewhat depends on how well we'd like to support these stacks. If we're okay with simply allocating a fixed amount of space for each stack, we can do that. This may mean though that one stack runs out of space, while the others are nearly empty.

Alternatively, we can be flexible in our space allocation, but this significantly increases the complexity of the problem.

Approach 1: Fixed Division

We can divide the array in three equal parts and allow the individual stack to grow in that limited space. Note: We will use the notation "[" to mean inclusive of an end point and "(" to mean exclusive of an end point.

- For stack 1, we will use $[0, \frac{n}{3})$.
- For stack 2, we will use $[\frac{n}{3}, \frac{2n}{3})$.
- For stack 3, we will use $[\frac{2n}{3}, n)$.

The code for this solution is below.

```
class FixedMultiStack {
  private int numberOfStacks = 3;
  private int stackCapacity;
  private int[] values;
  private int[] sizes;

  public FixedMultiStack(int stackSize) {
    stackCapacity = stackSize;
    values = new int[stackSize * numberOfStacks];
    sizes = new int[numberOfStacks];
  }

  /* Push value onto stack. */
  public void push(int stackNum, int value) throws FullStackException {
    /* Check that we have space for the next element */
    if (isFull(stackNum)) {
      throw new FullStackException();
```

```
        }

        /* Increment stack pointer and then update top value. */
        sizes[stackNum]++;
        values[indexOfTop(stackNum)] = value;
    }

    /* Pop item from top stack. */
    public int pop(int stackNum) {
        if (isEmpty(stackNum)) {
            throw new EmptyStackException();
        }

        int topIndex = indexOfTop(stackNum);
        int value = values[topIndex]; // Get top
        values[topIndex] = 0; // Clear
        sizes[stackNum]--; // Shrink
        return value;
    }

    /* Return top element. */
    public int peek(int stackNum) {
        if (isEmpty(stackNum)) {
            throw new EmptyStackException();
        }
        return values[indexOfTop(stackNum)];
    }

    /* Return if stack is empty. */
    public boolean isEmpty(int stackNum) {
        return sizes[stackNum] == 0;
    }

    /* Return if stack is full. */
    public boolean isFull(int stackNum) {
        return sizes[stackNum] == stackCapacity;
    }

    /* Returns index of the top of the stack. */
    private int indexOfTop(int stackNum) {
        int offset = stackNum * stackCapacity;
        int size = sizes[stackNum];
        return offset + size - 1;
    }
}
```

If we had additional information about the expected usages of the stacks, then we could modify this algorithm accordingly. For example, if we expected Stack 1 to have many more elements than Stack 2, we could allocate more space to Stack 1 and less space to Stack 2.

Approach 2: Flexible Divisions

A second approach is to allow the stack blocks to be flexible in size. When one stack exceeds its initial capacity, we grow the allowable capacity and shift elements as necessary.

We will also design our array to be circular, such that the final stack may start at the end of the array and wrap around to the beginning.

Please note that the code for this solution is far more complex than would be appropriate for an interview. You could be responsible for pseudocode, or perhaps the code of individual components, but the entire implementation would be far too much work.

```
public class MultiStack {
  /* StackInfo is a simple class that holds a set of data about each stack. It
   * does not hold the actual items in the stack. We could have done this with
   * just a bunch of individual variables, but that's messy and doesn't gain us
   * much. */
  private class StackInfo {
    public int start, size, capacity;
    public StackInfo(int start, int capacity) {
      this.start = start;
      this.capacity = capacity;
    }

    /* Check if an index on the full array is within the stack boundaries. The
     * stack can wrap around to the start of the array. */
    public boolean isWithinStackCapacity(int index) {
      /* If outside of bounds of array, return false. */
      if (index < 0 || index >= values.length) {
        return false;
      }

      /* If index wraps around, adjust it. */
      int contiguousIndex = index < start ? index + values.length : index;
      int end = start + capacity;
      return start <= contiguousIndex && contiguousIndex < end;
    }

    public int lastCapacityIndex() {
      return adjustIndex(start + capacity - 1);
    }

    public int lastElementIndex() {
      return adjustIndex(start + size - 1);
    }

    public boolean isFull() { return size == capacity; }
    public boolean isEmpty() { return size == 0; }
  }

  private StackInfo[] info;
  private int[] values;

  public MultiStack(int numberOfStacks, int defaultSize) {
    /* Create metadata for all the stacks. */
    info = new StackInfo[numberOfStacks];
    for (int i = 0; i < numberOfStacks; i++) {
      info[i] = new StackInfo(defaultSize * i, defaultSize);
    }
    values = new int[numberOfStacks * defaultSize];
  }

  /* Push value onto stack num, shifting/expanding stacks as necessary. Throws
   * exception if all stacks are full. */
  public void push(int stackNum, int value) throws FullStackException {
```

```
    if (allStacksAreFull()) {
      throw new FullStackException();
    }

    /* If this stack is full, expand it. */
    StackInfo stack = info[stackNum];
    if (stack.isFull()) {
      expand(stackNum);
    }

    /* Find the index of the top element in the array + 1, and increment the
     * stack pointer */
    stack.size++;
    values[stack.lastElementIndex()] = value;
  }

  /* Remove value from stack. */
  public int pop(int stackNum) throws Exception {
    StackInfo stack = info[stackNum];
    if (stack.isEmpty()) {
      throw new EmptyStackException();
    }

    /* Remove last element. */
    int value = values[stack.lastElementIndex()];
    values[stack.lastElementIndex()] = 0; // Clear item
    stack.size--; // Shrink size
    return value;
  }

  /* Get top element of stack.*/
  public int peek(int stackNum) {
    StackInfo stack = info[stackNum];
    return values[stack.lastElementIndex()];
  }
  /* Shift items in stack over by one element. If we have available capacity, then
   * we'll end up shrinking the stack by one element. If we don't have available
   * capacity, then we'll need to shift the next stack over too. */
  private void shift(int stackNum) {
    System.out.println("/// Shifting " + stackNum);
    StackInfo stack = info[stackNum];

    /* If this stack is at its full capacity, then you need to move the next
     * stack over by one element. This stack can now claim the freed index. */
    if (stack.size >= stack.capacity) {
      int nextStack = (stackNum + 1) % info.length;
      shift(nextStack);
      stack.capacity++; // claim index that next stack lost
    }

    /* Shift all elements in stack over by one. */
    int index = stack.lastCapacityIndex();
    while (stack.isWithinStackCapacity(index)) {
      values[index] = values[previousIndex(index)];
      index = previousIndex(index);
    }
```

```

    /* Adjust stack data. */
    values[stack.start] = 0; // Clear item
    stack.start = nextIndex(stack.start); // move start
    stack.capacity--; // Shrink capacity
  }

  /* Expand stack by shifting over other stacks */
  private void expand(int stackNum) {
    shift((stackNum + 1) % info.length);
    info[stackNum].capacity++;
  }

  /* Returns the number of items actually present in stack. */
  public int numberOfElements() {
    int size = 0;
    for (StackInfo sd : info) {
      size += sd.size;
    }
    return size;
  }

  /* Returns true is all the stacks are full. */
  public boolean allStacksAreFull() {
    return numberOfElements() == values.length;
  }

  /* Adjust index to be within the range of 0 -> length - 1. */
  private int adjustIndex(int index) {
    /* Java's mod operator can return neg values. For example, (-11 % 5) will
     * return -1, not 4. We actually want the value to be 4 (since we're wrapping
     * around the index). */
    int max = values.length;
    return ((index % max) + max) % max;
  }

  /* Get index after this index, adjusted for wrap around. */
  private int nextIndex(int index) {
    return adjustIndex(index + 1);
  }

  /* Get index before this index, adjusted for wrap around. */
  private int previousIndex(int index) {
    return adjustIndex(index - 1);
  }
}
```

In problems like this, it's important to focus on writing clean, maintainable code. You should use additional classes, as we did with `StackInfo`, and pull chunks of code into separate methods. Of course, this advice applies to the "real world" as well.

3.2 Stack Min: How would you design a stack which, in addition to `push` and `pop`, has a function `min` which returns the minimum element? `Push`, `pop` and `min` should all operate in `O(1)` time.

pg 98

SOLUTION

The thing with minimums is that they don't change very often. They only change when a smaller element is added.

One solution is to have just a single `int` value, `minValue`, that's a member of the `Stack` class. When `minValue` is popped from the stack, we search through the stack to find the new minimum. Unfortunately, this would break the constraint that `push` and `pop` operate in `O(1)` time.

To further understand this question, let's walk through it with a short example:

```
push(5); // stack is {5}, min is 5
push(6); // stack is {6, 5}, min is 5
push(3); // stack is {3, 6, 5}, min is 3
push(7); // stack is {7, 3, 6, 5}, min is 3
pop(); // pops 7. stack is {3, 6, 5}, min is 3
pop(); // pops 3. stack is {6, 5}. min is 5.
```

Observe how once the stack goes back to a prior state (`{6, 5}`), the minimum also goes back to its prior state (5). This leads us to our second solution.

If we kept track of the minimum at each state, we would be able to easily know the minimum. We can do this by having each node record what the minimum beneath itself is. Then, to find the `min`, you just look at what the top element thinks is the min.

When you push an element onto the stack, the element is given the current minimum. It sets its "`local min`" to be the `min`.

```
public class StackWithMin extends Stack<NodeWithMin> {
   public void push(int value) {
      int newMin = Math.min(value, min());
      super.push(new NodeWithMin(value, newMin));
   }

   public int min() {
      if (this.isEmpty()) {
         return Integer.MAX_VALUE; // Error value
      } else {
         return peek().min;
      }
   }
}

class NodeWithMin {
   public int value;
   public int min;
   public NodeWithMin(int v, int min){
      value = v;
      this.min = min;
   }
}
```

There's just one issue with this: if we have a large stack, we waste a lot of space by keeping track of the `min` for every single element. Can we do better?

We can (maybe) do a bit better than this by using an additional stack which keeps track of the `mins`.

```
public class StackWithMin2 extends Stack<Integer> {
   Stack<Integer> s2;
   public StackWithMin2() {
      s2 = new Stack<Integer>();
   }

   public void push(int value){
      if (value <= min()) {
         s2.push(value);
      }
      super.push(value);
   }

   public Integer pop() {
      int value = super.pop();
      if (value == min()) {
         s2.pop();
      }
      return value;
   }

   public int min() {
      if (s2.isEmpty()) {
         return Integer.MAX_VALUE;
      } else {
         return s2.peek();
      }
   }
}
```

Why might this be more space efficient? Suppose we had a very large stack and the first element inserted happened to be the minimum. In the first solution, we would be keeping n integers, where n is the size of the stack. In the second solution though, we store just a few pieces of data: a second stack with one element and the members within this stack.

3.3 **Stack of Plates:** Imagine a (literal) stack of plates. If the stack gets too high, it might topple. Therefore, in real life, we would likely start a new stack when the previous stack exceeds some threshold. Implement a data structure `SetOfStacks` that mimics this. `SetOfStacks` should be composed of several stacks and should create a new stack once the previous one exceeds capacity. `SetOfStacks.push()` and `SetOfStacks.pop()` should behave identically to a single stack (that is, `pop()` should return the same values as it would if there were just a single stack).

FOLLOW UP

Implement a function `popAt(int index)` which performs a pop operation on a specific sub-stack.

pg 99

SOLUTION

In this problem, we've been told what our data structure should look like:

```
class SetOfStacks {
   ArrayList<Stack> stacks = new ArrayList<Stack>();
   public void push(int v) { ... }
```

```
    public int pop() { ... }
}
```

We know that push() should behave identically to a single stack, which means that we need push() to call push() on the last stack in the array of stacks. We have to be a bit careful here though: if the last stack is at capacity, we need to create a new stack. Our code should look something like this:

```
void push(int v) {
   Stack last = getLastStack();
   if (last != null && !last.isFull()) { // add to last stack
      last.push(v);
   } else { // must create new stack
      Stack stack = new Stack(capacity);
      stack.push(v);
      stacks.add(stack);
   }
}
```

What should pop() do? It should behave similarly to push() in that it should operate on the last stack. If the last stack is empty (after popping), then we should remove the stack from the list of stacks.

```
int pop() {
   Stack last = getLastStack();
   if (last == null) throw new EmptyStackException();
   int v = last.pop();
   if (last.size == 0) stacks.remove(stacks.size() - 1);
   return v;
}
```

Follow Up: Implement popAt(int index)

This is a bit trickier to implement, but we can imagine a "rollover" system. If we pop an element from stack 1, we need to remove the *bottom* of stack 2 and push it onto stack 1. We then need to rollover from stack 3 to stack 2, stack 4 to stack 3, etc.

You could make an argument that, rather than "rolling over," we should be okay with some stacks not being at full capacity. This would improve the time complexity (by a fair amount, with a large number of elements), but it might get us into tricky situations later on if someone assumes that all stacks (other than the last) operate at full capacity. There's no "right answer" here; you should discuss this trade-off with your interviewer.

```
public class SetOfStacks {
   ArrayList<Stack> stacks = new ArrayList<Stack>();
   public int capacity;
   public SetOfStacks(int capacity) {
      this.capacity = capacity;
   }

   public Stack getLastStack() {
      if (stacks.size() == 0) return null;
      return stacks.get(stacks.size() - 1);
   }

   public void push(int v) { /* see earlier code */ }
   public int pop() { /* see earlier code */ }
   public boolean isEmpty() {
      Stack last = getLastStack();
      return last == null || last.isEmpty();
   }
```

```

   public int popAt(int index) {
      return leftShift(index, true);
   }

   public int leftShift(int index, boolean removeTop) {
      Stack stack = stacks.get(index);
      int removed_item;
      if (removeTop) removed_item = stack.pop();
      else removed_item = stack.removeBottom();
      if (stack.isEmpty()) {
         stacks.remove(index);
      } else if (stacks.size() > index + 1) {
         int v = leftShift(index + 1, false);
         stack.push(v);
      }
      return removed_item;
   }
}

public class Stack {
   private int capacity;
   public Node top, bottom;
   public int size = 0;

   public Stack(int capacity) { this.capacity = capacity; }
   public boolean isFull() { return capacity == size; }

   public void join(Node above, Node below) {
      if (below != null) below.above = above;
      if (above != null) above.below = below;
   }

   public boolean push(int v) {
      if (size >= capacity) return false;
      size++;
      Node n = new Node(v);
      if (size == 1) bottom = n;
      join(n, top);
      top = n;
      return true;
   }

   public int pop() {
      Node t = top;
      top = top.below;
      size--;
      return t.value;
   }

   public boolean isEmpty() {
      return size == 0;
   }

   public int removeBottom() {
      Node b = bottom;
```

```
        bottom = bottom.above;
        if (bottom != null) bottom.below = null;
        size--;
        return b.value;
    }
}
```

This problem is not conceptually that tough, but it requires a lot of code to implement it fully. Your interviewer would not ask you to implement the entire code.

A good strategy on problems like this is to separate code into other methods, like a `leftShift` method that `popAt` can call. This will make your code cleaner and give you the opportunity to lay down the skeleton of the code before dealing with some of the details.

3.4 Queue via Stacks: Implement a `MyQueue` class which implements a queue using two stacks.

pg 99

SOLUTION

Since the major difference between a queue and a stack is the order (first-in first-out vs. last-in first-out), we know that we need to modify `peek()` and `pop()` to go in reverse order. We can use our second stack to reverse the order of the elements (by popping `s1` and pushing the elements on to `s2`). In such an implementation, on each `peek()` and `pop()` operation, we would pop everything from `s1` onto `s2`, perform the `peek` / `pop` operation, and then `push` everything back.

This will work, but if two pop / `peeks` are performed back-to-back, we're needlessly moving elements. We can implement a "lazy" approach where we let the elements sit in `s2` until we absolutely must reverse the elements.

In this approach, `stackNewest` has the newest elements on top and `stackOldest` has the oldest elements on top. When we dequeue an element, we want to remove the oldest element first, and so we dequeue from `stackOldest`. If `stackOldest` is empty, then we want to transfer all elements from `stackNewest` into this stack in reverse order. To insert an element, we push onto `stackNewest`, since it has the newest elements on top.

The code below implements this algorithm.

```
public class MyQueue<T> {
   Stack<T> stackNewest, stackOldest;

   public MyQueue() {
      stackNewest = new Stack<T>();
      stackOldest = new Stack<T>();
   }

   public int size() {
      return stackNewest.size() + stackOldest.size();
   }

   public void add(T value) {
      /* Push onto stackNewest, which always has the newest elements on top */
      stackNewest.push(value);
   }

   /* Move elements from stackNewest into stackOldest. This is usually done so that
    * we can do operations on stackOldest. */
```

```
    private void shiftStacks() {
      if (stackOldest.isEmpty()) {
        while (!stackNewest.isEmpty()) {
          stackOldest.push(stackNewest.pop());
        }
      }
    }

    public T peek() {
      shiftStacks(); // Ensure stackOldest has the current elements
      return stackOldest.peek(); // retrieve the oldest item.
    }

    public T remove() {
      shiftStacks(); // Ensure stackOldest has the current elements
      return stackOldest.pop(); // pop the oldest item.
    }
}
```

During your actual interview, you may find that you forget the exact API calls. Don't stress too much if that happens to you. Most interviewers are okay with your asking for them to refresh your memory on little details. They're much more concerned with your big picture understanding.

3.5 **Sort Stack:** Write a program to sort a stack such that the smallest items are on the top. You can use an additional temporary stack, but you may not copy the elements into any other data structure (such as an array). The stack supports the following operations: `push`, `pop`, `peek`, and `isEmpty`.

pg 99

SOLUTION

One approach is to implement a rudimentary sorting algorithm. We search through the entire stack to find the minimum element and then push that onto a new stack. Then, we find the new minimum element and push that. This will actually require a total of three stacks: `s1` is the original stack, `s2` is the final sorted stack, and `s3` acts as a buffer during our searching of `s1`. To search `s1` for each minimum, we need to pop elements from `s1` and push them onto the buffer, `s3`.

Unfortunately, this requires two additional stacks, and we can only use one. Can we do better? Yes.

Rather than searching for the minimum repeatedly, we can sort `s1` by inserting each element from `s1` in order into `s2`. How would this work?

Imagine we have the following stacks, where `s2` is "sorted" and `s1` is not:

s1	s2
	12
5	8
10	3
7	1

When we pop 5 from `s1`, we need to find the right place in `s2` to insert this number. In this case, the correct place is on `s2` just above 3. How do we get it there? We can do this by popping 5 from `s1` and holding it in a temporary variable. Then, we move 12 and 8 over to `s1` (by popping them from `s2` and pushing them onto `s1`) and then push 5 onto `s2`.

Step 1

s1	s2
	12
	8
10	3
7	1

tmp = 5

->

Step 2

s1	s2
8	
12	
10	3
7	1

tmp = 5

->

Step 3

s1	s2
8	
12	5
10	3
7	1

tmp = --

Note that 8 and 12 are still in `s1`—and that's okay! We just repeat the same steps for those two numbers as we did for 5, each time popping off the top of `s1` and putting it into the "right place" on `s2`. (Of course, since 8 and 12 were moved from `s2` to `s1` precisely *because* they were larger than 5, the "right place" for these elements will be right on top of 5. We won't need to muck around with `s2`'s other elements, and the inside of the below `while` loop will not be run when `tmp` is 8 or 12.)

```
void sort(Stack<Integer> s) {
   Stack<Integer> r = new Stack<Integer>();
   while(!s.isEmpty()) {
      /* Insert each element in s in sorted order into r. */
      int tmp = s.pop();
      while(!r.isEmpty() && r.peek() > tmp) {
         s.push(r.pop());
      }
      r.push(tmp);
   }

   /* Copy the elements from r back into s. */
   while (!r.isEmpty()) {
      s.push(r.pop());
   }
}
```

This algorithm is $O(N^2)$ time and $O(N)$ space.

If we were allowed to use unlimited stacks, we could implement a modified quicksort or mergesort.

With the mergesort solution, we would create two extra stacks and divide the stack into two parts. We would recursively sort each stack, and then merge them back together in sorted order into the original stack. Note that this would require the creation of two additional stacks per level of recursion.

With the quicksort solution, we would create two additional stacks and divide the stack into the two stacks based on a pivot element. The two stacks would be recursively sorted, and then merged back together into the original stack. Like the earlier solution, this one involves creating two additional stacks per level of recursion.

3.6 **Animal Shelter:** An animal shelter, which holds only dogs and cats, operates on a strictly "first in, first out" basis. People must adopt either the "oldest" (based on arrival time) of all animals at the shelter, or they can select whether they would prefer a dog or a cat (and will receive the oldest animal of that type). They cannot select which specific animal they would like. Create the data structures to maintain this system and implement operations such as enqueue, dequeueAny, dequeueDog, and dequeueCat. You may use the built-in LinkedList data structure.

pg 99

SOLUTION

We could explore a variety of solutions to this problem. For instance, we could maintain a single queue. This would make dequeueAny easy, but dequeueDog and dequeueCat would require iteration through the queue to find the first dog or cat. This would increase the complexity of the solution and decrease the efficiency.

An alternative approach that is simple, clean and efficient is to simply use separate queues for dogs and cats, and to place them within a wrapper class called AnimalQueue. We then store some sort of timestamp to mark when each animal was enqueued. When we call dequeueAny, we peek at the heads of both the dog and cat queue and return the oldest.

```
abstract class Animal {
   private int order;
   protected String name;
   public Animal(String n) { name = n; }
   public void setOrder(int ord) { order = ord; }
   public int getOrder() { return order; }

   /* Compare orders of animals to return the older item. */
   public boolean isOlderThan(Animal a) {
      return this.order < a.getOrder();
   }
}

class AnimalQueue {
   LinkedList<Dog> dogs = new LinkedList<Dog>();
   LinkedList<Cat> cats = new LinkedList<Cat>();
   private int order = 0; // acts as timestamp

   public void enqueue(Animal a) {
      /* Order is used as a sort of timestamp, so that we can compare the insertion
       * order of a dog to a cat. */
      a.setOrder(order);
      order++;

      if (a instanceof Dog) dogs.addLast((Dog) a);
      else if (a instanceof Cat) cats.addLast((Cat)a);
   }

   public Animal dequeueAny() {
      /* Look at tops of dog and cat queues, and pop the queue with the oldest
       * value. */
      if (dogs.size() == 0) {
         return dequeueCats();
      } else if (cats.size() == 0) {
         return dequeueDogs();
      }
```

```java

    Dog dog = dogs.peek();
    Cat cat = cats.peek();
    if (dog.isOlderThan(cat)) {
      return dequeueDogs();
    } else {
      return dequeueCats();
    }
  }

  public Dog dequeueDogs() {
    return dogs.poll();
  }

  public Cat dequeueCats() {
    return cats.poll();
  }
}

public class Dog extends Animal {
  public Dog(String n) { super(n); }
}

public class Cat extends Animal {
  public Cat(String n) { super(n); }
}
```

It is important that Dog and `Cat` both inherit from an `Animal` class since `dequeueAny()` needs to be able to support returning both Dog and `Cat` objects.

If we wanted, `order` could be a true timestamp with the actual date and time. The advantage of this is that we wouldn't have to set and maintain the numerical order. If we somehow wound up with two animals with the same timestamp, then (by definition) we don't have an older animal and we could return either one.

4

Solutions to Trees and Graphs

4.1 **Route Between Nodes:** Given a directed graph, design an algorithm to find out whether there is a route between two nodes.

pg 109

SOLUTION

This problem can be solved by just simple graph traversal, such as depth-first search or breadth-first search. We start with one of the two nodes and, during traversal, check if the other node is found. We should mark any node found in the course of the algorithm as "already visited" to avoid cycles and repetition of the nodes.

The code below provides an iterative implementation of breadth-first search.

```
enum State { Unvisited, Visited, Visiting; }

boolean search(Graph g, Node start, Node end) {
  if (start == end) return true;

  // operates as Queue
  LinkedList<Node> q = new LinkedList<Node>();

  for (Node u : g.getNodes()) {
     u.state = State.Unvisited;
  }
  start.state = State.Visiting;
  q.add(start);
  Node u;
  while (!q.isEmpty()) {
     u = q.removeFirst(); // i.e., dequeue()
     if (u != null) {
        for (Node v : u.getAdjacent()) {
           if (v.state == State.Unvisited) {
              if (v == end) {
                 return true;
              } else {
                 v.state = State.Visiting;
                 q.add(v);
              }
           }
        }
        u.state = State.Visited;
     }
```

```
    }
    return false;
}
```

It may be worth discussing with your interviewer the tradeoffs between breadth-first search and depth-first search for this and other problems. For example, depth-first search is a bit simpler to implement since it can be done with simple recursion. Breadth-first search can also be useful to find the shortest path, whereas depth-first search may traverse one adjacent node very deeply before ever going onto the immediate neighbors.

4.2 **Minimal Tree:** Given a sorted (increasing order) array with unique integer elements, write an algorithm to create a binary search tree with minimal height.

pg 109

SOLUTION

To create a tree of minimal height, we need to match the number of nodes in the left subtree to the number of nodes in the right subtree as much as possible. This means that we want the root to be the middle of the array, since this would mean that half the elements would be less than the root and half would be greater than it.

We proceed with constructing our tree in a similar fashion. The middle of each subsection of the array becomes the root of the node. The left half of the array will become our left subtree, and the right half of the array will become the right subtree.

One way to implement this is to use a simple `root.insertNode(int v)` method which inserts the value `v` through a recursive process that starts with the root node. This will indeed construct a tree with minimal height but it will not do so very efficiently. Each insertion will require traversing the tree, giving a total cost of `O(N log N)` to the tree.

Alternatively, we can cut out the extra traversals by recursively using the `createMinimalBST` method. This method is passed just a subsection of the array and returns the root of a minimal tree for that array.

The algorithm is as follows:

1. Insert into the tree the middle element of the array.
2. Insert (into the left subtree) the left subarray elements.
3. Insert (into the right subtree) the right subarray elements.
4. Recurse.

The code below implements this algorithm.

```
TreeNode createMinimalBST(int array[]) {
   return createMinimalBST(array, 0, array.length - 1);
}

TreeNode createMinimalBST(int arr[], int start, int end) {
   if (end < start) {
      return null;
   }
   int mid = (start + end) / 2;
   TreeNode n = new TreeNode(arr[mid]);
   n.left = createMinimalBST(arr, start, mid - 1);
   n.right = createMinimalBST(arr, mid + 1, end);
   return n;
```

```
}
```

Although this code does not seem especially complex, it can be very easy to make little off-by-one errors. Be sure to test these parts of the code very thoroughly.

4.3 **List of Depths:** Given a binary tree, design an algorithm which creates a linked list of all the nodes at each depth (e.g., if you have a tree with depth D, you'll have D linked lists).

pg 109

SOLUTION

Though we might think at first glance that this problem requires a level-by-level traversal, this isn't actually necessary. We can traverse the graph any way that we'd like, provided we know which level we're on as we do so.

We can implement a simple modification of the pre-order traversal algorithm, where we pass in `level + 1` to the next recursive call. The code below provides an implementation using depth-first search.

```
void createLevelLinkedList(TreeNode root, ArrayList<LinkedList<TreeNode>> lists,
                           int level) {
  if (root == null) return; // base case

  LinkedList<TreeNode> list = null;
  if (lists.size() == level) { // Level not contained in list
    list = new LinkedList<TreeNode>();
    /* Levels are always traversed in order. So, if this is the first time we've
     * visited level i, we must have seen levels 0 through i - 1. We can
     * therefore safely add the level at the end. */
    lists.add(list);
  } else {
    list = lists.get(level);
  }
  list.add(root);
  createLevelLinkedList(root.left, lists, level + 1);
  createLevelLinkedList(root.right, lists, level + 1);
}

ArrayList<LinkedList<TreeNode>> createLevelLinkedList(TreeNode root) {
  ArrayList<LinkedList<TreeNode>> lists = new ArrayList<LinkedList<TreeNode>>();
  createLevelLinkedList(root, lists, 0);
  return lists;
}
```

Alternatively, we can also implement a modification of breadth-first search. With this implementation, we want to iterate through the root first, then level 2, then level 3, and so on.

With each level `i`, we will have already fully visited all nodes on level `i - 1`. This means that to get which nodes are on level `i`, we can simply look at all children of the nodes of level `i - 1`.

The code below implements this algorithm.

```
ArrayList<LinkedList<TreeNode>> createLevelLinkedList(TreeNode root) {
  ArrayList<LinkedList<TreeNode>> result = new ArrayList<LinkedList<TreeNode>>();
  /* "Visit" the root */
  LinkedList<TreeNode> current = new LinkedList<TreeNode>();
  if (root != null) {
    current.add(root);
  }
```

```

    while (current.size() > 0) {
      result.add(current); // Add previous level
      LinkedList<TreeNode> parents = current; // Go to next level
      current = new LinkedList<TreeNode>();
      for (TreeNode parent : parents) {
        /* Visit the children */
        if (parent.left != null) {
          current.add(parent.left);
        }
        if (parent.right != null) {
          current.add(parent.right);
        }
      }
    }
    return result;
  }
```

One might ask which of these solutions is more efficient. Both run in O(N) time, but what about the space efficiency? At first, we might want to claim that the second solution is more space efficient.

In a sense, that's correct. The first solution uses O(log N) recursive calls (in a balanced tree), each of which adds a new level to the stack. The second solution, which is iterative, does not require this extra space.

However, both solutions require returning O(N) data. The extra O(log N) space usage from the recursive implementation is dwarfed by the O(N) data that must be returned. So while the first solution may actually use more data, they are equally efficient when it comes to "big O."

4.4 Check Balanced: Implement a function to check if a binary tree is balanced. For the purposes of this question, a balanced tree is defined to be a tree such that the heights of the two subtrees of any node never differ by more than one.

pg 110

SOLUTION

In this question, we've been fortunate enough to be told exactly what balanced means: that for each node, the two subtrees differ in height by no more than one. We can implement a solution based on this definition. We can simply recurse through the entire tree, and for each node, compute the heights of each subtree.

```
int getHeight(TreeNode root) {
  if (root == null) return -1; // Base case
  return Math.max(getHeight(root.left), getHeight(root.right)) + 1;
}

boolean isBalanced(TreeNode root) {
  if (root == null) return true; // Base case

  int heightDiff = getHeight(root.left) - getHeight(root.right);
  if (Math.abs(heightDiff) > 1) {
    return false;
  } else { // Recurse
    return isBalanced(root.left) && isBalanced(root.right);
  }
}
```

Although this works, it's not very efficient. On each node, we recurse through its entire subtree. This means that `getHeight` is called repeatedly on the same nodes. The algorithm is `O(N log N)` since each node is "touched" once per node above it.

We need to cut out some of the calls to `getHeight`.

If we inspect this method, we may notice that `getHeight` could actually check if the tree is balanced at the same time as it's checking heights. What do we do when we discover that the subtree isn't balanced? Just return an error code.

This improved algorithm works by checking the height of each subtree as we recurse down from the root. On each node, we recursively get the heights of the left and right subtrees through the `checkHeight` method. If the subtree is balanced, then `checkHeight` will return the actual height of the subtree. If the subtree is not balanced, then `checkHeight` will return an error code. We will immediately break and return an error code from the current call.

> What do we use for an error code? The height of a null tree is generally defined to be -1, so that's not a great idea for an error code. Instead, we'll use `Integer.MIN_VALUE`.

The code below implements this algorithm.

```
int checkHeight(TreeNode root) {
  if (root == null) return -1;

  int leftHeight = checkHeight(root.left);
  if (leftHeight == Integer.MIN_VALUE) return Integer.MIN_VALUE; // Pass error up

  int rightHeight = checkHeight(root.right);
  if (rightHeight == Integer.MIN_VALUE) return Integer.MIN_VALUE; // Pass error up

  int heightDiff = leftHeight - rightHeight;
  if (Math.abs(heightDiff) > 1) {
    return Integer.MIN_VALUE; // Found error -> pass it back
  } else {
    return Math.max(leftHeight, rightHeight) + 1;
  }
}

boolean isBalanced(TreeNode root) {
  return checkHeight(root) != Integer.MIN_VALUE;
}
```

This code runs in `O(N)` time and `O(H)` space, where H is the height of the tree.

4.5 Validate BST: Implement a function to check if a binary tree is a binary search tree.

pg 110

SOLUTION

We can implement this solution in two different ways. The first leverages the in-order traversal, and the second builds off the property that `left <= current < right`.

Solution #1: In-Order Traversal

Our first thought might be to do an in-order traversal, copy the elements to an array, and then check to see if the array is sorted. This solution takes up a bit of extra memory, but it works—mostly.

The only problem is that it can't handle duplicate values in the tree properly. For example, the algorithm cannot distinguish between the two trees below (one of which is invalid) since they have the same in-order traversal.

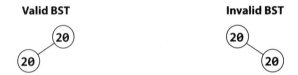

However, if we assume that the tree cannot have duplicate values, then this approach works. The pseudocode for this method looks something like:

```
int index = 0;
void copyBST(TreeNode root, int[] array) {
  if (root == null) return;
  copyBST(root.left, array);
  array[index] = root.data;
  index++;
  copyBST(root.right, array);
}

boolean checkBST(TreeNode root) {
  int[] array = new int[root.size];
  copyBST(root, array);
  for (int i = 1; i < array.length; i++) {
    if (array[i] <= array[i - 1]) return false;
  }
  return true;
}
```

Note that it is necessary to keep track of the logical "end" of the array, since it would be allocated to hold all the elements.

When we examine this solution, we find that the array is not actually necessary. We never use it other than to compare an element to the previous element. So why not just track the last element we saw and compare it as we go?

The code below implements this algorithm.

```
Integer last_printed = null;
boolean checkBST(TreeNode n) {
  if (n == null) return true;

  // Check / recurse left
  if (!checkBST(n.left)) return false;

  // Check current
  if (last_printed != null && n.data <= last_printed) {
    return false;
  }
  last_printed = n.data;

  // Check / recurse right
```

```
    if (!checkBST(n.right)) return false;

    return true; // All good!
}
```

We've used an `Integer` instead of `int` so that we can know when `last_printed` has been set to a value.

If you don't like the use of static variables, then you can tweak this code to use a wrapper class for the integer, as shown below.

```
class WrapInt {
  public int value;
}
```

Or, if you're implementing this in C++ or another language that supports passing integers by reference, then you can simply do that.

Solution #2: The Min / Max Solution

In the second solution, we leverage the definition of the binary search tree.

What does it mean for a tree to be a binary search tree? We know that it must, of course, satisfy the condition `left.data <= current.data < right.data` for each node, but this isn't quite sufficient. Consider the following small tree:

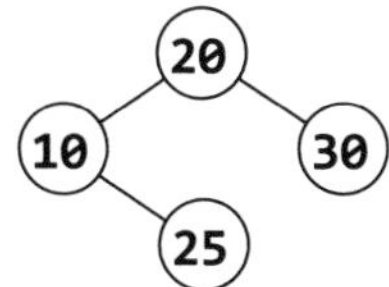

Although each node is bigger than its left node and smaller than its right node, this is clearly not a binary search tree since 25 is in the wrong place.

More precisely, the condition is that *all* left nodes must be less than or equal to the current node, which must be less than all the right nodes.

Using this thought, we can approach the problem by passing down the min and max values. As we iterate through the tree, we verify against progressively narrower ranges.

Consider the following sample tree:

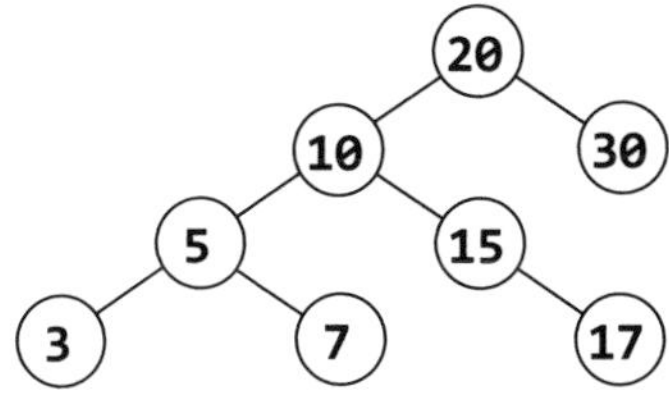

We start with a range of `(min = NULL, max = NULL)`, which the root obviously meets. (NULL indicates that there is no min or max.) We then branch left, checking that these nodes are within the range `(min = NULL, max = 20)`. Then, we branch right, checking that the nodes are within the range `(min = 20, max = NULL)`.

We proceed through the tree with this approach. When we branch left, the max gets updated. When we branch right, the min gets updated. If anything fails these checks, we stop and return false.

The time complexity for this solution is O(N), where N is the number of nodes in the tree. We can prove that this is the best we can do, since any algorithm must touch all N nodes.

Due to the use of recursion, the space complexity is O(log N) on a balanced tree. There are up to O(log N) recursive calls on the stack since we may recurse up to the depth of the tree.

The recursive code for this is as follows:

```
boolean checkBST(TreeNode n) {
  return checkBST(n, null, null);
}

boolean checkBST(TreeNode n, Integer min, Integer max) {
  if (n == null) {
    return true;
  }
  if ((min != null && n.data <= min) || (max != null && n.data > max)) {
    return false;
  }

  if (!checkBST(n.left, min, n.data) || !checkBST(n.right, n.data, max)) {
    return false;
  }
  return true;
}
```

Remember that in recursive algorithms, you should always make sure that your base cases, as well as your null cases, are well handled.

4.6 **Successor:** Write an algorithm to find the "next" node (i.e., in-order successor) of a given node in a binary search tree. You may assume that each node has a link to its parent.

pg 110

SOLUTION

Recall that an in-order traversal traverses the left subtree, then the current node, then the right subtree. To approach this problem, we need to think very, very carefully about what happens.

Let's suppose we have a hypothetical node. We know that the order goes left subtree, then current side, then right subtree. So, the next node we visit should be on the right side.

But which node on the right subtree? It should be the first node we'd visit if we were doing an in-order traversal of that subtree. This means that it should be the leftmost node on the right subtree. Easy enough!

But what if the node doesn't have a right subtree? This is where it gets a bit trickier.

If a node n doesn't have a right subtree, then we are done traversing n's subtree. We need to pick up where we left off with n's parent, which we'll call q.

If n was to the left of q, then the next node we should traverse should be q (again, since `left -> current -> right`).

If n were to the right of q, then we have fully traversed q's subtree as well. We need to traverse upwards from q until we find a node x that we have *not* fully traversed. How do we know that we have not fully traversed a node x? We know we have hit this case when we move from a left node to its parent. The left node is fully traversed, but its parent is not.

The pseudocode looks like this:

```
Node inorderSucc(Node n) {
  if (n has a right subtree) {
    return leftmost child of right subtree
  } else {
    while (n is a right child of n.parent) {
      n = n.parent; // Go up
    }
    return n.parent; // Parent has not been traversed
  }
}
```

But wait—what if we traverse all the way up the tree before finding a left child? This will happen only when we hit the very end of the in-order traversal. That is, if we're *already* on the far right of the tree, then there is no in-order successor. We should return `null`.

The code below implements this algorithm (and properly handles the null case).

```
TreeNode inorderSucc(TreeNode n) {
  if (n == null) return null;

  /* Found right children -> return leftmost node of right subtree. */
  if (n.right != null) {
    return leftMostChild(n.right);
  } else {
    TreeNode q = n;
    TreeNode x = q.parent;
    // Go up until we're on left instead of right
    while (x != null && x.left != q) {
      q = x;
      x = x.parent;
    }
    return x;
  }
}

TreeNode leftMostChild(TreeNode n) {
  if (n == null) {
    return null;
  }
  while (n.left != null) {
    n = n.left;
  }
  return n;
}
```

This is not the most algorithmically complex problem in the world, but it can be tricky to code perfectly. In a problem like this, it's useful to sketch out pseudocode to carefully outline the different cases.

4.7 **Build Order:** You are given a list of projects and a list of dependencies (which is a list of pairs of projects, where the second project is dependent on the first project). All of a project's dependencies must be built before the project is. Find a build order that will allow the projects to be built. If there is no valid build order, return an error.

EXAMPLE

Input:

```
projects: a, b, c, d, e, f
dependencies: (a, d), (f, b), (b, d), (f, a), (d, c)
```

Output: `f, e, a, b, d, c`

pg 110

SOLUTION

Visualizing the information as a graph probably works best. Be careful with the direction of the arrows. In the graph below, an arrow from d to g means that d must be compiled before g. You can also draw them in the opposite direction, but you need to consistent and clear about what you mean. Let's draw a fresh example.

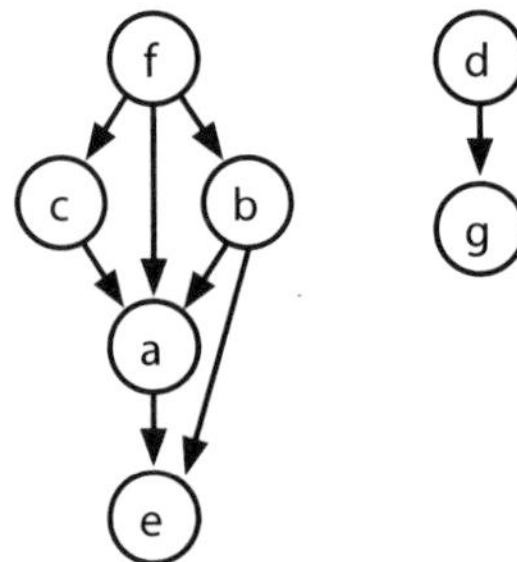

In drawing this example (which is *not* the example from the problem description), I looked for a few things.

- I wanted the nodes labeled somewhat randomly. If I had instead put a at the top, with b and c as children, then d and e, it could be misleading. The alphabetical order would match the compile order.
- I wanted a graph with multiple parts/components, since a connected graph is a bit of a special case.
- I wanted a graph where a node links to a node that cannot immediately follow it. For example, `f` links to a but a cannot immediately follow it (since b and c must come before a and after `f`).
- I wanted a larger graph since I need to figure out the pattern.
- I wanted nodes with multiple dependencies.

Now that we have a good example, let's get started with an algorithm.

Solution #1

Where do we start? Are there any nodes that we can definitely compile immediately?

Yes. Nodes with no incoming edges can be built immediately since they don't depend on anything. Let's add all such nodes to the build order. In the earlier example, this means we have an order of `f`, d (or d, `f`).

Once we've done that, it's irrelevant that some nodes are dependent on d and `f` since d and `f` have already been built. We can reflect this new state by removing d and `f`'s outgoing edges.

```
build order: f, d
```

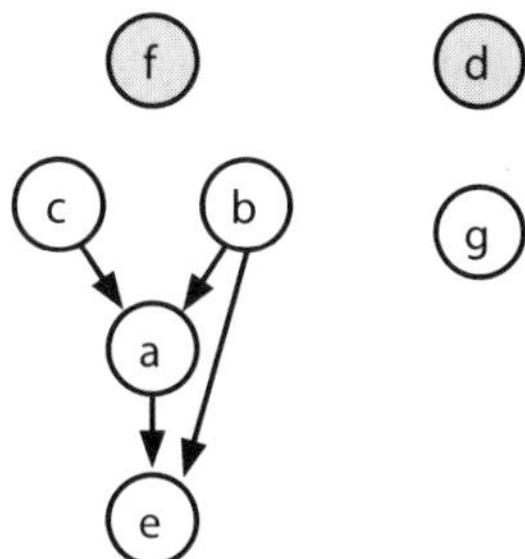

Next, we know that c, b, and g are free to build since they have no incoming edges. Let's build those and then remove their outgoing edges.

```
build order: f, d, c, b, g
```

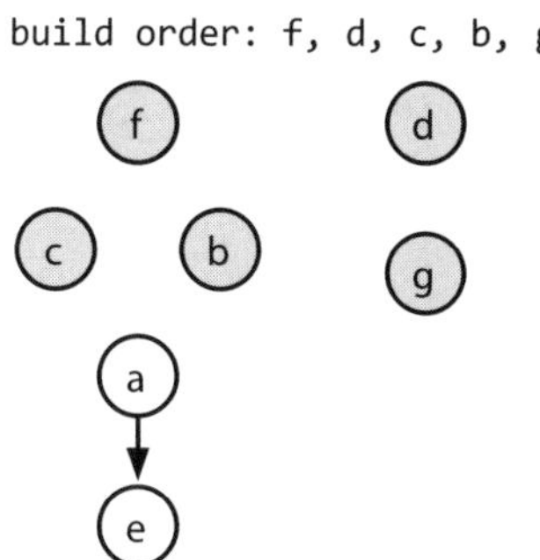

Project a can be built next, so let's do that and remove its outgoing edges. This leaves just e. We build that next, giving us a complete build order.

```
build order: f, d, c, b, g, a, e
```

Did this algorithm work, or did we just get lucky? Let's think about the logic.

1. We first added the nodes with no incoming edges. If the set of projects can be built, there must be some "first" project, and that project can't have any dependencies. If a project has no dependencies (incoming edges), then we certainly can't break anything by building it first.
2. We removed all outgoing edges from these roots. This is reasonable. Once those root projects were built, it doesn't matter if another project depends on them.
3. After that, we found the nodes that *now* have no incoming edges. Using the same logic from steps 1 and 2, it's okay if we build these. Now we just repeat the same steps: find the nodes with no dependencies, add them to the build order, remove their outgoing edges, and repeat.
4. What if there are nodes remaining, but all have dependencies (incoming edges)? This means there's no way to build the system. We should return an error.

The implementation follows this approach very closely.

Initialization and setup:

1. Build a graph where each project is a node and its outgoing edges represent the projects that depend on it. That is, if A has an edge to B (A -> B), it means B has a dependency on A and therefore A must be built before B. Each node also tracks the number of *incoming* edges.
2. Initialize a `buildOrder` array. Once we determine a project's build order, we add it to the array. We also continue to iterate through the array, using a `toBeProcessed` pointer to point to the next node to be fully processed.

3. Find all the nodes with zero incoming edges and add those to a `buildOrder` array. Set a `toBeProcessed` pointer to the beginning of the array.

Repeat until `toBeProcessed` is at the end of the `buildOrder`:

1. Read node at `toBeProcessed`.
   » If node is `null`, then all remaining nodes have a dependency and we have detected a cycle.
2. For each child of node:
   » Decrement `child.dependencies` (the number of incoming edges).
   » If `child.dependencies` is zero, add `child` to end of `buildOrder`.
3. Increment `toBeProcessed`.

The code below implements this algorithm.

```
/* Find a correct build order. */
Project[] findBuildOrder(String[] projects, String[][] dependencies) {
  Graph graph = buildGraph(projects, dependencies);
  return orderProjects(graph.getNodes());
}

/* Build the graph, adding the edge (a, b) if b is dependent on a. Assumes a pair
 * is listed in "build order". The pair (a, b) in dependencies indicates that b
 * depends on a and a must be built before b. */
Graph buildGraph(String[] projects, String[][] dependencies) {
  Graph graph = new Graph();
  for (String project : projects) {
    graph.createNode(project);
  }

  for (String[] dependency : dependencies) {
    String first = dependency[0];
    String second = dependency[1];
    graph.addEdge(first, second);
  }

  return graph;
}

/* Return a list of the projects a correct build order.*/
Project[] orderProjects(ArrayList<Project> projects) {
  Project[] order = new Project[projects.size()];

  /* Add "roots" to the build order first.*/
  int endOfList = addNonDependent(order, projects, 0);

  int toBeProcessed = 0;
  while (toBeProcessed < order.length) {
    Project current = order[toBeProcessed];

    /* We have a circular dependency since there are no remaining projects with
     * zero dependencies. */
    if (current == null) {
      return null;
    }

```

```
      /* Remove myself as a dependency. */
      ArrayList<Project> children = current.getChildren();
      for (Project child : children) {
        child.decrementDependencies();
      }

      /* Add children that have no one depending on them. */
      endOfList = addNonDependent(order, children, endOfList);
      toBeProcessed++;
    }

    return order;
  }

  /* A helper function to insert projects with zero dependencies into the order
   * array, starting at index offset. */
  int addNonDependent(Project[] order, ArrayList<Project> projects, int offset) {
    for (Project project : projects) {
      if (project.getNumberDependencies() == 0) {
        order[offset] = project;
        offset++;
      }
    }
    return offset;
  }

  public class Graph {
    private ArrayList<Project> nodes = new ArrayList<Project>();
    private HashMap<String, Project> map = new HashMap<String, Project>();

    public Project getOrCreateNode(String name) {
      if (!map.containsKey(name)) {
        Project node = new Project(name);
        nodes.add(node);
        map.put(name, node);
      }

      return map.get(name);
    }

    public void addEdge(String startName, String endName) {
      Project start = getOrCreateNode(startName);
      Project end = getOrCreateNode(endName);
      start.addNeighbor(end);
    }

    public ArrayList<Project> getNodes() { return nodes; }
  }

  public class Project {
    private ArrayList<Project> children = new ArrayList<Project>();
    private HashMap<String, Project> map = new HashMap<String, Project>();
    private String name;
    private int dependencies = 0;

    public Project(String n) { name = n; }
```

```
	
	public void addNeighbor(Project node) {
		if (!map.containsKey(node.getName())) {
			children.add(node);
			map.put(node.getName(), node);
			node.incrementDependencies();
		}
	}
	
	public void incrementDependencies() { dependencies++; }
	public void decrementDependencies() { dependencies--; }
	
	public String getName() { return name; }
	public ArrayList<Project> getChildren() { return children; }
	public int getNumberDependencies() { return dependencies; }
}
```

This solution takes O(P + D) time, where P is the number of projects and D is the number of dependency pairs.

> **Note:** You might recognize this as the topological sort algorithm on page 632. We've rederived this from scratch. Most people won't know this algorithm and it's reasonable for an interviewer to expect you to be able to derive it.

Solution #2

Alternatively, we can use depth-first search (DFS) to find the build path.

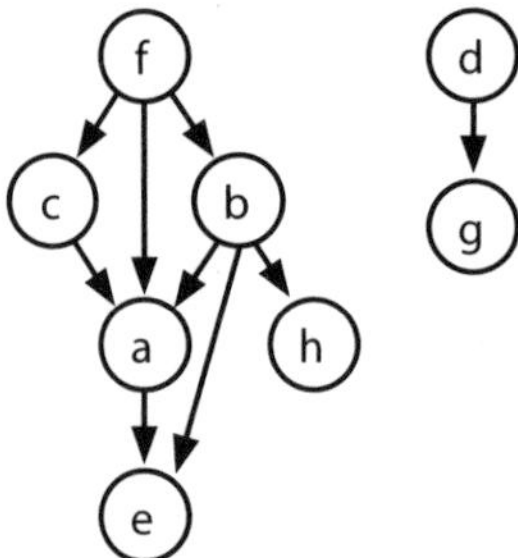

Suppose we picked an arbitrary node (say b) and performed a depth-first search on it. When we get to the end of a path and can't go any further (which will happen at h and e), we know that those terminating nodes can be the last projects to be built. No projects depend on them.

```
DFS(b)                              // Step 1
    DFS(h)                          // Step 2
        build order = ..., h        // Step 3
    DFS(a)                          // Step 4
        DFS(e)                      // Step 5
            build order = ..., e, h // Step 6
        ...                         // Step 7+
    ...
```

Now, consider what happens at node a when we return from the DFS of e. We know a's children need to appear after a in the build order. So, once we return from searching a's children (and therefore they have been added), we can choose to add a to the front of the build order.

Once we return from a, and complete the DFS of b's other children, then everything that must appear after b is in the list. Add b to the front.

```
DFS(b)                              // Step 1
    DFS(h)                          // Step 2
        build order = ..., h        // Step 3
    DFS(a)                          // Step 4
        DFS(e)                      // Step 5
            build order = ..., e, h     // Step 6
        build order = ..., a, e, h  // Step 7
    DFS(e) -> return                // Step 8
    build order = ..., b, a, e, h   // Step 9
```

Let's mark these nodes as having been built too, just in case someone else needs to build them.

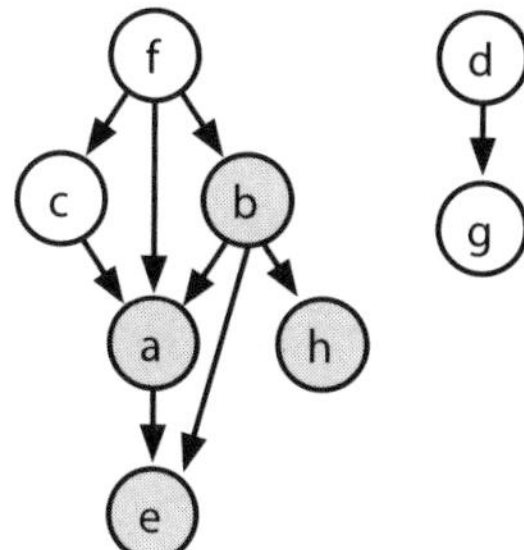

Now what? We can start with any old node again, doing a DFS on it and then adding the node to the front of the build queue when the DFS is completed.

```
DFS(d)
    DFS(g)
        build order = ..., g, b, a, e, h
    build order = ..., d, g, b, a, e, h

DFS(f)
    DFS(c)
        build order = ..., c, d, g, b, a, e, h
    build order = f, c, d, g, b, a, e, h
```

In an algorithm like this, we should think about the issue of cycles. There is no possible build order if there is a cycle. But still, we don't want to get stuck in an infinite loop just because there's no possible solution.

A cycle will happen if, while doing a DFS on a node, we run back into the same path. What we need therefore is a signal that indicates "I'm still processing this node, so if you see the node again, we have a problem."

What we can do for this is to mark each node as a "`partial`" (or "`is visiting`") state just before we start the DFS on it. If we see any node whose state is `partial`, then we know we have a problem. When we're done with this node's DFS, we need to update the state.

We also need a state to indicate "I've already processed/built this node" so we don't re-build the node. Our state therefore can have three options: `COMPLETED`, `PARTIAL`, and `BLANK`.

The code below implements this algorithm.

```
Stack<Project> findBuildOrder(String[] projects, String[][] dependencies) {
  Graph graph = buildGraph(projects, dependencies);
  return orderProjects(graph.getNodes());
}
```

```
Stack<Project> orderProjects(ArrayList<Project> projects) {
  Stack<Project> stack = new Stack<Project>();
  for (Project project : projects) {
    if (project.getState() == Project.State.BLANK) {
      if (!doDFS(project, stack)) {
        return null;
      }
    }
  }
  return stack;
}

boolean doDFS(Project project, Stack<Project> stack) {
  if (project.getState() == Project.State.PARTIAL) {
    return false; // Cycle
  }

  if (project.getState() == Project.State.BLANK) {
    project.setState(Project.State.PARTIAL);
    ArrayList<Project> children = project.getChildren();
    for (Project child : children) {
      if (!doDFS(child, stack)) {
        return false;
      }
    }
    project.setState(Project.State.COMPLETE);
    stack.push(project);
  }
  return true;
}

/* Same as before */
Graph buildGraph(String[] projects, String[][] dependencies) {...}
public class Graph {}

/* Essentially equivalent to earlier solution, with state info added and
 * dependency count removed. */
public class Project {
  public enum State {COMPLETE, PARTIAL, BLANK};
  private State state = State.BLANK;
  public State getState() { return state; }
  public void setState(State st) { state = st; }
  /* Duplicate code removed for brevity */
}
```

Like the earlier algorithm, this solution is `O(P+D)` time, where P is the number of projects and D is the number of dependency pairs.

By the way, this problem is called **topological sort**: linearly ordering the vertices in a graph such that for every edge `(a, b)`, a appears before b in the linear order.

4.8 First Common Ancestor: Design an algorithm and write code to find the first common ancestor of two nodes in a binary tree. Avoid storing additional nodes in a data structure. NOTE: This is not necessarily a binary search tree.

pg 110

SOLUTION

If this were a binary search tree, we could modify the `find` operation for the two nodes and see where the paths diverge. Unfortunately, this is not a binary search tree, so we must try other approaches.

Let's assume we're looking for the common ancestor of nodes p and q. One question to ask here is if each node in our tree has a link to its parents.

Solution #1: With Links to Parents

If each node has a link to its parent, we could trace p and q's paths up until they intersect. This is essentially the same problem as question 2.7 which find the intersection of two linked lists. The "linked list" in this case is the path from each node up to the root. (Review this solution on page 221.)

```
TreeNode commonAncestor(TreeNode p, TreeNode q) {
   int delta = depth(p) - depth(q); // get difference in depths
   TreeNode first = delta > 0 ? q : p; // get shallower node
   TreeNode second = delta > 0 ? p : q; // get deeper node
   second = goUpBy(second, Math.abs(delta)); // move deeper node up

   /* Find where paths intersect. */
   while (first != second && first != null && second != null) {
      first = first.parent;
      second = second.parent;
   }
   return first == null || second == null ? null : first;
}

TreeNode goUpBy(TreeNode node, int delta) {
   while (delta > 0 && node != null) {
      node = node.parent;
      delta--;
   }
   return node;
}

int depth(TreeNode node) {
   int depth = 0;
   while (node != null) {
      node = node.parent;
      depth++;
   }
   return depth;
}
```

This approach will take `O(d)` time, where d is the depth of the deeper node.

Solution #2: With Links to Parents (Better Worst-Case Runtime)

Similar to the earlier approach, we could trace p's path upwards and check if any of the nodes cover q. The first node that covers q (we already know that every node on this path will cover p) must be the first common ancestor.

Observe that we don't need to re-check the entire subtree. As we move from a node x to its parent y, all the nodes under x have already been checked for q. Therefore, we only need to check the new nodes "uncovered", which will be the nodes under x's sibling.

For example, suppose we're looking for the first common ancestor of node `p = 7` and node `q = 17`. When we go to `p.parent` (5), we uncover the subtree rooted at 3. We therefore need to search this subtree for q.

Next, we go to node 10, uncovering the subtree rooted at 15. We check this subtree for node 17 and—voila—there it is.

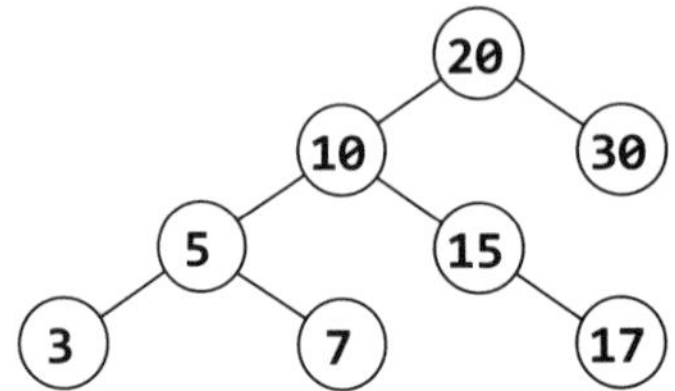

To implement this, we can just traverse upwards from p, storing the `parent` and the `sibling` node in a variable. (The `sibling` node is always a child of `parent` and refers to the newly uncovered subtree.) At each iteration, `sibling` gets set to the old `parent`'s sibling node and `parent` gets set to `parent.parent`.

```
TreeNode commonAncestor(TreeNode root, TreeNode p, TreeNode q) {
   /* Check if either node is not in the tree, or if one covers the other. */
   if (!covers(root, p) || !covers(root, q)) {
      return null;
   } else if (covers(p, q)) {
      return p;
   } else if (covers(q, p)) {
      return q;
   }

   /* Traverse upwards until you find a node that covers q. */
   TreeNode sibling = getSibling(p);
   TreeNode parent = p.parent;
   while (!covers(sibling, q)) {
      sibling = getSibling(parent);
      parent = parent.parent;
   }
   return parent;
}

boolean covers(TreeNode root, TreeNode p) {
   if (root == null) return false;
   if (root == p) return true;
   return covers(root.left, p) || covers(root.right, p);
}

TreeNode getSibling(TreeNode node) {
   if (node == null || node.parent == null) {
      return null;
   }

   TreeNode parent = node.parent;
```

```
    return parent.left == node ? parent.right : parent.left;
}
```

This algorithm takes O(t) time, where t is the size of the subtree for the first common ancestor. In the worst case, this will be O(n), where n is the number of nodes in the tree. We can derive this runtime by noticing that each node in that subtree is searched once.

Solution #3: Without Links to Parents

Alternatively, you could follow a chain in which p and q are on the same side. That is, if p and q are both on the left of the node, branch left to look for the common ancestor. If they are both on the right, branch right to look for the common ancestor. When p and q are no longer on the same side, you must have found the first common ancestor.

The code below implements this approach.

```
TreeNode commonAncestor(TreeNode root, TreeNode p, TreeNode q) {
  /* Error check - one node is not in the tree. */
  if (!covers(root, p) || !covers(root, q)) {
    return null;
  }
  return ancestorHelper(root, p, q);
}

TreeNode ancestorHelper(TreeNode root, TreeNode p, TreeNode q) {
  if (root == null || root == p || root == q) {
    return root;
  }

  boolean pIsOnLeft = covers(root.left, p);
  boolean qIsOnLeft = covers(root.left, q);
  if (pIsOnLeft != qIsOnLeft) { // Nodes are on different side
    return root;
  }
  TreeNode childSide = pIsOnLeft ? root.left : root.right;
  return ancestorHelper(childSide, p, q);
}

boolean covers(TreeNode root, TreeNode p) {
  if (root == null) return false;
  if (root == p) return true;
  return covers(root.left, p) || covers(root.right, p);
}
```

This algorithm runs in O(n) time on a balanced tree. This is because covers is called on 2n nodes in the first call (n nodes for the left side, and n nodes for the right side). After that, the algorithm branches left or right, at which point covers will be called on $\frac{2n}{2}$ nodes, then $\frac{2n}{4}$, and so on. This results in a runtime of O(n).

We know at this point that we cannot do better than that in terms of the asymptotic runtime since we need to potentially look at every node in the tree. However, we may be able to improve it by a constant multiple.

Solution #4: Optimized

Although Solution #3 is optimal in its runtime, we may recognize that there is still some inefficiency in how it operates. Specifically, covers searches all nodes under root for p and q, including the nodes in each subtree (root.left and root.right). Then, it picks one of those subtrees and searches all of its nodes. Each subtree is searched over and over again.

We may recognize that we should only need to search the entire tree once to find p and q. We should then be able to "bubble up" the findings to earlier nodes in the stack. The basic logic is the same as the earlier solution.

We recurse through the entire tree with a function called `commonAncestor(TreeNode root, TreeNode p, TreeNode q)`. This function returns values as follows:

- Returns p, if `root`'s subtree includes p (and not q).
- Returns q, if `root`'s subtree includes q (and not p).
- Returns `null`, if neither p nor q are in `root`'s subtree.
- Else, returns the common ancestor of p and q.

Finding the common ancestor of p and q in the final case is easy. When `commonAncestor(n.left, p, q)` and `commonAncestor(n.right, p, q)` both return non-`null` values (indicating that p and q were found in different subtrees), then n will be the common ancestor.

The code below offers an initial solution, but it has a bug. Can you find it?

```
/* The below code has a bug. */
TreeNode commonAncestor(TreeNode root, TreeNode p, TreeNode q) {
   if (root == null) return null;
   if (root == p && root == q) return root;

   TreeNode x = commonAncestor(root.left, p, q);
   if (x != null && x != p && x != q) { // Already found ancestor
      return x;
   }

   TreeNode y = commonAncestor(root.right, p, q);
   if (y != null && y != p && y != q) { // Already found ancestor
      return y;
   }

   if (x != null && y != null) { // p and q found in diff. subtrees
      return root; // This is the common ancestor
   } else if (root == p || root == q) {
      return root;
   } else {
      return x == null ? y : x; /* return the non-null value */
   }
}
```

The problem with this code occurs in the case where a node is not contained in the tree. For example, look at the following tree:

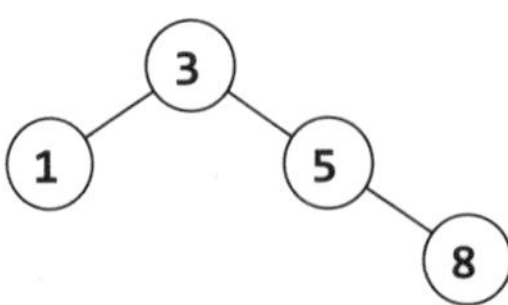

Suppose we call `commonAncestor(node 3, node 5, node 7)`. Of course, `node 7` does not exist—and that's where the issue will come in. The calling order looks like:

```
commonAnc(node 3, node 5, node 7)              // --> 5
   calls commonAnc(node 1, node 5, node 7)     // --> null
```

```
  calls commonAnc(node 5, node 5, node 7)      // --> 5
    calls commonAnc(node 8, node 5, node 7)   // --> null
```

In other words, when we call `commonAncestor` on the right subtree, the code will return node 5, just as it should. The problem is that, in finding the common ancestor of p and q, the calling function can't distinguish between the two cases:

- Case 1: p is a child of q (or, q is a child of p)
- Case 2: p is in the tree and q is not (or, q is in the tree and p is not)

In either of these cases, `commonAncestor` will return p. In the first case, this is the correct return value, but in the second case, the return value should be `null`.

We somehow need to distinguish between these two cases, and this is what the code below does. This code solves the problem by returning two values: the node itself and a flag indicating whether this node is actually the common ancestor.

```
class Result {
  public TreeNode node;
  public boolean isAncestor;
  public Result(TreeNode n, boolean isAnc) {
    node = n;
    isAncestor = isAnc;
  }
}

TreeNode commonAncestor(TreeNode root, TreeNode p, TreeNode q) {
  Result r = commonAncestorHelper(root, p, q);
  if (r.isAncestor) {
    return r.node;
  }
  return null;
}

Result commonAncHelper(TreeNode root, TreeNode p, TreeNode q) {
  if (root == null) return new Result(null, false);

  if (root == p && root == q) {
    return new Result(root, true);
  }

  Result rx = commonAncHelper(root.left, p, q);
  if (rx.isAncestor) { // Found common ancestor
    return rx;
  }

  Result ry = commonAncHelper(root.right, p, q);
  if (ry.isAncestor) { // Found common ancestor
    return ry;
  }

  if (rx.node != null && ry.node != null) {
    return new Result(root, true); // This is the common ancestor
  } else if (root == p || root == q) {
    /* If we're currently at p or q, and we also found one of those nodes in a
     * subtree, then this is truly an ancestor and the flag should be true. */
    boolean isAncestor = rx.node != null || ry.node != null;
```

```
        return new Result(root, isAncestor);
    } else {
        return new Result(rx.node!=null ? rx.node : ry.node, false);
    }
}
```

Of course, as this issue only comes up when p or q is not actually in the tree, an alternative solution would be to first search through the entire tree to make sure that both nodes exist.

4.9 **BST Sequences:** A binary search tree was created by traversing through an array from left to right and inserting each element. Given a binary search tree with distinct elements, print all possible arrays that could have led to this tree.

EXAMPLE

Input:

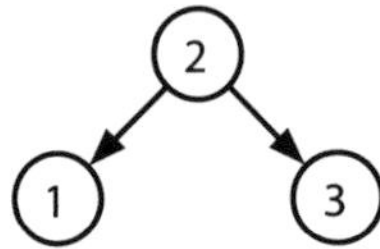

Output: `{2, 1, 3}`, `{2, 3, 1}`

pg 110

SOLUTION

It's useful to kick off this question with a good example.

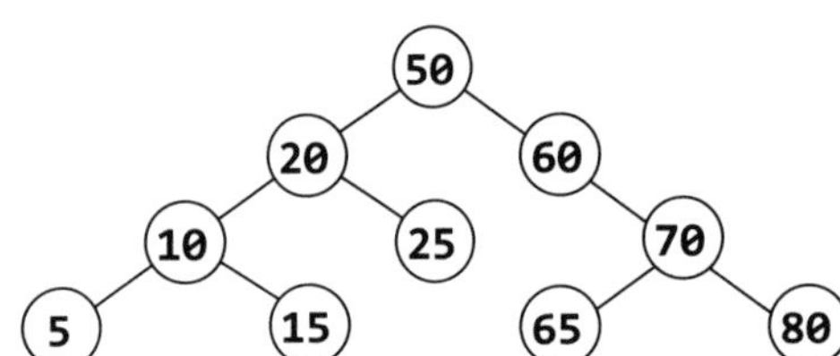

We should also think about the ordering of items in a binary search tree. Given a node, all nodes on its left must be less than all nodes on its right. Once we reach a place without a node, we insert the new value there.

What this means is that the very first element in our array must have been a 50 in order to create the above tree. If it were anything else, then that value would have been the root instead.

What else can we say? Some people jump to the conclusion that everything on the left must have been inserted before elements on the right, but that's not actually true. In fact, the reverse is true: the order of the left or right items doesn't matter.

Once the 50 is inserted, all items less than 50 will be routed to the left and all items greater than 50 will be routed to the right. The 60 or the 20 could be inserted first, and it wouldn't matter.

Let's think about this problem recursively. If we had all arrays that could have created the subtree rooted at 20 (call this `arraySet20`), and all arrays that could have created the subtree rooted at 60 (call this `arraySet60`), how would that give us the full answer? We could just "weave" each array from `arraySet20` with each array from `arraySet60`—and then prepend each array with a 50.

Here's what we mean by weaving. We are merging two arrays in all possible ways, while keeping the elements within each array in the same relative order.

```
array1: {1, 2}
array2: {3, 4}
weaved: {1, 2, 3, 4}, {1, 3, 2, 4}, {1, 3, 4, 2},
        {3, 1, 2, 4}, {3, 1, 4, 2}, {3, 4, 1, 2}
```

Note that, as long as there aren't any duplicates in the original array sets, we won't have to worry that weaving will create duplicates.

The last piece to talk about here is how the weaving works. Let's think recursively about how to weave `{1, 2, 3}` and `{4, 5, 6}`. What are the subproblems?

- Prepend a 1 to all weaves of `{2, 3}` and `{4, 5, 6}`.
- Prepend a 4 to all weaves of `{1, 2, 3}` and `{5, 6}`.

To implement this, we'll store each as linked lists. This will make it easy to add and remove elements. When we recurse, we'll push the prefixed elements down the recursion. When `first` or `second` are empty, we add the remainder to `prefix` and store the result.

It works something like this:

```
weave(first, second, prefix):
    weave({1, 2}, {3, 4}, {})
        weave({2}, {3, 4}, {1})
            weave({}, {3, 4}, {1, 2})
                {1, 2, 3, 4}
            weave({2}, {4}, {1, 3})
                weave({}, {4}, {1, 3, 2})
                    {1, 3, 2, 4}
                weave({2}, {}, {1, 3, 4})
                    {1, 3, 4, 2}
        weave({1, 2}, {4}, {3})
            weave({2}, {4}, {3, 1})
                weave({}, {4}, {3, 1, 2})
                    {3, 1, 2, 4}
                weave({2}, {}, {3, 1, 4})
                    {3, 1, 4, 2}
            weave({1, 2}, {}, {3, 4})
                {3, 4, 1, 2}
```

Now, let's think through the implementation of removing, say, 1 from `{1, 2}` and recursing. We need to be careful about modifying this list, since a later recursive call (e.g., `weave({1, 2}, {4}, {3})`) might need the 1 still in `{1, 2}`.

We could clone the list when we recurse, so that we only modify the recursive calls. Or, we could modify the list, but then "revert" the changes after we're done with recursing.

We've chosen to implement it the latter way. Since we're keeping the same reference to `first`, `second`, and `prefix` the entire way down the recursive call stack, then we'll need to clone `prefix` just before we store the complete result.

```
ArrayList<LinkedList<Integer>> allSequences(TreeNode node) {
  ArrayList<LinkedList<Integer>> result = new ArrayList<LinkedList<Integer>>();

  if (node == null) {
    result.add(new LinkedList<Integer>());
    return result;
```

```
    }

    LinkedList<Integer> prefix = new LinkedList<Integer>();
    prefix.add(node.data);

    /* Recurse on left and right subtrees. */
    ArrayList<LinkedList<Integer>> leftSeq = allSequences(node.left);
    ArrayList<LinkedList<Integer>> rightSeq = allSequences(node.right);

    /* Weave together each list from the left and right sides. */
    for (LinkedList<Integer> left : leftSeq) {
      for (LinkedList<Integer> right : rightSeq) {
        ArrayList<LinkedList<Integer>> weaved =
          new ArrayList<LinkedList<Integer>>();
        weaveLists(left, right, weaved, prefix);
        result.addAll(weaved);
      }
    }
    return result;
}

/* Weave lists together in all possible ways. This algorithm works by removing the
 * head from one list, recursing, and then doing the same thing with the other
 * list. */
void weaveLists(LinkedList<Integer> first, LinkedList<Integer> second,
          ArrayList<LinkedList<Integer>> results, LinkedList<Integer> prefix) {
    /* One list is empty. Add remainder to [a cloned] prefix and store result. */
    if (first.size() == 0 || second.size() == 0) {
      LinkedList<Integer> result = (LinkedList<Integer>) prefix.clone();
      result.addAll(first);
      result.addAll(second);
      results.add(result);
      return;
    }

    /* Recurse with head of first added to the prefix. Removing the head will damage
     * first, so we'll need to put it back where we found it afterwards. */
    int headFirst = first.removeFirst();
    prefix.addLast(headFirst);
    weaveLists(first, second, results, prefix);
    prefix.removeLast();
    first.addFirst(headFirst);

    /* Do the same thing with second, damaging and then restoring the list.*/
    int headSecond = second.removeFirst();
    prefix.addLast(headSecond);
    weaveLists(first, second, results, prefix);
    prefix.removeLast();
    second.addFirst(headSecond);
}
```

Some people struggle with this problem because there are two different recursive algorithms that must be designed and implemented. They get confused with how the algorithms should interact with each other and they try to juggle both in their heads.

If this sounds like you, try this: *trust and focus*. *Trust* that one method does the right thing when implementing an independent method, and *focus* on the one thing that this independent method needs to do.

Look at `weaveLists`. It has a specific job: to weave two lists together and return a list of all possible weaves. The existence of `allSequences` is irrelevant. Focus on the task that `weaveLists` has to do and design this algorithm.

As you're implementing `allSequences` (whether you do this before or after `weaveLists`), trust that `weaveLists` will do the right thing. Don't concern yourself with the particulars of how `weaveLists` operates while implementing something that is essentially independent. Focus on what you're doing while you're doing it.

In fact, this is good advice in general when you're confused during whiteboard coding. Have a good understanding of what a particular function should do ("okay, this function is going to return a list of ____"). You should verify that it's really doing what you think. But when you're not dealing with that function, focus on the one you are dealing with and trust that the others do the right thing. It's often too much to keep the implementations of multiple algorithms straight in your head.

4.10 Check Subtree: T1 and T2 are two very large binary trees, with T1 much bigger than T2. Create an algorithm to determine if T2 is a subtree of T1.

A tree *T2* is a subtree of *T1* if there exists a node *n* in *T1* such that the subtree of *n* is identical to *T2*. That is, if you cut off the tree at node *n*, the two trees would be identical.

pg 111

SOLUTION

In problems like this, it's useful to attempt to solve the problem assuming that there is just a small amount of data. This will give us a basic idea of an approach that might work.

The Simple Approach

In this smaller, simpler problem, we could consider comparing string representations of traversals of each tree. If T2 is a subtree of T1, then T2's traversal should be a substring of T1. Is the reverse true? If so, should we use an in-order traversal or a pre-order traversal?

An in-order traversal will definitely not work. After all, consider a scenario in which we were using binary search trees. A binary search tree's in-order traversal always prints out the values in sorted order. Therefore, two binary search trees with the same values will always have the same in-order traversals, even if their structure is different.

What about a pre-order traversal? This is a bit more promising. At least in this case we know certain things, like the first element in the pre-order traversal is the root node. The left and right elements will follow.

Unfortunately, trees with different structures could still have the same pre-order traversal.

There's a simple fix though. We can store NULL nodes in the pre-order traversal string as a special character, like an 'X'. (We'll assume that the binary trees contain only integers.) The left tree would have the traversal `{3, 4, X}` and the right tree will have the traversal `{3, X, 4}`.

Observe that, as long as we represent the NULL nodes, the pre-order traversal of a tree is unique. That is, if two trees have the same pre-order traversal, then we know they are identical trees in values and structure.

To see this, consider reconstructing a tree from its pre-order traversal (with NULL nodes indicated). For example: 1, 2, 4, X, X, X, 3, X, X.

The root is 1, and its left node, 2, follows it. 2.left must be 4. 4 must have two NULL nodes (since it is followed by two Xs). 4 is complete, so we move back up to its parent, 2. 2.right is another X (NULL). 1's left subtree is now complete, so we move to 1's right child. We place a 3 with two NULL children there. The tree is now complete.

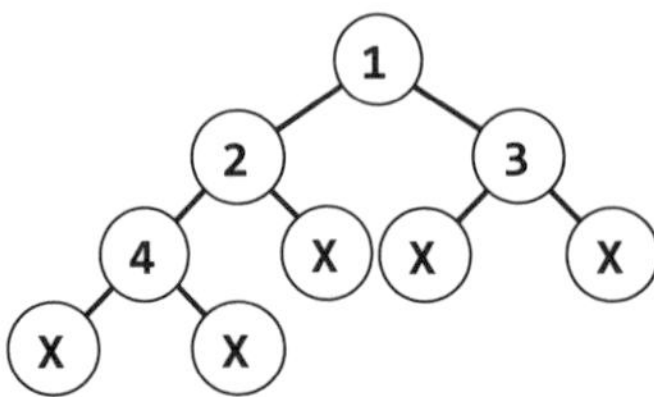

This whole process was deterministic, as it will be on any other tree. A pre-order traversal always starts at the root and, from there, the path we take is entirely defined by the traversal. Therefore, two trees are identical if they have the same pre-order traversal.

Now consider the subtree problem. If T2's pre-order traversal is a substring of T1's pre-order traversal, then T2's root element must be found in T1. If we do a pre-order traversal from this element in T1, we will follow an identical path to T2's traversal. Therefore, T2 is a subtree of T1.

Implementing this is quite straightforward. We just need to construct and compare the pre-order traversals.

```
boolean containsTree(TreeNode t1, TreeNode t2) {
   StringBuilder string1 = new StringBuilder();
   StringBuilder string2 = new StringBuilder();

   getOrderString(t1, string1);
   getOrderString(t2, string2);

   return string1.indexOf(string2.toString()) != -1;
}

void getOrderString(TreeNode node, StringBuilder sb) {
   if (node == null) {
      sb.append("X");             // Add null indicator
      return;
   }
   sb.append(node.data + " ");     // Add root
   getOrderString(node.left, sb);  // Add left
   getOrderString(node.right, sb); // Add right
}
```

This approach takes `O(n + m)` time and `O(n + m)` space, where `n` and `m` are the number of nodes in `T1` and `T2`, respectively. Given millions of nodes, we might want to reduce the space complexity.

The Alternative Approach

An alternative approach is to search through the larger tree, `T1`. Each time a node in `T1` matches the root of `T2`, call `matchTree`. The `matchTree` method will compare the two subtrees to see if they are identical.

Analyzing the runtime is somewhat complex. A naive answer would be to say that it is `O(nm)` time, where `n` is the number of nodes in `T1` and `m` is the number of nodes in `T2`. While this is technically correct, a little more thought can produce a tighter bound.

We do not actually call `matchTree` on every node in `T1`. Rather, we call it k times, where k is the number of occurrences of T2's root in `T1`. The runtime is closer to `O(n + km)`.

In fact, even that overstates the runtime. Even if the root were identical, we exit `matchTree` when we find a difference between `T1` and `T2`. We therefore probably do not actually look at `m` nodes on each call of `matchTree`.

The code below implements this algorithm.

```
boolean containsTree(TreeNode t1, TreeNode t2) {
  if (t2 == null) return true; // The empty tree is always a subtree
  return subTree(t1, t2);
}

boolean subTree(TreeNode r1, TreeNode r2) {
  if (r1 == null) {
    return false; // big tree empty & subtree still not found.
  } else if (r1.data == r2.data && matchTree(r1, r2)) {
    return true;
  }
  return subTree(r1.left, r2) || subTree(r1.right, r2);
}

boolean matchTree(TreeNode r1, TreeNode r2) {
  if (r1 == null && r2 == null) {
    return true; // nothing left in the subtree
  } else if (r1 == null || r2 == null) {
    return false; // exactly tree is empty, therefore trees don't match
  } else if (r1.data != r2.data) {
    return false;  // data doesn't match
  } else {
    return matchTree(r1.left, r2.left) && matchTree(r1.right, r2.right);
  }
}
```

When might the simple solution be better, and when might the alternative approach be better? This is a great conversation to have with your interviewer. Here are a few thoughts on that matter:

1. The simple solution takes `O(n + m)` memory. The alternative solution takes `O(log(n) + log(m))` memory. Remember: memory usage can be a very big deal when it comes to scalability.
2. The simple solution is `O(n + m)` time and the alternative solution has a worst case time of `O(nm)`. However, the worst case time can be deceiving; we need to look deeper than that.
3. A slightly tighter bound on the runtime, as explained earlier, is `O(n + km)`, where k is the number of occurrences of T2's root in `T1`. Let's suppose the node data for `T1` and `T2` were random numbers picked between 0 and p. The value of k would be approximately n/p. Why? Because each of n nodes in `T1` has a $1/p$ chance of equaling the root, so approximately n/p nodes in `T1` should equal `T2.root`. So, let's say `p = 1000`, `n = 1000000` and `m = 100`. We would do somewhere around 1,100,000 node checks ($1100000 = 1000000 + \frac{100*1000000}{1000}$).
4. More complex mathematics and assumptions could get us an even tighter bound. We assumed in #3 above that if we call `matchTree`, we would end up traversing all `m` nodes of T2. It's far more likely, though, that we will find a difference very early on in the tree and will then exit early.

In summary, the alternative approach is certainly more optimal in terms of space and is likely more optimal in terms of time as well. It all depends on what assumptions you make and whether you prioritize reducing the average case runtime at the expense of the worst case runtime. This is an excellent point to make to your interviewer.

4.11 Random Node: You are implementing a binary search tree class from scratch, which, in addition to `insert`, `find`, and `delete`, has a method `getRandomNode()` which returns a random node from the tree. All nodes should be equally likely to be chosen. Design and implement an algorithm for `getRandomNode`, and explain how you would implement the rest of the methods.

pg 111

SOLUTION

Let's draw an example.

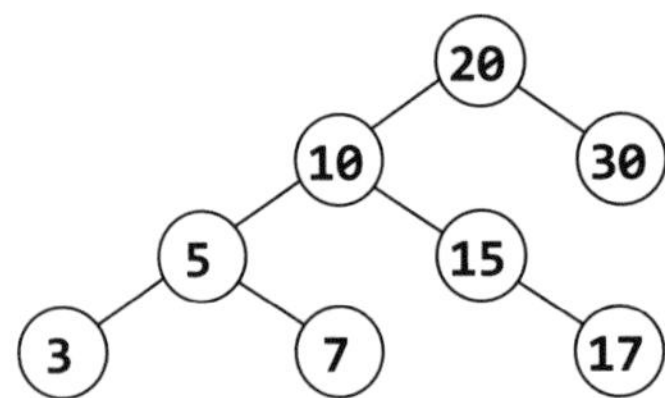

We're going to explore many solutions until we get to an optimal one that works.

One thing we should realize here is that the question was phrased in a very interesting way. The interviewer did not simply say, "Design an algorithm to return a random node from a binary tree." We were told that this is a class that we're building from scratch. There is a reason the question was phrased that way. We probably need access to some part of the internals of the data structure.

Option #1 [Slow & Working]

One solution is to copy all the nodes to an array and return a random element in the array. This solution will take `O(N)` time and `O(N)` space, where `N` is the number of nodes in the tree.

We can guess our interviewer is probably looking for something more optimal, since this is a little too straightforward (and should make us wonder why the interviewer gave us a binary tree, since we don't need that information).

We should keep in mind as we develop this solution that we probably need to know something about the internals of the tree. Otherwise, the question probably wouldn't specify that we're developing the tree class from scratch.

Option #2 [Slow & Working]

Returning to our original solution of copying the nodes to an array, we can explore a solution where we maintain an array at all times that lists all the nodes in the tree. The problem is that we'll need to remove nodes from this array as we delete them from the tree, and that will take `O(N)` time.

Option #3 [Slow & Working]

We could label all the nodes with an index from 1 to `N` and label them in binary search tree order (that is, according to its inorder traversal). Then, when we call `getRandomNode`, we generate a random index between 1 and `N`. If we apply the label correctly, we can use a binary search tree search to find this index.

However, this leads to a similar issue as earlier solutions. When we insert a node or a delete a node, all of the indices might need to be updated. This can take `O(N)` time.

Option #4 [Fast & Not Working]

What if we knew the depth of the tree? (Since we're building our own class, we can ensure that we know this. It's an easy enough piece of data to track.)

We could pick a random depth, and then traverse left/right randomly until we go to that depth. This wouldn't actually ensure that all nodes are equally likely to be chosen though.

First, the tree doesn't necessarily have an equal number of nodes at each level. This means that nodes on levels with fewer nodes might be more likely to be chosen than nodes on a level with more nodes.

Second, the random path we take might end up terminating before we get to the desired level. Then what? We could just return the last node we find, but that would mean unequal probabilities at each node.

Option #5 [Fast & Not Working]

We could try just a simple approach: traverse randomly down the tree. At each node:

- With $1/3$ odds, we return the current node.
- With $1/3$ odds, we traverse left.
- With $1/3$ odds, we traverse right.

This solution, like some of the others, does not distribute the probabilities evenly across the nodes. The root has a $1/3$ probability of being selected—the same as all the nodes in the left put together.

Option #6 [Fast & Working]

Rather than just continuing to brainstorm new solutions, let's see if we can fix some of the issues in the previous solutions. To do so, we must diagnose—deeply—the root problem in a solution.

Let's look at Option #5. It fails because the probabilities aren't evenly distributed across the options. Can we fix that while keeping the basic algorithm the same?

We can start with the root. With what probability should we return the root? Since we have N nodes, we must return the root node with $1/N$ probability. (In fact, we must return each node with $1/N$ probability. After all, we have N nodes and each must have equal probability. The total must be 1 (100%), therefore each must have $1/N$ probability.)

We've resolved the issue with the root. Now what about the rest of the problem? With what probability should we traverse left versus right? It's not 50/50. Even in a balanced tree, the number of nodes on each side might not be equal. If we have more nodes on the left than the right, then we need to go left more often.

One way to think about it is that the odds of picking something—anything—from the left must be the sum of each individual probability. Since each node must have probability $1/N$, the odds of picking something from the left must have probability `LEFT_SIZE *` $1/N$. This should therefore be the odds of going left.

Likewise, the odds of going right should be `RIGHT_SIZE *` $1/N$.

This means that each node must know the size of the nodes on the left and the size of the nodes on the right. Fortunately, our interviewer has told us that we're building this tree class from scratch. It's easy to keep track of this size information on inserts and deletes. We can just store a `size` variable in each node. Increment `size` on inserts and decrement it on deletes.

```
class TreeNode {
  private int data;
  public TreeNode left;
  public TreeNode right;
  private int size = 0;

  public TreeNode(int d) {
    data = d;
    size = 1;
  }

  public TreeNode getRandomNode() {
    int leftSize = left == null ? 0 : left.size();
    Random random = new Random();
    int index = random.nextInt(size);
    if (index < leftSize) {
      return left.getRandomNode();
    } else if (index == leftSize) {
      return this;
    } else {
      return right.getRandomNode();
    }
  }

  public void insertInOrder(int d) {
    if (d <= data) {
      if (left == null) {
        left = new TreeNode(d);
      } else {
        left.insertInOrder(d);
      }
    } else {
      if (right == null) {
        right = new TreeNode(d);
      } else {
        right.insertInOrder(d);
      }
    }
    size++;
  }

  public int size() { return size; }
  public int data() { return data; }

  public TreeNode find(int d) {
    if (d == data) {
      return this;
    } else if (d <= data) {
      return left != null ? left.find(d) : null;
    } else if (d > data) {
      return right != null ? right.find(d) : null;
    }
    return null;
  }
}
```

In a balanced tree, this algorithm will be `O(log N)`, where N is the number of nodes.

Option #7 [Fast & Working]

Random number calls can be expensive. If we'd like, we can reduce the number of random number calls substantially.

Imagine we called `getRandomNode` on the tree below, and then traversed left.

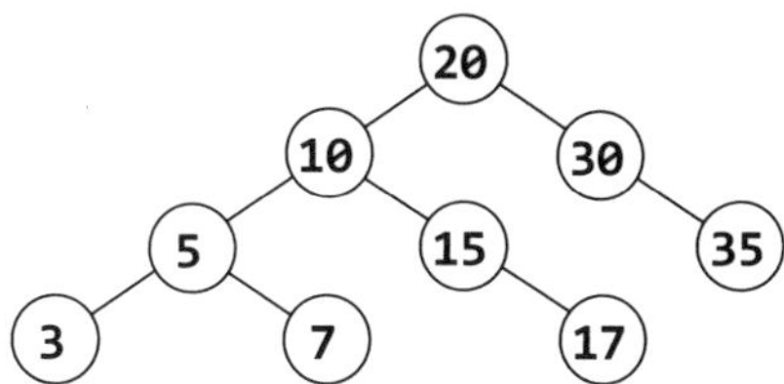

We traversed left because we picked a number between 0 and 5 (inclusive). When we traverse left, we again pick a random number between 0 and 5. Why re-pick? The first number will work just fine.

But what if we went right instead? We have a number between 7 and 8 (inclusive) but we would need a number between 0 and 1 (inclusive). That's easy to fix: just subtract out `LEFT_SIZE + 1`.

Another way to think about what we're doing is that the initial random number call indicates which node (`i`) to return, and then we're locating the `i`th node in an in-order traversal. Subtracting `LEFT_SIZE + 1` from `i` reflects that, when we go right, we skip over `LEFT_SIZE + 1` nodes in the in-order traversal.

```
class Tree {
  TreeNode root = null;

  public int size() { return root == null ? 0 : root.size(); }

  public TreeNode getRandomNode() {
    if (root == null) return null;

    Random random = new Random();
    int i = random.nextInt(size());
    return root.getIthNode(i);
  }

  public void insertInOrder(int value) {
    if (root == null) {
      root = new TreeNode(value);
    } else {
      root.insertInOrder(value);
    }
  }
}

class TreeNode {
  /* constructor and variables are the same. */

  public TreeNode getIthNode(int i) {
    int leftSize = left == null ? 0 : left.size();
    if (i < leftSize) {
      return left.getIthNode(i);
    } else if (i == leftSize) {
      return this;
    } else {
```

```
            /* Skipping over leftSize + 1 nodes, so subtract them. */
            return right.getIthNode(i - (leftSize + 1));
        }
    }

    public void insertInOrder(int d) { /* same */ }
    public int size() { return size; }
    public TreeNode find(int d) { /* same */ }
}
```

Like the previous algorithm, this algorithm takes `O(log N)` time in a balanced tree. We can also describe the runtime as `O(D)`, where D is the max depth of the tree. Note that `O(D)` is an accurate description of the runtime whether the tree is balanced or not.

4.12 Paths with Sum: You are given a binary tree in which each node contains an integer value (which might be positive or negative). Design an algorithm to count the number of paths that sum to a given value. The path does not need to start or end at the root or a leaf, but it must go downwards (traveling only from parent nodes to child nodes).

pg 111

SOLUTION

Let's pick a potential sum—say, 8—and then draw a binary tree based on this. This tree intentionally has a number of paths with this sum.

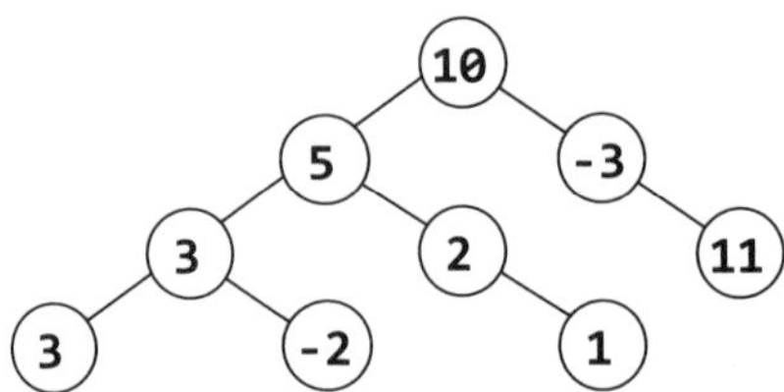

One option is the brute force approach.

Solution #1: Brute Force

In the brute force approach, we just look at all possible paths. To do this, we traverse to each node. At each node, we recursively try all paths downwards, tracking the sum as we go. As soon as we hit our target sum, we increment the total.

```
int countPathsWithSum(TreeNode root, int targetSum) {
    if (root == null) return 0;

    /* Count paths with sum starting from the root. */
    int pathsFromRoot = countPathsWithSumFromNode(root, targetSum, 0);

    /* Try the nodes on the left and right. */
    int pathsOnLeft = countPathsWithSum(root.left, targetSum);
    int pathsOnRight = countPathsWithSum(root.right, targetSum);

    return pathsFromRoot + pathsOnLeft + pathsOnRight;
}

/* Returns the number of paths with this sum starting from this node. */
```

```
int countPathsWithSumFromNode(TreeNode node, int targetSum, int currentSum) {
  if (node == null) return 0;

  currentSum += node.data;

  int totalPaths = 0;
  if (currentSum == targetSum) { // Found a path from the root
    totalPaths++;
  }

  totalPaths += countPathsWithSumFromNode(node.left, targetSum, currentSum);
  totalPaths += countPathsWithSumFromNode(node.right, targetSum, currentSum);
  return totalPaths;
}
```

What is the time complexity of this algorithm?

Consider that node at depth d will be "touched" (via `countPathsWithSumFromNode`) by d nodes above it.

In a balanced binary tree, d will be no more than approximately `log N`. Therefore, we know that with N nodes in the tree, `countPathsWithSumFromNode` will be called `O(N log N)` times. The runtime is O(N log N).

We can also approach this from the other direction. At the root node, we traverse to all `N - 1` nodes beneath it (via `countPathsWithSumFromNode`). At the second level (where there are two nodes), we traverse to `N - 3` nodes. At the third level (where there are four nodes, plus three above those), we traverse to `N - 7` nodes. Following this pattern, the total work is roughly:

```
(N - 1) + (N - 3) + (N - 7) + (N - 15) + (N - 31) + ... + (N - N)
```

To simplify this, notice that the left side of each term is always N and the right side is one less than a power of two. The number of terms is the depth of the tree, which is `O(log N)`. For the right side, we can ignore the fact that it's one less than a power of two. Therefore, we really have this:

```
O(N * [number of terms] - [sum of powers of two from 1 through N])
O(N log N - N)
O(N log N)
```

If the value of the sum of powers of two from 1 through N isn't obvious to you, think about what the powers of two look like in binary:

```
  0001
+ 0010
+ 0100
+ 1000
= 1111
```

Therefore, the runtime is `O(N log N)` in a balanced tree.

In an unbalanced tree, the runtime could be much worse. Consider a tree that is just a straight line down. At the root, we traverse to `N - 1` nodes. At the next level (with just a single node), we traverse to `N - 2` nodes. At the third level, we traverse to `N - 3` nodes, and so on. This leads us to the sum of numbers between 1 and N, which is $O(N^2)$.

Solution #2: Optimized

In analyzing the last solution, we may realize that we repeat some work. For a path such as `10 -> 5 -> 3 -> -2`, we traverse this path (or parts of it) repeatedly. We do it when we start with node 10, then when we go to node 5 (looking at 5, then 3, then -2), then when we go to node 3, and then finally when we go to node -2. Ideally, we'd like to reuse this work.

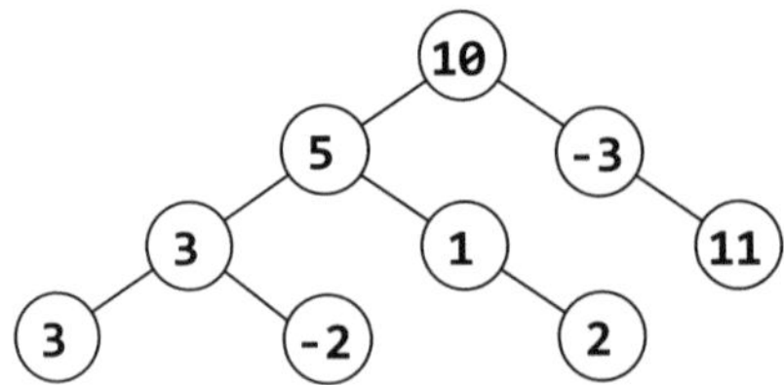

Let's isolate a given path and treat it as just an array. Consider a (hypothetical, extended) path like:

```
10 -> 5 -> 1 -> 2 -> -1 -> -1 -> 7 -> 1 -> 2
```

What we're really saying then is: How many contiguous subsequences in this array sum to a target sum such as 8? In other words, for each y, we're trying to find the x values below. (Or, more accurately, the number of x values below.)

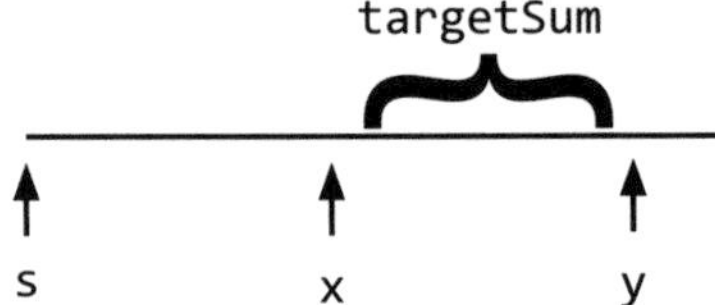

If each value knows its running sum (the sum of values from s through itself), then we can find this pretty easily. We just need to leverage this simple equation: $\texttt{runningSum}_x = \texttt{runningSum}_y - \texttt{targetSum}$. We then look for the values of x where this is true.

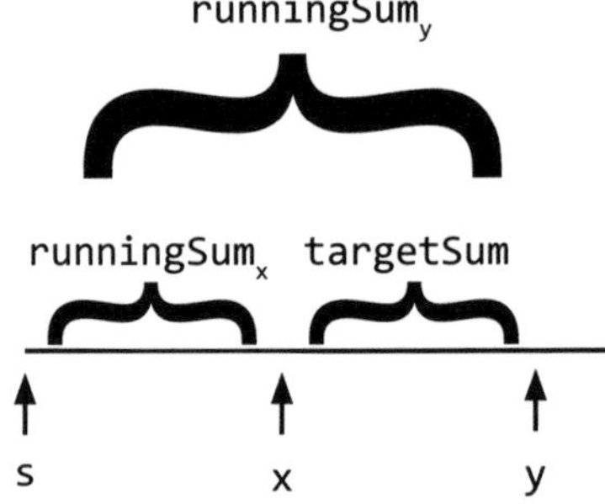

Since we're just looking for the number of paths, we can use a hash table. As we iterate through the array, build a hash table that maps from a runningSum to the number of times we've seen that sum. Then, for each y, look up $\texttt{runningSum}_y$ - targetSum in the hash table. The value in the hash table will tell you the number of paths with sum targetSum that end at y.

For example:

```
index:  0    1    2    3     4     5    6    7    8
value:  10 -> 5 -> 1 -> 2 -> -1 -> -1 -> 7 -> 1 -> 2
sum:    10   15   16   18    17    16   23   24   26
```

The value of $\texttt{runningSum}_7$ is 24. If targetSum is 8, then we'd look up 16 in the hash table. This would have a value of 2 (originating from index 2 and index 5). As we can see above, indexes 3 through 7 and indexes 6 through 7 have sums of 8.

Now that we've settled the algorithm for an array, let's review this on a tree. We take a similar approach.

We traverse through the tree using depth-first search. As we visit each node:

1. Track its `runningSum`. We'll take this in as a parameter and immediately increment it by `node.value`.
2. Look up `runningSum - targetSum` in the hash table. The value there indicates the total number. Set `totalPaths` to this value.
3. If `runningSum == targetSum`, then there's one additional path that starts at the root. Increment `totalPaths`.
4. Add `runningSum` to the hash table (incrementing the value if it's already there).
5. Recurse left and right, counting the number of paths with sum `targetSum`.
6. After we're done recursing left and right, decrement the value of `runningSum` in the hash table. This is essentially backing out of our work; it reverses the changes to the hash table so that other nodes don't use it (since we're now done with `node`).

Despite the complexity of deriving this algorithm, the code to implement this is relatively simple.

```
int countPathsWithSum(TreeNode root, int targetSum) {
  return countPathsWithSum(root, targetSum, 0, new HashMap<Integer, Integer>());
}

int countPathsWithSum(TreeNode node, int targetSum, int runningSum,
                      HashMap<Integer, Integer> pathCount) {
  if (node == null) return 0; // Base case

  /* Count paths with sum ending at the current node. */
  runningSum += node.data;
  int sum = runningSum - targetSum;
  int totalPaths = pathCount.getOrDefault(sum, 0);

  /* If runningSum equals targetSum, then one additional path starts at root.
   * Add in this path.*/
  if (runningSum == targetSum) {
    totalPaths++;
  }

  /* Increment pathCount, recurse, then decrement pathCount. */
  incrementHashTable(pathCount, runningSum, 1); // Increment pathCount
  totalPaths += countPathsWithSum(node.left, targetSum, runningSum, pathCount);
  totalPaths += countPathsWithSum(node.right, targetSum, runningSum, pathCount);
  incrementHashTable(pathCount, runningSum, -1); // Decrement pathCount

  return totalPaths;
}

void incrementHashTable(HashMap<Integer, Integer> hashTable, int key, int delta) {
  int newCount = hashTable.getOrDefault(key, 0) + delta;
  if (newCount == 0) { // Remove when zero to reduce space usage
    hashTable.remove(key);
  } else {
    hashTable.put(key, newCount);
  }
}
```

The runtime for this algorithm is `O(N)`, where `N` is the number of nodes in the tree. We know it is `O(N)` because we travel to each node just once, doing `O(1)` work each time. In a balanced tree, the space complexity is `O(log N)` due to the hash table. The space complexity can grow to `O(n)` in an unbalanced tree.

5

Solutions to Bit Manipulation

5.1 **Insertion:** You are given two 32-bit numbers, N and M, and two bit positions, `i` and `j`. Write a method to insert M into N such that M starts at bit `j` and ends at bit `i`. You can assume that the bits `j` through `i` have enough space to fit all of M. That is, if M = `10011`, you can assume that there are at least 5 bits between `j` and `i`. You would not, for example, have `j` = 3 and `i` = 2, because M could not fully fit between bit 3 and bit 2.

EXAMPLE

Input: `N = 10000000000, M = 10011, i = 2, j = 6`

Output: `N = 10001001100`

pg 115

SOLUTION

This problem can be approached in three key steps:

1. Clear the bits `j` through `i` in N
2. Shift M so that it lines up with bits `j` through `i`
3. Merge M and N.

The trickiest part is Step 1. How do we clear the bits in N? We can do this with a mask. This mask will have all 1s, except for 0s in the bits `j` through `i`. We create this mask by creating the left half of the mask first, and then the right half.

```
int updateBits(int n, int m, int i, int j) {
  /* Create a mask to clear bits i through j in n. EXAMPLE: i = 2, j = 4. Result
   * should be 11100011. For simplicity, we'll use just 8 bits for the example. */
  int allOnes = ~0; // will equal sequence of all 1s

  // 1s before position j, then 0s. left = 11100000
  int left = allOnes << (j + 1);

  // 1's after position i. right = 00000011
  int right = ((1 << i) - 1);

  // All 1s, except for 0s between i and j. mask = 11100011
  int mask = left | right;

  /* Clear bits j through i then put m in there */
  int n_cleared = n & mask; // Clear bits j through i.
  int m_shifted = m << i; // Move m into correct position.
```

```
    return n_cleared | m_shifted; // OR them, and we're done!
}
```

In a problem like this (and many bit manipulation problems), you should make sure to thoroughly test your code. It's extremely easy to wind up with off-by-one errors.

5.2 **Binary to String:** Given a real number between 0 and 1 (e.g., 0.72) that is passed in as a double, print the binary representation. If the number cannot be represented accurately in binary with at most 32 characters, print "ERROR."

pg 116

SOLUTION

NOTE: When otherwise ambiguous, we'll use the subscripts x_2 and x_{10} to indicate whether x is in base 2 or base 10.

First, let's start off by asking ourselves what a non-integer number in binary looks like. By analogy to a decimal number, the binary number 0.101_2 would look like:

$$0.101_2 = 1 * \frac{1}{2^1} + 0 * \frac{1}{2^2} + 1 * \frac{1}{2^3}.$$

To print the decimal part, we can multiply by 2 and check if 2n is greater than or equal to 1. This is essentially "shifting" the fractional sum. That is:

$$\begin{aligned} r &= 2_{10} * n \\ &= 2_{10} * 0.101_2 \\ &= 1 * \frac{1}{2^0} + 0 * \frac{1}{2^1} + 1 * \frac{1}{2^2} \\ &= 1.01_2 \end{aligned}$$

If `r >= 1`, then we know that n had a 1 right after the decimal point. By doing this continuously, we can check every digit.

```
String printBinary(double num) {
   if (num >= 1 || num <= 0) {
      return "ERROR";
   }

   StringBuilder binary = new StringBuilder();
   binary.append(".");
   while (num > 0) {
      /* Setting a limit on length: 32 characters */
      if (binary.length() >= 32) {
         return "ERROR";
      }

      double r = num * 2;
      if (r >= 1) {
         binary.append(1);
         num = r - 1;
      } else {
         binary.append(0);
         num = r;
      }
   }
   return binary.toString();
}
```

Alternatively, rather than multiplying the number by two and comparing it to 1, we can compare the number to .5, then .25, and so on. The code below demonstrates this approach.

```
String printBinary2(double num) {
   if (num >= 1 || num <= 0) {
      return "ERROR";
   }

   StringBuilder binary = new StringBuilder();
   double frac = 0.5;
   binary.append(".");
   while (num > 0) {
      /* Setting a limit on length: 32 characters */
      if (binary.length() > 32) {
         return "ERROR";
      }
      if (num >= frac) {
         binary.append(1);
         num -= frac;
      } else {
         binary.append(0);
      }
      frac /= 2;
   }
   return binary.toString();
}
```

Both approaches are equally good; choose the one you feel most comfortable with.

Either way, you should make sure to prepare thorough test cases for this problem—and to actually run through them in your interview.

5.3 Flip Bit to Win: You have an integer and you can flip exactly one bit from a 0 to a 1. Write code to find the length of the longest sequence of 1s you could create.

EXAMPLE

Input: 1775 (or: 11011101111)

Output: 8

pg 116

SOLUTION

We can think about each integer as being an alternating sequence of 0s and 1s. Whenever a 0s sequence has length one, we can potentially merge the adjacent 1s sequences.

Brute Force

One approach is to convert an integer into an array that reflects the lengths of the 0s and 1s sequences. For example, 11011101111 would be (reading from right to left) $[0_0, 4_1, 1_0, 3_1, 1_0, 2_1, 21_0]$. The subscript reflects whether the integer corresponds to a 0s sequence or a 1s sequence, but the actual solution doesn't need this. It's a strictly alternating sequence, always starting with the 0s sequence.

Once we have this, we just walk through the array. At each 0s sequence, then we consider merging the adjacent 1s sequences if the 0s sequence has length 1.

```
int longestSequence(int n) {
```

```
    if (n == -1) return Integer.BYTES * 8;
    ArrayList<Integer> sequences = getAlternatingSequences(n);
    return findLongestSequence(sequences);
}

/* Return a list of the sizes of the sequences. The sequence starts off with the
     number of 0s (which might be 0) and then alternates with the counts of each
     value.*/
ArrayList<Integer> getAlternatingSequences(int n) {
    ArrayList<Integer> sequences = new ArrayList<Integer>();

    int searchingFor = 0;
    int counter = 0;

    for (int i = 0; i < Integer.BYTES * 8; i++) {
        if ((n & 1) != searchingFor) {
            sequences.add(counter);
            searchingFor = n & 1; // Flip 1 to 0 or 0 to 1
            counter = 0;
        }
        counter++;
        n >>>= 1;
    }
    sequences.add(counter);

    return sequences;
}

/* Given the lengths of alternating sequences of 0s and 1s, find the longest one
 * we can build. */
int findLongestSequence(ArrayList<Integer> seq) {
    int maxSeq = 1;

    for (int i = 0; i < seq.size(); i += 2) {
        int zerosSeq = seq.get(i);
        int onesSeqRight = i - 1 >= 0 ? seq.get(i - 1) : 0;
        int onesSeqLeft = i + 1 < seq.size() ? seq.get(i + 1) : 0;

        int thisSeq = 0;
        if (zerosSeq == 1) { // Can merge
            thisSeq = onesSeqLeft + 1 + onesSeqRight;
        } if (zerosSeq > 1) { // Just add a zero to either side
            thisSeq = 1 + Math.max(onesSeqRight, onesSeqLeft);
        } else if (zerosSeq == 0) { // No zero, but take either side
            thisSeq = Math.max(onesSeqRight, onesSeqLeft);
        }
        maxSeq = Math.max(thisSeq, maxSeq);
    }

    return maxSeq;
}
```

This is pretty good. It's O(b) time and O(b) memory, where b is the length of the sequence.

> Be careful with how you express the runtime. For example, if you say the runtime is O(n), what is n? It is not correct to say that this algorithm is O(value of the integer). This algorithm is O(number of bits). For this reason, when you have potential ambiguity in what n might mean, it's best just to not use n. Then neither you nor your interviewer will be confused. Pick a different variable name. We used "b", for the number of bits. Something logical works well.

Can we do better? Recall the concept of Best Conceivable Runtime. The B.C.R. for this algorithm is O(b) (since we'll always have to read through the sequence), so we know we can't optimize the time. We can, however, reduce the memory usage.

Optimal Algorithm

To reduce the space usage, note that we don't need to hang on to the length of each sequence the entire time. We only need it long enough to compare each 1s sequence to the immediately preceding 1s sequence.

Therefore, we can just walk through the integer doing this, tracking the current 1s sequence length and the previous 1s sequence length. When we see a zero, update `previousLength`:

- If the next bit is a 1, `previousLength` should be set to `currentLength`.
- If the next bit is a 0, then we can't merge these sequences together. So, set `previousLength` to 0.

Update `maxLength` as we go.

```
int flipBit(int a) {
   /* If all 1s, this is already the longest sequence. */
   if (~a == 0) return Integer.BYTES * 8;

   int currentLength = 0;
   int previousLength = 0;
   int maxLength = 1; // We can always have a sequence of at least one 1
   while (a != 0) {
      if ((a & 1) == 1) { // Current bit is a 1
         currentLength++;
      } else if ((a & 1) == 0) { // Current bit is a 0
         /* Update to 0 (if next bit is 0) or currentLength (if next bit is 1). */
         previousLength = (a & 2) == 0 ? 0 : currentLength;
         currentLength = 0;
      }
      maxLength = Math.max(previousLength + currentLength + 1, maxLength);
      a >>>= 1;
   }
   return maxLength;
}
```

The runtime of this algorithm is still O(b), but we use only O(1) additional memory.

5.4 Next Number: Given a positive integer, print the next smallest and the next largest number that have the same number of 1 bits in their binary representation.

pg 116

SOLUTION

There are a number of ways to approach this problem, including using brute force, using bit manipulation, and using clever arithmetic. Note that the arithmetic approach builds on the bit manipulation approach. You'll want to understand the bit manipulation approach before going on to the arithmetic one.

> The terminology can be confusing for this problem. We'll call `getNext` the bigger number and `getPrev` the smaller number.

The Brute Force Approach

An easy approach is simply brute force: count the number of 1s in n, and then increment (or decrement) until you find a number with the same number of 1s. Easy—but not terribly interesting. Can we do something a bit more optimal? Yes!

Let's start with the code for `getNext`, and then move on to `getPrev`.

Bit Manipulation Approach for Get Next Number

If we think about what the next number *should* be, we can observe the following. Given the number 13948, the binary representation looks like:

1	1	0	1	1	0	0	1	1	1	1	1	0	0
13	12	11	10	9	8	7	6	5	4	3	2	1	0

We want to make this number bigger (but not *too* big). We also need to keep the same number of ones.

Observation: Given a number n and two bit locations `i` and `j`, suppose we flip bit `i` from a `1` to a `0`, and bit `j` from a `0` to a `1`. If `i > j`, then n will have decreased. If `i < j`, then n will have increased.

We know the following:

1. If we flip a zero to a one, we must flip a one to a zero.
2. When we do that, the number will be bigger if and only if the zero-to-one bit was to the left of the one-to-zero bit.
3. We want to make the number bigger, but not unnecessarily bigger. Therefore, we need to flip the rightmost zero which has ones on the right of it.

To put this in a different way, we are flipping the rightmost non-trailing zero. That is, using the above example, the trailing zeros are in the `0`th and `1`st spot. The rightmost non-trailing zero is at bit 7. Let's call this position p.

Step 1: Flip rightmost non-trailing zero

1	1	0	1	1	0	1	1	1	1	1	1	0	0
13	12	11	10	9	8	7	6	5	4	3	2	1	0

With this change, we have increased the size of n. But, we also have one too many ones, and one too few zeros. We'll need to shrink the size of our number as much as possible while keeping that in mind.

We can shrink the number by rearranging all the bits to the right of bit p such that the `0`s are on the left and the `1`s are on the right. As we do this, we want to replace one of the 1s with a `0`.

A relatively easy way of doing this is to count how many ones are to the right of p, clear all the bits from 0 until p, and then add back in `c1-1` ones. Let `c1` be the number of ones to the right of p and `c0` be the number of zeros to the right of p.

Let's walk through this with an example.

Step 2: Clear bits to the right of p. From before, `c0 = 2`. `c1 = 5`. `p = 7`.

1	1	0	1	1	0	1	0	0	0	0	0	0	0
13	12	11	10	9	8	7	6	5	4	3	2	1	0

To clear these bits, we need to create a mask that is a sequence of ones, followed by p zeros. We can do this as follows:

```
a = 1 << p; // all zeros except for a 1 at position p.
b = a - 1;    // all zeros, followed by p ones.
mask = ~b;    // all ones, followed by p zeros.
n = n & mask; // clears rightmost p bits.
```

Or, more concisely, we do:

```
n &= ~((1 << p) - 1).
```

Step 3: Add in `c1 - 1` *ones.*

1	1	0	1	1	0	1	0	0	0	1	1	1	1
13	12	11	10	9	8	7	6	5	4	3	2	1	0

To insert `c1 - 1` ones on the right, we do the following:

```
a = 1 << (c1 - 1); // 0s with a 1 at position c1 - 1
b = a - 1;         // 0s with 1s at positions 0 through c1 - 1
n = n | b;         // inserts 1s at positions 0 through c1 - 1
```

Or, more concisely:

```
n |= (1 << (c1 - 1)) - 1;
```

We have now arrived at the smallest number bigger than n with the same number of ones.

The code for `getNext` is below.

```
int getNext(int n) {
   /* Compute c0 and c1 */
   int c = n;
   int c0 = 0;
   int c1 = 0;
   while (((c & 1) == 0) && (c != 0)) {
      c0++;
      c >>= 1;
   }

   while ((c & 1) == 1) {
      c1++;
      c >>= 1;
   }

   /* Error: if n == 11..1100...00, then there is no bigger number with the same
    * number of 1s. */
   if (c0 + c1 == 31 || c0 + c1 == 0) {
      return -1;
   }

   int p = c0 + c1; // position of rightmost non-trailing zero

   n |= (1 << p); // Flip rightmost non-trailing zero
   n &= ~((1 << p) - 1); // Clear all bits to the right of p
   n |= (1 << (c1 - 1)) - 1; // Insert (c1-1) ones on the right.
```

```
  return n;
}
```

Bit Manipulation Approach for Get Previous Number

To implement `getPrev`, we follow a very similar approach.

1. Compute `c0` and `c1`. Note that `c1` is the number of trailing ones, and `c0` is the size of the block of zeros immediately to the left of the trailing ones.
2. Flip the rightmost non-trailing one to a zero. This will be at position `p = c1 + c0`.
3. Clear all bits to the right of bit p.
4. Insert `c1 + 1` ones immediately to the right of position p.

Note that Step 2 sets bit p to a zero and Step 3 sets bits `0` through `p-1` to a zero. We can merge these steps.

Let's walk through this with an example.

Step 1: Initial Number. `p = 7. c1 = 2. c0 = 5.`

1	0	0	1	1	1	1	0	0	0	0	0	1	1
13	12	11	10	9	8	7	6	5	4	3	2	1	0

Steps 2 & 3: Clear bits `0` through p.

1	0	0	1	1	1	0	0	0	0	0	0	0	0
13	12	11	10	9	8	7	6	5	4	3	2	1	0

We can do this as follows:

```
int a = ~0;              // Sequence of 1s
int b = a << (p + 1);    // Sequence of 1s followed by p + 1 zeros.
n &= b;                  // Clears bits 0 through p.
```

Steps 4: Insert `c1 + 1` *ones immediately to the right of position* p.

1	0	0	1	1	1	0	1	1	1	0	0	0	0
13	12	11	10	9	8	7	6	5	4	3	2	1	0

Note that since `p = c1 + c0`, the `(c1 + 1)` ones will be followed by `(c0 - 1)` zeros.

We can do this as follows:

```
int a = 1 << (c1 + 1); // 0s with 1 at position (c1 + 1)
int b = a - 1;         // 0s followed by c1 + 1 ones
int c = b << (c0 - 1); // c1+1 ones followed by c0-1 zeros.
n |= c;
```

The code to implement this is below.

```
int getPrev(int n) {
  int temp = n;
  int c0 = 0;
  int c1 = 0;
  while (temp & 1 == 1) {
    c1++;
    temp >>= 1;
  }

```

```
    if (temp == 0) return -1;

    while (((temp & 1) == 0) && (temp != 0)) {
       c0++;
       temp >>= 1;
    }

    int p = c0 + c1; // position of rightmost non-trailing one
    n &= ((~0) << (p + 1)); // clears from bit p onwards

    int mask = (1 << (c1 + 1)) - 1; // Sequence of (c1+1) ones
    n |= mask << (c0 - 1);

    return n;
}
```

Arithmetic Approach to Get Next Number

If `c0` is the number of trailing zeros, `c1` is the size of the one block immediately following, and `p = c0 + c1`, we can word our solution from earlier as follows:

1. Set the pth bit to 1.
2. Set all bits following p to `0`.
3. Set bits `0` through `c1 - 2` to 1. This will be `c1 - 1` total bits.

A quick and dirty way to perform steps 1 and 2 is to set the trailing zeros to 1 (giving us p trailing ones), and then add 1. Adding one will flip all trailing ones, so we wind up with a 1 at bit p followed by p zeros. We can perform this arithmetically.

```
n += 2^c0 - 1;   // Sets trailing 0s to 1, giving us p trailing 1s
n += 1;          // Flips first p 1s to 0s, and puts a 1 at bit p.
```

Now, to perform Step 3 arithmetically, we just do:

```
n += 2^(c1 - 1) - 1; // Sets trailing c1 - 1 zeros to ones.
```

This math reduces to:

$$
\begin{aligned}
next &= n + (2^{c0} - 1) + 1 + (2^{c1-1} - 1) \\
&= n + 2^{c0} + 2^{c1-1} - 1
\end{aligned}
$$

The best part is that, using a little bit manipulation, it's simple to code.

```
int getNextArith(int n) {
   /* ... same calculation for c0 and c1 as before ... */
   return n + (1 << c0) + (1 << (c1 - 1)) - 1;
}
```

Arithmetic Approach to Get Previous Number

If c_1 is the number of trailing ones, c_0 is the size of the zero block immediately following, and $p = c_0 + c_1$, we can word the initial `getPrev` solution as follows:

1. Set the pth bit to `0`
2. Set all bits following p to 1
3. Set bits 0 through $c_0 - 1$ to `0`.

We can implement this arithmetically as follows. For clarity in the example, we will assume n = `10000011`. This makes $c_1 = 2$ and $c_0 = 5$.

```
n -= 2^c1 - 1;        // Removes trailing 1s. n is now 10000000.
n -= 1;               // Flips trailing 0s. n is now 01111111.
n -= 2^(c0 - 1) - 1;  // Flips last (c0-1) 0s. n is now 01110000.
```

This reduces mathematically to:

```
next    = n - (2^c1 - 1) - 1 - (2^(c0 - 1) - 1).
        = n - 2^c1 - 2^(c0 - 1) + 1
```

Again, this is very easy to implement.

```
int getPrevArith(int n) {
  /* ... same calculation for c0 and c1 as before ... */
  return n - (1 << c1) - (1 << (c0 - 1)) + 1;
}
```

Whew! Don't worry, you wouldn't be expected to get all this in an interview—at least not without a lot of help from the interviewer.

5.5 **Debugger:** Explain what the following code does: ((n & (n-1)) == 0).

pg 116

SOLUTION

We can work backwards to solve this question.

What does it mean if A & B == 0?

It means that A and B never have a 1 bit in the same place. So if `n & (n-1) == 0`, then n and `n-1` never share a 1.

What does n-1 look like (as compared with n)?

Try doing subtraction by hand (in base 2 or 10). What happens?

```
  1101011000 [base 2]           593100 [base 10]
-          1                  -      1
= 1101010111 [base 2]         = 593099 [base 10]
```

When you subtract 1 from a number, you look at the least significant bit. If it's a 1 you change it to 0, and you are done. If it's a zero, you must "borrow" from a larger bit. So, you go to increasingly larger bits, changing each bit from a 0 to a 1, until you find a 1. You flip that 1 to a 0 and you are done.

Thus, `n-1` will look like n, except that n's initial 0s will be 1s in `n-1`, and n's least significant 1 will be a 0 in `n-1`. That is:

```
if     n = abcde1000
then n-1 = abcde0111
```

So what does n & (n-1) == 0 indicate?

n and `n-1` must have no 1s in common. Given that they look like this:

```
if     n = abcde1000
then n-1 = abcde0111
```

`abcde` must be all `0`s, which means that n must look like this: `00001000`. The value n is therefore a power of two.

So, we have our answer: `((n & (n-1)) == 0)` checks if n is a power of 2 (or if n is 0).

5.6 **Conversion:** Write a function to determine the number of bits you would need to flip to convert integer A to integer B.

EXAMPLE

Input: `29 (or: 11101), 15 (or: 01111)`

Output: 2

pg 116

SOLUTION

This seemingly complex problem is actually rather straightforward. To approach this, ask yourself how you would figure out which bits in two numbers are different. Simple: with an XOR.

Each **1** in the XOR represents a bit that is different between A and B. Therefore, to check the number of bits that are different between A and B, we simply need to count the number of bits in A^B that are **1**.

```
int bitSwapRequired(int a, int b) {
   int count = 0;
   for (int c = a ^ b; c != 0; c = c >>> 1) {
      count += c & 1;
   }
   return count;
}
```

This code is good, but we can make it a bit better. Rather than simply shifting `c` repeatedly while checking the least significant bit, we can continuously flip the least significant bit and count how long it takes `c` to reach 0. The operation `c = c & (c - 1)` will clear the least significant bit in `c`.

The code below utilizes this approach.

```
int bitSwapRequired(int a, int b) {
   int count = 0;
   for (int c = a ^ b; c != 0; c = c & (c-1)) {
      count++;
   }
   return count;
}
```

The above code is one of those bit manipulation problems that comes up sometimes in interviews. Though it'd be hard to come up with it on the spot if you've never seen it before, it is useful to remember the trick for your interviews.

5.7 **Pairwise Swap:** Write a program to swap odd and even bits in an integer with as few instructions as possible (e.g., bit 0 and bit 1 are swapped, bit 2 and bit 3 are swapped, and so on).

pg 116

SOLUTION

Like many of the previous problems, it's useful to think about this problem in a different way. Operating on individual pairs of bits would be difficult, and probably not that efficient either. So how else can we think about this problem?

We can approach this as operating on the odds bits first, and then the even bits. Can we take a number n and move the odd bits over by 1? Sure. We can mask all odd bits with **10101010** in binary (which is **0xAA**), then shift them right by 1 to put them in the even spots. For the even bits, we do an equivalent operation. Finally, we merge these two values.

This takes a total of five instructions. The code below implements this approach.

```
int swapOddEvenBits(int x) {
  return ( ((x & 0xaaaaaaaa) >>> 1) | ((x & 0x55555555) << 1) );
}
```

Note that we use the logical right shift, instead of the arithmetic right shift. This is because we want the sign bit to be filled with a zero.

We've implemented the code above for 32-bit integers in Java. If you were working with 64-bit integers, you would need to change the mask. The logic, however, would remain the same.

5.8 Draw Line: A monochrome screen is stored as a single array of bytes, allowing eight consecutive pixels to be stored in one byte. The screen has width `w`, where `w` is divisible by 8 (that is, no byte will be split across rows). The height of the screen, of course, can be derived from the length of the array and the width. Implement a function that draws a horizontal line from (x1, y) to (x2, y).

The method signature should look something like:

`drawLine(byte[] screen, int width, int x1, int x2, int y)`

pg 116

SOLUTION

A naive solution to the problem is straightforward: iterate in a for loop from `x1` to `x2`, setting each pixel along the way. But that's hardly any fun, is it? (Nor is it very efficient.)

A better solution is to recognize that if `x1` and `x2` are far away from each other, several full bytes will be contained between them. These full bytes can be set one at a time by doing `screen[byte_pos] = 0xFF`. The residual start and end of the line can be set using masks.

```
void drawLine(byte[] screen, int width, int x1, int x2, int y) {
  int start_offset = x1 % 8;
  int first_full_byte = x1 / 8;
  if (start_offset != 0) {
    first_full_byte++;
  }

  int end_offset = x2 % 8;
  int last_full_byte = x2 / 8;
  if (end_offset != 7) {
    last_full_byte--;
  }

  // Set full bytes
  for (int b = first_full_byte; b <= last_full_byte; b++) {
    screen[(width / 8) * y + b] = (byte) 0xFF;
  }

  // Create masks for start and end of line
  byte start_mask = (byte) (0xFF >> start_offset);
  byte end_mask = (byte) ~(0xFF >> (end_offset + 1));

  // Set start and end of line
  if ((x1 / 8) == (x2 / 8)) { // x1 and x2 are in the same byte
```

```
      byte mask = (byte) (start_mask & end_mask);
      screen[(width / 8) * y + (x1 / 8)] |= mask;
   } else {
      if (start_offset != 0) {
         int byte_number = (width / 8) * y + first_full_byte - 1;
         screen[byte_number] |= start_mask;
      }
      if (end_offset != 7) {
         int byte_number = (width / 8) * y + last_full_byte + 1;
         screen[byte_number] |= end_mask;
      }
   }
}
```

Be careful on this problem; there are a lot of "gotchas" and special cases. For example, you need to consider the case where x1 and x2 are in the same byte. Only the most careful candidates can implement this code bug-free.

6

Solutions to Math and Logic Puzzles

6.1 The Heavy Pill: You have 20 bottles of pills. 19 bottles have 1.0 gram pills, but one has pills of weight 1.1 grams. Given a scale that provides an exact measurement, how would you find the heavy bottle? You can only use the scale once.

pg 122

SOLUTION

Sometimes, tricky constraints can be a clue. This is the case with the constraint that we can only use the scale once.

Because we can only use the scale once, we know something interesting: we must weigh multiple pills at the same time. In fact, we know we must weigh pills from at least 19 bottles at the same time. Otherwise, if we skipped two or more bottles entirely, how could we distinguish between those missed bottles? Remember that we only have *one* chance to use the scale.

So how can we weigh pills from more than one bottle and discover which bottle has the heavy pills? Let's suppose there were just two bottles, one of which had heavier pills. If we took one pill from each bottle, we would get a weight of 2.1 grams, but we wouldn't know which bottle contributed the extra 0.1 grams. We know we must treat the bottles differently somehow.

If we took one pill from Bottle #1 and two pills from Bottle #2, what would the scale show? It depends. If Bottle #1 were the heavy bottle, we would get 3.1 grams. If Bottle #2 were the heavy bottle, we would get 3.2 grams. And that is the trick to this problem.

We know the "expected" weight of a bunch of pills. The difference between the expected weight and the actual weight will indicate which bottle contributed the heavier pills, *provided* we select a different number of pills from each bottle.

We can generalize this to the full solution: take one pill from Bottle #1, two pills from Bottle #2, three pills from Bottle #3, and so on. Weigh this mix of pills. If all pills were one gram each, the scale would read 210 grams (`1 + 2 + ... + 20 = 20 * 21 / 2 = 210`). Any "overage" must come from the extra 0.1 gram pills.

This formula will tell you the bottle number:

$$\frac{\texttt{weight - 210 grams}}{\texttt{0.1 grams}}.$$

So, if the set of pills weighed 211.3 grams, then Bottle #13 would have the heavy pills.

6.2 **Basketball:** You have a basketball hoop and someone says that you can play one of two games.

Game 1: You get one shot to make the hoop.

Game 2: You get three shots and you have to make two of three shots.

If p is the probability of making a particular shot, for which values of p should you pick one game or the other?

pg 123

SOLUTION

To solve this problem, we can apply straightforward probability laws by comparing the probabilities of winning each game.

Probability of winning Game 1:

The probability of winning Game 1 is p, by definition.

Probability of winning Game 2:

Let `s(k,n)` be the probability of making exactly k shots out of n. The probability of winning Game 2 is the probability of making exactly two shots out of three OR making all three shots. In other words:

```
P(winning) = s(2,3) + s(3,3)
```

The probability of making all three shots is:

$$s(3,3) = p^3$$

The probability of making exactly two shots is:

```
P(making 1 and 2, and missing 3)
        + P(making 1 and 3, and missing 2)
        + P(missing 1, and making 2 and 3)
    = p * p * (1 - p) + p * (1 - p) * p + (1 - p) * p * p
```

$$= 3 (1 - p) p^2$$

Adding these together, we get:

$$= p^3 + 3 (1 - p) p^2$$
$$= p^3 + 3p^2 - 3p^3$$
$$= 3p^2 - 2p^3$$

Which game should you play?

You should play Game 1 if `P(Game 1) > P(Game 2)`:

$$p > 3p^2 - 2p^3.$$
$$1 > 3p - 2p^2$$
$$2p^2 - 3p + 1 > 0$$
$$(2p - 1)(p - 1) > 0$$

Both terms must be positive, or both must be negative. But we know $p < 1$, so $p - 1 < 0$. This means both terms must be negative.

$$2p - 1 < 0$$
$$2p < 1$$
$$p < .5$$

So, we should play Game 1 if $0 < p < .5$ and Game 2 if $.5 < p < 1$.

If $p = 0, 0.5$, or 1, then `P(Game 1) = P(Game 2)`, so it doesn't matter which game we play.

6.3 **Dominos:** There is an 8x8 chessboard in which two diagonally opposite corners have been cut off. You are given 31 dominos, and a single domino can cover exactly two squares. Can you use the 31 dominos to cover the entire board? Prove your answer (by providing an example or showing why it's impossible).

pg 123

SOLUTION

At first, it seems like this should be possible. It's an 8 x 8 board, which has 64 squares, but two have been cut off, so we're down to 62 squares. A set of 31 dominoes should be able to fit there, right?

When we try to lay down dominoes on row 1, which only has 7 squares, we may notice that one domino must stretch into the row 2. Then, when we try to lay down dominoes onto row 2, again we need to stretch a domino into row 3.

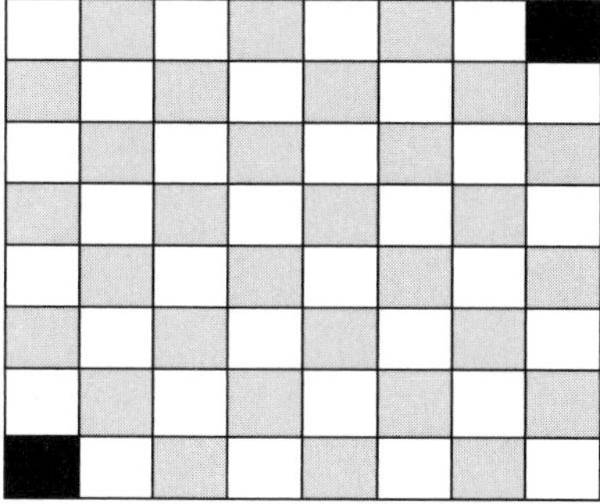

For each row we place, we'll always have one domino that needs to poke into the next row. No matter how many times and ways we try to solve this issue, we won't be able to successfully lay down all the dominoes.

There's a cleaner, more solid proof for why it won't work. The chessboard initially has 32 black and 32 white squares. By removing opposite corners (which must be the same color), we're left with 30 of one color and 32 of the other color. Let's say, for the sake of argument, that we have 30 black and 32 white squares.

Each domino we set on the board will always take up one white and one black square. Therefore, 31 dominos will take up 31 white squares and 31 black squares exactly. On this board, however, we must have 30 black squares and 32 white squares. Hence, it is impossible.

6.4 **Ants on a Triangle:** There are three ants on different vertices of a triangle. What is the probability of collision (between any two or all of them) if they start walking on the sides of the triangle? Assume that each ant randomly picks a direction, with either direction being equally likely to be chosen, and that they walk at the same speed.

Similarly, find the probability of collision with n ants on an n-vertex polygon.

pg 123

SOLUTION

The ants will collide if any of them are moving towards each other. So, the only way that they won't collide is if they are all moving in the same direction (clockwise or counterclockwise). We can compute this probability and work backwards from there.

Since each ant can move in two directions, and there are three ants, the probability is:

$$P(\text{clockwise}) = (1/2)^3$$
$$P(\text{counter clockwise}) = (1/2)^3$$
$$P(\text{same direction}) = (1/2)^3 + (1/2)^3 = 1/4$$

The probability of collision is therefore the probability of the ants *not* moving in the same direction:

$$P(\text{collision}) = 1 - P(\text{same direction}) = 1 - 1/4 = 3/4$$

To generalize this to an n-vertex polygon: there are still only two ways in which the ants can move to avoid a collision, but there are 2^n ways they can move in total. Therefore, in general, probability of collision is:

$$P(\text{clockwise}) = (1/2)^n$$
$$P(\text{counter}) = (1/2)^n$$
$$P(\text{same direction}) = 2(1/2)^n = (1/2)^{n-1}$$
$$P(\text{collision}) = 1 - P(\text{same direction}) = 1 - (1/2)^{n-1}$$

6.5 **Jugs of Water:** You have a five-quart jug, a three-quart jug, and an unlimited supply of water (but no measuring cups). How would you come up with exactly four quarts of water? Note that the jugs are oddly shaped, such that filling up exactly "half" of the jug would be impossible.

pg 123

SOLUTION

If we just play with the jugs, we'll find that we can pour water back and forth between them as follows:

5 Quart	3 Quart	Action
5	0	Filled 5-quart jug.
2	3	Filled 3-quart with 5-quart's contents.
2	0	Dumped 3-quart.
0	2	Fill 3-quart with 5-quart's contents.
5	2	Filled 5-quart.
4	3	Fill remainder of 3-quart with 5-quart.
4		Done! We have 4 quarts.

This question, like many puzzle questions, has a math/computer science root. If the two jug sizes are relatively prime, you can measure any value between one and the sum of the jug sizes.

6.6 Blue-Eyed Island: A bunch of people are living on an island, when a visitor comes with a strange order: all blue-eyed people must leave the island as soon as possible. There will be a flight out at 8:00pm every evening. Each person can see everyone else's eye color, but they do not know their own (nor is anyone allowed to tell them). Additionally, they do not know how many people have blue eyes, although they do know that at least one person does. How many days will it take the blue-eyed people to leave?

pg 123

SOLUTION

Let's apply the Base Case and Build approach. Assume that there are n people on the island and c of them have blue eyes. We are explicitly told that `c > 0`.

Case c = 1: Exactly one person has blue eyes.

Assuming all the people are intelligent, the blue-eyed person should look around and realize that no one else has blue eyes. Since he knows that at least one person has blue eyes, he must conclude that it is he who has blue eyes. Therefore, he would take the flight that evening.

Case c = 2: Exactly two people have blue eyes.

The two blue-eyed people see each other, but are unsure whether c is 1 or 2. They know, from the previous case, that if c = 1, the blue-eyed person would leave on the first night. Therefore, if the other blue-eyed person is still there, he must deduce that c = 2, which means that he himself has blue eyes. Both men would then leave on the second night.

Case c > 2: The General Case.

As we increase c, we can see that this logic continues to apply. If c = 3, then those three people will immediately know that there are either 2 or 3 people with blue eyes. If there were two people, then those two people would have left on the second night. So, when the others are still around after that night, each person would conclude that c = 3 and that they, therefore, have blue eyes too. They would leave that night.

This same pattern extends up through any value of c. Therefore, if c men have blue eyes, it will take c nights for the blue-eyed men to leave. All will leave on the same night.

6.7 The Apocalypse: In the new post-apocalyptic world, the world queen is desperately concerned about the birth rate. Therefore, she decrees that all families should ensure that they have one girl or else they face massive fines. If all families abide by this policy—that is, they have continue to have children until they have one girl, at which point they immediately stop—what will the gender ratio of the new generation be? (Assume that the odds of someone having a boy or a girl on any given pregnancy is equal.) Solve this out logically and then write a computer simulation of it.

pg 123

SOLUTION

If each family abides by this policy, then each family will have a sequence of zero or more boys followed by a single girl. That is, if "G" indicates a girl and "B" indicates a boy, the sequence of children will look like one of: G; BG; BBG; BBBG; BBBBG; and so on.

We can solve this problem multiple ways.

Mathematically

We can work out the probability for each gender sequence.

- P(G) = $1/2$. That is, 50% of families will have a girl first. The others will go on to have more children.
- P(BG) = $1/4$. Of those who have a second child (which is 50%), 50% of them will have a girl the next time.
- P(BBG) = $1/8$. Of those who have a third child (which is 25%), 50% of them will have a girl the next time.

And so on.

We know that every family has exactly one girl. How many boys does each family have, on average? To compute this, we can look at the expected value of the number of boys. The expected value of the number of boys is the probability of each sequence multiplied by the number of boys in that sequence.

Sequence	Number of Boys	Probability	Number of Boys * Probability
G	0	$1/2$	0
BG	1	$1/4$	$1/4$
BBG	2	$1/8$	$2/8$
BBBG	3	$1/16$	$3/16$
BBBBG	4	$1/32$	$4/32$
BBBBBG	5	$1/64$	$5/64$
BBBBBBG	6	$1/128$	$6/128$

Or in other words, this is the sum of `i` to infinity of i divided by 2^i.

$$\sum_{i=0}^{\infty} \frac{i}{2^{i+1}}$$

You probably won't know this off the top of your head, but we can try to estimate it. Let's try converting the above values to a common denominator of 128 (2^6).

$1/4 = 32/128$ $\quad$ $4/32 = 16/128$

$2/8 = 32/128$ $\quad$ $5/64 = 10/128$

$3/16 = 24/128$ $\quad$ $6/128 = 6/128$

$$\frac{32 + 32 + 24 + 16 + 10 + 6}{128} = \frac{120}{128}$$

This looks like it's going to inch closer to $128/128$ (which is of course 1). This "looks like" intuition is valuable, but it's not exactly a mathematical concept. It's a clue though and we can turn to logic here. Should it be 1?

Logically

If the earlier sum is 1, this would mean that the gender ratio is even. Families contribute exactly one girl and on average one boy. The birth policy is therefore ineffective. Does this make sense?

At first glance, this seems wrong. The policy is designed to favor girls as it ensures that all families have a girl.

On the other hand, the families that keep having children contribute (potentially) multiple boys to the population. This could offset the impact of the "one girl" policy.

One way to think about this is to imagine that we put all the gender sequence of each family into one giant string. So if family 1 has BG, family 2 has BBG, and family 3 has G, we would write BGBBGG.

In fact, we don't really care about the groupings of families because we're concerned about the population as a whole. As soon as a child is born, we can just append its gender (B or G) to the string.

What are the odds of the next character being a G? Well, if the odds of having a boy and girl is the same, then the odds of the next character being a G is 50%. Therefore, roughly half of the string should be Gs and half should be Bs, giving an even gender ratio.

This actually makes a lot of sense. Biology hasn't been changed. Half of newborn babies are girls and half are boys. Abiding by some rule about when to stop having children doesn't change this fact.

Therefore, the gender ratio is 50% girls and 50% boys.

Simulation

We'll write this in a simple way that directly corresponds to the problem.

```
double runNFamilies(int n) {
   int boys = 0;
   int girls = 0;
   for (int i = 0; i < n; i++) {
      int[] genders = runOneFamily();
      girls += genders[0];
      boys += genders[1];
   }
   return girls / (double) (boys + girls);
}

int[] runOneFamily() {
   Random random = new Random();
   int boys = 0;
   int girls = 0;
   while (girls == 0) { // until we have a girl
      if (random.nextBoolean()) { // girl
         girls += 1;
      } else { // boy
         boys += 1;
      }
   }
   int[] genders = {girls, boys};
   return genders;
}
```

Sure enough, if you run this on large values of n, you should get something very close to 0.5.

6.8 The Egg Drop Problem: There is a building of 100 floors. If an egg drops from the Nth floor or above, it will break. If it's dropped from any floor below, it will not break. You're given two eggs. Find N, while minimizing the number of drops for the worst case.

pg 124

SOLUTION

We may observe that, regardless of how we drop Egg 1, Egg 2 must do a linear search (from lowest to highest) between the "breaking floor" and the next highest non-breaking floor. For example, if Egg 1 is dropped from floors 5 and 10 without breaking, but it breaks when it's dropped from floor 15, then Egg 2 must be dropped, in the worst case, from floors 11, 12, 13, and 14.

The Approach

As a first try, suppose we drop an egg from the 10th floor, then the 20th, ...

- If Egg 1 breaks on the first drop (floor 10), then we have at most 10 drops total.
- If Egg 1 breaks on the last drop (floor 100), then we have at most 19 drops total (floors 10, 20, ...,90, 100, then 91 through 99).

That's pretty good, but all we've considered is the absolute worst case. We should do some "load balancing" to make those two cases more even.

Our goal is to create a system for dropping Egg 1 such that the number of drops is as consistent as possible, whether Egg 1 breaks on the first drop or the last drop.

1. A perfectly load-balanced system would be one in which `Drops(Egg 1) + Drops(Egg 2)` is always the same, regardless of where Egg 1 breaks.
2. For that to be the case, since each drop of Egg 1 takes one more step, Egg 2 is allowed one fewer step.
3. We must, therefore, reduce the number of steps potentially required by Egg 2 by one drop each time. For example, if Egg 1 is dropped on floor 20 and then floor 30, Egg 2 is potentially required to take 9 steps. When we drop Egg 1 again, we must reduce potential Egg 2 steps to only 8. That is, we must drop Egg 1 at floor 39.
4. Therefore, Egg 1 must start at floor X, then go up by `X-1` floors, then `X-2`, ..., until it gets to 100.
5. Solve for X.

$$X + (X - 1) + (X - 2) + ... + 1 = 100$$

$$X(X+1)/2 = 100$$

$$X \approx 13.65$$

X clearly needs to be an integer. Should we round X up or down?

- If we round X up to 14, then we would go up by 14, then 13, then 12, and so on. The last increment would be 4, and it would happen on floor 99. If Egg 1 broke on any of the prior floors, we know we've balanced the eggs such that the number of drops of Egg 1 and Egg 2 always sum to the same thing: 14. If Egg 1 hasn't broken by floor 99, then we just need one more drop to determine if it will break at floor 100. Either way, the number of drops is no more than 14.
- If we round X down to 13, then we would go up by 13, then 12, then 11, and so on. The last increment will be 1 and it will happen at floor 91. This is after 13 drops. Floors 92 through 100 have not been covered yet. We can't cover those floors in just one drop (which would be necessary to merely tie the

"round up" case).

Therefore, we should round X up to 14. That is, we go to floor 14, then 27, then 39, ... This takes 14 steps in the worse case.

As in many other maximizing / minimizing problems, the key in this problem is "worst case balancing."

The following code simulates this approach.

```
int breakingPoint = ...;
int countDrops = 0;

boolean drop(int floor) {
  countDrops++;
  return floor >= breakingPoint;
}

int findBreakingPoint(int floors) {
  int interval = 14;
  int previousFloor = 0;
  int egg1 = interval;

  /* Drop egg1 at decreasing intervals. */
  while (!drop(egg1) && egg1 <= floors) {
    interval -= 1;
    previousFloor = egg1;
    egg1 += interval;
  }

  /* Drop egg2 at 1 unit increments. */
  int egg2 = previousFloor + 1;
  while (egg2 < egg1 && egg2 <= floors && !drop(egg2)) {
    egg2 += 1;
  }

  /* If it didn't break, return -1. */
  return egg2 > floors ? -1 : egg2;
}
```

If we want to generalize this code for more building sizes, then we can solve for x in:

$$x(x+1)/2 = \text{number of floors}$$

This will involve the quadratic formula.

6.9 100 Lockers: There are 100 closed lockers in a hallway. A man begins by opening all 100 lockers. Next, he closes every second locker. Then, on his third pass, he toggles every third locker (closes it if it is open or opens it if it is closed). This process continues for 100 passes, such that on each pass `i`, the man toggles every `i`th locker. After his 100th pass in the hallway, in which he toggles only locker #100, how many lockers are open?

pg 124

SOLUTION

We can tackle this problem by thinking through what it means for a door to be toggled. This will help us deduce which doors at the very end will be left opened.

Question: For which rounds is a door toggled (open or closed)?

A door n is toggled once for each factor of n, including itself and 1. That is, door 15 is toggled on rounds 1, 3, 5, and 15.

Question: When would a door be left open?

A door is left open if the number of factors (which we will call x) is odd. You can think about this by pairing factors off as an open and a close. If there's one remaining, the door will be open.

Question: When would x be odd?

The value x is odd if n is a perfect square. Here's why: pair n's factors by their complements. For example, if n is 36, the factors are (1, 36), (2, 18), (3, 12), (4, 9), (6, 6). Note that (6, 6) only contributes one factor, thus giving n an odd number of factors.

Question: How many perfect squares are there?

There are 10 perfect squares. You could count them (1, 4, 9, 16, 25, 36, 49, 64, 81, 100), or you could simply realize that you can take the numbers 1 through 10 and square them:

```
1*1, 2*2, 3*3, ..., 10*10
```

Therefore, there are 10 lockers open at the end of this process.

6.10 **Poison**: You have 1000 bottles of soda, and exactly one is poisoned. You have 10 test strips which can be used to detect poison. A single drop of poison will turn the test strip positive permanently. You can put any number of drops on a test strip at once and you can reuse a test strip as many times as you'd like (as long as the results are negative). However, you can only run tests once per day and it takes seven days to return a result. How would you figure out the poisoned bottle in as few days as possible?

Follow up: Write code to simulate your approach.

pg 124

SOLUTION

Observe the wording of the problem. Why seven days? Why not have the results just return immediately?

The fact that there's such a lag between starting a test and reading the results likely means that we'll be doing something else in the meantime (running additional tests). Let's hold on to that thought, but start off with a simple approach just to wrap our heads around the problem.

Naive Approach (28 days)

A simple approach is to divide the bottles across the 10 test strips, first in groups of 100. Then, we wait seven days. When the results come back, we look for a positive result across the test strips. We select the bottles associated with the positive test strip, "toss" (i.e., ignore) all the other bottles, and repeat the process. We perform this operation until there is only one bottle left in the test set.

1. Divide bottles across available test strips, one drop per test strip.
2. After seven days, check the test strips for results.
3. On the positive test strip: select the bottles associated with it into a new set of bottles. If this set size is 1,

we have located the poisoned bottle. If it's greater than one, go to step 1.

To simulate this, we'll build classes for `Bottle` and `TestStrip` that mirror the problem's functionality.

```
class Bottle {
  private boolean poisoned = false;
  private int id;

  public Bottle(int id) { this.id = id; }
  public int getId() { return id; }
  public void setAsPoisoned() { poisoned = true; }
  public boolean isPoisoned() { return poisoned; }
}

class TestStrip {
  public static int DAYS_FOR_RESULT = 7;
  private ArrayList<ArrayList<Bottle>> dropsByDay =
    new ArrayList<ArrayList<Bottle>>();
  private int id;

  public TestStrip(int id) { this.id = id; }
  public int getId() { return id; }

  /* Resize list of days/drops to be large enough. */
  private void sizeDropsForDay(int day) {
    while (dropsByDay.size() <= day) {
      dropsByDay.add(new ArrayList<Bottle>());
    }
  }

  /* Add drop from bottle on specific day. */
  public void addDropOnDay(int day, Bottle bottle) {
    sizeDropsForDay(day);
    ArrayList<Bottle> drops = dropsByDay.get(day);
    drops.add(bottle);
  }

  /* Checks if any of the bottles in the set are poisoned. */
  private boolean hasPoison(ArrayList<Bottle> bottles) {
    for (Bottle b : bottles) {
      if (b.isPoisoned()) {
        return true;
      }
    }
    return false;
  }

  /* Gets bottles used in the test DAYS_FOR_RESULT days ago. */
  public ArrayList<Bottle> getLastWeeksBottles(int day) {
    if (day < DAYS_FOR_RESULT) {
      return null;
    }
    return dropsByDay.get(day - DAYS_FOR_RESULT);
  }

  /* Checks for poisoned bottles since before DAYS_FOR_RESULT */
  public boolean isPositiveOnDay(int day) {
```

```
      int testDay = day - DAYS_FOR_RESULT;
      if (testDay < 0 || testDay >= dropsByDay.size()) {
         return false;
      }
      for (int d = 0; d <= testDay; d++) {
         ArrayList<Bottle> bottles = dropsByDay.get(d);
         if (hasPoison(bottles)) {
            return true;
         }
      }
      return false;
   }
}
```

This is just one way of simulating the behavior of the bottles and test strips, and each has its pros and cons.

With this infrastructure built, we can now implement code to test our approach.

```
int findPoisonedBottle(ArrayList<Bottle> bottles, ArrayList<TestStrip> strips) {
   int today = 0;

   while (bottles.size() > 1 && strips.size() > 0) {
      /* Run tests. */
      runTestSet(bottles, strips, today);

      /* Wait for results. */
      today += TestStrip.DAYS_FOR_RESULT;

      /* Check results. */
      for (TestStrip strip : strips) {
         if (strip.isPositiveOnDay(today)) {
            bottles = strip.getLastWeeksBottles(today);
            strips.remove(strip);
            break;
         }
      }
   }

   if (bottles.size() == 1) {
      return bottles.get(0).getId();
   }
   return -1;
}

/* Distribute bottles across test strips evenly. */
void runTestSet(ArrayList<Bottle> bottles, ArrayList<TestStrip> strips, int day) {
   int index = 0;
   for (Bottle bottle : bottles) {
      TestStrip strip = strips.get(index);
      strip.addDropOnDay(day, bottle);
      index = (index + 1) % strips.size();
   }
}

/* The complete code can be found in the downloadable code attachment. */
```

Note that this approach makes the assumption that there will always be multiple test strips at each round. This assumption is valid for 1000 bottles and 10 test strips.

If we can't assume this, we can implement a fail-safe. If we have just one test strip remaining, we start doing one bottle at a time: test a bottle, wait a week, test another bottle. This approach will take at most 28 days.

Optimized Approach (10 days)

As noted in the beginning of the solution, it might be more optimal to run multiple tests at once.

If we divide the bottles up into 10 groups (with bottles 0 - 99 going to strip 0, bottles 100 - 199 going to strip 1, bottles 200 - 299 going to strip 2, and so on), then day 7 will reveal the first digit of the bottle number. A positive result on strip `i` at day 7 shows that the first digit (100's digit) of the bottle number is `i`.

Dividing the bottles in a different way can reveal the second or third digit. We just need to run these tests on different days so that we don't confuse the results.

	Day 0 -> 7	Day 1 -> 8	Day 2 -> 9
Strip 0	0xx	x0x	xx0
Strip 1	1xx	x1x	xx1
Strip 2	2xx	x2x	xx2
Strip 3	3xx	x3x	xx3
Strip 4	4xx	x4x	xx4
Strip 5	5xx	x5x	xx5
Strip 6	6xx	x6x	xx6
Strip 7	7xx	x7x	xx7
Strip 8	8xx	x8x	xx8
Strip 9	9xx	x9x	xx9

For example, if day 7 showed a positive result on strip 4, day 8 showed a positive result on strip 3, and day 9 showed a positive result on strip 8, then this would map to bottle #438.

This mostly works, except for one edge case: what happens if the poisoned bottle has a duplicate digit? For example, bottle #882 or bottle #383.

In fact, these cases are quite different. If day 8 doesn't have any "new" positive results, then we can conclude that digit 2 equals digit 1.

The bigger issue is what happens if day 9 doesn't have any new positive results. In this case, all we know is that digit 3 equals either digit 1 or digit 2. We could not distinguish between bottle #383 and bottle #388. They will both have the same pattern of test results.

We will need to run one additional test. We could run this at the end to clear up ambiguity, but we can also run it at day 3, just in case there's any ambiguity. All we need to do is shift the final digit so that it winds up in a different place than day 2's results.

	Day 0 -> 7	Day 1 -> 8	Day 2 -> 9	Day 3 -> 10
Strip 0	0xx	x0x	xx0	xx9
Strip 1	1xx	x1x	xx1	xx0
Strip 2	2xx	x2x	xx2	xx1
Strip 3	3xx	x3x	xx3	xx2
Strip 4	4xx	x4x	xx4	xx3
Strip 5	5xx	x5x	xx5	xx4

	Day 0 -> 7	Day 1 -> 8	Day 2 -> 9	Day 3 -> 10
Strip 6	6xx	x6x	xx6	xx5
Strip 7	7xx	x7x	xx7	xx6
Strip 8	8xx	x8x	xx8	xx7
Strip 9	9xx	x9x	xx9	xx8

Now, bottle #383 will see (Day 7 = #3, Day 8 -> #8, Day 9 -> [NONE], Day 10 -> #4), while bottle #388 will see (Day 7 = #3, Day 8 -> #8, Day 9 -> [NONE], Day 10 -> #9). We can distinguish between these by "reversing" the shifting on day 10's results.

What happens, though, if day 10 still doesn't see any new results? Could this happen?

Actually, yes. Bottle #898 would see (Day 7 = #8, Day 8 -> #9, Day 9 -> [NONE], Day 10 -> [NONE]). That's okay, though. We just need to distinguish bottle #898 from #899. Bottle #899 will see (Day 7 = #8, Day 8 -> #9, Day 9 -> [NONE], Day 10 -> #0).

The "ambiguous" bottles from day 9 will always map to different values on day 10. The logic is:

- If Day 3->10's test reveals a new test result, "unshift" this value to derive the third digit.
- Otherwise, we know that the third digit equals either the first digit or the second digit *and* that the third digit, when shifted, still equals either the first digit or the second digit. Therefore, we just need to figure out whether the first digit "shifts" into the second digit or the other way around. In the former case, the third digit equals the first digit. In the latter case, the third digit equals the second digit.

Implementing this requires some careful work to prevent bugs.

```
int findPoisonedBottle(ArrayList<Bottle> bottles, ArrayList<TestStrip> strips) {
  if (bottles.size() > 1000 || strips.size() < 10) return -1;

  int tests = 4; // three digits, plus one extra
  int nTestStrips = strips.size();

  /* Run tests. */
  for (int day = 0; day < tests; day++) {
    runTestSet(bottles, strips, day);
  }

  /* Get results. */
  HashSet<Integer> previousResults = new HashSet<Integer>();
  int[] digits = new int[tests];
  for (int day = 0; day < tests; day++) {
    int resultDay = day + TestStrip.DAYS_FOR_RESULT;
    digits[day] = getPositiveOnDay(strips, resultDay, previousResults);
    previousResults.add(digits[day]);
  }

  /* If day 1's results matched day 0's, update the digit. */
  if (digits[1] == -1) {
    digits[1] = digits[0];
  }

  /* If day 2 matched day 0 or day 1, check day 3. Day 3 is the same as day 2, but
   * incremented by 1. */
  if (digits[2] == -1) {
```

```
        if (digits[3] == -1) { /* Day 3 didn't give new result */
           /* Digit 2 equals digit 0 or digit 1. But, digit 2, when incremented also
            * matches digit 0 or digit 1. This means that digit 0 incremented matches
            * digit 1, or the other way around. */
           digits[2] = ((digits[0] + 1) % nTestStrips) == digits[1] ?
                       digits[0] : digits[1];
        } else {
           digits[2] = (digits[3] - 1 + nTestStrips) % nTestStrips;
        }
     }

     return digits[0] * 100 + digits[1] * 10 + digits[2];
  }

  /* Run set of tests for this day. */
  void runTestSet(ArrayList<Bottle> bottles, ArrayList<TestStrip> strips, int day) {
     if (day > 3) return; // only works for 3 days (digits) + one extra

     for (Bottle bottle : bottles) {
        int index = getTestStripIndexForDay(bottle, day, strips.size());
        TestStrip testStrip = strips.get(index);
        testStrip.addDropOnDay(day, bottle);
     }
  }

  /* Get strip that should be used on this bottle on this day. */
  int getTestStripIndexForDay(Bottle bottle, int day, int nTestStrips) {
     int id = bottle.getId();
     switch (day) {
        case 0: return id /100;
        case 1: return (id % 100) / 10;
        case 2: return id % 10;
        case 3: return (id % 10 + 1) % nTestStrips;
        default: return -1;
     }
  }

  /* Get results that are positive for a particular day, excluding prior results. */
  int getPositiveOnDay(ArrayList<TestStrip> testStrips, int day,
                       HashSet<Integer> previousResults) {
     for (TestStrip testStrip : testStrips) {
        int id = testStrip.getId();
        if (testStrip.isPositiveOnDay(day) && !previousResults.contains(id)) {
           return testStrip.getId();
        }
     }
     return -1;
  }
```

It will take 10 days in the worst case to get a result with this approach.

Optimal Approach (7 days)

We can actually optimize this slightly more, to return a result in just seven days. This is of course the minimum number of days possible.

Notice what each test strip really means. It's a binary indicator for poisoned or unpoisoned. Is it possible to map 1000 keys to 10 binary values such that each key is mapped to a unique configuration of values? Yes, of course. This is what a binary number is.

We can take each bottle number and look at its binary representation. If there's a 1 in the `i`th digit, then we will add a drop of this bottle's contents to test strip `i`. Observe that 2^{10} is 1024, so 10 test strips will be enough to handle up to 1024 bottles.

We wait seven days, and then read the results. If test strip `i` is positive, then set bit `i` of the result value. Reading all the test strips will give us the ID of the poisoned bottle.

```
int findPoisonedBottle(ArrayList<Bottle> bottles, ArrayList<TestStrip> strips) {
  runTests(bottles, strips);
  ArrayList<Integer> positive = getPositiveOnDay(strips, 7);
  return setBits(positive);
}

/* Add bottle contents to test strips */
void runTests(ArrayList<Bottle> bottles, ArrayList<TestStrip> testStrips) {
  for (Bottle bottle : bottles) {
    int id = bottle.getId();
    int bitIndex = 0;
    while (id > 0) {
      if ((id & 1) == 1) {
        testStrips.get(bitIndex).addDropOnDay(0, bottle);
      }
      bitIndex++;
      id >>= 1;
    }
  }
}

/* Get test strips that are positive on a particular day. */
ArrayList<Integer> getPositiveOnDay(ArrayList<TestStrip> testStrips, int day) {
  ArrayList<Integer> positive = new ArrayList<Integer>();
  for (TestStrip testStrip : testStrips) {
    int id = testStrip.getId();
    if (testStrip.isPositiveOnDay(day)) {
      positive.add(id);
    }
  }
  return positive;
}

/* Create number by setting bits with indices specified in positive. */
int setBits(ArrayList<Integer> positive) {
  int id = 0;
  for (Integer bitIndex : positive) {
    id |= 1 << bitIndex;
  }
  return id;
}
```

This approach will work as long as $2^T >= B$, where T is the number of test strips and B is the number of bottles.

7

Solutions to Object-Oriented Design

7.1 Deck of Cards: Design the data structures for a generic deck of cards. Explain how you would subclass the data structures to implement blackjack.

pg 127

SOLUTION

First, we need to recognize that a "generic" deck of cards can mean many things. Generic could mean a standard deck of cards that can play a poker-like game, or it could even stretch to Uno or Baseball cards. It is important to ask your interviewer what she means by generic.

Let's assume that your interviewer clarifies that the deck is a standard 52-card set, like you might see used in a blackjack or poker game. If so, the design might look like this:

```
public enum Suit {
  Club (0), Diamond (1), Heart (2), Spade (3);
  private int value;
  private Suit(int v) { value = v; }
  public int getValue() { return value; }
  public static Suit getSuitFromValue(int value) { ... }
}

public class Deck <T extends Card> {
  private ArrayList<T> cards; // all cards, dealt or not
  private int dealtIndex = 0; // marks first undealt card

  public void setDeckOfCards(ArrayList<T> deckOfCards) { ... }

  public void shuffle() { ... }
  public int remainingCards() {
    return cards.size() - dealtIndex;
  }
  public T[] dealHand(int number) { ... }
  public T dealCard() { ... }
}

public abstract class Card {
  private boolean available = true;

  /* number or face that's on card - a number 2 through 10, or 11 for Jack, 12 for
   * Queen, 13 for King, or 1 for Ace */
  protected int faceValue;
  protected Suit suit;
```

```

  public Card(int c, Suit s) {
    faceValue = c;
    suit = s;
  }

  public abstract int value();
  public Suit suit() { return suit; }

  /* Checks if the card is available to be given out to someone */
  public boolean isAvailable() { return available; }
  public void markUnavailable() { available = false; }
  public void markAvailable() { available = true; }
}

public class Hand <T extends Card> {
  protected ArrayList<T> cards = new ArrayList<T>();

  public int score() {
    int score = 0;
    for (T card : cards) {
      score += card.value();
    }
    return score;
  }

  public void addCard(T card) {
    cards.add(card);
  }
}
```

In the above code, we have implemented Deck with generics but restricted the type of T to Card. We have also implemented Card as an abstract class, since methods like value() don't make much sense without a specific game attached to them. (You could make a compelling argument that they should be implemented anyway, by defaulting to standard poker rules.)

Now, let's say we're building a blackjack game, so we need to know the value of the cards. Face cards are 10 and an ace is 11 (most of the time, but that's the job of the Hand class, not the following class).

```
public class BlackJackHand extends Hand<BlackJackCard> {
  /* There are multiple possible scores for a blackjack hand, since aces have
   * multiple values. Return the highest possible score that's under 21, or the
   * lowest score that's over. */
  public int score() {
    ArrayList<Integer> scores = possibleScores();
    int maxUnder = Integer.MIN_VALUE;
    int minOver = Integer.MAX_VALUE;
    for (int score : scores) {
      if (score > 21 && score < minOver) {
        minOver = score;
      } else if (score <= 21 && score > maxUnder) {
        maxUnder = score;
      }
    }
    return maxUnder == Integer.MIN_VALUE ? minOver : maxUnder;
  }

```

```
  /* return a list of all possible scores this hand could have (evaluating each
   * ace as both 1 and 11 */
  private ArrayList<Integer> possibleScores() { ... }

  public boolean busted() { return score() > 21; }
  public boolean is21() { return score() == 21; }
  public boolean isBlackJack() { ... }
}

public class BlackJackCard extends Card {
  public BlackJackCard(int c, Suit s) { super(c, s); }
  public int value() {
    if (isAce()) return 1;
    else if (faceValue >= 11 && faceValue <= 13) return 10;
    else return faceValue;
  }

  public int minValue() {
    if (isAce()) return 1;
    else return value();
  }

  public int maxValue() {
    if (isAce()) return 11;
    else return value();
  }

  public boolean isAce() {
    return faceValue == 1;
  }

  public boolean isFaceCard() {
    return faceValue >= 11 && faceValue <= 13;
  }
}
```

This is just one way of handling aces. We could, alternatively, create a class of type `Ace` that extends `BlackJackCard`.

An executable, fully automated version of blackjack is provided in the downloadable code attachment.

7.2 Call Center: Imagine you have a call center with three levels of employees: respondent, manager, and director. An incoming telephone call must be first allocated to a respondent who is free. If the respondent can't handle the call, he or she must escalate the call to a manager. If the manager is not free or not able to handle it, then the call should be escalated to a director. Design the classes and data structures for this problem. Implement a method `dispatchCall()` which assigns a call to the first available employee.

pg 127

SOLUTION

All three ranks of employees have different work to be done, so those specific functions are profile specific. We should keep these things within their respective class.

There are a few things which are common to them, like address, name, job title, and age. These things can be kept in one class and can be extended or inherited by others.

Finally, there should be one `CallHandler` class which would route the calls to the correct person.

Note that on any object-oriented design question, there are many ways to design the objects. Discuss the trade-offs of different solutions with your interviewer. You should usually design for long-term code flexibility and maintenance.

We'll go through each of the classes below in detail.

`CallHandler` represents the body of the program, and all calls are funneled first through it.

```
public class CallHandler {
   /* 3 levels of employees: respondents, managers, directors. */
   private final int LEVELS = 3;

   /* Initialize 10 respondents, 4 managers, and 2 directors. */
   private final int NUM_RESPONDENTS = 10;
   private final int NUM_MANAGERS = 4;
   private final int NUM_DIRECTORS = 2;

   /* List of employees, by level.
    * employeeLevels[0] = respondents
    * employeeLevels[1] = managers
    * employeeLevels[2] = directors
    */
   List<List<Employee>> employeeLevels;

   /* queues for each call's rank */
   List<List<Call>> callQueues;

   public CallHandler() { ... }

   /* Gets the first available employee who can handle this call.*/
   public Employee getHandlerForCall(Call call) { ... }

   /* Routes the call to an available employee, or saves in a queue if no employee
    * is available. */
   public void dispatchCall(Caller caller) {
      Call call = new Call(caller);
      dispatchCall(call);
   }

   /* Routes the call to an available employee, or saves in a queue if no employee
    * is available. */
   public void dispatchCall(Call call) {
      /* Try to route the call to an employee with minimal rank. */
      Employee emp = getHandlerForCall(call);
      if (emp != null) {
         emp.receiveCall(call);
         call.setHandler(emp);
      } else {
         /* Place the call into corresponding call queue according to its rank. */
         call.reply("Please wait for free employee to reply");
         callQueues.get(call.getRank().getValue()).add(call);
      }
   }
```

```

    /* An employee got free. Look for a waiting call that employee can serve. Return
     * true if we assigned a call, false otherwise. */
    public boolean assignCall(Employee emp) { ... }
}
```

Call represents a call from a user. A call has a minimum rank and is assigned to the first employee who can handle it.

```
public class Call {
    /* Minimal rank of employee who can handle this call. */
    private Rank rank;

    /* Person who is calling. */
    private Caller caller;

    /* Employee who is handling call. */
    private Employee handler;

    public Call(Caller c) {
        rank = Rank.Responder;
        caller = c;
    }

    /* Set employee who is handling call. */
    public void setHandler(Employee e) { handler = e; }

    public void reply(String message) { ... }
    public Rank getRank() { return rank; }
    public void setRank(Rank r) { rank = r; }
    public Rank incrementRank() { ... }
    public void disconnect() { ... }
}
```

Employee is a super class for the Director, Manager, and Respondent classes. It is implemented as an abstract class since there should be no reason to instantiate an Employee type directly.

```
abstract class Employee {
    private Call currentCall = null;
    protected Rank rank;

    public Employee(CallHandler handler) { ... }

    /* Start the conversation */
    public void receiveCall(Call call) { ... }

    /* the issue is resolved, finish the call */
    public void callCompleted() { ... }

    /* The issue has not been resolved. Escalate the call, and assign a new call to
     * the employee. */
    public void escalateAndReassign() { ... }

    /* Assign a new call to an employee, if the employee is free. */
    public boolean assignNewCall() { ... }

    /* Returns whether or not the employee is free. */
    public boolean isFree() { return currentCall == null; }

```

```
    public Rank getRank() { return rank; }
}

```

The Respondent, Director, and Manager classes are now just simple extensions of the Employee class.

```
class Director extends Employee {
    public Director() {
        rank = Rank.Director;
    }
}

class Manager extends Employee {
    public Manager() {
        rank = Rank.Manager;
    }
}

class Respondent extends Employee {
    public Respondent() {
        rank = Rank.Responder;
    }
}
```

This is just one way of designing this problem. Note that there are many other ways that are equally good.

This may seem like an awful lot of code to write in an interview, and it is. We've been much more thorough here than you would need. In a real interview, you would likely be much lighter on some of the details until you have time to fill them in.

7.3 **Jukebox:** Design a musical jukebox using object-oriented principles.

pg 127

SOLUTION

In any object-oriented design question, you first want to start off with asking your interviewer some questions to clarify design constraints. Is this jukebox playing CDs? Records? MP3s? Is it a simulation on a computer, or is it supposed to represent a physical jukebox? Does it take money, or is it free? And if it takes money, which currency? And does it deliver change?

Unfortunately, we don't have an interviewer here that we can have this dialogue with. Instead, we'll make some assumptions. We'll assume that the jukebox is a computer simulation that closely mirrors physical jukeboxes, and we'll assume that it's free.

Now that we have that out of the way, we'll outline the basic system components:

- Jukebox
- CD
- Song
- Artist
- Playlist
- Display (displays details on the screen)

Now, let's break this down further and think about the possible actions.

- Playlist creation (includes add, delete, and shuffle)
- CD selector
- Song selector
- Queuing up a song
- Get next song from playlist

A user also can be introduced:

- Adding
- Deleting
- Credit information

Each of the main system components translates roughly to an object, and each action translates to a method. Let's walk through one potential design.

The `Jukebox` class represents the body of the problem. Many of the interactions between the components of the system, or between the system and the user, are channeled through here.

```
public class Jukebox {
   private CDPlayer cdPlayer;
   private User user;
   private Set<CD> cdCollection;
   private SongSelector ts;

   public Jukebox(CDPlayer cdPlayer, User user, Set<CD> cdCollection,
                  SongSelector ts) { ... }

   public Song getCurrentSong() { return ts.getCurrentSong(); }
   public void setUser(User u) { this.user = u; }
}
```

Like a real CD player, the `CDPlayer` class supports storing just one CD at a time. The CDs that are not in play are stored in the jukebox.

```
public class CDPlayer {
   private Playlist p;
   private CD c;

   /* Constructors. */
   public CDPlayer(CD c, Playlist p) { ... }
   public CDPlayer(Playlist p) { this.p = p; }
   public CDPlayer(CD c) { this.c = c; }

   /* Play song */
   public void playSong(Song s) { ... }

   /* Getters and setters */
   public Playlist getPlaylist() { return p; }
   public void setPlaylist(Playlist p) { this.p = p; }

   public CD getCD() { return c; }
   public void setCD(CD c) { this.c = c; }
}
```

The `Playlist` manages the current and next songs to play. It is essentially a wrapper class for a queue and offers some additional methods for convenience.

```
public class Playlist {
   private Song song;
   private Queue<Song> queue;
   public Playlist(Song song, Queue<Song> queue) {
      ...
   }
   public Song getNextSToPlay() {
      return queue.peek();
   }
   public void queueUpSong(Song s) {
      queue.add(s);
   }
}
```

The classes for CD, Song, and `User` are all fairly straightforward. They consist mainly of member variables and getters and setters.

```
public class CD { /* data for id, artist, songs, etc */ }

public class Song { /* data for id, CD (could be null), title, length, etc */ }

public class User {
   private String name;
   public String getName() { return name; }
   public void setName(String name) {   this.name = name; }
   public long getID() { return ID; }
   public void setID(long iD) { ID = iD; }
   private long ID;
   public User(String name, long iD) { ... }
   public User getUser() { return this; }
   public static User addUser(String name, long iD) { ... }
}
```

This is by no means the only "correct" implementation. The interviewer's responses to initial questions, as well as other constraints, will shape the design of the jukebox classes.

7.4 Parking Lot: Design a parking lot using object-oriented principles.

pg 127

SOLUTION

The wording of this question is vague, just as it would be in an actual interview. This requires you to have a conversation with your interviewer about what types of vehicles it can support, whether the parking lot has multiple levels, and so on.

For our purposes right now, we'll make the following assumptions. We made these specific assumptions to add a bit of complexity to the problem without adding too much. If you made different assumptions, that's totally fine.

- The parking lot has multiple levels. Each level has multiple rows of spots.
- The parking lot can park motorcycles, cars, and buses.
- The parking lot has motorcycle spots, compact spots, and large spots.
- A motorcycle can park in any spot.
- A car can park in either a single compact spot or a single large spot.

- A bus can park in five large spots that are consecutive and within the same row. It cannot park in small spots.

In the below implementation, we have created an abstract class `Vehicle`, from which `Car`, `Bus`, and `Motorcycle` inherit. To handle the different parking spot sizes, we have just one class `ParkingSpot` which has a member variable indicating the size.

```
public enum VehicleSize { Motorcycle, Compact,   Large }

public abstract class Vehicle {
  protected ArrayList<ParkingSpot> parkingSpots = new ArrayList<ParkingSpot>();
  protected String licensePlate;
  protected int spotsNeeded;
  protected VehicleSize size;

  public int getSpotsNeeded() { return spotsNeeded; }
  public VehicleSize getSize() { return size; }

  /* Park vehicle in this spot (among others, potentially) */
  public void parkInSpot(ParkingSpot s) { parkingSpots.add(s); }

  /* Remove car from spot, and notify spot that it's gone */
  public void clearSpots() { ... }

  /* Checks if the spot is big enough for the vehicle (and is available). This
   * compares the SIZE only. It does not check if it has enough spots. */
  public abstract boolean canFitInSpot(ParkingSpot spot);
}

public class Bus extends Vehicle {
  public Bus() {
    spotsNeeded = 5;
    size = VehicleSize.Large;
  }

  /* Checks if the spot is a Large. Doesn't check num of spots */
  public boolean canFitInSpot(ParkingSpot spot) { ... }
}

public class Car extends Vehicle {
  public Car() {
    spotsNeeded = 1;
    size = VehicleSize.Compact;
  }

  /* Checks if the spot is a Compact or a Large. */
  public boolean canFitInSpot(ParkingSpot spot) { ... }
}

public class Motorcycle extends Vehicle {
  public Motorcycle() {
    spotsNeeded = 1;
    size = VehicleSize.Motorcycle;
  }

  public boolean canFitInSpot(ParkingSpot spot) { ... }
}
```

The ParkingLot class is essentially a wrapper class for an array of Levels. By implementing it this way, we are able to separate out logic that deals with actually finding free spots and parking cars out from the broader actions of the ParkingLot. If we didn't do it this way, we would need to hold parking spots in some sort of double array (or hash table which maps from a level number to the list of spots). It's cleaner to just separate ParkingLot from Level.

```
public class ParkingLot {
  private Level[] levels;
  private final int NUM_LEVELS = 5;

  public ParkingLot() { ... }

  /* Park the vehicle in a spot (or multiple spots). Return false if failed. */
  public boolean parkVehicle(Vehicle vehicle) { ... }
}

/* Represents a level in a parking garage */
public class Level {
  private int floor;
  private ParkingSpot[] spots;
  private int availableSpots = 0; // number of free spots
  private static final int SPOTS_PER_ROW = 10;

  public Level(int flr, int numberSpots) { ... }

  public int availableSpots() { return availableSpots; }

  /* Find a place to park this vehicle. Return false if failed. */
  public boolean parkVehicle(Vehicle vehicle) { ... }

  /* Park a vehicle starting at the spot spotNumber, and continuing until
   * vehicle.spotsNeeded. */
  private boolean parkStartingAtSpot(int num, Vehicle v) { ... }

  /* Find a spot to park this vehicle. Return index of spot, or -1 on failure. */
  private int findAvailableSpots(Vehicle vehicle) { ... }

  /* When a car was removed from the spot, increment availableSpots */
  public void spotFreed() { availableSpots++; }
}
```

The ParkingSpot is implemented by having just a variable which represents the size of the spot. We could have implemented this by having classes for LargeSpot, CompactSpot, and MotorcycleSpot which inherit from ParkingSpot, but this is probably overkill. The spots probably do not have different behaviors, other than their sizes.

```
public class ParkingSpot {
  private Vehicle vehicle;
  private VehicleSize spotSize;
  private int row;
  private int spotNumber;
  private Level level;

  public ParkingSpot(Level lvl, int r, int n, VehicleSize s) {...}

  public boolean isAvailable() { return vehicle == null; }

```

```
    /* Check if the spot is big enough and is available */
    public boolean canFitVehicle(Vehicle vehicle) { ... }

    /* Park vehicle in this spot. */
    public boolean park(Vehicle v) { ... }

    public int getRow() { return row; }
    public int getSpotNumber() { return spotNumber; }

    /* Remove vehicle from spot, and notify level that a new spot is available */
    public void removeVehicle() { ... }
}
```

A full implementation of this code, including executable test code, is provided in the downloadable code attachment.

7.5 Online Book Reader: Design the data structures for an online book reader system.

pg 127

SOLUTION

Since the problem doesn't describe much about the functionality, let's assume we want to design a basic online reading system which provides the following functionality:

- User membership creation and extension.
- Searching the database of books.
- Reading a book.
- Only one active user at a time
- Only one active book by this user.

To implement these operations we may require many other functions, like `get`, `set`, `update`, and so on. The objects required would likely include `User`, `Book`, and `Library`.

The class `OnlineReaderSystem` represents the body of our program. We could implement the class such that it stores information about all the books, deals with user management, and refreshes the display, but that would make this class rather hefty. Instead, we've chosen to tear off these components into `Library`, `UserManager`, and `Display` classes.

```
public class OnlineReaderSystem {
   private Library library;
   private UserManager userManager;
   private Display display;

   private Book activeBook;
   private User activeUser;

   public OnlineReaderSystem() {
      userManager = new UserManager();
      library = new Library();
      display = new Display();
   }

   public Library getLibrary() { return library;  }
   public UserManager getUserManager() { return userManager; }
```

```
    public Display getDisplay() { return display; }

    public Book getActiveBook() { return activeBook; }
    public void setActiveBook(Book book) {
        activeBook = book;
        display.displayBook(book);
    }

    public User getActiveUser() { return activeUser; }
    public void setActiveUser(User user) {
        activeUser = user;
        display.displayUser(user);
    }
}
```

We then implement separate classes to handle the user manager, the library, and the display components.

```
public class Library {
    private HashMap<Integer, Book> books;

    public Book addBook(int id, String details) {
        if (books.containsKey(id)) {
            return null;
        }
        Book book = new Book(id, details);
        books.put(id, book);
        return book;
    }

    public boolean remove(Book b) { return remove(b.getID()); }
    public boolean remove(int id) {
        if (!books.containsKey(id)) {
            return false;
        }
        books.remove(id);
        return true;
    }

    public Book find(int id) {
        return books.get(id);
    }
}

public class UserManager {
    private HashMap<Integer, User> users;

    public User addUser(int id, String details, int accountType) {
        if (users.containsKey(id)) {
            return null;
        }
        User user = new User(id, details, accountType);
        users.put(id, user);
        return user;
    }

    public User find(int id) { return users.get(id); }
    public boolean remove(User u) { return remove(u.getID()); }
    public boolean remove(int id) {
```

```
    if (!users.containsKey(id)) {
      return false;
    }
    users.remove(id);
    return true;
  }
}

public class Display {
  private Book activeBook;
  private User activeUser;
  private int pageNumber = 0;

  public void displayUser(User user) {
    activeUser = user;
    refreshUsername();
  }

  public void displayBook(Book book) {
    pageNumber = 0;
    activeBook = book;

    refreshTitle();
    refreshDetails();
    refreshPage();
  }

  public void turnPageForward() {
    pageNumber++;
    refreshPage();
  }

  public void turnPageBackward() {
    pageNumber--;
    refreshPage();
  }

  public void refreshUsername() { /* updates username display */ }
  public void refreshTitle() { /* updates title display */ }
  public void refreshDetails() { /* updates details display */   }
  public void refreshPage() { /* updated page display */ }
}
```

The classes for User and Book simply hold data and provide little true functionality.

```
public class Book {
  private int bookId;
  private String details;

  public Book(int id, String det) {
    bookId = id;
    details = det;
  }

  public int getID() { return bookId;  }
  public void setID(int id) { bookId = id; }
  public String getDetails() { return details; }
  public void setDetails(String d) { details = d; }
```

```
}

public class User {
   private int userId;
   private String details;
   private int accountType;

   public void renewMembership() {  }

   public User(int id, String details, int accountType) {
      userId = id;
      this.details = details;
      this.accountType = accountType;
   }

   /* Getters and setters */
   public int getID() { return userId; }
   public void setID(int id) { userId = id; }
   public String getDetails() {
      return details;
   }

   public void setDetails(String details) {
      this.details = details;
   }
   public int getAccountType() { return accountType; }
   public void setAccountType(int t) { accountType = t; }
}
```

The decision to tear off user management, library, and display into their own classes, when this functionality could have been in the general `OnlineReaderSystem` class, is an interesting one. On a very small system, making this decision could make the system overly complex. However, as the system grows, and more and more functionality gets added to `OnlineReaderSystem`, breaking off such components prevents this main class from getting overwhelmingly lengthy.

7.6 **Jigsaw:** Implement an NxN jigsaw puzzle. Design the data structures and explain an algorithm to solve the puzzle. You can assume that you have a `fitsWith` method which, when passed two puzzle edges, returns true if the two edges belong together.

pg 128

SOLUTION

We have a traditional jigsaw puzzle. The puzzle is grid-like, with rows and columns. Each piece is located in a single row and column and has four edges. Each edge comes in one of three types: inner, outer, and flat. A corner piece, for example, will have two flat edges and two other edges, which could be inner or outer.

As we solve the jigsaw puzzle (manually or algorithmically), we'll need to store the position of each piece. We could think about the position as absolute or relative:

- *Absolute Position:* "This piece is located at position (12, 23)."
- *Relative Position:* "I don't know where this piece is actually located, but I know it is next to this other piece."

For our solution, we will use the absolute position.

We'll need classes to represent `Puzzle`, `Piece`, and `Edge`. Additionally, we'll want enums for the different shapes (`inner`, `outer`, `flat`) and the orientations of the edges (`left`, `top`, `right`, `bottom`).

`Puzzle` will start off with a list of the pieces. When we solve the puzzle, we'll fill in an NxN `solution` matrix of pieces.

`Piece` will have a hash table that maps from an orientation to the appropriate edge. Note that we might rotate the piece at some point, so the hash table could change. The orientation of the edges will be arbitrarily assigned at first.

`Edge` will have just its shape and a pointer back to its parent piece. It will not keep its orientation.

A potential object-oriented design looks like the following:

```
public enum Orientation {
   LEFT, TOP, RIGHT, BOTTOM; // Should stay in this order

   public Orientation getOpposite() {
      switch (this) {
         case LEFT: return RIGHT;
         case RIGHT: return LEFT;
         case TOP: return BOTTOM;
         case BOTTOM: return TOP;
         default: return null;
      }
   }
}

public enum Shape {
   INNER, OUTER, FLAT;

   public Shape getOpposite() {
      switch (this) {
         case INNER: return OUTER;
         case OUTER: return INNER;
         default: return null;
```

```
    }
  }
}

public class Puzzle {
  private LinkedList<Piece> pieces; /* Remaining pieces to put away. */
  private Piece[][] solution;
  private int size;

  public Puzzle(int size, LinkedList<Piece> pieces) { ... }


  /* Put piece into the solution, turn it appropriately, and remove from list. */
  private void setEdgeInSolution(LinkedList<Piece> pieces, Edge edge, int row,
                                 int column, Orientation orientation) {
    Piece piece = edge.getParentPiece();
    piece.setEdgeAsOrientation(edge, orientation);
    pieces.remove(piece);
    solution[row][column] = piece;
  }

  /* Find the matching piece in piecesToSearch and insert it at row, column. */
  private boolean fitNextEdge(LinkedList<Piece> piecesToSearch, int row, int col);

  /* Solve puzzle. */
  public boolean solve() { ... }
}

public class Piece {
  private HashMap<Orientation, Edge> edges = new HashMap<Orientation, Edge>();

  public Piece(Edge[] edgeList) { ... }

  /* Rotate edges by "numberRotations". */
  public void rotateEdgesBy(int numberRotations) { ... }

  public boolean isCorner() { ... }
  public boolean isBorder() { ... }
}

public class Edge {
  private Shape shape;
  private Piece parentPiece;
  public Edge(Shape shape) { ... }
  public boolean fitsWith(Edge edge) { ... }
}
```

Algorithm to Solve the Puzzle

Just as a kid might in solving a puzzle, we'll start with grouping the pieces into corner pieces, border pieces, and inside pieces.

Once we've done that, we'll pick an arbitrary corner piece and put it in the top left corner. We will then walk through the puzzle in order, filling in piece by piece. At each location, we search through the correct group of pieces to find the matching piece. When we insert the piece into the puzzle, we need to rotate the piece to fit correctly.

The code below outlines this algorithm.

```
/* Find the matching piece within piecesToSearch and insert it at row, column. */
boolean fitNextEdge(LinkedList<Piece> piecesToSearch, int row, int column) {
  if (row == 0 && column == 0) { // On top left corner, just put in a piece
    Piece p = piecesToSearch.remove();
    orientTopLeftCorner(p);
    solution[0][0] = p;
  } else {
    /* Get the right edge and list to match. */
    Piece pieceToMatch = column == 0 ? solution[row - 1][0] :
                                       solution[row][column - 1];
    Orientation orientationToMatch = column == 0 ? Orientation.BOTTOM :
                                                   Orientation.RIGHT;
    Edge edgeToMatch = pieceToMatch.getEdgeWithOrientation(orientationToMatch);

    /* Get matching edge. */
    Edge edge = getMatchingEdge(edgeToMatch, piecesToSearch);
    if (edge == null) return false; // Can't solve

    /* Insert piece and edge. */
    Orientation orientation = orientationToMatch.getOpposite();
    setEdgeInSolution(piecesToSearch, edge, row, column, orientation);
  }
  return true;
}

boolean solve() {
  /* Group pieces. */
  LinkedList<Piece> cornerPieces = new LinkedList<Piece>();
  LinkedList<Piece> borderPieces = new LinkedList<Piece>();
  LinkedList<Piece> insidePieces = new LinkedList<Piece>();
  groupPieces(cornerPieces, borderPieces, insidePieces);

  /* Walk through puzzle, finding the piece that joins the previous one. */
  solution = new Piece[size][size];
  for (int row = 0; row < size; row++) {
    for (int column = 0; column < size; column++) {
      LinkedList<Piece> piecesToSearch = getPieceListToSearch(cornerPieces,
        borderPieces, insidePieces, row, column);
      if (!fitNextEdge(piecesToSearch, row, column)) {
        return false;
      }
    }
  }

  return true;
}
```

The full code for this solution can be found in the downloadable code attachment.

7.7 **Chat Server:** Explain how you would design a chat server. In particular, provide details about the various backend components, classes, and methods. What would be the hardest problems to solve?

pg 128

SOLUTION

Designing a chat server is a huge project, and it is certainly far beyond the scope of what could be completed in an interview. After all, teams of many people spend months or years creating a chat server. Part of your job, as a candidate, is to focus on an aspect of the problem that is reasonably broad, but focused enough that you could accomplish it during an interview. It need not match real life exactly, but it should be a fair representation of an actual implementation.

For our purposes, we'll focus on the core user management and conversation aspects: adding a user, creating a conversation, updating one's status, and so on. In the interest of time and space, we will not go into the networking aspects of the problem, or how the data actually gets pushed out to the clients.

We will assume that "friending" is mutual; I am only your contact if you are mine. Our chat system will support both group chat and one-on-one (private) chats. We will not worry about voice chat, video chat, or file transfer.

What specific actions does it need to support?

This is also something to discuss with your interviewer, but here are some ideas:

- Signing online and offline.
- Add requests (sending, accepting, and rejecting).
- Updating a status message.
- Creating private and group chats.
- Adding new messages to private and group chats.

This is just a partial list. If you have more time, you can add more actions.

What can we learn about these requirements?

We must have a concept of users, add request status, online status, and messages.

What are the core components of the system?

The system would likely consist of a database, a set of clients, and a set of servers. We won't include these parts in our object-oriented design, but we can discuss the overall view of the system.

The database will be used for more permanent storage, such as the user list or chat archives. A SQL database is a good bet, or, if we need more scalability, we could potentially use BigTable or a similar system.

For communication between the client and servers, using XML will work well. Although it's not the most compressed format (and you should point this out to your interviewer), it's nice because it's easy for both computers and humans to read. Using XML will make your debugging efforts easier—and that matters a lot.

The server will consist of a set of machines. Data will be split across machines, requiring us to potentially hop from machine to machine. When possible, we will try to replicate some data across machines to minimize the lookups. One major design constraint here is to prevent having a single point of failure. For instance, if one machine controlled all the user sign-ins, then we'd cut off millions of users potentially if a single machine lost network connectivity.

What are the key objects and methods?

The key objects of the system will be a concept of users, conversations, and status messages. We've implemented a `UserManager` class. If we were looking more at the networking aspects of the problem, or a different component, we might have instead dived into those objects.

```
/* UserManager serves as a central place for core user actions. */
public class UserManager {
   private static UserManager instance;
   /* maps from a user id to a user */
   private HashMap<Integer, User> usersById;

   /* maps from an account name to a user */
   private HashMap<String, User> usersByAccountName;

   /* maps from the user id to an online user */
   private HashMap<Integer, User> onlineUsers;

   public static UserManager getInstance() {
      if (instance == null) instance = new UserManager();
      return instance;
   }

   public void addUser(User fromUser, String toAccountName) { ... }
   public void approveAddRequest(AddRequest req) { ... }
   public void rejectAddRequest(AddRequest req) { ... }
   public void userSignedOn(String accountName) { ... }
   public void userSignedOff(String accountName) { ... }
}
```

The method `receivedAddRequest`, in the `User` class, notifies User B that User A has requested to add him. User B approves or rejects the request (via `UserManager.approveAddRequest` or `rejectAddRequest`), and the `UserManager` takes care of adding the users to each other's contact lists.

The method `sentAddRequest` in the `User` class is called by `UserManager` to add an `AddRequest` to User A's list of requests. So the flow is:

1. User A clicks "add user" on the client, and it gets sent to the server.
2. User A calls `requestAddUser(User B)`.
3. This method calls `UserManager.addUser`.
4. `UserManager` calls both `User A.sentAddRequest` and `User B.receivedAddRequest`.

Again, this is just *one* way of designing these interactions. It is not the only way, or even the only "good" way.

```
public class User {
   private int id;
   private UserStatus status = null;

   /* maps from the other participant's user id to the chat */
   private HashMap<Integer, PrivateChat> privateChats;

   /* list of group chats */
```

```
    private ArrayList<GroupChat> groupChats;

    /* maps from the other person's user id to the add request */
    private HashMap<Integer, AddRequest> receivedAddRequests;

    /* maps from the other person's user id to the add request */
    private HashMap<Integer, AddRequest> sentAddRequests;

    /* maps from the user id to user object */
    private HashMap<Integer, User> contacts;

    private String accountName;
    private String fullName;

    public User(int id, String accountName, String fullName) { ... }
    public boolean sendMessageToUser(User to, String content){ ... }
    public boolean sendMessageToGroupChat(int id, String cnt){...}
    public void setStatus(UserStatus status) { ... }
    public UserStatus getStatus() { ... }
    public boolean addContact(User user) { ... }
    public void receivedAddRequest(AddRequest req) { ...}
    public void sentAddRequest(AddRequest req) { ... }
    public void removeAddRequest(AddRequest req) { ... }
    public void requestAddUser(String accountName) { ... }
    public void addConversation(PrivateChat conversation) { ... }
    public void addConversation(GroupChat conversation) { ... }
    public int getId() { ... }
    public String getAccountName() { ... }
    public String getFullName() { ... }
}
```

The `Conversation` class is implemented as an abstract class, since all `Conversations` must be either a `GroupChat` or a `PrivateChat`, and since these two classes each have their own functionality.

```
public abstract class Conversation {
    protected ArrayList<User> participants;
    protected int id;
    protected ArrayList<Message> messages;

    public ArrayList<Message> getMessages() { ... }
    public boolean addMessage(Message m) { ... }
    public int getId() { ... }
}

public class GroupChat extends Conversation {
    public void removeParticipant(User user) { ... }
    public void addParticipant(User user) { ... }
}

public class PrivateChat extends Conversation {
    public PrivateChat(User user1, User user2) { ...
    public User getOtherParticipant(User primary) { ... }
}

public class Message {
    private String content;
    private Date date;
    public Message(String content, Date date) { ... }
```

```
    public String getContent() { ... }
    public Date getDate() { ... }
}
```

AddRequest and UserStatus are simple classes with little functionality. Their main purpose is to group data that other classes will act upon.

```
public class AddRequest {
    private User fromUser;
    private User toUser;
    private Date date;
    RequestStatus status;

    public AddRequest(User from, User to, Date date) { ... }
    public RequestStatus getStatus() { ... }
    public User getFromUser() { ... }
    public User getToUser() { ... }
    public Date getDate() { ... }
}

public class UserStatus {
     private String message;
     private UserStatusType type;
     public UserStatus(UserStatusType type, String message) { ... }
     public UserStatusType getStatusType() { ... }
     public String getMessage() { ... }
}

public enum UserStatusType {
    Offline, Away, Idle, Available, Busy
}

public enum RequestStatus {
    Unread, Read, Accepted, Rejected
}
```

The downloadable code attachment provides a more detailed look at these methods, including implementations for the methods shown above.

What problems would be the hardest to solve (or the most interesting)?

The following questions may be interesting to discuss with your interviewer further.

Q1: How do we know if someone is online—I mean, really, really know?

While we would like users to tell us when they sign off, we can't know for sure. A user's connection might have died, for example. To make sure that we know when a user has signed off, we might try regularly pinging the client to make sure it's still there.

Q2: How do we deal with conflicting information?

We have some information stored in the computer's memory and some in the database. What happens if they get out of sync? Which one is "right"?

Q3: How do we make our server scale?

While we designed out chat server without worrying—too much– about scalability, in real life this would be a concern. We'd need to split our data across many servers, which would increase our concern about out-of-sync data.

Q4: How we do prevent denial of service attacks?

Clients can push data to us—what if they try to DOS (denial of service) us? How do we prevent that?

7.8 **Othello:** Othello is played as follows: Each Othello piece is white on one side and black on the other. When a piece is surrounded by its opponents on both the left and right sides, or both the top and bottom, it is said to be captured and its color is flipped. On your turn, you must capture at least one of your opponent's pieces. The game ends when either user has no more valid moves. The win is assigned to the person with the most pieces. Implement the object-oriented design for Othello.

pg 128

SOLUTION

Let's start with an example. Suppose we have the following moves in an Othello game:

1. Initialize the board with two black and two white pieces in the center. The black pieces are placed at the upper left hand and lower right hand corners.
2. Play a black piece at (row 6, column 4). This flips the piece at (row 5, column 4) from white to black.
3. Play a white piece at (row 4, column 3). This flips the piece at (row 4, column 4) from black to white.

This sequence of moves leads to the board below.

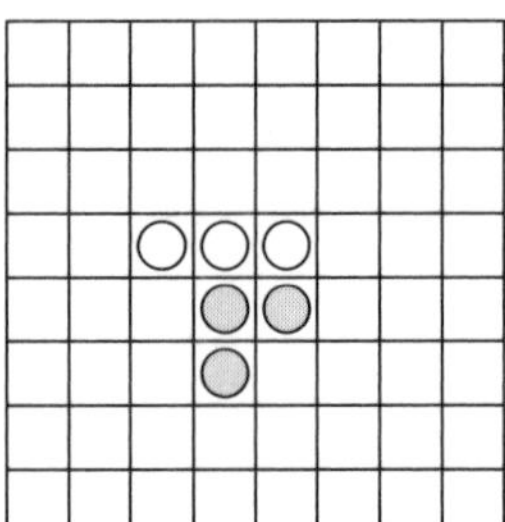

The core objects in Othello are probably the game, the board, the pieces (black or white), and the players. How do we represent these with elegant object-oriented design?

Should BlackPiece and WhitePiece be classes?

At first, we might think we want to have a `BlackPiece` class and a `WhitePiece` class, which inherit from an abstract `Piece`. However, this is probably not a great idea. Each piece may flip back and forth between colors frequently, so continuously destroying and creating what is really the same object is probably not wise. It may be better to just have a `Piece` class, with a flag in it representing the current color.

Do we need separate Board and Game classes?

Strictly speaking, it may not be necessary to have both a `Game` object and a `Board` object. Keeping the objects separate allows us to have a logical separation between the board (which contains just logic involving placing pieces) and the game (which involves times, game flow, etc.). However, the drawback is that we are adding extra layers to our program. A function may call out to a method in Game, only to have it immediately call Board. We have made the choice below to keep Game and Board separate, but you should discuss this with your interviewer.

Who keeps score?

We know we should probably have some sort of score keeping for the number of black and white pieces. But who should maintain this information? One could make a strong argument for either Game or Board maintaining this information, and possibly even for Piece (in static methods). We have implemented this with Board holding this information, since it can be logically grouped with the board. It is updated by Piece or Board calling the colorChanged and colorAdded methods within Board.

Should Game be a Singleton class?

Implementing Game as a singleton class has the advantage of making it easy for anyone to call a method within Game, without having to pass around references to the Game object.

However, making Game a singleton means it can only be instantiated once. Can we make this assumption? You should discuss this with your interviewer.

One possible design for Othello is below.

```
public enum Direction {
  left, right, up, down
}

public enum Color {
  White, Black
}

public class Game {
  private Player[] players;
  private static Game instance;
  private Board board;
  private final int ROWS = 10;
  private final int COLUMNS = 10;

  private Game() {
    board = new Board(ROWS, COLUMNS);
    players = new Player[2];
    players[0] = new Player(Color.Black);
    players[1] = new Player(Color.White);
  }

  public static Game getInstance() {
    if (instance == null) instance = new Game();
    return instance;
  }

  public Board getBoard() {
    return board;
  }
}
```

The Board class manages the actual pieces themselves. It does not handle much of the game play, leaving that up to the Game class.

```
public class Board {
   private int blackCount = 0;
   private int whiteCount = 0;
   private Piece[][] board;

   public Board(int rows, int columns) {
      board = new Piece[rows][columns];
   }

   public void initialize() {
      /* initialize center black and white pieces */
   }

   /* Attempt to place a piece of color color at (row, column). Return true if we
    * were successful. */
   public boolean placeColor(int row, int column, Color color) {
      ...
   }

   /* Flips pieces starting at (row, column) and proceeding in direction d. */
   private int flipSection(int row, int column, Color color, Direction d) { ... }

   public int getScoreForColor(Color c) {
      if (c == Color.Black) return blackCount;
      else return whiteCount;
   }

   /* Update board with additional newPieces pieces of color newColor. Decrease
    * score of opposite color. */
   public void updateScore(Color newColor, int newPieces) { ... }
}
```

As described earlier, we implement the black and white pieces with the Piece class, which has a simple Color variable representing whether it is a black or white piece.

```
public class Piece {
   private Color color;
   public Piece(Color c) { color = c; }

   public void flip() {
      if (color == Color.Black) color = Color.White;
      else color = Color.Black;
   }

   public Color getColor() { return color; }
}
```

The Player holds only a very limited amount of information. It does not even hold its own score, but it does have a method one can call to get the score. Player.getScore() will call out to the Game object to retrieve this value.

```
public class Player {
   private Color color;
   public Player(Color c) { color = c; }

   public int getScore() { ... }
```

```

    public boolean playPiece(int r, int c) {
       return Game.getInstance().getBoard().placeColor(r, c, color);
    }

    public Color getColor() { return color; }
 }
```

A fully functioning (automated) version of this code can be found in the downloadable code attachment.

Remember that in many problems, what you did is less important than *why* you did it. Your interviewer probably doesn't care much whether you chose to implement Game as a singleton or not, but she probably does care that you took the time to think about it and discuss the trade-offs.

7.9 Circular Array: Implement a `CircularArray` class that supports an array-like data structure which can be efficiently rotated. If possible, the class should use a generic type (also called a template), and should support iteration via the standard `for (Obj o : circularArray)` notation.

pg 128

SOLUTION

This problem really has two parts to it. First, we need to implement the `CircularArray` class. Second, we need to support iteration. We will address these parts separately.

Implementing the CircularArray class

One way to implement the `CircularArray` class is to actually shift the elements each time we call `rotate(int shiftRight)`. Doing this is, of course, not very efficient.

Instead, we can just create a member variable head which points to what should be *conceptually* viewed as the start of the circular array. Rather than shifting around the elements in the array, we just increment head by `shiftRight`.

The code below implements this approach.

```
public class CircularArray<T> {
   private T[] items;
   private int head = 0;

   public CircularArray(int size) {
      items = (T[]) new Object[size];
   }

   private int convert(int index) {
      if (index < 0) {
         index += items.length;
      }
      return (head + index) % items.length;
   }

   public void rotate(int shiftRight) {
      head = convert(shiftRight);
   }

   public T get(int i) {
      if (i < 0 || i >= items.length) {
```

```
            throw new java.lang.IndexOutOfBoundsException("...");
        }
        return items[convert(i)];
    }

    public void set(int i, T item) {
        items[convert(i)] = item;
    }
}
```

There are a number of things here which are easy to make mistakes on, such as:

- In Java, we cannot create an array of the generic type. Instead, we must either cast the array or define `items` to be of type `List<T>`. For simplicity, we have done the former.
- The % operator will return a negative value when we do `negValue % posVal`. For example, `-8 % 3` is `-2`. This is different from how mathematicians would define the modulus function. We must add `items.length` to a negative index to get the correct positive result.
- We need to be sure to consistently convert the raw index to the rotated index. For this reason, we have implemented a `convert` function that is used by other methods. Even the `rotate` function uses `convert`. This is a good example of code reuse.

Now that we have the basic code for `CircularArray` out of the way, we can focus on implementing an iterator.

Implementing the Iterator Interface

The second part of this question asks us to implement the `CircularArray` class such that we can do the following:

```
CircularArray<String> array = ...
for (String s : array) { ... }
```

Implementing this requires implementing the `Iterator` interface. The details of this implementation apply to Java, but similar things can be implemented in other languages.

To implement the `Iterator` interface, we need to do the following:

- Modify the `CircularArray<T>` definition to add `implements Iterable<T>`. This will also require us to add an `iterator()` method to `CircularArray<T>`.
- Create a `CircularArrayIterator<T>` which implements `Iterator<T>`. This will also require us to implement, in the `CircularArrayIterator`, the methods `hasNext()`, `next()`, and `remove()`.

Once we've done the above items, the for loop will "magically" work.

In the code below, we have removed the aspects of `CircularArray` which were identical to the earlier implementation.

```
public class CircularArray<T> implements Iterable<T> {
    ...
    public Iterator<T> iterator() {
        return new CircularArrayIterator();
    }

    private class CircularArrayIterator implements Iterator<T> {
        private int _current = -1;

        public CircularArrayIterator() { }
```

```

      @Override
      public boolean hasNext() {
         return _current < items.length - 1;
      }

      @Override
      public T next() {
         _current++;
         return (T) items[convert(_current)];
      }

      @Override
      public void remove() {
         throw new UnsupportedOperationException("Remove is not supported");
      }
   }
}
```

In the above code, note that the first iteration of the for loop will call `hasNext()` and then `next()`. Be very sure that your implementation will return the correct values here.

When you get a problem like this one in an interview, there's a good chance you don't remember exactly what the various methods and interfaces are called. In this case, work through the problem as well as you can. If you can reason out what sorts of methods one might need, that alone will show a good degree of competency.

7.10 Minesweeper: Design and implement a text-based Minesweeper game. Minesweeper is the classic single-player computer game where an NxN grid has B mines (or bombs) hidden across the grid. The remaining cells are either blank or have a number behind them. The numbers reflect the number of bombs in the surrounding eight cells. The user then uncovers a cell. If it is a bomb, the player loses. If it is a number, the number is exposed. If it is a blank cell, this cell and all adjacent blank cells (up to and including the surrounding numeric cells) are exposed. The player wins when all non-bomb cells are exposed. The player can also flag certain places as potential bombs. This doesn't affect game play, other than to block the user from accidentally clicking a cell that is thought to have a bomb. (Tip for the reader: if you're not familiar with this game, please play a few rounds online first.)

This is a fully exposed board with 3 bombs. This is not shown to the user.

	1	1	1			
	1	*	1			
	2	2	2			
	1	*	1			
	1	1	1			
			1	1	1	
			1	*	1	

The player initially sees a board with nothing exposed.

?	?	?	?	?	?	?
?	?	?	?	?	?	?
?	?	?	?	?	?	?
?	?	?	?	?	?	?
?	?	?	?	?	?	?
?	?	?	?	?	?	?
?	?	?	?	?	?	?

Clicking on cell (row = 1, col = 0) would expose this:

	1	?	?	?	?	?
	1	?	?	?	?	?
	2	?	?	?	?	?
	1	?	?	?	?	?
	1	1	1	?	?	?
			1	?	?	?
			1	?	?	?

The user wins when everything other than bombs has been exposed.

	1	1	1			
	1	?	1			
	2	2	2			
	1	?	1			
	1	1	1			
			1	1	1	
			1	?	1	

pg 129

SOLUTION

Writing an entire game—even a text-based one—would take far longer than the allotted time you have in an interview. This doesn't mean that it's not fair game as a question. It just means that your interviewer's expectation will not be that you actually write all of this in an interview. It also means that you need to focus on getting the key ideas—or structure—out.

Let's start with what the classes are. We certainly want a `Cell` class as well as a `Board` class. We also probably want to have a `Game` class.

> We could potentially merge `Board` and `Game` together, but it's probably best to keep them separate. Err towards more organization, not less. `Board` can hold the list of `Cell` objects and do some basic moves with flipping over cells. `Game` will hold the game state and handle user input.

Design: Cell

Cell will need to have knowledge of whether it's a bomb, a number, or a blank. We could potentially subclass Cell to hold this data, but I'm not sure that offers us much benefit.

We could also have an enum TYPE {BOMB, NUMBER, BLANK} to describe the type of cell. We've chosen not to do this because BLANK is really a type of NUMBER cell, where the number is 0. It's sufficient to just have an isBomb flag.

It's okay to have made different choices here. These aren't the only good choices. Explain the choices you make and their tradeoffs with your interviewer.

We also need to store state for whether the cell is exposed or not. We probably do not want to subclass Cell for ExposedCell and UnexposedCell. This is a bad idea because Board holds a reference to the cells, and we'd have to change the reference when we flip a cell. And then what if other objects reference the instance of Cell?

It's better to just have a boolean flag for isExposed. We'll do a similar thing for isGuess.

```
public class Cell {
  private int row;
  private int column;
  private boolean isBomb;
  private int number;
  private boolean isExposed = false;
  private boolean isGuess = false;

  public Cell(int r, int c) { ... }

  /* Getters and setters for above variables. */
  ...

  public boolean flip() {
    isExposed = true;
    return !isBomb;
  }

  public boolean toggleGuess() {
    if (!isExposed) {
      isGuess = !isGuess;
    }
    return isGuess;
  }

  /* Full code can be found in downloadable code solutions. */
}
```

Design: Board

Board will need to have an array of all the Cell objects. A two-dimension array will work just fine.

We'll probably want Board to keep state of how many unexposed cells there are. We'll track this as we go, so we don't have to continuously count it.

Board will also handle some of the basic algorithms:

- Initializing the board and laying out the bombs.
- Flipping a cell.

- Expanding blank areas.

It will receive the game plays from the Game object and carry them out. It will then need to return the result of the play, which could be any of {clicked a bomb and lost, clicked out of bounds, clicked an already exposed area, clicked a blank area and still playing, clicked a blank area and won, clicked a number and won}. This is really two different items that need to be returned: successful (whether or not the play was successfully made) and a game state (won, lost, playing). We'll use an additional `GamePlayResult` to return this data.

We'll also use a `GamePlay` class to hold the move that the player plays. We need to use a row, column, and then a flag to indicate whether this was an actual flip or the user was just marking this as a "guess" at a possible bomb.

The basic skeleton of this class might look something like this:

```
public class Board {
  private int nRows;
  private int nColumns;
  private int nBombs = 0;
  private Cell[][] cells;
  private Cell[] bombs;
  private int numUnexposedRemaining;

  public Board(int r, int c, int b) { ... }

  private void initializeBoard() { ... }
  private boolean flipCell(Cell cell) { ... }
  public void expandBlank(Cell cell) { ... }
  public UserPlayResult playFlip(UserPlay play) { ... }
  public int getNumRemaining() { return numUnexposedRemaining; }
}

public class UserPlay {
  private int row;
  private int column;
  private boolean isGuess;
  /* constructor, getters, setters. */
}

public class UserPlayResult {
  private boolean successful;
  private Game.GameState resultingState;
  /* constructor, getters, setters. */
}
```

Design: Game

The Game class will store references to the board and hold the game state. It also takes the user input and sends it off to `Board`.

```
public class Game {
  public enum GameState { WON, LOST, RUNNING }

  private Board board;
  private int rows;
  private int columns;
  private int bombs;
  private GameState state;
```

```

    public Game(int r, int c, int b) { ... }

    public boolean initialize() { ... }
    public boolean start() { ... }
    private boolean playGame() { ... } // Loops until game is over.
}
```

Algorithms

This is the basic object-oriented design in our code. Our interviewer might ask us now to implement a few of the most interesting algorithms.

In this case, the three interesting algorithms is the initialization (placing the bombs randomly), setting the values of the numbered cells, and expanding the blank region.

Placing the Bombs

To place the bombs, we could randomly pick a cell and then place a bomb if it's still available, and otherwise pick a different location for it. The problem with this is that if there are a lot of bombs, it could get very slow. We could end up in a situation where we repeatedly pick cells with bombs.

To get around this, we could take an approach similar to the card deck shuffling problem (pg 531). We could place the K bombs in the first K cells and then shuffle all the cells around.

Shuffling an array operates by iterating through the array from `i = 0` through `N-1`. For each `i`, we pick a random index between `i` and `N-1` and swap it with that index.

To shuffle a grid, we do a very similar thing, just converting the index into a row and column location.

```
void shuffleBoard() {
   int nCells = nRows * nColumns;
   Random random = new Random();
   for (int index1 = 0; index1 < nCells; index1++) {
      int index2 = index1 + random.nextInt(nCells - index1);
      if (index1 != index2) {
         /* Get cell at index1. */
         int row1 = index1 / nColumns;
         int column1 = (index1 - row1 * nColumns) % nColumns;
         Cell cell1 = cells[row1][column1];

         /* Get cell at index2. */
         int row2 = index2 / nColumns;
         int column2 = (index2 - row2 * nColumns) % nColumns;
         Cell cell2 = cells[row2][column2];

         /* Swap. */
         cells[row1][column1] = cell2;
         cell2.setRowAndColumn(row1, column1);
         cells[row2][column2] = cell1;
         cell1.setRowAndColumn(row2, column2);
      }
   }
}
```

Setting the Numbered Cells

Once the bombs have been placed, we need to set the values of the numbered cells. We could go through each cell and check how many bombs are around it. This would work, but it's actually a bit slower than is necessary.

Instead, we can go to each bomb and increment each cell around it. For example, cells with 3 bombs will get `incrementNumber` called three times on them and will wind up with a number of 3.

```
/* Set the cells around the bombs to the right number. Although the bombs have
 * been shuffled, the reference in the bombs array is still to same object. */
void setNumberedCells() {
  int[][] deltas = { // Offsets of 8 surrounding cells
      {-1, -1}, {-1, 0}, {-1, 1},
      { 0, -1},          { 0, 1},
      { 1, -1}, { 1, 0}, { 1, 1}
  };
  for (Cell bomb : bombs) {
    int row = bomb.getRow();
    int col = bomb.getColumn();
    for (int[] delta : deltas) {
      int r = row + delta[0];
      int c = col + delta[1];
      if (inBounds(r, c)) {
        cells[r][c].incrementNumber();
      }
    }
  }
}
```

Expanding a Blank Region

Expanding the blank region could be done either iteratively or recursively. We implemented it iteratively.

You can think about this algorithm like this: each blank cell is surrounded by either blank cells or numbered cells (never a bomb). All need to be flipped. But, if you're flipping a blank cell, you also need to add the blank cells to a queue, to flip their neighboring cells.

```
void expandBlank(Cell cell) {
  int[][] deltas = {
      {-1, -1}, {-1, 0}, {-1, 1},
      { 0, -1},          { 0, 1},
      { 1, -1}, { 1, 0}, { 1, 1}
  };

  Queue<Cell> toExplore = new LinkedList<Cell>();
  toExplore.add(cell);

  while (!toExplore.isEmpty()) {
    Cell current = toExplore.remove();

    for (int[] delta : deltas) {
      int r = current.getRow() + delta[0];
      int c = current.getColumn() + delta[1];

      if (inBounds(r, c)) {
        Cell neighbor = cells[r][c];
        if (flipCell(neighbor) && neighbor.isBlank()) {
          toExplore.add(neighbor);
```

```
                }
            }
        }
    }
}
```

You could instead implement this algorithm recursively. In this algorithm, rather than adding the cell to a queue, you would make a recursive call.

Your implementation of these algorithms could vary substantially depending on your class design.

7.11 File System: Explain the data structures and algorithms that you would use to design an in-memory file system. Illustrate with an example in code where possible.

pg 129

SOLUTION

Many candidates may see this problem and instantly panic. A file system seems so low level!

However, there's no need to panic. If we think through the components of a file system, we can tackle this problem just like any other object-oriented design question.

A file system, in its most simplistic version, consists of `Files` and `Directories`. Each `Directory` contains a set of `Files` and `Directories`. Since `Files` and `Directories` share so many characteristics, we've implemented them such that they inherit from the same class, `Entry`.

```
public abstract class Entry {
   protected Directory parent;
   protected long created;
   protected long lastUpdated;
   protected long lastAccessed;
   protected String name;

   public Entry(String n, Directory p) {
      name = n;
      parent = p;
      created = System.currentTimeMillis();
      lastUpdated = System.currentTimeMillis();
      lastAccessed = System.currentTimeMillis();
   }

   public boolean delete() {
      if (parent == null) return false;
      return parent.deleteEntry(this);
   }

   public abstract int size();

   public String getFullPath() {
      if (parent == null) return name;
      else return parent.getFullPath() + "/" + name;
   }

   /* Getters and setters. */
   public long getCreationTime() { return created; }
   public long getLastUpdatedTime() { return lastUpdated; }
   public long getLastAccessedTime() { return lastAccessed; }
```

```
    public void changeName(String n) { name = n; }
    public String getName() { return name; }
}

public class File extends Entry {
    private String content;
    private int size;

    public File(String n, Directory p, int sz) {
        super(n, p);
        size = sz;
    }

    public int size() { return size; }
    public String getContents() { return content; }
    public void setContents(String c) { content = c; }
}

public class Directory extends Entry {
    protected ArrayList<Entry> contents;

    public Directory(String n, Directory p) {
        super(n, p);
        contents = new ArrayList<Entry>();
    }

    public int size() {
        int size = 0;
        for (Entry e : contents) {
            size += e.size();
        }
        return size;
    }

    public int numberOfFiles() {
        int count = 0;
        for (Entry e : contents) {
            if (e instanceof Directory) {
                count++; // Directory counts as a file
                Directory d = (Directory) e;
                count += d.numberOfFiles();
            } else if (e instanceof File) {
                count++;
            }
        }
        return count;
    }

    public boolean deleteEntry(Entry entry) {
        return contents.remove(entry);
    }

    public void addEntry(Entry entry) {
        contents.add(entry);
    }

```

```
    protected ArrayList<Entry> getContents() { return contents; }
}
```

Alternatively, we could have implemented `Directory` such that it contains separate lists for files and subdirectories. This makes the `numberOfFiles()` method a bit cleaner, since it doesn't need to use the `instanceof` operator, but it does prohibit us from cleanly sorting files and directories by dates or names.

7.12 Hash Table: Design and implement a hash table which uses chaining (linked lists) to handle collisions.

pg 129

SOLUTION

Suppose we are implementing a hash table that looks like `Hash<K, V>`. That is, the hash table maps from objects of type K to objects of type V.

At first, we might think our data structure would look something like this:

```
class Hash<K, V> {
  LinkedList<V>[] items;
  public void put(K key, V value) { ... }
  public V get(K key) { ... }
}
```

Note that `items` is an array of linked lists, where `items[i]` is a linked list of all objects with keys that map to index `i` (that is, all the objects that collided at `i`).

This would seem to work until we think more deeply about collisions.

Suppose we have a very simple hash function that uses the string length.

```
int hashCodeOfKey(K key) {
  return key.toString().length() % items.length;
}
```

The keys `jim` and `bob` will map to the same index in the array, even though they are different keys. We need to search through the linked list to find the actual object that corresponds to these keys. But how would we do that? All we've stored in the linked list is the value, not the original key.

This is why we need to store both the value and the original key.

One way to do that is to create another object called `LinkedListNode` which pairs keys and values. With this implementation, our linked list is of type `LinkedListNode`.

The code below uses this implementation.

```
public class Hasher<K, V> {
  /* Linked list node class. Used only within hash table. No one else should get
   * access to this. Implemented as doubly linked list. */
  private static class LinkedListNode<K, V> {
    public LinkedListNode<K, V> next;
    public LinkedListNode<K, V> prev;
    public K key;
    public V value;
    public LinkedListNode(K k, V v) {
      key = k;
      value = v;
    }
  }

```

```
    private ArrayList<LinkedListNode<K, V>> arr;
    public Hasher(int capacity) {
       /* Create list of linked lists at a particular size. Fill list with null
        * values, as it's the only way to make the array the desired size. */
       arr = new ArrayList<LinkedListNode<K, V>>();
       arr.ensureCapacity(capacity); // Optional optimization
       for (int i = 0; i < capacity; i++) {
          arr.add(null);
       }
    }

    /* Insert key and value into hash table and return old value. */
    public V put(K key, V value) {
       LinkedListNode<K, V> node = getNodeForKey(key);
       if (node != null) {
          V oldValue = node.value;
          node.value = value; // just update the value.
          return oldValue;
       }

       node = new LinkedListNode<K, V>(key, value);
       int index = getIndexForKey(key);
       if (arr.get(index) != null) {
          node.next = arr.get(index);
          node.next.prev = node;
       }
       arr.set(index, node);
       return null;
    }

    /* Remove node for key and return value. */
    public V remove(K key) {
       LinkedListNode<K, V> node = getNodeForKey(key);
       if (node == null) {
          return null;
       }

       if (node.prev != null) {
          node.prev.next = node.next;
       } else {
          /* Removing head - update. */
          int hashKey = getIndexForKey(key);
          arr.set(hashKey, node.next);
       }

       if (node.next != null) {
          node.next.prev = node.prev;
       }
       return node.value;
    }

    /* Get value for key. */
    public V get(K key) {
       if (key == null) return null;
       LinkedListNode<K, V> node = getNodeForKey(key);
       return node == null ? null : node.value;
```

```
    }

    /* Get linked list node associated with a given key. */
    private LinkedListNode<K, V> getNodeForKey(K key) {
       int index = getIndexForKey(key);
       LinkedListNode<K, V> current = arr.get(index);
       while (current != null) {
          if (current.key == key) {
             return current;
          }
          current = current.next;
       }
       return null;
    }

    /* Really naive function to map a key to an index. */
    public int getIndexForKey(K key) {
       return Math.abs(key.hashCode() % arr.size());
    }
 }
```

Alternatively, we could implement a similar data structure (a key->value lookup) with a binary search tree as the underlying data structure. Retrieving an element will no longer be `O(1)` (although, technically, this implementation is not `O(1)` if there are many collisions), but it prevents us from creating an unnecessarily large array to hold items.

Solutions to Recursion and Dynamic Programming

8.1 Triple Step: A child is running up a staircase with n steps and can hop either 1 step, 2 steps, or 3 steps at a time. Implement a method to count how many possible ways the child can run up the stairs.

pg 134

SOLUTION

Let's think about this with the following question: What is the very last step that is done?

The very last hop the child makes—the one that lands her on the nth step—was either a 3-step hop, a 2-step hop, or a 1-step hop.

How many ways then are there to get up to the nth step? We don't know yet, but we can relate it to some subproblems.

If we thought about all of the paths to the nth step, we could just build them off the paths to the three previous steps. We can get up to the nth step by any of the following:

- Going to the (n-1)st step and hopping 1 step.
- Going to the (n-2)nd step and hopping 2 steps.
- Going to the (n-3)rd step and hopping 3 steps.

Therefore, we just need to add the number of these paths together.

Be very careful here. A lot of people want to multiply them. Multiplying one path with another would signify taking one path and then taking the other. That's not what's happening here.

Brute Force Solution

This is a fairly straightforward algorithm to implement recursively. We just need to follow logic like this:

```
countWays(n-1) + countWays(n-2) + countWays(n-3)
```

The one tricky bit is defining the base case. If we have 0 steps to go (we're currently standing on the step), are there zero paths to that step or one path?

That is, what is `countWays(0)`? Is it 1 or 0?

You could define it either way. There is no "right" answer here.

However, it's a lot easier to define it as 1. If you defined it as 0, then you would need some additional base cases (or else you'd just wind up with a series of 0s getting added).

A simple implementation of this code is below.

```
int countWays(int n) {
  if (n < 0) {
    return 0;
  } else if (n == 0) {
    return 1;
  } else {
    return countWays(n-1) + countWays(n-2) + countWays(n-3);
  }
}
```

Like the Fibonacci problem, the runtime of this algorithm is exponential (roughly $O(3^n)$), since each call branches out to three more calls.

Memoization Solution

The previous solution for `countWays` is called many times for the same values, which is unnecessary. We can fix this through memoization.

Essentially, if we've seen this value of n before, return the cached value. Each time we compute a fresh value, add it to the cache.

Typically we use a `HashMap<Integer, Integer>` for a cache. In this case, the keys will be exactly `1` through n. It's more compact to use an integer array.

```
int countWays(int n) {
  int[] memo = new int[n + 1];
  Arrays.fill(memo, -1);
  return countWays(n, memo);
}

int countWays(int n, int[] memo) {
  if (n < 0) {
    return 0;
  } else if (n == 0) {
    return 1;
  } else if (memo[n] > -1) {
    return memo[n];
  } else {
    memo[n] = countWays(n - 1, memo) + countWays(n - 2, memo) +
              countWays(n - 3, memo);
    return memo[n];
  }
}
```

Regardless of whether or not you use memoization, note that the number of ways will quickly overflow the bounds of an integer. By the time you get to just n = 37, the result has already overflowed. Using a `long` will delay, but not completely solve, this issue.

It is great to communicate this issue to your interviewer. He probably won't ask you to work around it (although you could, with a `BigInteger` class), but it's nice to demonstrate that you think about these issues.

8.2 **Robot in a Grid:** Imagine a robot sitting on the upper left corner of grid with r rows and c columns. The robot can only move in two directions, right and down, but certain cells are "off limits" such that the robot cannot step on them. Design an algorithm to find a path for the robot from the top left to the bottom right.

pg 135

SOLUTION

If we picture this grid, the only way to move to spot `(r,c)` is by moving to one of the adjacent spots: `(r-1,c)` or `(r,c-1)`. So, we need to find a path to either `(r-1,c)` or `(r,c-1)`.

How do we find a path to those spots? To find a path to `(r-1,c)` or `(r,c-1)`, we need to move to one of its adjacent cells. So, we need to find a path to a spot adjacent to `(r-1,c)`, which are coordinates `(r-2,c)` and `(r-1,c-1)`, or a spot adjacent to `(r,c-1)`, which are spots `(r-1,c-1)` and `(r,c-2)`. Observe that we list the point `(r-1,c-1)` twice; we'll discuss that issue later.

> Tip: A lot of people use the variable names x and y when dealing with two-dimensional arrays. This can actually cause some bugs. People tend to think about x as the first coordinate in the matrix and y as the second coordinate (e.g., `matrix[x][y]`). But, this isn't really correct. The first coordinate is usually thought of as the row number, which is in fact the y value (it goes vertically!). You should write `matrix[y][x]`. Or, just make your life easier by using r (row) and c (column) instead.

So then, to find a path from the origin, we just work backwards like this. Starting from the last cell, we try to find a path to each of its adjacent cells. The recursive code below implements this algorithm.

```
ArrayList<Point> getPath(boolean[][] maze) {
   if (maze == null || maze.length == 0) return null;
   ArrayList<Point> path = new ArrayList<Point>();
   if (getPath(maze, maze.length - 1, maze[0].length - 1, path)) {
      return path;
   }
   return null;
}

boolean getPath(boolean[][] maze, int row, int col, ArrayList<Point> path) {
   /* If out of bounds or not available, return.*/
   if (col < 0 || row < 0 || !maze[row][col]) {
      return false;
   }

   boolean isAtOrigin = (row == 0) && (col == 0);

   /* If there's a path from the start to here, add my location. */
   if (isAtOrigin || getPath(maze, row, col - 1, path) ||
        getPath(maze, row - 1, col, path)) {
      Point p = new Point(row, col);
      path.add(p);
      return true;
   }

   return false;
}
```

This solution is $O(2^{r+c})$, since each path has r+c steps and there are two choices we can make at each step.

We should look for a faster way.

Often, we can optimize exponential algorithms by finding duplicate work. What work are we repeating?

If we walk through the algorithm, we'll see that we are visiting squares multiple times. In fact, we visit each square many, many times. After all, we have `rc` squares but we're doing $O(2^{r+c})$ work. If we were only visiting each square once, we would probably have an algorithm that was `O(rc)` (unless we were somehow doing a lot of work during each visit).

How does our current algorithm work? To find a path to `(r,c)`, we look for a path to an adjacent coordinate: `(r-1,c)` or `(r,c-1)`. Of course, if one of those squares is off limits, we ignore it. Then, we look at their adjacent coordinates: `(r-2,c)`, `(r-1,c-1)`, `(r-1,c-1)`, and `(r,c-2)`. The spot `(r-1,c-1)` appears twice, which means that we're duplicating effort. Ideally, we should remember that we already visited `(r-1,c-1)` so that we don't waste our time.

This is what the dynamic programming algorithm below does.

```
ArrayList<Point> getPath(boolean[][] maze) {
  if (maze == null || maze.length == 0) return null;
  ArrayList<Point> path = new ArrayList<Point>();
  HashSet<Point> failedPoints = new HashSet<Point>();
  if (getPath(maze, maze.length - 1, maze[0].length - 1, path, failedPoints)) {
    return path;
  }
  return null;
}

boolean getPath(boolean[][] maze, int row, int col, ArrayList<Point> path,
                HashSet<Point> failedPoints) {
  /* If out of bounds or not available, return.*/
  if (col < 0 || row < 0 || !maze[row][col]) {
    return false;
  }

  Point p = new Point(row, col);

  /* If we've already visited this cell, return. */
  if (failedPoints.contains(p)) {
    return false;
  }

  boolean isAtOrigin = (row == 0) && (col == 0);

  /* If there's a path from start to my current location, add my location.*/
  if (isAtOrigin || getPath(maze, row, col - 1, path, failedPoints) ||
      getPath(maze, row - 1, col, path, failedPoints)) {
    path.add(p);
    return true;
  }

  failedPoints.add(p); // Cache result
  return false;
}
```

This simple change will make our code run substantially faster. The algorithm will now take `O(rc)` time because we hit each cell just once.

8.3 Magic Index: A magic index in an array `A[1...n-1]` is defined to be an index such that `A[i] = i`. Given a sorted array of distinct integers, write a method to find a magic index, if one exists, in array A.

FOLLOW UP

What if the values are not distinct?

pg 135

SOLUTION

Immediately, the brute force solution should jump to mind—and there's no shame in mentioning it. We simply iterate through the array, looking for an element which matches this condition.

```
int magicSlow(int[] array) {
   for (int i = 0; i < array.length; i++) {
      if (array[i] == i) {
         return i;
      }
   }
   return -1;
}
```

Given that the array is sorted, though, it's very likely that we're supposed to use this condition.

We may recognize that this problem sounds a lot like the classic binary search problem. Leveraging the Pattern Matching approach for generating algorithms, how might we apply binary search here?

In binary search, we find an element k by comparing it to the middle element, x, and determining if k would land on the left or the right side of x.

Building off this approach, is there a way that we can look at the middle element to determine where a magic index might be? Let's look at a sample array:

-40	-20	-1	1	2	3	5	7	9	12	13
0	1	2	3	4	5	6	7	8	9	10

When we look at the middle element `A[5] = 3`, we know that the magic index must be on the right side, since `A[mid] < mid`.

Why couldn't the magic index be on the left side? Observe that when we move from `i` to `i-1`, the value at this index must decrease by at least 1, if not more (since the array is sorted and all the elements are distinct). So, if the middle element is already too small to be a magic index, then when we move to the left, subtracting k indexes and (at least) k values, all subsequent elements will also be too small.

We continue to apply this recursive algorithm, developing code that looks very much like binary search.

```
int magicFast(int[] array) {
   return magicFast(array, 0, array.length - 1);
}

int magicFast(int[] array, int start, int end) {
   if (end < start) {
      return -1;
   }
   int mid = (start + end) / 2;
   if (array[mid] == mid) {
      return mid;
   } else if (array[mid] > mid){
```

```
      return magicFast(array, start, mid - 1);
    } else {
      return magicFast(array, mid + 1, end);
    }
}
```

Follow Up: What if the elements are not distinct?

If the elements are not distinct, then this algorithm fails. Consider the following array:

-10	-5	2	2	2	3	4	7	9	12	13
0	1	2	3	4	5	6	7	8	9	10

When we see that `A[mid] < mid`, we cannot conclude which side the magic index is on. It could be on the right side, as before. Or, it could be on the left side (as it, in fact, is).

Could it be *anywhere* on the left side? Not exactly. Since `A[5] = 3`, we know that `A[4]` couldn't be a magic index. `A[4]` would need to be 4 to be the magic index, but `A[4]` must be less than or equal to `A[5]`.

In fact, when we see that `A[5] = 3`, we'll need to recursively search the right side as before. But, to search the left side, we can skip a bunch of elements and only recursively search elements `A[0]` through `A[3]`. `A[3]` is the first element that could be a magic index.

The general pattern is that we compare `midIndex` and `midValue` for equality first. Then, if they are not equal, we recursively search the left and right sides as follows:

- Left side: search indices `start` through `Math.min(midIndex - 1, midValue)`.
- Right side: search indices `Math.max(midIndex + 1, midValue)` through end.

The code below implements this algorithm.

```
int magicFast(int[] array) {
  return magicFast(array, 0, array.length - 1);
}

int magicFast(int[] array, int start, int end) {
  if (end < start) return -1;

  int midIndex = (start + end) / 2;
  int midValue = array[midIndex];
  if (midValue == midIndex) {
    return midIndex;
  }

  /* Search left */
  int leftIndex = Math.min(midIndex - 1, midValue);
  int left = magicFast(array, start, leftIndex);
  if (left >= 0) {
    return left;
  }

  /* Search right */
  int rightIndex = Math.max(midIndex + 1, midValue);
  int right = magicFast(array, rightIndex, end);

  return right;
}
```

Note that in the above code, if the elements are all distinct, the method operates almost identically to the first solution.

8.4 Power Set: Write a method to return all subsets of a set.

pg 135

SOLUTION

We should first have some reasonable expectations of our time and space complexity.

How many subsets of a set are there? When we generate a subset, each element has the "choice" of either being in there or not. That is, for the first element, there are two choices: it is either in the set, or it is not. For the second, there are two, etc. So, doing `{2 * 2 * ... }` n times gives us 2^n subsets.

Assuming that we're going to be returning a list of subsets, then our best case time is actually the total number of elements across all of those subsets. There are 2^n subsets and each of the n elements will be contained in half of the subsets (which 2^{n-1} subsets). Therefore, the total number of elements across all of those subsets is $n * 2^{n-1}$.

We will not be able to beat $O(n2^n)$ in space or time complexity.

The subsets of $\{a_1, a_2, \ldots, a_n\}$ are also called the powerset, $P(\{a_1, a_2, \ldots, a_n\})$, or just $P(n)$.

Solution #1: Recursion

This problem is a good candidate for the Base Case and Build approach. Imagine that we are trying to find all subsets of a set like $S = \{a_1, a_2, \ldots, a_n\}$. We can start with the Base Case.

Base Case: n = 0.

There is just one subset of the empty set: {}.

Case: n = 1.

There are two subsets of the set $\{a_1\}$: {}, $\{a_1\}$.

Case: n = 2.

There are four subsets of the set $\{a_1, a_2\}$: {}, $\{a_1\}$, $\{a_2\}$, $\{a_1, a_2\}$.

Case: n = 3.

Now here's where things get interesting. We want to find a way of generating the solution for n = 3 based on the prior solutions.

What is the difference between the solution for n = 3 and the solution for n = 2? Let's look at this more deeply:

$$P(2) = \{\}, \{a_1\}, \{a_2\}, \{a_1, a_2\}$$
$$P(3) = \{\}, \{a_1\}, \{a_2\}, \{a_3\}, \{a_1, a_2\}, \{a_1, a_3\}, \{a_2, a_3\}, \{a_1, a_2, a_3\}$$

The difference between these solutions is that P(2) is missing all the subsets containing a_3.

$$P(3) - P(2) = \{a_3\}, \{a_1, a_3\}, \{a_2, a_3\}, \{a_1, a_2, a_3\}$$

How can we use P(2) to create P(3)? We can simply clone the subsets in P(2) and add a_3 to them:

$$P(2) = \{\}, \{a_1\}, \{a_2\}, \{a_1, a_2\}$$
$$P(2) + a_3 = \{a_3\}, \{a_1, a_3\}, \{a_2, a_3\}, \{a_1, a_2, a_3\}$$

When merged together, the lines above make P(3).

Case: n > 0

Generating P(n) for the general case is just a simple generalization of the above steps. We compute P(n-1), clone the results, and then add a_n to each of these cloned sets.

The following code implements this algorithm:

```
ArrayList<ArrayList<Integer>> getSubsets(ArrayList<Integer> set, int index) {
  ArrayList<ArrayList<Integer>> allsubsets;
  if (set.size() == index) { // Base case - add empty set
    allsubsets = new ArrayList<ArrayList<Integer>>();
    allsubsets.add(new ArrayList<Integer>()); // Empty set
  } else {
    allsubsets = getSubsets(set, index + 1);
    int item = set.get(index);
    ArrayList<ArrayList<Integer>> moresubsets =
      new ArrayList<ArrayList<Integer>>();
    for (ArrayList<Integer> subset : allsubsets) {
      ArrayList<Integer> newsubset = new ArrayList<Integer>();
      newsubset.addAll(subset); //
      newsubset.add(item);
      moresubsets.add(newsubset);
    }
    allsubsets.addAll(moresubsets);
  }
  return allsubsets;
}
```

This solution will be $O(n2^n)$ in time and space, which is the best we can do. For a slight optimization, we could also implement this algorithm iteratively.

Solution #2: Combinatorics

While there's nothing wrong with the above solution, there's another way to approach it.

Recall that when we're generating a set, we have two choices for each element: (1) the element is in the set (the "yes" state) or (2) the element is not in the set (the "no" state). This means that each subset is a sequence of yeses / nos—e.g., "yes, yes, no, no, yes, no"

This gives us 2^n possible subsets. How can we iterate through all possible sequences of "yes" / "no" states for all elements? If each "yes" can be treated as a 1 and each "no" can be treated as a 0, then each subset can be represented as a binary string.

Generating all subsets, then, really just comes down to generating all binary numbers (that is, all integers). We iterate through all numbers from 0 to 2^n (exclusive) and translate the binary representation of the numbers into a set. Easy!

```
ArrayList<ArrayList<Integer>> getSubsets2(ArrayList<Integer> set) {
  ArrayList<ArrayList<Integer>> allsubsets = new ArrayList<ArrayList<Integer>>();
  int max = 1 << set.size(); /* Compute 2^n */
  for (int k = 0; k < max; k++) {
    ArrayList<Integer> subset = convertIntToSet(k, set);
    allsubsets.add(subset);
  }
  return allsubsets;
}
```

```

ArrayList<Integer> convertIntToSet(int x, ArrayList<Integer> set) {
   ArrayList<Integer> subset = new ArrayList<Integer>();
   int index = 0;
   for (int k = x; k > 0; k >>= 1) {
      if ((k & 1) == 1) {
         subset.add(set.get(index));
      }
      index++;
   }
   return subset;
}
```

There's nothing substantially better or worse about this solution compared to the first one.

8.5 Recursive Multiply: Write a recursive function to multiply two positive integers without using the * operator (or / operator). You can use addition, subtraction, and bit shifting, but you should minimize the number of those operations.

pg 135

SOLUTION

Let's pause for a moment and think about what it means to do multiplication.

> This is a good approach for a lot of interview questions. It's often useful to think about what it really means to do something, even when it's pretty obvious.

We can think about multiplying 8x7 as doing 8+8+8+8+8+8+8 (or adding 7 eight times). We can also think about it as the number of squares in an 8x7 grid.

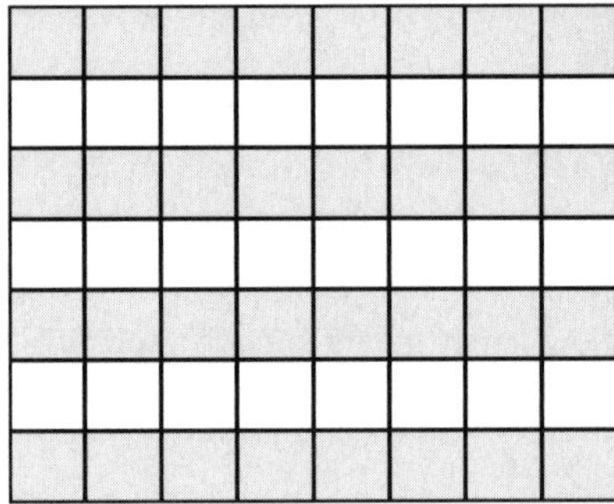

Solution #1

How would we count the number of squares in this grid? We could just count each cell. That's pretty slow, though.

Alternatively, we could count half the squares and then double it (by adding this count to itself). To count half the squares, we repeat the same process.

Of course, this "doubling" only works if the number is in fact even. When it's not even, we need to do the counting/summing from scratch.

```
int minProduct(int a, int b) {
   int bigger = a < b ? b : a;
```

```
  int smaller = a < b ? a : b;
  return minProductHelper(smaller, bigger);
}

int minProductHelper(int smaller, int bigger) {
  if (smaller == 0) { // 0 x bigger = 0
    return 0;
  } else if (smaller == 1) { // 1 x bigger = bigger
    return bigger;
  }

  /* Compute half. If uneven, compute other half. If even, double it. */
  int s = smaller >> 1; // Divide by 2
  int side1 = minProductHelper(s, bigger);
  int side2 = side1;
  if (smaller % 2 == 1) {
    side2 = minProductHelper(smaller - s, bigger);
  }

  return side1 + side2;
}
```

Can we do better? Yes.

Solution #2

If we observe how the recursion operates, we'll notice that we have duplicated work. Consider this example:

```
minProduct(17, 23)
      minProduct(8, 23)
          minProduct(4, 23) * 2
              ...
    + minProduct(9, 23)
          minProduct(4, 23)
              ...
        + minProduct(5, 23)
              ...
```

The second call to `minProduct(4, 23)` is unaware of the prior call, and so it repeats the same work. We should cache these results.

```
int minProduct(int a, int b) {
  int bigger = a < b ? b : a;
  int smaller = a < b ? a : b;

  int memo[] = new int[smaller + 1];
  return minProduct(smaller, bigger, memo);
}

int minProduct(int smaller, int bigger, int[] memo) {
  if (smaller == 0) {
    return 0;
  } else if (smaller == 1) {
    return bigger;
  } else if (memo[smaller] > 0) {
    return memo[smaller];
  }

  /* Compute half. If uneven, compute other half. If even, double it. */
```

```
    int s = smaller >> 1; // Divide by 2
    int side1 = minProduct(s, bigger, memo); // Compute half
    int side2 = side1;
    if (smaller % 2 == 1) {
       side2 = minProduct(smaller - s, bigger, memo);
    }

    /* Sum and cache.*/
    memo[smaller] = side1 + side2;
    return memo[smaller];
}
```

We can still make this a bit faster.

Solution #3

One thing we might notice when we look at this code is that a call to `minProduct` on an even number is much faster than one on an odd number. For example, if we call `minProduct(30, 35)`, then we'll just do `minProduct(15, 35)` and double the result. However, if we do `minProduct(31, 35)`, then we'll need to call `minProduct(15, 35)` and `minProduct(16, 35)`.

This is unnecessary. Instead, we can do:

```
minProduct(31, 35) = 2 * minProduct(15, 35) + 35
```

After all, since `31 = 2*15+1`, then `31x35 = 2*15*35+35`.

The logic in this final solution is that, on even numbers, we just divide `smaller` by 2 and double the result of the recursive call. On odd numbers, we do the same, but then we also add `bigger` to this result.

In doing so, we have an unexpected "win." Our `minProduct` function just recurses straight downwards, with increasingly small numbers each time. It will never repeat the same call, so there's no need to cache any information.

```
int minProduct(int a, int b) {
   int bigger = a < b ? b : a;
   int smaller = a < b ? a : b;
   return minProductHelper(smaller, bigger);
}

int minProductHelper(int smaller, int bigger) {
   if (smaller == 0) return 0;
   else if (smaller == 1) return bigger;

   int s = smaller >> 1; // Divide by 2
   int halfProd = minProductHelper(s, bigger);

   if (smaller % 2 == 0) {
      return halfProd + halfProd;
   } else {
      return halfProd + halfProd + bigger;
   }
}
```

This algorithm will run in `O(log s)` time, where `s` is the smaller of the two numbers.

8.6 **Towers of Hanoi:** In the classic problem of the Towers of Hanoi, you have 3 towers and N disks of different sizes which can slide onto any tower. The puzzle starts with disks sorted in ascending order of size from top to bottom (i.e., each disk sits on top of an even larger one). You have the following constraints:

(1) Only one disk can be moved at a time.

(2) A disk is slid off the top of one tower onto another tower.

(3) A disk cannot be placed on top of a smaller disk.

Write a program to move the disks from the first tower to the last using Stacks.

pg 135

SOLUTION

This problem sounds like a good candidate for the Base Case and Build approach.

Let's start with the smallest possible example: `n = 1`.

Case `n = 1`. Can we move Disk 1 from Tower 1 to Tower 3? Yes.

1. We simply move Disk 1 from Tower 1 to Tower 3.

Case `n = 2`. Can we move Disk 1 and Disk 2 from Tower 1 to Tower 3? Yes.

1. Move Disk 1 from Tower 1 to Tower 2
2. Move Disk 2 from Tower 1 to Tower 3
3. Move Disk 1 from Tower 2 to Tower 3

Note how in the above steps, Tower 2 acts as a buffer, holding a disk while we move other disks to Tower 3.

Case `n = 3`. Can we move Disk 1, 2, and 3 from Tower 1 to Tower 3? Yes.

1. We know we can move the top two disks from one tower to another (as shown earlier), so let's assume we've already done that. But instead, let's move them to Tower 2.
2. Move Disk 3 to Tower 3.
3. Move Disk 1 and Disk 2 to Tower 3. We already know how to do this—just repeat what we did in Step 1.

Case `n = 4`. Can we move Disk 1, 2, 3 and 4 from Tower 1 to Tower 3? Yes.

1. Move Disks 1, 2, and 3 to Tower 2. We know how to do that from the earlier examples.
2. Move Disk 4 to Tower 3.
3. Move Disks 1, 2 and 3 back to Tower 3.

Remember that the labels of Tower 2 and Tower 3 aren't important. They're equivalent towers. So, moving disks to Tower 3 with Tower 2 serving as a buffer is equivalent to moving disks to Tower 2 with Tower 3 serving as a buffer.

This approach leads to a natural recursive algorithm. In each part, we are doing the following steps, outlined below with pseudocode:

```
moveDisks(int n, Tower origin, Tower destination, Tower buffer) {
   /* Base case */
   if (n <= 0) return;

   /* move top n - 1 disks from origin to buffer, using destination as a buffer. */
   moveDisks(n - 1, origin, buffer, destination);

   /* move top from origin to destination
   moveTop(origin, destination);

   /* move top n - 1 disks from buffer to destination, using origin as a buffer. */
   moveDisks(n - 1, buffer, destination, origin);
}
```

The following code provides a more detailed implementation of this algorithm, using concepts of object-oriented design.

```
void main(String[] args) {
   int n = 3;
   Tower[] towers = new Tower[n];
   for (int i = 0; i < 3; i++) {
      towers[i] = new Tower(i);
   }

   for (int i = n - 1; i >= 0; i--) {
      towers[0].add(i);
   }
   towers[0].moveDisks(n, towers[2], towers[1]);
}

class Tower {
   private Stack<Integer> disks;
   private int index;
   public Tower(int i) {
      disks = new Stack<Integer>();
      index = i;
   }

   public int index() {
      return index;
   }

   public void add(int d) {
      if (!disks.isEmpty() && disks.peek() <= d) {
         System.out.println("Error placing disk " + d);
      } else {
         disks.push(d);
      }
   }

   public void moveTopTo(Tower t) {
      int top = disks.pop();
      t.add(top);
   }

```

```
    public void moveDisks(int n, Tower destination, Tower buffer) {
      if (n > 0) {
        moveDisks(n - 1, buffer, destination);
        moveTopTo(destination);
        buffer.moveDisks(n - 1, destination, this);
      }
    }
}
```

Implementing the towers as their own objects is not strictly necessary, but it does help to make the code cleaner in some respects.

8.7 Permutations without Dups: Write a method to compute all permutations of a string of unique characters.

pg 135

SOLUTION

Like in many recursive problems, the Base Case and Build approach will be useful. Assume we have a string S represented by the characters $a_1a_2...a_n$.

Approach 1: Building from permutations of first n-1 characters.

Base Case: permutations of first character substring

The only permutation of a_1 is the string a_1. So:

$P(a_1) = a_1$

Case: permutations of a_1a_2

$P(a_1a_2) = a_1a_2$ and a_2a_1

Case: permutations of $a_1a_2a_3$

$P(a_1a_2a_3) = a_1a_2a_3, a_1a_3a_2, a_2a_1a_3, a_2a_3a_1, a_3a_1a_2, a_3a_2a_1,$

Case: permutations of $a_1a_2a_3a_4$

This is the first interesting case. How can we generate permutations of $a_1a_2a_3a_4$ from $a_1a_2a_3$?

Each permutation of $a_1a_2a_3a_4$ represents an ordering of $a_1a_2a_3$. For example, $a_2a_4a_1a_3$ represents the order $a_2a_1a_3$.

Therefore, if we took all the permutations of $a_1a_2a_3$ and added a_4 into all possible locations, we would get all permutations of $a_1a_2a_3a_4$.

$a_1a_2a_3$ -> $a_4a_1a_2a_3$, $a_1a_4a_2a_3$, $a_1a_2a_4a_3$, $a_1a_2a_3a_4$
$a_1a_3a_2$ -> $a_4a_1a_3a_2$, $a_1a_4a_3a_2$, $a_1a_3a_4a_2$, $a_1a_3a_2a_4$
$a_3a_1a_2$ -> $a_4a_3a_1a_2$, $a_3a_4a_1a_2$, $a_3a_1a_4a_2$, $a_3a_1a_2a_4$
$a_2a_1a_3$ -> $a_4a_2a_1a_3$, $a_2a_4a_1a_3$, $a_2a_1a_4a_3$, $a_2a_1a_3a_4$
$a_2a_3a_1$ -> $a_4a_2a_3a_1$, $a_2a_4a_3a_1$, $a_2a_3a_4a_1$, $a_2a_3a_1a_4$
$a_3a_2a_1$ -> $a_4a_3a_2a_1$, $a_3a_4a_2a_1$, $a_3a_2a_4a_1$, $a_3a_2a_1a_4$

We can now implement this algorithm recursively.

```
ArrayList<String> getPerms(String str) {
  if (str == null) return null;

  ArrayList<String> permutations = new ArrayList<String>();
  if (str.length() == 0) { // base case
    permutations.add(“”);
```

```
        return permutations;
    }

    char first = str.charAt(0); // get the first char
    String remainder = str.substring(1); // remove the first char
    ArrayList<String> words = getPerms(remainder);
    for (String word : words) {
        for (int j = 0; j <= word.length(); j++) {
            String s = insertCharAt(word, first, j);
            permutations.add(s);
        }
    }
    return permutations;
}

/* Insert char c at index i in word. */
String insertCharAt(String word, char c, int i) {
    String start = word.substring(0, i);
    String end = word.substring(i);
    return start + c + end;
}
```

Approach 2: Building from permutations of all n-1 character substrings.

Base Case: single-character strings

The only permutation of a_1 is the string a_1. So:

$$P(a_1) = a_1$$

Case: two-character strings

$P(a_1a_2) = a_1a_2$ and a_2a_1.
$P(a_2a_3) = a_2a_3$ and a_3a_2.
$P(a_1a_3) = a_1a_3$ and a_3a_1.

Case: three-character strings

Here is where the cases get more interesting. How can we generate all permutations of three-character strings, such as $a_1a_2a_3$, given the permutations of two-character strings?

Well, in essence, we just need to "try" each character as the first character and then append the permutations.

$P(a_1a_2a_3) = \{a_1 + P(a_2a_3)\} + a_2 + P(a_1a_3)\} + \{a_3 + P(a_1a_2)\}$
$\{a_1 + P(a_2a_3)\}$ -> $a_1a_2a_3$, $a_1a_3a_2$
$\{a_2 + P(a_1a_3)\}$ -> $a_2a_1a_3$, $a_2a_3a_1$
$\{a_3 + P(a_1a_2)\}$ -> $a_3a_1a_2$, $a_3a_2a_1$

Now that we can generate all permutations of three-character strings, we can use this to generate permutations of four-character strings.

$$P(a_1a_2a_3a_4) = \{a_1 + P(a_2a_3a_4)\} + \{a_2 + P(a_1a_3a_4)\} + \{a_3 + P(a_1a_2a_4)\} + \{a_4 + P(a_1a_2a_3)\}$$

This is now a fairly straightforward algorithm to implement.

```
ArrayList<String> getPerms(String remainder) {
    int len = remainder.length();
    ArrayList<String> result = new ArrayList<String>();

    /* Base case. */
```

```
    if (len == 0) {
        result.add(“”); // Be sure to return empty string!
        return result;
    }


    for (int i = 0; i < len; i++) {
        /* Remove char i and find permutations of remaining chars.*/
        String before = remainder.substring(0, i);
        String after = remainder.substring(i + 1, len);
        ArrayList<String> partials = getPerms(before + after);

        /* Prepend char i to each permutation.*/
        for (String s : partials) {
            result.add(remainder.charAt(i) + s);
        }
    }

    return result;
}
```

Alternatively, instead of passing the permutations back up the stack, we can push the prefix down the stack. When we get to the bottom (base case), `prefix` holds a full permutation.

```
ArrayList<String> getPerms(String str) {
    ArrayList<String> result = new ArrayList<String>();
    getPerms(“”, str, result);
    return result;
}

void getPerms(String prefix, String remainder, ArrayList<String> result) {
    if (remainder.length() == 0) result.add(prefix);

    int len = remainder.length();
    for (int i = 0; i < len; i++) {
        String before = remainder.substring(0, i);
        String after = remainder.substring(i + 1, len);
        char c = remainder.charAt(i);
        getPerms(prefix + c, before + after, result);
    }
}
```

For a discussion of the runtime of this algorithm, see Example 12 on page 51.

8.8 Permutations with Duplicates: Write a method to compute all permutations of a string whose characters are not necessarily unique. The list of permutations should not have duplicates.

pg 135

SOLUTION

This is very similar to the previous problem, except that now we could potentially have duplicate characters in the word.

One simple way of handling this problem is to do the same work to check if a permutation has been created before and then, if not, add it to the list. A simple hash table will do the trick here. This solution will take `O(n!)` time in the worst case (and, in fact, in all cases).

While it's true that we can't beat this worst case time, we should be able to design an algorithm to beat this in many cases. Consider a string with all duplicate characters, like aaaaaaaaaaaaa. This will take an extremely long time (since there are over 6 billion permutations of a 13-character string), even though there is only one unique permutation.

Ideally, we would like to only create the unique permutations, rather than creating every permutation and then ruling out the duplicates.

We can start with computing the count of each letter (easy enough to get this—just use a hash table). For a string such as aabbbbc, this would be:

```
a->2 | b->4 | c->1
```

Let's imagine generating a permutation of this string (now represented as a hash table). The first choice we make is whether to use an a, b, or c as the first character. After that, we have a subproblem to solve: find all permutations of the remaining characters, and append those to the already picked "prefix."

```
P(a->2 | b->4 | c->1) = {a + P(a->1 | b->4 | c->1)} +
                        {b + P(a->2 | b->3 | c->1)} +
                        {c + P(a->2 | b->4 | c->0)}
   P(a->1 | b->4 | c->1) = {a + P(a->0 | b->4 | c->1)} +
                           {b + P(a->1 | b->3 | c->1)} +
                           {c + P(a->1 | b->4 | c->0)}
   P(a->2 | b->3 | c->1) = {a + P(a->1 | b->3 | c->1)} +
                           {b + P(a->2 | b->2 | c->1)} +
                           {c + P(a->2 | b->3 | c->0)}
   P(a->2 | b->4 | c->0) = {a + P(a->1 | b->4 | c->0)} +
                           {b + P(a->2 | b->3 | c->0)}
```

Eventually, we'll get down to no more characters remaining.

The code below implements this algorithm.

```
ArrayList<String> printPerms(String s) {
  ArrayList<String> result = new ArrayList<String>();
  HashMap<Character, Integer> map = buildFreqTable(s);
  printPerms(map, “”, s.length(), result);
  return result;
}

HashMap<Character, Integer> buildFreqTable(String s) {
  HashMap<Character, Integer> map = new HashMap<Character, Integer>();
  for (char c : s.toCharArray()) {
    if (!map.containsKey(c)) {
      map.put(c, 0);
    }
    map.put(c, map.get(c) + 1);
  }
  return map;
}

void printPerms(HashMap<Character, Integer> map, String prefix, int remaining,
                ArrayList<String> result) {
  /* Base case. Permutation has been completed. */
  if (remaining == 0) {
    result.add(prefix);
    return;
  }

  /* Try remaining letters for next char, and generate remaining permutations. */
```

```
    for (Character c : map.keySet()) {
       int count = map.get(c);
       if (count > 0) {
          map.put(c,  count - 1);
          printPerms(map, prefix + c, remaining - 1, result);
          map.put(c,  count);
       }
    }
 }
```

In situations where the string has many duplicates, this algorithm will run a lot faster than the earlier algorithm.

8.9 **Parens:** Implement an algorithm to print all valid (i.e., properly opened and closed) combinations of n pairs of parentheses.

EXAMPLE

Input: 3

Output: `((()))`, `(()())`, `(())()`, `()(())`, `()()()`

pg 136

SOLUTION

Our first thought here might be to apply a recursive approach where we build the solution for `f(n)` by adding pairs of parentheses to `f(n-1)`. That's certainly a good instinct.

Let's consider the solution for `n = 3`:

```
   (()())     ((()))     ()(())     (())()     ()()()
```

How might we build this from `n = 2`?

```
   (())     ()()
```

We can do this by inserting a pair of parentheses inside every existing pair of parentheses, as well as one at the beginning of the string. Any other places that we could insert parentheses, such as at the end of the string, would reduce to the earlier cases.

So, we have the following:

```
   (()) -> (()()) /* inserted pair after 1st left paren */
        -> ((())) /* inserted pair after 2nd left paren */
        -> ()(()) /* inserted pair at beginning of string */
   ()() -> (())() /* inserted pair after 1st left paren */
        -> ()(()) /* inserted pair after 2nd left paren */
        -> ()()() /* inserted pair at beginning of string */
```

But wait—we have some duplicate pairs listed. The string `()(())` is listed twice.

If we're going to apply this approach, we'll need to check for duplicate values before adding a string to our list.

```
Set<String> generateParens(int remaining) {
   Set<String> set = new HashSet<String>();
   if (remaining == 0) {
      set.add("");
   } else {
      Set<String> prev = generateParens(remaining - 1);
      for (String str : prev) {
         for (int i = 0; i < str.length(); i++) {
```

```
            if (str.charAt(i) == ‘(‘) {
               String s = insertInside(str, i);
               /* Add s to set if it’s not already in there. Note:  HashSet
                * automatically checks for duplicates before adding, so an explicit
                * check is not necessary. */
               set.add(s);
            }
         }
         set.add(“()” + str);
      }
   }
   return set;
}

String insertInside(String str, int leftIndex) {
   String left = str.substring(0, leftIndex + 1);
   String right = str.substring(leftIndex + 1, str.length());
   return left + “()” + right;
}
```

This works, but it's not very efficient. We waste a lot of time coming up with the duplicate strings.

We can avoid this duplicate string issue by building the string from scratch. Under this approach, we add left and right parens, as long as our expression stays valid.

On each recursive call, we have the index for a particular character in the string. We need to select either a left or a right paren. When can we use a left paren, and when can we use a right paren?

1. *Left Paren:* As long as we haven't used up all the left parentheses, we can always insert a left paren.
2. *Right Paren:* We can insert a right paren as long as it won't lead to a syntax error. When will we get a syntax error? We will get a syntax error if there are more right parentheses than left.

So, we simply keep track of the number of left and right parentheses allowed. If there are left parens remaining, we'll insert a left paren and recurse. If there are more right parens remaining than left (i.e., if there are more left parens in use than right parens), then we'll insert a right paren and recurse.

```
void addParen(ArrayList<String> list, int leftRem, int rightRem, char[] str,
              int index) {
   if (leftRem < 0 || rightRem < leftRem) return; // invalid state

   if (leftRem == 0 && rightRem == 0) { /* Out of left and right parentheses */
      list.add(String.copyValueOf(str));
   } else {
      str[index] = '('; // Add left and recurse
      addParen(list, leftRem - 1, rightRem, str, index + 1);

      str[index] = ')'; // Add right and recurse
      addParen(list, leftRem, rightRem - 1, str, index + 1);
   }
}

ArrayList<String> generateParens(int count) {
   char[] str = new char[count*2];
   ArrayList<String> list = new ArrayList<String>();
   addParen(list, count, count, str, 0);
   return list;
}
```

Because we insert left and right parentheses at each index in the string, and we never repeat an index, each string is guaranteed to be unique.

8.10 **Paint Fill:** Implement the "paint fill" function that one might see on many image editing programs. That is, given a screen (represented by a two-dimensional array of colors), a point, and a new color, fill in the surrounding area until the color changes from the original color.

pg 136

SOLUTION

First, let's visualize how this method works. When we call `paintFill` (i.e., "click" paint fill in the image editing application) on, say, a green pixel, we want to "bleed" outwards. Pixel by pixel, we expand outwards by calling `paintFill` on the surrounding pixel. When we hit a pixel that is not green, we stop.

We can implement this algorithm recursively:

```
enum Color { Black, White, Red, Yellow, Green }

boolean PaintFill(Color[][] screen, int r, int c, Color ncolor) {
  if (screen[r][c] == ncolor) return false;
  return PaintFill(screen, r, c, screen[r][c], ncolor);
}

boolean PaintFill(Color[][] screen, int r, int c, Color ocolor, Color ncolor) {
  if (r < 0 || r >= screen.length || c < 0 || c >= screen[0].length) {
    return false;
  }

  if (screen[r][c] == ocolor) {
    screen[r][c] = ncolor;
    PaintFill(screen, r - 1, c, ocolor, ncolor); // up
    PaintFill(screen, r + 1, c, ocolor, ncolor); // down
    PaintFill(screen, r, c - 1, ocolor, ncolor); // left
    PaintFill(screen, r, c + 1, ocolor, ncolor); // right
  }
  return true;
}
```

If you used the variable names x and y to implement this, be careful about the ordering of the variables in `screen[y][x]`. Because x represents the *horizontal* axis (that is, it's left to right), it actually corresponds to the column number, not the row number. The value of y equals the number of rows. This is a very easy place to make a mistake in an interview, as well as in your daily coding. It's typically clearer to use `row` and `column` instead, as we've done here.

Does this algorithm seem familiar? It should! This is essentially depth-first search on a graph. At each pixel, we are searching outwards to each surrounding pixel. We stop once we've fully traversed all the surrounding pixels of this color.

We could alternatively implement this using breadth-first search.

8.11 Coins: Given an infinite number of quarters (25 cents), dimes (10 cents), nickels (5 cents), and pennies (1 cent), write code to calculate the number of ways of representing n cents.

pg 136

SOLUTION

This is a recursive problem, so let's figure out how to compute `makeChange(n)` using prior solutions (i.e., subproblems).

Let's say `n = 100`. We want to compute the number of ways of making change for 100 cents. What is the relationship between this problem and its subproblems?

We know that making change for 100 cents will involve either 0, 1, 2, 3, or 4 quarters. So:

```
makeChange(100) = makeChange(100 using 0 quarters) +
                  makeChange(100 using 1 quarter)  +
                  makeChange(100 using 2 quarters) +
                  makeChange(100 using 3 quarters) +
                  makeChange(100 using 4 quarters)
```

Inspecting this further, we can see that some of these problems reduce. For example, `makeChange(100 using 1 quarter)` will equal `makeChange(75 using 0 quarters)`. This is because, if we must use exactly one quarter to make change for 100 cents, then our only remaining choices involve making change for the remaining 75 cents.

We can apply the same logic to `makeChange(100 using 2 quarters)`, `makeChange(100 using 3 quarters)` and `makeChange(100 using 4 quarters)`. We have thus reduced the above statement to the following.

```
makeChange(100) = makeChange(100 using 0 quarters) +
                  makeChange(75 using 0 quarters) +
                  makeChange(50 using 0 quarters) +
                  makeChange(25 using 0 quarters) +
                  1
```

Note that the final statement from above, `makeChange(100 using 4 quarters)`, equals 1. We call this "fully reduced."

Now what? We've used up all our quarters, so now we can start applying our next biggest denomination: dimes.

Our approach for quarters applies to dimes as well, but we apply this for *each* of the four of five parts of the above statement. So, for the first part, we get the following statements:

```
makeChange(100 using 0 quarters) = makeChange(100 using 0 quarters, 0 dimes) +
                                   makeChange(100 using 0 quarters, 1 dime)  +
                                   makeChange(100 using 0 quarters, 2 dimes) +
                                   ...
                                   makeChange(100 using 0 quarters, 10 dimes)

makeChange(75 using 0 quarters) = makeChange(75 using 0 quarters, 0 dimes) +
                                  makeChange(75 using 0 quarters, 1 dime)  +
                                  makeChange(75 using 0 quarters, 2 dimes) +
                                  ...
                                  makeChange(75 using 0 quarters, 7 dimes)

makeChange(50 using 0 quarters) = makeChange(50 using 0 quarters, 0 dimes) +
                                  makeChange(50 using 0 quarters, 1 dime)  +
                                  makeChange(50 using 0 quarters, 2 dimes) +
```

```
                                          ...
                                          makeChange(50 using 0 quarters, 5 dimes)

makeChange(25 using 0 quarters) = makeChange(25 using 0 quarters, 0 dimes) +
                                  makeChange(25 using 0 quarters, 1 dime)  +
                                  makeChange(25 using 0 quarters, 2 dimes)
```

Each one of these, in turn, expands out once we start applying nickels. We end up with a tree-like recursive structure where each call expands out to four or more calls.

The base case of our recursion is the fully reduced statement. For example, `makeChange(50 using 0 quarters, 5 dimes)` is fully reduced to 1, since 5 dimes equals 50 cents.

This leads to a recursive algorithm that looks like this:

```
int makeChange(int amount, int[] denoms, int index) {
  if (index >= denoms.length - 1) return 1; // last denom
  int denomAmount = denoms[index];
  int ways = 0;
  for (int i = 0; i * denomAmount <= amount; i++) {
    int amountRemaining = amount - i * denomAmount;
    ways += makeChange(amountRemaining, denoms, index + 1);
  }
  return ways;
}

int makeChange(int n) {
  int[] denoms = {25, 10, 5, 1};
  return makeChange(n, denoms, 0);
}
```

This works, but it's not as optimal as it could be. The issue is that we will be recursively calling `makeChange` several times for the same values of `amount` and `index`.

We can resolve this issue by storing the previously computed values. We'll need to store a mapping from each pair `(amount, index)` to the precomputed result.

```
int makeChange(int n) {
  int[] denoms = {25, 10, 5, 1};
  int[][] map = new int[n + 1][denoms.length]; // precomputed vals
  return makeChange(n, denoms, 0, map);
}

int makeChange(int amount, int[] denoms, int index, int[][] map) {
  if (map[amount][index] > 0) { // retrieve value
    return map[amount][index];
  }
  if (index >= denoms.length - 1) return 1; // one denom remaining
  int denomAmount = denoms[index];
  int ways = 0;
  for (int i = 0; i * denomAmount <= amount; i++) {
    // go to next denom, assuming i coins of denomAmount
    int amountRemaining = amount - i * denomAmount;
    ways += makeChange(amountRemaining, denoms, index + 1, map);
  }
  map[amount][index] = ways;
  return ways;
}
```

Note that we've used a two-dimensional array of integers to store the previously computed values. This is simpler, but takes up a little extra space. Alternatively, we could use an actual hash table that maps from `amount` to a new hash table, which then maps from `denom` to the precomputed value. There are other alternative data structures as well.

8.12 Eight Queens: Write an algorithm to print all ways of arranging eight queens on an 8x8 chess board so that none of them share the same row, column, or diagonal. In this case, "diagonal" means all diagonals, not just the two that bisect the board.

pg 136

SOLUTION

We have eight queens which must be lined up on an 8x8 chess board such that none share the same row, column or diagonal. So, we know that each row and column (and diagonal) must be used exactly once.

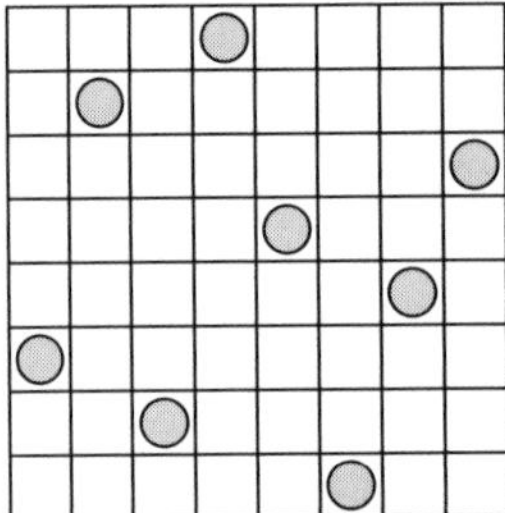

A "Solved" Board with 8 Queens

Picture the queen that is placed last, which we'll assume is on row 8. (This is an okay assumption to make since the ordering of placing the queens is irrelevant.) On which cell in row 8 is this queen? There are eight possibilities, one for each column.

So if we want to know all the valid ways of arranging 8 queens on an 8x8 chess board, it would be:

```
ways to arrange 8 queens on an 8x8 board =
   ways to arrange 8 queens on an 8x8 board with queen at (7, 0) +
   ways to arrange 8 queens on an 8x8 board with queen at (7, 1) +
   ways to arrange 8 queens on an 8x8 board with queen at (7, 2) +
   ways to arrange 8 queens on an 8x8 board with queen at (7, 3) +
   ways to arrange 8 queens on an 8x8 board with queen at (7, 4) +
   ways to arrange 8 queens on an 8x8 board with queen at (7, 5) +
   ways to arrange 8 queens on an 8x8 board with queen at (7, 6) +
   ways to arrange 8 queens on an 8x8 board with queen at (7, 7)
```

We can compute each one of these using a very similar approach:

```
ways to arrange 8 queens on an 8x8 board with queen at (7, 3) =
   ways to ... with queens at (7, 3) and (6, 0) +
   ways to ... with queens at (7, 3) and (6, 1) +
   ways to ... with queens at (7, 3) and (6, 2) +
   ways to ... with queens at (7, 3) and (6, 4) +
   ways to ... with queens at (7, 3) and (6, 5) +
   ways to ... with queens at (7, 3) and (6, 6) +
   ways to ... with queens at (7, 3) and (6, 7)
```

Note that we don't need to consider combinations with queens at `(7, 3)` and `(6, 3)`, since this is a violation of the requirement that every queen is in its own row, column and diagonal.

Implementing this is now reasonably straightforward.

```
int GRID_SIZE = 8;

void placeQueens(int row, Integer[] columns, ArrayList<Integer[]> results) {
  if (row == GRID_SIZE) { // Found valid placement
    results.add(columns.clone());
  } else {
    for (int col = 0; col < GRID_SIZE; col++) {
      if (checkValid(columns, row, col)) {
        columns[row] = col;  // Place queen
        placeQueens(row + 1, columns, results);
      }
    }
  }
}

/* Check if (row1, column1) is a valid spot for a queen by checking if there is a
 * queen in the same column or diagonal. We don't need to check it for queens in
 * the same row because the calling placeQueen only attempts to place one queen at
 * a time. We know this row is empty. */
boolean checkValid(Integer[] columns, int row1, int column1) {
  for (int row2 = 0; row2 < row1; row2++) {
    int column2 = columns[row2];
    /* Check if (row2, column2) invalidates (row1, column1) as a
     * queen spot. */

    /* Check if rows have a queen in the same column */
    if (column1 == column2) {
      return false;
    }

    /* Check diagonals: if the distance between the columns equals the distance
     * between the rows, then they're in the same diagonal. */
    int columnDistance = Math.abs(column2 - column1);

    /* row1 > row2, so no need for abs */
    int rowDistance = row1 - row2;
    if (columnDistance == rowDistance) {
      return false;
    }
  }
  return true;
}
```

Observe that since each row can only have one queen, we don't need to store our board as a full 8x8 matrix. We only need a single array where `column[r] = c` indicates that row `r` has a queen at column `c`.

8.13 Stack of Boxes: You have a stack of n boxes, with widths w_i, heights h_i, and depths d_i. The boxes cannot be rotated and can only be stacked on top of one another if each box in the stack is strictly larger than the box above it in width, height, and depth. Implement a method to compute the height of the tallest possible stack. The height of a stack is the sum of the heights of each box.

pg 136

SOLUTION

To tackle this problem, we need to recognize the relationship between the different subproblems.

Solution #1

Imagine we had the following boxes: b_1, b_2, ..., b_n. The biggest stack that we can build with all the boxes equals the max of (biggest stack with bottom b_1, biggest stack with bottom b_2, ..., biggest stack with bottom b_n). That is, if we experimented with each box as a bottom and built the biggest stack possible with each, we would find the biggest stack possible.

But, how would we find the biggest stack with a particular bottom? Essentially the same way. We experiment with different boxes for the second level, and so on for each level.

Of course, we only experiment with valid boxes. If b_5 is bigger than b_1, then there's no point in trying to build a stack that looks like {b_1, b_5 , ...}. We already know b_1 can't be below b_5.

We can perform a small optimization here. The requirements of this problem stipulate that the lower boxes must be strictly greater than the higher boxes in all dimensions. Therefore, if we sort (descending order) the boxes on a dimension—any dimension—then we know we don't have to look backwards in the list. The box b_1 cannot be on top of box b_5, since its height (or whatever dimension we sorted on) is greater than b_5's height.

The code below implements this algorithm recursively.

```
int createStack(ArrayList<Box> boxes) {
   /* Sort in decending order by height. */
   Collections.sort(boxes, new BoxComparator());
   int maxHeight = 0;
   for (int i = 0; i < boxes.size(); i++) {
      int height = createStack(boxes, i);
      maxHeight = Math.max(maxHeight, height);
   }
   return maxHeight;
}

int createStack(ArrayList<Box> boxes, int bottomIndex) {
   Box bottom = boxes.get(bottomIndex);
   int maxHeight = 0;
   for (int i = bottomIndex + 1; i < boxes.size(); i++) {
      if (boxes.get(i).canBeAbove(bottom)) {
         int height = createStack(boxes, i);
         maxHeight = Math.max(height, maxHeight);
      }
   }
   maxHeight += bottom.height;
   return maxHeight;
}

class BoxComparator implements Comparator<Box> {
```

```
    @Override
    public int compare(Box x, Box y){
        return y.height - x.height;
    }
}
```

The problem in this code is that it gets very inefficient. We try to find the best solution that looks like {b_3, b_4, ...} even though we may have already found the best solution with b_4 at the bottom. Instead of generating these solutions from scratch, we can cache these results using memoization.

```
int createStack(ArrayList<Box> boxes) {
    Collections.sort(boxes, new BoxComparator());
    int maxHeight = 0;
    int[] stackMap = new int[boxes.size()];
    for (int i = 0; i < boxes.size(); i++) {
        int height = createStack(boxes, i, stackMap);
        maxHeight = Math.max(maxHeight, height);
    }
    return maxHeight;
}

int createStack(ArrayList<Box> boxes, int bottomIndex, int[] stackMap) {
    if (bottomIndex < boxes.size() && stackMap[bottomIndex] > 0) {
        return stackMap[bottomIndex];
    }

    Box bottom = boxes.get(bottomIndex);
    int maxHeight = 0;
    for (int i = bottomIndex + 1; i < boxes.size(); i++) {
        if (boxes.get(i).canBeAbove(bottom)) {
            int height = createStack(boxes, i, stackMap);
            maxHeight = Math.max(height, maxHeight);
        }
    }
    maxHeight += bottom.height;
    stackMap[bottomIndex] = maxHeight;
    return maxHeight;
}
```

Because we're only mapping from an index to a height, we can just use an integer array for our "hash table."

Be very careful here with what each spot in the hash table represents. In this code, `stackMap[i]` represents the tallest stack with box `i` at the bottom. Before pulling the value from the hash table, you have to ensure that box `i` can be placed on top of the current bottom.

It helps to keep the line that recalls from the hash table symmetric with the one that inserts. For example, in this code, we recall from the hash table with `bottomIndex` at the start of the method. We insert into the hash table with `bottomIndex` at the end.

Solution #2

Alternatively, we can think about the recursive algorithm as making a choice, at each step, whether to put a particular box in the stack. (We will again sort our boxes in descending order by a dimension, such as height.)

First, we choose whether or not to put box 0 in the stack. Take one recursive path with box 0 at the bottom and one recursive path without box 0. Return the better of the two options.

Then, we choose whether or not to put box 1 in the stack. Take one recursive path with box 1 at the bottom and one path without box 1. Return the better of the two options.

We will again use memoization to cache the height of the tallest stack with a particular bottom.

```
1   int createStack(ArrayList<Box> boxes) {
2     Collections.sort(boxes, new BoxComparator());
3     int[] stackMap = new int[boxes.size()];
4     return createStack(boxes, null, 0, stackMap);
5   }
6
7   int createStack(ArrayList<Box> boxes, Box bottom, int offset, int[] stackMap) {
8     if (offset >= boxes.size()) return 0; // Base case
9
10    /* height with this bottom */
11    Box newBottom = boxes.get(offset);
12    int heightWithBottom = 0;
13    if (bottom == null || newBottom.canBeAbove(bottom)) {
14      if (stackMap[offset] == 0) {
15        stackMap[offset] = createStack(boxes, newBottom, offset + 1, stackMap);
16        stackMap[offset] += newBottom.height;
17      }
18      heightWithBottom = stackMap[offset];
19    }
20
21    /* without this bottom */
22    int heightWithoutBottom = createStack(boxes, bottom, offset + 1, stackMap);
23
24    /* Return better of two options. */
25    return Math.max(heightWithBottom, heightWithoutBottom);
26  }
```

Again, pay close attention to when you recall and insert values into the hash table. It's typically best if these are symmetric, as they are in lines 15 and 16-18.

8.14 Boolean Evaluation: Given a boolean expression consisting of the symbols `0` (false), `1` (true), `&` (AND), `|` (OR), and `^` (XOR), and a desired boolean result value `result`, implement a function to count the number of ways of parenthesizing the expression such that it evaluates to `result`. The expression should be fully parenthesized (e.g., `(0)^(1)`) but not extraneously (e.g., `(((0))^(1))`).

EXAMPLE

```
countEval("1^0|0|1", false) -> 2
countEval("0&0&0&1^1|0", true) -> 10
```

pg 136

SOLUTION

As in other recursive problems, the key to this problem is to figure out the relationship between a problem and its subproblems.

Brute Force

Consider an expression like `0^0&0^1|1` and the target result `true`. How can we break down `countEval(0^0&0^1|1, true)` into smaller problems?

We could just essentially iterate through each possible place to put a parenthesis.

```
countEval(0^0&0^1|1, true) =
   countEval(0^0&0^1|1 where paren around char 1, true)
 + countEval(0^0&0^1|1 where paren around char 3, true)
 + countEval(0^0&0^1|1 where paren around char 5, true)
 + countEval(0^0&0^1|1 where paren around char 7, true)
```

Now what? Let's look at just one of those expressions—the paren around char 3. This gives us `(0^0)&(0^1)`.

In order to make that expression true, both the left and right sides must be true. So:

```
left = "0^0"
right = "0^1|1"
countEval(left & right, true) = countEval(left, true) * countEval(right, true)
```

The reason we multiply the results of the left and right sides is that each result from the two sides can be paired up with each other to form a unique combination.

Each of those terms can now be decomposed into smaller problems in a similar process.

What happens when we have an "|" (OR)? Or an "^" (XOR)?

If it's an OR, then either the left or the right side must be true—or both.

```
countEval(left | right, true) = countEval(left, true)  * countEval(right, false)
                              + countEval(left, false) * countEval(right, true)
                              + countEval(left, true)  * countEval(right, true)
```

If it's an XOR, then the left or the right side can be true, but not both.

```
countEval(left ^ right, true) = countEval(left, true) * countEval(right, false)
                              + countEval(left, false) * countEval(right, true)
```

What if we were trying to make the result `false` instead? We can switch up the logic from above:

```
countEval(left & right, false) = countEval(left, true)  * countEval(right, false)
                               + countEval(left, false) * countEval(right, true)
                               + countEval(left, false) * countEval(right, false)
countEval(left | right, false) = countEval(left, false) * countEval(right, false)
countEval(left ^ right, false) = countEval(left, false) * countEval(right, false)
                               + countEval(left, true)  * countEval(right, true)
```

Alternatively, we can just use the same logic from above and subtract it out from the total number of ways of evaluating the expression.

```
totalEval(left) = countEval(left, true) + countEval(left, false)
totalEval(right) = countEval(right, true) + countEval(right, false)
totalEval(expression) = totalEval(left) * totalEval(right)
countEval(expression, false) = totalEval(expression) - countEval(expression, true)
```

This makes the code a bit more concise.

```
int countEval(String s, boolean result) {
  if (s.length() == 0) return 0;
  if (s.length() == 1) return stringToBool(s) == result ? 1 : 0;

  int ways = 0;
  for (int i = 1; i < s.length(); i += 2) {
    char c = s.charAt(i);
    String left = s.substring(0, i);
    String right = s.substring(i + 1, s.length());

    /* Evaluate each side for each result. */
    int leftTrue = countEval(left, true);
    int leftFalse = countEval(left, false);
    int rightTrue = countEval(right, true);
```

```
      int rightFalse = countEval(right, false);
      int total = (leftTrue + leftFalse) * (rightTrue + rightFalse);

      int totalTrue = 0;
      if (c == '^') { // required: one true and one false
        totalTrue = leftTrue * rightFalse + leftFalse * rightTrue;
      } else if (c == '&') { // required: both true
        totalTrue = leftTrue * rightTrue;
      } else if (c == '|') { // required: anything but both false
        totalTrue = leftTrue * rightTrue + leftFalse * rightTrue +
                    leftTrue * rightFalse;
      }

      int subWays = result ? totalTrue : total - totalTrue;
      ways += subWays;
    }

    return ways;
  }

  boolean stringToBool(String c) {
    return c.equals("1") ? true : false;
  }
```

Note that the tradeoff of computing the `false` results from the `true` ones, and of computing the `{leftTrue, rightTrue, leftFalse, and rightFalse}` values upfront, is a small amount of extra work in some cases. For example, if we're looking for the ways that an AND (&) can result in `true`, we never would have needed the `leftFalse` and `rightFalse` results. Likewise, if we're looking for the ways that an OR (|) can result in `false`, we never would have needed the `leftTrue` and `rightTrue` results.

Our current code is blind to what we do and don't actually need to do and instead just computes all of the values. This is probably a reasonable tradeoff to make (especially given the constraints of whiteboard coding) as it makes our code substantially shorter and less tedious to write. Whichever approach you make, you should discuss the tradeoffs with your interviewer.

That said, there are more important optimizations we can make.

Optimized Solutions

If we follow the recursive path, we'll note that we end up doing the same computation repeatedly.

Consider the expression `0^0&0^1|1` and these recursion paths:

- Add parens around char 1. `(0)^(0&0^1|1)`
  - » Add parens around char 3. `(0)^((0)&(0^1|1))`
- Add parens around char 3. `(0^0)&(0^1|1)`
  - » Add parens around char 1. `((0)^(0))&(0^1|1)`

Although these two expressions are different, they have a similar component: `(0^1|1)`. We should reuse our effort on this.

We can do this by using memoization, or a hash table. We just need to store the result of `countEval(expression, result)` for each expression and result. If we see an expression that we've calculated before, we just return it from the cache.

```
int countEval(String s, boolean result, HashMap<String, Integer> memo) {
  if (s.length() == 0) return 0;
  if (s.length() == 1) return stringToBool(s) == result ? 1 : 0;
```

```
    if (memo.containsKey(result + s)) return memo.get(result + s);

    int ways = 0;

    for (int i = 1; i < s.length(); i += 2) {
      char c = s.charAt(i);
      String left = s.substring(0, i);
      String right = s.substring(i + 1, s.length());
      int leftTrue = countEval(left, true, memo);
      int leftFalse = countEval(left, false, memo);
      int rightTrue = countEval(right, true, memo);
      int rightFalse = countEval(right, false, memo);
      int total = (leftTrue + leftFalse) * (rightTrue + rightFalse);

      int totalTrue = 0;
      if (c == '^') {
        totalTrue = leftTrue * rightFalse + leftFalse * rightTrue;
      } else if (c == '&') {
        totalTrue = leftTrue * rightTrue;
      } else if (c == '|') {
        totalTrue = leftTrue * rightTrue + leftFalse * rightTrue +
                    leftTrue * rightFalse;
      }

      int subWays = result ? totalTrue : total - totalTrue;
      ways += subWays;
    }

    memo.put(result + s, ways);
    return ways;
}
```

The added benefit of this is that we could actually end up with the same substring in multiple parts of the expression. For example, an expression like `0^1^0&0^1^0` has two instances of `0^1^0`. By caching the result of the substring value in a memoization table, we'll get to reuse the result for the right part of the expression after computing it for the left.

There is one further optimization we can make, but it's far beyond the scope of the interview. There *is* a closed form expression for the number of ways of parenthesizing an expression, but you wouldn't be expected to know it. It is given by the Catalan numbers, where n is the number of operators:

$$C_n = \frac{(2n)!}{(n+1)!n!}$$

We could use this to compute the total ways of evaluating the expression. Then, rather than computing `leftTrue` and `leftFalse`, we just compute one of those and calculate the other using the Catalan numbers. We would do the same thing for the right side.

Solutions to System Design and Scalability

9.1 Stock Data: Imagine you are building some sort of service that will be called by up to 1,000 client applications to get simple end-of-day stock price information (open, close, high, low). You may assume that you already have the data, and you can store it in any format you wish. How would you design the client-facing service that provides the information to client applications? You are responsible for the development, rollout, and ongoing monitoring and maintenance of the feed. Describe the different methods you considered and why you would recommend your approach. Your service can use any technologies you wish, and can distribute the information to the client applications in any mechanism you choose.

pg 144

SOLUTION

From the statement of the problem, we want to focus on how we actually distribute the information to clients. We can assume that we have some scripts that magically collect the information.

We want to start off by thinking about what the different aspects we should consider in a given proposal are:

- *Client Ease of Use:* We want the service to be easy for the clients to implement and useful for them.
- *Ease for Ourselves:* This service should be as easy as possible for us to implement, as we shouldn't impose unnecessary work on ourselves. We need to consider in this not only the cost of implementing, but also the cost of maintenance.
- *Flexibility for Future Demands:* This problem is stated in a "what would you do in the real world" way, so we should think like we would in a real-world problem. Ideally, we do not want to overly constrain ourselves in the implementation, such that we can't be flexible if the requirements or demands change.
- *Scalability and Efficiency:* We should be mindful of the efficiency of our solution, so as not to overly burden our service.

With this framework in mind, we can consider various proposals.

Proposal #1

One option is that we could keep the data in simple text files and let clients download the data through some sort of FTP server. This would be easy to maintain in some sense, since files can be easily viewed and backed up, but it would require more complex parsing to do any sort of query. And, if additional data were added to our text file, it might break the clients' parsing mechanism.

Proposal #2

We could use a standard SQL database, and let the clients plug directly into that. This would provide the following benefits:

- Facilitates an easy way for the clients to do query processing over the data, in case there are additional features we need to support. For example, we could easily and efficiently perform a query such as "return all stocks having an open price greater than N and a closing price less than M."
- Rolling back, backing up data, and security could be provided using standard database features. We don't have to "reinvent the wheel," so it's easy for us to implement.
- Reasonably easy for the clients to integrate into existing applications. SQL integration is a standard feature in software development environments.

What are the disadvantages of using a SQL database?

- It's much heavier weight than we really need. We don't necessarily need all the complexity of a SQL backend to support a feed of a few bits of information.
- It's difficult for humans to be able to read it, so we'll likely need to implement an additional layer to view and maintain the data. This increases our implementation costs.
- Security: While a SQL database offers pretty well defined security levels, we would still need to be very careful to not give clients access that they shouldn't have. Additionally, even if clients aren't doing anything "malicious," they might perform expensive and inefficient queries, and our servers would bear the costs of that.

These disadvantages don't mean that we shouldn't provide SQL access. Rather, they mean that we should be aware of the disadvantages.

Proposal #3

XML is another great option for distributing the information. Our data has fixed format and fixed size: `company_name`, `open`, `high`, `low`, `closing price`. The XML could look like this:

```
<root>
  <date value="2008-10-12">
    <company name="foo">
      <open>126.23</open>
      <high>130.27</high>
      <low>122.83</low>
      <closingPrice>127.30</closingPrice>
    </company>
    <company name="bar">
      <open>52.73</open>
      <high>60.27</high>
      <low>50.29</low>
      <closingPrice>54.91</closingPrice>
    </company>
  </date>
  <date value="2008-10-11"> . . . </date>
</root>
```

The advantages of this approach include the following:

- It's very easy to distribute, and it can also be easily read by both machines and humans. This is one reason that XML is a standard data model to share and distribute data.
- Most languages have a library to perform XML parsing, so it's reasonably easy for clients to implement.

- We can add new data to the XML file by adding additional nodes. This would not break the client's parser (provided they have implemented their parser in a reasonable way).
- Since the data is being stored as XML files, we can use existing tools for backing up the data. We don't need to implement our own backup tool.

The disadvantages may include:

- This solution sends the clients all the information, even if they only want part of it. It is inefficient in that way.
- Performing any queries on the data requires parsing the entire file.

Regardless of which solution we use for data storage, we could provide a web service (e.g., SOAP) for client data access. This adds a layer to our work, but it can provide additional security, and it may even make it easier for clients to integrate the system.

However—and this is a pro and a con—clients will be limited to grabbing the data only how we expect or want them to. By contrast, in a pure SQL implementation, clients could query for the highest stock price, even if this wasn't a procedure we "expected" them to need.

So which one of these would we use? There's no clear answer. The pure text file solution is probably a bad choice, but you can make a compelling argument for the SQL or XML solution, with or without a web service.

The goal of a question like this is not to see if you get the "correct" answer (there is no single correct answer). Rather, it's to see how you design a system, and how you evaluate trade-offs.

9.2 Social Network: How would you design the data structures for a very large social network like Facebook or LinkedIn? Describe how you would design an algorithm to show the shortest path between two people (e.g., Me -> Bob -> Susan -> Jason -> You).

pg 145

SOLUTION

A good way to approach this problem is to remove some of the constraints and solve it for that situation first.

Step 1: Simplify the Problem—Forget About the Millions of Users

First, let's forget that we're dealing with millions of users. Design this for the simple case.

We can construct a graph by treating each person as a node and letting an edge between two nodes indicate that the two users are friends.

If I wanted to find the path between two people, I could start with one person and do a simple breadth-first search.

Why wouldn't a depth-first search work well? First, depth-first search would just find a path. It wouldn't necessarily find the shortest path. Second, even if we just needed any path, it would be very inefficient. Two users might be only one degree of separation apart, but I could search millions of nodes in their "subtrees" before finding this relatively immediate connection.

Alternatively, I could do what's called a bidirectional breadth-first search. This means doing two breadth-first searches, one from the source and one from the destination. When the searches collide, we know we've found a path.

In the implementation, we'll use two classes to help us. BFSData holds the data we need for a breadth-first search, such as the isVisited hash table and the toVisit queue. PathNode will represent the path as we're searching it, storing each Person and the previousNode we visited in this path.

```
LinkedList<Person> findPathBiBFS(HashMap<Integer, Person> people, int source,
                                 int destination) {
  BFSData sourceData = new BFSData(people.get(source));
  BFSData destData = new BFSData(people.get(destination));

  while (!sourceData.isFinished() && !destData.isFinished()) {
    /* Search out from source. */
    Person collision = searchLevel(people, sourceData, destData);
    if (collision != null) {
      return mergePaths(sourceData, destData, collision.getID());
    }

    /* Search out from destination. */
    collision = searchLevel(people, destData, sourceData);
    if (collision != null) {
      return mergePaths(sourceData, destData, collision.getID());
    }
  }
  return null;
}

/* Search one level and return collision, if any. */
Person searchLevel(HashMap<Integer, Person> people, BFSData primary,
                   BFSData secondary) {
  /* We only want to search one level at a time. Count how many nodes are
   * currently in the primary's level and only do that many nodes. We'll continue
   * to add nodes to the end. */
  int count = primary.toVisit.size();
  for (int i = 0; i < count; i++) {
    /* Pull out first node. */
    PathNode pathNode = primary.toVisit.poll();
    int personId = pathNode.getPerson().getID();

    /* Check if it's already been visited. */
    if (secondary.visited.containsKey(personId)) {
      return pathNode.getPerson();
    }

    /* Add friends to queue. */
    Person person = pathNode.getPerson();
    ArrayList<Integer> friends = person.getFriends();
    for (int friendId : friends) {
      if (!primary.visited.containsKey(friendId)) {
        Person friend = people.get(friendId);
        PathNode next = new PathNode(friend, pathNode);
        primary.visited.put(friendId, next);
        primary.toVisit.add(next);
      }
    }
  }
  return null;
}

```

```
/* Merge paths where searches met at connection. */
LinkedList<Person> mergePaths(BFSData bfs1, BFSData bfs2, int connection) {
  PathNode end1 = bfs1.visited.get(connection); // end1 -> source
  PathNode end2 = bfs2.visited.get(connection); // end2 -> dest
  LinkedList<Person> pathOne = end1.collapse(false);
  LinkedList<Person> pathTwo = end2.collapse(true); // reverse
  pathTwo.removeFirst(); // remove connection
  pathOne.addAll(pathTwo); // add second path
  return pathOne;
}

class PathNode {
  private Person person = null;
  private PathNode previousNode = null;
  public PathNode(Person p, PathNode previous) {
    person = p;
    previousNode = previous;
  }

  public Person getPerson() { return person; }

  public LinkedList<Person> collapse(boolean startsWithRoot) {
    LinkedList<Person> path = new LinkedList<Person>();
    PathNode node = this;
    while (node != null) {
      if (startsWithRoot) {
        path.addLast(node.person);
      } else {
        path.addFirst(node.person);
      }
      node = node.previousNode;
    }
    return path;
  }
}

class BFSData {
  public Queue<PathNode> toVisit = new LinkedList<PathNode>();
  public HashMap<Integer, PathNode> visited =
    new HashMap<Integer, PathNode>();

  public BFSData(Person root) {
    PathNode sourcePath = new PathNode(root, null);
    toVisit.add(sourcePath);
    visited.put(root.getID(), sourcePath);
  }

  public boolean isFinished() {
    return toVisit.isEmpty();
  }
}
```

Many people are surprised that this is faster. Some quick math can explain why.

Suppose every person has k friends, and node S and node D have a friend C in common.

- Traditional breadth-first search from S to D: We go through roughly k+k*k nodes: each of S's k friends, and then each of their k friends.

- Bidirectional breadth-first search: We go through 2k nodes: each of S's k friends and each of D's k friends.

Of course, 2k is much less than k+k*k.

Generalizing this to a path of length q, we have this:

- BFS: $O(k^q)$
- Bidirectional BFS: $O(k^{q/2} + k^{q/2})$, which is just $O(k^{q/2})$

If you imagine a path like A->B->C->D->E where each person has 100 friends, this is a big difference. BFS will require looking at 100 million (100^4) nodes. A bidirectional BFS will require looking at only 20,000 nodes (2×100^2).

A bidirectional BFS will generally be faster than the traditional BFS. However, it requires actually having access to both the source node and the destination nodes, which is not always the case.

Step 2: Handle the Millions of Users

When we deal with a service the size of LinkedIn or Facebook, we cannot possibly keep all of our data on one machine. That means that our simple `Person` data structure from above doesn't quite work—our friends may not live on the same machine as we do. Instead, we can replace our list of friends with a list of their IDs, and traverse as follows:

1. For each friend ID: `int machine_index = getMachineIDForUser(personID);`
2. Go to machine `#machine_index`
3. On that machine, do: `Person friend = getPersonWithID(person_id);`

The code below outlines this process. We've defined a class `Server`, which holds a list of all the machines, and a class `Machine`, which represents a single machine. Both classes have hash tables to efficiently lookup data.

```
class Server {
   HashMap<Integer, Machine> machines = new HashMap<Integer, Machine>();
   HashMap<Integer, Integer> personToMachineMap = new HashMap<Integer, Integer>();

   public Machine getMachineWithId(int machineID) {
      return machines.get(machineID);
   }

   public int getMachineIDForUser(int personID) {
      Integer machineID = personToMachineMap.get(personID);
      return machineID == null ? -1 : machineID;
   }

   public Person getPersonWithID(int personID) {
      Integer machineID = personToMachineMap.get(personID);
      if (machineID == null) return null;

      Machine machine = getMachineWithId(machineID);
      if (machine == null) return null;

      return machine.getPersonWithID(personID);
   }
}

class Person {
```

```
    private ArrayList<Integer> friends = new ArrayList<Integer>();
    private int personID;
    private String info;

    public Person(int id) { this.personID = id; }
    public String getInfo() { return info; }
    public void setInfo(String info) { this.info = info; }
    public ArrayList<Integer> getFriends() { return friends; }
    public int getID() { return personID; }
    public void addFriend(int id) { friends.add(id); }
}
```

There are more optimizations and follow-up questions here than we could possibly discuss, but here are just a few possibilities.

Optimization: Reduce machine jumps

Jumping from one machine to another is expensive. Instead of randomly jumping from machine to machine with each friend, try to batch these jumps—e.g., if five of my friends live on one machine, I should look them up all at once.

Optimization: Smart division of people and machines

People are much more likely to be friends with people who live in the same country as they do. Rather than randomly dividing people across machines, try to divide them by country, city, state, and so on. This will reduce the number of jumps.

Question: Breadth-first search usually requires "marking" a node as visited. How do you do that in this case?

Usually, in BFS, we mark a node as visited by setting a `visited` flag in its node class. Here, we don't want to do that. There could be multiple searches going on at the same time, so it's a bad idea to just edit our data.

Instead, we could mimic the marking of nodes with a hash table to look up a node id and determine whether it's been visited.

Other Follow-Up Questions:

- In the real world, servers fail. How does this affect you?
- How could you take advantage of caching?
- Do you search until the end of the graph (infinite)? How do you decide when to give up?
- In real life, some people have more friends of friends than others, and are therefore more likely to make a path between you and someone else. How could you use this data to pick where to start traversing?

These are just a few of the follow-up questions you or the interviewer could raise. There are many others.

9.3 Web Crawler: If you were designing a web crawler, how would you avoid getting into infinite loops?

pg 145

SOLUTION

The first thing to ask ourselves in this problem is how an infinite loop might occur. The simplest answer is that, if we picture the web as a graph of links, an infinite loop will occur when a cycle occurs.

To prevent infinite loops, we just need to detect cycles. One way to do this is to create a hash table where we set `hash[v]` to `true` after we visit page `v`.

We can crawl the web using breadth-first search. Each time we visit a page, we gather all its links and insert them at the end of a queue. If we've already visited a page, we ignore it.

This is great—but what does it mean to visit page `v`? Is page `v` defined based on its content or its URL?

If it's defined based on its URL, we must recognize that URL parameters might indicate a completely different page. For example, the page `www.careercup.com/page?pid=microsoft-interview-questions` is totally different from the page `www.careercup.com/page?pid=google-interview-questions`. But, we can also append URL parameters arbitrarily to any URL without truly changing the page, provided it's not a parameter that the web application recognizes and handles. The page `www.careercup.com?foobar=hello` is the same as `www.careercup.com`.

"Okay, then," you might say, "let's define it based on its content." That sounds good too, at first, but it also doesn't quite work. Suppose I have some randomly generated content on the careercup.com home page. Is it a different page each time you visit it? Not really.

The reality is that there is probably no perfect way to define a "different" page, and this is where this problem gets tricky.

One way to tackle this is to have some sort of estimation for degree of similarity. If, based on the content and the URL, a page is deemed to be sufficiently similar to other pages, we *deprioritize* crawling its children. For each page, we would come up with some sort of signature based on snippets of the content and the page's URL.

Let's see how this would work.

We have a database which stores a list of items we need to crawl. On each iteration, we select the highest priority page to crawl. We then do the following:

1. Open up the page and create a signature of the page based on specific subsections of the page and its URL.
2. Query the database to see whether anything with this signature has been crawled recently.
3. If something with this signature has been recently crawled, insert this page back into the database at a low priority.
4. If not, crawl the page and insert its links into the database.

Under the above implementation, we never "complete" crawling the web, but we will avoid getting stuck in a loop of pages. If we want to allow for the possibility of "finishing" crawling the web (which would clearly happen only if the "web" were actually a smaller system, like an intranet), then we can set a minimum priority that a page must have to be crawled.

This is just one, simplistic solution, and there are many others that are equally valid. A problem like this will more likely resemble a conversation with your interviewer which could take any number of paths. In fact, the discussion of this problem could have taken the path of the very next problem.

9.4 **Duplicate URLs:** You have 10 billion URLs. How do you detect the duplicate documents? In this case, assume "duplicate" means that the URLs are identical.

pg 145

SOLUTION

Just how much space do 10 billion URLs take up? If each URL is an average of 100 characters, and each character is 4 bytes, then this list of 10 billion URLs will take up about 4 terabytes. We are probably not going to hold that much data in memory.

But, let's just pretend for a moment that we were miraculously holding this data in memory, since it's useful to first construct a solution for the simple version. Under this version of the problem, we would just create a hash table where each URL maps to `true` if it's already been found elsewhere in the list. (As an alternative solution, we could sort the list and look for the duplicate values that way. That will take a bunch of extra time and offers few advantages.)

Now that we have a solution for the simple version, what happens when we have all 4000 gigabytes of data and we can't store it all in memory? We could solve this either by storing some of the data on disk or by splitting up the data across machines.

Solution #1: Disk Storage

If we stored all the data on one machine, we would do two passes of the document. The first pass would split the list of URLs into 4000 chunks of 1 GB each. An easy way to do that might be to store each URL u in a file named `<x>.txt` where `x = hash(u) % 4000`. That is, we divide up the URLs based on their hash value (modulo the number of chunks). This way, all URLs with the same hash value would be in the same file.

In the second pass, we would essentially implement the simple solution we came up with earlier: load each file into memory, create a hash table of the URLs, and look for duplicates.

Solution #2: Multiple Machines

The other solution is to perform essentially the same procedure, but to use multiple machines. In this solution, rather than storing the data in file `<x>.txt`, we would send the URL to machine `x`.

Using multiple machines has pros and cons.

The main pro is that we can parallelize the operation, such that all 4000 chunks are processed simultaneously. For large amounts of data, this might result in a faster solution.

The disadvantage though is that we are now relying on 4000 different machines to operate perfectly. That may not be realistic (particularly with more data and more machines), and we'll need to start considering how to handle failure. Additionally, we have increased the complexity of the system simply by involving so many machines.

Both are good solutions, though, and both should be discussed with your interviewer.

9.5 **Cache:** Imagine a web server for a simplified search engine. This system has 100 machines to respond to search queries, which may then call out using `processSearch(string query)` to another cluster of machines to actually get the result. The machine which responds to a given query is chosen at random, so you cannot guarantee that the same machine will always respond to the same request. The method `processSearch` is very expensive. Design a caching mechanism to cache the results of the most recent queries. Be sure to explain how you would update the cache when data changes.

pg 145

SOLUTION

Before getting into the design of this system, we first have to understand what the question means. Many of the details are somewhat ambiguous, as is expected in questions like this. We will make reasonable assumptions for the purposes of this solution, but you should discuss these details—in depth—with your interviewer.

Assumptions

Here are a few of the assumptions we make for this solution. Depending on the design of your system and how you approach the problem, you may make other assumptions. Remember that while some approaches are better than others, there is no one "correct" approach.

- Other than calling out to `processSearch` as necessary, all query processing happens on the initial machine that was called.
- The number of queries we wish to cache is large (millions).
- Calling between machines is relatively quick.
- The result for a given query is an ordered list of URLs, each of which has an associated 50 character title and 200 character summary.
- The most popular queries are extremely popular, such that they would always appear in the cache.

Again, these aren't the *only* valid assumptions. This is just one reasonable set of assumptions.

System Requirements

When designing the cache, we know we'll need to support two primary functions:

- Efficient lookups given a key.
- Expiration of old data so that it can be replaced with new data.

In addition, we must also handle updating or clearing the cache when the results for a query change. Because some queries are very common and may permanently reside in the cache, we cannot just wait for the cache to naturally expire.

Step 1: Design a Cache for a Single System

A good way to approach this problem is to start by designing it for a single machine. So, how would you create a data structure that enables you to easily purge old data and also efficiently look up a value based on a key?

- A linked list would allow easy purging of old data, by moving "fresh" items to the front. We could implement it to remove the last element of the linked list when the list exceeds a certain size.

- A hash table allows efficient lookups of data, but it wouldn't ordinarily allow easy data purging.

How can we get the best of both worlds? By merging the two data structures. Here's how this works:

Just as before, we create a linked list where a node is moved to the front every time it's accessed. This way, the end of the linked list will always contain the stalest information.

In addition, we have a hash table that maps from a query to the corresponding node in the linked list. This allows us to not only efficiently return the cached results, but also to move the appropriate node to the front of the list, thereby updating its "freshness."

For illustrative purposes, abbreviated code for the cache is below. The code attachment provides the full code for this part. Note that in your interview, it is unlikely that you would be asked to write the full code for this as well as perform the design for the larger system.

```
public class Cache {
   public static int MAX_SIZE = 10;
   public Node head, tail;
   public HashMap<String, Node> map;
   public int size = 0;

   public Cache() {
      map = new HashMap<String, Node>();
   }

   /* Moves node to front of linked list */
   public void moveToFront(Node node) { ... }
   public void moveToFront(String query) { ... }

   /* Removes node from linked list */
   public void removeFromLinkedList(Node node) { ... }

   /* Gets results from cache, and updates linked list */
   public String[] getResults(String query) {
      if (!map.containsKey(query)) return null;

      Node node = map.get(query);
      moveToFront(node); // update freshness
      return node.results;
   }

   /* Inserts results into linked list and hash */
   public void insertResults(String query, String[] results) {
      if (map.containsKey(query)) { // update values
         Node node = map.get(query);
         node.results = results;
         moveToFront(node); // update freshness
         return;
      }

      Node node = new Node(query, results);
      moveToFront(node);
      map.put(query, node);

      if (size > MAX_SIZE) {
         map.remove(tail.query);
         removeFromLinkedList(tail);
      }
```

```
    }
}
```

Step 2: Expand to Many Machines

Now that we understand how to design this for a single machine, we need to understand how we would design this when queries could be sent to many different machines. Recall from the problem statement that there's no guarantee that a particular query will be consistently sent to the same machine.

The first thing we need to decide is to what extent the cache is shared across machines. We have several options to consider.

Option 1: Each machine has its own cache.

A simple option is to give each machine its own cache. This means that if "foo" is sent to machine 1 twice in a short amount of time, the result would be recalled from the cache on the second time. But, if "foo" is sent first to machine 1 and then to machine 2, it would be treated as a totally fresh query both times.

This has the advantage of being relatively quick, since no machine-to-machine calls are used. The cache, unfortunately, is somewhat less effective as an optimization tool as many repeat queries would be treated as fresh queries.

Option 2: Each machine has a copy of the cache.

On the other extreme, we could give each machine a complete copy of the cache. When new items are added to the cache, they are sent to all machines. The entire data structure—linked list and hash table—would be duplicated.

This design means that common queries would nearly always be in the cache, as the cache is the same everywhere. The major drawback however is that updating the cache means firing off data to N different machines, where N is the size of the response cluster. Additionally, because each item effectively takes up N times as much space, our cache would hold much less data.

Option 3: Each machine stores a segment of the cache.

A third option is to divide up the cache, such that each machine holds a different part of it. Then, when machine `i` needs to look up the results for a query, machine `i` would figure out which machine holds this value, and then ask this other machine (machine `j`) to look up the query in `j`'s cache.

But how would machine `i` know which machine holds this part of the hash table?

One option is to assign queries based on the formula `hash(query) % N`. Then, machine `i` only needs to apply this formula to know that machine `j` should store the results for this query.

So, when a new query comes in to machine `i`, this machine would apply the formula and call out to machine `j`. Machine `j` would then return the value from its cache or call `processSearch(query)` to get the results. Machine `j` would update its cache and return the results back to `i`.

Alternatively, you could design the system such that machine `j` just returns `null` if it doesn't have the `query` in its current cache. This would require machine `i` to call `processSearch` and then forward the results to machine `j` for storage. This implementation actually increases the number of machine-to-machine calls, with few advantages.

Step 3: Updating results when contents change

Recall that some queries may be so popular that, with a sufficiently large cache, they would permanently be cached. We need some sort of mechanism to allow cached results to be refreshed, either periodically or "on-demand" when certain content changes.

To answer this question, we need to consider when results would change (and you need to discuss this with your interviewer). The primary times would be when:

1. The content at a URL changes (or the page at that URL is removed).
2. The ordering of results change in response to the rank of a page changing.
3. New pages appear related to a particular query.

To handle situations #1 and #2, we could create a separate hash table that would tell us which cached queries are tied to a specific URL. This could be handled completely separately from the other caches, and reside on different machines. However, this solution may require a lot of data.

Alternatively, if the data doesn't require instant refreshing (which it probably doesn't), we could periodically crawl through the cache stored on each machine to purge queries tied to the updated URLs.

Situation #3 is substantially more difficult to handle. We could update single word queries by parsing the content at the new URL and purging these one-word queries from the caches. But, this will only handle the one-word queries.

A good way to handle Situation #3 (and likely something we'd want to do anyway) is to implement an "automatic time-out" on the cache. That is, we'd impose a time out where *no* query, regardless of how popular it is, can sit in the cache for more than `x` minutes. This will ensure that all data is periodically refreshed.

Step 4: Further Enhancements

There are a number of improvements and tweaks you could make to this design depending on the assumptions you make and the situations you optimize for.

One such optimization is to better support the situation where some queries are very popular. For example, suppose (as an extreme example) a particular string constitutes 1% of all queries. Rather than machine `i` forwarding the request to machine `j` every time, machine `i` could forward the request just once to `j`, and then `i` could store the results in its own cache as well.

Alternatively, there may also be some possibility of doing some sort of re-architecture of the system to assign queries to machines based on their hash value (and therefore the location of the cache), rather than randomly. However, this decision may come with its own set of trade-offs.

Another optimization we could make is to the "automatic time out" mechanism. As initially described, this mechanism purges any data after X minutes. However, we may want to update some data (like current news) much more frequently than other data (like historical stock prices). We could implement timeouts based on topic or based on URLs. In the latter situation, each URL would have a time out value based on how frequently the page has been updated in the past. The time out for the query would be the minimum of the time outs for each URL.

These are just a few of the enhancements we can make. Remember that in questions like this, there is no single correct way to solve the problem. These questions are about having a discussion with your interviewer about design criteria and demonstrating your general approach and methodology.

9.6 **Sales Rank**: A large eCommerce company wishes to list the best-selling products, overall and by category. For example, one product might be the #1056th best-selling product overall but the #13th best-selling product under "Sports Equipment" and the #24th best-selling product under "Safety." Describe how you would design this system.

pg 145

SOLUTION

Let's first start off by making some assumptions to define the problem.

Step 1: Scope the Problem

First, we need to define what exactly we're building.

- We'll assume that we're only being asked to design the components relevant to this question, and not the entire eCommerce system. In this case, we might touch the design of the frontend and purchase components, but only as it impacts the sales rank.
- We should also define what the sales rank means. Is it total sales over all time? Sales in the last month? Last week? Or some more complicated function (such as one involving some sort of exponential decay of sales data)? This would be something to discuss with your interviewer. We will assume that it is simply the total sales over the past week.
- We will assume that each product can be in multiple categories, and that there is no concept of "subcategories."

This part just gives us a good idea of what the problem, or scope of features, is.

Step 2: Make Reasonable Assumptions

These are the sorts of things you'd want to discuss with your interviewer. Because we don't have an interviewer in front of us, we'll have to make some assumptions.

- We will assume that the stats do not need to be 100% up-to-date. Data can be up to an hour old for the most popular items (for example, top 100 in each category), and up to one day old for the less popular items. That is, few people would care if the #2,809,132th best-selling item should have actually been listed as #2,789,158th instead.
- Precision is important for the most popular items, but a small degree of error is okay for the less popular items.
- We will assume that the data should be updated every hour (for the most popular items), but the time range for this data does not need to be precisely the last seven days (168 hours). If it's sometimes more like 150 hours, that's okay.

The important thing is not so much which decision you made at each possible issue, but whether it occurred to you that these are assumptions. We should get out as many of these assumptions as possible in the beginning. It's possible you will need to make other assumptions along the way.

Step 3: Draw the Major Components

We should now design just a basic, naive system that describes the major components. This is where you would go up to a whiteboard.

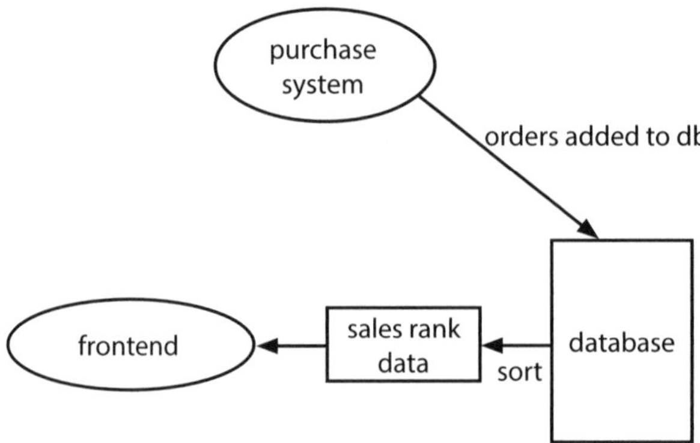

In this simple design, we store every order as soon as it comes into the database. Every hour or so, we pull sales data from the database by category, compute the total sales, sort it, and store it in some sort of sales rank data cache (which is probably held in memory). The frontend just pulls the sales rank from this table, rather than hitting the standard database and doing its own analytics.

Step 4: Identify the Key Issues

Analytics are Expensive

In the naive system, we periodically query the database for the number of sales in the past week for each product. This will be fairly expensive. That's running a query over all sales for all time.

Our database just needs to track the total sales. We'll assume (as noted in the beginning of the solution) that the general storage for purchase history is taken care of in other parts of the system, and we just need to focus on the sales data analytics.

Instead of listing every purchase in our database, we'll store just the total sales from the last week. Each purchase will just update the total weekly sales.

Tracking the total sales takes a bit of thought. If we just use a single column to track the total sales over the past week, then we'll need to re-compute the total sales every day (since the specific days covered in the last seven days change with each day). That is unnecessarily expensive.

Instead, we'll just use a table like this.

Prod ID	Total	Sun	Mon	Tues	Wed	Thurs	Fri	Sat

This is essentially like a circular array. Each day, we clear out the corresponding day of the week. On each purchase, we update the total sales count for that product on that day of the week, as well as the total count.

We will also need a separate table to store the associations of product IDs and categories.

Prod ID	Category ID

To get the sales rank per category, we'll need to join these tables.

Database Writes are Very Frequent

Even with this change, we'll still be hitting the database very frequently. With the amount of purchases that could come in every second, we'll probably want to batch up the database writes.

Instead of immediately committing each purchase to the database, we could store purchases in some sort of in-memory cache (as well as to a log file as a backup). Periodically, we'll process the log / cache data, gather the totals, and update the database.

> We should quickly think about whether or not it's feasible to hold this in memory. If there are 10 million products in the system, can we store each (along with a count) in a hash table? Yes. If each product ID is four bytes (which is big enough to hold up to 4 billion unique IDs) and each count is four bytes (more than enough), then such a hash table would only take about 40 megabytes. Even with some additional overhead and substantial system growth, we would still be able to fit this all in memory.

After updating the database, we can re-run the sales rank data.

We need to be a bit careful here, though. If we process one product's logs before another's, and re-run the stats in between, we could create a bias in the data (since we're including a larger timespan for one product than its "competing" product).

We can resolve this by either ensuring that the sales rank doesn't run until all the stored data is processed (difficult to do when more and more purchases are coming in), or by dividing up the in-memory cache by some time period. If we update the database for all the stored data up to a particular moment in time, this ensures that the database will not have biases.

Joins are Expensive

We have potentially tens of thousands of product categories. For each category, we'll need to first pull the data for its items (possibly through an expensive join) and then sort those.

Alternatively, we could just do one join of products and categories, such that each product will be listed once per category. Then, if we sorted that on category and then product ID, we could just walk the results to get the sales rank for each category.

Prod ID	Category	Total	Sun	Mon	Tues	Wed	Thurs	Fri	Sat
1423	sportseq	13	4	1	4	19	322	32	232
1423	safety	13	4	1	4	19	322	32	232

Rather than running thousands of queries (one for each category), we could sort the data on the category first and then the sales volume. Then, if we walked those results, we would get the sales rank for each category. We would also need to do one sort of the entire table on just sales number, to get the overall rank.

We could also just keep the data in a table like this from the beginning, rather than doing joins. This would require us to update multiple rows for each product.

Database Queries Might Still Be Expensive

Alternatively, if the queries and writes get very expensive, we could consider forgoing a database entirely and just using log files. This would allow us to take advantage of something like MapReduce.

Under this system, we would write a purchase to a simple text file with the product ID and time stamp. Each category has its own directory, and each purchase gets written to all the categories associated with that product.

We would run frequent jobs to merge files together by product ID and time ranges, so that eventually all purchases in a given day (or possibly hour) were grouped together.

```
/sportsequipment
    1423,Dec 13 08:23-Dec 13 08:23,1
    4221,Dec 13 15:22-Dec 15 15:45,5
    ...
/safety
    1423,Dec 13 08:23-Dec 13 08:23,1
    5221,Dec 12 03:19-Dec 12 03:28,19
...
```

To get the best-selling products within each category, we just need to sort each directory.

How do we get the overall ranking? There are two good approaches:

- We could treat the general category as just another directory, and write every purchase to that directory. That would mean a lot of files in this directory.
- Or, since we'll already have the products sorted by sales volume order for each category, we can also do an N-way merge to get the overall rank.

Alternatively, we can take advantage of the fact that the data doesn't need (as we assumed earlier) to be 100% up-to-date. We just need the most popular items to be up-to-date.

We can merge the most popular items from each category in a pairwise fashion. So, two categories get paired together and we merge the most popular items (the first 100 or so). After we have 100 items in this sorted order, we stop merging this pair and move onto the next pair.

To get the ranking for all products, we can be much lazier and only run this work once a day.

One of the advantages of this is that it scales nicely. We can easily divide up the files across multiple servers, as they aren't dependent on each other.

Follow Up Questions

The interviewer could push this design in any number of directions.

- Where do you think you'd hit the next bottlenecks? What would you do about that?
- What if there were subcategories as well? So items could be listed under "Sports" and "Sports Equipment" (or even "Sports" > "Sports Equipment" > "Tennis" > "Rackets")?
- What if data needed to be more accurate? What if it needed to be accurate within 30 minutes for all products?

Think through your design carefully and analyze it for the tradeoffs. You might also be asked to go into more detail on any specific aspect of the product.

9.7 Personal Financial Manager: Explain how you would design a personal financial manager (like Mint.com). This system would connect to your bank accounts, analyze your spending habits, and make recommendations.

pg 145

SOLUTION

The first thing we need to do is define what it is exactly that we are building.

Step 1: Scope the Problem

Ordinarily, you would clarify this system with your interviewer. We'll scope the problem as follows:

- You create an account and add your bank accounts. You can add multiple bank accounts. You can also add them at a later point in time.
- It pulls in all your financial history, or as much of it as your bank will allow.
- This financial history includes outgoing money (things you bought or paid for), incoming money (salary and other payments), and your current money (what's in your bank account and investments).
- Each payment transaction has a "category" associated with it (food, travel, clothing, etc.).
- There is some sort of data source provided that tells the system, with some reliability, which category a transaction is associated with. The user might, in some cases, override the category when it's improperly assigned (e.g., eating at the cafe of a department store getting assigned to "clothing" rather than "food").
- Users will use the system to get recommendations on their spending. These recommendations will come from a mix of "typical" users ("people generally shouldn't spend more than X% of their income on clothing"), but can be overridden with custom budgets. This will not be a primary focus right now.
- We assume this is just a website for now, although we could potentially talk about a mobile app as well.
- We probably want email notifications either on a regular basis, or on certain conditions (spending over a certain threshold, hitting a budget max, etc.).
- We'll assume that there's no concept of user-specified rules for assigning categories to transactions.
- We will assume that the categorizations are based strictly on the origin of the transaction (i.e., the seller's name), not the price or date.

This gives us a basic goal for what we want to build.

Step 2: Make Reasonable Assumptions

Now that we have the basic goal for the system, we should define some further assumptions about the characteristics of the system.

- Adding or removing bank accounts is relatively unusual.
- The system is write-heavy. A typical user may make several new transactions daily, although few users would access the website more than once a week. In fact, for many users, their primary interaction might be through email alerts.
- Once a transaction is assigned to a category, it will only be changed if the user asks to change it. The system will never reassign a transaction to a different category "behind the scenes", even if the rules change. This means that two otherwise identical transactions could be assigned to different categories if the rules changed in between each transaction's date. We do this because it may confuse users if their spending per category changes with no action on their part.
- The banks probably won't push data to our system. Instead, we will need to pull data from the banks.
- Alerts on users exceeding budgets probably do not need to be sent instantaneously. (That wouldn't be realistic anyway, since we won't get the transaction data instantaneously.) It's probably pretty safe for them to be up to 24 hours delayed.

It's okay to make different assumptions here, but you should explicitly state them to your interviewer.

Step 3: Draw the Major Components

The most naive system would be one that pulls bank data on each login, categorizes all the data, and then analyzes the user's budget. This wouldn't quite fit the requirements, though, as we want email notifications on particular events.

We can do a bit better.

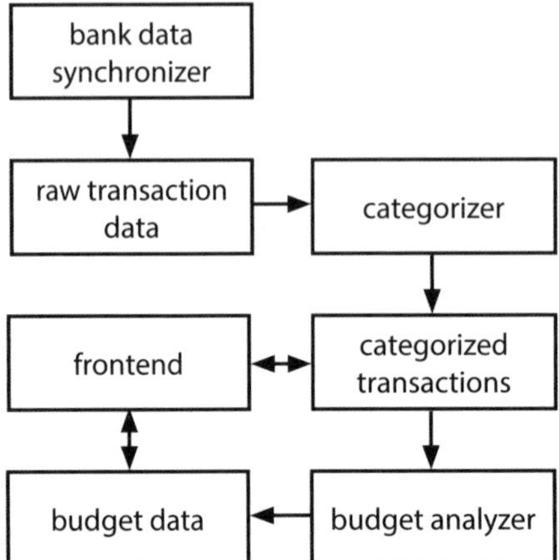

With this basic architecture, the bank data is pulled at periodic times (hourly or daily). The frequency may depend on the behavior of the users. Less active users may have their accounts checked less frequently.

Once new data arrives, it is stored in some list of raw, unprocessed transactions. This data is then pushed to the categorizer, which assigns each transaction to a category and stores these categorized transactions in another datastore.

The budget analyzer pulls in the categorized transactions, updates each user's budget per category, and stores the user's budget.

The frontend pulls data from both the categorized transactions datastore as well as from the budget datastore. Additionally, a user could also interact with the frontend by changing the budget or the categorization of their transactions.

Step 4: Identify the Key Issues

We should now reflect on what the major issues here might be.

This will be a very data-heavy system. We want it to feel snappy and responsive, though, so we'll want as much processing as possible to be asynchronous.

We will almost certainly want at least one task queue, where we can queue up work that needs to be done. This work will include tasks such as pulling in new bank data, re-analyzing budgets, and categorizing new bank data. It would also include re-trying tasks that failed.

These tasks will likely have some sort of priority associated with them, as some need to be performed more often than others. We want to build a task queue system that can prioritize some task types over others, while still ensuring that all tasks will be performed eventually. That is, we wouldn't want a low priority task to essentially "starve" because there are always higher priority tasks.

One important part of the system that we haven't yet addressed will be the email system. We could use a task to regularly crawl user's data to check if they're exceeding their budget, but that means checking every single user daily. Instead, we'll want to queue a task whenever a transaction occurs that potentially exceeds a budget. We can store the current budget totals by category to make it easy to understand if a new transaction exceeds the budget.

We should also consider incorporating the knowledge (or assumption) that a system like this will probably have a large number of inactive users—users who signed up once and then haven't touched the system since. We may want to either remove them from the system entirely or deprioritize their accounts. We'll want some system to track their account activity and associate priority with their accounts.

The biggest bottleneck in our system will likely be the massive amount of data that needs to be pulled and analyzed. We should be able to fetch the bank data asynchronously and run these tasks across many servers. We should drill a bit deeper into how the categorizer and budget analyzer work.

Categorizer and Budget Analyzer

One thing to note is that transactions are not dependent on each other. As soon as we get a transaction for a user, we can categorize it and integrate this data. It might be inefficient to do so, but it won't cause any inaccuracies.

Should we use a standard database for this? With lots of transactions coming in at once, that might not be very efficient. We certainly don't want to do a bunch of joins.

It may be better instead to just store the transactions to a set of flat text files. We assumed earlier that the categorizations are based on the seller's name alone. If we're assuming a lot of users, then there will be a lot of duplicates across the sellers. If we group the transaction files by seller's name, we can take advantage of these duplicates.

The categorizer can do something like this:

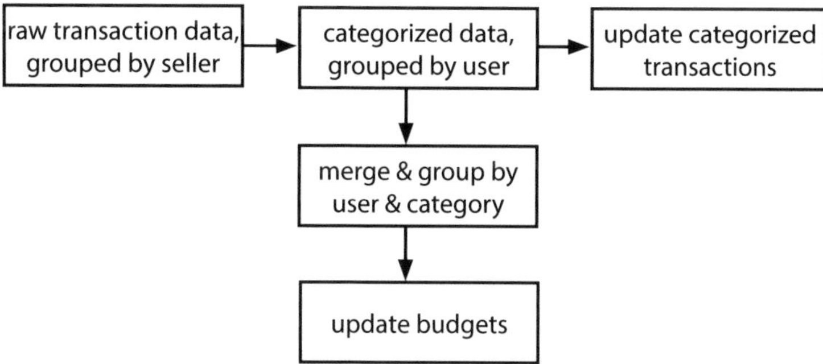

It first gets the raw transaction data, grouped by seller. It picks the appropriate category for the seller (which might be stored in a cache for the most common sellers), and then applies that category to all those transactions.

After applying the category, it re-groups all the transactions by user. Then, those transactions are inserted into the datastore for this user.

before categorizer	after categorizer

`amazon/`
`   user121,$5.43,Aug 13`
`   user922,$15.39,Aug 27`
`   ...`
`comcast/`
`   user922,$9.29,Aug 24`
`   user248,$40.13,Aug 18`
`   ...`
	`user121/`
	`   amazon,shopping,$5.43,Aug 13`
	`   ...`
	`user922/`
	`   amazon,shopping,$15.39,Aug 27`
	`   comcast,utilities,$9.29,Aug 24`
	`   ...`
	`user248/`
	`   comcast,utilities,$40.13,Aug 18`
	`   ...`

Then, the budget analyzer comes in. It takes the data grouped by user, merges it across categories (so all Shopping tasks for this user in this timespan are merged), and then updates the budget.

Most of these tasks will be handled in simple log files. Only the final data (the categorized transactions and the budget analysis) will be stored in a database. This minimizes writing and reading from the database.

User Changing Categories

The user might selectively override particular transactions to assign them to a different category. In this case, we would update the datastore for the categorized transactions. It would also signal a quick recomputation of the budget to decrement the item from the old category and increment the item in the other category.

We could also just recompute the budget from scratch. The budget analyzer is fairly quick as it just needs to look over the past few weeks of transactions for a single user.

Follow Up Questions

- How would this change if you also needed to support a mobile app?
- How would you design the component which assigns items to each category?
- How would you design the recommended budgets feature?
- How would you change this if the user could develop rules to categorize all transactions from a particular seller differently than the default?

9.8 **Pastebin**: Design a system like Pastebin, where a user can enter a piece of text and get a randomly generated URL for public access.

pg 145

SOLUTION

We can start with clarifying the specifics of this system.

Step 1: Scope the Problem

- The system does not support user accounts or editing documents.
- The system tracks analytics of how many times each page is accessed.
- Old documents get deleted after not being accessed for a sufficiently long period of time.
- While there isn't true authentication on accessing documents, users should not be able to "guess" docu-

ment URLs easily.

- The system has a frontend as well as an API.
- The analytics for each URL can be accessed through a "stats" link on each page. It is not shown by default, though.

Step 2: Make Reasonable Assumptions

- The system gets heavy traffic and contains many millions of documents.
- Traffic is not equally distributed across documents. Some documents get much more access than others.

Step 3: Draw the Major Components

We can sketch out a simple design. We'll need to keep track of URLs and the files associated with them, as well as analytics for how often the files have been accessed.

How should we store the documents? We have two options: we can store them in a database or we can store them on a file. Since the documents can be large and it's unlikely we need searching capabilities, storing them on a file is probably the better choice.

A simple design like this might work well:

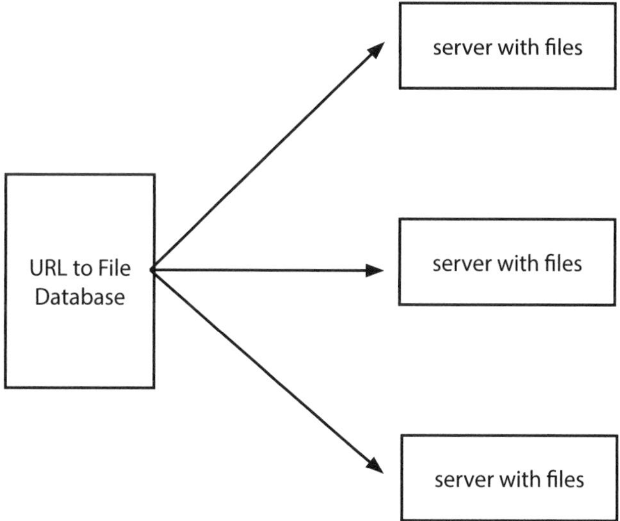

Here, we have a simple database that looks up the location (server and path) of each file. When we have a request for a URL, we look up the location of the URL within the datastore and then access the file.

Additionally, we will need a database that tracks analytics. We can do this with a simple datastore that adds each visit (including timestamp, IP address, and location) as a row in a database. When we need to access the stats of each visit, we pull the relevant data in from this database.

Step 4: Identify the Key Issues

The first issue that comes to mind is that some documents will be accessed much more frequently than others. Reading data from the filesystem is relatively slow compared with reading from data in memory. Therefore, we probably want to use a cache to store the most recently accessed documents. This will ensure that items accessed very frequently (or very recently) will be quickly accessible. Since documents cannot be edited, we will not need to worry about invalidating this cache.

We should also potentially consider sharding the database. We can shard it using some mapping from the URL (for example, the URL's hash code modulo some integer), which will allow us to quickly locate the database which contains this file.

In fact, we could even take this a step further. We could skip the database entirely and just let a hash of the URL indicate which server contains the document. The URL itself could reflect the location of the document. One potential issue from this is that if we need to add servers, it could be difficult to redistribute the documents.

Generating URLs

We have not yet discussed how to actually generate the URLs. We probably do not want a monotonically increasing integer value, as this would be easy for a user to "guess." We want URLs to be difficult to access without being provided the link.

One simple path is to generate a random GUID (e.g., 5d50e8ac-57cb-4a0d-8661-bcdee2548979). This is a 128-bit value that, while not strictly guaranteed to be unique, has low enough odds of a collision that we can treat it as unique. The drawback of this plan is that such a URL is not very "pretty" to the user. We could hash it to a smaller value, but then that increases the odds of collision.

We could do something very similar, though. We could just generate a 10-character sequence of letters and numbers, which gives us 36^{10} possible strings. Even with a billion URLs, the odds of a collision on any specific URL are very low.

> This is not to say that the odds of a collision over the whole system are low. They are not. Any one specific URL is unlikely to collide. However, after storing a billion URLs, we are very likely to have a collision at some point.

Assuming that we aren't okay with periodic (even if unusual) data loss, we'll need to handle these collisions. We can either check the datastore to see if the URL exists yet or, if the URL maps to a specific server, just detect whether a file already exists at the destination.

When a collision occurs, we can just generate a new URL. With 36^{10} possible URLs, collisions would be rare enough that the lazy approach here (detect collisions and retry) is sufficient.

Analytics

The final component to discuss is the analytics piece. We probably want to display the number of visits, and possibly break this down by location or time.

We have two options here:

- Store the raw data from each visit.
- Store just the data we know we'll use (number of visits, etc.).

You can discuss this with your interviewer, but it probably makes sense to store the raw data. We never know what features we'll add to the analytics down the road. The raw data allows us flexibility.

This does not mean that the raw data needs to be easily searchable or even accessible. We can just store a log of each visit in a file, and back this up to other servers.

One issue here is that this amount of data could be substantial. We could potentially reduce the space usage considerably by storing data only probabilistically. Each URL would have a `storage_probability` associated with it. As the popularity of a site goes up, the `storage_probability` goes down. For example, a popular document might have data logged only one out of every ten times, at random. When we look up the number of visits for the site, we'll need to adjust the value based on the probability (for example, by multiplying it by 10). This will of course lead to a small inaccuracy, but that may be acceptable.

The log files are not designed to be used frequently. We will want to also store this precomputed data in a datastore. If the analytics just displays the number of visits plus a graph over time, this could be kept in a separate database.

URL	Month and Year	Visits
`12ab31b92p`	`December 2013`	`242119`
`12ab31b92p`	`January 2014`	`429918`
...	...	...

Every time a URL is visited, we can increment the appropriate row and column. This datastore can also be sharded by the URL.

As the stats are not listed on the regular pages and would generally be of less interest, it should not face as heavy of a load. We could still cache the generated HTML on the frontend servers, so that we don't continuously reaccess the data for the most popular URLs.

Follow-Up Questions

- How would you support user accounts?
- How would you add a new piece of analytics (e.g., referral source) to the stats page?
- How would your design change if the stats were shown with each document?

10

Solutions to Sorting and Searching

10.1 Sorted Merge: You are given two sorted arrays, A and B, where A has a large enough buffer at the end to hold B. Write a method to merge B into A in sorted order.

pg 149

SOLUTION

Since we know that A has enough buffer at the end, we won't need to allocate additional space. Our logic should involve simply comparing elements of A and B and inserting them in order, until we've exhausted all elements in A and in B.

The only issue with this is that if we insert an element into the front of A, then we'll have to shift the existing elements backwards to make room for it. It's better to insert elements into the back of the array, where there's empty space.

The code below does just that. It works from the back of A and B, moving the largest elements to the back of A.

```
void merge(int[] a, int[] b, int lastA, int lastB) {
   int indexA = lastA - 1; /* Index of last element in array a */
   int indexB = lastB - 1; /* Index of last element in array b */
   int indexMerged = lastB + lastA - 1; /* end of merged array */

   /* Merge a and b, starting from the last element in each */
   while (indexB >= 0) {
      /* end of a is > than end of b */
      if (indexA >= 0 && a[indexA] > b[indexB]) {
         a[indexMerged] = a[indexA]; // copy element
         indexA--;
      } else {
         a[indexMerged] = b[indexB]; // copy element
         indexB--;
      }
      indexMerged--; // move indices
   }
}
```

Note that you don't need to copy the contents of A after running out of elements in B. They are already in place.

10.2 Group Anagrams: Write a method to sort an array of strings so that all the anagrams are next to each other.

pg 150

SOLUTION

This problem asks us to group the strings in an array such that the anagrams appear next to each other. Note that no specific ordering of the words is required, other than this.

We need a quick and easy way of determining if two strings are anagrams of each other. What defines if two words are anagrams of each other? Well, anagrams are words that have the same characters but in different orders. It follows then that if we can put the characters in the same order, we can easily check if the new words are identical.

One way to do this is to just apply any standard sorting algorithm, like merge sort or quick sort, and modify the comparator. This comparator will be used to indicate that two strings which are anagrams of each other are equivalent.

What's the easiest way of checking if two words are anagrams? We could count the occurrences of the distinct characters in each string and return `true` if they match. Or, we could just sort the string. After all, two words which are anagrams will look the same once they're sorted.

The code below implements the comparator.

```
class AnagramComparator implements Comparator<String> {
  private String sortChars(String s) {
    char[] content = s.toCharArray();
    Arrays.sort(content);
    return new String(content);
  }

  public int compare(String s1, String s2) {
    return sortChars(s1).compareTo(sortChars(s2));
  }
}
```

Now, just sort the arrays using this `compareTo` method instead of the usual one.

```
Arrays.sort(array, new AnagramComparator());
```

This algorithm will take `O(n log(n))` time.

This may be the best we can do for a general sorting algorithm, but we don't actually need to fully sort the array. We only need to *group* the strings in the array by anagram.

We can do this by using a hash table which maps from the sorted version of a word to a list of its anagrams. So, for example, `acre` will map to the list `{acre, race, care}`. Once we've grouped all the words into these lists by anagram, we can then put them back into the array.

The code below implements this algorithm.

```
void sort(String[] array) {
  HashMapList<String, String> mapList = new HashMapList<String, String>();

  /* Group words by anagram */
  for (String s : array) {
    String key = sortChars(s);
    mapList.put(key, s);
  }
```

```

    /* Convert hash table to array */
    int index = 0;
    for (String key : mapList.keySet()) {
       ArrayList<String> list = mapList.get(key);
       for (String t : list) {
          array[index] = t;
          index++;
       }
    }
 }

 String sortChars(String s) {
    char[] content = s.toCharArray();
    Arrays.sort(content);
    return new String(content);
 }

 /* HashMapList<String, String> is a HashMap that maps from Strings to
  * ArrayList<String>. See appendix for implementation. */
```

You may notice that the algorithm above is a modification of bucket sort.

10.3 Search in Rotated Array: Given a sorted array of n integers that has been rotated an unknown number of times, write code to find an element in the array. You may assume that the array was originally sorted in increasing order.

EXAMPLE

Input: find 5 in `{15, 16, 19, 20, 25, 1, 3, 4, 5, 7, 10, 14}`

Output: 8 (the index of 5 in the array)

pg 150

SOLUTION

If this problem smells like binary search to you, you're right!

In classic binary search, we compare x with the midpoint to figure out if x belongs on the left or the right side. The complication here is that the array is rotated and may have an inflection point. Consider, for example, the following two arrays:

```
Array1: {10, 15, 20,  0,  5}
Array2: {50,  5, 20, 30, 40}
```

Note that both arrays have a midpoint of 20, but 5 appears on the left side of one and on the right side of the other. Therefore, comparing x with the midpoint is insufficient.

However, if we look a bit deeper, we can see that one half of the array must be ordered normally (in increasing order). We can therefore look at the normally ordered half to determine whether we should search the left or right half.

For example, if we are searching for 5 in `Array1`, we can look at the left element (10) and middle element (20). Since 10 < 20, the left half must be ordered normally. And, since 5 is not between those, we know that we must search the right half.

In `Array2`, we can see that since 50 > 20, the right half must be ordered normally. We turn to the middle (20) and right (40) element to check if 5 would fall between them. The value 5 would not; therefore, we search the left half.

The tricky condition is if the left and the middle are identical, as in the example array `{2, 2, 2, 3, 4, 2}`. In this case, we can check if the rightmost element is different. If it is, we can search just the right side. Otherwise, we have no choice but to search both halves.

```
int search(int a[], int left, int right, int x) {
   int mid = (left + right) / 2;
   if (x == a[mid]) { // Found element
      return mid;
   }
   if (right < left) {
      return -1;
   }

   /* Either the left or right half must be normally ordered. Find out which side
    * is normally ordered, and then use the normally ordered half to figure out
    * which side to search to find x. */
   if (a[left] < a[mid]) { // Left is normally ordered.
      if (x >= a[left] && x < a[mid]) {
         return search(a, left, mid - 1, x); // Search left
      } else {
         return search(a, mid + 1, right, x); // Search right
      }
   } else if (a[mid] < a[left]) { // Right is normally ordered.
      if (x > a[mid] && x <= a[right]) {
         return search(a, mid + 1, right, x); // Search right
      } else {
         return search(a, left, mid - 1, x); // Search left
      }
   } else if (a[left] == a[mid]) { // Left or right half is all repeats
      if (a[mid] != a[right]) { // If right is different, search it
         return search(a, mid + 1, right, x); // search right
      } else { // Else, we have to search both halves
         int result = search(a, left, mid - 1, x); // Search left
         if (result == -1) {
            return search(a, mid + 1, right, x); // Search right
         } else {
            return result;
         }
      }
   }
   return -1;
}
```

This code will run in `O(log n)` if all the elements are unique. However, with many duplicates, the algorithm is actually `O(n)`. This is because with many duplicates, we will often have to search both the left and right sides of the array (or subarrays).

Note that while this problem is not conceptually very complex, it is actually very difficult to implement flawlessly. Don't feel bad if you had trouble implementing it without a few bugs. Because of the ease of making off-by-one and other minor errors, you should make sure to test your code very thoroughly.

10.4 Sorted Search, No Size: You are given an array-like data structure `Listy` which lacks a size method. It does, however, have an `elementAt(i)` method that returns the element at index `i` in `O(1)` time. If `i` is beyond the bounds of the data structure, it returns `-1`. (For this reason, the data structure only supports positive integers.) Given a `Listy` which contains sorted, positive integers, find the index at which an element x occurs. If x occurs multiple times, you may return any index.

pg 150

SOLUTION

Our first thought here should be binary search. The problem is that binary search requires us knowing the length of the list, so that we can compare it to the midpoint. We don't have that here.

Could we compute the length? Yes!

We know that `elementAt` will return `-1` when `i` is too large. We can therefore just try bigger and bigger values until we exceed the size of the list.

But how much bigger? If we just went through the list linearly—1, then 2, then 3, then 4, and so on—we'd wind up with a linear time algorithm. We probably want something faster than this. Otherwise, why would the interviewer have specified the list is sorted?

It's better to back off exponentially. Try 1, then 2, then 4, then 8, then 16, and so on. This ensures that, if the list has length n, we'll find the length in at most `O(log n)` time.

> Why `O(log n)`? Imagine we start with pointer q at q = 1. At each iteration, this pointer q doubles, until q is bigger than the length n. How many times can q double in size before it's bigger than n? Or, in other words, for what value of k does $2^k = n$? This expression is equal when k = `log` n, as this is precisely what `log` means. Therefore, it will take `O(log n)` steps to find the length.

Once we find the length, we just perform a (mostly) normal binary search. I say "mostly" because we need to make one small tweak. If the mid point is -1, we need to treat this as a "too big" value and search left. This is on line 16 below.

There's one more little tweak. Recall that the way we figure out the length is by calling `elementAt` and comparing it to -1. If, in the process, the element is bigger than the value x (the one we're searching for), we'll jump over to the binary search part early.

```
1  int search(Listy list, int value) {
2     int index = 1;
3     while (list.elementAt(index) != -1 && list.elementAt(index) < value) {
4        index *= 2;
5     }
6     return binarySearch(list, value, index / 2, index);
7  }
8
9  int binarySearch(Listy list, int value, int low, int high) {
10    int mid;
11
12    while (low <= high) {
13       mid = (low + high) / 2;
14       int middle = list.elementAt(mid);
15       if (middle > value || middle == -1) {
16          high = mid - 1;
17       } else if (middle < value) {
```

```
            low = mid + 1;
        } else {
            return mid;
        }
    }
    return -1;
}
```

It turns out that not knowing the length didn't impact the runtime of the search algorithm. We find the length in O(log n) time and then do the search in O(log n) time. Our overall runtime is O(log n), just as it would be in a normal array.

10.5 Sparse Search: Given a sorted array of strings that is interspersed with empty strings, write a method to find the location of a given string.

EXAMPLE

Input: ball, {"at", "", "", "", "ball", "", "", "car", "", "", "dad", "", ""}

Output: 4

pg 150

SOLUTION

If it weren't for the empty strings, we could simply use binary search. We would compare the string to be found, str, with the midpoint of the array, and go from there.

With empty strings interspersed, we can implement a simple modification of binary search. All we need to do is fix the comparison against mid, in case mid is an empty string. We simply move mid to the closest non-empty string.

The recursive code below to solve this problem can easily be modified to be iterative. We provide such an implementation in the code attachment.

```
int search(String[] strings, String str, int first, int last) {
    if (first > last) return -1;
    /* Move mid to the middle */
    int mid = (last + first) / 2;

    /* If mid is empty, find closest non-empty string. */
    if (strings[mid].isEmpty()) {
        int left = mid - 1;
        int right = mid + 1;
        while (true) {
            if (left < first && right > last) {
                return -1;
            } else if (right <= last && !strings[right].isEmpty()) {
                mid = right;
                break;
            } else if (left >= first && !strings[left].isEmpty()) {
                mid = left;
                break;
            }
            right++;
            left--;
        }
    }
```

```
    /* Check for string, and recurse if necessary */
    if (str.equals(strings[mid])) { // Found it!
       return mid;
    } else if (strings[mid].compareTo(str) < 0) { // Search right
       return search(strings, str, mid + 1, last);
    } else { // Search left
       return search(strings, str, first, mid - 1);
    }
 }

 int search(String[] strings, String str) {
    if (strings == null || str == null || str == "") {
       return -1;
    }
    return search(strings, str, 0, strings.length - 1);
 }
```

The worst-case runtime for this algorithm is O(n). In fact, it's impossible to have an algorithm for this problem that is better than O(n) in the worst case. After all, you could have an array of all empty strings except for one non-empty string. There is no "smart" way to find this non-empty string. In the worst case, you will need to look at every element in the array.

Careful consideration should be given to the situation when someone searches for the empty string. Should we find the location (which is an O(n) operation)? Or should we handle this as an error?

There's no correct answer here. This is an issue you should raise with your interviewer. Simply asking this question will demonstrate that you are a careful coder.

10.6 Sort Big File: Imagine you have a 20 GB file with one string per line. Explain how you would sort the file.

pg 150

SOLUTION

When an interviewer gives a size limit of 20 gigabytes, it should tell you something. In this case, it suggests that they don't want you to bring all the data into memory.

So what do we do? We only bring part of the data into memory.

We'll divide the file into chunks, which are x megabytes each, where x is the amount of memory we have available. Each chunk is sorted separately and then saved back to the file system.

Once all the chunks are sorted, we merge the chunks, one by one. At the end, we have a fully sorted file.

This algorithm is known as external sort.

10.7 Missing Int: Given an input file with four billion non-negative integers, provide an algorithm to generate an integer that is not contained in the file. Assume you have 1 GB of memory available for this task.

FOLLOW UP

What if you have only 10 MB of memory? Assume that all the values are distinct and we now have no more than one billion non-negative integers.

pg 150

SOLUTION

There are a total of 2^{32}, or 4 billion, distinct integers possible and 2^{31} non-negative integers. Therefore, we know the input file (assuming it is `ints` rather than `longs`) contains some duplicates.

We have 1 GB of memory, or 8 billion bits. Thus, with 8 billion bits, we can map all possible integers to a distinct bit with the available memory. The logic is as follows:

1. Create a bit vector (BV) with 4 billion bits. Recall that a bit vector is an array that compactly stores boolean values by using an array of ints (or another data type). Each int represents 32 boolean values.
2. Initialize BV with all 0s.
3. Scan all numbers (num) from the file and call `BV.set(num, 1)`.
4. Now scan again BV from the 0th index.
5. Return the first index which has a value of 0.

The following code demonstrates our algorithm.

```
long numberOfInts = ((long) Integer.MAX_VALUE) + 1;
byte[] bitfield = new byte [(int) (numberOfInts / 8)];
String filename = ...

void findOpenNumber() throws FileNotFoundException {
  Scanner in = new Scanner(new FileReader(filename));
  while (in.hasNextInt()) {
    int n = in.nextInt ();
    /* Finds the corresponding number in the bitfield by using the OR operator to
     * set the nth bit of a byte (e.g., 10 would correspond to bit 2 of
     * index 1 in the byte array). */
    bitfield[n / 8] |= 1 << (n % 8);
  }

  for (int i = 0; i < bitfield.length; i++) {
    for (int j = 0; j < 8; j++) {
      /* Retrieves the individual bits of each byte. When 0 bit is found, print
       * the corresponding value. */
      if ((bitfield[i] & (1 << j)) == 0) {
        System.out.println (i * 8 + j);
        return;
      }
    }
  }
}
```

Follow Up: What if we have only 10 MB memory?

It's possible to find a missing integer with two passes of the data set. We can divide up the integers into blocks of some size (we'll discuss how to decide on a size later). Let's just assume that we divide up the integers into blocks of 1000. So, block 0 represents the numbers 0 through 999, block 1 represents numbers 1000 - 1999, and so on.

Since all the values are distinct, we know how many values we *should* find in each block. So, we search through the file and count how many values are between 0 and 999, how many are between 1000 and 1999, and so on. If we count only 999 values in a particular range, then we know that a missing int must be in that range.

In the second pass, we'll actually look for which number in that range is missing. We use the bit vector approach from the first part of this problem. We can ignore any number outside of this specific range.

The question, now, is what is the appropriate block size? Let's define some variables as follows:

- Let `rangeSize` be the size of the ranges that each block in the first pass represents.
- Let `arraySize` represent the number of blocks in the first pass. Note that `arraySize` = $2^{31}/\texttt{rangeSize}$ since there are 2^{31} non-negative integers.

We need to select a value for `rangeSize` such that the memory from the first pass (the array) and the second pass (the bit vector) fit.

First Pass: The Array

The array in the first pass can fit in 10 megabytes, or roughly 2^{23} bytes, of memory. Since each element in the array is an int, and an int is 4 bytes, we can hold an array of at most about 2^{21} elements. So, we can deduce the following:

$$\texttt{arraySize} = \frac{2^{31}}{\texttt{rangeSize}} \leq 2^{21}$$

$$\texttt{rangeSize} \geq \frac{2^{31}}{2^{21}}$$

$$\texttt{rangeSize} \geq 2^{10}$$

Second Pass: The Bit Vector

We need to have enough space to store `rangeSize` bits. Since we can fit 2^{23} bytes in memory, we can fit 2^{26} bits in memory. Therefore, we can conclude the following:

$$2^{10} <= \texttt{rangeSize} <= 2^{26}$$

These conditions give us a good amount of "wiggle room," but the nearer to the middle that we pick, the less memory will be used at any given time.

The below code provides one implementation for this algorithm.

```
int findOpenNumber(String filename) throws FileNotFoundException {
  int rangeSize = (1 << 20); // 2^20 bits (2^17 bytes)

  /* Get count of number of values within each block. */
  int[] blocks = getCountPerBlock(filename, rangeSize);

  /* Find a block with a missing value. */
  int blockIndex = findBlockWithMissing(blocks, rangeSize);
  if (blockIndex < 0) return -1;
```

```

    /* Create bit vector for items within this range. */
    byte[] bitVector = getBitVectorForRange(filename, blockIndex, rangeSize);

    /* Find a zero in the bit vector */
    int offset = findZero(bitVector);
    if (offset < 0) return -1;

    /* Compute missing value. */
    return blockIndex * rangeSize + offset;
 }

 /* Get count of items within each range. */
 int[] getCountPerBlock(String filename, int rangeSize)
       throws FileNotFoundException {
    int arraySize = Integer.MAX_VALUE / rangeSize + 1;
    int[] blocks = new int[arraySize];

    Scanner in = new Scanner (new FileReader(filename));
    while (in.hasNextInt()) {
        int value = in.nextInt();
        blocks[value / rangeSize]++;
    }
    in.close();
    return blocks;
 }

 /* Find a block whose count is low. */
 int findBlockWithMissing(int[] blocks, int rangeSize) {
    for (int i = 0; i < blocks.length; i++) {
       if (blocks[i] < rangeSize){
          return i;
       }
    }
    return -1;
 }

 /* Create a bit vector for the values within a specific range. */
 byte[] getBitVectorForRange(String filename, int blockIndex, int rangeSize)
       throws FileNotFoundException {
    int startRange = blockIndex * rangeSize;
    int endRange = startRange + rangeSize;
    byte[] bitVector = new byte[rangeSize/Byte.SIZE];

    Scanner in = new Scanner(new FileReader(filename));
    while (in.hasNextInt()) {
       int value = in.nextInt();
       /* If the number is inside the block that's missing numbers, we record it */
       if (startRange <= value && value < endRange) {
          int offset = value - startRange;
          int mask = (1 << (offset % Byte.SIZE));
          bitVector[offset / Byte.SIZE] |= mask;
       }
    }
    in.close();
    return bitVector;
```

```
}

/* Find bit index that is 0 within byte. */
int findZero(byte b) {
   for (int i = 0; i < Byte.SIZE; i++) {
      int mask = 1 << i;
      if ((b & mask) == 0) {
         return i;
      }
   }
   return -1;
}

/* Find a zero within the bit vector and return the index. */
int findZero(byte[] bitVector) {
   for (int i = 0; i < bitVector.length; i++) {
      if (bitVector[i] != ~0) { // If not all 1s
         int bitIndex = findZero(bitVector[i]);
         return i * Byte.SIZE + bitIndex;
      }
   }
   return -1;
}
```

What if, as a follow up question, you are asked to solve the problem with even less memory? In this case, we can do repeated passes using the approach from the first step. We'd first check to see how many integers are found within each sequence of a million elements. Then, in the second pass, we'd check how many integers are found in each sequence of a thousand elements. Finally, in the third pass, we'd apply the bit vector.

10.8 Find Duplicates: You have an array with all the numbers from 1 to N, where N is at most 32,000. The array may have duplicate entries and you do not know what N is. With only 4 kilobytes of memory available, how would you print all duplicate elements in the array?

pg 151

SOLUTION

We have 4 kilobytes of memory which means we can address up to $8 * 4 * 2^{10}$ bits. Note that $32 * 2^{10}$ bits is greater than 32000. We can create a bit vector with 32000 bits, where each bit represents one integer.

Using this bit vector, we can then iterate through the array, flagging each element v by setting bit v to 1. When we come across a duplicate element, we print it.

```
void checkDuplicates(int[] array) {
   BitSet bs = new BitSet(32000);
   for (int i = 0; i < array.length; i++) {
      int num = array[i];
      int num0 = num - 1; // bitset starts at 0, numbers start at 1
      if (bs.get(num0)) {
         System.out.println(num);
      } else {
         bs.set(num0);
      }
   }
}

class BitSet {
```

```
    int[] bitset;

    public BitSet(int size) {
       bitset = new int[(size >> 5) + 1]; // divide by 32
    }

    boolean get(int pos) {
       int wordNumber = (pos >> 5); // divide by 32
       int bitNumber = (pos & 0x1F); // mod 32
       return (bitset[wordNumber] & (1 << bitNumber)) != 0;
    }

    void set(int pos) {
       int wordNumber = (pos >> 5); // divide by 32
       int bitNumber = (pos & 0x1F); // mod 32
       bitset[wordNumber] |= 1 << bitNumber;
    }
 }
```

Note that while this isn't an especially difficult problem, it's important to implement this cleanly. This is why we defined our own bit vector class to hold a large bit vector. If our interviewer lets us (she may or may not), we could have of course used Java's built in `BitSet` class.

10.9 Sorted Matrix Search: Given an `M x N` matrix in which each row and each column is sorted in ascending order, write a method to find an element.

pg 151

SOLUTION

We can approach this in two ways: a more naive solution that only takes advantage of part of the sorting, and a more optimal way that takes advantage of both parts of the sorting.

Solution #1: Naive Solution

As a first approach, we can do binary search on every row to find the element. This algorithm will be `O(M log(N))`, since there are `M` rows and it takes `O(log(N))` time to search each one. This is a good approach to mention to your interviewer before you proceed with generating a better algorithm.

To develop an algorithm, let's start with a simple example.

15	20	40	85
20	35	80	95
30	55	95	105
40	80	100	120

Suppose we are searching for the element 55. How can we identify where it is?

If we look at the start of a row or the start of a column, we can start to deduce the location. If the start of a column is greater than 55, we know that 55 can't be in that column, since the start of the column is always the minimum element. Additionally, we know that 55 can't be in any columns on the right, since the first element of each column must increase in size from left to right. Therefore, if the start of the column is greater than the element `x` that we are searching for, we know that we need to move further to the left.

For rows, we use identical logic. If the start of a row is bigger than `x`, we know we need to move upwards.

Observe that we can also make a similar conclusion by looking at the ends of columns or rows. If the end of a column or row is less than x, then we know that we must move down (for rows) or to the right (for columns) to find x. This is because the end is always the maximum element.

We can bring these observations together into a solution. The observations are the following:

- If the start of a column is greater than x, then x is to the left of the column.
- If the end of a column is less than x, then x is to the right of the column.
- If the start of a row is greater than x, then x is above that row.
- If the end of a row is less than x, then x is below that row.

We can begin in any number of places, but let's begin with looking at the starts of columns.

We need to start with the greatest column and work our way to the left. This means that our first element for comparison is `array[0][c-1]`, where c is the number of columns. By comparing the start of columns to x (which is 55), we'll find that x must be in columns 0, 1, or 2. We will have stopped at `array[0][2]`.

This element may not be the end of a row in the full matrix, but it is an end of a row of a submatrix. The same conditions apply. The value at `array[0][2]`, which is 40, is less than 55, so we know we can move downwards.

We now have a submatrix to consider that looks like the following (the gray squares have been eliminated).

15	20	40	85
20	35	80	95
30	55	95	105
40	80	100	120

We can repeatedly apply these conditions to search for 55. Note that the only conditions we actually use are conditions 1 and 4.

The code below implements this elimination algorithm.

```
boolean findElement(int[][] matrix, int elem) {
   int row = 0;
   int col = matrix[0].length - 1;
   while (row < matrix.length && col >= 0) {
      if (matrix[row][col] == elem) {
         return true;
      } else if (matrix[row][col] > elem) {
         col--;
      } else {
         row++;
      }
   }
   return false;
}
```

Alternatively, we can apply a solution that more directly looks like binary search. The code is considerably more complicated, but it applies many of the same learnings.

Solution #2: Binary Search

Let's again look at a simple example.

15	20	70	85
20	35	80	95
30	55	95	105
40	80	100	120

We want to be able to leverage the sorting property to more efficiently find an element. So, we might ask ourselves, what does the unique ordering property of this matrix imply about where an element might be located?

We are told that every row and column is sorted. This means that element `a[i][j]` will be greater than the elements in row `i` between columns 0 and `j - 1` and the elements in column `j` between rows 0 and `i - 1`.

Or, in other words:

```
a[i][0] <= a[i][1] <= ... <= a[i][j-1] <= a[i][j]
a[0][j] <= a[1][j] <= ... <= a[i-1][j] <= a[i][j]
```

Looking at this visually, the dark gray element below is bigger than all the light gray elements.

15	20	70	85
20	35	80	95
30	55	95	105
40	80	100	120

The light gray elements also have an ordering to them: each is bigger than the elements to the left of it, as well as the elements above it. So, by transitivity, the dark gray element is bigger than the entire square.

15	20	70	85
20	35	80	95
30	55	95	105
40	80	100	120

This means that for any rectangle we draw in the matrix, the bottom right hand corner will always be the biggest.

Likewise, the top left hand corner will always be the smallest. The colors below indicate what we know about the ordering of elements (light gray < dark gray < black):

15	20	70	85
20	35	80	95
30	55	95	105
40	80	120	120

Let's return to the original problem: suppose we were searching for the value 85. If we look along the diagonal, we'll find the elements 35 and 95. What does this tell us about the location of 85?

15	20	70	85
25	35	80	95
30	55	95	105
40	80	120	120

85 can't be in the black area, since 95 is in the upper left hand corner and is therefore the smallest element in that square.

85 can't be in the light gray area either, since 35 is in the lower right hand corner of that square.

85 must be in one of the two white areas.

So, we partition our grid into four quadrants and recursively search the lower left quadrant and the upper right quadrant. These, too, will get divided into quadrants and searched.

Observe that since the diagonal is sorted, we can efficiently search it using binary search.

The code below implements this algorithm.

```
Coordinate findElement(int[][] matrix, Coordinate origin, Coordinate dest, int x){
   if (!origin.inbounds(matrix) || !dest.inbounds(matrix)) {
      return null;
   }
   if (matrix[origin.row][origin.column] == x) {
      return origin;
   } else if (!origin.isBefore(dest)) {
      return null;
   }

   /* Set start to start of diagonal and end to the end of the diagonal. Since the
    * grid may not be square, the end of the diagonal may not equal dest. */
   Coordinate start = (Coordinate) origin.clone();
   int diagDist = Math.min(dest.row - origin.row, dest.column - origin.column);
   Coordinate end = new Coordinate(start.row + diagDist, start.column + diagDist);
   Coordinate p = new Coordinate(0, 0);

   /* Do binary search on the diagonal, looking for the first element > x */
   while (start.isBefore(end)) {
      p.setToAverage(start, end);
      if (x > matrix[p.row][p.column]) {
         start.row = p.row + 1;
         start.column = p.column + 1;
      } else {
         end.row = p.row - 1;
         end.column = p.column - 1;
      }
   }

   /* Split the grid into quadrants. Search the bottom left and the top right. */
   return partitionAndSearch(matrix, origin, dest, start, x);
}

Coordinate partitionAndSearch(int[][] matrix, Coordinate origin, Coordinate dest,
                              Coordinate pivot, int x) {
   Coordinate lowerLeftOrigin = new Coordinate(pivot.row, origin.column);
   Coordinate lowerLeftDest = new Coordinate(dest.row, pivot.column - 1);
   Coordinate upperRightOrigin = new Coordinate(origin.row, pivot.column);
   Coordinate upperRightDest = new Coordinate(pivot.row - 1, dest.column);

   Coordinate lowerLeft = findElement(matrix, lowerLeftOrigin, lowerLeftDest, x);
   if (lowerLeft == null) {
      return findElement(matrix, upperRightOrigin, upperRightDest, x);
   }
```

```
    return lowerLeft;
}

Coordinate findElement(int[][] matrix, int x) {
    Coordinate origin = new Coordinate(0, 0);
    Coordinate dest = new Coordinate(matrix.length - 1, matrix[0].length - 1);
    return findElement(matrix, origin, dest, x);
}

public class Coordinate implements Cloneable {
    public int row, column;
    public Coordinate(int r, int c) {
        row = r;
        column = c;
    }

    public boolean inbounds(int[][] matrix) {
        return  row >= 0 && column >= 0 &&
                row < matrix.length && column < matrix[0].length;
    }

    public boolean isBefore(Coordinate p) {
        return row <= p.row && column <= p.column;
    }

    public Object clone() {
        return new Coordinate(row, column);
    }

    public void setToAverage(Coordinate min, Coordinate max) {
        row = (min.row + max.row) / 2;
        column = (min.column + max.column) / 2;
    }
}
```

If you read all this code and thought, "there's no way I could do all this in an interview!" you're probably right. You couldn't. But, your performance on any problem is evaluated compared to other candidates on the same problem. So while you couldn't implement all this, neither could they. You are at no disadvantage when you get a tricky problem like this.

You help yourself out a bit by separating code out into other methods. For example, by pulling `partitionAndSearch` out into its own method, you will have an easier time outlining key aspects of the code. You can then come back to fill in the body for `partitionAndSearch` if you have time.

10.10 Rank from Stream: Imagine you are reading in a stream of integers. Periodically, you wish to be able to look up the rank of a number x (the number of values less than or equal to x). Implement the data structures and algorithms to support these operations. That is, implement the method `track(int x)`, which is called when each number is generated, and the method `getRankOfNumber(int x)`, which returns the number of values less than or equal to x (not including x itself).

EXAMPLE

Stream (in order of appearance): `5, 1, 4, 4, 5, 9, 7, 13, 3`

`getRankOfNumber(1) = 0`

`getRankOfNumber(3) = 1`

`getRankOfNumber(4) = 3`

pg 151

SOLUTION

A relatively easy way to implement this would be to have an array that holds all the elements in sorted order. When a new element comes in, we would need to shift the other elements to make room. Implementing `getRankOfNumber` would be quite efficient, though. We would simply perform a binary search for n, and return the index.

However, this is very inefficient for inserting elements (that is, the `track(int x)` function). We need a data structure which is good at keeping relative ordering, as well as updating when we insert new elements. A binary search tree can do just that.

Instead of inserting elements into an array, we insert elements into a binary search tree. The method `track(int x)` will run in `O(log n)` time, where n is the size of the tree (provided, of course, that the tree is balanced).

To find the rank of a number, we could do an in-order traversal, keeping a counter as we traverse. The goal is that, by the time we find x, `counter` will equal the number of elements less than x.

As long as we're moving left during searching for x, the counter won't change. Why? Because all the values we're skipping on the right side are greater than x. After all, the very smallest element (with rank of 1) is the leftmost node.

When we move to the right though, we skip over a bunch of elements on the left. All of these elements are less than x, so we'll need to increment `counter` by the number of elements in the left subtree.

Rather than counting the size of the left subtree (which would be inefficient), we can track this information as we add new elements to the tree.

Let's walk through an example on the following tree. In the below example, the value in parentheses indicates the number of nodes in the left subtree (or, in other words, the rank of the node *relative* to its subtree).

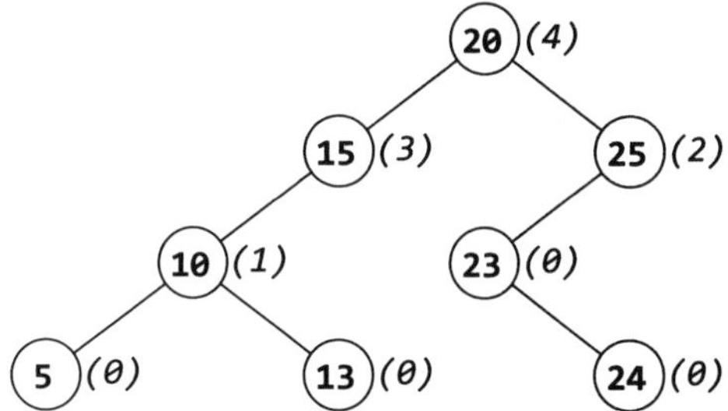

Suppose we want to find the rank of 24 in the tree above. We would compare 24 with the root, 20, and find that 24 must reside on the right. The root has 4 nodes in its left subtree, and when we include the root itself, this gives us five total nodes smaller than 24. We set `counter` to 5.

Then, we compare 24 with node 25 and find that 24 must be on the left. The value of `counter` does not update, since we're not "passing over" any smaller nodes. The value of `counter` is still 5.

Next, we compare 24 with node 23, and find that 24 must be on the right. `Counter` gets incremented by just 1 (to 6), since 23 has no left nodes.

Finally, we find 24 and we return `counter`: 6.

Recursively, the algorithm is the following:

```
int getRank(Node node, int x) {
  if x is node.data, return node.leftSize()
  if x is on left of node, return getRank(node.left, x)
  if x is on right of node, return node.leftSize() + 1 + getRank(node.right, x)
}
```

The full code for this is below.

```
RankNode root = null;

void track(int number) {
  if (root == null) {
    root = new RankNode(number);
  } else {
    root.insert(number);
  }
}

int getRankOfNumber(int number) {
  return root.getRank(number);
}


public class RankNode {
  public int left_size = 0;
  public RankNode left, right;
  public int data = 0;
  public RankNode(int d) {
    data = d;
  }

  public void insert(int d) {
    if (d <= data) {
```

```
            if (left != null) left.insert(d);
            else left = new RankNode(d);
            left_size++;
        } else {
            if (right != null) right.insert(d);
            else right = new RankNode(d);
        }
    }

    public int getRank(int d) {
        if (d == data) {
            return left_size;
        } else if (d < data) {
            if (left == null) return -1;
            else return left.getRank(d);
        } else {
            int right_rank = right == null ? -1 : right.getRank(d);
            if (right_rank == -1) return -1;
            else return left_size + 1 + right_rank;
        }
    }
}
```

The `track` method and the `getRankOfNumber` method will both operate in `O(log N)` on a balanced tree and `O(N)` on an unbalanced tree.

Note how we've handled the case in which d is not found in the tree. We check for the -1 return value, and, when we find it, return -1 up the tree. It is important that you handle cases like this.

10.11 Peaks and Valleys: In an array of integers, a "peak" is an element which is greater than or equal to the adjacent integers and a "valley" is an element which is less than or equal to the adjacent integers. For example, in the array {5, 8, 6, 2, 3, 4, 6}, {8, 6} are peaks and {5, 2} are valleys. Given an array of integers, sort the array into an alternating sequence of peaks and valleys.

EXAMPLE

Input: {5, 3, 1, 2, 3}

Output: {5, 1, 3, 2, 3}

pg 151

SOLUTION

Since this problem asks us to sort the array in a particular way, one thing we can try is doing a normal sort and then "fixing" the array into an alternating sequence of peaks and valleys.

Suboptimal Solution

Imagine we were given an unsorted array and then sort it to become the following:

```
0   1   4   7   8   9
```

We now have an ascending list of integers.

How can we rearrange this into a proper alternating sequence of peaks and valleys? Let's walk through it and try to do that.

- The `0` is okay.

- The 1 is in the wrong place. We can swap it with either the 0 or 4. Let's swap it with the 0.

```
1  0  4  7  8  9
```

- The 4 is okay.
- The 7 is in the wrong place. We can swap it with either the 4 or the 8. Let's swap it with the 4.

```
1  0  7  4  8  9
```

- The 9 is in the wrong place. Let's swap it with the 8.

```
1  0  7  4  9  8
```

Observe that there's nothing special about the array having these values. The relative order of the elements matters, but all sorted arrays will have the same relative order. Therefore, we can take this same approach on any sorted array.

Before coding, we should clarify the exact algorithm, though.

1. Sort the array in ascending order.
2. Iterate through the elements, starting from index 1 (not 0) and jumping two elements at a time.
3. At each element, swap it with the previous element. Since every three elements appear in the order `small <= medium <= large`, swapping these elements will always put medium as a peak: `medium <= small <= large`.

This approach will ensure that the peaks are in the right place: indexes 1, 3, 5, and so on. As long as the odd-numbered elements (the peaks) are bigger than the adjacent elements, then the even-numbered elements (the valleys) must be smaller than the adjacent elements.

The code to implement this is below.

```java
void sortValleyPeak(int[] array) {
  Arrays.sort(array);
  for (int i = 1; i < array.length; i += 2) {
    swap(array, i - 1, i);
  }
}

void swap(int[] array, int left, int right) {
  int temp = array[left];
  array[left] = array[right];
  array[right] = temp;
}
```

This algorithm runs in `O(n log n)` time.

Optimal Solution

To optimize past the prior solution, we need to cut out the sorting step. The algorithm must operate on an unsorted array.

Let's revisit an example.

```
9  1  0  4  8  7
```

For each element, we'll look at the adjacent elements. Let's imagine some sequences. We'll just use the numbers 0, 1 and 2. The specific values don't matter.

```
0  1  2
0  2  1      // peak
1  0  2
1  2  0      // peak
2  1  0
```

```
2  0  1
```

If the center element needs to be a peak, then two of those sequences work. Can we fix the other ones to make the center element a peak?

Yes. We can fix this sequence by swapping the center element with the largest adjacent element.

```
0  1  2  -> 0  2  1
0  2  1     // peak
1  0  2  -> 1  2  0
1  2  0  // peak
2  1  0  -> 1  2  0
2  0  1  -> 0  2  1
```

As we noted before, if we make sure the peaks are in the right place then we know the valleys are in the right place.

> We should be a little cautious here. Is it possible that one of these swaps could "break" an earlier part of the sequence that we'd already processed? This is a good thing to worry about, but it's not an issue here. If we're swapping `middle` with `left`, then `left` is currently a valley. `Middle` is smaller than `left`, so we're putting an even smaller element as a valley. Nothing will break. All is good!

The code to implement this is below.

```
void sortValleyPeak(int[] array) {
   for (int i = 1; i < array.length; i += 2) {
      int biggestIndex = maxIndex(array, i - 1, i, i + 1);
      if (i != biggestIndex) {
         swap(array, i, biggestIndex);
      }
   }
}

int maxIndex(int[] array, int a, int b, int c) {
   int len = array.length;
   int aValue = a >= 0 && a < len ? array[a] : Integer.MIN_VALUE;
   int bValue = b >= 0 && b < len ? array[b] : Integer.MIN_VALUE;
   int cValue = c >= 0 && c < len ? array[c] : Integer.MIN_VALUE;

   int max = Math.max(aValue, Math.max(bValue, cValue));
   if (aValue == max) return a;
   else if (bValue == max) return b;
   else return c;
}
```

This algorithm takes O(n) time.

11

Solutions to Testing

11.1 Mistake: Find the mistake(s) in the following code:

```
unsigned int i;
for (i = 100; i >= 0; --i)
    printf("%d\n", i);
```

pg 157

SOLUTION

There are two mistakes in this code.

First, note that an `unsigned int` is, by definition, always greater than or equal to zero. The for loop condition will therefore always be true, and it will loop infinitely.

The correct code to print all numbers from 100 to 1, is `i > 0`. If we truly wanted to print zero, we could add an additional `printf` statement after the for loop.

```
unsigned int i;
for (i = 100; i > 0; --i)
    printf("%d\n", i);
```

One additional correction is to use %u in place of %d, as we are printing `unsigned int`.

```
unsigned int i;
for (i = 100; i > 0; --i)
    printf("%u\n", i);
```

This code will now correctly print the list of all numbers from 100 to 1, in descending order.

11.2 Random Crashes: You are given the source to an application which crashes when it is run. After running it ten times in a debugger, you find it never crashes in the same place. The application is single threaded, and uses only the C standard library. What programming errors could be causing this crash? How would you test each one?

pg 157

SOLUTION

The question largely depends on the type of application being diagnosed. However, we can give some general causes of random crashes.

1. *"Random Variable:"* The application may use some random number or variable component that may not be fixed for every execution of the program. Examples include user input, a random number generated by the program, or the time of day.

2. *Uninitialized Variable:* The application could have an uninitialized variable which, in some languages, may cause it to take on an arbitrary value. The values of this variable could result in the code taking a slightly different path each time.
3. *Memory Leak:* The program may have run out of memory. Other culprits are totally random for each run since it depends on the number of processes running at that particular time. This also includes heap overflow or corruption of data on the stack.
4. *External Dependencies:* The program may depend on another application, machine, or resource. If there are multiple dependencies, the program could crash at any point.

To track down the issue, we should start with learning as much as possible about the application. Who is running it? What are they doing with it? What kind of application is it?

Additionally, although the application doesn't crash in exactly the same place, it's possible that it is linked to specific components or scenarios. For example, it could be that the application never crashes if it's simply launched and left untouched, and that crashes only appear at some point after loading a file. Or, it may be that all the crashes take place within the lower level components, such as file I/O.

It may be useful to approach this by elimination. Close down all other applications on the system. Track resource use very carefully. If there are parts of the program we can disable, do so. Run it on a different machine and see if we experience the same issue. The more we can eliminate (or change), the easier we can track down the issue.

Additionally, we may be able to use tools to check for specific situations. For example, to investigate issue #2, we can utilize runtime tools which check for uninitialized variables.

These problems are as much about your brainstorming ability as they are about your approach. Do you jump all over the place, shouting out random suggestions? Or do you approach it in a logical, structured manner? Hopefully, it's the latter.

11.3 Chess Test: We have the following method used in a chess game: boolean `canMoveTo(int x, int y)`. This method is part of the `Piece` class and returns whether or not the piece can move to position `(x, y)`. Explain how you would test this method.

pg 157

SOLUTION

In this problem, there are two primary types of testing: extreme case validation (ensuring that the program doesn't crash on bad input), and general case testing. We'll start with the first type.

Testing Type #1: Extreme Case Validation

We need to ensure that the program handles bad or unusual input gracefully. This means checking the following conditions:

- Test with negative numbers for x and y
- Test with x larger than the width
- Test with y larger than the height
- Test with a completely full board
- Test with an empty or nearly empty board
- Test with far more white pieces than black

- Test with far more black pieces than white

For the error cases above, we should ask our interviewer whether we want to return false or throw an exception, and we should test accordingly.

Testing Type #2: General Testing:

General testing is much more expansive. Ideally, we would test every possible board, but there are far too many boards. We can, however, perform a reasonable coverage of different boards.

There are 6 pieces in chess, so we can test each piece against every other piece, in every possible direction. This would look something like the below code:

```
foreach piece a:
   for each other type of piece b (6 types + empty space)
      foreach direction d
         Create a board with piece a.
         Place piece b in direction d.
         Try to move - check return value.
```

The key to this problem is recognizing that we can't test every possible scenario, even if we would like to. So, instead, we must focus on the essential areas.

11.4 No Test Tools: How would you load test a webpage without using any test tools?

pg 157

SOLUTION

Load testing helps to identify a web application's maximum operating capacity, as well as any bottlenecks that may interfere with its performance. Similarly, it can check how an application responds to variations in load.

To perform load testing, we must first identify the performance critical scenarios and the metrics which fulfill our performance objectives. Typical criteria include:

- Response time
- Throughput
- Resource utilization
- Maximum load that the system can bear.

Then, we design tests to simulate the load, taking care to measure each of these criteria.

In the absence of formal testing tools, we can basically create our own. For example, we could simulate concurrent users by creating thousands of virtual users. We would write a multi-threaded program with thousands of threads, where each thread acts as a real-world user loading the page. For each user, we would programmatically measure response time, data I/O, etc.

We would then analyze the results based on the data gathered during the tests and compare it with the accepted values.

11.5 Test a Pen: How would you test a pen?

pg 157

SOLUTION

This problem is largely about understanding the constraints and approaching the problem in a structured manner.

To understand the constraints, you should ask a lot of questions to understand the "who, what, where, when, how and why" of a problem (or as many of those as apply to the problem). Remember that a good tester understands exactly what he is testing before starting the work.

To illustrate the technique in this problem, let us guide you through a mock conversation.

- **Interviewer:** How would you test a pen?
- **Candidate:** Let me find out a bit about the pen. Who is going to use the pen?
- **Interviewer:** Probably children.
- **Candidate:** Okay, that's interesting. What will they be doing with it? Will they be writing, drawing, or doing something else with it?
- **Interviewer:** Drawing.
- **Candidate:** Okay, great. On what? Paper? Clothing? Walls?
- **Interviewer:** On clothing.
- **Candidate:** Great. What kind of tip does the pen have? Felt? Ballpoint? Is it intended to wash off, or is it intended to be permanent?
- **Interviewer:** It's intended to wash off.

Many questions later, you may get to this:

- **Candidate:** Okay, so as I understand it, we have a pen that is being targeted at 5 to 10-year-olds. The pen has a felt tip and comes in red, green, blue and black. It's intended to wash off when clothing is washed. Is that correct?

The candidate now has a problem that is significantly different from what it initially seemed to be. This is not uncommon. In fact, many interviewers intentionally give a problem that seems clear (everyone knows what a pen is!), only to let you discover that it's quite a different problem from what it seemed. Their belief is that users do the same thing, though users do so accidentally.

Now that you understand what you're testing, it's time to come up with a plan of attack. The key here is *structure.*

Consider what the different components of the object or problem, and go from there. In this case, the components might be:

- *Fact check:* Verify that the pen is felt tip and that the ink is one of the allowed colors.
- *Intended use:* Drawing. Does the pen write properly on clothing?
- *Intended use:* Washing. Does it wash off of clothing (even if it's been there for an extended period of time)? Does it wash off in hot, warm and cold water?
- *Safety:* Is the pen safe (non-toxic) for children?
- *Unintended uses:* How else might children use the pen? They might write on other surfaces, so you need to check whether the behavior there is correct. They might also stomp on the pen, throw it, and so on.

You'll need to make sure that the pen holds up under these conditions.

Remember that in any testing question, you need to test both the intended and unintended scenarios. People don't always use the product the way you want them to.

11.6 Test an ATM: How would you test an ATM in a distributed banking system?

pg 157

SOLUTION

The first thing to do on this question is to clarify assumptions. Ask the following questions:

- Who is going to use the ATM? Answers might be "anyone," or it might be "blind people," or any number of other answers.
- What are they going to use it for? Answers might be "withdrawing money," "transferring money," "checking their balance," or many other answers.
- What tools do we have to test? Do we have access to the code, or just to the ATM?

Remember: a good tester makes sure she knows what she's testing!

Once we understand what the system looks like, we'll want to break down the problem into different testable components. These components include:

- Logging in
- Withdrawing money
- Depositing money
- Checking balance
- Transferring money

We would probably want to use a mix of manual and automated testing.

Manual testing would involve going through the steps above, making sure to check for all the error cases (low balance, new account, nonexistent account, and so on).

Automated testing is a bit more complex. We'll want to automate all the standard scenarios, as shown above, and we also want to look for some very specific issues, such as race conditions. Ideally, we would be able to set up a closed system with fake accounts and ensure that, even if someone withdraws and deposits money rapidly from different locations, he never gets money or loses money that he shouldn't.

Above all, we need to prioritize security and reliability. People's accounts must always be protected, and we must make sure that money is always properly accounted for. No one wants to unexpectedly lose money! A good tester understands the system priorities.

12

Solutions to C and C++

12.1 Last K Lines: Write a method to print the last K lines of an input file using C++.

pg 163

SOLUTION

One brute force way could be to count the number of lines (N) and then print from N-K to Nth line. But this requires two reads of the file, which is unnecessarily costly. We need a solution which allows us to read just once and be able to print the last K lines.

We can allocate an array for all K lines and the last K lines we've read in the array. , and so on. Each time that we read a new line, we purge the oldest line from the array.

But—you might ask—wouldn't this require shifting elements in the array, which is also very expensive? No, not if we do it correctly. Instead of shifting the array each time, we will use a circular array.

With a circular array, we always replace the oldest item when we read a new line. The oldest item is tracked in a separate variable, which adjusts as we add new items.

The following is an example of a circular array:

```
step 1 (initially): array = {a, b, c, d, e, f}. p = 0
step 2 (insert g):  array = {g, b, c, d, e, f}. p = 1
step 3 (insert h):  array = {g, h, c, d, e, f}. p = 2
step 4 (insert i):  array = {g, h, i, d, e, f}. p = 3
```

The code below implements this algorithm.

```
void printLast10Lines(char* fileName) {
  const int K = 10;
  ifstream file (fileName);
  string L[K];
  int size = 0;

  /* read file line by line into circular array */
  /* peek() so an EOF following a line ending is not considered a separate line */
  while (file.peek() != EOF) {
    getline(file, L[size % K]);
    size++;
  }

  /* compute start of circular array, and the size of it */
  int start = size > K ? (size % K) : 0;
  int count = min(K, size);

```

```
    /* print elements in the order they were read */
    for (int i = 0; i < count; i++) {
       cout << L[(start + i) % K] << endl;
    }
}
```

This solution will require reading in the whole file, but only ten lines will be in memory at any given point.

12.2 Reverse String: Implement a function void reverse(char* str) in C or C++ which reverses a null-terminated string.

pg 163

SOLUTION

This is a classic interview question. The only "gotcha" is to try to do it in place, and to be careful for the `null` character.

We will implement this in C.

```
void reverse(char *str) {
   char* end = str;
   char tmp;
   if (str) {
      while (*end) { /* find end of the string */
         ++end;
      }
      --end; /* set one char back, since last char is null */

      /* swap characters from start of string with the end of the string, until the
       * pointers meet in middle. */
      while (str < end) {
         tmp = *str;
         *str++ = *end;
         *end-- = tmp;
      }
   }
}
```

This is just one of many ways to implement this solution. We could even implement this code recursively (but we wouldn't recommend it).

12.3 Hash Table vs STL Map: Compare and contrast a hash table and an STL map. How is a hash table implemented? If the number of inputs is small, which data structure options can be used instead of a hash table?

pg 163

SOLUTION

In a hash table, a value is stored by calling a hash function on a key. Values are not stored in sorted order. Additionally, since hash tables use the key to find the index that will store the value, an insert or lookup can be done in amortized `O(1)` time (assuming few collisions in the hash table). In a hash table, one must also handle potential collisions. This is often done by chaining, which means to create a linked list of all the values whose keys map to a particular index.

An STL map inserts the key/value pairs into a binary search tree based on the keys. There is no need to handle collisions, and, since the tree is balanced, the insert and lookup time is guaranteed to be `O(log N)`.

How is a hash table implemented?

A hash table is traditionally implemented with an array of linked lists. When we want to insert a key/value pair, we map the key to an index in the array using a hash function. The value is then inserted into the linked list at that position.

Note that the elements in a linked list at a particular index of the array do not have the same key. Rather, `hashFunction(key)` is the same for these values. Therefore, in order to retrieve the value for a specific key, we need to store in each node both the exact key and the value.

To summarize, the hash table will be implemented with an array of linked lists, where each node in the linked list holds two pieces of data: the value and the original key. In addition, we will want to note the following design criteria:

1. We want to use a good hash function to ensure that the keys are well distributed. If they are not well distributed, then we would get a lot of collisions and the speed to find an element would decline.
2. No matter how good our hash function is, we will still have collisions, so we need a method for handling them. This often means chaining via a linked list, but it's not the only way.
3. We may also wish to implement methods to dynamically increase or decrease the hash table size depending on capacity. For example, when the ratio of the number of elements to the table size exceeds a certain threshold, we may wish to increase the hash table size. This would mean creating a new hash table and transferring the entries from the old table to the new table. Because this is an expensive operation, we want to be careful to not do it too often.

What can be used instead of a hash table, if the number of inputs is small?

You can use an STL map or a binary tree. Although this takes `O(log(n))` time, the number of inputs may be small enough to make this time negligible.

12.4 Virtual Functions: How do virtual functions work in C++?

pg 164

SOLUTION

A virtual function depends on a "vtable" or "Virtual Table." If any function of a class is declared to be virtual, a vtable is constructed which stores addresses of the virtual functions of this class. The compiler also adds a hidden `vptr` variable in all such classes which points to the vtable of that class. If a virtual function is not overridden in the derived class, the vtable of the derived class stores the address of the function in its parent class. The vtable is used to resolve the address of the function when the virtual function is called. Dynamic binding in C++ is performed through the vtable mechanism.

Thus, when we assign the derived class object to the base class pointer, the `vptr` variable points to the vtable of the derived class. This assignment ensures that the most derived virtual function gets called.

Consider the following code.

```
class Shape {
  public:
   int edge_length;
   virtual int circumference () {
```

```
        cout << "Circumference of Base Class\n";
        return 0;
    }
};

class Triangle: public Shape {
  public:
  int circumference () {
     cout<< "Circumference of Triangle Class\n";
     return 3 * edge_length;
  }
};

void main() {
  Shape * x = new Shape();
  x->circumference(); // "Circumference of Base Class"
  Shape *y = new Triangle();
  y->circumference(); // "Circumference of Triangle Class"
}
```

In the previous example, `circumference` is a virtual function in the `Shape` class, so it becomes virtual in each of the derived classes (`Triangle`, etc). C++ non-virtual function calls are resolved at compile time with static binding, while virtual function calls are resolved at runtime with dynamic binding.

12.5 Shallow vs Deep Copy: What is the difference between deep copy and shallow copy? Explain how you would use each.

pg 164

SOLUTION

A shallow copy copies all the member values from one object to another. A deep copy does all this and also deep copies any pointer objects.

An example of shallow and deep copy is below.

```
struct Test {
  char * ptr;
};

void shallow_copy(Test & src, Test & dest) {
  dest.ptr = src.ptr;
}

void deep_copy(Test & src, Test & dest) {
  dest.ptr = (char*)malloc(strlen(src.ptr) + 1);
  strcpy(dest.ptr, src.ptr);
}
```

Note that `shallow_copy` may cause a lot of programming runtime errors, especially with the creation and deletion of objects. Shallow copy should be used very carefully and only when a programmer really understands what he wants to do. In most cases, shallow copy is used when there is a need to pass information about a complex structure without actual duplication of data. One must also be careful with destruction of objects in a shallow copy.

In real life, shallow copy is rarely used. Deep copy should be used in most cases, especially when the size of the copied structure is small.

12.6 Volatile: What is the significance of the keyword "volatile" in C?

pg 164

SOLUTION

The keyword `volatile` informs the compiler that the value of variable it is applied to can change from the outside, without any update done by the code. This may be done by the operating system, the hardware, or another thread. Because the value can change unexpectedly, the compiler will therefore reload the value each time from memory.

A volatile integer can be declared by either of the following statements:

```
int volatile x;
volatile int x;
```

To declare a pointer to a volatile integer, we do the following:

```
volatile int * x;
int volatile * x;
```

A volatile pointer to non-volatile data is rare, but can be done.

```
int * volatile x;
```

If you wanted to declare a volatile variable pointer for volatile memory (both pointer address and memory contained are volatile), you would do the following:

```
int volatile * volatile x;
```

Volatile variables are not optimized, which can be very useful. Imagine this function:

```
int opt = 1;
void Fn(void) {
   start:
      if (opt == 1) goto start;
      else return;
}
```

At first glance, our code appears to loop infinitely. The compiler may try to optimize it to:

```
void Fn(void) {
   start:
      int opt = 1;
      if (true)
      goto start;
}
```

This becomes an infinite loop. However, an external operation might write '0' to the location of variable `opt`, thus breaking the loop.

To prevent the compiler from performing such optimization, we want to signal that another element of the system could change the variable. We do this using the `volatile` keyword, as shown below.

```
volatile int opt = 1;
void Fn(void) {
   start:
      if (opt == 1) goto start;
      else return;
}
```

Volatile variables are also useful when multi-threaded programs have global variables and any thread can modify these shared variables. We may not want optimization on these variables.

12.7 Virtual Base Class: Why does a destructor in base class need to be declared virtual?

pg 164

SOLUTION

Let's think about why we have virtual methods to start with. Suppose we have the following code:

```
class Foo {
 public:
  void f();
};

class Bar : public Foo {
 public:
  void f();
};

Foo * p = new Bar();
p->f();
```

Calling `p->f()` will result in a call to `Foo::f()`. This is because p is a pointer to Foo, and `f()` is not virtual.

To ensure that `p->f()` will invoke the most derived implementation of `f()`, we need to declare `f()` to be a virtual function.

Now, let's go back to our destructor. Destructors are used to clean up memory and resources. If Foo's destructor were not virtual, then Foo's destructor would be called, even when p is *really* of type Bar.

This is why we declare destructors to be virtual; we want to ensure that the destructor for the most derived class is called.

12.8 Copy Node: Write a method that takes a pointer to a Node structure as a parameter and returns a complete copy of the passed in data structure. The Node data structure contains two pointers to other Nodes.

pg 164

SOLUTION

The algorithm will maintain a mapping from a node address in the original structure to the corresponding node in the new structure. This mapping will allow us to discover previously copied nodes during a traditional depth-first traversal of the structure. Traversals often mark visited nodes—the mark can take many forms and does not necessarily need to be stored in the node.

Thus, we have a simple recursive algorithm:

```
typedef map<Node*, Node*> NodeMap;

Node * copy_recursive(Node * cur, NodeMap & nodeMap) {
  if (cur == NULL) {
    return NULL;
  }

  NodeMap::iterator i = nodeMap.find(cur);
  if (i != nodeMap.end()) {
    // we've been here before, return the copy
    return i->second;
  }
```

```

    Node * node = new Node;
    nodeMap[cur] = node; // map current before traversing links
    node->ptr1 = copy_recursive(cur->ptr1, nodeMap);
    node->ptr2 = copy_recursive(cur->ptr2, nodeMap);
    return node;
}

Node * copy_structure(Node * root) {
    NodeMap nodeMap; // we will need an empty map
    return copy_recursive(root, nodeMap);
}
```

12.9 **Smart Pointer:** Write a smart pointer class. A smart pointer is a data type, usually implemented with templates, that simulates a pointer while also providing automatic garbage collection. It automatically counts the number of references to a *SmartPointer<T*>* object and frees the object of type T when the reference count hits zero.

pg 164

SOLUTION

A smart pointer is the same as a normal pointer, but it provides safety via automatic memory management. It avoids issues like dangling pointers, memory leaks and allocation failures. The smart pointer must maintain a single reference count for all references to a given object.

This is one of those problems that seems at first glance pretty overwhelming, especially if you're not a C++ expert. One useful way to approach the problem is to divide the problem into two parts: (1) outline the pseudocode and approach and then (2) implement the detailed code.

In terms of the approach, we need a reference count variable that is incremented when we add a new reference to the object and decremented when we remove a reference. The code should look something like the below pseudocode:

```
template <class T> class SmartPointer {
   /* The smart pointer class needs pointers to both the object itself and to the
    * ref count. These must be pointers, rather than the actual object or ref count
    * value, since the goal of a smart pointer is that the reference count is
    * tracked across multiple smart pointers to one object. */
   T * obj;
   unsigned * ref_count;
}
```

We know we need constructors and a single destructor for this class, so let's add those first.

```
SmartPointer(T * object) {
   /* We want to set the value of T * obj, and set the reference counter to 1. */
}

SmartPointer(SmartPointer<T>& sptr) {
   /* This constructor creates a new smart pointer that points to an existing
    * object. We will need to first set obj and ref_count to pointer to sptr's obj
    * and ref_count. Then, because we created a new reference to obj, we need to
    * increment ref_count. */
}

~SmartPointer(SmartPointer<T> sptr) {
   /* We are destroying a reference to the object. Decrement ref_count. If
```

```
    * ref_count is 0, then free the memory created by the integer and destroy the
    * object. */
}
```

There's one additional way that references can be created: by setting one `SmartPointer` equal to another. We'll want to override the `equal` operator to handle this, but for now, let's sketch the code like this.

```
onSetEquals(SmartPoint<T> ptr1, SmartPoint<T> ptr2) {
   /* If ptr1 has an existing value, decrement its reference count. Then, copy the
    * pointers to obj and ref_count over. Finally, since we created a new
    * reference, we need to increment ref_count. */
}
```

Getting just the approach, even without filling in the complicated C++ syntax, would count for a lot. Finishing out the code is now just a matter of filling the details.

```
template <class T> class SmartPointer {
 public:
   SmartPointer(T * ptr) {
      ref = ptr;
      ref_count = (unsigned*)malloc(sizeof(unsigned));
      *ref_count = 1;
   }

   SmartPointer(SmartPointer<T> & sptr) {
      ref = sptr.ref;
      ref_count = sptr.ref_count;
      ++(*ref_count);
   }

   /* Override the equal operator, so that when you set one smart pointer equal to
    * another the old smart pointer has its reference count decremented and the new
    * smart pointer has its reference count incremenented. */
   SmartPointer<T> & operator=(SmartPointer<T> & sptr) {
      if (this == &sptr) return *this;

      /* If already assigned to an object, remove one reference. */
      if (*ref_count > 0) {
         remove();
      }

      ref = sptr.ref;
      ref_count = sptr.ref_count;
      ++(*ref_count);
      return *this;
   }

   ~SmartPointer() {
      remove(); // Remove one reference to object.
   }

   T getValue() {
      return *ref;
   }

 protected:
   void remove() {
      --(*ref_count);
      if (*ref_count == 0) {
```

```
            delete ref;
            free(ref_count);
            ref = NULL;
            ref_count = NULL;
        }
    }

    T * ref;
    unsigned * ref_count;
};
```

The code for this problem is complicated, and you probably wouldn't be expected to complete it flawlessly.

12.10 Malloc: Write an aligned malloc and free function that supports allocating memory such that the memory address returned is divisible by a specific power of two.

EXAMPLE

`align_malloc(1000,128)` will return a memory address that is a multiple of 128 and that points to memory of size 1000 bytes.

`aligned_free()` will free memory allocated by `align_malloc`.

pg 164

SOLUTION

Typically, with `malloc`, we do not have control over where the memory is allocated within the heap. We just get a pointer to a block of memory which could start at any memory address within the heap.

We need to work with these constraints by requesting enough memory that we can return a memory address which is divisible by the desired value.

Suppose we are requesting a 100-byte chunk of memory, and we want it to start at a memory address that is a multiple of 16. How much extra memory would we need to allocate to ensure that we can do so? We would need to allocate an extra 15 bytes. With these 15 bytes, plus another 100 bytes right after that sequence, we know that we would have a memory address divisible by 16 with space for 100 bytes.

We could then do something like:

```
1  void* aligned_malloc(size_t required_bytes, size_t alignment) {
2    int offset = alignment - 1;
3    void* p = (void*) malloc(required_bytes + offset);
4    void* q = (void*) (((size_t)(p) + offset) & ~(alignment - 1));
5    return q;
6  }
```

Line 4 is a bit tricky, so let's discuss it. Suppose `alignment` is 16. We know that one of the first 16 memory address in the block at p must be divisible by 16. With `(p + 15) & 11...10000` we advance as need to this address. ANDing the last four bits of `p + 15` with `0000` guarantees that this new value will be divisible by 16 (either at the original p or in one of the following 15 addresses).

This solution is *almost* perfect, except for one big issue: how do we free the memory?

We've allocated an extra 15 bytes, in the above example, and we need to free them when we free the "real" memory.

We can do this by storing, in this "extra" memory, the address of where the full memory block begins. We will store this immediately before the aligned memory block. Of course, this means that we now need to allocate even *more* extra memory to ensure that we have enough space to store this pointer.

Therefore, to guarantee both an aligned address and space for this pointer, we will need to allocate an additional `alignment - 1 + sizeof(void*)` bytes.

The code below implements this approach.

```
1  void* aligned_malloc(size_t required_bytes, size_t alignment) {
2    void* p1; // initial block
3    void* p2; // aligned block inside initial block
4    int offset = alignment - 1 + sizeof(void*);
5    if ((p1 = (void*)malloc(required_bytes + offset)) == NULL) {
6      return NULL;
7    }
8    p2 = (void*)(((size_t)(p1) + offset) & ~(alignment - 1));
9    ((void **)p2)[-1] = p1;
10   return p2;
11 }
12
13 void aligned_free(void *p2) {
14   /* for consistency, we use the same names as aligned_malloc*/
15   void* p1 = ((void**)p2)[-1];
16   free(p1);
17 }
```

Let's look at the pointer arithmetic in lines 9 and 15. If we treat p2 as a `void**` (or an array of `void*`'s), we can just look at the index `- 1` to retrieve p1.

In `aligned_free`, we take p2 as the same p2 returned from `aligned_malloc`. As before, we know that the value of p1 (which points to the beginning of the full memory block) was stored just before p2. By freeing p1, we deallocate the whole memory block.

12.11 2D Alloc: Write a function in C called `my2DAlloc` which allocates a two-dimensional array. Minimize the number of calls to `malloc` and make sure that the memory is accessible by the notation `arr[i][j]`.

pg 164

SOLUTION

As you may know, a two-dimensional array is essentially an array of arrays. Since we use pointers with arrays, we can use double pointers to create a double array.

The basic idea is to create a one-dimensional array of pointers. Then, for each array index, we create a new one-dimensional array. This gives us a two-dimensional array that can be accessed via array indices.

The code below implements this.

```
int** my2DAlloc(int rows, int cols) {
  int** rowptr;
  int i;
  rowptr = (int**) malloc(rows * sizeof(int*));
  for (i = 0; i < rows; i++) {
    rowptr[i] = (int*) malloc(cols * sizeof(int));
  }
   return rowptr;
}
```

Observe how, in the above code, we've told `rowptr` where exactly each index should point. The following diagram represents how this memory is allocated.

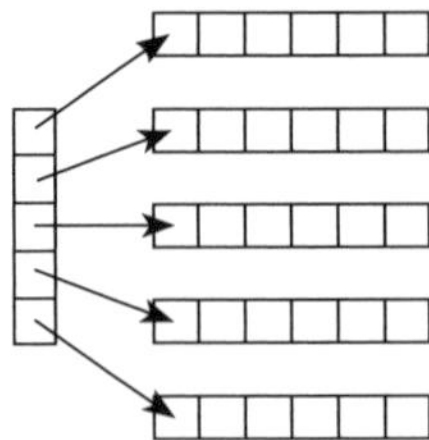

To free this memory, we cannot simply call `free` on `rowptr`. We need to make sure to free not only the memory from the first `malloc` call, but also each subsequent call.

```
void my2DDealloc(int** rowptr, int rows) {
   for (i = 0; i < rows; i++) {
      free(rowptr[i]);
   }
   free(rowptr);
}
```

Rather than allocating the memory in many different blocks (one block for each row, plus one block to specify *where* each row is located), we can allocate this in a consecutive block of memory. Conceptually, for a two-dimensional array with five rows and six columns, this would look like the following.

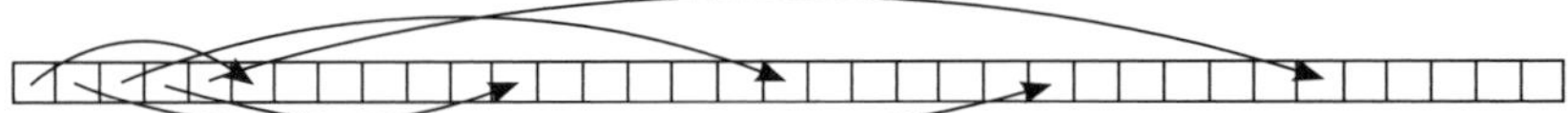

If it seems strange to view the 2D array like this (and it probably does), remember that this is fundamentally no different than the first diagram. The only difference is that the memory is in a contiguous block, so our first five (in this example) elements point elsewhere in the same block of memory.

To implement this solution, we do the following.

```
1  int** my2DAlloc(int rows, int cols) {
2     int i;
3     int header = rows * sizeof(int*);
4     int data = rows * cols * sizeof(int);
5     int** rowptr = (int**)malloc(header + data);
6     if (rowptr == NULL) return NULL;
7
8     int* buf = (int*) (rowptr + rows);
9     for (i = 0; i < rows; i++) {
10       rowptr[i] = buf + i * cols;
11    }
12    return rowptr;
13 }
```

You should carefully observe what is happening on lines 11 through 13. If there are five rows of six columns each, `array[0]` will point to `array[5]`, `array[1]` will point to `array[11]`, and so on.

Then, when we actually call `array[1][3]`, the computer looks up `array[1]`, which is a pointer to another spot in memory—specifically, a pointer to `array[5]`. This element is treated as its own array, and we then get the third (zero-indexed) element from it.

Constructing the array in a single call to `malloc` has the added benefit of allowing disposal of the array with a single `free` call rather than using a special function to free the remaining data blocks.

13

Solutions to Java

13.1 Private Constructor: In terms of inheritance, what is the effect of keeping a constructor private?

pg 167

SOLUTION

Declaring a constructor `private` on class A means that you can only access the (private) constructor if you could also access A's private methods. Who, other than A, can access A's private methods and constructor? A's inner classes can. Additionally, if A is an inner class of Q, then Q's other inner classes can.

This has direct implications for inheritance, since a subclass calls its parent's constructor. The class A can be inherited, but only by its own or its parent's inner classes.

13.2 Return from Finally: In Java, does the finally block get executed if we insert a return statement inside the try block of a try-catch-finally?

pg 167

SOLUTION

Yes, it will get executed. The `finally` block gets executed when the `try` block exits. Even when we attempt to exit within the `try` block (via a `return` statement, a `continue` statement, a `break` statement or any exception), the `finally` block will still be executed.

Note that there are some cases in which the `finally` block will not get executed, such as the following:

- If the virtual machine exits during `try/catch` block execution.
- If the thread which is executing during the `try/catch` block gets killed.

13.3 Final, etc.: What is the difference between `final`, `finally`, and `finalize`?

pg 167

SOLUTIONS

Despite their similar sounding names, `final`, `finally` and `finalize` have very different purposes. To speak in very general terms, `final` is used to control whether a variable, method, or class is "changeable." The `finally` keyword is used in a `try/ catch` block to ensure that a segment of code is always executed. The `finalize()` method is called by the garbage collector once it determines that no more references exist.

Further detail on these keywords and methods is provided below.

final

The final statement has a different meaning depending on its context.

- When applied to a variable (primitive): The value of the variable cannot change.
- When applied to a variable (reference): The reference variable cannot point to any other object on the heap.
- When applied to a method: The method cannot be overridden.
- When applied to a class: The class cannot be subclassed.

finally keyword

There is an optional `finally` block after the `try` block or after the `catch` block. Statements in the `finally` block will always be executed, even if an exception is thrown (except if Java Virtual Machine exits from the `try` block). The `finally` block is often used to write the clean-up code. It will be executed after the `try` and `catch` blocks, but before control transfers back to its origin.

Watch how this plays out in the example below.

```
public static String lem() {
   System.out.println(“lem”);
   return “return from lem”;
}

public static String foo() {
   int x = 0;
   int y = 5;
   try {
      System.out.println(“start try”);
      int b = y / x;
      System.out.println(“end try”);
      return “returned from try”;
   } catch (Exception ex) {
      System.out.println(“catch”);
      return lem() + “ | returned from catch”;
   } finally {
      System.out.println(“finally”);
   }
}

public static void bar() {
   System.out.println(“start bar”);
   String v = foo();
   System.out.println(v);
   System.out.println(“end bar”);
}

public static void main(String[] args) {
   bar();
}
```

The output for this code is the following:

```
start bar
```

```
2   start try
3   catch
4   lem
5   finally
6   return from lem | returned from catch
7   end bar
```

Look carefully at lines 3 to 5 in the output. The `catch` block is fully executed (including the function call in the `return` statement), then the `finally` block, and then the function actually returns.

finalize()

The automatic garbage collector calls the `finalize()` method just before actually destroying the object. A class can therefore override the `finalize()` method from the `Object` class in order to define custom behavior during garbage collection.

```
protected void finalize() throws Throwable {
  /* Close open files, release resources, etc */
}
```

13.4 Generics vs. Templates: Explain the difference between templates in C++ and generics in Java.

pg 167

SOLUTION

Many programmers consider templates and generics to be essentially equivalent because both allow you to do something like `List<String>`. But, *how* each language does this, and *why*, varies significantly.

The implementation of Java generics is rooted in an idea of "type erasure." This technique eliminates the parameterized types when source code is translated to the Java Virtual Machine (JVM) byte code.

For example, suppose you have the Java code below:

```
Vector<String>  vector = new Vector<String>();
vector.add(new String("hello"));
String  str = vector.get(0);
```

During compilation, this code is re-written into:

```
Vector vector = new Vector();
vector.add(new String("hello"));
String  str = (String) vector.get(0);
```

The use of Java generics didn't really change much about our capabilities; it just made things a bit prettier. For this reason, Java generics are sometimes called "syntactic sugar."

This is quite different from C++. In C++, templates are essentially a glorified macro set, with the compiler creating a new copy of the template code for each type. Proof of this is in the fact that an instance of `MyClass<Foo>` will not share a static variable with `MyClass<Bar>`. Two instances of `MyClass<Foo>`, however, will share a static variable.

To illustrate this, consider the code below:

```
/*** MyClass.h ***/
template<class T> class MyClass {
 public:
  static int val;
  MyClass(int v) { val = v; }
};
```

```
/*** MyClass.cpp ***/
template<typename T>
int MyClass<T>::bar;

template class MyClass<Foo>;
template class MyClass<Bar>;

/*** main.cpp ***/
MyClass<Foo> * foo1 = new MyClass<Foo>(10);
MyClass<Foo> * foo2 = new MyClass<Foo>(15);
MyClass<Bar> * bar1 = new MyClass<Bar>(20);
MyClass<Bar> * bar2 = new MyClass<Bar>(35);

int f1 = foo1->val; // will equal 15
int f2 = foo2->val; // will equal 15
int b1 = bar1->val; // will equal 35
int b2 = bar2->val; // will equal 35
```

In Java, static variables are shared across instances of `MyClass`, regardless of the different type parameters.

Java generics and C++ templates have a number of other differences. These include:

- C++ templates can use primitive types, like `int`. Java cannot and must instead use `Integer`.
- In Java, you can restrict the template's type parameters to be of a certain type. For instance, you might use generics to implement a `CardDeck` and specify that the type parameter must extend from `CardGame`.
- In C++, the type parameter can be instantiated, whereas Java does not support this.
- In Java, the type parameter (i.e., the `Foo` in `MyClass<Foo>`) cannot be used for static methods and variables, since these would be shared between `MyClass<Foo>` and `MyClass<Bar>`. In C++, these classes are different, so the type parameter can be used for static methods and variables.
- In Java, all instances of `MyClass`, regardless of their type parameters, are the same type. The type parameters are erased at runtime. In C++, instances with different type parameters are different types.

Remember: Although Java generics and C++ templates look the same in many ways, they are very different.

13.5 TreeMap, HashMap, LinkedHashMap: Explain the differences between `TreeMap`, `HashMap`, and `LinkedHashMap`. Provide an example of when each one would be best.

pg 167

SOLUTION

All offer a key->value map and a way to iterate through the keys. The most important distinction between these classes is the time guarantees and the ordering of the keys.

- `HashMap` offers `O(1)` lookup and insertion. If you iterate through the keys, though, the ordering of the keys is essentially arbitrary. It is implemented by an array of linked lists.
- `TreeMap` offers `O(log N)` lookup and insertion. Keys are ordered, so if you need to iterate through the keys in sorted order, you can. This means that keys must implement the `Comparable` interface. `TreeMap` is implemented by a Red-Black Tree.
- `LinkedHashMap` offers `O(1)` lookup and insertion. Keys are ordered by their insertion order. It is implemented by doubly-linked buckets.

Imagine you passed an empty `TreeMap`, `HashMap`, and `LinkedHashMap` into the following function:

```
void insertAndPrint(AbstractMap<Integer, String> map) {
  int[] array = {1, -1, 0};
  for (int x : array) {
    map.put(x, Integer.toString(x));
  }

  for (int k : map.keySet()) {
    System.out.print(k + ", ");
  }
}
```

The output for each will look like the results below.

HashMap	LinkedHashMap	TreeMap
(any ordering)	{1, -1, 0}	{-1, 0, 1}

Very important: The output of `LinkedHashMap` and `TreeMap` must look like the above. For `HashMap`, the output was, in my own tests, `{0, 1, -1}`, but it could be any ordering. There is no *guarantee* on the ordering.

When might you need ordering in real life?

- Suppose you were creating a mapping of names to `Person` objects. You might want to periodically output the people in alphabetical order by name. A `TreeMap` lets you do this.
- A `TreeMap` also offers a way to, given a name, output the next 10 people. This could be useful for a "More" function in many applications.
- A `LinkedHashMap` is useful whenever you need the ordering of keys to match the ordering of insertion. This might be useful in a caching situation, when you want to delete the oldest item.

Generally, unless there is a reason not to, you would use `HashMap`. That is, if you need to get the keys back in insertion order, then use `LinkedHashMap`. If you need to get the keys back in their true/natural order, then use `TreeMap`. Otherwise, `HashMap` is probably best. It is typically faster and requires less overhead.

13.6 Object Reflection: Explain what object reflection is in Java and why it is useful.

pg 168

SOLUTION

Object Reflection is a feature in Java that provides a way to get reflective information about Java classes and objects, and perform operations such as:

1. Getting information about the methods and fields present inside the class at runtime.
2. Creating a new instance of a class.
3. Getting and setting the object fields directly by getting field reference, regardless of what the access modifier is.

The code below offers an example of object reflection.

```
/* Parameters */
Object[] doubleArgs = new Object[] { 4.2, 3.9 };

/* Get class */
Class rectangleDefinition = Class.forName("MyProj.Rectangle");

```

```
/* Equivalent: Rectangle rectangle = new Rectangle(4.2, 3.9); */
Class[] doubleArgsClass = new Class[] {double.class, double.class};
Constructor doubleArgsConstructor =
   rectangleDefinition.getConstructor(doubleArgsClass);
Rectangle rectangle = (Rectangle) doubleArgsConstructor.newInstance(doubleArgs);

/* Equivalent: Double area = rectangle.area(); */
Method m = rectangleDefinition.getDeclaredMethod(“area”);
Double area = (Double) m.invoke(rectangle);
```

This code does the equivalent of:

```
Rectangle rectangle = new Rectangle(4.2, 3.9);
Double area = rectangle.area();
```

Why Is Object Reflection Useful?

Of course, it doesn't seem very useful in the above example, but reflection can be very useful in some cases. Three main reasons are:

1. It can help you observe or manipulate the runtime behavior of applications.
2. It can help you debug or test programs, as you have direct access to methods, constructors, and fields.
3. You can call methods by name when you don't know the method in advance. For example, we may let the user pass in a class name, parameters for the constructor, and a method name. We can then use this information to create an object and call a method. Doing these operations without reflection would require a complex series of if-statements, if it's possible at all.

13.7 Lambda Expressions: There is a class `Country` that has methods `getContinent()` and `getPopulation()`. Write a function `int getPopulation(List<Country> countries, String continent)` that computes the total population of a given continent, given a list of all countries and the name of a continent.

pg 168

SOLUTION

This question really comes in two parts. First, we need to generate a list of the countries in North America. Then, we need to compute their total population.

Without lambda expressions, this is fairly straightforward to do.

```
int getPopulation(List<Country> countries, String continent) {
   int sum = 0;
   for (Country c : countries) {
      if (c.getContinent().equals(continent)) {
         sum += c.getPopulation();
      }
   }
   return sum;
}
```

To implement this with lambda expressions, let's break this up into multiple parts.

First, we use `filter` to get a list of the countries in the specified continent.

```
Stream<Country> northAmerica = countries.stream().filter(
   country -> { return country.getContinent().equals(continent);}
```

```
);
```

Second, we convert this into a list of populations using `map`.

```
Stream<Integer> populations = northAmerica.map(
  c -> c.getPopulation()
);
```

Third and finally, we compute the sum using `reduce`.

```
int population = populations.reduce(0, (a, b) -> a + b);
```

This function puts it all together.

```
int getPopulation(List<Country> countries, String continent) {
  /* Filter countries. */
  Stream<Country> sublist = countries.stream().filter(
    country -> { return country.getContinent().equals(continent);}
  );

  /* Convert to list of populations. */
  Stream<Integer> populations = sublist.map(
    c -> c.getPopulation()
  );

  /* Sum list. */
  int population = populations.reduce(0, (a, b) -> a + b);
  return population;
}
```

Alternatively, because of the nature of this specific problem, we can actually remove the `filter` entirely. The `reduce` operation can have logic that maps the population of countries not in the right continent to zero. The sum will effectively disregard countries not within `continent`.

```
int getPopulation(List<Country> countries, String continent) {
  Stream<Integer> populations = countries.stream().map(
    c -> c.getContinent().equals(continent) ? c.getPopulation() : 0);
  return populations.reduce(0, (a, b) -> a + b);
}
```

Lambda functions were new to Java 8, so if you don't recognize them, that's probably why. Now is a great time to learn about them, though!

13.8 Lambda Random: Using Lambda expressions, write a function `List<Integer> getRandomSubset(List<Integer> list)` that returns a random subset of arbitrary size. All subsets (including the empty set) should be equally likely to be chosen.

pg 439

SOLUTION

It's tempting to approach this problem by picking a subset size from `0` to N and then generating a random subset of that size.

That creates two issues:

1. We'd have to weight those probabilities. If `N > 1`, there are more subsets of size `N/2` than there are of subsets of size N (of which there is always only one).
2. It's actually more difficult to generate a subset of a restricted size (e.g., specifically 10) than it is to generate a subset of any size.

Instead, rather than generating a subset based on sizes, let's think about it based on elements. (The fact that we're told to use lambda expressions is also a hint that we should think about some sort of iteration or processing through the elements.)

Imagine we were iterating through `{1, 2, 3}` to generate a subset. Should 1 be in this subset?

We've got two choices: yes or no. We need to weight the probability of "yes" vs. "no" based on the percent of subsets that contain 1. So, what percent of elements contain 1?

For any specific element, there are as many subsets that contain the element as do not contain it. Consider the following:

```
{}          {1}
{2}         {1, 2}
{3}         {1, 3}
{2, 3}      {1, 2, 3}
```

Note how the difference between the subsets on the left and the subsets on the right is the existence of 1. The left and right sides must have the same number of subsets because we can convert from one to the other by just adding an element.

This means that we can generate a random subset by iterating through the list and flipping a coin (i.e., deciding on a 50/50 chance) to pick whether or not each element will be in it.

Without lambda expressions, we can write something like this:

```
List<Integer> getRandomSubset(List<Integer> list) {
   List<Integer> subset = new ArrayList<Integer>();
   Random random = new Random();
   for (int item : list) {
      /* Flip coin. */
      if (random.nextBoolean()) {
         subset.add(item);
      }
   }
   return subset;
}
```

To implement this approach using lambda expressions, we can do the following:

```
List<Integer> getRandomSubset(List<Integer> list) {
   Random random = new Random();
   List<Integer> subset = list.stream().filter(
      k -> { return random.nextBoolean(); /* Flip coin. */
   }).collect(Collectors.toList());
   return subset;
}
```

Or, we can use a predicate (defined within the class or within the function):

```
Random random = new Random();
Predicate<Object> flipCoin = o -> {
   return random.nextBoolean();
};

List<Integer> getRandomSubset(List<Integer> list) {
   List<Integer> subset = list.stream().filter(flipCoin).
      collect(Collectors.toList());
   return subset;
}
```

The nice thing about this implementation is that now we can apply the `flipCoin` predicate in other places.

14

Solutions to Databases

Questions 1 through 3 refer to the following database schema:

Apartments	
AptID	int
UnitNumber	varchar(10)
BuildingID	int

Buildings	
BuildingID	int
ComplexID	int
BuildingName	varchar(100)
Address	varchar(500)

Requests	
RequestID	int
Status	varchar(100)
AptID	int
Description	varchar(500)

Complexes	
ComplexID	int
ComplexName	varchar(100)

AptTenants	
TenantID	int
AptID	int

Tenants	
TenantID	int
TenantName	varchar(100)

Note that each apartment can have multiple tenants, and each tenant can have multiple apartments. Each apartment belongs to one building, and each building belongs to one complex.

14.1 Multiple Apartments: Write a SQL query to get a list of tenants who are renting more than one apartment.

pg 172

SOLUTION

To implement this, we can use the HAVING and GROUP BY clauses and then perform an INNER JOIN with Tenants.

```
SELECT TenantName
FROM Tenants
INNER JOIN
   (SELECT TenantID FROM AptTenants GROUP BY TenantID HAVING count(*) > 1) C
ON Tenants.TenantID = C.TenantID
```

Whenever you write a GROUP BY clause in an interview (or in real life), make sure that anything in the SELECT clause is either an aggregate function or contained within the GROUP BY clause.

14.2 Open Requests: Write a SQL query to get a list of all buildings and the number of open requests (Requests in which status equals 'Open').

pg 173

SOLUTION

This problem uses a straightforward join of Requests and Apartments to get a list of building IDs and the number of open requests. Once we have this list, we join it again with the Buildings table.

```
SELECT BuildingName, ISNULL(Count, 0) as 'Count'
FROM Buildings
LEFT JOIN
   (SELECT Apartments.BuildingID, count(*) as 'Count'
    FROM Requests INNER JOIN Apartments
    ON Requests.AptID = Apartments.AptID
    WHERE Requests.Status = 'Open'
    GROUP BY Apartments.BuildingID) ReqCounts
ON ReqCounts.BuildingID = Buildings.BuildingID
```

Queries like this that utilize sub-queries should be thoroughly tested, even when coding by hand. It may be useful to test the inner part of the query first, and then test the outer part.

14.3 Close All Requests: Building #11 is undergoing a major renovation. Implement a query to close all requests from apartments in this building.

pg 173

SOLUTION

UPDATE queries, like SELECT queries, can have WHERE clauses. To implement this query, we get a list of all apartment IDs within building #11 and the list of update requests from those apartments.

```
UPDATE Requests
SET Status = 'Closed'
WHERE AptID IN (SELECT AptID FROM Apartments WHERE BuildingID = 11)
```

14.4 Joins: What are the different types of joins? Please explain how they differ and why certain types are better in certain situations.

pg 173

SOLUTION

JOIN is used to combine the results of two tables. To perform a JOIN, each of the tables must have at least one field that will be used to find matching records from the other table. The join type defines which records will go into the result set.

Let's take for example two tables: one table lists the "regular" beverages, and another lists the calorie-free beverages. Each table has two fields: the beverage name and its product code. The "code" field will be used to perform the record matching.

Regular Beverages:

Name	Code
Budweiser	BUDWEISER
Coca-Cola	COCACOLA

Name	**Code**
`Pepsi`	`PEPSI`

Calorie-Free Beverages:

Name	**Code**
`Diet Coca-Cola`	`COCACOLA`
`Fresca`	`FRESCA`
`Diet Pepsi`	`PEPSI`
`Pepsi Light`	`PEPSI`
`Purified Water`	`Water`

If we wanted to join `Beverage` with `Calorie-Free Beverages`, we would have many options. These are discussed below.

- `INNER JOIN`: The result set would contain only the data where the criteria match. In our example, we would get three records: one with a `COCACOLA` code and two with `PEPSI` codes.
- `OUTER JOIN`: An `OUTER JOIN` will always contain the results of `INNER JOIN`, but it may also contain some records that have no matching record in the other table. `OUTER JOIN`s are divided into the following subtypes:
  - `LEFT OUTER JOIN`, or simply `LEFT JOIN`: The result will contain all records from the left table. If no matching records were found in the right table, then its fields will contain the `NULL` values. In our example, we would get four records. In addition to `INNER JOIN` results, `BUDWEISER` would be listed, because it was in the left table.
  - `RIGHT OUTER JOIN`, or simply `RIGHT JOIN`: This type of join is the opposite of `LEFT JOIN`. It will contain every record from the right table; the missing fields from the left table will be `NULL`. Note that if we have two tables, `A` and `B`, then we can say that the statement `A LEFT JOIN B` is equivalent to the statement `B RIGHT JOIN A`. In our example above, we will get five records. In addition to `INNER JOIN` results, `FRESCA` and `WATER` records will be listed.
  - `FULL OUTER JOIN`: This type of join combines the results of the `LEFT` and `RIGHT JOINS`. All records from both tables will be included in the result set, regardless of whether or not a matching record exists in the other table. If no matching record was found, then the corresponding result fields will have a `NULL` value. In our example, we will get six records.

14.5 Denormalization: What is denormalization? Explain the pros and cons.

pg 173

SOLUTION

Denormalization is a database optimization technique in which we add redundant data to one or more tables. This can help us avoid costly joins in a relational database.

By contrast, in a traditional normalized database, we store data in separate logical tables and attempt to minimize redundant data. We may strive to have only one copy of each piece of data in the database.

For example, in a normalized database, we might have a `Courses` table and a `Teachers` table. Each entry in `Courses` would store the `teacherID` for a `Course` but not the `teacherName`. When we need to retrieve a list of all `Courses` with the `Teacher` name, we would do a join between these two tables.

In some ways, this is great; if a teacher changes his or her name, we only have to update the name in one place.

The drawback, however, is that if the tables are large, we may spend an unnecessarily long time doing joins on tables.

Denormalization, then, strikes a different compromise. Under denormalization, we decide that we're okay with some redundancy and some extra effort to update the database in order to get the efficiency advantages of fewer joins.

Cons of Denormalization	**Pros of Denormalization**
Updates and inserts are more expensive.	Retrieving data is faster since we do fewer joins.
Denormalization can make update and insert code harder to write.	Queries to retrieve can be simpler (and therefore less likely to have bugs), since we need to look at fewer tables.
Data may be inconsistent. Which is the "correct" value for a piece of data?	
Data redundancy necessitates more storage.	

In a system that demands scalability, like that of any major tech companies, we almost always use elements of both normalized and denormalized databases.

14.6 Entity-Relationship Diagram: Draw an entity-relationship diagram for a database with companies, people, and professionals (people who work for companies).

pg 173

SOLUTION

People who work for `Companies` are `Professionals`. So, there is an `ISA` ("is a") relationship between `People` and `Professionals` (or we could say that a `Professional` is derived from `People`).

Each `Professional` has additional information such as degree and work experiences in addition to the properties derived from `People`.

A `Professional` works for one company at a time (probably—you might want to validate this assumption), but `Companies` can hire many `Professionals`. So, there is a many-to-one relationship between `Professionals` and `Companies`. This "Works For" relationship can store attributes such as an employee's start date and salary. These attributes are defined only when we relate a `Professional` with a `Company`.

A `Person` can have multiple phone numbers, which is why Phone is a multi-valued attribute.

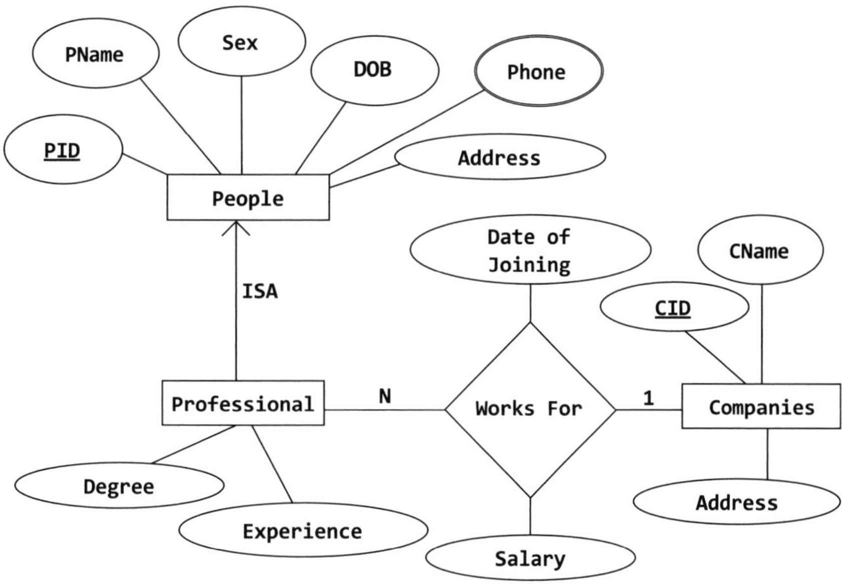

14.7 Design Grade Database: Imagine a simple database storing information for students' grades. Design what this database might look like and provide a SQL query to return a list of the honor roll students (top 10%), sorted by their grade point average.

pg 173

SOLUTION

In a simplistic database, we'll have at least three objects: `Students`, `Courses`, and `CourseEnrollment`. `Students` will have at least a student name and ID and will likely have other personal information. `Courses` will contain the course name and ID and will likely contain the course description, professor, and other information. `CourseEnrollment` will pair `Students` and `Courses` and will also contain a field for `CourseGrade`.

Students	
StudentID	int
StudentName	varchar(100)
Address	varchar(500)

Courses	
CourseID	int
CourseName	varchar(100)
ProfessorID	int

CourseEnrollment	
CourseID	int
StudentID	int
Grade	float
Term	int

This database could get arbitrarily more complicated if we wanted to add in professor information, billing information, and other data.

Using the Microsoft SQL Server `TOP ... PERCENT` function, we might (incorrectly) first try a query like this:

```
SELECT TOP 10 PERCENT AVG(CourseEnrollment.Grade) AS GPA,
                                                     CourseEnrollment.StudentID
FROM CourseEnrollment
GROUP BY CourseEnrollment.StudentID
ORDER BY AVG(CourseEnrollment.Grade)
```

The problem with the above code is that it will return literally the top 10% of rows, when sorted by GPA. Imagine a scenario in which there are 100 students, and the top 15 students all have 4.0 GPAs. The above function will only return 10 of those students, which is not really what we want. In case of a tie, we want to include the students who tied for the top 10% -- even if this means that our honor roll includes more than 10% of the class.

To correct this issue, we can build something similar to this query, but instead first get the GPA cut off.

```
DECLARE @GPACutOff float;
SET @GPACutOff = (SELECT min(GPA) as 'GPAMin' FROM (
     SELECT TOP 10 PERCENT AVG(CourseEnrollment.Grade) AS GPA
     FROM CourseEnrollment
     GROUP BY CourseEnrollment.StudentID
     ORDER BY GPA desc) Grades);
```

Then, once we have `@GPACutOff` defined, selecting the students with at least this GPA is reasonably straightforward.

```
SELECT StudentName, GPA
FROM (SELECT AVG(CourseEnrollment.Grade) AS GPA, CourseEnrollment.StudentID
      FROM CourseEnrollment
      GROUP BY CourseEnrollment.StudentID
      HAVING AVG(CourseEnrollment.Grade) >= @GPACutOff) Honors
INNER JOIN Students ON Honors.StudentID = Student.StudentID
```

Be very careful about what implicit assumptions you make. If you look at the above database description, what potentially incorrect assumption do you see? One is that each course can only be taught by one professor. At some schools, courses may be taught by multiple professors.

However, you *will* need to make some assumptions, or you'd drive yourself crazy. Which assumptions you make is less important than just recognizing *that* you made assumptions. Incorrect assumptions, both in the real world and in an interview, can be dealt with *as long as they are acknowledged.*

Remember, additionally, that there's a trade-off between flexibility and complexity. Creating a system in which a course can have multiple professors does increase the database's flexibility, but it also increases its complexity. If we tried to make our database flexible to every possible situation, we'd wind up with something hopelessly complex.

Make your design reasonably flexible, and state any other assumptions or constraints. This goes for not just database design, but object-oriented design and programming in general.

15

Solutions to Threads and Locks

15.1 Thread vs. Process: What's the difference between a thread and a process?

pg 179

SOLUTION

Processes and threads are related to each other but are fundamentally different.

A process can be thought of as an instance of a program in execution. A process is an independent entity to which system resources (e.g., CPU time and memory) are allocated. Each process is executed in a separate address space, and one process cannot access the variables and data structures of another process. If a process wishes to access another process' resources, inter-process communications have to be used. These include pipes, files, sockets, and other forms.

A thread exists within a process and shares the process' resources (including its heap space). Multiple threads within the same process will share the same heap space. This is very different from processes, which cannot directly access the memory of another process. Each thread still has its own registers and its own stack, but other threads can read and write the heap memory.

A thread is a particular execution path of a process. When one thread modifies a process resource, the change is immediately visible to sibling threads.

15.2 Context Switch: How would you measure the time spent in a context switch?

pg 179

SOLUTION

This is a tricky question, but let's start with a possible solution.

A context switch is the time spent switching between two processes (i.e., bringing a waiting process into execution and sending an executing process into waiting/terminated state). This happens in multitasking. The operating system must bring the state information of waiting processes into memory and save the state information of the currently running process.

In order to solve this problem, we would like to record the timestamps of the last and first instruction of the swapping processes. The context switch time is the difference in the timestamps between the two processes.

Let's take an easy example: Assume there are only two processes, P_1 and P_2.

P_1 is executing and P_2 is waiting for execution. At some point, the operating system must swap P_1 and P_2—let's assume it happens at the Nth instruction of P_1. If $t_{x,k}$ indicates the timestamp in microseconds of the kth instruction of process x, then the context switch would take $t_{2,1} - t_{1,n}$ microseconds.

The tricky part is this: how do we know when this swapping occurs? We cannot, of course, record the timestamp of every instruction in the process.

Another issue is that swapping is governed by the scheduling algorithm of the operating system and there may be many kernel level threads which are also doing context switches. Other processes could be contending for the CPU or the kernel handling interrupts. The user does not have any control over these extraneous context switches. For instance, if at time $t_{1,n}$ the kernel decides to handle an interrupt, then the context switch time would be overstated.

In order to overcome these obstacles, we must first construct an environment such that after P_1 executes, the task scheduler immediately selects P_2 to run. This may be accomplished by constructing a data channel, such as a pipe, between P_1 and P_2 and having the two processes play a game of ping-pong with a data token.

That is, let's allow P_1 to be the initial sender and P_2 to be the receiver. Initially, P_2 is blocked (sleeping) as it awaits the data token. When P_1 executes, it delivers the token over the data channel to P_2 and immediately attempts to read a response token. However, since P_2 has not yet had a chance to run, no such token is available for P_1 and the process is blocked. This relinquishes the CPU.

A context switch results and the task scheduler must select another process to run. Since P_2 is now in a ready-to-run state, it is a desirable candidate to be selected by the task scheduler for execution. When P_2 runs, the roles of P_1 and P_2 are swapped. P_2 is now acting as the sender and P_1 as the blocked receiver. The game ends when P_2 returns the token to P_1.

To summarize, an iteration of the game is played with the following steps:

1. P_2 blocks awaiting data from P_1.
2. P_1 marks the start time.
3. P_1 sends token to P_2.
4. P_1 attempts to read a response token from P_2. This induces a context switch.
5. P_2 is scheduled and receives the token.
6. P_2 sends a response token to P_1.
7. P_2 attempts read a response token from P_1. This induces a context switch.
8. P_1 is scheduled and receives the token.
9. P_1 marks the end time.

The key is that the delivery of a data token induces a context switch. Let T_d and T_r be the time it takes to deliver and receive a data token, respectively, and let T_c be the amount of time spent in a context switch. At step 2, P_1 records the timestamp of the delivery of the token, and at step 9, it records the timestamp of the response. The amount of time elapsed, T, between these events may be expressed by:

$$T = 2 * (T_d + T_c + T_r)$$

This formula arises because of the following events: P_1 sends a token (3), the CPU context switches (4), P_2 receives it (5). P_2 then sends the response token (6), the CPU context switches (7), and finally P_1 receives it (8).

P_1 will be able to easily compute T, since this is just the time between events 3 and 8. So, to solve for T_c, we must first determine the value of $T_d + T_r$.

How can we do this? We can do this by measuring the length of time it takes P_1 to send and receive a token to itself. This will not induce a context switch since P_1 is running on the CPU at the time it sent the token and will not block to receive it.

The game is played a number of iterations to average out any variability in the elapsed time between steps 2 and 9 that may result from unexpected kernel interrupts and additional kernel threads contending for the CPU. We select the smallest observed context switch time as our final answer.

However, all we can ultimately say that this is an approximation which depends on the underlying system. For example, we make the assumption that P_2 is selected to run once a data token becomes available. However, this is dependent on the implementation of the task scheduler and we cannot make any guarantees.

That's okay; it's important in an interview to recognize when your solution might not be perfect.

15.3 Dining Philosophers: In the famous dining philosophers problem, a bunch of philosophers are sitting around a circular table with one chopstick between each of them. A philosopher needs both chopsticks to eat, and always picks up the left chopstick before the right one. A deadlock could potentially occur if all the philosophers reached for the left chopstick at the same time. Using threads and locks, implement a simulation of the dining philosophers problem that prevents deadlocks.

pg 180

SOLUTION

First, let's implement a simple simulation of the dining philosophers problem in which we don't concern ourselves with deadlocks. We can implement this solution by having `Philosopher` extend `Thread`, and `Chopstick` call `lock.lock()` when it is picked up and `lock.unlock()` when it is put down.

```
class Chopstick {
   private Lock lock;

   public Chopstick() {
      lock = new ReentrantLock();
   }

   public void pickUp() {
      void lock.lock();
   }

   public void putDown() {
      lock.unlock();
   }
}

class Philosopher extends Thread {
   private int bites = 10;
   private Chopstick left, right;

   public Philosopher(Chopstick left, Chopstick right) {
      this.left = left;
      this.right = right;
   }
```

```

  public void eat() {
    pickUp();
    chew();
    putDown();
  }

  public void pickUp() {
    left.pickUp();
    right.pickUp();
  }

  public void chew() { }

  public void putDown() {
    right.putDown();
    left.putDown();
  }

  public void run() {
    for (int i = 0; i < bites; i++) {
      eat();
    }
  }
}
```

Running the above code may lead to a deadlock if all the philosophers have a left chopstick and are waiting for the right one.

Solution #1: All or Nothing

To prevent deadlocks, we can implement a strategy where a philosopher will put down his left chopstick if he is unable to obtain the right one.

```
public class Chopstick {
  /* same as before */

  public boolean pickUp() {
    return lock.tryLock();
  }
}

public class Philosopher extends Thread {
  /* same as before */

  public void eat() {
    if (pickUp()) {
      chew();
      putDown();
    }
  }

  public boolean pickUp() {
    /* attempt to pick up */
    if (!left.pickUp()) {
      return false;
    }
    if (!right.pickUp()) {
```

```
            left.putDown();
            return false;
        }
        return true;
    }
}
```

In the above code, we need to be sure to release the left chopstick if we can't pick up the right one—and to not call `putDown()` on the chopsticks if we never had them in the first place.

One issue with this is that if all the philosophers were perfectly synchronized, they could simultaneously pick up their left chopstick, be unable to pick up the right one, and then put back down the left one—only to have the process repeated again.

Solution #2: Prioritized Chopsticks

Alternatively, we can label the chopsticks with a number from `0` to `N - 1`. Each philosopher attempts to pick up the lower numbered chopstick first. This essentially means that each philosopher goes for the left chopstick before right one (assuming that's the way you labeled it), except for the last philosopher who does this in reverse. This will break the cycle.

```
public class Philosopher extends Thread {
    private int bites = 10;
    private Chopstick lower, higher;
    private int index;
    public Philosopher(int i, Chopstick left, Chopstick right) {
        index = i;
        if (left.getNumber() < right.getNumber()) {
            this.lower = left;
            this.higher = right;
        } else {
            this.lower = right;
            this.higher = left;
        }
    }

    public void eat() {
        pickUp();
        chew();
        putDown();
    }

    public void pickUp() {
        lower.pickUp();
        higher.pickUp();
    }

    public void chew() { ... }

    public void putDown() {
        higher.putDown();
        lower.putDown();
    }

    public void run() {
        for (int i = 0; i < bites; i++) {
            eat();
```

```
      }
   }
}

public class Chopstick {
   private Lock lock;
   private int number;

   public Chopstick(int n) {
      lock = new ReentrantLock();
      this.number = n;
   }

   public void pickUp() {
      lock.lock();
   }

   public void putDown() {
      lock.unlock();
   }

   public int getNumber() {
      return number;
   }
}
```

With this solution, a philosopher can never hold the larger chopstick without holding the smaller one. This prevents the ability to have a cycle, since a cycle means that a higher chopstick would "point" to a lower one.

15.4 Deadlock-Free Class: Design a class which provides a lock only if there are no possible deadlocks.

pg 180

SOLUTION

There are several common ways to prevent deadlocks. One of the popular ways is to require a process to declare upfront what locks it will need. We can then verify if a deadlock would be created by issuing these locks, and we can fail if so.

With these constraints in mind, let's investigate how we can detect deadlocks. Suppose this was the order of locks requested:

```
A = {1, 2, 3, 4}
B = {1, 3, 5}
C = {7, 5, 9, 2}
```

This may create a deadlock because we could have the following scenario:

```
A locks 2, waits on 3
B locks 3, waits on 5
C locks 5, waits on 2
```

We can think about this as a graph, where 2 is connected to 3, 3 is connected to 5, and 5 is connected to 2. A deadlock is represented by a cycle. An edge `(w, v)` exists in the graph if a process declares that it will request lock v immediately after lock `w`. For the earlier example, the following edges would exist in the graph: `(1, 2), (2, 3), (3, 4), (1, 3), (3, 5), (7, 5), (5, 9), (9, 2)`. The "owner" of the edge does not matter.

This class will need a `declare` method, which threads and processes will use to declare what order they will request resources in. This declare method will iterate through the declare order, adding each contiguous pair of elements (v, w) to the graph. Afterwards, it will check to see if any cycles have been created. If any cycles have been created, it will backtrack, removing these edges from the graph, and then exit.

We have one final component to discuss: how do we detect a cycle? We can detect a cycle by doing a depth-first search through each connected component (i.e., each connected part of the graph). Complex algorithms exist to find all the connected components of a graph, but our work in this problem does not require this degree of complexity.

We know that if a cycle was created, one of our new edges must be to blame. Thus, as long as our depth-first search touches all of these edges at some point, then we know that we have fully searched for a cycle.

The pseudocode for this special case cycle detection looks like this:

```
boolean checkForCycle(locks[] locks) {
   touchedNodes = hash table(lock -> boolean)
   initialize touchedNodes to false for each lock in locks
   for each (lock x in process.locks) {
      if (touchedNodes[x] == false) {
         if (hasCycle(x, touchedNodes)) {
            return true;
         }
      }
   }
   return false;
}

boolean hasCycle(node x, touchedNodes) {
   touchedNodes[r] = true;
   if (x.state == VISITING) {
      return true;
   } else if (x.state == FRESH) {
      ... (see full code below)
   }
}
```

In the above code, note that we may do several depth-first searches, but `touchedNodes` is only initialized once. We iterate until all the values in `touchedNodes` are false.

The code below provides further details. For simplicity, we assume that all locks and processes (owners) are ordered sequentially.

```
class LockFactory {
   private static LockFactory instance;

   private int numberOfLocks = 5; /* default */
   private LockNode[] locks;

   /* Maps from a process or owner to the order that the owner claimed it would
    * call the locks in */
   private HashMap<Integer, LinkedList<LockNode>> lockOrder;

   private LockFactory(int count) { ... }
   public static LockFactory getInstance() { return instance; }

   public static synchronized LockFactory initialize(int count) {
      if (instance == null) instance = new LockFactory(count);
```

```
        return instance;
    }

    public boolean hasCycle(HashMap<Integer, Boolean> touchedNodes,
                            int[] resourcesInOrder) {
        /* check for a cycle */
        for (int resource : resourcesInOrder) {
            if (touchedNodes.get(resource) == false) {
                LockNode n = locks[resource];
                if (n.hasCycle(touchedNodes)) {
                    return true;
                }
            }
        }
        return false;
    }

    /* To prevent deadlocks, force the processes to declare upfront what order they
     * will need the locks in. Verify that this order does not create a deadlock (a
     * cycle in a directed graph) */
    public boolean declare(int ownerId, int[] resourcesInOrder) {
        HashMap<Integer, Boolean> touchedNodes = new HashMap<Integer, Boolean>();

        /* add nodes to graph */
        int index = 1;
        touchedNodes.put(resourcesInOrder[0], false);
        for (index = 1; index < resourcesInOrder.length; index++) {
            LockNode prev = locks[resourcesInOrder[index - 1]];
            LockNode curr = locks[resourcesInOrder[index]];
            prev.joinTo(curr);
            touchedNodes.put(resourcesInOrder[index], false);
        }

        /* if we created a cycle, destroy this resource list and return false */
        if (hasCycle(touchedNodes, resourcesInOrder)) {
            for (int j = 1; j < resourcesInOrder.length; j++) {
                LockNode p = locks[resourcesInOrder[j - 1]];
                LockNode c = locks[resourcesInOrder[j]];
                p.remove(c);
            }
            return false;
        }

        /* No cycles detected. Save the order that was declared, so that we can
         * verify that the process is really calling the locks in the order it said
         * it would. */
        LinkedList<LockNode> list = new LinkedList<LockNode>();
        for (int i = 0; i < resourcesInOrder.length; i++) {
            LockNode resource = locks[resourcesInOrder[i]];
            list.add(resource);
        }
        lockOrder.put(ownerId, list);

        return true;
    }

```

```
    /* Get the lock, verifying first that the process is really calling the locks in
     * the order it said it would. */
    public Lock getLock(int ownerId, int resourceID) {
       LinkedList<LockNode> list = lockOrder.get(ownerId);
       if (list == null) return null;

       LockNode head = list.getFirst();
       if (head.getId() == resourceID) {
          list.removeFirst();
          return head.getLock();
       }
       return null;
    }
 }

 public class LockNode {
    public enum VisitState { FRESH, VISITING, VISITED };

    private ArrayList<LockNode> children;
    private int lockId;
    private Lock lock;
    private int maxLocks;

    public LockNode(int id, int max) { ... }

    /* Join "this" to "node", checking that it doesn't create a cycle */
    public void joinTo(LockNode node) { children.add(node); }
    public void remove(LockNode node) { children.remove(node); }

    /* Check for a cycle by doing a depth-first-search. */
    public boolean hasCycle(HashMap<Integer, Boolean> touchedNodes) {
       VisitState[] visited = new VisitState[maxLocks];
       for (int i = 0; i < maxLocks; i++) {
          visited[i] = VisitState.FRESH;
       }
       return hasCycle(visited, touchedNodes);
    }

    private boolean hasCycle(VisitState[] visited,
                             HashMap<Integer, Boolean> touchedNodes) {
       if (touchedNodes.containsKey(lockId)) {
          touchedNodes.put(lockId, true);
       }

       if (visited[lockId] == VisitState.VISITING) {
          /* We looped back to this node while still visiting it, so we know there's
           * a cycle. */
          return true;
       } else if (visited[lockId] == VisitState.FRESH) {
          visited[lockId] = VisitState.VISITING;
          for (LockNode n : children) {
             if (n.hasCycle(visited, touchedNodes)) {
                return true;
             }
          }
          visited[lockId] = VisitState.VISITED;
```

```
        }
        return false;
    }

    public Lock getLock() {
        if (lock == null) lock = new ReentrantLock();
        return lock;
    }

    public int getId() { return lockId; }
}
```

As always, when you see code this complicated and lengthy, you wouldn't be expected to write all of it. More likely, you would be asked to sketch out pseudocode and possibly implement one of these methods.

15.5 Call In Order: Suppose we have the following code:

```
public class Foo {
    public Foo() { ... }
    public void first() { ... }
    public void second() { ... }
    public void third() { ... }
}
```

The same instance of Foo will be passed to three different threads. ThreadA will call first, threadB will call second, and threadC will call third. Design a mechanism to ensure that `first` is called before `second` and `second` is called before `third`.

pg 180

SOLUTION

The general logic is to check if `first()` has completed before executing `second()`, and if `second()` has completed before calling `third()`. Because we need to be very careful about thread safety, simple `boolean` flags won't do the job.

What about using a `lock` to do something like the below code?

```
public class FooBad {
    public int pauseTime = 1000;
    public ReentrantLock lock1, lock2;

    public FooBad() {
        try {
            lock1 = new ReentrantLock();
            lock2 = new ReentrantLock();

            lock1.lock();
            lock2.lock();
        } catch (...) { ... }
    }

    public void first() {
        try {
            ...
            lock1.unlock(); // mark finished with first()
        } catch (...) { ... }
    }
```

```

    public void second() {
       try {
          lock1.lock(); // wait until finished with first()
          lock1.unlock();
          ...

          lock2.unlock(); // mark finished with second()
       } catch (...) { ... }
    }

    public void third() {
       try {
          lock2.lock(); // wait until finished with third()
          lock2.unlock();
          ...
       } catch (...) { ... }
    }
 }
```

This code won't actually quite work due to the concept of *lock ownership*. One thread is actually performing the lock (in the FooBad constructor), but different threads attempt to unlock the locks. This is not allowed, and your code will raise an exception. A lock in Java is owned by the same thread which locked it.

Instead, we can replicate this behavior with semaphores. The logic is identical.

```
public class Foo {
   public Semaphore sem1, sem2;

   public Foo() {
      try {
         sem1 = new Semaphore(1);
         sem2 = new Semaphore(1);

         sem1.acquire();
         sem2.acquire();
      } catch (...) { ... }
   }

   public void first() {
      try {
         ...
         sem1.release();
      } catch (...) { ... }
   }

   public void second() {
      try {
         sem1.acquire();
         sem1.release();
         ...
         sem2.release();
      } catch (...) { ... }
   }

   public void third() {
      try {
         sem2.acquire();
```

```
            sem2.release();
            ...
        } catch (...) { ... }
    }
}
```

15.6 Synchronized Methods: You are given a class with `synchronized` method A and a normal method B. If you have two threads in one instance of a program, can they both execute A at the same time? Can they execute A and B at the same time?

pg 180

SOLUTION

By applying the word `synchronized` to a method, we ensure that two threads cannot execute synchronized methods *on the same object instance* at the same time.

So, the answer to the first part really depends. If the two threads have the same instance of the object, then no, they cannot simultaneously execute method A. However, if they have different instances of the object, then they can.

Conceptually, you can see this by considering locks. A synchronized method applies a "lock" on *all* synchronized methods in that instance of the object. This blocks other threads from executing synchronized methods within that instance.

In the second part, we're asked if `thread1` can execute synchronized method A while `thread2` is executing non-synchronized method B. Since B is not synchronized, there is nothing to block `thread1` from executing A while `thread2` is executing B. This is true regardless of whether `thread1` and `thread2` have the same instance of the object.

Ultimately, the key concept to remember is that only one synchronized method can be in execution per instance of that object. Other threads can execute non-synchronized methods on that instance, or they can execute any method on a different instance of the object.

15.7 FizzBuzz: In the classic problem FizzBuzz, you are told to print the numbers from 1 to n. However, when the number is divisible by 3, print "Fizz". When it is divisible by 5, print "Buzz". When it is divisible by 3 and 5, print "FizzBuzz". In this problem, you are asked to do this in a multithreaded way. Implement a multithreaded version of FizzBuzz with four threads. One thread checks for divisibility of 3 and prints "Fizz". Another thread is responsible for divisibility of 5 and prints "Buzz". A third thread is responsible for divisibility of 3 and 5 and prints "FizzBuzz". A fourth thread does the numbers.

pg 180

SOLUTION

Let's start off with implementing a single threaded version of FizzBuzz.

Single Threaded

Although this problem (in the single threaded version) shouldn't be hard, a lot of candidates overcomplicate it. They look for something "beautiful" that reuses the fact that the divisible by 3 and 5 case ("FizzBuzz") seems to resemble the individual cases ("Fizz" and "Buzz").

In actuality, the best way to do it, considering readability and efficiency, is just the straightforward way.

```
void fizzbuzz(int n) {
```

```
    for (int i = 1; i <= n; i++) {
       if (i % 3 == 0 && i % 5 == 0) {
          System.out.println("FizzBuzz");
       } else if (i % 3 == 0) {
          System.out.println("Fizz");
       } else if (i % 5 == 0) {
          System.out.println("Buzz");
       } else {
          System.out.println(i);
       }
    }
 }
```

The primary thing to be careful of here is the order of the statements. If you put the check for divisibility by 3 before the check for divisibility by 3 and 5, it won't print the right thing.

Multithreaded

To do this multithreaded, we want a structure that looks something like this:

FizzBuzz Thread	Fizz Thread

if i div by 3 && 5
   print FizzBuzz
   increment i
repeat until i > n
	if i div by only 3
	   print Fizz
	   increment i
	repeat until i > n

Buzz Thread	Number Thread

if i div by only 5
   print Buzz
   increment i
repeat until i > n
	if i not div by 3 or 5
	   print i
	   increment i
	repeat until i > n

The code for this will look something like:

```
1  while (true) {
2     if (current > max) {
3        return;
4     }
5     if (/* divisibility test */) {
6        System.out.println(/* print something */);
7        current++;
8     }
9  }
```

We'll need to add some synchronization in the loop. Otherwise, the value of `current` could change between lines 2 - 4 and lines 5 - 8, and we can inadvertently exceed the intended bounds of the loop. Additionally, incrementing is not thread-safe.

To actually implement this concept, there are many possibilities. One possibility is to have four entirely separate thread classes that share a reference to the current variable (which can be wrapped in an object).

The loop for each thread is substantially similar. They just have different target values for the divisibility checks, and different print values.

	FizzBuzz	Fizz	Buzz	Number
current % 3 == 0	true	true	false	false
current % 5 == 0	true	false	true	false
to print	FizzBuzz	Fizz	Buzz	current

For the most part, this can be handled by taking in "target" parameters and the value to print. The output for the `Number` thread needs to be overwritten, though, as it's not a simple, fixed string.

We can implement a `FizzBuzzThread` class which handles most of this. A `NumberThread` class can extend `FizzBuzzThread` and override the `print` method.

```
Thread[] threads = {new FizzBuzzThread(true, true, n, "FizzBuzz"),
                    new FizzBuzzThread(true, false, n, "Fizz"),
                    new FizzBuzzThread(false, true, n, "Buzz"),
                    new NumberThread(false, false, n)};
for (Thread thread : threads) {
  thread.start();
}

public class FizzBuzzThread extends Thread {
  private static Object lock = new Object();
  protected static int current = 1;
  private int max;
  private boolean div3, div5;
  private String toPrint;

  public FizzBuzzThread(boolean div3, boolean div5, int max, String toPrint) {
    this.div3 = div3;
    this.div5 = div5;
    this.max = max;
    this.toPrint = toPrint;
  }

  public void print() {
    System.out.println(toPrint);
  }

  public void run() {
    while (true) {
      synchronized (lock) {
        if (current > max) {
          return;
        }

        if ((current % 3 == 0) == div3 &&
            (current % 5 == 0) == div5) {
          print();
          current++;
        }
      }
    }
  }
}

public class NumberThread extends FizzBuzzThread {
```

```
   public NumberThread(boolean div3, boolean div5, int max) {
      super(div3, div5, max, null);
   }

   public void print() {
      System.out.println(current);
   }
}
```

Observe that we need to put the comparison of `current` and `max` before the if statement, to ensure the value will only get printed when `current` is less than or equal to `max`.

Alternatively, if we're working in a language which supports this (Java 8 and many other languages do), we can pass in a `validate` method and a `print` method as parameters.

```
int n = 100;
Thread[] threads = {
   new FBThread(i -> i % 3 == 0 && i % 5 == 0, i -> "FizzBuzz", n),
   new FBThread(i -> i % 3 == 0 && i % 5 != 0, i -> "Fizz", n),
   new FBThread(i -> i % 3 != 0 && i % 5 == 0, i -> "Buzz", n),
   new FBThread(i -> i % 3 != 0 && i % 5 != 0, i -> Integer.toString(i), n)};
for (Thread thread : threads) {
   thread.start();
}

public class FBThread extends Thread {
   private static Object lock = new Object();
   protected static int current = 1;
   private int max;
   private Predicate<Integer> validate;
   private Function<Integer, String> printer;
   int x = 1;

   public FBThread(Predicate<Integer> validate,
                   Function<Integer, String> printer, int max) {
      this.validate = validate;
      this.printer = printer;
      this.max = max;
   }

   public void run() {
      while (true) {
         synchronized (lock) {
            if (current > max) {
               return;
            }
            if (validate.test(current)) {
               System.out.println(printer.apply(current));
               current++;
            }
         }
      }
   }
}
```

There are of course many other ways of implementing this as well.

16

Solutions to Moderate

16.1 Number Swapper: Write a function to swap a number in place (that is, without temporary variables).

pg 181

SOLUTION

This is a classic interview problem, and it's a reasonably straightforward one. We'll walk through this using a_0 to indicate the original value of a and b_0 to indicate the original value of b. We'll also use `diff` to indicate the value of a_0 - b_0.

Let's picture these on a number line for the case where a > b.

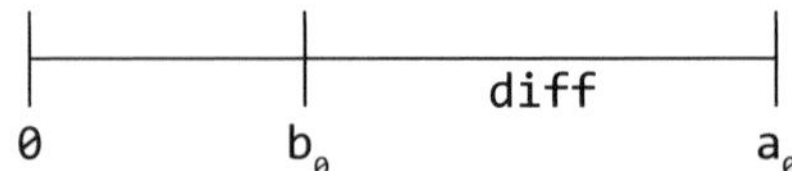

First, we briefly set a to `diff`, which is the right side of the above number line. Then, when we add b and `diff` (and store that value in b), we get a_0. We now have b = a_0 and a = `diff`. All that's left to do is to set a equal to a_0 - `diff`, which is just b - a.

The code below implements this.

```
// Example for a = 9, b = 4
a = a - b; // a = 9 - 4 = 5
b = a + b; // b = 5 + 4 = 9
a = b - a; // a = 9 - 5
```

We can implement a similar solution with bit manipulation. The benefit of this solution is that it works for more data types than just integers.

```
// Example for a = 101 (in binary) and b = 110
a = a^b; // a = 101^110 = 011
b = a^b; // b = 011^110 = 101
a = a^b; // a = 011^101 = 110
```

This code works by using XORs. The easiest way to see how this works is by focusing on a specific bit. If we can correctly swap two bits, then we know the entire operation works correctly.

Let's take two bits, x and y, and walk through this line by line.

1. `x = x ^ y`

   This line essentially checks if x and y have different values. It will result in 1 if and only if x != y.

2. `y = x ^ y`

Or: `y = {0 if originally same, 1 if different} ^ {original y}`

Observe that XORing a bit with 1 always flips the bit, whereas XORing with 0 will never change it.

Therefore, if we do `y = 1 ^ {original y}` when `x != y`, then y will be flipped and therefore have x's original value.

Otherwise, if `x == y`, then we do `y = 0 ^ {original y}` and the value of y does not change.

Either way, y will be equal to the original value of x.

3. `x = x ^ y`

   Or: `x = {0 if originally same, 1 if different} ^ {original x}`

   At this point, y is equal to the original value of x. This line is essentially equivalent to the line above it, but for different variables.

   If we do `x = 1 ^ {original x}` when the values are different, x will be flipped.

   If we do `x = 0 ^ {original x}` when the values are the same, x will not be changed.

This operation happens for each bit. Since it correctly swaps each bit, it will correctly swap the entire number.

16.2 Word Frequencies: Design a method to find the frequency of occurrences of any given word in a book. What if we were running this algorithm multiple times?

pg 181

SOLUTION

Let's start with the simple case.

Solution: Single Query

In this case, we simply go through the book, word by word, and count the number of times that a word appears. This will take O(n) time. We know we can't do better than that since we must look at every word in the book.

```
int getFrequency(String[] book, String word) {
   word = word.trim().toLowerCase();
   int count = 0;
   for (String w : book) {
      if (w.trim().toLowerCase().equals(word)) {
         count++;
      }
   }
   return count;
}
```

We have also converted the string to lowercase and trimmed it. You can discuss with your interviewer if this is necessary (or even desired).

Solution: Repetitive Queries

If we're doing the operation repeatedly, then we can probably afford to take some time and extra memory to do pre-processing on the book. We can create a hash table which maps from a word to its frequency. The frequency of any word can be easily looked up in O(1) time. The code for this is below.

```
HashMap<String, Integer> setupDictionary(String[] book) {
   HashMap<String, Integer> table =
```

```
        new HashMap<String, Integer>();
    for (String word : book) {
        word = word.toLowerCase();
        if (word.trim() != “”) {
            if (!table.containsKey(word)) {
                table.put(word, 0);
            }
            table.put(word, table.get(word) + 1);
        }
    }
    return table;
}

int getFrequency(HashMap<String, Integer> table, String word) {
    if (table == null || word == null) return -1;
    word = word.toLowerCase();
    if (table.containsKey(word)) {
        return table.get(word);
    }
    return 0;
}
```

Note that a problem like this is actually relatively easy. Thus, the interviewer is going to be looking heavily at how careful you are. Did you check for error conditions?

16.3 Intersection: Given two straight line segments (represented as a start point and an end point), compute the point of intersection, if any.

pg 181

SOLUTION

We first need to think about what it means for two line segments to intersect.

For two infinite lines to intersect, they only have to have different slopes. If they have the same slope, then they must be the exact same line (same y-intercept). That is:

```
slope 1 != slope 2
OR
slope 1 == slope 2 AND intersect 1 == intersect 2
```

For two straight lines to intersect, the condition above must be true, *plus* the point of intersection must be within the ranges of each line segment.

```
extended infinite segments intersect
AND
intersection is within line segment 1 (x and y coordinates)
AND
intersection is within line segment 2 (x and y coordinates)
```

What if the two segments represent the same infinite line? In this case, we have to ensure that some portion of their segments overlap. If we order the line segments by their x locations (start is before end, point 1 is before point 2), then an intersection occurs only if:

```
Assume:
    start1.x < start2.x && start1.x < end1.x && start2.x < end2.x
Then intersection occurs if:
    start2 is between start1 and end1
```

We can now go ahead and implement this algorithm.

```
Point intersection(Point start1, Point end1, Point start2, Point end2) {
  /* Rearranging these so that, in order of x values: start is before end and
   * point 1 is before point 2. This will make some of the later logic simpler. */
  if (start1.x > end1.x) swap(start1, end1);
  if (start2.x > end2.x) swap(start2, end2);
  if (start1.x > start2.x) {
    swap(start1, start2);
    swap(end1, end2);
  }

  /* Compute lines (including slope and y-intercept). */
  Line line1 = new Line(start1, end1);
  Line line2 = new Line(start2, end2);

  /* If the lines are parallel, they intercept only if they have the same y
   * intercept and start 2 is on line 1. */
  if (line1.slope == line2.slope) {
    if (line1.yintercept == line2.yintercept &&
        isBetween(start1, start2, end1)) {
      return start2;
    }
    return null;
  }

  /* Get intersection coordinate. */
  double x = (line2.yintercept - line1.yintercept) / (line1.slope - line2.slope);
  double y = x * line1.slope + line1.yintercept;
  Point intersection = new Point(x, y);

  /* Check if within line segment range. */
  if (isBetween(start1, intersection, end1) &&
      isBetween(start2, intersection, end2)) {
    return intersection;
  }
  return null;
}

/* Checks if middle is between start and end. */
boolean isBetween(double start, double middle, double end) {
  if (start > end) {
    return end <= middle && middle <= start;
  } else {
    return start <= middle && middle <= end;
  }
}

/* Checks if middle is between start and end. */
boolean isBetween(Point start, Point middle, Point end) {
  return isBetween(start.x, middle.x, end.x) &&
         isBetween(start.y, middle.y, end.y);
}

/* Swap coordinates of point one and two. */
void swap(Point one, Point two) {
  double x = one.x;
  double y = one.y;
```

```
    one.setLocation(two.x, two.y);
    two.setLocation(x, y);
}

public class Line {
    public double slope, yintercept;

    public Line(Point start, Point end) {
        double deltaY = end.y - start.y;
        double deltaX = end.x - start.x;
        slope = deltaY / deltaX; // Will be Infinity (not exception) when deltaX = 0
        yintercept = end.y - slope * end.x;
    }

public class Point {
    public double x, y;
    public Point(double x, double y) {
        this.x = x;
        this.y = y;
    }

    public void setLocation(double x, double y) {
        this.x = x;
        this.y = y;
    }
}
```

For simplicity and compactness (it really makes the code easier to read), we've chosen to make the variables within `Point` and `Line` `public`. You can discuss with your interviewer the advantages and disadvantages of this choice.

16.4 Tic Tac Win: Design an algorithm to figure out if someone has won a game of tic-tac-toe.

pg 181

SOLUTION

At first glance, this problem seems really straightforward. We're just checking a tic-tac-toe board; how hard could it be? It turns out that the problem is a bit more complex, and there is no single "perfect" answer. The optimal solution depends on your preferences.

There are a few major design decisions to consider:

1. Will `hasWon` be called just once or many times (for instance, as part of a tic-tac-toe website)? If the latter is the case, we may want to add pre-processing time to optimize the runtime of `hasWon`.
2. Do we know the last move that was made?
3. Tic-tac-toe is usually on a 3x3 board. Do we want to design for just that, or do we want to implement it as an NxN solution?
4. In general, how much do we prioritize compactness of code versus speed of execution vs. clarity of code? Remember: The most efficient code may not always be the best. Your ability to understand and maintain the code matters, too.

Solution #1: If hasWon is called many times

There are only 3^9, or about 20,000, tic-tac-toe boards (assuming a 3x3 board). Therefore, we can represent our tic-tac-toe board as an `int`, with each digit representing a piece (0 means Empty, 1 means Red, 2 means Blue). We set up a hash table or array in advance with all possible boards as keys and the value indicating who has won. Our function then is simply this:

```
Piece hasWon(int board) {
  return winnerHashtable[board];
}
```

To convert a board (represented by a char array) to an `int`, we can use what is essentially a "base 3" representation. Each board is represented as $3^0v_0 + 3^1v_1 + 3^2v_2 + \ldots + 3^8v_8$, where v_i is a `0` if the space is empty, a `1` if it's a "red spot" and a 2 if it's a "blue spot."

```
enum Piece { Empty, Red, Blue };

int convertBoardToInt(Piece[][] board) {
  int sum = 0;
  for (int i = 0; i < board.length; i++) {
    for (int j = 0; j < board[i].length; j++) {
      /* Each value in enum has an integer associated with it. We
       * can just use that. */
      int value = board[i][j].ordinal();
      sum = sum * 3 + value;
    }
  }
  return sum;
}
```

Now looking up the winner of a board is just a matter of looking it up in a hash table.

Of course, if we need to convert a board into this format every time we want to check for a winner, we haven't saved ourselves any time compared with the other solutions. But, if we can store the board this way from the very beginning, then the lookup process will be very efficient.

Solution #2: If we know the last move

If we know the very last move that was made (and we've been checking for a winner up until now), then we only need to check the row, column, and diagonal that overlaps with this position.

```
Piece hasWon(Piece[][] board, int row, int column) {
  if (board.length != board[0].length) return Piece.Empty;

  Piece piece = board[row][column];

  if (piece == Piece.Empty) return Piece.Empty;

  if (hasWonRow(board, row) || hasWonColumn(board, column)) {
    return piece;
  }

  if (row == column && hasWonDiagonal(board, 1)) {
    return piece;
  }

  if (row == (board.length - column - 1) && hasWonDiagonal(board, -1)) {
    return piece;
  }
```

```
	return Piece.Empty;
}

boolean hasWonRow(Piece[][] board, int row) {
	for (int c = 1; c < board[row].length; c++) {
		if (board[row][c] != board[row][0]) {
			return false;
		}
	}
	return true;
}

boolean hasWonColumn(Piece[][] board, int column) {
	for (int r = 1; r < board.length; r++) {
		if (board[r][column] != board[0][column]) {
			return false;
		}
	}
	return true;
}

boolean hasWonDiagonal(Piece[][] board, int direction) {
	int row = 0;
	int column = direction == 1 ? 0 : board.length - 1;
	Piece first = board[0][column];
	for (int i = 0; i < board.length; i++) {
		if (board[row][column] != first) {
			return false;
		}
		row += 1;
		column += direction;
	}
	return true;
}
```

There is actually a way to clean up this code to remove some of the duplicated code. We'll see this approach in a later function.

Solution #3: Designing for just a 3x3 board

If we really only want to implement a solution for a 3x3 board, the code is relatively short and simple. The only complex part is trying to be clean and organized, without writing too much duplicated code.

The code below checks each row, column, and diagonal to see if there is a winner.

```
Piece hasWon(Piece[][] board) {
	for (int i = 0; i < board.length; i++) {
		/* Check Rows */
		if (hasWinner(board[i][0], board[i][1], board[i][2])) {
			return board[i][0];
		}

		/* Check Columns */
		if (hasWinner(board[0][i], board[1][i], board[2][i])) {
			return board[0][i];
		}
```

```
  }

  /* Check Diagonal */
  if (hasWinner(board[0][0], board[1][1], board[2][2])) {
    return board[0][0];
  }

  if (hasWinner(board[0][2], board[1][1], board[2][0])) {
    return board[0][2];
  }

  return Piece.Empty;
}

boolean hasWinner(Piece p1, Piece p2, Piece p3) {
  if (p1 == Piece.Empty) {
    return false;
  }
  return p1 == p2 && p2 == p3;
}
```

This is an okay solution in that it's relatively easy to understand what is going on. The problem is that the values are hard coded. It's easy to accidentally type the wrong indices.

Additionally, it won't be easy to scale this to an NxN board.

Solution #4: Designing for an NxN board

There are a number of ways to implement this on an NxN board.

Nested For-Loops

The most obvious way is through a series of nested for-loops.

```
Piece hasWon(Piece[][] board) {
  int size = board.length;
  if (board[0].length != size) return Piece.Empty;
  Piece first;

  /* Check rows. */
  for (int i = 0; i < size; i++) {
    first = board[i][0];
    if (first == Piece.Empty) continue;
    for (int j = 1; j < size; j++) {
      if (board[i][j] != first) {
        break;
      } else if (j == size - 1) { // Last element
        return first;
      }
    }
  }

  /* Check columns. */
  for (int i = 0; i < size; i++) {
    first = board[0][i];
    if (first == Piece.Empty) continue;
    for (int j = 1; j < size; j++) {
      if (board[j][i] != first) {
```

```
                break;
            } else if (j == size - 1) { // Last element
                return first;
            }
        }
    }

    /* Check diagonals. */
    first = board[0][0];
    if (first != Piece.Empty) {
        for (int i = 1; i < size; i++) {
            if (board[i][i] != first) {
                break;
            } else if (i == size - 1) { // Last element
                return first;
            }
        }
    }

    first = board[0][size - 1];
    if (first != Piece.Empty) {
        for (int i = 1; i < size; i++) {
            if (board[i][size - i - 1] != first) {
                break;
            } else if (i == size - 1) { // Last element
                return first;
            }
        }
    }

    return Piece.Empty;
}
```

This is, to the say the least, pretty ugly. We're doing nearly the same work each time. We should look for a way of reusing the code.

Increment and Decrement Function

One way that we can reuse the code better is to just pass in the values to another function that increments/decrements the rows and columns. The `hasWon` function now just needs the starting position and the amount to increment the row and column by.

```
class Check {
    public int row, column;
    private int rowIncrement, columnIncrement;
    public Check(int row, int column, int rowI, int colI) {
        this.row = row;
        this.column = column;
        this.rowIncrement = rowI;
        this.columnIncrement = colI;
    }

    public void increment() {
        row += rowIncrement;
        column += columnIncrement;
    }

    public boolean inBounds(int size) {
```

```
      return row >= 0 && column >= 0 && row < size && column < size;
    }
}

Piece hasWon(Piece[][] board) {
  if (board.length != board[0].length) return Piece.Empty;
  int size = board.length;

  /* Create list of things to check. */
  ArrayList<Check> instructions = new ArrayList<Check>();
  for (int i = 0; i < board.length; i++) {
    instructions.add(new Check(0, i, 1, 0));
    instructions.add(new Check(i, 0, 0, 1));
  }
  instructions.add(new Check(0, 0, 1, 1));
  instructions.add(new Check(0, size - 1, 1, -1));

  /* Check them. */
  for (Check instr : instructions) {
    Piece winner = hasWon(board, instr);
    if (winner != Piece.Empty) {
        return winner;
    }
  }
  return Piece.Empty;
}

Piece hasWon(Piece[][] board, Check instr) {
  Piece first = board[instr.row][instr.column];
  while (instr.inBounds(board.length)) {
    if (board[instr.row][instr.column] != first) {
      return Piece.Empty;
    }
    instr.increment();
  }
  return first;
}
```

The Check function is essentially operating as an iterator.

Iterator

Another way of doing it is, of course, to actually build an iterator.

```
Piece hasWon(Piece[][] board) {
  if (board.length != board[0].length) return Piece.Empty;
  int size = board.length;

  ArrayList<PositionIterator> instructions = new ArrayList<PositionIterator>();
  for (int i = 0; i < board.length; i++) {
    instructions.add(new PositionIterator(new Position(0, i), 1, 0, size));
    instructions.add(new PositionIterator(new Position(i, 0), 0, 1, size));
  }
  instructions.add(new PositionIterator(new Position(0, 0), 1, 1, size));
  instructions.add(new PositionIterator(new Position(0, size - 1), 1, -1, size));

  for (PositionIterator iterator : instructions) {
    Piece winner = hasWon(board, iterator);
```

```
      if (winner != Piece.Empty) {
         return winner;
      }
   }
   return Piece.Empty;
}

Piece hasWon(Piece[][] board, PositionIterator iterator) {
   Position firstPosition = iterator.next();
   Piece first = board[firstPosition.row][firstPosition.column];
   while (iterator.hasNext()) {
      Position position = iterator.next();
      if (board[position.row][position.column] != first) {
         return Piece.Empty;
      }
   }
   return first;
}

class PositionIterator implements Iterator<Position> {
   private int rowIncrement, colIncrement, size;
   private Position current;

   public PositionIterator(Position p, int rowIncrement,
                           int colIncrement, int size) {
      this.rowIncrement = rowIncrement;
      this.colIncrement = colIncrement;
      this.size = size;
      current = new Position(p.row - rowIncrement, p.column - colIncrement);
   }

   @Override
   public boolean hasNext() {
      return current.row + rowIncrement < size &&
             current.column + colIncrement < size;
   }

   @Override
   public Position next() {
      current = new Position(current.row + rowIncrement,
                             current.column + colIncrement);
      return current;
   }
}

public class Position {
   public int row, column;
   public Position(int row, int column) {
      this.row = row;
      this.column = column;
   }
}
```

All of this is potentially overkill, but it's worth discussing the options with your interviewer. The point of this problem is to assess your understanding of how to code in a clean and maintainable way.

16.5 Factorial Zeros: Write an algorithm which computes the number of trailing zeros in n factorial.

pg 181

SOLUTION

A simple approach is to compute the factorial, and then count the number of trailing zeros by continuously dividing by ten. The problem with this though is that the bounds of an `int` would be exceeded very quickly. To avoid this issue, we can look at this problem mathematically.

Consider a factorial like `19!`:

```
19! = 1*2*3*4*5*6*7*8*9*10*11*12*13*14*15*16*17*18*19
```

A trailing zero is created with multiples of 10, and multiples of 10 are created with pairs of 5-multiples and 2-multiples.

For example, in 19!, the following terms create the trailing zeros:

```
19! = 2 * ... * 5 * ... * 10 * ... * 15 * 16 * ...
```

Therefore, to count the number of zeros, we only need to count the pairs of multiples of 5 and 2. There will always be more multiples of 2 than 5, though, so simply counting the number of multiples of 5 is sufficient.

One "gotcha" here is 15 contributes a multiple of 5 (and therefore one trailing zero), while 25 contributes two (because `25 = 5 * 5`).

There are two different ways to write this code.

The first way is to iterate through all the numbers from 2 through n, counting the number of times that 5 goes into each number.

```
/* If the number is a 5 of five, return which power of 5. For example: 5 -> 1,
 * 25-> 2, etc. */
int factorsOf5(int i) {
  int count = 0;
  while (i % 5 == 0) {
    count++;
    i /= 5;
  }
  return count;
}

int countFactZeros(int num) {
  int count = 0;
  for (int i = 2; i <= num; i++) {
    count += factorsOf5(i);
  }
  return count;
}
```

This isn't bad, but we can make it a little more efficient by directly counting the factors of 5. Using this approach, we would first count the number of multiples of 5 between 1 and n (which is $n/5$), then the number of multiples of 25 ($n/25$), then 125, and so on.

To count how many multiples of `m` are in n, we can just divide n by `m`.

```
int countFactZeros(int num) {
  int count = 0;
  if (num < 0) {
    return -1;
  }
```

```
    for (int i = 5; num / i > 0; i *= 5) {
       count += num / i;
    }
    return count;
 }
```

This problem is a bit of a brainteaser, but it can be approached logically (as shown above). By thinking through what exactly will contribute a zero, you can come up with a solution. You should be very clear in your rules upfront so that you can implement it correctly.

16.6 **Smallest Difference**: Given two arrays of integers, compute the pair of values (one value in each array) with the smallest (non-negative) difference. Return the difference.

EXAMPLE

Input: {1, 3, 15, 11, 2}, {23, 127, 235, 19, 8}

Output: 3. That is, the pair (11, 8).

pg 181

SOLUTION

Let's start first with a brute force solution.

Brute Force

The simple brute force way is to just iterate through all pairs, compute the difference, and compare it to the current minimum difference.

```
int findSmallestDifference(int[] array1, int[] array2) {
   if (array1.length == 0 || array2.length == 0) return -1;

   int min = Integer.MAX_VALUE;
   for (int i = 0; i < array1.length; i++) {
      for (int j = 0; j < array2.length; j++) {
         if (Math.abs(array1[i] - array2[j]) < min) {
            min = Math.abs(array1[i] - array2[j]);
         }
      }
   }
   return min;
}
```

One minor optimization we could perform from here is to return immediately if we find a difference of zero, since this is the smallest difference possible. However, depending on the input, this might actually be slower.

This will only be faster if there's a pair with difference zero early in the list of pairs. But to add this optimization, we need to execute an additional line of code each time. There's a tradeoff here; it's faster for some inputs and slower for others. Given that it adds complexity in reading the code, it may be best to leave it out.

With or without this "optimization," the algorithm will take O(AB) time.

Optimal

A more optimal approach is to sort the arrays. Once the arrays are sorted, we can find the minimum difference by iterating through the array.

Consider the following two arrays:

```
A: {1, 2, 11, 15}
B: {4, 12, 19, 23, 127, 235}
```

Try the following approach:

1. Suppose a pointer a points to the beginning of A and a pointer b points to the beginning of B. The current difference between a and b is 3. Store this as the `min`.
2. How can we (potentially) make this difference smaller? Well, the value at b is bigger than the value at a, so moving b will only make the difference larger. Therefore, we want to move a.
3. Now a points to 2 and b (still) points to 4. This difference is 2, so we should update `min`. Move a, since it is smaller.
4. Now a points to 11 and b points to 4. Move b.
5. Now a points to 11 and b points to 12. Update `min` to 1. Move b.

And so on.

```
int findSmallestDifference(int[] array1, int[] array2) {
  Arrays.sort(array1);
  Arrays.sort(array2);
  int a = 0;
  int b = 0;
  int difference = Integer.MAX_VALUE;
  while (a < array1.length && b < array2.length) {
    if (Math.abs(array1[a] - array2[b]) < difference) {
      difference = Math.abs(array1[a] - array2[b]);
    }

    /* Move smaller value. */
    if (array1[a] < array2[b]) {
      a++;
    } else {
      b++;
    }
  }
  return difference;
}
```

This algorithm takes `O(A log A + B log B)` time to sort and `O(A + B)` time to find the minimum difference. Therefore, the overall runtime is `O(A log A + B log B)`.

16.7 Number Max: Write a method that finds the maximum of two numbers. You should not use if-else or any other comparison operator.

pg 181

SOLUTION

A common way of implementing a `max` function is to look at the sign of `a - b`. In this case, we can't use a comparison operator on this sign, but we *can* use multiplication.

Let k equal the sign of `a - b` such that if `a - b >= 0`, then k is 1. Else, `k = 0`. Let q be the inverse of k.

We can then implement the code as follows:

```
/* Flips a 1 to a 0 and a 0 to a 1 */
int flip(int bit) {
```

```
    return 1^bit;
}

/* Returns 1 if a is positive, and 0 if a is negative */
int sign(int a) {
    return flip((a >> 31) & 0x1);
}

int getMaxNaive(int a, int b) {
    int k = sign(a - b);
    int q = flip(k);
    return a * k + b * q;
}
```

This code almost works. It fails, unfortunately, when a - b overflows. Suppose, for example, that a is `INT_MAX - 2` and b is `-15`. In this case, a - b will be greater than `INT_MAX` and will overflow, resulting in a negative value.

We can implement a solution to this problem by using the same approach. Our goal is to maintain the condition where k is 1 when a > b. We will need to use more complex logic to accomplish this.

When does a - b overflow? It will overflow only when a is positive and b is negative, or the other way around. It may be difficult to specially detect the overflow condition, but we *can* detect when a and b have different signs. Note that if a and b have different signs, then we want k to equal `sign(a)`.

The logic looks like:

```
if a and b have different signs:
    // if a > 0, then b < 0, and k = 1.
    // if a < 0, then b > 0, and k = 0.
    // so either way, k = sign(a)
    let k = sign(a)
else
    let k = sign(a - b) // overflow is impossible
```

The code below implements this, using multiplication instead of if-statements.

```
int getMax(int a, int b) {
    int c = a - b;

    int sa = sign(a); // if a >= 0, then 1 else 0
    int sb = sign(b); // if b >= 0, then 1 else 0
    int sc = sign(c); // depends on whether or not a - b overflows

    /* Goal: define a value k which is 1 if a > b and 0 if a < b.
     * (if a = b, it doesn't matter what value k is) */

    // If a and b have different signs, then k = sign(a)
    int use_sign_of_a = sa ^ sb;

    // If a and b have the same sign, then k = sign(a - b)
    int use_sign_of_c = flip(sa ^ sb);

    int k = use_sign_of_a * sa + use_sign_of_c * sc;
    int q = flip(k); // opposite of k

    return a * k + b * q;
}
```

Note that for clarity, we split up the code into many different methods and variables. This is certainly not the most compact or efficient way to write it, but it does make what we're doing much cleaner.

16.8 English Int: Given any integer, print an English phrase that describes the integer (e.g., "One Thousand, Two Hundred Thirty Four").

pg 182

SOLUTION

This is not an especially challenging problem, but it is a somewhat tedious one. The key is to be organized in how you approach the problem—and to make sure you have good test cases.

We can think about converting a number like 19,323,984 as converting each of three 3-digit segments of the number, and inserting "thousands" and "millions" in between as appropriate. That is,

```
convert(19,323,984) = convert(19) + “ million ” + convert(323) + “ thousand ” +
                      convert(984)
```

The code below implements this algorithm.

```
String[] smalls = {“Zero”, “One”, “Two”, “Three”, “Four”, “Five”, “Six”, “Seven”,
  “Eight”, “Nine”, “Ten”, “Eleven”, “Twelve”, “Thirteen”, “Fourteen”, “Fifteen”,
  “Sixteen”, “Seventeen”, “Eighteen”, “Nineteen”};
String[] tens = {“”, “”, “Twenty”, “Thirty”, “Forty”, “Fifty”, “Sixty”, “Seventy”,
  “Eighty”, “Ninety”};
String[] bigs = {“”, “Thousand”, “Million”, “Billion”};
String hundred = “Hundred”;
String negative = “Negative”;

String convert(int num) {
  if (num == 0) {
    return smalls[0];
  } else if (num < 0) {
    return negative + “ ” + convert(-1 * num);
  }

  LinkedList<String> parts = new LinkedList<String>();
  int chunkCount = 0;

  while (num > 0) {
    if (num % 1000 != 0) {
      String chunk = convertChunk(num % 1000) + “ ” + bigs[chunkCount];
      parts.addFirst(chunk);
    }
    num /= 1000; // shift chunk
    chunkCount++;
  }

  return listToString(parts);
}

String convertChunk(int number) {
  LinkedList<String> parts = new LinkedList<String>();

  /* Convert hundreds place */
  if (number >= 100) {
    parts.addLast(smalls[number / 100]);
```

```
            parts.addLast(hundred);
            number %= 100;
        }

        /* Convert tens place */
        if (number >= 10 && number <= 19) {
            parts.addLast(smalls[number]);
        } else if (number >= 20) {
            parts.addLast(tens[number / 10]);
            number %= 10;
        }

        /* Convert ones place */
        if (number >= 1 && number <= 9) {
            parts.addLast(smalls[number]);
        }

        return listToString(parts);
    }
    /* Convert a linked list of strings to a string, dividing it up with spaces. */
    String listToString(LinkedList<String> parts) {
        StringBuilder sb = new StringBuilder();
        while (parts.size() > 1) {
            sb.append(parts.pop());
            sb.append(" ");
        }
        sb.append(parts.pop());
        return sb.toString();
    }
```

The key in a problem like this is to make sure you consider all the special cases. There are a lot of them.

16.9 Operations: Write methods to implement the multiply, subtract, and divide operations for integers. The results of all of these are integers. Use only the add operator.

pg 182

SOLUTION

The only operation we have to work with is the add operator. In each of these problems, it's useful to think in depth about what these operations really do or how to phrase them in terms of other operations (either add or operations we've already completed).

Subtraction

How can we phrase subtraction in terms of addition? This one is pretty straightforward. The operation `a - b` is the same thing as `a + (-1) * b`. However, because we are not allowed to use the * (multiply) operator, we must implement a `negate` function.

```
/* Flip a positive sign to negative or negative sign to pos. */
int negate(int a) {
    int neg = 0;
    int newSign = a < 0 ? 1 : -1;
    while (a != 0) {
        neg += newSign;
        a += newSign;
    }
```

```
    return neg;
}

/* Subtract two numbers by negating b and adding them */
int minus(int a, int b) {
    return a + negate(b);
}
```

The negation of the value k is implemented by adding -1 k times. Observe that this will take O(k) time.

If optimizing is something we value here, we can try to get a to zero faster. (For this explanation, we'll assume that a is positive.) To do this, we can first reduce a by 1, then 2, then 4, then 8, and so on. We'll call this value delta. We want a to reach exactly zero. When reducing a by the next delta would change the sign of a, we reset delta back to 1 and repeat the process.

For example:

```
a:      29   28   26   22   14   13   11    7    6    4    0
delta:    -1   -2   -4   -8   -1   -2   -4   -1   -2   -4
```

The code below implements this algorithm.

```
int negate(int a) {
    int neg = 0;
    int newSign = a < 0 ? 1 : -1;
    int delta = newSign;
    while (a != 0) {
        boolean differentSigns = (a + delta > 0) != (a > 0);
        if (a + delta != 0 && differentSigns) { // If delta is too big, reset it.
            delta = newSign;
        }
        neg += delta;
        a += delta;
        delta += delta; // Double the delta
    }
    return neg;
}
```

Figuring out the runtime here takes a bit of calculation.

Observe that reducing a by half takes O(log a) work. Why? For each round of "reduce a by half", the absolute values of a and delta always add up to the same number. The values of delta and a will converge at $\frac{a}{2}$. Since delta is being doubled each time, it will take O(log a) steps to reach half of a.

We do O(log a) rounds.

1. Reducing a to $\frac{a}{2}$ takes $O(\log a)$ time.
2. Reducing $\frac{a}{2}$ to $\frac{a}{4}$ takes $O(\log \frac{a}{2})$ time.
3. Reducing $\frac{a}{4}$ to $\frac{a}{8}$ takes $O(\log \frac{a}{4})$ time.

... As so on, for O(log a) rounds.

The runtime therefore is $O(\log a + \log(\frac{a}{2}) + \log(\frac{a}{4}) + \ldots)$, with O(log a) terms in the expression.

Recall two rules of logs:

- $\log(xy) = \log x + \log y$
- $\log(\frac{x}{y}) = \log x - \log y$.

If we apply this to the above expression, we get:

1. $O(\log a + \log(\frac{a}{2}) + \log(\frac{a}{4}) + \ldots)$
2. $O(\log a + (\log a - \log 2) + (\log a - \log 4) + (\log a - \log 8) + \ldots$
3. $O((\log a)*(\log a) - (\log 2 + \log 4 + \log 8 + \ldots + \log a))$ // $O(\log a)$ terms
4. $O((\log a)*(\log a) - (1 + 2 + 3 + \ldots + \log a))$ // computing the values of logs
5. $O((\log a)*(\log a) - \frac{(\log a)(1+\log a)}{2})$ // apply equation for sum of 1 through k
6. $O((\log a)^2)$ // drop second term from step 5

Therefore, the runtime is $O((\log a)^2)$.

This math is considerably more complicated than most people would be able to do (or expected to do) in an interview. You could make a simplification: You do `O(log a)` rounds and the longest round takes `O(log a)` work. Therefore, as an upper bound, `negate` takes $O((\log a)^2)$ time. In this case, the upper bound happens to be the true time.

There are some faster solutions too. For example, rather than resetting `delta` to 1 at each round, we could change `delta` to its previous value. This would have the effect of `delta` "counting up" by multiples of two, and then "counting down" by multiples of two. The runtime of this approach would be `O(log a)`. However, this implementation would require a stack, division, or bit shifting—any of which might violate the spirit of the problem. You could certainly discuss those implementations with your interviewer though.

Multiplication

The connection between addition and multiplication is equally straightforward. To multiply a by b, we just add a to itself b times.

```
/* Multiply a by b by adding a to itself b times */
int multiply(int a, int b) {
   if (a < b) {
      return multiply(b, a); // algorithm is faster if b < a
   }
   int sum = 0;
   for (int i = abs(b); i > 0; i = minus(i, 1)) {
      sum += a;
   }
   if (b < 0) {
      sum = negate(sum);
   }
   return sum;
}

/* Return absolute value */
int abs(int a) {
   if (a < 0) {
      return negate(a);
   } else {
      return a;
   }
}
```

The one thing we need to be careful of in the above code is to properly handle multiplication of negative numbers. If b is negative, we need to flip the value of `sum`. So, what this code really does is:

```
multiply(a, b) <-- abs(b) * a * (-1 if b < 0).
```

We also implemented a simple abs function to help.

Division

Of the three operations, division is certainly the hardest. The good thing is that we can use the `multiply`, `subtract`, and `negate` methods now to implement `divide`.

We are trying to compute x where $x = \frac{a}{b}$. Or, to put this another way, find x where a = bx. We've now changed the problem into one that can be stated with something we know how to do: multiplication.

We could implement this by multiplying b by progressively higher values, until we reach a. That would be fairly inefficient, particularly given that our implementation of `multiply` involves a lot of adding.

Alternatively, we can look at the equation a = xb to see that we can compute x by adding b to itself repeatedly until we reach a. The number of times we need to do that will equal x.

Of course, a might not be evenly divisible by b, and that's okay. Integer division, which is what we've been asked to implement, is supposed to truncate the result.

The code below implements this algorithm.

```
int divide(int a, int b) throws java.lang.ArithmeticException {
  if (b == 0) {
    throw new java.lang.ArithmeticException("ERROR");
  }
  int absa = abs(a);
  int absb = abs(b);

  int product = 0;
  int x = 0;
  while (product + absb <= absa) { /* don't go past a */
    product += absb;
    x++;
  }

  if ((a < 0 && b < 0) || (a > 0 && b > 0)) {
    return x;
  } else {
    return negate(x);
  }
}
```

In tackling this problem, you should be aware of the following:

- A logical approach of going back to what exactly multiplication and division do comes in handy. Remember that. All (good) interview problems can be approached in a logical, methodical way!
- The interviewer is looking for this sort of logical work-your-way-through-it approach.
- This is a great problem to demonstrate your ability to write clean code—specifically, to show your ability to reuse code. For example, if you were writing this solution and didn't put `negate` in its own method, you should move it into its own method once you see that you'll use it multiple times.
- Be careful about making assumptions while coding. Don't assume that the numbers are all positive or that a is bigger than b.

16.10 Living People: Given a list of people with their birth and death years, implement a method to compute the year with the most number of people alive. You may assume that all people were born between 1900 and 2000 (inclusive). If a person was alive during any portion of that year, they should be included in that year's count. For example, Person (birth = 1908, death = 1909) is included in the counts for both 1908 and 1909.

pg 182

SOLUTION

The first thing we should do is outline what this solution will look like. The interview question hasn't specified the exact form of input. In a real interview, we could ask the interviewer how the input is structured. Alternatively, you can explicitly state your (reasonable) assumptions.

Here, we'll need to make our own assumptions. We will assume that we have an array of simple `Person` objects:

```
public class Person {
   public int birth;
   public int death;
   public Person(int birthYear, int deathYear) {
      birth = birthYear;
      death = deathYear;
   }
}
```

We could have also given `Person` a `getBirthYear()` and `getDeathYear()` objects. Some would argue that's better style, but for compactness and clarity, we'll just keep the variables public.

The important thing here is to actually use a `Person` object. This shows better style than, say, having an integer array for birth years and an integer array for death years (with an implicit association of `births[i]` and `deaths[i]` being associated with the same person). You don't get a lot of chances to demonstrate great coding style, so it's valuable to take the ones you get.

With that in mind, let's start with a brute force algorithm.

Brute Force

The brute force algorithm falls directly out from the wording of the problem. We need to find the year with the most number of people alive. Therefore, we go through each year and check how many people are alive in that year.

```
int maxAliveYear(Person[] people, int min, int max) {
   int maxAlive = 0;
   int maxAliveYear = min;

   for (int year = min; year <= max; year++) {
      int alive = 0;
      for (Person person : people) {
         if (person.birth <= year && year <= person.death) {
            alive++;
         }
      }
      if (alive > maxAlive) {
         maxAlive = alive;
         maxAliveYear = year;
      }
   }
```

```

    return maxAliveYear;
}
```

Note that we have passed in the values for the min year (1900) and max year (2000). We shouldn't hard code these values.

The runtime of this is O(RP), where R is the range of years (100 in this case) and P is the number of people.

Slightly Better Brute Force

A slightly better way of doing this is to create an array where we track the number of people born in each year. Then, we iterate through the list of people and increment the array for each year they are alive.

```
1  int maxAliveYear(Person[] people, int min, int max) {
2     int[] years = createYearMap(people, min, max);
3     int best = getMaxIndex(years);
4     return best + min;
5  }
6  
7  /* Add each person's years to a year map. */
8  int[] createYearMap(Person[] people, int min, int max) {
9     int[] years = new int[max - min + 1];
10    for (Person person : people) {
11       incrementRange(years, person.birth - min, person.death - min);
12    }
13    return years;
14 }
15 
16 /* Increment array for each value between left and right. */
17 void incrementRange(int[] values, int left, int right) {
18    for (int i = left; i <= right; i++) {
19       values[i]++;
20    }
21 }
22 
23 /* Get index of largest element in array. */
24 int getMaxIndex(int[] values) {
25    int max = 0;
26    for (int i = 1; i < values.length; i++) {
27       if (values[i] > values[max]) {
28          max = i;
29       }
30    }
31    return max;
32 }
```

Be careful on the size of the array in line 9. If the range of years is 1900 to 2000 inclusive, then that's 101 years, not 100. That is why the array has size `max - min + 1`.

Let's think about the runtime by breaking this into parts.

- We create an R-sized array, where R is the min and max years.
- Then, for P people, we iterate through the years (Y) that the person is alive.
- Then, we iterate through the R-sized array again.

The total runtime is O(PY + R). In the worst case, Y is R and we have done no better than we did in the first algorithm.

More Optimal

Let's create an example. (In fact, an example is really helpful in almost all problems. Ideally, you've already done this.) Each column below is matched, so that the items correspond to the same person. For compactness, we'll just write the last two digits of the year.

```
birth: 12  20  10  01  10  23  13  90  83  75
death: 15  90  98  72  98  82  98  98  99  94
```

It's worth noting that it doesn't really matter whether these years are matched up. Every birth adds a person and every death removes a person.

Since we don't actually need to match up the births and deaths, let's sort both. A sorted version of the years might help us solve the problem.

```
birth: 01  10  10  12  13  20  23  75  83  90
death: 15  72  82  90  94  98  98  98  98  99
```

We can try walking through the years.

- At year 0, no one is alive.
- At year 1, we see one birth.
- At years 2 through 9, nothing happens.
- Let's skip ahead until year 10, when we have two births. We now have three people alive.
- At year 15, one person dies. We are now down to two people alive.
- And so on.

If we walk through the two arrays like this, we can track the number of people alive at each point.

```
int maxAliveYear(Person[] people, int min, int max) {
   int[] births = getSortedYears(people, true);
   int[] deaths = getSortedYears(people, false);

   int birthIndex = 0;
   int deathIndex = 0;
   int currentlyAlive = 0;
   int maxAlive = 0;
   int maxAliveYear = min;

   /* Walk through arrays. */
   while (birthIndex < births.length) {
      if (births[birthIndex] <= deaths[deathIndex]) {
         currentlyAlive++; // include birth
         if (currentlyAlive > maxAlive) {
            maxAlive = currentlyAlive;
            maxAliveYear = births[birthIndex];
         }
         birthIndex++; // move birth index
      } else if (births[birthIndex] > deaths[deathIndex]) {
         currentlyAlive--; // include death
         deathIndex++; // move death index
      }
   }

   return maxAliveYear;
}

/* Copy birth years or death years (depending on the value of copyBirthYear into
```

```
30   * integer array, then sort array. */
31  int[] getSortedYears(Person[] people, boolean copyBirthYear) {
32    int[] years = new int[people.length];
33    for (int i = 0; i < people.length; i++) {
34      years[i] = copyBirthYear ? people[i].birth : people[i].death;
35    }
36    Arrays.sort(years);
37    return years;
38  }
```

There are some very easy things to mess up here.

On line 13, we need to think carefully about whether this should be a less than (<) or a less than or equals (<=). The scenario we need to worry about is that you see a birth and death in the same year. (It doesn't matter whether the birth and death is from the same person.)

When we see a birth and death from the same year, we want to include the birth *before* we include the death, so that we count this person as alive for that year. That is why we use a <= on line 13.

We also need to be careful about where we put the updating of `maxAlive` and `maxAliveYear`. It needs to be after the `currentAlive++`, so that it takes into account the updated total. But it needs to be before `birthIndex++`, or we won't have the right year.

This algorithm will take `O(P log P)` time, where P is the number of people.

More Optimal (Maybe)

Can we optimize this further? To optimize this, we'd need to get rid of the sorting step. We're back to dealing with unsorted values:

```
birth: 12  20  10  01  10  23  13  90  83  75
death: 15  90  98  72  98  82  98  98  99  94
```

Earlier, we had logic that said that a birth is just adding a person and a death is just subtracting a person. Therefore, let's represent the data using the logic:

```
01: +1      10: +1      10: +1      12: +1      13: +1
15: -1      20: +1      23: +1      72: -1      75: +1
82: -1      83: +1      90: +1      90: -1      94: -1
98: -1      98: -1      98: -1      98: -1      99: -1
```

We can create an array of the years, where the value at `array[year]` indicates how the population changed in that year. To create this array, we walk through the list of people and increment when they're born and decrement when they die.

Once we have this array, we can walk through each of the years, tracking the current population as we go (adding the value at `array[year]` each time).

This logic is reasonably good, but we should think about it more. Does it really work?

One edge case we should consider is when a person dies the same year that they're born. The increment and decrement operations will cancel out to give 0 population change. According to the wording of the problem, this person should be counted as living in that year.

In fact, the "bug" in our algorithm is broader than that. This same issue applies to all people. People who die in 1908 shouldn't be removed from the population count until 1909.

There's a simple fix: instead of decrementing `array[deathYear]`, we should decrement `array[deathYear + 1]`.

```
int maxAliveYear(Person[] people, int min, int max) {
```

```
    /* Build population delta array. */
    int[] populationDeltas = getPopulationDeltas(people, min, max);
    int maxAliveYear = getMaxAliveYear(populationDeltas);
    return maxAliveYear + min;
  }

  /* Add birth and death years to deltas array. */
  int[] getPopulationDeltas(Person[] people, int min, int max) {
    int[] populationDeltas = new int[max - min + 2];
    for (Person person : people) {
      int birth = person.birth - min;
      populationDeltas[birth]++;

      int death = person.death - min;
      populationDeltas[death + 1]--;
    }
    return populationDeltas;
  }

  /* Compute running sums and return index with max. */
  int getMaxAliveYear(int[] deltas) {
    int maxAliveYear = 0;
    int maxAlive = 0;
    int currentlyAlive = 0;
    for (int year = 0; year < deltas.length; year++) {
      currentlyAlive += deltas[year];
      if (currentlyAlive > maxAlive) {
        maxAliveYear = year;
        maxAlive = currentlyAlive;
      }
    }

    return maxAliveYear;
  }
```

This algorithm takes `O(R + P)` time, where R is the range of years and P is the number of people. Although `O(R + P)` might be faster than `O(P log P)` for many expected inputs, you cannot directly compare the speeds to say that one is faster than the other.

16.11 Diving Board: You are building a diving board by placing a bunch of planks of wood end-to-end. There are two types of planks, one of length `shorter` and one of length `longer`. You must use exactly K planks of wood. Write a method to generate all possible lengths for the diving board.

pg 182

SOLUTION

One way to approach this is to think about the choices we make as we're building a diving board. This leads us to a recursive algorithm.

Recursive Solution

For a recursive solution, we can imagine ourselves building a diving board. We make K decisions, each time choosing which plank we will put on next. Once we've put on K planks, we have a complete diving board and we can add this to the list (assuming we haven't seen this length before).

We can follow this logic to write recursive code. Note that we don't need to track the sequence of planks. All we need to know is the current length and the number of planks remaining.

```
HashSet<Integer> allLengths(int k, int shorter, int longer) {
  HashSet<Integer> lengths = new HashSet<Integer>();
  getAllLengths(k, 0, shorter, longer, lengths);
  return lengths;
}

void getAllLengths(int k, int total, int shorter, int longer,
                   HashSet<Integer> lengths) {
  if (k == 0) {
    lengths.add(total);
    return;
  }
  getAllLengths(k - 1, total + shorter, shorter, longer, lengths);
  getAllLengths(k - 1, total + longer, shorter, longer, lengths);
}
```

We've added each length to a hash set. This will automatically prevent adding duplicates.

This algorithm takes $O(2^K)$ time, since there are two choices at each recursive call and we recurse to a depth of K.

Memoization Solution

As in many recursive algorithms (especially those with exponential runtimes), we can optimize this through memorization (a form of dynamic programming).

Observe that some of the recursive calls will be essentially equivalent. For example, picking plank 1 and then plank 2 is equivalent to picking plank 2 and then plank 1.

Therefore, if we've seen this `(total, plank count)` pair before then we stop this recursive path. We can do this using a `HashSet` with a key of `(total, plank count)`.

> Many candidates will make a mistake here. Rather than stopping only when they've seen `(total, plank count)`, they'll stop whenever they've seen just `total` before. This is incorrect. Seeing two planks of length 1 is not the same thing as one plank of length 2, because there are different numbers of planks remaining. In memoization problems, be very careful about what you choose for your key.

The code for this approach is very similar to the earlier approach.

```
HashSet<Integer> allLengths(int k, int shorter, int longer) {
  HashSet<Integer> lengths = new HashSet<Integer>();
  HashSet<String> visited = new HashSet<String>();
  getAllLengths(k, 0, shorter, longer, lengths, visited);
  return lengths;
}

void getAllLengths(int k, int total, int shorter, int longer,
                   HashSet<Integer> lengths, HashSet<String> visited) {
  if (k == 0) {
    lengths.add(total);
    return;
  }
  String key = k + " " + total;
```

```
    if (visited.contains(key)) { // If we've seen this before, then just exit
       return;
    }
    getAllLengths(k - 1, total + shorter, shorter, longer, lengths, visited);
    getAllLengths(k - 1, total + longer, shorter, longer, lengths, visited);
    visited.add(key); // Record that we've seen this before
}
```

For simplicity, we've set the key to be a string representation of `total` and the current plank count. Some people may argue it's better to use a data structure to represent this pair. There are benefits to this, but there are drawbacks as well. It's worth discussing this tradeoff with your interviewer.

The runtime of this algorithm is a bit tricky to figure out.

One way we can think about the runtime is by understanding that we're basically filling in a table of SUMS x PLANK COUNTS. The biggest possible sum is K * LONGER and the biggest possible plank count is K. Therefore, the runtime will be no worse than $O(K^2 * LONGER)$.

Of course, a bunch of those sums will never actually be reached. How many unique sums can we get? Observe that any path with the same number of each type of planks will have the same sum. Since we can have at most K planks of each type, there are only K+1 different sums we can make. Therefore, the table really has $(K+1)^2$ cells, and the runtime is $O(K^2)$.

Optimal Solution

If you re-read the prior paragraph, you might notice something interesting. There are only K distinct sums we can get. Isn't that the whole point of the problem—to find all possible sums?

We don't actually need to go through all arrangements of planks. We just need to go through all unique sets of K planks (sets, not orders!). There are only K+1 ways of picking K planks if we only have two possible types: {0 of type A, K of type B}, {1 of type A, K-1 of type B}, {2 of type A, K-2 of type B}, ...

This can be done in just a simple for loop. At each "sequence", we just compute the sum.

```
HashSet<Integer> allLengths(int k, int shorter, int longer) {
   HashSet<Integer> lengths = new HashSet<Integer>();
   for (int nShorter = 0; nShorter <= k; nShorter++) {
      int nLonger = k - nShorter;
      int length = nShorter * shorter + nLonger * longer;
      lengths.add(length);
   }
   return lengths;
}
```

We've used a `HashSet` here for consistency with the prior solutions. This isn't really necessary though, since we shouldn't get any duplicates. We could instead use an `ArrayList`. If we do this, though, we just need to handle an edge case where the two types of planks are the same length. In this case, we would just return an `ArrayList` of size 1.

16.12 XML Encoding: Since XML is very verbose, you are given a way of encoding it where each tag gets mapped to a pre-defined integer value. The language/grammar is as follows:

```
Element   --> Tag Attributes END Children END
Attribute --> Tag Value
END       --> 0
Tag       --> some predefined mapping to int
Value     --> string value
```

For example, the following XML might be converted into the compressed string below (assuming a mapping of `family -> 1, person ->2, firstName -> 3, lastName -> 4, state -> 5`).

```
<family lastName="McDowell" state="CA">
  <person firstName="Gayle">Some Message</person>
</family>
```

Becomes:

```
1 4 McDowell 5 CA 0 2 3 Gayle 0 Some Message 0 0
```

Write code to print the encoded version of an XML element (passed in `Element` and `Attribute` objects).

pg 182

SOLUTION

Since we know the element will be passed in as an `Element` and `Attribute`, our code is reasonably simple. We can implement this by applying a tree-like approach.

We repeatedly call `encode()` on parts of the XML structure, handling the code in slightly different ways depending on the type of the XML element.

```
void encode(Element root, StringBuilder sb) {
  encode(root.getNameCode(), sb);
  for (Attribute a : root.attributes) {
    encode(a, sb);
  }
  encode(“0”, sb);
  if (root.value != null && root.value != “”) {
    encode(root.value, sb);
  } else {
    for (Element e : root.children) {
      encode(e, sb);
    }
  }
  encode(“0”, sb);
}

void encode(String v, StringBuilder sb) {
  sb.append(v);
  sb.append(“ “);
}

void encode(Attribute attr, StringBuilder sb) {
  encode(attr.getTagCode(), sb);
  encode(attr.value, sb);
}

```

```
27 String encodeToString(Element root) {
28    StringBuilder sb = new StringBuilder();
29    encode(root, sb);
30    return sb.toString();
31 }
```

Observe in line 17, the use of the very simple `encode` method for a string. This is somewhat unnecessary; all it does is insert the string and a space following it. However, using this method is a nice touch as it ensures that every element will be inserted with a space surrounding it. Otherwise, it might be easy to break the encoding by forgetting to append the empty string.

16.13 Bisect Squares: Given two squares on a two-dimensional plane, find a line that would cut these two squares in half. Assume that the top and the bottom sides of the square run parallel to the x-axis.

pg 182

SOLUTION

Before we start, we should think about what exactly this problem means by a "line." Is a line defined by a slope and a y-intercept? Or by any two points on the line? Or, should the line be really a line segment, which starts and ends at the edges of the squares?

We will assume, since it makes the problem a bit more interesting, that we mean the third option: that the line should end at the edges of the squares. In an interview situation, you should discuss this with your interviewer.

This line that cuts two squares in half must connect the two middles. We can easily calculate the slope, knowing that `slope` $= \frac{y1 - y2}{x1 - x2}$. Once we calculate the slope using the two middles, we can use the same equation to calculate the start and end points of the line segment.

In the below code, we will assume the origin `(0, 0)` is in the upper left-hand corner.

```
public class Square {
   ...
   public Point middle() {
      return new Point((this.left + this.right) / 2.0,
                       (this.top + this.bottom) / 2.0);
   }

   /* Return the point where the line segment connecting mid1 and mid2 intercepts
    * the edge of square 1. That is, draw a line from mid2 to mid1, and continue it
    * out until the edge of the square. */
   public Point extend(Point mid1, Point mid2, double size) {
      /* Find what direction the line mid2 -> mid1 goes. */
      double xdir = mid1.x < mid2.x ? -1 : 1;
      double ydir = mid1.y < mid2.y ? -1 : 1;

      /* If mid1 and mid2 have the same x value, then the slope calculation will
       * throw a divide by 0 exception. So, we compute this specially. */
      if (mid1.x == mid2.x) {
         return new Point(mid1.x, mid1.y + ydir * size / 2.0);
      }

      double slope = (mid1.y - mid2.y) / (mid1.x - mid2.x);
      double x1 = 0;
      double y1 = 0;

```

```
    /* Calculate slope using the equation (y1 - y2) / (x1 - x2).
     * Note: if the slope is "steep" (>1) then the end of the line segment will
     * hit size / 2 units away from the middle on the y axis. If the slope is
     * "shallow" (<1) the end of the line segment will hit size / 2 units away
     * from the middle on the x axis. */
    if (Math.abs(slope) == 1) {
      x1 = mid1.x + xdir * size / 2.0;
      y1 = mid1.y + ydir * size / 2.0;
    } else if (Math.abs(slope) < 1) { // shallow slope
      x1 = mid1.x + xdir * size / 2.0;
      y1 = slope * (x1 - mid1.x) + mid1.y;
    } else { // steep slope
      y1 = mid1.y + ydir * size / 2.0;
      x1 = (y1 - mid1.y) / slope + mid1.x;
    }
    return new Point(x1, y1);
  }

  public Line cut(Square other) {
    /* Calculate where a line between each middle would collide with the edges of
     * the squares */
    Point p1 = extend(this.middle(), other.middle(), this.size);
    Point p2 = extend(this.middle(), other.middle(), -1 * this.size);
    Point p3 = extend(other.middle(), this.middle(), other.size);
    Point p4 = extend(other.middle(), this.middle(), -1 * other.size);

    /* Of above points, find start and end of lines. Start is farthest left (with
     * top most as a tie breaker) and end is farthest right (with bottom most as
     * a tie breaker. */
    Point start = p1;
    Point end = p1;
    Point[] points = {p2, p3, p4};
    for (int i = 0; i < points.length; i++) {
      if (points[i].x < start.x ||
         (points[i].x == start.x && points[i].y < start.y)) {
        start = points[i];
      } else if (points[i].x > end.x ||
              (points[i].x == end.x && points[i].y > end.y)) {
        end = points[i];
      }
    }

    return new Line(start, end);
  }
```

The main goal of this problem is to see how careful you are about coding. It's easy to glance over the special cases (e.g., the two squares having the same middle). You should make a list of these special cases before you start the problem and make sure to handle them appropriately. This is a question that requires careful and thorough testing.

16.14 Best Line: Given a two-dimensional graph with points on it, find a line which passes the most number of points.

pg 183

SOLUTION

This solution seems quite straightforward at first. And it is—sort of.

We just "draw" an infinite line (that is, not a line segment) between every two points and, using a hash table, track which line is the most common. This will take $O(N^2)$ time, since there are N^2 line segments.

We will represent a line as a slope and y-intercept (as opposed to a pair of points), which allows us to easily check to see if the line from `(x1, y1)` to `(x2, y2)` is equivalent to the line from `(x3, y3)` to `(x4, y4)`.

To find the most common line then, we just iterate through all lines segments, using a hash table to count the number of times we've seen each line. Easy enough!

However, there's one little complication. We're defining two lines to be equal if the lines have the same slope and y-intercept. We are then, furthermore, hashing the lines based on these values (specifically, based on the slope). The problem is that floating point numbers cannot always be represented accurately in binary. We resolve this by checking if two floating point numbers are within an `epsilon` value of each other.

What does this mean for our hash table? It means that two lines with "equal" slopes may not be hashed to the same value. To solve this, we will round the slope down to the next epsilon and use this `flooredSlope` as the hash key. Then, to retrieve all lines that are *potentially* equal, we will search the hash table at three spots: `flooredSlope`, `flooredSlope - epsilon`, and `flooredSlope + epsilon`. This will ensure that we've checked out all lines that might be equal.

```
/* Find line that goes through most number of points. */
Line findBestLine(GraphPoint[] points) {
  HashMapList<Double, Line> linesBySlope = getListOfLines(points);
  return getBestLine(linesBySlope);
}

/* Add each pair of points as a line to the list. */
HashMapList<Double, Line> getListOfLines(GraphPoint[] points) {
  HashMapList<Double, Line> linesBySlope = new HashMapList<Double, Line>();
  for (int i = 0; i < points.length; i++) {
    for (int j = i + 1; j < points.length; j++) {
      Line line = new Line(points[i], points[j]);
      double key = Line.floorToNearestEpsilon(line.slope);
      linesBySlope.put(key, line);
    }
  }
  return linesBySlope;
}

/* Return the line with the most equivalent other lines. */
Line getBestLine(HashMapList<Double, Line> linesBySlope) {
  Line bestLine = null;
  int bestCount = 0;

  Set<Double> slopes = linesBySlope.keySet();

  for (double slope : slopes) {
```

```
      ArrayList<Line> lines = linesBySlope.get(slope);
      for (Line line : lines) {
         /* count lines that are equivalent to current line */
         int count = countEquivalentLines(linesBySlope, line);

         /* if better than current line, replace it */
         if (count > bestCount) {
            bestLine = line;
            bestCount = count;
            bestLine.Print();
            System.out.println(bestCount);
         }
      }
   }
   return bestLine;
}

/* Check hashmap for lines that are equivalent. Note that we need to check one
 * epsilon above and below the actual slope since we're defining two lines as
 * equivalent if they're within an epsilon of each other. */
int countEquivalentLines(HashMapList<Double, Line> linesBySlope, Line line) {
   double key = Line.floorToNearestEpsilon(line.slope);
   int count = countEquivalentLines(linesBySlope.get(key), line);
   count += countEquivalentLines(linesBySlope.get(key - Line.epsilon), line);
   count += countEquivalentLines(linesBySlope.get(key + Line.epsilon), line);
   return count;
}

/* Count lines within an array of lines which are "equivalent" (slope and
 * y-intercept are within an epsilon value) to a given line */
int countEquivalentLines(ArrayList<Line> lines, Line line) {
   if (lines == null) return 0;

   int count = 0;
   for (Line parallelLine : lines) {
      if (parallelLine.isEquivalent(line)) {
         count++;
      }
   }
   return count;
}

public class Line {
   public static double epsilon = .0001;
   public double slope, intercept;
   private boolean infinite_slope = false;

   public Line(GraphPoint p, GraphPoint q) {
      if (Math.abs(p.x - q.x) > epsilon) { // if x's are different
         slope = (p.y - q.y) / (p.x - q.x); // compute slope
         intercept = p.y - slope * p.x; // y intercept from y=mx+b
      } else {
         infinite_slope = true;
         intercept = p.x; // x-intercept, since slope is infinite
      }
   }
```

```
    public static double floorToNearestEpsilon(double d) {
        int r = (int) (d / epsilon);
        return ((double) r) * epsilon;
    }

    public boolean isEquivalent(double a, double b) {
        return (Math.abs(a - b) < epsilon);
    }

    public boolean isEquivalent(Object o) {
        Line l = (Line) o;
        if (isEquivalent(l.slope, slope) && isEquivalent(l.intercept, intercept) &&
            (infinite_slope == l.infinite_slope)) {
            return true;
        }
        return false;
    }
}

/* HashMapList<String, Integer> is a HashMap that maps from Strings to
 * ArrayList<Integer>. See appendix for implementation. */
```

We need to be careful about the calculation of the slope of a line. The line might be completely vertical, which means that it doesn't have a y-intercept and its slope is infinite. We can keep track of this in a separate flag (`infinite_slope`). We need to check this condition in the equals method.

16.15 Master Mind: The Game of Master Mind is played as follows:

The computer has four slots, and each slot will contain a ball that is red (R), yellow (Y), green (G) or blue (B). For example, the computer might have RGGB (Slot #1 is red, Slots #2 and #3 are green, Slot #4 is blue).

You, the user, are trying to guess the solution. You might, for example, guess YRGB.

When you guess the correct color for the correct slot, you get a "hit." If you guess a color that exists but is in the wrong slot, you get a "pseudo-hit." Note that a slot that is a hit can never count as a pseudo-hit.

For example, if the actual solution is RGBY and you guess GGRR, you have one hit and one pseudo-hit.

Write a method that, given a guess and a solution, returns the number of hits and pseudo-hits.

pg 183

SOLUTION

This problem is straightforward, but it's surprisingly easy to make little mistakes. You should check your code *extremely* thoroughly, on a variety of test cases.

We'll implement this code by first creating a frequency array which stores how many times each character occurs in `solution`, excluding times when the slot is a "hit." Then, we iterate through `guess` to count the number of pseudo-hits.

The code below implements this algorithm.

```
class Result {
    public int hits = 0;
```

```
    public int pseudoHits = 0;

    public String toString() {
       return "(" + hits + ", " + pseudoHits + ")";
    }
 }

 int code(char c) {
    switch (c) {
    case 'B':
       return 0;
    case 'G':
       return 1;
    case 'R':
       return 2;
    case 'Y':
       return 3;
    default:
       return -1;
    }
 }

 int MAX_COLORS = 4;

 Result estimate(String guess, String solution) {
    if (guess.length() != solution.length()) return null;

    Result res = new Result();
    int[] frequencies = new int[MAX_COLORS];

    /* Compute hits and build frequency table */
    for (int i = 0; i < guess.length(); i++) {
       if (guess.charAt(i) == solution.charAt(i)) {
          res.hits++;
       } else {
          /* Only increment the frequency table (which will be used for pseudo-hits)
           * if it's not a hit. If it's a hit, the slot has already been "used." */
          int code = code(solution.charAt(i));
          frequencies[code]++;
       }
    }

    /* Compute pseudo-hits */
    for (int i = 0; i < guess.length(); i++) {
       int code = code(guess.charAt(i));
       if (code >= 0 && frequencies[code] > 0 &&
           guess.charAt(i) != solution.charAt(i)) {
          res.pseudoHits++;
          frequencies[code]--;
       }
    }
    return res;
 }
```

Note that the easier the algorithm for a problem is, the more important it is to write clean and correct code. In this case, we've pulled `code(char c)` into its own method, and we've created a `Result` class to hold the result, rather than just printing it.

16.16 Sub Sort: Given an array of integers, write a method to find indices m and n such that if you sorted elements m through n, the entire array would be sorted. Minimize n - m (that is, find the smallest such sequence).

EXAMPLE

Input: `1, 2, 4, 7, 10, 11, 7, 12, 6, 7, 16, 18, 19`

Output: `(3, 9)`

pg 183

SOLUTION

Before we begin, let's make sure we understand what our answer will look like. If we're looking for just two indices, this indicates that some middle section of the array will be sorted, with the start and end of the array already being in order.

Now, let's approach this problem by looking at an example.

```
1, 2, 4, 7, 10, 11, 8, 12, 5, 6, 16, 18, 19
```

Our first thought might be to just find the longest increasing subsequence at the beginning and the longest increasing subsequence at the end.

```
left:   1, 2, 4, 7, 10, 11
middle: 8, 12
right:  5, 6, 16, 18, 19
```

These subsequences are easy to generate. We just start from the left and the right sides, and work our way inward. When an element is out of order, then we have found the end of our increasing/decreasing subsequence.

In order to solve our problem, though, we would need to be able to sort the middle part of the array and, by doing just that, get all the elements in the array in order. Specifically, the following would have to be true:

```
/* all items on left are smaller than all items in middle */
min(middle) > end(left)

/* all items in middle are smaller than all items in right */
max(middle) < start(right)
```

Or, in other words, for all elements:

```
left < middle < right
```

In fact, this condition will *never* be met. The middle section is, by definition, the elements that were out of order. That is, it is *always* the case that `left.end > middle.start` and `middle.end > right.start`. Thus, you cannot sort the middle to make the entire array sorted.

But, what we can do is *shrink* the left and right subsequences until the earlier conditions are met. We need the left part to be smaller than all the elements in the middle and right side, and the right part to be bigger than all the elements on the left and right side.

Let `min` equal `min(middle and right side)` and `max` equal `max(middle and left side)`. Observe that since the right and left sides are already in sorted order, we only actually need to check their start or end point.

On the left side, we start with the end of the subsequence (value 11, at element 5) and move to the left. The value `min` equals 5. Once we find an element `i` such that `array[i] < min`, we know that we could sort the middle and have that part of the array appear in order.

Then, we do a similar thing on the right side. The value max equals 12. So, we begin with the start of the right subsequence (value 5) and move to the right. We compare the max of 12 to 6, then 16. When reach 16, we know that no elements smaller than 12 could be after it (since it's an increasing subsequence). Thus, the middle of the array could now be sorted to make the entire array sorted.

The following code implements this algorithm.

```
void findUnsortedSequence(int[] array) {
  // find left subsequence
  int end_left = findEndOfLeftSubsequence(array);
  if (end_left >= array.length - 1) return; // Already sorted

  // find right subsequence
  int start_right = findStartOfRightSubsequence(array);

  // get min and max
  int max_index = end_left; // max of left side
  int min_index = start_right; // min of right side
  for (int i = end_left + 1; i < start_right; i++) {
    if (array[i] < array[min_index]) min_index = i;
    if (array[i] > array[max_index]) max_index = i;
  }

  // slide left until less than array[min_index]
  int left_index = shrinkLeft(array, min_index, end_left);

  // slide right until greater than array[max_index]
  int right_index = shrinkRight(array, max_index, start_right);

  System.out.println(left_index + " " + right_index);
}

int findEndOfLeftSubsequence(int[] array) {
  for (int i = 1; i < array.length; i++) {
    if (array[i] < array[i - 1]) return i - 1;
  }
  return array.length - 1;
}

int findStartOfRightSubsequence(int[] array) {
  for (int i = array.length - 2; i >= 0; i--) {
    if (array[i] > array[i + 1]) return i + 1;
  }
  return 0;
}

int shrinkLeft(int[] array, int min_index, int start) {
  int comp = array[min_index];
  for (int i = start - 1; i >= 0; i--) {
    if (array[i] <= comp) return i + 1;
  }
  return 0;
}

int shrinkRight(int[] array, int max_index, int start) {
  int comp = array[max_index];
  for (int i = start; i < array.length; i++) {
```

```
        if (array[i] >= comp) return i - 1;
    }
    return array.length - 1;
}
```

Note the use of other methods in this solution. Although we could have jammed it all into one method, it would have made the code a lot harder to understand, maintain, and test. In your interview coding, you should prioritize these aspects.

16.17 Contiguous Sequence: You are given an array of integers (both positive and negative). Find the contiguous sequence with the largest sum. Return the sum.

EXAMPLE

Input: `2, -8, 3, -2, 4, -10`

Output: 5 `(i.e., {3, -2, 4})`

pg 183

SOLUTION

This is a challenging problem, but an extremely common one. Let's approach this by looking at an example:

```
2   3   -8   -1   2   4   -2   3
```

If we think about our array as having alternating sequences of positive and negative numbers, we can observe that we would never include only part of a negative subsequence or part of a positive sequence. Why would we? Including part of a negative subsequence would make things unnecessarily negative, and we should just instead not include that negative sequence at all. Likewise, including only part of a positive subsequence would be strange, since the sum would be even bigger if we included the whole thing.

For the purposes of coming up with our algorithm, we can think about our array as being a sequence of alternating negative and positive numbers. Each number corresponds to the sum of a subsequence of positive numbers of a subsequence of negative numbers. For the array above, our new reduced array would be:

```
5   -9   6   -2   3
```

This doesn't give away a great algorithm immediately, but it does help us to better understand what we're working with.

Consider the array above. Would it ever make sense to have `{5, -9}` in a subsequence? No. These numbers sum to `-4`, so we're better off not including either number, or possibly just having the sequence be just `{5}`).

When would we want negative numbers included in a subsequence? Only if it allows us to join two positive subsequences, each of which have a sum greater than the negative value.

We can approach this in a step-wise manner, starting with the first element in the array.

When we look at 5, this is the biggest sum we've seen so far. We set `maxSum` to 5, and `sum` to 5. Then, we consider -9. If we added it to `sum`, we'd get a negative value. There's no sense in extending the subsequence from 5 to -9 (which "reduces" to a sequence of just -4), so we just reset the value of `sum`.

Now, we consider 6. This subsequence is greater than 5, so we update both `maxSum` and `sum`.

Next, we look at -2. Adding this to 6 will set `sum` to 4. Since this is still a "value add" (when adjoined to another, bigger sequence), we *might* want `{6, -2}` in our max subsequence. We'll update `sum`, but not `maxSum`.

Finally, we look at 3. Adding 3 to `sum` (4) gives us 7, so we update `maxSum`. The max subsequence is therefore the sequence `{6, -2, 3}`.

When we look at this in the fully expanded array, our logic is identical. The code below implements this algorithm.

```
int getMaxSum(int[] a) {
   int maxsum = 0;
   int sum = 0;
   for (int i = 0; i < a.length; i++) {
      sum += a[i];
      if (maxsum < sum) {
         maxsum = sum;
      } else if (sum < 0) {
         sum = 0;
      }
   }
   return maxsum;
}
```

If the array is all negative numbers, what is the correct behavior? Consider this simple array: `{-3, -10, -5}`. You could make a good argument that the maximum sum is either:

1. -3 (if you assume the subsequence can't be empty)
2. 0 (the subsequence has length 0)
3. `MINIMUM_INT` (essentially, the error case).

We went with option #2 (`maxSum = 0`), but there's no "correct" answer. This is a great thing to discuss with your interviewer; it will show how detail-oriented you are.

16.18 Pattern Matching: You are given two strings, `pattern` and `value`. The `pattern` string consists of just the letters a and b, describing a pattern within a string. For example, the string `catcatgocatgo` matches the pattern `aabab` (where `cat` is a and go is b). It also matches patterns like a, ab, and b. Write a method to determine if `value` matches `pattern`.

pg 183

SOLUTION

As always, we can start with a simple brute force approach.

Brute Force

A brute force algorithm is to just try all possible values for a and b and then check if this works.

We could do this by iterating through all substrings for a and all possible substrings for b. There are $O(n^2)$ substrings in a string of length n, so this will actually take $O(n^4)$ time. But then, for each value of a and b, we need to build the new string of this length and compare it for equality. This building/comparison step takes $O(n)$ time, giving an overall runtime of $O(n^5)$.

```
for each possible substring a
   for each possible substring b
      candidate = buildFromPattern(pattern, a, b)
      if candidate equals value
         return true
```

Ouch.

One easy optimization is to notice that if the pattern starts with 'a', then the a string must start at the beginning of `value`. (Otherwise, the b string must start at the beginning of `value`.) Therefore, there aren't $O(n^2)$ possible values for a; there are $O(n)$.

The algorithm then is to check if the pattern starts with a or b. If it starts with b, we can "invert" it (flipping each 'a' to a 'b' and each 'b' to an 'a') so that it starts with 'a'. Then, iterate through all possible substrings for a (each of which must begin at index 0) and all possible substrings for b (each of which must begin at some character after the end of a). As before, we then compare the string for this pattern with the original string.

This algorithm now takes $O(n^4)$ time.

There's one more minor (optional) optimization we can make. We don't actually need to do this "inversion" if the string starts with 'b' instead of 'a'. The `buildFromPattern` method can take care of this. We can think about the first character in the pattern as the "main" item and the other character as the alternate character. The `buildFromPattern` method can build the appropriate string based on whether 'a' is the main character or alternate character.

```
boolean doesMatch(String pattern, String value) {
   if (pattern.length() == 0) return value.length() == 0;

   int size = value.length();
   for (int mainSize = 0; mainSize < size; mainSize++) {
      String main = value.substring(0, mainSize);
      for (int altStart = mainSize; altStart <= size; altStart++) {
         for (int altEnd = altStart; altEnd <= size; altEnd++) {
            String alt = value.substring(altStart, altEnd);
            String cand = buildFromPattern(pattern, main, alt);
            if (cand.equals(value)) {
               return true;
            }
         }
      }
   }
   return false;
}

String buildFromPattern(String pattern, String main, String alt) {
   StringBuffer sb = new StringBuffer();
   char first = pattern.charAt(0);
   for (char c : pattern.toCharArray()) {
      if (c == first) {
         sb.append(main);
      } else {
         sb.append(alt);
      }
   }
   return sb.toString();
}
```

We should look for a more optimal algorithm.

Optimized

Let's think through our current algorithm. Searching through all values for the main string is fairly fast (it takes $O(n)$ time). It's the alternate string that is so slow: $O(n^2)$ time. We should study how to optimize that.

Suppose we have a pattern like aabab and we're comparing it to the string catcatgocatgo. Once we've picked "cat" as the value for a to try, then the a strings are going to take up nine characters (three a strings with length three each). Therefore, the b strings must take up the remaining four characters, with each having length two. Moreover, we actually know exactly where they must occur, too. If a is cat, and the pattern is aabab, then b must be go.

In other words, once we've picked a, we've picked b too. There's no need to iterate. Gathering some basic stats on pattern (number of as, number of bs, first occurrence of each) and iterating through values for a (or whichever the main string is) will be sufficient.

```
boolean doesMatch(String pattern, String value) {
  if (pattern.length() == 0) return value.length() == 0;

  char mainChar = pattern.charAt(0);
  char altChar = mainChar == 'a' ? 'b' : 'a';
  int size = value.length();

  int countOfMain = countOf(pattern, mainChar);
  int countOfAlt = pattern.length() - countOfMain;
  int firstAlt = pattern.indexOf(altChar);
  int maxMainSize = size / countOfMain;

  for (int mainSize = 0; mainSize <= maxMainSize; mainSize++) {
    int remainingLength = size - mainSize * countOfMain;
    String first = value.substring(0, mainSize);
    if (countOfAlt == 0 || remainingLength % countOfAlt == 0) {
      int altIndex = firstAlt * mainSize;
      int altSize = countOfAlt == 0 ? 0 : remainingLength / countOfAlt;
      String second = countOfAlt == 0 ? "" :
                      value.substring(altIndex, altSize + altIndex);

      String cand = buildFromPattern(pattern, first, second);
      if (cand.equals(value)) {
        return true;
      }
    }
  }
  return false;
}

int countOf(String pattern, char c) {
  int count = 0;
  for (int i = 0; i < pattern.length(); i++) {
    if (pattern.charAt(i) == c) {
      count++;
    }
  }
  return count;
}

String buildFromPattern(...) {  /* same as before */ }
```

This algorithm takes $O(n^2)$, since we iterate through O(n) possibilities for the main string and do O(n) work to build and compare the strings.

Observe that we've also cut down the possibilities for the main string that we try. If there are three instances of the main string, then its length cannot be any more than one third of value.

Optimized (Alternate)

If you don't like the work of building a string only to compare it (and then destroy it), we can eliminate this.

Instead, we can iterate through the values for a and b as before. But this time, to check if the string matches the pattern (given those values for a and b), we walk through `value`, comparing each substring to the first instance of the a and b strings.

```
boolean doesMatch(String pattern, String value) {
  if (pattern.length() == 0) return value.length() == 0;

  char mainChar = pattern.charAt(0);
  char altChar = mainChar == 'a' ? 'b' : 'a';
  int size = value.length();

  int countOfMain = countOf(pattern, mainChar);
  int countOfAlt = pattern.length() - countOfMain;
  int firstAlt = pattern.indexOf(altChar);
  int maxMainSize = size / countOfMain;

  for (int mainSize = 0; mainSize <= maxMainSize; mainSize++) {
    int remainingLength = size - mainSize * countOfMain;
    if (countOfAlt == 0 || remainingLength % countOfAlt == 0) {
      int altIndex = firstAlt * mainSize;
      int altSize = countOfAlt == 0 ? 0 : remainingLength / countOfAlt;
      if (matches(pattern, value, mainSize, altSize, altIndex)) {
        return true;
      }
    }
  }
  return false;
}

/* Iterates through pattern and value. At each character within pattern, checks if
 * this is the main string or the alternate string. Then checks if the next set of
 * characters in value match the original set of those characters (either the main
 * or the alternate. */
boolean matches(String pattern, String value, int mainSize, int altSize,
                int firstAlt) {
  int stringIndex = mainSize;
  for (int i = 1; i < pattern.length(); i++) {
    int size = pattern.charAt(i) == pattern.charAt(0) ? mainSize : altSize;
    int offset = pattern.charAt(i) == pattern.charAt(0) ? 0 : firstAlt;
    if (!isEqual(value, offset, stringIndex, size)) {
      return false;
    }
    stringIndex += size;
  }
  return true;
}

/* Checks if two substrings are equal, starting at given offsets and continuing to
 * size. */
boolean isEqual(String s1, int offset1, int offset2, int size) {
  for (int i = 0; i < size; i++) {
    if (s1.charAt(offset1 + i) != s1.charAt(offset2 + i)) {
      return false;
```

```
        }
    }
    return true;
}
```

This algorithm will still take $O(n^2)$ time, but the benefit is that it can short circuit when matches fail early (which they usually will). The previous algorithm must go through all the work to build the string before it can learn that it has failed.

16.19 Pond Sizes: You have an integer matrix representing a plot of land, where the value at that location represents the height above sea level. A value of zero indicates water. A pond is a region of water connected vertically, horizontally, or diagonally. The size of the pond is the total number of connected water cells. Write a method to compute the sizes of all ponds in the matrix.

EXAMPLE

Input:

```
0 2 1 0
0 1 0 1
1 1 0 1
0 1 0 1
```

Output: 2, 4, 1 (in any order)

pg 184

SOLUTION

The first thing we can try is just walking through the array. It's easy enough to find water: when it's a zero, that's water.

Given a water cell, how can we compute the amount of water nearby? If the cell is not adjacent to any zero cells, then the size of this pond is 1. If it is, then we need to add in the adjacent cells, plus any water cells adjacent to those cells. We need to, of course, be careful to not recount any cells. We can do this with a modified breadth-first or depth-first search. Once we visit a cell, we permanently mark it as visited.

For each cell, we need to check eight adjacent cells. We could do this by writing in lines to check up, down, left, right, and each of the four diagonal cells. It's even easier, though, to do this with a loop.

```
ArrayList<Integer> computePondSizes(int[][] land) {
   ArrayList<Integer> pondSizes = new ArrayList<Integer>();
   for (int r = 0; r < land.length; r++) {
      for (int c = 0; c < land[r].length; c++) {
         if (land[r][c] == 0) { // Optional. Would return anyway.
            int size = computeSize(land, r, c);
            pondSizes.add(size);
         }
      }
   }
   return pondSizes;
}

int computeSize(int[][] land, int row, int col) {
   /* If out of bounds or already visited. */
   if (row < 0 || col < 0 || row >= land.length || col >= land[row].length ||
        land[row][col] != 0) { // visited or not water
      return 0;
   }
```

```
    int size = 1;
    land[row][col] = -1; // Mark visited
    for (int dr = -1; dr <= 1; dr++) {
       for (int dc = -1; dc <= 1; dc++) {
          size += computeSize(land, row + dr, col + dc);
       }
    }
    return size;
}
```

In this case, we marked a cell as visited by setting its value to -1. This allows us to check, in one line (`land[row][col] != 0`), if the value is valid dry land or visited. In either case, the value will be zero.

You might also notice that the for loop iterates through nine cells, not eight. It includes the current cell. We could add a line in there to not recurse if `dr == 0` and `dc == 0`. This really doesn't save us much. We'll execute this if-statement in eight cells unnecessarily, just to avoid one recursive call. The recursive call returns immediately since the cell is marked as visited.

If you don't like modifying the input matrix, you can create a secondary `visited` matrix.

```
ArrayList<Integer> computePondSizes(int[][] land) {
   boolean[][] visited = new boolean[land.length][land[0].length];
   ArrayList<Integer> pondSizes = new ArrayList<Integer>();
   for (int r = 0; r < land.length; r++) {
      for (int c = 0; c < land[r].length; c++) {
         int size = computeSize(land, visited, r, c);
         if (size > 0) {
            pondSizes.add(size);
         }
      }
   }
   return pondSizes;
}

int computeSize(int[][] land, boolean[][] visited, int row, int col) {
   /* If out of bounds or already visited. */
   if (row < 0 || col < 0 || row >= land.length || col >= land[row].length ||
       visited[row][col] || land[row][col] != 0) {
      return 0;
   }
   int size = 1;
   visited[row][col] = true;
   for (int dr = -1; dr <= 1; dr++) {
      for (int dc = -1; dc <= 1; dc++) {
         size += computeSize(land, visited, row + dr, col + dc);
      }
   }
   return size;
}
```

Both implementations are O(WH), where W is the width of the matrix and H is the height.

> Note: Many people say "O(N)" or "O(N^2)", as though N has some inherent meaning. It doesn't. Suppose this were a square matrix. You could describe the runtime as O(N) or O(N^2). Both are correct, depending on what you mean by N. The runtime is O(N^2), where N is the length of one side. Or, if N is the number of cells, it is O(N). Be careful by what you mean by N. In fact, it might be safer to just not use N at all when there's any ambiguity as to what it could mean.

Some people will miscompute the runtime to be $O(N^4)$, reasoning that the computeSize method could take as long as $O(N^2)$ time and you might call it as much as $O(N^2)$ times (and apparently assuming an **NxN** matrix, too). While those are both basically correct statements, you can't just multiply them together. That's because as a single call to computeSize gets more expensive, the number of times it is called goes down.

For example, suppose the very first call to computeSize goes through the entire matrix. That might take $O(N^2)$ time, but then we never call computeSize again.

Another way to compute this is to think about how many times each cell is "touched" by either call. Each cell will be touched once by the computePondSizes function. Additionally, a cell might be touched once by each of its adjacent cells. This is still a constant number of touches per cell. Therefore, the overall runtime is $O(N^2)$ on an NxN matrix or, more generally, $O(WH)$.

16.20 **T9:** On old cell phones, users typed on a numeric keypad and the phone would provide a list of words that matched these numbers. Each digit mapped to a set of 0 - 4 letters. Implement an algorithm to return a list of matching words, given a sequence of digits. You are provided a list of valid words (provided in whatever data structure you'd like). The mapping is shown in the diagram below:

1	**2** abc	**3** def
4 ghi	**5** jkl	**6** mno
7 pqrs	**8** tuv	**9** wxyz
	0	

EXAMPLE

Input: 8733

Output: tree, used

pg 184

SOLUTION

We could approach this in a couple of ways. Let's start with a brute force algorithm.

Brute Force

Imagine how you would solve the problem if you had to do it by hand. You'd probably try every possible value for each digit with all other possible values.

This is exactly what we do algorithmically. We take the first digit and run through all the characters that map to that digit. For each character, we add it to a prefix variable and recurse, passing the prefix downward. Once we run out of characters, we print prefix (which now contains the full word) if the string is a valid word.

We will assume the list of words is passed in as a HashSet. A HashSet operates similarly to a hash table, but rather than offering key->value lookups, it can tell us if a word is contained in the set in $O(1)$ time.

```
ArrayList<String> getValidT9Words(String number, HashSet<String> wordList) {
  ArrayList<String> results = new ArrayList<String>();
  getValidWords(number, 0, "", wordList, results);
  return results;
}

```

```
void getValidWords(String number, int index, String prefix,
                   HashSet<String> wordSet, ArrayList<String> results) {
  /* If it's a complete word, print it. */
  if (index == number.length() && wordSet.contains(prefix)) {
    results.add(prefix);
    return;
  }

  /* Get characters that match this digit. */
  char digit = number.charAt(index);
  char[] letters = getT9Chars(digit);

  /* Go through all remaining options. */
  if (letters != null) {
    for (char letter : letters) {
      getValidWords(number, index + 1, prefix + letter, wordSet, results);
    }
  }
}

/* Return array of characters that map to this digit. */
char[] getT9Chars(char digit) {
  if (!Character.isDigit(digit)) {
    return null;
  }
  int dig = Character.getNumericValue(digit) - Character.getNumericValue('0');
  return t9Letters[dig];
}

/* Mapping of digits to letters. */
char[][] t9Letters = {null, null, {'a', 'b', 'c'}, {'d', 'e', 'f'},
  {'g', 'h', 'i'}, {'j', 'k', 'l'}, {'m', 'n', 'o'}, {'p', 'q', 'r', 's'},
  {'t', 'u', 'v'},  {'w', 'x', 'y', 'z'}
};
```

This algorithm runs in $O(4^N)$ time, where N is the length of the string. This is because we recursively branch four times for each call to `getValidWords`, and we recurse until a call stack depth of N.

This is very, very slow on large strings.

Optimized

Let's return to thinking about how you would do this, if you were doing it by hand. Imagine the example of `33835676368` (which corresponds to `development`). If you were doing this by hand, I bet you'd skip over solutions that start with `fftf` [3383], as no valid words start with those characters.

Ideally, we'd like our program to make the same sort of optimization: stop recursing down paths which will obviously fail. Specifically, if there are no words in the dictionary that start with `prefix`, stop recursing.

The `Trie` data structure (see "Tries (Prefix Trees)" on page 105) can do this for us. Whenever we reach a string which is not a valid prefix, we exit.

```
ArrayList<String> getValidT9Words(String number, Trie trie) {
  ArrayList<String> results = new ArrayList<String>();
  getValidWords(number, 0, "", trie.getRoot(), results);
  return results;
}

```

```
void getValidWords(String number, int index, String prefix, TrieNode trieNode,
                   ArrayList<String> results) {
  /* If it's a complete word, print it. */
  if (index == number.length()) {
    if (trieNode.terminates()) { // Is complete word
      results.add(prefix);
    }
    return;
  }

  /* Get characters that match this digit */
  char digit = number.charAt(index);
  char[] letters = getT9Chars(digit);

  /* Go through all remaining options. */
  if (letters != null) {
    for (char letter : letters) {
      TrieNode child = trieNode.getChild(letter);
      /* If there are words that start with prefix + letter,
       * then continue recursing. */
      if (child != null) {
        getValidWords(number, index + 1, prefix + letter, child, results);
      }
    }
  }
}
```

It's difficult to describe the runtime of this algorithm since it depends on what the language looks like. However, this "short-circuiting" will make it run much, much faster in practice.

Most Optimal

Believe or not, we can actually make it run even faster. We just need to do a little bit of preprocessing. That's not a big deal though. We were doing that to build the trie anyway.

This problem is asking us to list all the words represented by a particular number in T9. Instead of trying to do this "on the fly" (and going through a lot of possibilities, many of which won't actually work), we can just do this in advance.

Our algorithm now has a few steps:

Pre-Computation:

1. Create a hash table that maps from a sequence of digits to a list of strings.
2. Go through each word in the dictionary and convert it to its T9 representation (e.g., `APPLE -> 27753`). Store each of these in the above hash table. For example, 8733 would map to `{used, tree}`.

Word Lookup:

1. Just look up the entry in the hash table and return the list.

That's it!

```
/* WORD LOOKUP */
ArrayList<String> getValidT9Words(String numbers,
                                  HashMapList<String, String> dictionary) {
  return dictionary.get(numbers);
}

```

```java
/* PRECOMPUTATION */

/* Create a hash table that maps from a number to all words that have this
 * numerical representation. */
HashMapList<String, String> initializeDictionary(String[] words) {
  /* Create a  hash table that maps from a letter to the digit */
  HashMap<Character, Character> letterToNumberMap = createLetterToNumberMap();

  /* Create word -> number map. */
  HashMapList<String, String> wordsToNumbers = new HashMapList<String, String>();
  for (String word : words) {
    String numbers = convertToT9(word, letterToNumberMap);
    wordsToNumbers.put(numbers, word);
  }
  return wordsToNumbers;
}

/* Convert mapping of number->letters into letter->number. */
HashMap<Character, Character> createLetterToNumberMap() {
  HashMap<Character, Character> letterToNumberMap =
    new HashMap<Character, Character>();
  for (int i = 0; i < t9Letters.length; i++) {
    char[] letters = t9Letters[i];
    if (letters != null) {
      for (char letter : letters) {
        char c = Character.forDigit(i, 10);
        letterToNumberMap.put(letter, c);
      }
    }
  }
  return letterToNumberMap;
}

/* Convert from a string to its T9 representation. */
String convertToT9(String word, HashMap<Character, Character> letterToNumberMap) {
  StringBuilder sb = new StringBuilder();
  for (char c : word.toCharArray()) {
    if (letterToNumberMap.containsKey(c)) {
      char digit = letterToNumberMap.get(c);
      sb.append(digit);
    }
  }
  return sb.toString();
}

char[][] t9Letters = /* Same as before */

/* HashMapList<String, Integer> is a HashMap that maps from Strings to
 * ArrayList<Integer>. See appendix for implementation. */
```

Getting the words that map to this number will run in O(N) time, where N is the number of digits. The O(N) comes in during the hash table look up (we need to convert the number to a hash table). If you know the words are never longer than a certain max size, then you could also describe the runtime as O(1).

Note that it's easy to think, "Oh, linear—that's not that fast." But it depends what it's linear *on*. Linear on the length of the word is extremely fast. Linear on the length of the dictionary is not so fast.

16.21 Sum Swap: Given two arrays of integers, find a pair of values (one value from each array) that you can swap to give the two arrays the same sum.

EXAMPLE

Input: `{4, 1, 2, 1, 1, 2}` and `{3, 6, 3, 3}`

Output: `{1, 3}`

pg 184

SOLUTION

We should start by trying to understand what exactly we're looking for.

We have two arrays and their sums. Although we likely aren't given their sums upfront, we can just act like we are for now. After all, computing the sum is an O(N) operation and we know we can't beat O(N) anyway. Computing the sum, therefore, won't impact the runtime.

When we move a (positive) value a from array A to array B, then the sum of A drops by a and the sum of B increases by a.

We are looking for two values, a and b, such that:

```
sumA - a + b = sumB - b + a
```

Doing some quick math:

```
2a - 2b = sumA - sumB
a - b = (sumA - sumB) / 2
```

Therefore, we're looking for two values that have a specific target difference: `(sumA - sumB) / 2`.

Observe that because that the target must be an integer (after all, you can't swap two integers to get a non-integer difference), we can conclude that the difference between the sums must be even to have a valid pair.

Brute Force

A brute force algorithm is simple enough. We just iterate through the arrays and check all pairs of values.

We can either do this the "naive" way (compare the new sums) or by looking for a pair with that difference.

Naive approach:

```
int[] findSwapValues(int[] array1, int[] array2) {
   int sum1 = sum(array1);
   int sum2 = sum(array2);

   for (int one : array1) {
      for (int two : array2) {
         int newSum1 = sum1 - one + two;
         int newSum2 = sum2 - two + one;
         if (newSum1 == newSum2) {
            int[] values = {one, two};
            return values;
         }
      }
   }

   return null;
}
```

Target approach:

```
int[] findSwapValues(int[] array1, int[] array2) {
```

```
    Integer target = getTarget(array1, array2);
    if (target == null) return null;

    for (int one : array1) {
       for (int two : array2) {
          if (one - two == target) {
             int[] values = {one, two};
             return values;
          }
       }
    }

    return null;
 }

 Integer getTarget(int[] array1, int[] array2) {
    int sum1 = sum(array1);
    int sum2 = sum(array2);

    if ((sum1 - sum2) % 2 != 0) return null;
    return (sum1 - sum2) / 2;
 }
```

We've used an `Integer` (a boxed data type) as the return value for `getTarget`. This allows us to distinguish an "error" case.

This algorithm takes O(AB) time.

Optimal Solution

This problem reduces to finding a pair of values that have a particular difference. With that in mind, let's revisit what the brute force does.

In the brute force, we're looping through A and then, for each element, looking for an element in B which gives us the "right" difference. If the value in A is 5 and the target is 3, then we must be looking for the value 2. That's the only value that could fulfill the goal.

That is, rather than writing `one - two == target`, we could have written `two == one - target`. How can we more quickly find an element in B that equals `one - target`?

We can do this very quickly with a hash table. We just throw all the elements in B into a hash table. Then, iterate through A and look for the appropriate element in B.

```
int[] findSwapValues(int[] array1, int[] array2) {
   Integer target = getTarget(array1, array2);
   if (target == null) return null;
   return findDifference(array1, array2, target);
}

/* Find a pair of values with a specific difference. */
int[] findDifference(int[] array1, int[] array2, int target) {
   HashSet<Integer> contents2 = getContents(array2);
   for (int one : array1) {
      int two = one - target;
      if (contents2.contains(two)) {
         int[] values = {one, two};
         return values;
      }
```

```
  }

  return null;
}

/* Put contents of array into hash set. */
HashSet<Integer> getContents(int[] array) {
  HashSet<Integer> set = new HashSet<Integer>();
  for (int a : array) {
    set.add(a);
  }
  return set;
}
```

This solution will take O(A+B) time. This is the Best Conceivable Runtime (BCR), since we have to at least touch every element in the two arrays.

Alternate Solution

If the arrays are sorted, we can iterate through them to find an appropriate pair. This will require less space.

```
int[] findSwapValues(int[] array1, int[] array2) {
  Integer target = getTarget(array1, array2);
  if (target == null) return null;
  return findDifference(array1, array2, target);
}

int[] findDifference(int[] array1, int[] array2, int target) {
  int a = 0;
  int b = 0;

  while (a < array1.length && b < array2.length) {
    int difference = array1[a] - array2[b];
    /* Compare difference to target. If difference is too small, then make it
     * bigger by moving a to a bigger value. If it is too big, then make it
     * smaller by moving b to a bigger value. If it's just right, return this
     * pair. */
    if (difference == target) {
      int[] values = {array1[a], array2[b]};
      return values;
    } else if (difference < target) {
      a++;
    } else {
      b++;
    }
  }

  return null;
}
```

This algorithm takes O(A + B) time but requires the arrays to be sorted. If the arrays aren't sorted, we can still apply this algorithm but we'd have to sort the arrays first. The overall runtime would be O(A log A + B log B).

16.22 Langton's Ant: An ant is sitting on an infinite grid of white and black squares. Initially, the grid is all white and the ant faces right. At each step, it does the following:

(1) At a white square, flip the color of the square, turn 90 degrees right (clockwise), and move forward one unit.

(2) At a black square, flip the color of the square, turn 90 degrees left (counter-clockwise), and move forward one unit.

Write a program to simulate the first K moves that the ant makes and print the final board as a grid. Note that you are not provided with the data structure to represent the grid. This is something you must design yourself. The only input to your method is K. You should print the final grid and return nothing. The method signature might be something like `void printKMoves(int K)`.

pg 185

SOLUTION

At first glance, this problem seems very straightforward: create a grid, remember the ant's position and orientation, flip the cells, turn, and move. The interesting part comes in how to handle an infinite grid.

Solution #1: Fixed Array

Technically, since we're only running the first K moves, we do have a max size for the grid. The ant cannot move more than K moves in either direction. If we create a grid that has width 2K and height 2K (and place the ant at the center), we know it will be big enough.

The problem with this is that it's not very extensible. If you run K moves and then want to run another K moves, you might be out of luck.

Additionally, this solution wastes a good amount of space. The max might be K moves in a particular dimension, but the ant is probably going in circles a bit. You probably won't need all this space.

Solution #2: Resizable Array

One thought is to use a resizable array, such as Java's `ArrayList` class. This allows us to grow an array as necessary, while still offering `O(1)` amortized insertion.

The problem is that our grid needs to grow in two dimensions, but the `ArrayList` is only a single array. Additionally, we need to grow "backward" into negative values. The `ArrayList` class doesn't support this.

However, we take a similar approach by building our own resizable grid. Each time the ant hits an edge, we double the size of the grid in that dimension.

What about the negative expansions? While conceptually we can talk about something being at negative positions, we cannot actually access array indices with negative values.

One way we can handle this is to create "fake indices." Let us treat the ant as being at coordinates `(-3, -10)`, but track some sort of offset or delta to translate these coordinates into array indices.

This is actually unnecessary, though. The ant's location does not need to be publicly exposed or consistent (unless, of course, indicated by the interviewer). When the ant travels into negative coordinates, we can double the size of the array and just move the ant and all cells into the positive coordinates. Essentially, we are relabeling all the indices.

This relabeling will not impact the big O time since we have to create a new matrix anyway.

```
public class Grid {
  private boolean[][] grid;
```

```
  private Ant ant = new Ant();

  public Grid() {
    grid = new boolean[1][1];
  }

  /* Copy old values into new array, with an offset/shift applied to the row and
   * columns. */
  private void copyWithShift(boolean[][] oldGrid, boolean[][] newGrid,
                             int shiftRow, int shiftColumn) {
    for (int r = 0; r < oldGrid.length; r++) {
      for (int c = 0; c < oldGrid[0].length; c++) {
        newGrid[r + shiftRow][c + shiftColumn] = oldGrid[r][c];
      }
    }
  }

  /* Ensure that the given position will fit on the array. If necessary, double
   * the size of the matrix, copy the old values over, and adjust the ant's
   * position so that it's in a positive range. */
  private void ensureFit(Position position) {
    int shiftRow = 0;
    int shiftColumn = 0;

    /* Calculate new number of rows. */
    int numRows = grid.length;
    if (position.row < 0) {
      shiftRow = numRows;
      numRows *= 2;
    } else if (position.row >= numRows) {
      numRows *= 2;
    }

    /* Calculate new number of columns. */
    int numColumns = grid[0].length;
    if (position.column < 0) {
      shiftColumn = numColumns;
      numColumns *= 2;
    } else if (position.column >= numColumns) {
      numColumns *= 2;
    }

    /* Grow array, if necessary. Shift ant's position too. */
    if (numRows != grid.length || numColumns != grid[0].length) {
      boolean[][] newGrid = new boolean[numRows][numColumns];
      copyWithShift(grid, newGrid, shiftRow, shiftColumn);
      ant.adjustPosition(shiftRow, shiftColumn);
      grid = newGrid;
    }
  }

  /* Flip color of cells. */
  private void flip(Position position) {
    int row = position.row;
    int column = position.column;
    grid[row][column] = grid[row][column] ? false : true;
```

```
    }

    /* Move ant. */
    public void move() {
       ant.turn(grid[ant.position.row][ant.position.column]);
       flip(ant.position);
       ant.move();
       ensureFit(ant.position); // grow
    }

    /* Print board. */
    public String toString() {
       StringBuilder sb = new StringBuilder();
       for (int r = 0; r < grid.length; r++) {
          for (int c = 0; c < grid[0].length; c++) {
             if (r == ant.position.row && c == ant.position.column) {
                sb.append(ant.orientation);
             } else if (grid[r][c]) {
                sb.append("X");
             } else {
                sb.append("_");
             }
          }
          sb.append("\n");
       }
       sb.append("Ant: " + ant.orientation + ". \n");
       return sb.toString();
    }
 }
```

We pulled the Ant code into a separate class. The nice thing about this is that if we need to have multiple ants for some reason, we can easily extend the code to support this.

```
public class Ant {
   public Position position = new Position(0, 0);
   public Orientation orientation = Orientation.right;

   public void turn(boolean clockwise) {
      orientation = orientation.getTurn(clockwise);
   }

   public void move() {
      if (orientation == Orientation.left) {
         position.column--;
      } else if (orientation == Orientation.right) {
         position.column++;
      } else if (orientation == Orientation.up) {
         position.row--;
      } else if (orientation == Orientation.down) {
         position.row++;
      }
   }

   public void adjustPosition(int shiftRow, int shiftColumn) {
      position.row += shiftRow;
      position.column += shiftColumn;
   }
}
```

`Orientation` is also its own `enum`, with a few useful functions.

```
public enum Orientation {
  left, up, right, down;

  public Orientation getTurn(boolean clockwise) {
    if (this == left) {
      return clockwise ? up : down;
    } else if (this == up) {
      return clockwise ? right : left;
    } else if (this == right) {
      return clockwise ? down : up;
    } else { // down
      return clockwise ? left : right;
    }
  }

  @Override
  public String toString() {
    if (this == left) {
      return "\u2190";
    } else if (this == up) {
      return "\u2191";
    } else if (this == right) {
      return "\u2192";
    } else { // down
      return "\u2193";
    }
  }
}
```

We've also put `Position` into its own simple class. We could just as easily track the row and column separately.

```
public class Position {
  public int row;
  public int column;

  public Position(int row, int column) {
    this.row = row;
    this.column = column;
  }
}
```

This works, but it's actually more complicated than is necessary.

Solution #3: HashSet

Although it may seem "obvious" that we would use a matrix to represent a grid, it's actually easier not to do that. All we actually need is a list of the white squares (as well as the ant's location and orientation).

We can do this by using a HashSet of the white squares. If a position is in the hash set, then the square is white. Otherwise, it is black.

The one tricky bit is how to print the board. Where do we start printing? Where do we end?

Since we will need to print a grid, we can track what should be top-left and bottom-right corner of the grid. Each time the ant moves, we compare the ant's position to the most top-left position and most bottom-right position, updating them if necessary.

```
public class Board {
  private HashSet<Position> whites = new HashSet<Position>();
  private Ant ant = new Ant();
  private Position topLeftCorner = new Position(0, 0);
  private Position bottomRightCorner = new Position(0, 0);

  public Board() { }

  /* Move ant. */
  public void move() {
    ant.turn(isWhite(ant.position)); // Turn
    flip(ant.position); // flip
    ant.move(); // move
    ensureFit(ant.position);
  }

  /* Flip color of cells. */
  private void flip(Position position) {
    if (whites.contains(position)) {
      whites.remove(position);
    } else {
      whites.add(position.clone());
    }
  }

  /* Grow grid by tracking the most top-left and bottom-right positions.*/
  private void ensureFit(Position position) {
    int row = position.row;
    int column = position.column;

    topLeftCorner.row = Math.min(topLeftCorner.row, row);
    topLeftCorner.column = Math.min(topLeftCorner.column, column);

    bottomRightCorner.row = Math.max(bottomRightCorner.row, row);
    bottomRightCorner.column = Math.max(bottomRightCorner.column, column);
  }

  /* Check if cell is white. */
  public boolean isWhite(Position p) {
    return whites.contains(p);
  }

  /* Check if cell is white. */
  public boolean isWhite(int row, int column) {
    return whites.contains(new Position(row, column));
  }

  /* Print board. */
  public String toString() {
    StringBuilder sb = new StringBuilder();
    int rowMin = topLeftCorner.row;
    int rowMax = bottomRightCorner.row;
    int colMin = topLeftCorner.column;
    int colMax = bottomRightCorner.column;
    for (int r = rowMin; r <= rowMax; r++) {
      for (int c = colMin; c <= colMax; c++) {
```

```
            if (r == ant.position.row && c == ant.position.column) {
               sb.append(ant.orientation);
            } else if (isWhite(r, c)) {
               sb.append("X");
            } else {
               sb.append("_");
            }
         }
         sb.append("\n");
      }
      sb.append("Ant: " + ant.orientation + ". \n");
      return sb.toString();
   }
```

The implementation of Ant and Orientation is the same.

The implementation of Position gets updated slightly, in order to support the HashSet functionality. The position will be the key, so we need to implement a hashCode() function.

```
public class Position {
   public int row;
   public int column;

   public Position(int row, int column) {
      this.row = row;
      this.column = column;
   }

   @Override
   public boolean equals(Object o) {
      if (o instanceof Position) {
         Position p = (Position) o;
         return p.row == row && p.column == column;
      }
      return false;
   }

   @Override
   public int hashCode() {
      /* There are many options for hash functions. This is one. */
      return (row * 31) ^ column;
   }

   public Position clone() {
      return new Position(row, column);
   }
}
```

The nice thing about this implementation is that if we do need to access a particular cell elsewhere, we have consistent row and column labeling.

16.23 Rand7 from Rand5: Implement a method `rand7()` given `rand5()`. That is, given a method that generates a random integer between 0 and 4 (inclusive), write a method that generates a random integer between 0 and 6 (inclusive).

pg 186

SOLUTION

To implement this function correctly, we must have each of the values between 0 and 6 returned with 1/7th probability.

First Attempt (Fixed Number of Calls)

As a first attempt, we might try generating all numbers between 0 and 9, and then mod the resulting value by 7. Our code for it might look something like this:

```
int rand7() {
   int v = rand5() + rand5();
   return v % 7;
}
```

Unfortunately, the above code will not generate the values with equal probability. We can see this by looking at the results of each call to `rand5()` an d the return result of the `rand7()` function.

1st Call	2nd Call	Result
0	0	0
0	1	1
0	2	2
0	3	3
0	4	4
1	0	1
1	1	2
1	2	3
1	3	4
1	4	5
2	0	2
2	1	3
2	2	4
2	3	5
2	4	6
3	0	3
3	1	4
3	2	5
3	3	6
3	4	0
4	0	4
4	1	5
4	2	6
4	3	0
4	4	1

Each individual row has a 1 in 25 chance of occurring, since there are two calls to `rand5()` and each distributes its results with $\frac{1}{5}$th probability. If you count up the number of times each number occurs, you'll note that this `rand7()` function will return 4 with $\frac{5}{25}$th probability but return 0 with just $\frac{3}{25}$th probability. This means that our function has failed; the results do not have probability $\frac{1}{7}$th.

Now, imagine we modify our function to add an if-statement, to change the constant multiplier, or to insert a new call to `rand5()`. We will still wind up with a similar looking table, and the probability of getting any one of those rows will be $\frac{1}{5^k}$, where k is the number of calls to `rand5()` in that row. Different rows may have different number of calls.

The probability of winding up with the result of the `rand7()` function being, say, 6 would be the sum of the probabilities of all rows that result in 6. That is:

$$P(\texttt{rand7()} = 6) = \frac{1}{5^i} + \frac{1}{5^j} + \ldots + \frac{1}{5^m}$$

We know that, in order for our function to be correct, this probability must equal $\frac{1}{7}$. This is impossible though. Because 5 and 7 are relatively prime, no series of reciprocal powers of 5 will result in $\frac{1}{7}$.

Does this mean the problem is impossible? Not exactly. Strictly speaking, it means that, as long as we can list out the combinations of `rand5()` results that will result in a particular value of `rand7()`, the function will not give well distributed results.

We can still solve this problem. We just have to use a while loop, and realize that there's no telling just how many turns will be required to return a result.

Second Attempt (Nondeterministic Number of Calls)

As soon as we've allowed for a while loop, our work gets much easier. We just need to generate a range of values where each value is equally likely (and where the range has at least seven elements). If we can do this, then we can discard the elements greater than the previous multiple of 7, and mod the rest of them by 7. This will get us a value within the range of 0 to 6, with each value being equally likely.

In the below code, we generate the range 0 through 24 by doing `5 * rand5() + rand5()`. Then, we discard the values between 21 and 24, since they would otherwise make `rand7()` unfairly weighted towards 0 through 3. Finally, we mod by 7 to give us the values in the range 0 to 6 with equal probability.

Note that because we discard values in this approach, we have no guarantee on the number of `rand5()` calls it may take to return a value. This is what is meant by a *nondeterministic* number of calls.

```
int rand7() {
  while (true) {
    int num = 5 * rand5() + rand5();
    if (num < 21) {
      return num % 7;
    }
  }
}
```

Observe that doing `5 * rand5() + rand5()` gives us exactly one way of getting each number in its range (0 to 24). This ensures that each value is equally probable.

Could we instead do `2 * rand5() + rand5()`? No, because the values wouldn't be equally distributed. For example, there would be three ways of getting a 6 (`6 = 2 * 1 + 4`, `6 = 2 * 2 + 2`, and `6 = 2 * 3 + 0`) but only one way of getting a 0 (`0=2*0+0`). The values in the range are not equally probable.

There *is* a way that we can use `2 * rand5()` and still get an identically distributed range, but it's much more complicated. See below.

```
int rand7() {
  while (true) {
    int r1 = 2 * rand5(); /* evens between 0 and 9 */
    int r2 = rand5(); /* used later to generate a 0 or 1 */
    if (r2 != 4) { /* r2 has extra even num-discard the extra */
      int rand1 = r2 % 2; /* Generate 0 or 1 */
      int num = r1 + rand1; /* will be in the range 0 to 9 */
      if (num < 7) {
        return num;
      }
    }
  }
}
```

In fact, there is an infinite number of ranges we can use. The key is to make sure that the range is big enough and that all values are equally likely.

16.24 Pairs with Sum: Design an algorithm to find all pairs of integers within an array which sum to a specified value.

pg 185

SOLUTION

Let's start with a definition. If we're trying to find a pair of numbers that sums to z, the *complement* of x will be z - x (that is, the number that can be added to x to make z). For example, if we're trying to find a pair of numbers that sums to 12, the complement of –5 would be 17.

Brute Force

A brute force solution is to just iterate through all pairs and print the pair if its sum matches the target sum.

```
ArrayList<Pair> printPairSums(int[] array, int sum) {
   ArrayList<Pair> result = new ArrayList<Pair>();
   for (int i = 0 ; i < array.length; i++) {
      for (int j = i + 1; j < array.length; j++) {
         if (array[i] + array[j] == sum) {
            result.add(new Pair(array[i], array[j]));
         }
      }
   }
   return result;
}
```

If there are duplicates in the array (e.g., `{5, 6, 5}`), it might print the same sum twice. You should discuss this with your interviewer.

Optimized Solution

We can optimize this with a hash map, where the value in the hash map reflects the number of "unpaired" instances of a key. We walk through the array. At each element x, check how many unpaired instances of x's complement preceded it in the array. If the count is at least one, then there is an unpaired instance of x's complement. We add this pair and decrement x's complement to signify that this element has been paired. If the count is zero, then increment the value of x in the hash table to signify that x is unpaired.

```
ArrayList<Pair> printPairSums(int[] array, int sum) {
   ArrayList<Pair> result = new ArrayList<Pair>();
   HashMap<Integer, Integer> unpairedCount = new HashMap<Integer, Integer>();
   for (int x : array) {
      int complement = sum - x;
      if (unpairedCount.getOrDefault(complement, 0) > 0) {
         result.add(new Pair(x, complement));
         adjustCounterBy(unpairedCount, complement, -1); // decrement complement
      } else {
         adjustCounterBy(unpairedCount, x, 1); // increment count
      }
   }
   return result;
}
```

```java
void adjustCounterBy(HashMap<Integer, Integer> counter, int key, int delta) {
  counter.put(key, counter.getOrDefault(key, 0) + delta);
}
```

This solution will print duplicate pairs, but will not reuse the same instance of an element. It will take `O(N)` time and `O(N)` space.

Alternate Solution

Alternatively, we can sort the array and then find the pairs in a single pass. Consider this array:

`{-2, -1, 0, 3, 5, 6, 7, 9, 13, 14}.`

Let `first` point to the head of the array and `last` point to the end of the array. To find the complement of `first`, we just move `last` backwards until we find it. If `first + last < sum`, then there is no complement for `first`. We can therefore move `first` forward. We stop when `first` is greater than `last`.

Why must this find all complements for `first`? Because the array is sorted and we're trying progressively smaller numbers. When the sum of `first` and `last` is less than the sum, we know that trying even smaller numbers (as `last`) won't help us find a complement.

Why must this find all complements for `last`? Because all pairs must be made up of a `first` and a `last`. We've found all complements for `first`, therefore we've found all complements of `last`.

```java
void printPairSums(int[] array, int sum) {
  Arrays.sort(array);
  int first = 0;
  int last = array.length - 1;
  while (first < last) {
    int s = array[first] + array[last];
    if (s == sum) {
      System.out.println(array[first] + " " + array[last]);
      first++;
      last--;
    } else {
      if (s < sum) first++;
      else last--;
    }
  }
}
```

This algorithm takes `O(N log N)` time to sort and `O(N)` time to find the pairs.

Note that since the array is presumably unsorted, it would be equally fast in terms of big O to just do a binary search at each element for its complement. This would give us a two-step algorithm, where each step is `O(N log N)`.

16.25 LRU Cache: Design and build a "least recently used" cache, which evicts the least recently used item. The cache should map from keys to values (allowing you to insert and retrieve a value associated with a particular key) and be initialized with a max size. When it is full, it should evict the least recently used item. You can assume the keys are integers and the values are strings.

pg 185

SOLUTION

We should start off by defining the scope of the problem. What exactly do we need to achieve?

- **Inserting Key, Value Pair:** We need to be able to insert a (key, value) pair.

- **Retrieving Value by Key:** We need to be able to retrieve the value using the key.
- **Finding Least Recently Used:** We need to know the least recently used item (and, likely, the usage ordering of all items).
- **Updating Most Recently Used:** When we retrieve a value by key, we need to update the order to be the most recently used item.
- **Eviction:** The cache should have a max capacity and should remove the least recently used item when it hits capacity.

The (key, value) mapping suggests a hash table. This would make it easy to look up the value associated with a particular key.

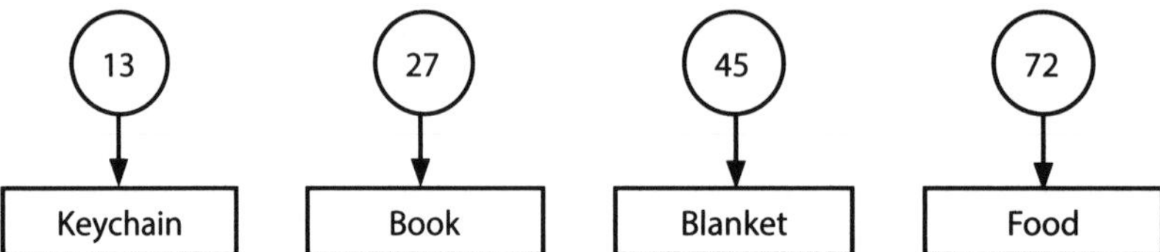

Unfortunately, a hash table usually would not offer a quick way to remove the most recently used item. We could mark each item with a timestamp and iterate through the hash table to remove the item with the lowest timestamp, but that can get quite slow (`O(N)` for insertions).

Instead, we could use a linked list, ordered by the most recently used. This would make it easy to mark an item as the most recently used (just put it in the front of the list) or to remove the least recently used item (remove the end).

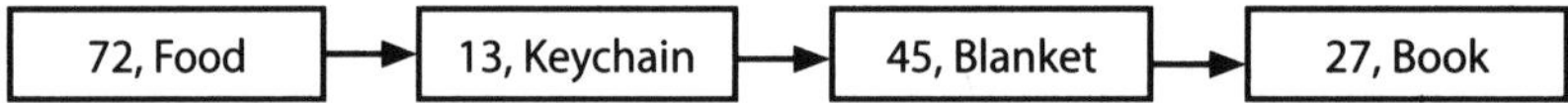

Unfortunately, this does not offer a quick way to look up an item by its key. We could iterate through the linked list and find the item by key. But this could get very slow (`O(N)` for retrieval).

Each approach does half of the problem (different halves) very well, but neither approach does both parts well.

Can we get the best parts of each? Yes. By using both!

The linked list looks as it did in the earlier example, but now it's a doubly linked list. This allows us to easily remove an element from the middle of the linked list. The hash table now maps to each linked list node rather than the value.

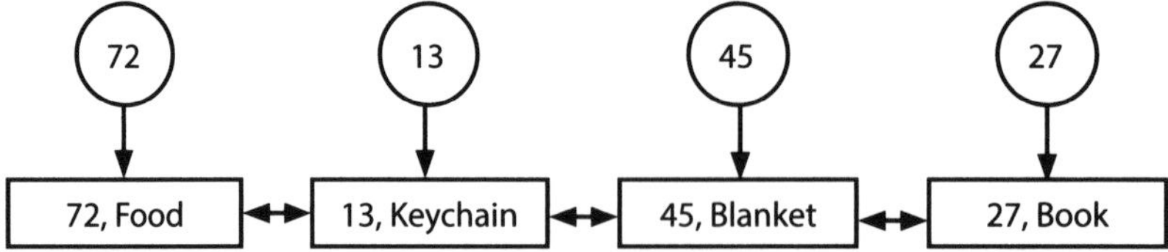

The algorithms now operate as follows:

- **Inserting Key, Value Pair:** Create a linked list node with key, value. Insert into head of linked list. Insert key -> node mapping into hash table.
- **Retrieving Value by Key:** Look up node in hash table and return value. Update most recently used item

(see below).

- **Finding Least Recently Used:** Least recently used item will be found at the end of the linked list.
- **Updating Most Recently Used:** Move node to front of linked list. Hash table does not need to be updated.
- **Eviction:** Remove tail of linked list. Get key from linked list node and remove key from hash table.

The code below implements these classes and algorithms.

```
public class Cache {
  private int maxCacheSize;
  private HashMap<Integer, LinkedListNode> map =
    new HashMap<Integer, LinkedListNode>();
  private LinkedListNode listHead = null;
  public LinkedListNode listTail = null;

  public Cache(int maxSize) {
    maxCacheSize = maxSize;
  }

  /* Get value for key and mark as most recently used. */
  public String getValue(int key) {
    LinkedListNode item = map.get(key);
    if (item == null) return null;

    /* Move to front of list to mark as most recently used. */
    if (item != listHead) {
      removeFromLinkedList(item);
      insertAtFrontOfLinkedList(item);
    }
    return item.value;
  }

  /* Remove node from linked list. */
  private void removeFromLinkedList(LinkedListNode node) {
    if (node == null)  return;

    if (node.prev != null) node.prev.next = node.next;
    if (node.next != null) node.next.prev = node.prev;
    if (node == listTail) listTail = node.prev;
    if (node == listHead) listHead = node.next;
  }

  /* Insert node at front of linked list. */
  private void insertAtFrontOfLinkedList(LinkedListNode node) {
    if (listHead == null) {
      listHead = node;
      listTail = node;
    } else {
      listHead.prev = node;
      node.next = listHead;
      listHead = node;
    }
  }

  /* Remove key/value pair from cache, deleting from hashtable and linked list. */
  public boolean removeKey(int key) {
```

```
        LinkedListNode node = map.get(key);
        removeFromLinkedList(node);
        map.remove(key);
        return true;
    }

    /* Put key, value pair in cache. Removes old value for key if necessary. Inserts
     * pair into linked list and hash table.*/
    public void setKeyValue(int key, String value) {
        /* Remove if already there. */
        removeKey(key);

        /* If full, remove least recently used item from cache. */
        if (map.size() >= maxCacheSize && listTail != null) {
            removeKey(listTail.key);
        }

        /* Insert new node. */
        LinkedListNode node = new LinkedListNode(key, value);
        insertAtFrontOfLinkedList(node);
        map.put(key, node);
    }

    private static class LinkedListNode {
        private LinkedListNode next, prev;
        public int key;
        public String value;
        public LinkedListNode(int k, String v) {
            key = k;
            value = v;
        }
    }
}
```

Note that we've chosen to make `LinkedListNode` an inner class of `Cache`, since no other classes should need access to this class and really should only exist within the scope of `Cache`.

16.26 Calculator: Given an arithmetic equation consisting of positive integers, +, -, * and / (no parentheses), compute the result.

EXAMPLE

Input: `2*3+5/6*3+15`

Output: `23.5`

pg 185

SOLUTION

The first thing we should realize is that the dumb thing—just applying each operator left to right—won't work. Multiplication and division are considered "higher priority" operations, which means that they have to happen before addition.

For example, if you have the simple expression 3+6*2, the multiplication must be performed first, and then the addition. If you just processed the equation left to right, you would end up with the incorrect result, 18, rather than the correct one, 15. You know all of this, of course, but it's worth really spelling out what it means.

Solution #1

We can still process the equation from left to right; we just have to be a little smarter about how we do it. Multiplication and division need to be grouped together such that whenever we see those operations, we perform them immediately on the surrounding terms.

For example, suppose we have this expression:

```
2 - 6 - 7*8/2 + 5
```

It's fine to compute 2 - 6 immediately and store it into a `result` variable. But, when we see `7*(something)`, we know we need to fully process that term before adding it to the result.

We can do this by reading left to right and maintaining two variables.

- The first is `processing`, which maintains the result of the current cluster of terms (both the operator and the value). In the case of addition and subtraction, the cluster will be just the current term. In the case of multiplication and division, it will be the full sequence (until you get to the next addition or subtraction).
- The second is the `result` variable. If the next term is an addition or subtraction (or there is no next term), then `processing` is applied to `result`.

On the above example, we would do the following:

1. Read +2. Apply it to `processing`. Apply processing to `result`. Clear `processing`.
```
processing = {+, 2} --> null
result = 0          --> 2
```
2. Read -6. Apply it to `processing`. Apply processing to `result`. Clear `processing`.
```
processing = {-, 6} --> null
result = 2          --> -4
```
3. Read -7. Apply it to `processing`. Observe next sign is a *. Continue.
```
processing = {-, 7}
result = -4
```
4. Read *8. Apply it to `processing`. Observe next sign is a /. Continue.
```
processing = {-, 56}
result = -4
```
5. Read /2. Apply it to `processing`. Observe next sign is a +, which terminates this multiplication and division cluster. Apply processing to `result`. Clear `processing`.
```
processing = {-, 28}    --> null
result = -4           --> -32
```
6. Read +5. Apply it to `processing`. Apply processing to `result`. Clear `processing`.
```
processing = {+, 5} --> null
result = -32        --> -27
```

The code below implements this algorithm.

```
/* Compute the result of the arithmetic sequence. This works by reading left to
 * right and applying each term to a result. When we see a multiplication or
 * division, we instead apply this sequence to a temporary variable. */
double compute(String sequence) {
  ArrayList<Term> terms = Term.parseTermSequence(sequence);
  if (terms == null) return Integer.MIN_VALUE;

  double result = 0;
  Term processing = null;
  for (int i = 0; i < terms.size(); i++) {
```

```
      Term current = terms.get(i);
      Term next = i + 1 < terms.size() ? terms.get(i + 1) : null;

      /* Apply the current term to "processing". */
      processing = collapseTerm(processing, current);

      /* If next term is + or -, then this cluster is done and we should apply
       * "processing" to "result". */
      if (next == null || next.getOperator() == Operator.ADD
          || next.getOperator() == Operator.SUBTRACT) {
        result = applyOp(result, processing.getOperator(), processing.getNumber());
        processing = null;
      }
    }

    return result;
  }

  /* Collapse two terms together using the operator in secondary and the numbers
   * from each. */
  Term collapseTerm(Term primary, Term secondary) {
    if (primary == null) return secondary;
    if (secondary == null) return primary;

    double value = applyOp(primary.getNumber(), secondary.getOperator(),
                   secondary.getNumber());
    primary.setNumber(value);
    return primary;
  }

  double applyOp(double left, Operator op, double right) {
    if (op == Operator.ADD) return left + right;
    else if (op == Operator.SUBTRACT) return left - right;
    else if (op == Operator.MULTIPLY) return left * right;
    else if (op == Operator.DIVIDE) return left / right;
    else return right;
  }

  public class Term {
    public enum Operator {
      ADD, SUBTRACT, MULTIPLY, DIVIDE, BLANK
    }

    private double value;
    private Operator operator = Operator.BLANK;

    public Term(double v, Operator op) {
      value = v;
      operator = op;
    }

    public double getNumber() { return value; }
    public Operator getOperator() { return operator; }
    public void setNumber(double v) { value = v; }

    /* Parses arithmetic sequence into a list of Terms. For example, 3-5*6 becomes
```

```
     * something like: [{BLANK,3}, {SUBTRACT, 5}, {MULTIPLY, 6}].
     * If improperly formatted, returns null. */
    public static ArrayList<Term> parseTermSequence(String sequence) {
       /* Code can be found in downloadable solutions. */
    }
}
```

This takes `O(N)` time, where `N` is the length of the initial string.

Solution #2

Alternatively, we can solve this problem using two stacks: one for numbers and one for operators.

`2 - 6 - 7 * 8 / 2 + 5`

The processing works as follows:

- Each time we see a number, it gets pushed onto `numberStack`.
- Operators get pushed onto `operatorStack`—as long as the operator has higher priority than the current top of the stack. If `priority(currentOperator) <= priority(operatorStack.top())`, then we "collapse" the top of the stacks:
  - » Collapsing: pop two elements off `numberStack`, pop an operator off `operatorStack`, apply the operator, and push the result onto `numberStack`.
  - » Priority: addition and subtraction have equal priority, which is lower than the priority of multiplication and division (also equal priority).

  This collapsing continues until the above inequality is broken, at which point `currentOperator` is pushed onto `operatorStack`.
- At the very end, we collapse the stack.

Let's see this with an example: `2 - 6 - 7 * 8 / 2 + 5`

	action	numberStack	operatorStack
2	numberStack.push(2)	2	[empty]
-	operatorStack.push(-)	2	-
6	numberStack.push(6)	6, 2	-
-	collapseStacks [2 - 6] operatorStack.push(-)	-4 -4	[empty] -
7	numberStack.push(7)	7, -4	-
*	operatorStack.push(*)	7, -4	*, -
8	numberStack.push(8)	8, 7, -4	*, -
/	collapseStack [7 * 8] operatorStack.push(/)	56, -4 56, -4	- /, -
2	numberStack.push(2)	2, 56, -4	/, -
+	collapseStack [56 / 2] collapseStack [-4 - 28] operatorStack.push(+)	28, -4 -32 -32	- [empty] +
5	numberStack.push(5)	5, -32	+
	collapseStack [-32 + 5]	-27	[empty]
	return -27		

The code below implements this algorithm.

```
public enum Operator {
   ADD, SUBTRACT, MULTIPLY, DIVIDE, BLANK
}

double compute(String sequence) {
   Stack<Double> numberStack = new Stack<Double>();
   Stack<Operator> operatorStack = new Stack<Operator>();

   for (int i = 0; i < sequence.length(); i++) {
      try {
         /* Get number and push. */
         int value = parseNextNumber(sequence, i);
         numberStack.push((double) value);

         /* Move to the operator. */
         i += Integer.toString(value).length();
         if (i >= sequence.length()) {
            break;
         }

         /* Get operator, collapse top as needed, push operator. */
         Operator op = parseNextOperator(sequence, i);
         collapseTop(op, numberStack, operatorStack);
         operatorStack.push(op);
      } catch (NumberFormatException ex) {
         return Integer.MIN_VALUE;
      }
   }

   /* Do final collapse. */
   collapseTop(Operator.BLANK, numberStack, operatorStack);
   if (numberStack.size() == 1 && operatorStack.size() == 0) {
      return numberStack.pop();
   }
   return 0;
}

/* Collapse top until priority(futureTop) > priority(top). Collapsing means to pop
 * the top 2 numbers and apply the operator popped from the top of the operator
 * stack, and then push that onto the numbers stack.*/
void collapseTop(Operator futureTop, Stack<Double> numberStack,
                 Stack<Operator> operatorStack) {
   while (operatorStack.size() >= 1 && numberStack.size() >= 2) {
      if (priorityOfOperator(futureTop) <=
          priorityOfOperator(operatorStack.peek())) {
         double second = numberStack.pop();
         double first = numberStack.pop();
         Operator op = operatorStack.pop();
         double collapsed = applyOp(first, op, second);
         numberStack.push(collapsed);
      } else {
         break;
      }
   }
```

```
}

/* Return priority of operator. Mapped so that:
 *     addition == subtraction < multiplication == division. */
int priorityOfOperator(Operator op) {
  switch (op) {
    case ADD: return 1;
    case SUBTRACT: return 1;
    case MULTIPLY: return 2;
    case DIVIDE: return 2;
    case BLANK: return 0;
  }
  return 0;
}

/* Apply operator: left [op] right. */
double applyOp(double left, Operator op, double right) {
  if (op == Operator.ADD) return left + right;
  else if (op == Operator.SUBTRACT) return left - right;
  else if (op == Operator.MULTIPLY) return left * right;
  else if (op == Operator.DIVIDE) return left / right;
  else return right;
}

/* Return the number that starts at offset. */
int parseNextNumber(String seq, int offset) {
  StringBuilder sb = new StringBuilder();
  while (offset < seq.length() && Character.isDigit(seq.charAt(offset))) {
    sb.append(seq.charAt(offset));
    offset++;
  }
  return Integer.parseInt(sb.toString());
}

/* Return the operator that occurs as offset. */
Operator parseNextOperator(String sequence, int offset) {
  if (offset < sequence.length()) {
    char op = sequence.charAt(offset);
    switch(op) {
      case ‘+’: return Operator.ADD;
      case ‘-’: return Operator.SUBTRACT;
      case ‘*’: return Operator.MULTIPLY;
      case ‘/’: return Operator.DIVIDE;
    }
  }
  return Operator.BLANK;
}
```

This code also takes O(N) time, where N is the length of the string.

This solution involves a lot of annoying string parsing code. Remember that getting all these details out is not that important in an interview. In fact, your interviewer might even let you assume the expression is passed in pre-parsed into some sort of data structure.

Focus on modularizing your code from the beginning and "farming out" tedious or less interesting parts of the code to other functions. You want to focus on getting the core `compute` function working. The rest of the details can wait!

17

Solutions to Hard

17.1 Add Without Plus: Write a function that adds two numbers. You should not use + or any arithmetic operators.

pg 186

SOLUTION

Our first instinct in problems like these should be that we're going to have to work with bits. Why? Because when you take away the + sign, what other choice do we have? Plus, that's how computers do it!

Our next thought should be to deeply understand how addition works. We can walk through an addition problem to see if we can understand something new—some pattern—and then see if we can replicate that with code.

So let's do just that—let's walk through an addition problem. We'll work in base 10 so that it's easier to see.

To add 759 + 674, I would usually add `digit[0]` from each number, carry the one, add `digit[1]` from each number, carry the one, and so on. You could take the same approach in binary: add each digit, and carry the one as necessary.

Can we make this a little easier? Yes! Imagine I decided to split apart the "addition" and "carry" steps. That is, I do the following:

1. Add 759 + 674, but "forget" to carry. I then get 323.
2. Add 759 + 674 but only do the carrying, rather than the addition of each digit. I then get 1110.
3. Add the result of the first two operations (recursively, using the same process described in step 1 and 2): 1110 + 323 = 1433.

Now, how would we do this in binary?

1. If I add two binary numbers together, but forget to carry, the `i`th bit in the sum will be `0` only if a and b have the same `i`th bit (both `0` or both 1). This is essentially an XOR.
2. If I add two numbers together but *only* carry, I will have a 1 in the `i`th bit of the sum only if bits `i - 1` of a and b are both 1s. This is an AND, shifted.
3. Now, recurse until there's nothing to carry.

The following code implements this algorithm.

```
int add(int a, int b) {
  if (b == 0) return a;
  int sum = a ^ b; // add without carrying
  int carry = (a & b) << 1; // carry, but don't add
```

```
    return add(sum, carry); // recurse with sum + carry
}
```

Alternatively, you can implement this iteratively.

```
int add(int a, int b) {
  while (b != 0) {
    int sum = a ^ b; // add without carrying
    int carry = (a & b) << 1; // carry, but don't add
    a = sum;
    b = carry;
  }
  return a;
}
```

Problems requiring us to implement core operations like addition and subtraction are relatively common. The key in all of these problems is to dig into how these operations are usually implemented, so that we can re-implement them with the constraints of the given problem.

17.2 Shuffle: Write a method to shuffle a deck of cards. It must be a perfect shuffle—in other words, each of the 52! permutations of the deck has to be equally likely. Assume that you are given a random number generator which is perfect.

pg 186

SOLUTION

This is a very well known interview question, and a well known algorithm. If you aren't one of the lucky few to already know this algorithm, read on.

Let's imagine our n-element array. Suppose it looks like this:

```
[1] [2] [3] [4] [5]
```

Using our Base Case and Build approach, we can ask this question: suppose we had a method `shuffle(...)` that worked on `n - 1` elements. Could we use this to shuffle n elements?

Sure. In fact, that's quite easy. We would first shuffle the first n - 1 elements. Then, we would take the nth element and randomly swap it with an element in the array. That's it!

Recursively, that algorithm looks like this:

```
/* Random number between lower and higher, inclusive */
int rand(int lower, int higher) {
  return lower + (int)(Math.random() * (higher - lower + 1));
}

int[] shuffleArrayRecursively(int[] cards, int i) {
  if (i == 0) return cards;

  shuffleArrayRecursively(cards, i - 1); // Shuffle earlier part
  int k = rand(0, i); // Pick random index to swap with

  /* Swap element k and i */
  int temp = cards[k];
  cards[k] = cards[i];
  cards[i] = temp;

  /* Return shuffled array */
  return cards;
```

```
}
```

What would this algorithm look like iteratively? Let's think about it. All it does is moving through the array and, for each element `i`, swapping `array[i]` with a random element between `0` and `i`, inclusive.

This is actually a very clean algorithm to implement iteratively:

```
void shuffleArrayIteratively(int[] cards) {
   for (int i = 0; i < cards.length; i++) {
      int k = rand(0, i);
      int temp = cards[k];
      cards[k] = cards[i];
      cards[i] = temp;
   }
}
```

The iterative approach is usually how we see this algorithm written.

17.3 Random Set: Write a method to randomly generate a set of `m` integers from an array of size n. Each element must have equal probability of being chosen.

pg 186

SOLUTION

Like the prior problem which was similar, (problem 17.2 on page 531), we can look at this problem recursively using the Base Case and Build approach.

Suppose we have an algorithm that can pull a random set of `m` elements from an array of size `n - 1`. How can we use this algorithm to pull a random set of `m` elements from an array of size `n`?

We can first pull a random set of size `m` from the first `n - 1` elements. Then, we just need to decide if `array[n]` should be inserted into our subset (which would require pulling out a random element from it). An easy way to do this is to pick a random number k from `0` through n. If `k < m`, then insert `array[n]` into `subset[k]`. This will both "fairly" (i.e., with proportional probability) insert `array[n]` into the subset and "fairly" remove a random element from the subset.

The pseudocode for this recursive algorithm would look like this:

```
int[] pickMRecursively(int[] original, int m, int i) {
   if (i + 1 == m) { // Base case
      /* return first m elements of original */
   } else if (i + 1 > m) {
      int[] subset = pickMRecursively(original, m, i - 1);
      int k =  random value between 0 and i, inclusive
      if (k < m) {
         subset[k] = original[i];
      }
      return subset;
   }
   return null;
}
```

This is even cleaner to write iteratively. In this approach, we initialize an array `subset` to be the first `m` elements in `original`. Then, we iterate through the array, starting at element `m`, inserting `array[i]` into the subset at (random) position k whenever `k < m`.

```
int[] pickMIteratively(int[] original, int m) {
   int[] subset = new int[m];

```

```
    /* Fill in subset array with first part of original array */
    for (int i = 0; i < m ; i++) {
       subset[i] = original[i];
    }

    /* Go through rest of original array. */
    for (int i = m; i < original.length; i++) {
       int k = rand(0, i); // Random # between 0 and i, inclusive
       if (k < m) {
          subset[k] = original[i];
       }
    }

    return subset;
 }
```

Both solutions are, not surprisingly, very similar to the algorithm to shuffle an array.

17.4 Missing Number: An array A contains all the integers from 0 to n, except for one number which is missing. In this problem, we cannot access an entire integer in A with a single operation. The elements of A are represented in binary, and the only operation we can use to access them is "fetch the jth bit of A[i]," which takes constant time. Write code to find the missing integer. Can you do it in O(n) time?

pg 186

SOLUTION

You may have seen a very similar sounding problem: Given a list of numbers from 0 to n, with exactly one number removed, find the missing number. This problem can be solved by simply adding the list of numbers and comparing it to the actual sum of 0 through n, which is $\frac{n(n+1)}{2}$. The difference will be the missing number.

We could solve this by computing the value of each number, based on its binary representation, and calculating the sum.

The runtime of this solution is `n * length(n)`, when `length` is the number of bits in n. Note that `length(n)` = $\log_2$`(n)`. So, the runtime is actually `O(n log(n))`. Not quite good enough!

So how else can we approach it?

We can actually use a similar approach, but leverage the bit values more directly.

Picture a list of binary numbers (the `-----` indicates the value that was removed):

```
00000    00100    01000    01100
00001    00101    01001    01101
00010    00110    01010
-----    00111    01011
```

Removing the number above creates an imbalance of 1s and 0s in the least significant bit, which we'll call LSB_1. In a list of numbers from 0 to n, we would expect there to be the same number of 0s as 1s (if n is odd), or an additional 0 if n is even. That is:

```
if n % 2 == 1 then count(0s) = count(1s)
if n % 2 == 0 then count(0s) = 1 + count(1s)
```

Note that this means that `count(0s)` is always greater than or equal to `count(1s)`.

When we remove a value v from the list, we'll know immediately if v is even or odd just by looking at the least significant bits of all the other values in the list.

	n % 2 == 0 **count(0s) = 1 + count(1s)**	**n % 2 == 1** **count(0s) = count(1s)**
v % 2 == 0 **LSB_1(v) = 0**	a 0 is removed. count(0s) = count(1s)	a 0 is removed. count(0s) < count(1s)
v % 2 == 1 **LSB_1(v) = 1**	a 1 is removed. count(0s) > count(1s)	a 1 is removed. count(0s) > count(1s)

So, if `count(0s) <= count(1s)`, then v is even. If `count(0s) > count(1s)`, then v is odd.

We can now remove all the evens and focus on the odds, or remove all the odds and focus on the evens.

Okay, but how do we figure out what the next bit in v is? If v were contained in our (now smaller) list, then we should expect to find the following (where $count_2$ indicates the number of 0s or 1s in the second least significant bit):

$count_2$(0s) = $count_2$(1s)   OR $count_2$(0s) = 1 + $count_2$(1s)

As in the earlier example, we can deduce the value of the second least significant bit (LSB_2) of v.

	$count_2$(0s) = 1 + $count_2$(1s)	**$count_2$(0s) = $count_2$(1s)**
LSB_2(v) == 0	a 0 is removed. $count_2$(0s) = $count_2$(1s)	a 0 is removed. $count_2$(0s) < $count_2$(1s)
LSB_2(v) == 1	a 1 is removed. $count_2$(0s) > $count_2$(1s)	a 1 is removed. $count_2$(0s) > $count_2$(1s)

Again, we have the same conclusion:

- If $count_2$(0s) <= $count_2$(1s), then LSB_2(v) = 0.
- If $count_2$(0s) > $count_2$(1s), then LSB_2(v) = 1.

We can repeat this process for each bit. On each iteration, we count the number of 0s and 1s in bit `i` to check if LSB_i(v) is 0 or 1. Then, we discard the numbers where LSB_i(x) != LSB_i(v). That is, if v is even, we discard the odd numbers, and so on.

By the end of this process, we will have computed all bits in v. In each successive iteration, we look at n, then n / 2, then n / 4, and so on, bits. This results in a runtime of `O(N)`.

If it helps, we can also move through this more visually. In the first iteration, we start with all the numbers:

```
00000     00100     01000     01100
00001     00101     01001     01101
00010     00110     01010
-----     00111     01011
```

Since $count_1$(0s) > $count_1$(1s), we know that LSB_1(v) = 1. Now, discard all numbers x where LSB_1(x) != LSB_1(v).

```
~~00000~~     ~~00100~~     ~~01000~~     ~~01100~~
00001     00101     01001     01101
~~00010~~     ~~00110~~     ~~01010~~
-----     00111     01011
```

Now, $count_2$(0s) > $count_2$(1s), so we know that LSB_2(v) = 1. Now, discard all numbers x where LSB_2(x) != LSB_2(v).

~~00000~~ ~~00100~~ ~~01000~~ ~~01100~~
~~00001~~ ~~00101~~ ~~01001~~ ~~01101~~
~~00010~~ ~~00110~~ ~~01010~~
----- 00111 01011

This time, $\text{count}_3(0s) <= \text{count}_3(1s)$, we know that $\text{LSB}_3(v) = 0$. Now, discard all numbers x where $\text{LSB}_3(x) \;!= \text{LSB}_3(v)$.

~~00000~~ ~~00100~~ ~~01000~~ ~~01100~~
~~00001~~ ~~00101~~ ~~01001~~ ~~01101~~
~~00010~~ ~~00110~~ ~~01010~~
----- ~~00111~~ 01011

We're down to just one number. In this case, $\text{count}_4(0s) <= \text{count}_4(1s)$, so $\text{LSB}_4(v) = 0$.

When we discard all numbers where $\text{LSB}_4(x) \;!= 0$, we'll wind up with an empty list. Once the list is empty, then $\text{count}_i(0s) <= \text{count}_i(1s)$, so $\text{LSB}_i(v) = 0$. In other words, once we have an empty list, we can fill in the rest of the bits of v with 0.

This process will compute that, for the example above, v = 00011.

The code below implements this algorithm. We've implemented the discarding aspect by partitioning the array by bit value as we go.

```
1  int findMissing(ArrayList<BitInteger> array) {
2    /* Start from the least significant bit, and work our way up */
3    return findMissing(array, 0);
4  }
5
6  int findMissing(ArrayList<BitInteger> input, int column) {
7    if (column >= BitInteger.INTEGER_SIZE) { // We're done!
8      return 0;
9    }
10   ArrayList<BitInteger> oneBits = new ArrayList<BitInteger>(input.size()/2);
11   ArrayList<BitInteger> zeroBits = new ArrayList<BitInteger>(input.size()/2);
12
13   for (BitInteger t : input) {
14     if (t.fetch(column) == 0) {
15       zeroBits.add(t);
16     } else {
17       oneBits.add(t);
18     }
19   }
20   if (zeroBits.size() <= oneBits.size()) {
21     int v = findMissing(zeroBits, column + 1);
22     return (v << 1) | 0;
23   } else {
24     int v = findMissing(oneBits, column + 1);
25     return (v << 1) | 1;
26   }
27 }
```

In lines 24 and 27, we recursively calculate the other bits of v. Then, we insert either a 0 or 1, depending on whether or not $\text{count}_1(0s) <= \text{count}_1(1s)$.

17.5 Letters and Numbers: Given an array filled with letters and numbers, find the longest subarray with an equal number of letters and numbers.

pg 186

SOLUTION

In the introduction, we discussed the importance of creating a really good, general-purpose example. That's absolutely true. It's also important, though, to understand what matters.

In this case, we just want an equal number of letters and numbers. All letters are treated identically and all numbers are treated identically. Therefore, we can use an example with a single letter and a single number—or, for that matter, As and Bs, 0s and 1s, or `Thing1`s and `Thing2`s.

With that said, let's start with an example:

```
[A, B, A, A, A, B, B, B, A, B, A, A, B, B, A, A, A, A, A, A]
```

We're looking for the smallest subarray where `count(A, subarray) = count(B, subarray)`.

Brute Force

Let's start with the obvious solution. Just go through all subarrays, count the number of As and Bs (or letters and numbers), and find the longest one that is equal.

We can make one small optimization to this. We can start with the longest subarray and, as soon as we find one which fits this equality condition, return it.

```
/* Return the largest subarray with equal number of 0s and 1s. Look at each
 * subarray, starting from the longest. As soon as we find one that's equal, we
 * return.
char[] findLongestSubarray(char[] array) {
   for (int len = array.length; len > 1; len--) {
      for (int i = 0; i <= array.length - len; i++) {
         if (hasEqualLettersNumbers(array, i, i + len - 1)) {
            return extractSubarray(array, i, i + len - 1);
         }
      }
   }
   return null;
}

/* Check if subarray has equal number of letters and numbers. */
boolean hasEqualLettersNumbers(char[] array, int start, int end) {
   int counter = 0;
   for (int i = start; i <= end; i++) {
      if (Character.isLetter(array[i])) {
         counter++;
      } else if (Character.isDigit(array[i])) {
         counter--;
      }
   }
   return counter == 0;
}

/* Return subarray of array between start and end (inclusive). */
char[] extractSubarray(char[] array, int start, int end) {
   char[] subarray = new char[end - start + 1];
   for (int i = start; i <= end; i++) {
      subarray[i - start] = array[i];
```

```
    }
    return subarray;
}
```

Despite the one optimization we made, this algorithm is still $O(N^3)$, where N is the length of the array.

Optimal Solution

What we're trying to do is find a subarray where the count of letters equals the count of numbers. What if we just started from the beginning, counting the number of letters and numbers?

	a	a	a	a	1	1	a	1	1	a	a	1	a	a	1	a	a	a	a	a
#a	1	2	3	4	4	4	5	5	5	6	7	7	8	9	9	10	11	12	13	14
#1	0	0	0	0	1	2	2	3	4	4	4	5	5	5	6	6	6	6	6	6

Certainly, whenever the number of letters equals the number of numbers, we can say that from index 0 to that index is an "equal" subarray.

That will only tell us equal subarrays that start at index 0. How can we identify all equal subarrays?

Let's picture this. Suppose we inserted an equal subarray (like `a11a1a`) after an array like `a1aaa1`. How would that impact the counts?

	a	1	a	a	a	1	|	a	1	1	a	1	a
#a	1	1	2	3	4	4	|	5	5	5	6	6	7
#1	0	1	1	1	1	2	|	2	3	4	4	5	5

Study the numbers before the subarray (4, 2) and the end (7, 5). You might notice that, while the values aren't the same, the differences are: `4 - 2 = 7 - 5`. This makes sense. Since they've added the same number of letters and numbers, they should maintain the same difference.

> Observe that when the difference is the same, the subarray starts one after the initial matching index and continues through the final matching index. This explains line 10 in the code below.

Let's update the earlier array with the differences.

	a	a	a	a	1	1	a	1	1	a	a	1	a	a	1	a	a	a	a	a
#a	1	2	3	4	4	4	5	5	5	6	7	7	8	9	9	10	11	12	13	14
#1	0	0	0	0	1	2	2	3	4	4	4	5	5	5	6	6	6	6	6	6
-	1	2	3	4	3	2	3	2	1	2	3	2	3	4	3	4	5	6	7	8

Whenever we return the same difference, then we know we have found an equal subarray. To find the biggest subarray, we just have to find the two indices farthest apart with the same value.

To do so, we use a hash table to store the first time we see a particular difference. Then, each time we see the same difference, we see if this subarray (from first occurrence of this index to current index) is bigger than the current max. If so, we update the max.

```
1  char[] findLongestSubarray(char[] array) {
2    /* Compute deltas between count of numbers and count of letters. */
3    int[] deltas = computeDeltaArray(array);
4
5    /* Find pair in deltas with matching values and largest span. */
6    int[] match = findLongestMatch(deltas);
7
8    /* Return the subarray. Note that it starts one *after* the initial occurence of
9     * this delta. */
10   return extract(array, match[0] + 1, match[1]);
11 }
12
```

```
/* Compute the difference between the number of letters and numbers between the
 * beginning of the array and each index. */
int[] computeDeltaArray(char[] array) {
  int[] deltas = new int[array.length];
  int delta = 0;
  for (int i = 0; i < array.length; i++) {
    if (Character.isLetter(array[i])) {
      delta++;
    } else if (Character.isDigit(array[i])) {
      delta--;
    }
    deltas[i] = delta;
  }
  return deltas;
}

/* Find the matching pair of values in the deltas array with the largest
 * difference in indices. */
int[] findLongestMatch(int[] deltas) {
  HashMap<Integer, Integer> map = new HashMap<Integer, Integer>();
  map.put(0,  -1);
  int[] max = new int[2];
  for (int i = 0; i < deltas.length; i++) {
    if (!map.containsKey(deltas[i])) {
      map.put(deltas[i],  i);
    } else {
      int match = map.get(deltas[i]);
      int distance = i - match;
      int longest = max[1] - max[0];
      if (distance > longest) {
        max[1] = i;
        max[0] = match;
      }
    }
  }
  return max;
}

char[] extract(char[] array, int start, int end) { /* same */ }
```

This solution takes O(N) time, where N is size of the array.

17.6 Count of 2s: Write a method to count the number of 2s between 0 and n.

pg 186

SOLUTION

Our first approach to this problem can be—and probably should be—a brute force solution. Remember that interviewers want to see how you're approaching a problem. Offering a brute force solution is a great way to start.

```
/* Counts the number of '2' digits between 0 and n */
int numberOf2sInRange(int n) {
  int count = 0;
  for (int i = 2; i <= n; i++) { // Might as well start at 2
    count += numberOf2s(i);
```

```
    }
    return count;
}

/* Counts the number of '2' digits in a single number */
int numberOf2s(int n) {
    int count = 0;
    while (n > 0) {
        if (n % 10 == 2) {
            count++;
        }
        n = n / 10;
    }
    return count;
}
```

The only interesting part is that it's probably cleaner to separate out `numberOf2s` into a separate method. This demonstrates an eye for code cleanliness.

Improved Solution

Rather than looking at the problem by ranges of numbers, we can look at the problem digit by digit. Picture a sequence of numbers:

```
  0   1   2   3   4   5   6   7   8   9
 10  11  12  13  14  15  16  17  18  19
 20  21  22  23  24  25  26  27  28  29
...
110 111 112 113 114 115 116 117 118 119
```

We know that roughly one tenth of the time, the last digit will be a 2 since it happens once in any sequence of ten numbers. In fact, any digit is a 2 roughly one tenth of the time.

We say "roughly" because there are (very common) boundary conditions. For example, between 1 and 100, the 10's digit is a 2 exactly $\frac{1}{10}$ th of the time. However, between 1 and 37, the 10's digit is a 2 much more than $1/10^{th}$ of the time.

We can work out what exactly the ratio is by looking at the three cases individually: `digit < 2`, `digit = 2`, and `digit > 2`.

Case digit < 2

Consider the value `x = 61523` and `d = 3`, and observe that `x[d] = 1` (that is, the dth digit of x is 1). There are 2s at the 3rd digit in the ranges `2000 - 2999`, `12000 - 12999`, `22000 - 22999`, `32000 - 32999`, `42000 - 42999`, and `52000 - 52999`. We will not yet have hit the range `62000 - 62999`, so there are 6000 2s total in the 3rd digit. This is the same amount as if we were just counting all the 2s in the 3rd digit between 1 and 60000.

In other words, we can round *down* to the nearest 10^{d+1}, and then divide by 10, to compute the number of 2s in the dth digit.

```
if x[d] < 2: count2sInRangeAtDigit(x, d) =
    let y = round down to nearest 10^(d+1)
    return y / 10
```

Case digit > 2

Now, let's look at the case where dth digit of x is greater than 2 (`x[d] > 2`). We can apply almost the exact same logic to see that there are the same number of 2s in the 3rd digit in the range `0 - 63525` as there as in the range `0 - 70000`. So, rather than rounding down, we round up.

```
if x[d] > 2: count2sInRangeAtDigit(x, d) =
    let y = round up to nearest 10^(d+1)
    return y / 10
```

Case digit = 2

The final case may be the trickiest, but it follows from the earlier logic. Consider `x = 62523` and `d = 3`. We know that there are the same ranges of 2s from before (that is, the ranges `2000 - 2999`, `12000 - 12999`, ..., `52000 - 52999`). How many appear in the 3rd digit in the final, partial range from `62000 - 62523`? Well, that should be pretty easy. It's just 524 (`62000, 62001, ..., 62523`).

```
if x[d] = 2: count2sInRangeAtDigit(x, d) =
    let y = round down to nearest 10^(d+1)
    let z = right side of x (i.e., x % 10^d)
    return y / 10 + z + 1
```

Now, all you need is to iterate through each digit in the number. Implementing this code is reasonably straightforward.

```
int count2sInRangeAtDigit(int number, int d) {
   int powerOf10 = (int) Math.pow(10, d);
   int nextPowerOf10 = powerOf10 * 10;
   int right = number % powerOf10;

   int roundDown = number - number % nextPowerOf10;
   int roundUp = roundDown + nextPowerOf10;

   int digit = (number / powerOf10) % 10;
   if (digit < 2) { // if the digit in spot digit is
      return roundDown / 10;
   } else if (digit == 2) {
      return roundDown / 10 + right + 1;
   } else {
      return roundUp / 10;
   }
}

int count2sInRange(int number) {
   int count = 0;
   int len = String.valueOf(number).length();
   for (int digit = 0; digit < len; digit++) {
      count += count2sInRangeAtDigit(number, digit);
   }
   return count;
}
```

This question requires very careful testing. Make sure to generate a list of test cases, and to work through each of them.

17.7 Baby Names: Each year, the government releases a list of the 10,000 most common baby names and their frequencies (the number of babies with that name). The only problem with this is that some names have multiple spellings. For example, "John" and "Jon" are essentially the same name but would be listed separately in the list. Given two lists, one of names/frequencies and the other of pairs of equivalent names, write an algorithm to print a new list of the true frequency of each name. Note that if John and Jon are synonyms, and Jon and Johnny are synonyms, then John and Johnny are synonyms. (It is both transitive and symmetric.) In the final list, any name can be used as the "real" name.

EXAMPLE

Input:

Names: John (15), Jon (12), Chris (13), Kris (4), Christopher (19)

Synonyms: (Jon, John), (John, Johnny), (Chris, Kris), (Chris, Christopher)

Output: John (27), Kris (36)

pg 187

SOLUTION

Let's start off with a good example. We want an example with some names with multiple synonyms and some with none. Additionally, we want the synonym list to be diverse in which name is on the left side and which is on the right. For example, we wouldn't want Johnny to always be the name on the left side as we're creating the group of (John, Jonathan, Jon, and Johnny).

This list should work fairly well.

Name	Count
John	10
Jon	3
Davis	2
Kari	3
Johnny	11
Carlton	8
Carleton	2
Jonathan	9
Carrie	5

Name	Alternate
Jonathan	John
Jon	Johnny
Johnny	John
Kari	Carrie
Carleton	Carlton

The final list should be something like: John (33), Kari (8), Davis(2), Carleton (10).

Solution #1

Let's assume our baby names list is given to us as a hash table. (If not, it's easy enough to build one.)

We can start reading pairs in from the synonyms list. As we read the pair (Jonathan, John), we can merge the counts for Jonathan and John together. We'll need to remember, though, that we saw this pair, because, in the future, we could discover that Jonathan is equivalent to something else.

We can use a hash table (L1) that maps from a name to its "true" name. We'll also need to know, given a "true" name, all the names equivalent to it. This will be stored in a hash table L2. Note that L2 acts as a reverse lookup of L1.

```
READ (Jonathan, John)
```

```
        L1.ADD Jonathan -> John
        L2.ADD John -> Jonathan
    READ (Jon, Johnny)
        L1.ADD Jon -> Johnny
        L2.ADD Johnny -> Jon
    READ (Johnny, John)
        L1.ADD Johnny -> John
        L1.UPDATE Jon -> John
        L2.UPDATE John -> Jonathan, Johnny, Jon
```

If we later find that John is equivalent to, say, Jonny, we'll need to look up the names in L1 and L2 and merge together all the names that are equivalent to them.

This will work, but it's unnecessarily complicated to keep track of these two lists.

Instead, we can think of these names as "equivalence classes." When we find a pair (Jonathan, John), we put these in the same set (or equivalence classes). Each name maps to its equivalence class. All items in the set map to the same instance of the set.

If we need to merge two sets, then we copy one set into the other and update the hash table to point to the new set.

```
    READ (Jonathan, John)
        CREATE Set1 = Jonathan, John
        L1.ADD Jonathan -> Set1
        L1.ADD John -> Set1
    READ (Jon, Johnny)
        CREATE Set2 = Jon, Johnny
        L1.ADD Jon -> Set2
        L1.ADD Johnny -> Set2
    READ (Johnny, John)
        COPY Set2 into Set1.
            Set1 = Jonathan, John, Jon, Johnny
        L1.UPDATE Jon -> Set1
        L1.UPDATE Johnny -> Set1
```

In the last step above, we iterated through all items in Set2 and updated the reference to point to Set1. As we do this, we keep track of the total frequency of names.

```
HashMap<String, Integer> trulyMostPopular(HashMap<String, Integer> names,
                                           String[][] synonyms) {
  /* Parse list and initialize equivalence classes.*/
  HashMap<String, NameSet> groups = constructGroups(names);

  /* Merge equivalence classes together. */
  mergeClasses(groups, synonyms);

  /* Convert back to hash map. */
  return convertToMap(groups);
}

/* This is the core of the algorithm. Read through each pair. Merge their
 * equivalence classes and update the mapping of the secondary class to point to
 * the first set.*/
void mergeClasses(HashMap<String, NameSet> groups, String[][] synonyms) {
  for (String[] entry : synonyms) {
    String name1 = entry[0];
    String name2 = entry[1];
    NameSet set1 = groups.get(name1);
```

```
      NameSet set2 = groups.get(name2);
      if (set1 != set2) {
         /* Always merge the smaller set into the bigger one. */
         NameSet smaller = set2.size() < set1.size() ? set2 : set1;
         NameSet bigger = set2.size() < set1.size() ? set1 : set2;

         /* Merge lists */
         Set<String> otherNames = smaller.getNames();
         int frequency = smaller.getFrequency();
         bigger.copyNamesWithFrequency(otherNames, frequency);

         /* Update mapping */
         for (String name : otherNames) {
            groups.put(name,  bigger);
         }
      }
   }
}

/* Read through (name, frequency) pairs and initialize a mapping of names to
 * NameSets (equivalence classes).*/
HashMap<String, NameSet> constructGroups(HashMap<String, Integer> names) {
   HashMap<String, NameSet> groups = new HashMap<String, NameSet>();
   for (Entry<String, Integer> entry : names.entrySet()) {
      String name = entry.getKey();
      int frequency = entry.getValue();
      NameSet group = new NameSet(name, frequency);
      groups.put(name,  group);
   }
   return groups;
}

HashMap<String, Integer> convertToMap(HashMap<String, NameSet> groups) {
   HashMap<String, Integer> list = new HashMap<String, Integer>();
   for (NameSet group : groups.values()) {
      list.put(group.getRootName(), group.getFrequency());
   }
   return list;
}

public class NameSet {
   private Set<String> names = new HashSet<String>();
   private int frequency = 0;
   private String rootName;

   public NameSet(String name, int freq) {
      names.add(name);
      frequency = freq;
      rootName = name;
   }

   public void copyNamesWithFrequency(Set<String> more, int freq) {
      names.addAll(more);
      frequency += freq;
   }

```

```
    public Set<String> getNames() { return names; }
    public String getRootName() { return rootName; }
    public int getFrequency() { return frequency; }
    public int size() { return names.size(); }
}
```

The runtime of the algorithm is a bit tricky to figure out. One way to think about it is to think about what the worst case is.

For this algorithm, the worst case is where all names are equivalent—and we have to constantly merge sets together. Also, for the worst case, the merging should come in the worst possible way: repeated pairwise merging of sets. Each merging requires copying the set's elements into an existing set and updating the pointers from those items. It's slowest when the sets are larger.

If you notice the parallel with merge sort (where you have to merge single-element arrays into two-element arrays, and then two-element arrays into four-element arrays, until finally having a full array), you might guess it's `O(N log N)`. That is correct.

If you don't notice that parallel, here's another way to think about it.

Imagine we had the names (a, b, c, d, `...`, z). In our worst case, we'd first pair up the items into equivalence classes: (a, b), (c, d), (e, f), `...`, (y, z). Then, we'd merge pairs of those: (a, b, c, d), (e, f, g, h), `...`, (w, x, y, z). We'd continue doing this until we wind up with just one class.

At each "sweep" through the list where we merge sets together, half of the items get moved into a new set. This takes `O(N)` work per sweep. (There are fewer sets to merge, but each set has grown larger.)

How many sweeps do we do? At each sweep, we have half as many sets as we did before. Therefore, we do `O(log N)` sweeps.

Since we're doing `O(log N)` sweeps and `O(N)` work per sweep, the total runtime is `O(N log N)`.

This is pretty good, but let's see if we can make it even faster.

Optimized Solution

To optimize the old solution, we should think about what exactly makes it slow. Essentially, it's the merging and updating of pointers.

So what if we just didn't do that? What if we marked that there was an equivalence relationship between two names, but didn't actually do anything with the information yet?

In this case, we'd be building essentially a graph.

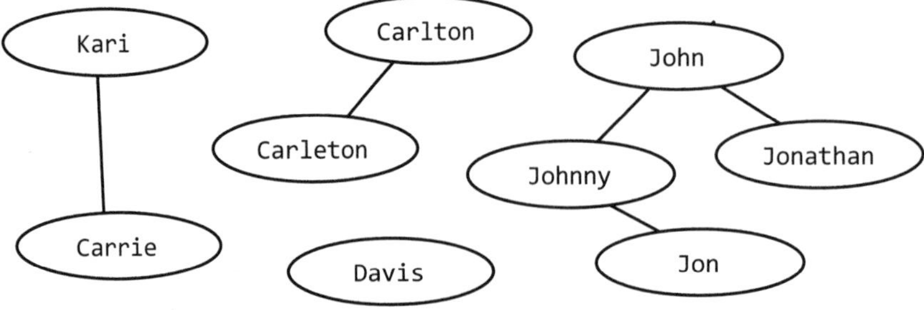

Now what? Visually, it seems easy enough. Each component is an equivalent set of names. We just need to group the names by their component, sum up their frequencies, and return a list with one arbitrarily chosen name from each group.

In practice, how does this work? We could pick a name and do a depth-first (or breadth-first) search to sum the frequencies of all the names in one component. We would have to make sure that we hit each component exactly once. That's easy enough to achieve: mark a node as `visited` after it's discovered in the graph search, and only start the search for nodes where `visited` is false.

```
HashMap<String, Integer> trulyMostPopular(HashMap<String, Integer> names,
                                          String[][] synonyms) {
  /* Create data. */
  Graph graph = constructGraph(names);
  connectEdges(graph, synonyms);

  /* Find components. */
  HashMap<String, Integer> rootNames = getTrueFrequencies(graph);
  return rootNames;
}

/* Add all names to graph as nodes. */
Graph constructGraph(HashMap<String, Integer> names) {
  Graph graph = new Graph();
  for (Entry<String, Integer> entry : names.entrySet()) {
      String name = entry.getKey();
      int frequency = entry.getValue();
      graph.createNode(name, frequency);
  }
  return graph;
}

/* Connect synonymous spellings. */
void connectEdges(Graph graph, String[][] synonyms) {
  for (String[] entry : synonyms) {
      String name1 = entry[0];
      String name2 = entry[1];
      graph.addEdge(name1,  name2);
  }
}

/* Do DFS of each component. If a node has been visited before, then its component
 * has already been computed. */
HashMap<String, Integer> getTrueFrequencies(Graph graph) {
  HashMap<String, Integer> rootNames = new HashMap<String, Integer>();
  for (GraphNode node : graph.getNodes()) {
     if (!node.isVisited()) { // Already visited this component
        int frequency = getComponentFrequency(node);
        String name = node.getName();
        rootNames.put(name, frequency);
     }
  }
  return rootNames;
}

/* Do depth-first search to find the total frequency of this component, and mark
 * each node as visited.*/
int getComponentFrequency(GraphNode node) {
  if (node.isVisited()) return 0; // Already visited

  node.setIsVisited(true);
  int sum = node.getFrequency();
```

```
    for (GraphNode child : node.getNeighbors()) {
       sum += getComponentFrequency(child);
    }
    return sum;
 }

 /* Code for GraphNode and Graph is fairly self-explanatory, but can be found in
  * the downloadable code solutions.*/
```

To analyze the efficiency, we can think about the efficiency of each part of the algorithm.

- Reading in the data is linear with respect to the size of the data, so it takes `O(B + P)` time, where B is the number of baby names and P is the number of pairs of synonyms. This is because we only do a constant amount of work per piece of input data.
- To compute the frequencies, each edge gets "touched" exactly once across all of the graph searches and each node gets touched exactly once to check if it's been visited. The time of this part is `O(B + P)`.

Therefore, the total time of the algorithm is `O(B + P)`. We know we cannot do better than this since we must at least read in the `B + P` pieces of data.

17.8 Circus Tower: A circus is designing a tower routine consisting of people standing atop one another's shoulders. For practical and aesthetic reasons, each person must be both shorter and lighter than the person below him or her. Given the heights and weights of each person in the circus, write a method to compute the largest possible number of people in such a tower.

pg 187

SOLUTION

When we cut out all the "fluff" to this problem, we can understand that the problem is really the following.

We have a list of pairs of items. Find the longest sequence such that both the first and second items are in non-decreasing order.

One thing we might first try is sorting the items on an attribute. This is useful actually, but it won't get us all the way there.

By sorting the items by height, we have a relative order the items must appear in. We still need to find the longest increasing subsequence of weight though.

Solution 1: Recursive

One approach is to essentially try all possibilities. After sorting by height, we iterate through the array. At each element, we branch into two choices: add this element to the subsequence (if it's valid) or do not.

```
ArrayList<HtWt> longestIncreasingSeq(ArrayList<HtWt> items) {
   Collections.sort(items);
   return bestSeqAtIndex(items, new ArrayList<HtWt>(), 0);
}

ArrayList<HtWt> bestSeqAtIndex(ArrayList<HtWt> array, ArrayList<HtWt> sequence,
                               int index) {
   if (index >= array.size()) return sequence;

   HtWt value = array.get(index);

```

```
  ArrayList<HtWt> bestWith = null;
  if (canAppend(sequence, value)) {
    ArrayList<HtWt> sequenceWith = (ArrayList<HtWt>) sequence.clone();
    sequenceWith.add(value);
    bestWith = bestSeqAtIndex(array, sequenceWith, index + 1);
  }

  ArrayList<HtWt> bestWithout = bestSeqAtIndex(array, sequence, index + 1);
  return max(bestWith, bestWithout);
}

boolean canAppend(ArrayList<HtWt> solution, HtWt value) {
  if (solution == null) return false;
  if (solution.size() == 0) return true;

  HtWt last = solution.get(solution.size() - 1);
  return last.isBefore(value);
}

ArrayList<HtWt> max(ArrayList<HtWt> seq1, ArrayList<HtWt> seq2) {
  if (seq1 == null) {
    return seq2;
  } else if (seq2 == null) {
    return seq1;
  }
  return seq1.size() > seq2.size() ? seq1 : seq2;
}

public class HtWt implements Comparable<HtWt> {
  private int height;
  private int weight;
  public HtWt(int h, int w) { height = h; weight = w; }

  public int compareTo(HtWt second) {
    if (this.height != second.height) {
      return ((Integer)this.height).compareTo(second.height);
    } else {
      return ((Integer)this.weight).compareTo(second.weight);
    }
  }

  /* Returns true if "this" should be lined up before "other". Note that it's
   * possible that this.isBefore(other) and other.isBefore(this) are both false.
   * This is different from the compareTo method, where if a < b then b > a. */
  public boolean isBefore(HtWt other) {
    if (height < other.height && weight < other.weight) {
      return true;
    } else {
      return false;
    }
  }
}
```

This algorithm will take $O(2^n)$ time. We can optimize it using memoization (that is, caching the best sequences).

There's a cleaner way to do this though.

Solution #2: Iterative

Imagine we had the longest subsequence that terminates with each element, A[0] through A[3]. Could we use this to find the longest subsequence that terminates with A[4]?

```
Array: 13, 14, 10, 11, 12
Longest(ending with A[0]): 13
Longest(ending with A[1]): 13, 14
Longest(ending with A[2]): 10
Longest(ending with A[3]): 10, 11
Longest(ending with A[4]): 10, 11, 12
```

Sure. We just append A[4] on to the longest subsequence that it can be appended to.

This is now fairly straightforward to implement.

```
ArrayList<HtWt> longestIncreasingSeq(ArrayList<HtWt> array) {
  Collections.sort(array);

  ArrayList<ArrayList<HtWt>> solutions =  new ArrayList<ArrayList<HtWt>>();
  ArrayList<HtWt> bestSequence = null;

  /* Find the longest subsequence that terminates with each element. Track the
   * longest overall subsequence as we go. */
  for (int i = 0; i < array.size(); i++) {
    ArrayList<HtWt> longestAtIndex = bestSeqAtIndex(array, solutions, i);
    solutions.add(i, longestAtIndex);
    bestSequence = max(bestSequence, longestAtIndex);
  }

  return bestSequence;
}

/* Find the longest subsequence which terminates with this element. */
ArrayList<HtWt> bestSeqAtIndex(ArrayList<HtWt> array,
    ArrayList<ArrayList<HtWt>> solutions, int index) {
  HtWt value = array.get(index);

  ArrayList<HtWt> bestSequence = new ArrayList<HtWt>();

  /* Find the longest subsequence that we can append this element to. */
  for (int i = 0; i < index; i++) {
    ArrayList<HtWt> solution = solutions.get(i);
    if (canAppend(solution, value)) {
      bestSequence = max(solution, bestSequence);
    }
  }

  /* Append element. */
  ArrayList<HtWt> best = (ArrayList<HtWt>) bestSequence.clone();
  best.add(value);

  return best;
}
```

This algorithm operates in $O(n^2)$ time. An O(n log(n)) algorithm does exist, but it is considerably more complicated and it is highly unlikely that you would derive this in an interview—even with some help. However, if you are interested in exploring this solution, a quick internet search will turn up a number of explanations of this solution.

17.9 Kth Multiple: Design an algorithm to find the kth number such that the only prime factors are 3, 5, and 7. Note that 3, 5, and 7 do not have to be factors, but it should not have any other prime factors. For example, the first several multiples would be (in order) 1, 3, 5, 7, 9, 15, 21.

pg 187

SOLUTION

Let's first understand what this problem is asking for. It's asking for the kth smallest number that is in the form $3^a * 5^b * 7^c$. Let's start with a brute force way of finding this.

Brute Force

We know that biggest this kth number could be is $3^k * 5^k * 7^k$. So, the "stupid" way of doing this is to compute $3^a * 5^b * 7^c$ for all values of a, b, and c between 0 and k. We can throw them all into a list, sort the list, and then pick the kth smallest value.

```
int getKthMagicNumber(int k) {
  ArrayList<Integer> possibilities = allPossibleKFactors(k);
  Collections.sort(possibilities);
  return possibilities.get(k);
}

ArrayList<Integer> allPossibleKFactors(int k) {
  ArrayList<Integer> values = new ArrayList<Integer>();
  for (int a = 0; a <= k; a++) { // loop 3
    int powA = (int) Math.pow(3,  a);
    for (int b = 0; b <= k; b++) { // loop 5
      int powB = (int) Math.pow(5,  b);
      for (int c = 0; c <= k; c++) { // loop 7
        int powC = (int) Math.pow(7, c);
        int value = powA * powB * powC;

        /* Check for overflow. */
        if (value < 0 || powA == Integer.MAX_VALUE ||
            powB == Integer.MAX_VALUE ||
            powC == Integer.MAX_VALUE) {
          value = Integer.MAX_VALUE;
        }
        values.add(value);
      }
    }
  }
  return values;
}
```

What is the runtime of this approach? We have nested for loops, each of which runs for k iterations. The runtime of the `allPossibleKFactors` is $O(k^3)$. Then, we sort the k^3 results in $O(k^3 \log (k^3))$ time (which is equivalent to $O(k^3 \log k)$. This gives us a runtime of $O(k^3 \log k)$.

There are a number of optimizations you could make to this (and better ways of handling the integer overflow), but honestly this algorithm is fairly slow. We should instead focus on reworking the algorithm.

Improved

Let's picture what our results will look like.

1	-	$3^0 * 5^0 * 7^0$
3	3	$3^1 * 5^0 * 7^0$
5	5	$3^0 * 5^1 * 7^0$
7	7	$3^0 * 5^0 * 7^1$
9	3*3	$3^2 * 5^0 * 7^0$
15	3*5	$3^1 * 5^1 * 7^0$
21	3*7	$3^1 * 5^0 * 7^1$
25	5*5	$3^0 * 5^2 * 7^0$
27	3*9	$3^3 * 5^0 * 7^0$
35	5*7	$3^0 * 5^1 * 7^1$
45	5*9	$3^2 * 5^1 * 7^0$
49	7*7	$3^0 * 5^0 * 7^2$
63	3*21	$3^2 * 5^0 * 7^1$

The question is: what is the next value in the list? The next value will be one of these:

- 3 * (some previous number in list)
- 5 * (some previous number in list)
- 7 * (some previous number in list)

If this doesn't immediately jump out at you, think about it this way: whatever the next value (let's call it nv) is, divide it by 3. Will that number have already appeared? As long as nv has factors of 3 in it, yes. The same can be said for dividing it by 5 and 7.

So, we know A_k can be expressed as (3, 5 or 7) * (some value in $\{A_1, \ldots, A_{k-1}\}$). We also know that A_k is, by definition, the next number in the list. Therefore, A_k will be the smallest "new" number (a number that it's already in $\{A_1, \ldots, A_{k-1}\}$) that can be formed by multiplying each value in the list by 3, 5 or 7.

How would we find A_k? Well, we could actually multiply each number in the list by 3, 5, and 7 and find the smallest element that has not yet been added to our list. This solution is $O(k^2)$. Not bad, but I think we can do better.

Rather than A_k trying to "pull" from a previous element in the list (by multiplying all of them by 3, 5 and 7), we can think about each previous value in the list as "pushing" out three subsequent values in the list. That is, each number A_i will eventually be used later in the list in the following forms:

- $3 * A_i$
- $5 * A_i$
- $7 * A_i$

We can use this thought to plan in advance. Each time we add a number A_i to the list, we hold on to the values $3A_i$, $5A_i$, and $7A_i$ in some sort of temporary list. To generate A_{i+1}, we search through this temporary list to find the smallest value.

Our code looks like this:

```
int removeMin(Queue<Integer> q) {
   int min = q.peek();
   for (Integer v : q) {
      if (min > v) {
         min = v;
      }
```

```
    }
    while (q.contains(min)) {
       q.remove(min);
    }
    return min;
 }

 void addProducts(Queue<Integer> q, int v) {
    q.add(v * 3);
    q.add(v * 5);
    q.add(v * 7);
 }

 int getKthMagicNumber(int k) {
    if (k < 0) return 0;

    int val = 1;
    Queue<Integer> q = new LinkedList<Integer>();
    addProducts(q, 1);
    for (int i = 0; i < k; i++) {
       val = removeMin(q);
       addProducts(q, val);
    }
    return val;
 }
```

This algorithm is certainly much, much better than our first algorithm, but it's still not quite perfect.

Optimal Algorithm

To generate a new element A_i, we are searching through a linked list where each element looks like one of:

- 3 * previous element
- 5 * previous element
- 7 * previous element

Where is there unnecessary work that we might be able to optimize out?

Let's imagine our list looks like:

$$q_6 = \{7A_1, 5A_2, 7A_2, 7A_3, 3A_4, 5A_4, 7A_4, 5A_5, 7A_5\}$$

When we search this list for the min, we check if $7A_1 < min$, and then later we check if $7A_5 < min$. That seems sort of silly, doesn't it? Since we know that $A_1 < A_5$, we should only need to check $7A_1$.

If we separated the list from the beginning by the constant factors, then we'd only need to check the first of the multiples of 3, 5 and 7. All subsequent elements would be bigger.

That is, our list above would look like:

$$Q36 = \{3A_4\}$$
$$Q56 = \{5A_2, 5A_4, 5A_5\}$$
$$Q76 = \{7A_1, 7A_2, 7A_3, 7A_4, 7A_5\}$$

To get the min, we only need to look at the fronts of each queue:

```
y = min(Q3.head(), Q5.head(), Q7.head())
```

Once we compute y, we need to insert 3y into Q3, 5y into Q5, and 7y into Q7. But, we only want to insert these elements if they aren't already in another list.

Why might, for example, 3y already be somewhere in the holding queues? Well, if y was pulled from Q7, then that means that y = 7x, for some smaller x. If 7x is the smallest value, we must have already seen 3x. And what did we do when we saw 3x? We inserted 7 * 3x into Q7. Note that 7 * 3x = 3 * 7x = 3y.

To put this another way, if we pull an element from Q7, it will look like 7 * `suffix`, and we know we have already handled 3 * `suffix` and 5 * `suffix`. In handling 3 * `suffix`, we inserted 7 * 3 * `suffix` into a Q7. And in handling 5 * `suffix`, we know we inserted 7 * 5 * `suffix` in Q7. The only value we haven't seen yet is 7 * 7 * suffix, so we just insert 7 * 7 * `suffix` into Q7.

Let's walk through this with an example to make it really clear.

```
initialize:
        Q3 = 3
        Q5 = 5
        Q7 = 7
remove min = 3. insert 3*3 in Q3, 5*3 into Q5, 7*3 into Q7.
        Q3 = 3*3
        Q5 = 5, 5*3
        Q7 = 7, 7*3
remove min = 5. 3*5 is a dup, since we already did 5*3. insert 5*5 into Q5, 7*5
into Q7.
        Q3 = 3*3
        Q5 = 5*3, 5*5
        Q7 = 7, 7*3, 7*5.
remove min = 7. 3*7 and 5*7 are dups, since we already did 7*3 and 7*5. insert 7*7
into Q7.
        Q3 = 3*3
        Q5 = 5*3, 5*5
        Q7 = 7*3, 7*5, 7*7
remove min = 3*3 = 9. insert 3*3*3 in Q3, 3*3*5 into Q5, 3*3*7 into Q7.
        Q3 = 3*3*3
        Q5 = 5*3, 5*5, 5*3*3
        Q7 = 7*3, 7*5, 7*7, 7*3*3
remove min = 5*3 = 15. 3*(5*3) is a dup, since we already did 5*(3*3). insert
5*5*3 in Q5, 7*5*3 into Q7.
        Q3 = 3*3*3
        Q5 = 5*5, 5*3*3, 5*5*3
        Q7 = 7*3, 7*5, 7*7, 7*3*3, 7*5*3
remove min = 7*3 = 21. 3*(7*3) and 5*(7*3) are dups, since we already did 7*(3*3)
and 7*(5*3). insert 7*7*3 into Q7.
        Q3 = 3*3*3
        Q5 = 5*5, 5*3*3, 5*5*3
        Q7 = 7*5, 7*7, 7*3*3, 7*5*3, 7*7*3
```

Our pseudocode for this problem is as follows:

1. Initialize `array` and queues Q3, Q5, and Q7
2. Insert 1 into `array`.
3. Insert `1*3`, `1*5` and `1*7` into Q3, Q5, and Q7 respectively.
4. Let x be the minimum element in Q3, Q5, and Q7. Append x to `magic`.
5. If x was found in:

   Q3 -> append `x*3`, `x*5` and `x*7` to Q3, Q5, and Q7. Remove x from Q3.

   Q5 -> append `x*5` and `x*7` to Q5 and Q7. Remove x from Q5.

   Q7 -> only append `x*7` to Q7. Remove x from Q7.

6. Repeat steps 4 - 6 until we've found k elements.

The code below implements this algorithm.

```
int getKthMagicNumber(int k) {
  if (k < 0) {
    return 0;
  }
  int val = 0;
  Queue<Integer> queue3 = new LinkedList<Integer>();
  Queue<Integer> queue5 = new LinkedList<Integer>();
  Queue<Integer> queue7 = new LinkedList<Integer>();
  queue3.add(1);

  /* Include 0th through kth iteration */
  for (int i = 0; i <= k; i++) {
    int v3 = queue3.size() > 0 ? queue3.peek() : Integer.MAX_VALUE;
    int v5 = queue5.size() > 0 ? queue5.peek() : Integer.MAX_VALUE;
    int v7 = queue7.size() > 0 ? queue7.peek() : Integer.MAX_VALUE;
    val = Math.min(v3, Math.min(v5, v7));
    if (val == v3) { // enqueue into queue 3, 5 and 7
      queue3.remove();
      queue3.add(3 * val);
      queue5.add(5 * val);
    } else if (val == v5) { // enqueue into queue 5 and 7
      queue5.remove();
      queue5.add(5 * val);
    } else if (val == v7) { // enqueue into Q7
      queue7.remove();
    }
    queue7.add(7 * val); // Always enqueue into Q7
  }
  return val;
}
```

When you get this question, do your best to solve it—even though it's really difficult. You can start with a brute force approach (challenging, but not quite as tricky), and then you can start trying to optimize it. Or, try to find a pattern in the numbers.

Chances are that your interviewer will help you along when you get stuck. Whatever you do, don't give up! Think out loud, wonder out loud, and explain your thought process. Your interviewer will probably jump in to guide you.

Remember, perfection on this problem is not expected. Your performance is evaluated in comparison to other candidates. Everyone struggles on a tricky problem.

17.10 Majority Element: A majority element is an element that makes up more than half of the items in an array. Given a positive integers array, find the majority element. If there is no majority element, return -1. Do this in O(N) time and O(1) space.

Input: `1 2 5 9 5 9 5 5 5`

Output: `5`

pg 187

SOLUTION

Let's start off with an example:

```
3 1 7 1 3 7 3 7 1 7 7
```

One thing we can notice here is that if the majority element (in this case 7) appears less often in the beginning, it must appear much more often toward the end. That's a good observation to make.

This interview question specifically requires us to do this in `O(N)` time and `O(1)` space. Nonetheless, sometimes it can be useful to relax one of those requirements and develop an algorithm. Let's try relaxing the time requirement but staying firm on the `O(1)` space requirement.

Solution #1 (Slow)

One simple way to do this is to just iterate through the array and check each element for whether it's the majority element. This takes $O(N^2)$ time and `O(1)` space.

```
int findMajorityElement(int[] array) {
   for (int x : array) {
      if (validate(array, x)) {
         return x;
      }
   }
   return -1;
}

boolean validate(int[] array, int majority) {
   int count = 0;
   for (int n : array) {
      if (n == majority) {
         count++;
      }
   }

   return count > array.length / 2;
}
```

This does not fit the time requirements of the problem, but it is potentially a starting point. We can think about optimizing this.

Solution #2 (Optimal)

Let's think about what that algorithm did on a particular example. Is there anything we can get rid of?

3	1	7	1	1	7	7	3	7	7	7
0	1	2	3	4	5	6	7	8	9	10

In the very first validation pass, we select 3 and validate it as the majority element by counting how many 3s appear after it. Several elements later, we've still counted just one 3 and several non-3 elements. Do we need to continue checking for 3?

On one hand, yes. 3 could redeem itself and be the majority element, if there are a bunch of 3s later in the array.

On the other hand, not really. If 3 does redeem itself, then we'll encounter those 3s later on, in a subsequent validation step. We could terminate this `validate(3)` step as soon as the number of "not 3s" (`countNo`) is at least as big as the number of 3s (`countYes`). That is, we terminate the `validate` operation when `countNo >= countYes`.

What do we do for the next elements? Well, since it worked for the first element, we can treat the second element like it's the start of a new array.

What would this look like?

```
validate(3) on [3, 1, 7, 1, 1, 7, 7, 3, 7, 7, 7]
    sees 3 -> countYes = 1, countNo = 0
    sees 1 -> countYes = 1, countNo = 1
    TERMINATE. 3 is not majority thus far.
validate(1) on [1, 7, 1, 1, 7, 7, 3, 7, 7, 7]
    sees 1 -> countYes = 0, countNo = 0
    sees 7 -> countYes = 1, countNo = 1
    TERMINATE. 1 is not majority thus far.
validate(7) on [7, 1, 1, 7, 7, 3, 7, 7, 7]
    sees 7 -> countYes = 1, countNo = 0
    sees 1 -> countYes = 1, countNo = 1
    TERMINATE. 7 is not majority thus far.
validate(1) on [1, 1, 7, 7, 3, 7, 7, 7]
    sees 1 -> countYes = 1, countNo = 0
    sees 1 -> countYes = 2, countNo = 0
    sees 7 -> countYes = 2, countNo = 1
    sees 7 -> countYes = 2, countNo = 1
    TERMINATE. 1 is not majority thus far.
validate(1) on [1, 7, 7, 3, 7, 7, 7]
    sees 1 -> countYes = 1, countNo = 0
    sees 7 -> countYes = 1, countNo = 1
    TERMINATE. 1 is not majority thus far.
validate(7) on [7, 7, 3, 7, 7, 7]
    sees 7 -> countYes = 1, countNo = 0
    sees 7 -> countYes = 2, countNo = 0
    sees 3 -> countYes = 2, countNo = 1
    sees 7 -> countYes = 3, countNo = 1
    sees 7 -> countYes = 4, countNo = 1
    sees 7 -> countYes = 5, countNo = 1
```

Do we know at this point that 7 is the majority element? Not necessarily. We have eliminated everything before that 7, and everything after it. But there could be no majority element. A quick `validate(7)` pass that starts from the beginning can confirm if 7 is actually the majority element. This `validate` step will be `O(N)` time, which is also our Best Conceivable Runtime. Therefore, this final `validate` step won't impact our total runtime.

This is pretty good, but let's see if we can make this a bit faster. We should notice that some elements are being "inspected" repeatedly. Can we get rid of this?

Look at the first `validate(3)`. This fails after the subarray `[3, 1]`, because 3 was not the majority element. But because `validate` fails the instant an element is not the majority element, it also means nothing else in that subarray was the majority element. By our earlier logic, we don't need to call `validate(1)`. We know that `1` did not appear more than half the time. If it is the majority element, it'll pop up later.

Let's try this again and see if it works out.

```
validate(3) on [3, 1, 7, 1, 1, 7, 7, 3, 7, 7, 7]
    sees 3 -> countYes = 1, countNo = 0
    sees 1 -> countYes = 1, countNo = 1
    TERMINATE. 3 is not majority thus far.
skip 1
validate(7) on [7, 1, 1, 7, 7, 3, 7, 7, 7]
    sees 7 -> countYes = 1, countNo = 0
    sees 1 -> countYes = 1, countNo = 1
    TERMINATE. 7 is not majority thus far.
skip 1
```

```
validate(1) on [1, 7, 7, 3, 7, 7, 7]
    sees 1 -> countYes = 1, countNo = 0
    sees 7 -> countYes = 1, countNo = 1
    TERMINATE. 1 is not majority thus far.
skip 7
validate(7) on [7, 3, 7, 7, 7]
    sees 7 -> countYes = 1, countNo = 0
    sees 3 -> countYes = 1, countNo = 1
    TERMINATE. 7 is not majority thus far.
skip 3
validate(7) on [7, 7, 7]
    sees 7 -> countYes = 1, countNo = 0
    sees 7 -> countYes = 2, countNo = 0
    sees 7 -> countYes = 3, countNo = 0
```

Good! We got the right answer. But did we just get lucky?

We should pause for a moment to think what this algorithm is doing.

1. We start off with `[3]` and we expand the subarray until 3 is no longer the majority element. We fail at `[3, 1]`. At the moment we fail, the subarray can have no majority element.
2. Then we go to `[7]` and expand until `[7, 1]`. Again, we terminate and nothing could be the majority element in that subarray.
3. We move to [1] and expand to `[1, 7]`. We terminate. Nothing there could be the majority element.
4. We go to `[7]` and expand to `[7, 3]`. We terminate. Nothing there could be the majority element.
5. We go to `[7]` and expand until the end of the array: `[7, 7, 7]`. We have found the majority element (and now we must validate that).

Each time we terminate the `validate` step, the subarray has no majority element. This means that there are at least as many non-7s as there are 7s. Although we're essentially removing this subarray from the original array, the majority element will still be found in the rest of the array—and will still have majority status. Therefore, at some point, we will discover the majority element.

Our algorithm can now be run in two passes: one to find the possible majority element and another to validate it. Rather than using two variables to count (`countYes` and `countNo`), we'll just use a single `count` variable that increments and decrements.

```
int findMajorityElement(int[] array) {
  int candidate = getCandidate(array);
  return validate(array, candidate) ? candidate : -1;
}

int getCandidate(int[] array) {
  int majority = 0;
  int count = 0;
  for (int n : array) {
    if (count == 0) { // No majority element in previous set.
      majority = n;
    }
    if (n == majority) {
      count++;
    } else {
      count--;
    }
  }
  return majority;
```

```
}

boolean validate(int[] array, int majority) {
  int count = 0;
  for (int n : array) {
    if (n == majority) {
      count++;
    }
  }

  return count > array.length / 2;
}
```

This algorithm runs in O(N) time and O(1) space.

17.11 Word Distance: You have a large text file containing words. Given any two words, find the shortest distance (in terms of number of words) between them in the file. If the operation will be repeated many times for the same file (but different pairs of words), can you optimize your solution?

pg 187

SOLUTION

We will assume for this question that it doesn't matter whether word1 or word2 appears first. This is a question you should ask your interviewer.

To solve this problem, we can traverse the file just once. We remember throughout our traversal where we've last seen word1 and word2, storing the locations in location1 and location2. If the current locations are better than our best known location, we update the best locations.

The code below implements this algorithm.

```
LocationPair findClosest(String[] words, String word1, String word2) {
  LocationPair best = new LocationPair(-1, -1);
  LocationPair current = new LocationPair(-1, -1);
  for (int i = 0; i < words.length; i++) {
    String word = words[i];
    if (word.equals(word1)) {
      current.location1 = i;
      best.updateWithMin(current);
    } else if (word.equals(word2)) {
      current.location2 = i;
      best.updateWithMin(current); // If shorter, update values
    }
  }
  return best;
}

public class LocationPair {
  public int location1, location2;
  public LocationPair(int first, int second) {
    setLocations(first, second);
  }

  public void setLocations(int first, int second) {
    this.location1 = first;
    this.location2 = second;
```

```
    }

    public void setLocations(LocationPair loc) {
        setLocations(loc.location1, loc.location2);
    }

    public int distance() {
        return Math.abs(location1 - location2);
    }

    public boolean isValid() {
        return location1 >= 0 && location2 >= 0;
    }

    public void updateWithMin(LocationPair loc) {
        if (!isValid() || loc.distance() < distance()) {
            setLocations(loc);
        }
    }
}
```

If we need to repeat the operation for other pairs of words, we can create a hash table that maps from each word to the locations where it occurs. We'll only need to read through the list of words once. After that point, we can do a very similar algorithm but just iterate through the locations directly.

Consider the following lists of locations.

```
listA: {1, 2, 9, 15, 25}
listB: {4, 10, 19}
```

Picture pointers pA and pB that point to the beginning of each list. Our goal is to make pA and pB point to values as close together as possible.

The first potential pair is `(1, 4)`.

What is the next pair we can find? If we moved pB, then the distance would definitely get larger. If we moved pA, though, we might get a better pair. Let's do that.

The second potential pair is `(2, 4)`. This is better than the previous pair, so let's record this as the best pair.

We move pA again and get `(9, 4)`. This is worse than we had before.

Now, since the value at pA is bigger than the one at pB, we move pB. We get `(9, 10)`.

Next we get `(15, 10)`, then `(15, 19)`, then `(25, 19)`.

We can implement this algorithm as shown below.

```
LocationPair findClosest(String word1, String word2,
                         HashMapList<String, Integer> locations) {
    ArrayList<Integer> locations1 = locations.get(word1);
    ArrayList<Integer> locations2 = locations.get(word2);
    return findMinDistancePair(locations1, locations2);
}

LocationPair findMinDistancePair(ArrayList<Integer> array1,
                                 ArrayList<Integer> array2) {
    if (array1 == null || array2 == null || array1.size() == 0 ||
        array2.size() == 0) {
        return null;
    }
```

```

    int index1 = 0;
    int index2 = 0;
    LocationPair best = new LocationPair(array1.get(0), array2.get(0));
    LocationPair current = new LocationPair(array1.get(0), array2.get(0));

    while (index1 < array1.size() && index2 < array2.size()) {
       current.setLocations(array1.get(index1), array2.get(index2));
       best.updateWithMin(current); // If shorter, update values
       if (current.location1 < current.location2) {
          index1++;
       } else {
          index2++;
       }
    }

    return best;
 }

 /* Precomputation. */
 HashMapList<String, Integer> getWordLocations(String[] words) {
    HashMapList<String, Integer> locations = new HashMapList<String, Integer>();
    for (int i = 0; i < words.length; i++) {
       locations.put(words[i], i);
    }
    return locations;
 }

 /* HashMapList<String, Integer> is a HashMap that maps from Strings to
  * ArrayList<Integer>. See appendix for implementation. */
```

The precomputation step of this algorithm will take O(N) time, where N is the number of words in the string.

Finding the closest pair of locations will take O(A + B) time, where A is the number of occurrences of the first word and B is the number of occurrences of the second word.

17.12 BiNode: Consider a simple data structure called BiNode, which has pointers to two other nodes. The data structure BiNode could be used to represent both a binary tree (where node1 is the left node and node2 is the right node) or a doubly linked list (where node1 is the previous node and node2 is the next node). Implement a method to convert a binary search tree (implemented with BiNode) into a doubly linked list. The values should be kept in order and the operation should be performed in place (that is, on the original data structure).

pg 188

SOLUTION

This seemingly complex problem can be implemented quite elegantly using recursion. You will need to understand recursion very well to solve it.

Picture a simple binary search tree:

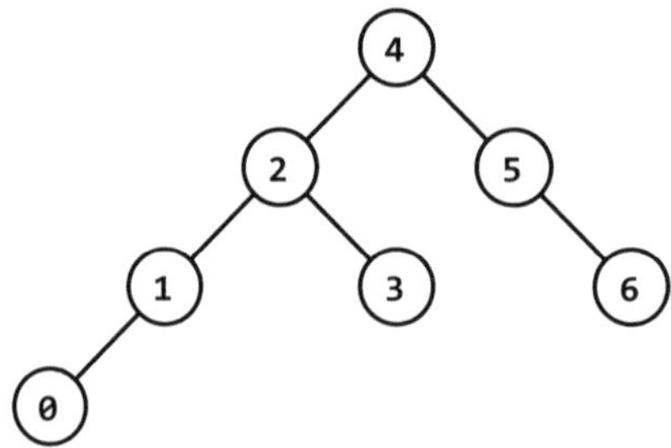

The `convert` method should transform it into the below doubly linked list:

```
0 <-> 1 <-> 2 <-> 3 <-> 4 <-> 5 <-> 6
```

Let's approach this recursively, starting with the root (node 4).

We know that the left and right halves of the tree form their own "sub-parts" of the linked list (that is, they appear consecutively in the linked list). So, if we recursively converted the left and right subtrees to a doubly linked list, could we build the final linked list from those parts?

Yes! We would simply merge the different parts.

The pseudocode looks something like:

```
BiNode convert(BiNode node) {
   BiNode left = convert(node.left);
   BiNode right = convert(node.right);
   mergeLists(left, node, right);
   return left; // front of left
}
```

To actually implement the nitty-gritty details of this, we'll need to get the head and tail of each linked list. We can do this several different ways.

Solution #1: Additional Data Structure

The first, and easier, approach is to create a new data structure called `NodePair` which holds just the head and tail of a linked list. The `convert` method can then return something of type `NodePair`.

The code below implements this approach.

```
private class NodePair {
   BiNode head, tail;

   public NodePair(BiNode head, BiNode tail) {
      this.head = head;
      this.tail = tail;
   }
}

public NodePair convert(BiNode root) {
   if (root == null) return null;

   NodePair part1 = convert(root.node1);
   NodePair part2 = convert(root.node2);

   if (part1 != null) {
      concat(part1.tail, root);
```

```
    }

    if (part2 != null) {
       concat(root, part2.head);
    }

    return new NodePair(part1 == null ? root : part1.head,
                        part2 == null ? root : part2.tail);
}

public static void concat(BiNode x, BiNode y) {
    x.node2 = y;
    y.node1 = x;
}
```

The above code still converts the BiNode data structure in place. We're just using NodePair as a way to return additional data. We could have alternatively used a two-element BiNode array to fulfill the same purposes, but it looks a bit messier (and we like clean code, especially in an interview).

It'd be nice, though, if we could do this without these extra data structures—and we can.

Solution #2: Retrieving the Tail

Instead of returning the head and tail of the linked list with NodePair, we can return just the head, and then we can use the head to find the tail of the linked list.

```
BiNode convert(BiNode root) {
   if (root == null) return null;

   BiNode part1 = convert(root.node1);
   BiNode part2 = convert(root.node2);

   if (part1 != null) {
      concat(getTail(part1), root);
   }

   if (part2 != null) {
      concat(root, part2);
   }

   return part1 == null ? root : part1;
}

public static BiNode getTail(BiNode node) {
   if (node == null) return null;
   while (node.node2 != null) {
      node = node.node2;
   }
   return node;
}
```

Other than a call to getTail, this code is almost identical to the first solution. It is not, however, very efficient. A leaf node at depth d will be "touched" by the getTail method d times (one for each node above it), leading to an $O(N^2)$ overall runtime, where N is the number of nodes in the tree.

Solution #3: Building a Circular Linked List

We can build our third and final approach off of the second one.

This approach requires returning the head and tail of the linked list with BiNode. We can do this by returning each list as the head of a *circular* linked list. To get the tail, then, we simply call head.node1.

```
BiNode convertToCircular(BiNode root) {
  if (root == null) return null;

  BiNode part1 = convertToCircular(root.node1);
  BiNode part3 = convertToCircular(root.node2);

  if (part1 == null && part3 == null) {
    root.node1 = root;
    root.node2 = root;
    return root;
  }
  BiNode tail3 = (part3 == null) ? null : part3.node1;

  /* join left to root */
  if (part1 == null) {
    concat(part3.node1, root);
  } else {
    concat(part1.node1, root);
  }

  /* join right to root */
  if (part3 == null) {
    concat(root, part1);
  } else {
    concat(root, part3);
  }

  /* join right to left */
  if (part1 != null && part3 != null) {
    concat(tail3, part1);
  }

  return part1 == null ? root : part1;
}

/* Convert list to a circular linked list, then break the circular connection. */
BiNode convert(BiNode root) {
  BiNode head = convertToCircular(root);
  head.node1.node2 = null;
  head.node1 = null;
  return head;
}
```

Observe that we have moved the main parts of the code into convertToCircular. The convert method calls this method to get the head of the circular linked list, and then breaks the circular connection.

The approach takes O(N) time, since each node is only touched an average of once (or, more accurately, O(1) times).

17.13 Re-Space: Oh, no! You have accidentally removed all spaces, punctuation, and capitalization in a lengthy document. A sentence like "`I reset the computer. It still didn't boot!`" became "`iresetthecomputeritstilldidntboot`". You'll deal with the punctuation and capitalization later; right now you need to re-insert the spaces. Most of the words are in a dictionary but a few are not. Given a dictionary (a list of strings) and the document (a string), design an algorithm to unconcatenate the document in a way that minimizes the number of unrecognized characters.

EXAMPLE

Input: `jesslookedjustliketimherbrother`

Output: `jess looked just like tim her brother` (7 unrecognized characters)

pg 188

SOLUTION

Some interviewers like to cut to the chase and give you the specific problems. Others, though, like to give you a lot of unnecessary context, like this problem has. It's useful in such cases to boil down the problem to what it's really all about.

In this case, the problem is really about finding a way to break up a string into separate words such that as few characters as possible are "left out" of the parsing.

Note that we do not attempt to "understand" the string. We could just as well parse "`thisisawesome`" to be "`this is a we some`" as we could "`this is awesome`."

Brute Force

The key to this problem is finding a way to define the solution (that is, parsed string) in terms of its subproblems. One way to do this is recursing through the string.

The very first choice we make is where to insert the first space. After the first character? Second character? Third character?

Let's imagine this in terms of a string like `thisismikesfavoritefood`. What is the first space we insert?

- If we insert a space after `t`, this gives us one invalid character.
- After `th` is two invalid characters.
- After `thi` is three invalid characters.
- At `this` we have a complete word. This is zero invalid characters.
- At `thisi` is five invalid characters.
- ... and so on.

After we choose the first space, we can recursively pick the second space, then the third space, and so on, until we are done with the string.

We take the best (fewest invalid characters) out of all these choices and return.

What should the function return? We need both the number of invalid characters in the recursive path as well as the actual parsing. Therefore, we just return both by using a custom-built `ParseResult` class.

```
String bestSplit(HashSet<String> dictionary, String sentence) {
  ParseResult r = split(dictionary, sentence, 0);
  return r == null ? null : r.parsed;
}

```

```
6  ParseResult split(HashSet<String> dictionary, String sentence, int start) {
7    if (start >= sentence.length()) {
8      return new ParseResult(0, “”);
9    }
10
11   int bestInvalid = Integer.MAX_VALUE;
12   String bestParsing = null;
13   String partial = “”;
14   int index = start;
15   while (index < sentence.length()) {
16     char c = sentence.charAt(index);
17     partial += c;
18     int invalid = dictionary.contains(partial) ? 0 : partial.length();
19     if (invalid < bestInvalid) { // Short circuit
20       /* Recurse, putting a space after this character. If this is better than
21        * the current best option, replace the best option. */
22       ParseResult result = split(dictionary, sentence, index + 1);
23       if (invalid + result.invalid < bestInvalid) {
24         bestInvalid = invalid + result.invalid;
25         bestParsing = partial + “ ” + result.parsed;
26         if (bestInvalid == 0) break; // Short circuit
27       }
28     }
29
30     index++;
31   }
32   return new ParseResult(bestInvalid, bestParsing);
33 }
34
35 public class ParseResult {
36   public int invalid = Integer.MAX_VALUE;
37   public String parsed = “ ”;
38   public ParseResult(int inv, String p) {
39     invalid = inv;
40     parsed = p;
41   }
42 }
```

We've applied two short circuits here.

- Line 19: If the number of current invalid characters exceeds the best known one, then we know this recursive path will not be ideal. There's no point in even taking it.
- Line 26: If we have a path with zero invalid characters, then we know we can't do better than this. We might as well accept this path.

What's the runtime of this? It's difficult to truly describe in practice as it depends on the (English) language.

One way of looking at it is to imagine a bizarre language where essentially all paths in the recursion are taken. In this case, we are making both choices at each character. If there are n characters, this is an $O(2^n)$ runtime.

Optimized

Commonly, when we have exponential runtimes for a recursive algorithm, we optimize them through memoization (that is, caching results). To do so, we need to find the common subproblems.

Where do recursive paths overlap? That is, where are the common subproblems?

Let's again imagine the string `thisismikesfavoritefood`. Again, imagine that everything is a valid word.

In this case, we attempt to insert the first space after `t` as well as after `th` (and many other choices). Think about what the next choice is.

```
split(thisismikesfavoritefood) ->
       t  + split(hisismikesfavoritefood)
    OR th + split(isismikesfavoritefood)
    OR ...

split(hisismikesfavoritefood) ->
       h + split(isismikesfavoritefood)
    OR ...

...
```

Adding a space after `t` and `h` leads to the same recursive path as inserting a space after `th`. There's no sense in computing `split(isismikesfavoritefood)` twice when it will lead to the same result.

We should instead cache the result. We do this using a hash table which maps from the current substring to the `ParseResult` object.

We don't actually need to make the current substring a key. The `start` index in the string sufficiently represents the substring. After all, if we were to use the substring, we'd really be using `sentence.substring(start, sentence.length)`. This hash table will map from a start index to the best parsing from that index to the end of the string.

And, since the start index is the key, we don't need a true hash table at all. We can just use an array of `ParseResult` objects. This will also serve the purpose of mapping from an index to an object.

The code is essentially identical to the earlier function, but now takes in a memo table (a cache). We look up when we first call the function and set it when we return.

```
String bestSplit(HashSet<String> dictionary, String sentence) {
  ParseResult[] memo = new ParseResult[sentence.length()];
  ParseResult r = split(dictionary, sentence, 0, memo);
  return r == null ? null : r.parsed;
}

ParseResult split(HashSet<String> dictionary, String sentence, int start,
                  ParseResult[] memo) {
  if (start >= sentence.length()) {
    return new ParseResult(0, “”);
  } if (memo[start] != null) {
    return memo[start];
  }

  int bestInvalid = Integer.MAX_VALUE;
  String bestParsing = null;
  String partial = “”;
  int index = start;
  while (index < sentence.length()) {
    char c = sentence.charAt(index);
    partial += c;
    int invalid = dictionary.contains(partial) ? 0 : partial.length();
    if (invalid < bestInvalid) { // Short circuit
      /* Recurse, putting a space after this character. If this is better than
       * the current best option, replace the best option. */
      ParseResult result = split(dictionary, sentence, index + 1, memo);
```

```
        if (invalid + result.invalid < bestInvalid) {
          bestInvalid = invalid + result.invalid;
          bestParsing = partial + " " + result.parsed;
          if (bestInvalid == 0) break; // Short circuit
        }
      }

      index++;
    }
    memo[start] = new ParseResult(bestInvalid, bestParsing);
    return memo[start];
  }
```

Understanding the runtime of this is even trickier than in the prior solution. Again, let's imagine the truly bizarre case, where essentially everything looks like a valid word.

One way we can approach it is to realize that `split(i)` will only be computed once for each value of `i`. What happens when we call `split(i)`, assuming we've already called `split(i+1)` through `split(n - 1)`?

```
split(i) -> calls:
    split(i + 1)
    split(i + 2)
    split(i + 3)
    split(i + 4)
    ...
    split(n - 1)
```

Each of the recursive calls has already been computed, so they just return immediately. Doing `n - i` calls at `O(1)` time each takes `O(n - i)` time. This means that `split(i)` takes `O(i)` time at most.

We can now apply the same logic to `split(i - 1)`, `split(i - 2)`, and so on. If we make 1 call to compute `split(n - 1)`, 2 calls to compute `split(n - 2)`, 3 calls to compute `split(n - 3)`, ..., n calls to compute `split(0)`, how many calls total do we do? This is basically the sum of the numbers from 1 through n, which is $O(n^2)$.

Therefore, the runtime of this function is $O(n^2)$.

17.14 Smallest K: Design an algorithm to find the smallest K numbers in an array.

pg 188

SOLUTION

There are a number of ways to approach this problem. We will go through three of them: sorting, max heap, and selection rank.

Some of these algorithms require modifying the array. This is something you should discuss with your interviewer. Note, though, that even if modifying the original array is not acceptable, you can always clone the array and modify the clone instead. This will not impact the overall big O time of any algorithm.

Solution 1: Sorting

We can sort the elements in ascending order and then take the first k numbers from that.

```
int[] smallestK(int[] array, int k) {
  if (k <= 0 || k > array.length) {
    throw new IllegalArgumentException();
```

```
    }

    /* Sort array. */
    Arrays.sort(array);

    /* Copy first k elements. */
    int[] smallest = new int[k];
    for (int i = 0; i < k; i++) {
       smallest[i] = array[i];
    }
    return smallest;
}
```

The time complexity is `O(n log(n))`.

Solution 2: Max Heap

We can use a max heap to solve this problem. We first create a max heap (largest element at the top) for the first k numbers.

Then, we traverse through the list. On each element, if it's smaller than the root, we insert it into the heap and delete the largest element (which will be the root).

At the end of the traversal, we will have a heap containing the smallest k numbers. This algorithm is `O(n log(k))`.

```
int[] smallestK(int[] array, int k) {
   if (k <= 0 || k > array.length) {
      throw new IllegalArgumentException();
   }

   PriorityQueue<Integer> heap = getKMaxHeap(array, k);
   return heapToIntArray(heap);
}

/* Create max heap of smallest k elements. */
PriorityQueue<Integer> getKMaxHeap(int[] array, int k) {
   PriorityQueue<Integer> heap =
      new PriorityQueue<Integer>(k, new MaxHeapComparator());
   for (int a : array) {
      if (heap.size() < k) { // If space remaining
         heap.add(a);
      } else if (a < heap.peek()) { // If full and top is small
         heap.poll(); // remove highest
         heap.add(a); // insert new element
      }
   }
   return heap;
}

/* Convert heap to int array. */
int[] heapToIntArray(PriorityQueue<Integer> heap) {
   int[] array = new int[heap.size()];
   while (!heap.isEmpty()) {
      array[heap.size() - 1] = heap.poll();
   }
   return array;
}
```

```

class MaxHeapComparator implements Comparator<Integer> {
    public int compare(Integer x, Integer y) {
        return y - x;
    }
}
```

Java's uses the `PriorityQueue` class to offer heap-like functionality. By default, it operates as a min heap, with the smallest element on the top. To switch it to the biggest element on the top, we can pass in a different comparator.

Approach 3: Selection Rank Algorithm (if elements are unique)

Selection Rank is a well-known algorithm in computer science to find the `ith` smallest (or largest) element in an array in linear time.

If the elements are unique, you can find the `ith` smallest element in expected `O(n)` time. The basic algorithm operates like this:

1. Pick a random element in the array and use it as a "pivot." Partition elements around the pivot, keeping track of the number of elements on the left side of the partition.
2. If there are exactly `i` elements on the left, then you just return the biggest element on the left.
3. If the left side is bigger than `i`, repeat the algorithm on just the left part of the array.
4. If the left side is smaller than `i`, repeat the algorithm on the right, but look for the element with rank `i - leftSize`.

Once you have found the `ith` smallest element, you know that all elements smaller than this will be to the left of this (since you've partitioned the array accordingly). You can now just return the first `i` elements.

The code below implements this algorithm.

```
int[] smallestK(int[] array, int k) {
   if (k <= 0 || k > array.length) {
      throw new IllegalArgumentException();
   }

   int threshold = rank(array, k - 1);
   int[] smallest = new int[k];
   int count = 0;
   for (int a : array) {
      if (a <= threshold) {
         smallest[count] = a;
         count++;
      }
   }
   return smallest;
}

/* Get element with rank. */
int rank(int[] array, int rank) {
   return rank(array, 0, array.length - 1, rank);
}

/* Get element with rank between left and right indices. */
int rank(int[] array, int left, int right, int rank) {
   int pivot = array[randomIntInRange(left, right)];
```

```
  int leftEnd = partition(array, left, right, pivot);
  int leftSize = leftEnd - left + 1;
  if (rank == leftSize - 1) {
    return max(array, left, leftEnd);
  } else if (rank < leftSize) {
    return rank(array, left, leftEnd, rank);
  } else {
    return rank(array, leftEnd + 1, right, rank - leftSize);
  }
}

/* Partition array around pivot such that all elements <= pivot come before all
 * elements > pivot. */
int partition(int[] array, int left, int right, int pivot) {
  while (left <= right) {
    if (array[left] > pivot) {
      /* Left is bigger than pivot. Swap it to the right side, where we know it
       * should be. */
      swap(array, left, right);
      right--;
    } else if (array[right] <= pivot) {
      /* Right is smaller than the pivot. Swap it to the left side, where we know
       * it should be. */
      swap(array, left, right);
      left++;
    } else {
      /* Left and right are in correct places. Expand both sides. */
      left++;
      right--;
    }
  }
  return left - 1;
}

/* Get random integer within range, inclusive. */
int randomIntInRange(int min, int max) {
  Random rand = new Random();
  return rand.nextInt(max + 1 - min) + min;
}

/* Swap values at index i and j. */
void swap(int[] array, int i, int j) {
  int t = array[i];
  array[i] = array[j];
  array[j] = t;
}

/* Get largest element in array between left and right indices. */
int max(int[] array, int left, int right) {
  int max = Integer.MIN_VALUE;
  for (int i = left; i <= right; i++) {
    max = Math.max(array[i], max);
  }
  return max;
}
```

If the elements are not unique, we can tweak this algorithm slightly to accommodate this.

Approach 4: Selection Rank Algorithm (if elements are not unique)

The major change that needs to be made is to the `partition` function. When we partition the array around a pivot element, we now partition it into three chunks: less than `pivot`, equal to `pivot`, and greater than `pivot`.

This requires minor tweaks to `rank` as well. We now compare the size of left and middle partitions to `rank`.

```
class PartitionResult {
  int leftSize, middleSize;
  public PartitionResult(int left, int middle) {
    this.leftSize = left;
    this.middleSize = middle;
  }
}

int[] smallestK(int[] array, int k) {
  if (k <= 0 || k > array.length) {
    throw new IllegalArgumentException();
  }

  /* Get item with rank k - 1. */
  int threshold = rank(array, k - 1);

  /* Copy elements smaller than the threshold element. */
  int[] smallest = new int[k];
  int count = 0;
  for (int a : array) {
    if (a < threshold) {
      smallest[count] = a;
      count++;
    }
  }

  /* If there's still room left, this must be for elements equal to the threshold
   * element. Copy those in. */
  while (count < k) {
    smallest[count] = threshold;
    count++;
  }

  return smallest;
}

/* Find value with rank k in array. */
int rank(int[] array, int k) {
  if (k >= array.length) {
    throw new IllegalArgumentException();
  }
  return rank(array, k, 0, array.length - 1);
}

/* Find value with rank k in sub array between start and end. */
int rank(int[] array, int k, int start, int end) {
  /* Partition array around an arbitrary pivot. */
  int pivot = array[randomIntInRange(start, end)];
  PartitionResult partition = partition(array, start, end, pivot);
```

```
    int leftSize = partition.leftSize;
    int middleSize = partition.middleSize;

    /* Search portion of array. */
    if (k < leftSize) { // Rank k is on left half
      return rank(array, k, start, start + leftSize - 1);
    } else if (k < leftSize + middleSize) { // Rank k is in middle
      return pivot; // middle is all pivot values
    } else { // Rank k is on right
      return rank(array, k - leftSize - middleSize, start + leftSize + middleSize,
                  end);
    }
  }

  /* Partition result into < pivot, equal to pivot -> bigger than pivot. */
  PartitionResult partition(int[] array, int start, int end, int pivot) {
    int left = start; /* Stays at (right) edge of left side. */
    int right = end;  /* Stays at (left) edge of right side. */
    int middle = start; /* Stays at (right) edge of middle. */
    while (middle <= right) {
      if (array[middle] < pivot) {
        /* Middle is smaller than the pivot. Left is either smaller or equal to
         * the pivot. Either way, swap them. Then middle and left should move by
         * one. */
        swap(array, middle, left);
        middle++;
        left++;
      } else if (array[middle] > pivot) {
        /* Middle is bigger than the pivot. Right could have any value. Swap them,
         * then we know that the new right is bigger than the pivot. Move right by
         * one. */
        swap(array, middle, right);
        right--;
      } else if (array[middle] == pivot) {
        /* Middle is equal to the pivot. Move by one. */
        middle++;
      }
    }

    /* Return sizes of left and middle. */
    return new PartitionResult(left - start, right - left + 1);
  }
```

Notice the change made to `smallestK` too. We can't simply copy all elements less than or equal to `threshold` into the array. Since we have duplicates, there could be many more than k elements that are less than or equal to `threshold`. (We also can't just say "okay, only copy k elements over." We could inadvertently fill up the array early on with "equal" elements, and not leave enough space for the smaller ones.)

The solution for this is fairly simple: only copy over the smaller elements first, then fill up the array with equal elements at the end.

17.15 Longest Word: Given a list of words, write a program to find the longest word made of other words in the list.

pg 188

SOLUTION

This problem seems complex, so let's simplify it. What if we just wanted to know the longest word made of *two* other words in the list?

We could solve this by iterating through the list, from the longest word to the shortest word. For each word, we would split it into all possible pairs and check if both the left and right side are contained in the list.

The pseudocode for this would look like the following:

```
String getLongestWord(String[] list) {
   String[] array = list.SortByLength();
   /* Create map for easy lookup */
   HashMap<String, Boolean> map = new HashMap<String, Boolean>;

   for (String str : array) {
      map.put(str, true);
   }

   for (String s : array) {
      // Divide into every possible pair
      for (int i = 1; i < s.length(); i++) {
         String left = s.substring(0, i);
         String right = s.substring(i);
         // Check if both sides are in the array
         if (map[left] == true && map[right] == true) {
            return s;
         }
      }
   }
   return str;
}
```

This works great for when we just want to know composites of two words. But what if a word could be formed by any number of other words?

In this case, we could apply a very similar approach, with one modification: rather than simply looking up if the right side is in the array, we would recursively see if we can build the right side from the other elements in the array.

The code below implements this algorithm:

```
String printLongestWord(String arr[]) {
   HashMap<String, Boolean> map = new HashMap<String, Boolean>();
   for (String str : arr) {
      map.put(str, true);
   }
   Arrays.sort(arr, new LengthComparator()); // Sort by length
   for (String s : arr) {
      if (canBuildWord(s, true, map)) {
         System.out.println(s);
         return s;
      }
   }
```

```
    return "";
}

boolean canBuildWord(String str, boolean isOriginalWord,
                     HashMap<String, Boolean> map) {
  if (map.containsKey(str) && !isOriginalWord) {
    return map.get(str);
  }
  for (int i = 1; i < str.length(); i++) {
    String left = str.substring(0, i);
    String right = str.substring(i);
    if (map.containsKey(left) && map.get(left) == true &&
        canBuildWord(right, false, map)) {
      return true;
    }
  }
  map.put(str, false);
  return false;
}
```

Note that in this solution we have performed a small optimization. We use a dynamic programming/memoization approach to cache the results between calls. This way, if we repeatedly need to check if there's any way to build "`testingtester`," we'll only have to compute it once.

A boolean flag `isOriginalWord` is used to complete the above optimization. The method `canBuildWord` is called for the original word and for each substring, and its first step is to check the cache for a previously calculated result. However, for the original words, we have a problem: `map` is initialized to `true` for them, but we don't want to return `true` (since a word cannot be composed solely of itself). Therefore, for the original word, we simply bypass this check using the `isOriginalWord` flag.

17.16 The Masseuse: A popular masseuse receives a sequence of back-to-back appointment requests and is debating which ones to accept. She needs a 15-minute break between appointments and therefore she cannot accept any adjacent requests. Given a sequence of back-to-back appointment requests (all multiples of 15 minutes, none overlap, and none can be moved), find the optimal (highest total booked minutes) set the masseuse can honor. Return the number of minutes.

EXAMPLE

Input: `{30, 15, 60, 75, 45, 15, 15, 45}`

Output: `180 minutes ({30, 60, 45, 45})`.

pg 188

SOLUTION

Let's start with an example. We'll draw it visually to get a better feel for the problem. Each number indicates the number of minutes in the appointment.

r_0 = 75	r_1 = 105	r_2 = 120	r_3 = 75	r_4 = 90	r_5 = 135

Alternatively, we could have also divided all the values (including the break) by 15 minutes, to give us the array `{5, 7, 8, 5, 6, 9}`. This would be equivalent, but now we would want a 1-minute break.

The best set of appointments for this problem has 330 minutes total, formed with {r_0 = 75, r_2 = 120, r_5 = 135}. Note that we've intentionally chosen an example in which the best sequence of appointments was not formed through a strictly alternating sequence.

We should also recognize that choosing the longest appointment first (the "greedy" strategy) would not necessarily be optimal. For example, a sequence like {45, 60, 45, 15} would not have 60 in the optimal set.

Solution #1: Recursion

The first thing that may come to mind is a recursive solution. We have essentially a sequence of choices as we walk down the list of appointments: Do we use this appointment or do we not? If we use appointment i, we must skip appointment i + 1 as we can't take back-to-back appointments. Appointment i + 2 is a possibility (but not necessarily the best choice).

```
int maxMinutes(int[] massages) {
  return maxMinutes(massages, 0);
}

int maxMinutes(int[] massages, int index) {
  if (index >= massages.length) { // Out of bounds
    return 0;
  }

  /* Best with this reservation. */
  int bestWith = massages[index] + maxMinutes(massages, index + 2);

  /* Best without this reservation. */
  int bestWithout = maxMinutes(massages, index + 1);

  /* Return best of this subarray, starting from index. */
  return Math.max(bestWith, bestWithout);
}
```

The runtime of this solution is $O(2^n)$ because at each element we're making two choices and we do this n times (where n is the number of massages).

The space complexity is $O(n)$ due to the recursive call stack.

We can also depict this through a recursive call tree on an array of length 5. The number in each node represents the index value in a call to maxMinutes. Observe that, for example, maxMinutes(massages, 0) calls maxMinutes(massages, 1) and maxMinutes(massages, 2).

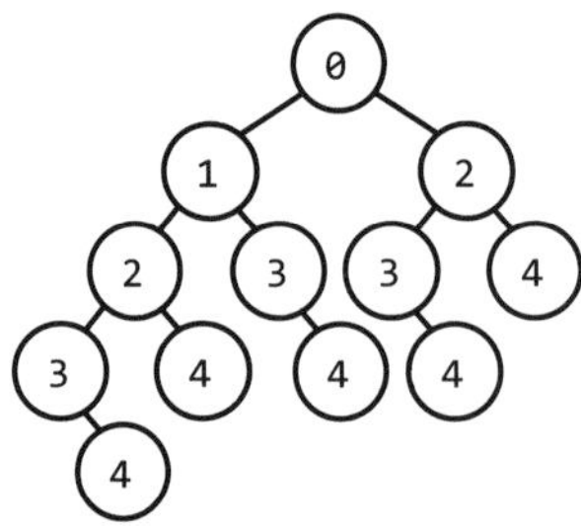

As with many recursive problems, we should evaluate if there's a possibility to memoize repeated subproblems. Indeed, there is.

Solution #2: Recursion + Memoization

We will repeatedly call `maxMinutes` on the same inputs. For example, we'll call it on index 2 when we're deciding whether to take appointment 0. We'll also call it on index 2 when we're deciding whether to take appointment 1. We should memoize this.

Our memo table is just a mapping from `index` to the max minutes. Therefore, a simple array will suffice.

```
int maxMinutes(int[] massages) {
   int[] memo = new int[massages.length];
   return maxMinutes(massages, 0, memo);
}

int maxMinutes(int[] massages, int index, int[] memo) {
   if (index >= massages.length) {
      return 0;
   }

   if (memo[index] == 0) {
      int bestWith = massages[index] + maxMinutes(massages, index + 2, memo);
      int bestWithout = maxMinutes(massages, index + 1, memo);
      memo[index] = Math.max(bestWith, bestWithout);
   }

   return memo[index];
}
```

To determine the runtime, we'll draw the same recursive call tree as before but gray-out the calls that will return immediately. The calls that will never happen will be deleted entirely.

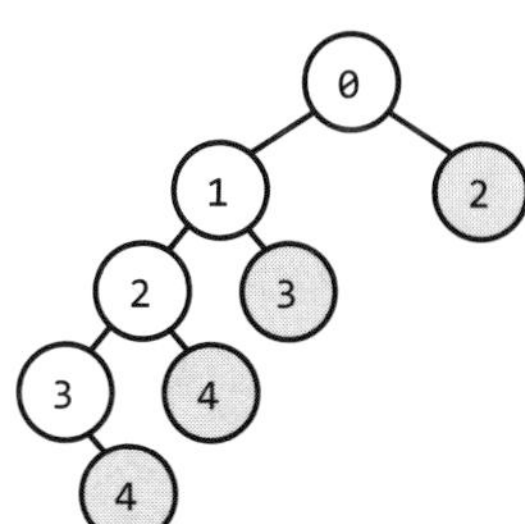

If we drew a bigger tree, we'd see a similar pattern. The tree looks very linear, with one branch down to the left. This gives us an `O(n)` runtime and `O(n)` space. The space usage comes from the recursive call stack as well as from the memo table.

Solution #3: Iterative

Can we do better? We certainly can't beat the time complexity since we have to look at each appointment. However, we might be able to beat the space complexity. This would mean not solving the problem recursively.

Let's look at our first example again.

r_0 = 30	r_1 = 15	r_2 = 60	r_3 = 75	r_4 = 45	r_5 = 15	r_6 = 15	r_7 = 45

As we noted in the problem statement, we cannot take adjacent appointments.

There's another observation, though, that we can make: We should never *skip* three consecutive appointments. That is, we might skip r_1 and r_2 if we wanted to take r_0 and r_3. But we would never skip r_1, r_2, and r_3. This would be suboptimal since we could always improve our set by grabbing that middle element.

This means that if we take r_0, we know we'll definitely skip r_1 and definitely take either r_2 or r_3. This substantially limits the options we need to evaluate and opens the door to an iterative solution.

Let's think about our recursive + memoization solution and try to reverse the logic; that is, let's try to approach it iteratively.

A useful way to do this is to approach it from the back and move toward the start of the array. At each point, we find the solution for the subarray.

- `best(7)`: What's the best option for {r_7 = 45}? We can get 45 min. if we take r_7, so `best(7) = 45`
- `best(6)`: What's the best option for {r_6 = 15, ...}? Still 45 min., so `best(6) = 45`.
- `best(5)`: What's the best option for {r_5 = 15, ...}? We can either:
  - » take r_5 = 15 and merge it with `best(7) = 45`, or:
  - » take `best(6) = 45`.

  The first gives us 60 minutes, `best(5) = 60`.
- `best(4)`: What's the best option for {r_4 = 45, ...}? We can either:
  - » take r_4 = 45 and merge it with `best(6) = 45`, or:
  - » take `best(5) = 60`.

  The first gives us 90 minutes, `best(4) = 90`.
- `best(3)`: What's the best option for {r_3 = 75, ...}? We can either:
  - » take r_3 = 75 and merge it with `best(5) = 60`, or:
  - » take `best(4) = 90`.

  The first gives us 135 minutes, `best(3) = 135`.
- `best(2)`: What's the best option for {r_2 = 60, ...}? We can either:
  - » take r_2 = 60 and merge it with `best(4) = 90`, or:
  - » take `best(3) = 135`.

  The first gives us 150 minutes, `best(2) = 150`.
- `best(1)`: What's the best option for {r_1 = 15, ...}? We can either:
  - » take r_1 = 15 and merge it with `best(3) = 135`, or:
  - » take `best(2) = 150`.

  Either way, `best(1) = 150`.
- `best(0)`: What's the best option for {r_0 = 30, ...}? We can either:
  - » take r_0 = 30 and merge it with `best(2) = 150`, or:
  - » take `best(1) = 150`.

  The first gives us 180 minutes, `best(0) = 180`.

Therefore, we return 180 minutes.

The code below implements this algorithm.

```
int maxMinutes(int[] massages) {
  /* Allocating two extra slots in the array so we don't have to do bounds
   * checking on lines 7 and 8. */
  int[] memo = new int[massages.length + 2];
```

```
    memo[massages.length] = 0;
    memo[massages.length + 1] = 0;
    for (int i = massages.length - 1; i >= 0; i--) {
       int bestWith = massages[i] + memo[i + 2];
       int bestWithout = memo[i + 1];
       memo[i] = Math.max(bestWith, bestWithout);
    }
    return memo[0];
 }
```

The runtime of this solution is O(n) and the space complexity is also O(n).

It's nice in some ways that it's iterative, but we haven't actually "won" anything here. The recursive solution had the same time and space complexity.

Solution #4: Iterative with Optimal Time and Space

In reviewing the last solution, we can recognize that we only use the values in the memo table for a short amount of time. Once we are several elements past an index, we never use that element's index again.

In fact, at any given index i, we only need to know the best value from i + 1 and i + 2. Therefore, we can get rid of the memo table and just use two integers.

```
int maxMinutes(int[] massages) {
   int oneAway = 0;
   int twoAway = 0;
   for (int i = massages.length - 1; i >= 0; i--) {
      int bestWith = massages[i] + twoAway;
      int bestWithout = oneAway;
      int current = Math.max(bestWith, bestWithout);
      twoAway = oneAway;
      oneAway = current;
   }
   return oneAway;
}
```

This gives us the most optimal time and space possible: O(n) time and O(1) space.

Why did we look backward? It's a common technique in many problems to walk backward through an array.

However, we can walk forward if we want. This is easier for some people to think about, and harder for others. In this case, rather than asking "What's the best set that starts with a[i]?", we would ask "What's the best set that ends with a[i]?"

17.17 Multi Search: Given a string b and an array of smaller strings T, design a method to search b for each small string in T.

pg 189

SOLUTION

Let's start with an example:

```
T = {"is", "ppi", "hi", "sis", "i", "ssippi"}
b = "mississippi"
```

Note that in our example, we made sure to have some strings (like "is") that appear multiple times in b.

Solution #1

The naive solution is reasonably straightforward. Just search through the bigger string for each instance of the smaller string.

```
HashMapList<String, Integer> searchAll(String big, String[] smalls) {
  HashMapList<String, Integer> lookup =
    new HashMapList<String, Integer>();
  for (String small : smalls) {
    ArrayList<Integer> locations = search(big, small);
    lookup.put(small, locations);
  }
  return lookup;
}

/* Find all locations of the smaller string within the bigger string. */
ArrayList<Integer> search(String big, String small) {
  ArrayList<Integer> locations = new ArrayList<Integer>();
  for (int i = 0; i < big.length() - small.length() + 1; i++) {
    if (isSubstringAtLocation(big, small, i)) {
      locations.add(i);
    }
  }
  return locations;
}

/* Check if small appears at index offset within big. */
boolean isSubstringAtLocation(String big, String small, int offset) {
  for (int i = 0; i < small.length(); i++) {
    if (big.charAt(offset + i) != small.charAt(i)) {
      return false;
    }
  }
  return true;
}

/* HashMapList<String, Integer> is a HashMap that maps from Strings to
 * ArrayList<Integer>. See appendix for implementation. */
```

We could have also used a `substring` and `equals` function, instead of writing `isSubstringAtLocation`. This is slightly faster (though not in terms of big O) because it doesn't require creating a bunch of substrings.

This will take `O(kbt)` time, where k is the length of the longest string in T, b is the length of the bigger string, and `t` is the number of smaller strings within T.

Solution #2

To optimize this, we should think about how we can tackle all the elements in T at once, or somehow re-use work.

One way is to create a trie-like data structure using each suffix in the bigger string. For the string `bibs`, the suffix list would be: `bibs`, `ibs`, `bs`, `s`.

The tree for this is below.

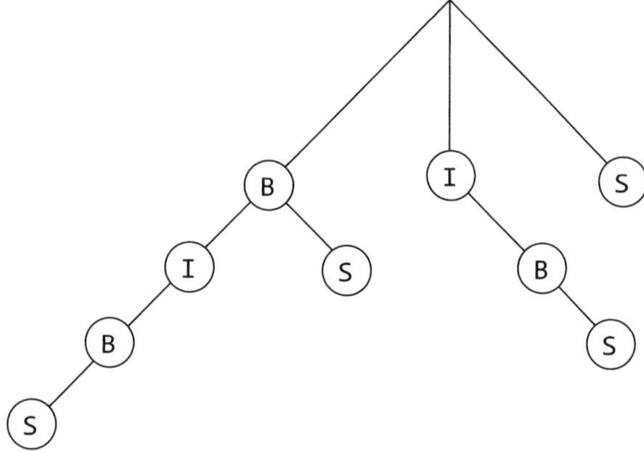

Then, all you need to do is search in the suffix tree for each string in T. Note that if "B" were a word, you would come up with two locations.

```
HashMapList<String, Integer> searchAll(String big, String[] smalls) {
  HashMapList<String, Integer> lookup = new HashMapList<String, Integer>();
  Trie tree = createTrieFromString(big);
  for (String s : smalls) {
    /* Get terminating location of each occurrence.*/
    ArrayList<Integer> locations = tree.search(s);

    /* Adjust to starting location. */
    subtractValue(locations, s.length());

    /* Insert. */
    lookup.put(s, locations);
  }
  return lookup;
}

Trie createTrieFromString(String s) {
  Trie trie = new Trie();
  for (int i = 0; i < s.length(); i++) {
    String suffix = s.substring(i);
    trie.insertString(suffix, i);
  }
  return trie;
}

void subtractValue(ArrayList<Integer> locations, int delta) {
  if (locations == null) return;
  for (int i = 0; i < locations.size(); i++) {
    locations.set(i, locations.get(i) - delta);
  }
}

public class Trie {
  private TrieNode root = new TrieNode();

  public Trie(String s) { insertString(s, 0); }
  public Trie() {}

```

```
  public ArrayList<Integer> search(String s) {
    return root.search(s);
  }

  public void insertString(String str, int location) {
    root.insertString(str, location);
  }

  public TrieNode getRoot() {
    return root;
  }
}

public class TrieNode {
  private HashMap<Character, TrieNode> children;
  private ArrayList<Integer> indexes;

  public TrieNode() {
    children = new HashMap<Character, TrieNode>();
    indexes = new ArrayList<Integer>();
  }

  public void insertString(String s, int index) {
    if (s == null) return;
    indexes.add(index);
    if (s.length() > 0) {
      char value = s.charAt(0);
      TrieNode child = null;
      if (children.containsKey(value)) {
        child = children.get(value);
      } else {
        child = new TrieNode();
        children.put(value, child);
      }
      String remainder = s.substring(1);
      child.insertString(remainder, index + 1);
    } else {
      children.put('\0', null); // Terminating character
    }
  }

  public ArrayList<Integer> search(String s) {
    if (s == null || s.length() == 0) {
      return indexes;
    } else {
      char first = s.charAt(0);
      if (children.containsKey(first)) {
        String remainder = s.substring(1);
        return children.get(first).search(remainder);
      }
    }
    return null;
  }

  public boolean terminates() {
    return children.containsKey('\0');
```

```
    }

    public TrieNode getChild(char c) {
       return children.get(c);
    }
}

/* HashMapList<String, Integer> is a HashMap that maps from Strings to
 * ArrayList<Integer>. See appendix for implementation. */
```

It takes $O(b^2)$ time to create the tree and O(kt) time to search for the locations.

> Reminder: k is the length of the longest string in T, b is the length of the bigger string, and t is the number of smaller strings within T.

The total runtime is $O(b^2 + kt)$.

Without some additional knowledge of the expected input, you cannot directly compare O(bkt), which was the runtime of the prior solution, to $O(b^2 + kt)$. If b is very large, then O(bkt) is preferable. But if you have a lot of smaller strings, then $O(b^2 + kt)$ might be better.

Solution #3

Alternatively, we can add all the smaller strings into a trie. For example, the strings {i, is, pp, ms} would look like the trie below. The asterisk (*) hanging from a node indicates that this node completes a word.

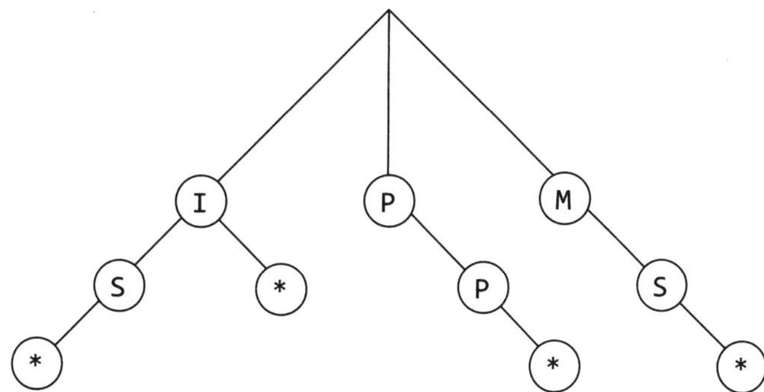

Now, when we want to find all words in mississippi, we search through this trie starting with each word.

- m: We would first look up in the trie starting with m, the first letter in mississippi. As soon as we go to mi, we terminate.
- i: Then, we go to i, the second character in mississippi. We see that i is a complete word, so we add it to the list. We also keep going with i over to is. The string is is also a complete word, so we add that to the list. This node has no more children, so we move onto the next character in mississippi.
- s: We now go to s. There is no upper-level node for s, so we go onto the next character.
- s: Another s. Go on to the next character.
- i: We see another i. We go to the i node in the trie. We see that i is a complete word, so we add it to the list. We also keep going with i over to is. The string is is also a complete word, so we add that to the list. This node has no more children, so we move onto the next character in mississippi.

- s: We go to s. There is no upper-level node for s.
- s: Another s. Go on to the next character.
- `i`: We go to the `i` node. We see that `i` is a complete word, so we add it to the list. The next character in `mississippi` is a p. There is no node p, so we break here.
- p: We see a p. There is no node p.
- p: Another p.
- `i`: We go to the `i` node. We see that `i` is a complete word, so we add it to the list. There are no more characters left in `mississippi`, so we are done.

Each time we find a complete "small" word, we add it to a list along with the location in the bigger word (`mississippi`) where we found the small word.

The code below implements this algorithm.

```
HashMapList<String, Integer> searchAll(String big, String[] smalls) {
   HashMapList<String, Integer> lookup = new HashMapList<String, Integer>();
   int maxLen = big.length();
   TrieNode root = createTreeFromStrings(smalls, maxLen).getRoot();

   for (int i = 0; i < big.length(); i++) {
      ArrayList<String> strings = findStringsAtLoc(root, big, i);
      insertIntoHashMap(strings, lookup, i);
   }

   return lookup;
}

/* Insert each string into trie (provided string is not longer than maxLen). */
Trie createTreeFromStrings(String[] smalls, int maxLen) {
   Trie tree = new Trie();
   for (String s : smalls) {
      if (s.length() <= maxLen) {
         tree.insertString(s, 0);
      }
   }
   return tree;
}

/* Find strings in trie that start at index "start" within big. */
ArrayList<String> findStringsAtLoc(TrieNode root, String big, int start) {
   ArrayList<String> strings = new ArrayList<String>();
   int index = start;
   while (index < big.length()) {
      root = root.getChild(big.charAt(index));
      if (root == null) break;
      if (root.terminates()) { // Is complete string, add to list
         strings.add(big.substring(start, index + 1));
      }
      index++;
   }
   return strings;
}

/* HashMapList<String, Integer> is a HashMap that maps from Strings to
```

```
 * ArrayList<Integer>. See appendix for implementation. */
```

This algorithm takes O(kt) time to create the trie and O(bk) time to search for all the strings.

> Reminder: k is the length of the longest string in T, b is the length of the bigger string, and t is the number of smaller strings within T.

The total time to solve the question is O(kt + bk).

Solution #1 was O(kbt). We know that O(kt + bk) will be faster than O(kbt).

Solution #2 was O(b^2 + kt). Since b will always be bigger than k (or if it's not, then we know this really long string k cannot be found in b), we know Solution #3 is also faster than Solution #2.

17.18 Shortest Supersequence: You are given two arrays, one shorter (with all distinct elements) and one longer. Find the shortest subarray in the longer array that contains all the elements in the shorter array. The items can appear in any order.

EXAMPLE

Input:

```
{1, 5, 9}
{7, 5, 9, 0, 2, 1, 3, 5, 7, 9, 1, 1, 5, 8, 8, 9, 7}
```

Output: `[7, 10] (the underlined portion above)`

pg 189

SOLUTIONS

As usual, a brute force approach is a good way to start. Try thinking about it as if you were doing it by hand. How would you do it?

Let's use the example from the problem to walk through this. We'll call the smaller array `smallArray` and the bigger array `bigArray`.

Brute Force

The slow, "easy" way to do this is to iterate through `bigArray` and do repeated small passes through it.

At each index in `bigArray`, scan forward to find the next occurrence of each element in `smallArray`. The largest of these next occurrences will tell us the shortest subarray that starts at that index. (We'll call this concept "closure." That is, the closure is the element that "closes" a complete subarray starting at that index. For example, the closure of index 3—which has value 0—in the example is index 9.)

By finding the closures for each index in the array, we can find the shortest subarray overall.

```
Range shortestSupersequence(int[] bigArray, int[] smallArray) {
  int bestStart = -1;
  int bestEnd = -1;
  for (int i = 0; i < bigArray.length; i++) {
    int end = findClosure(bigArray, smallArray, i);
    if (end == -1) break;
    if (bestStart == -1 || end - i < bestEnd - bestStart) {
      bestStart = i;
      bestEnd = end;
    }
  }
```

```
    return new Range(bestStart, bestEnd);
}

/* Given an index, find the closure (i.e., the element which terminates a complete
 * subarray containing all elements in smallArray). This will be the max of the
 * next locations of each element in smallArray. */
int findClosure(int[] bigArray, int[] smallArray, int index) {
   int max = -1;
   for (int i = 0; i < smallArray.length; i++) {
      int next = findNextInstance(bigArray, smallArray[i], index);
      if (next == -1) {
         return -1;
      }
      max = Math.max(next,  max);
   }
   return max;
}

/* Find next instance of element starting from index. */
int findNextInstance(int[] array, int element, int index) {
   for (int i = index; i < array.length; i++) {
      if (array[i] == element) {
         return i;
      }
   }
   return -1;
}

public class Range {
   private int start;
   private int end;
   public Range(int s, int e) {
      start = s;
      end = e;
   }

   public int length() { return end - start + 1; }
   public int getStart() { return start; }
   public int getEnd() { return end; }

   public boolean shorterThan(Range other) {
      return length() < other.length();
   }
}
```

This algorithm will potentially take $O(SB^2)$ time, where B is the length of `bigArray` and S is the length of `smallArray`. This is because at each of the B characters, we potentially do $O(SB)$ work: S scans of the rest of the string, which has potentially B characters.

Optimized

Let's think about how we can optimize this. The core reason why it's slow is the repeated searches. Is there a faster way that we can find, given an index, the next occurrence of a particular character?

Let's think about it with an example. Given the array below, is there a way we could quickly find the next 5 from each location?

```
7, 5, 9, 0, 2, 1, 3, 5, 7, 9, 1, 1, 5, 8, 8, 9, 7
```

Yes. Because we're going to have to do this repeatedly, we can precompute this information in just a single (backwards) sweep. Iterate through the array backwards, tracking the last (most recent) occurrence of 5.

value	7	5	9	0	2	1	3	5	7	9	1	1	5	8	8	9	7
index	0	1	2	3	4	5	6	7	8	9	10	11	12	13	14	15	16
next 5	1	1	7	7	7	7	7	7	12	12	12	12	12	x	x	x	x

Doing this for each of `{1, 5, 9}` takes just 3 backwards sweeps.

Some people want to merge this into one backwards sweep that handles all three values. It feels faster—but it's not really. Doing it in one backwards sweep means doing three comparisons at each iteration. N moves through the list with three comparisons at each move is no better than 3N moves and one comparison at each move. You might as well keep the code clean by doing it in separate sweeps.

value	7	5	9	0	2	1	3	5	7	9	1	1	5	8	8	9	7
index	0	1	2	3	4	5	6	7	8	9	10	11	12	13	14	15	16
next 1	5	5	5	5	5	5	10	10	10	10	10	11	x	x	x	x	x
next 5	1	1	7	7	7	7	7	7	12	12	12	12	12	x	x	x	x
next 9	2	2	2	9	9	9	9	9	9	9	15	15	15	15	15	15	x

The `findNextInstance` function can now just use this table to find the next occurrence, rather than doing a search.

But, actually, we can make it a bit simpler. Using the table above, we can quickly compute the closure of each index. It's just the max of the column. If a column has an x in it, then there is no closure, at this indicates that there's no next occurrence of that character.

The difference between the index and the closure is the smallest subarray starting at that index.

value	7	5	9	0	2	1	3	5	7	9	1	1	5	8	8	9	7
index	0	1	2	3	4	5	6	7	8	9	10	11	12	13	14	15	16
next 1	5	5	5	5	5	5	10	10	10	10	10	11	x	x	x	x	x
next 5	1	1	7	7	7	7	7	7	12	12	12	12	12	x	x	x	x
next 9	2	2	2	9	9	9	9	9	9	9	15	15	15	15	15	15	x
closure	5	5	7	9	9	9	10	10	12	12	15	15	x	x	x	x	x
diff.	5	4	5	6	5	4	4	3	4	3	5	4	x	x	x	x	x

Now, all we have to do is to find the minimum distance in this table.

```
Range shortestSupersequence(int[] big, int[] small) {
  int[][] nextElements = getNextElementsMulti(big, small);
  int[] closures = getClosures(nextElements);
  return getShortestClosure(closures);
}

/* Create table of next occurrences. */
int[][] getNextElementsMulti(int[] big, int[] small) {
  int[][] nextElements = new int[small.length][big.length];
  for (int i = 0; i < small.length; i++) {
    nextElements[i] = getNextElement(big, small[i]);
  }
  return nextElements;
}

/* Do backwards sweep to get a list of the next occurrence of value from each
```

```
 * index. */
int[] getNextElement(int[] bigArray, int value) {
  int next = -1;
  int[] nexts = new int[bigArray.length];
  for (int i = bigArray.length - 1; i >= 0; i--) {
    if (bigArray[i] == value) {
      next = i;
    }
    nexts[i] = next;
  }
  return nexts;
}

/* Get closure for each index. */
int[] getClosures(int[][] nextElements) {
  int[] maxNextElement = new int[nextElements[0].length];
  for (int i = 0; i < nextElements[0].length; i++) {
    maxNextElement[i] = getClosureForIndex(nextElements, i);
  }
  return maxNextElement;
}

/* Given an index and the table of next elements, find the closure for this index
 * (which will be the max of this column). */
int getClosureForIndex(int[][] nextElements, int index) {
  int max = -1;
  for (int i = 0; i < nextElements.length; i++) {
    if (nextElements[i][index] == -1) {
      return -1;
    }
    max = Math.max(max, nextElements[i][index]);
  }
  return max;
}

/* Get shortest closure. */
Range getShortestClosure(int[] closures) {
  int bestStart = -1;
  int bestEnd = -1;
  for (int i = 0; i < closures.length; i++) {
    if (closures[i] == -1) {
      break;
    }
    int current = closures[i] - i;
    if (bestStart == -1 || current < bestEnd - bestStart) {
      bestStart = i;
      bestEnd = closures[i];
    }
  }
  return new Range(bestStart, bestEnd);
}
```

This algorithm will potentially take O(SB) time, where B is the length of `bigArray` and S is the length of `smallArray`. This is because we do S sweeps through the array to build up the next occurrences table and each sweep takes O(B) time.

It uses O(SB) space.

More Optimized

While our solution is fairly optimal, we can reduce the space usage. Remember the table we created:

value	7	5	9	0	2	1	3	5	7	9	1	1	5	8	8	9	7
index	0	1	2	3	4	5	6	7	8	9	10	11	12	13	14	15	16
next 1	5	5	5	5	5	5	10	10	10	10	10	11	x	x	x	x	x
next 5	1	1	7	7	7	7	7	7	12	12	12	12	12	x	x	x	x
next 9	2	2	2	9	9	9	9	9	9	9	15	15	15	15	15	15	x
closure	5	5	7	9	9	9	10	10	12	12	15	15	x	x	x	x	x

In actuality, all we need is the closure row, which is the minimum of all the other rows. We don't need to store all the other next occurrence information the entire time.

Instead, as we do each sweep, we just update the closure row with the minimums. The rest of the algorithm works essentially the same way.

```
Range shortestSupersequence(int[] big, int[] small) {
  int[] closures = getClosures(big, small);
  return getShortestClosure(closures);
}

/* Get closure for each index. */
int[] getClosures(int[] big, int[] small) {
  int[] closure = new int[big.length];
  for (int i = 0; i < small.length; i++) {
    sweepForClosure(big, closure, small[i]);
  }
  return closure;
}

/* Do backwards sweep and update the closures list with the next occurrence of
 * value, if it's later than the current closure. */
void sweepForClosure(int[] big, int[] closures, int value) {
  int next = -1;
  for (int i = big.length - 1; i >= 0; i--) {
    if (big[i] == value) {
      next = i;
    }
    if ((next == -1 || closures[i] < next) &&
        (closures[i] != -1)) {
      closures[i] = next;
    }
  }
}

/* Get shortest closure. */
Range getShortestClosure(int[] closures) {
  Range shortest = new Range(0, closures[0]);
  for (int i = 1; i < closures.length; i++) {
    if (closures[i] == -1) {
      break;
    }
    Range range = new Range(i, closures[i]);
    if (!shortest.shorterThan(range)) {
      shortest = range;
```

```
        }
    }
    return shortest;
}
```

This still runs in O(SB) time, but it now only takes O(B) additional memory.

Alternative & More Optimal Solution

There's a totally different way to approach it. Let's suppose we had a list of the occurrences of each element in smallArray.

value	7	5	9	9	2	1	3	5	7	9	1	1	5	8	8	9	7
index	0	1	2	3	4	5	6	7	8	9	10	11	12	13	14	15	16

```
1 -> {5, 10, 11}
5 -> {1, 7, 12}
9 -> {2, 3, 9, 15}
```

What is the very first valid subsequence (which contains 1, 5, and 9)? We can just look at the heads of each list to tell us this. The minimum of the heads is the start of the range and the max of the heads is the end of the range. In this case, the first range is [1, 5]. This is currently our "best" subsequence.

How can we find the next one? Well, the next one will not include index 1, so let's remove that from the list.

```
1 -> {5, 10, 11}
5 -> {7, 12}
9 -> {2, 3, 9, 15}
```

The next subsequence is [2, 7]. This is worse than the earlier best, so we can toss it.

Now, what's the next subsequence? We can remove the min from earlier (2) and find out.

```
1 -> {5, 10, 11}
5 -> {7, 12}
9 -> {3, 9, 15}
```

The next subsequence is [3, 7], which is no better or worse than our current best.

We can continue down this path each time, repeating this process. We will end up iterating through all "minimal" subsequences that start from a given point.

1. Current subsequence is [min of heads, max of heads]. Compare to best subsequence and update if necessary.
2. Remove the minimum head.
3. Repeat.

This will give us an O(SB) time complexity. This is because for each of B elements, we are doing a comparison to the S other list heads to find the minimum.

This is pretty good, but let's see if we can make that minimum computation faster.

What we're doing in these repeated minimum calls is taking a bunch of elements, finding and removing the minimum, adding in one more element, and then finding the minimum again.

We can make this faster by using a min-heap. First, put each of the heads in a min-heap. Remove the minimum. Look up the list that this minimum came from and add back the new head. Repeat.

To get the list that the minimum element came from, we'll need to use a HeapNode class that stores both the locationWithinList (the index) and the listId. This way, when we remove the minimum, we can jump back to the correct list and add its new head to the heap.

```
Range shortestSupersequence(int[] array, int[] elements) {
  ArrayList<Queue<Integer>> locations = getLocationsForElements(array, elements);
  if (locations == null) return null;
  return getShortestClosure(locations);
}

/* Get list of queues (linked lists) storing the indices at which each element in
 * smallArray appears in bigArray. */
ArrayList<Queue<Integer>> getLocationsForElements(int[] big, int[] small) {
  /* Initialize hash map from item value to locations. */
  HashMap<Integer, Queue<Integer>> itemLocations =
    new HashMap<Integer, Queue<Integer>>();
  for (int s : small) {
    Queue<Integer> queue = new LinkedList<Integer>();
    itemLocations.put(s, queue);
  }

  /* Walk through big array, adding the item locations to hash map */
  for (int i = 0; i < big.length; i++) {
    Queue<Integer> queue = itemLocations.get(big[i]);
    if (queue != null) {
      queue.add(i);
    }
  }

  ArrayList<Queue<Integer>> allLocations = new ArrayList<Queue<Integer>>();
  allLocations.addAll(itemLocations.values());
  return allLocations;
}

Range getShortestClosure(ArrayList<Queue<Integer>> lists) {
  PriorityQueue<HeapNode> minHeap = new PriorityQueue<HeapNode>();
  int max = Integer.MIN_VALUE;

  /* Insert min element from each list. */
  for (int i = 0; i < lists.size(); i++) {
    int head = lists.get(i).remove();
    minHeap.add(new HeapNode(head, i));
    max = Math.max(max, head);
  }

  int min = minHeap.peek().locationWithinList;
  int bestRangeMin = min;
  int bestRangeMax = max;

  while (true) {
    /* Remove min node. */
    HeapNode n = minHeap.poll();
    Queue<Integer> list = lists.get(n.listId);

    /* Compare range to best range. */
    min = n.locationWithinList;
    if (max - min < bestRangeMax - bestRangeMin) {
      bestRangeMax = max;
      bestRangeMin = min;
    }
```

```
        /* If there are no more elements, then there's no more subsequences and we
         * can break. */
        if (list.size() == 0) {
           break;
        }

        /* Add new head of list to heap. */
        n.locationWithinList = list.remove();
        minHeap.add(n);
        max = Math.max(max, n.locationWithinList);
     }

     return new Range(bestRangeMin, bestRangeMax);
  }
```

We're going through B elements in `getShortestClosure`, and each time pass in the for loop will take `O(log S)` time (the time to insert/remove from the heap). This algorithm will therefore take `O(B log S)` time in the worst case.

17.19 Missing Two: You are given an array with all the numbers from 1 to N appearing exactly once, except for one number that is missing. How can you find the missing number in `O(N)` time and `O(1)` space? What if there were two numbers missing?

pg 189

SOLUTIONS

Let's start with the first part: find a missing number in `O(N)` time and `O(1)` space.

Part 1: Find One Missing Number

We have a very constrained problem here. We can't store all the values (that would take `O(N)` space) and yet, somehow, we need to have a "record" of them such that we can identify the missing number.

This suggests that we need to do some sort of computation with the values. What characteristics does this computation need to have?

- **Unique.** If this computation gives the same result on two arrays (which fit the description in the problem), then those arrays must be equivalent (same missing number). That is, the result of the computation must uniquely correspond to the specific array and missing number.
- **Reversible.** We need some way of getting from the result of the calculation to the missing number.
- **Constant Time:** The calculation can be slow, but it must be constant time per element in the array.
- **Constant Space:** The calculation can require additional memory, but it must be `O(1)` memory.

The "unique" requirement is the most interesting—and the most challenging. What calculations can be performed on a set of numbers such that the missing number will be discoverable?

There are actually a number of possibilities.

We could do something with prime numbers. For example, for each value `x` in the array, we multiply `result` by the `x`th prime. We would then get some value that is indeed unique (since two different sets of primes can't have the same product).

Is this reversible? Yes. We could take `result` and divide it by each prime number: 2, 3, 5, 7, and so on. When we get a non-integer for the `i`th prime, then we know `i` was missing from our array.

Is it constant time and space, though? Only if we had a way of getting the `i`th prime number in `O(1)` time and `O(1)` space. We don't have that.

What other calculations could we do? We don't even need to do all this prime number stuff. Why not just multiply all the numbers together?

- **Unique?** Yes. Picture `1*2*3*...*n`. Now, imagine crossing off one number. This will give us a different result than if we crossed off any other number.
- **Constant time and space?** Yes.
- **Reversible?** Let's think about this. If we compare what our product is to what it would have been without a number removed, can we find the missing number? Sure. We just divide `full_product` by `actual_product`. This will tell us which number was missing from `actual_product`.

There's just one issue: this product is really, really, really big. If n is 20, the product will be somewhere around 2,000,000,000,000,000,000.

We can still approach it this way, but we'll need to use the `BigInteger` class.

```
int missingOne(int[] array) {
  BigInteger fullProduct = productToN(array.length + 1);

  BigInteger actualProduct = new BigInteger("1");
  for (int i = 0; i < array.length; i++) {
    BigInteger value = new BigInteger(array[i] + "");
    actualProduct = actualProduct.multiply(value);
  }

  BigInteger missingNumber = fullProduct.divide(actualProduct);
  return Integer.parseInt(missingNumber.toString());
}

BigInteger productToN(int n) {
  BigInteger fullProduct = new BigInteger("1");
  for (int i = 2; i <= n; i++) {
    fullProduct = fullProduct.multiply(new BigInteger(i + ""));
  }
  return fullProduct;
}
```

There's no need for all of this, though. We can use the sum instead. It too will be unique.

Doing the sum has another benefit: there is already a closed form expression to compute the sum of numbers between 1 and n. This is $\frac{n(n+1)}{2}$.

> Most candidates probably won't remember the expression for the sum of numbers between 1 and n, and that's okay. Your interviewer might, however, ask you to derive it. Here's how to think about that: you can pair up the low and high values in the sequence of `0 + 1 + 2 + 3 + ... + n` to get: `(0, n) + (1, n-1) + (2, n-3)`, and so on. Each of those pairs has a sum of n and there are $\frac{n+1}{2}$ pairs. But what if n is even, such that $\frac{n+1}{2}$ is not an integer? In this case, pair up low and high values to get $n/2$ pairs with sum `n+1`. Either way, the math works out to $\frac{n(n+1)}{2}$.

Switching to a sum will delay the overflow issue substantially, but it won't wholly prevent it. You should discuss the issue with your interviewer to see how he/she would like you to handle it. Just mentioning it is plenty sufficient for many interviewers.

Part 2: Find Two Missing Numbers

This is substantially more difficult. Let's start with what our earlier approaches will tell us when we have two missing numbers.

- Sum: Using this approach will give us the sum of the two values that are missing.
- Product: Using this approach will give us the product of the two values that are missing.

Unfortunately, knowing the sum isn't enough. If, for example, the sum is 10, that could correspond to (1, 9), (2, 8), and a handful of other pairs. The same could be said for the product.

We're again at the same point we were in the first part of the problem. We need a calculation that can be applied such that the result is unique across all potential pairs of missing numbers.

Perhaps there is such a calculation (the prime one would work, but it's not constant time), but your interviewer probably doesn't expect you to know such math.

What else can we do? Let's go back to what we can do. We can get `x + y` and we can also get x * y. Each result leaves us with a number of possibilities. But using both of them narrows it down to the specific numbers.

$$
\begin{aligned}
x + y = sum &\rightarrow y = sum - x \\
x * y = product &\rightarrow x(sum - x) = product \\
& \quad x*sum - x^2 = product \\
& \quad x*sum - x^2 - product = 0 \\
& \quad -x^2 + x*sum - product = 0
\end{aligned}
$$

At this point, we can apply the quadratic formula to solve for x. Once we have x, we can then compute y.

There are actually a number of other calculations you can perform. In fact, almost any other calculation (other than "linear" calculations) will give us values for x and y.

For this part, let's use a different calculation. Instead of using the product of `1 * 2 * ... * n`, we can use the sum of the squares: $1^2 + 2^2 + ... + n^2$. This will make the `BigInteger` usage a little less critical, as the code will at least run on small values of n. We can discuss with our interviewer whether or not this is important.

$$
\begin{aligned}
x + y = s &\rightarrow y = s - x \\
x^2 + y^2 = t &\rightarrow x^2 + (s-x)^2 = t \\
& \quad 2x^2 - 2sx + s^2-t = 0
\end{aligned}
$$

Recall the quadratic formula:

$$x = [-b +- sqrt(b^2 - 4ac)] / 2a$$

where, in this case:

$$
\begin{aligned}
a &= 2 \\
b &= -2s \\
c &= s^2-t
\end{aligned}
$$

Implementing this is now somewhat straightforward.

```
int[] missingTwo(int[] array) {
  int max_value = array.length + 2;
  int rem_square = squareSumToN(max_value, 2);
  int rem_one = max_value * (max_value + 1) / 2;

```

```
    for (int i = 0; i < array.length; i++) {
      rem_square -= array[i] * array[i];
      rem_one -= array[i];
    }

    return solveEquation(rem_one, rem_square);
}

int squareSumToN(int n, int power) {
    int sum = 0;
    for (int i = 1; i <= n; i++) {
      sum += (int) Math.pow(i, power);
    }
    return sum;
}

int[] solveEquation(int r1, int r2) {
    /* ax^2 + bx + c
     * -->
     * x = [-b +- sqrt(b^2 - 4ac)] / 2a
     * In this case, it has to be a + not a - */
    int a = 2;
    int b = -2 * r1;
    int c = r1 * r1 - r2;

    double part1 = -1 * b;
    double part2 = Math.sqrt(b*b - 4 * a * c);
    double part3 = 2 * a;

    int solutionX = (int) ((part1 + part2) / part3);
    int solutionY = r1 - solutionX;

    int[] solution = {solutionX, solutionY};
    return solution;
}
```

You might notice that the quadratic formula usually gives us two answers (see the + or - part), yet in our code, we only use the (+) result. We never checked the (-) answer. Why is that?

The existence of the "alternate" solution doesn't mean that one is the correct solution and one is "fake." It means that there are exactly two values for x which will correctly fulfill our equation: $2x^2 - 2sx + (s^2-t) = 0$.

That's true. There are. What's the other one? The other value is y!

If this doesn't immediately make sense to you, remember that x and y are interchangeable. Had we solved for y earlier instead of x, we would have wound up with an identical equation: $2y^2 - 2sy + (s^2-t) = 0$. So of course y could fulfill x's equation and x could fulfill y's equation. They have the exact same equation. Since x and y are both solutions to equations that look like $2[\text{something}]^2 - 2s[\text{something}] + s^2-t = 0$, then the other `something` that fulfills that equation must be y.

Still not convinced? Okay, we can do some math. Let's say we took the alternate value for x: $[-b - \text{sqrt}(b^2 - 4ac)] / 2a$. What's y?

$$
\begin{aligned}
x + y &= r_1 \\
y &= r_1 - x \\
&= r_1 - [-b - \text{sqrt}(b^2 - 4ac)]/2a \\
&= [2a*r_1 + b + \text{sqrt}(b^2 - 4ac)]/2a
\end{aligned}
$$

Partially plug in values for a and b, but keep the rest of the equation as-is:

$$= [2(2)*r_1 + (-2r_1) + sqrt(b^2 - 4ac)]/2a$$
$$= [2r_1 + sqrt(b^2 - 4ac)]/2a$$

Recall that b = $-2r_1$. Now, we wind up with this equation:

$$= [-b + sqrt(b^2 - 4ac)]/2a$$

Therefore, if we use `x = (part1 + part2) / part3`, then we'll get `(part1 - part2) / part3` for the value for y.

We don't care which one we call x and which one we call y, so we can use either one. It'll work out the same in the end.

17.20 Continuous Median: Numbers are randomly generated and passed to a method. Write a program to find and maintain the median value as new values are generated.

pg 189

SOLUTIONS

One solution is to use two priority heaps: a max heap for the values below the median, and a min heap for the values above the median. This will divide the elements roughly in half, with the middle two elements as the top of the two heaps. This makes it trivial to find the median.

What do we mean by "roughly in half," though? "Roughly" means that, if we have an odd number of values, one heap will have an extra value. Observe that the following is true:

- If `maxHeap.size() > minHeap.size()`, `maxHeap.top()` will be the median.
- If `maxHeap.size() == minHeap.size()`, then the average of `maxHeap.top()` and `minHeap.top()` will be the median.

By the way in which we rebalance the heaps, we will ensure that it is always `maxHeap` with extra element.

The algorithm works as follows. When a new value arrives, it is placed in the `maxHeap` if the value is less than or equal to the median, otherwise it is placed into the `minHeap`. The heap sizes can be equal, or the `maxHeap` may have one extra element. This constraint can easily be restored by shifting an element from one heap to the other. The median is available in constant time, by looking at the top element(s). Updates take `O(log(n))` time.

```
Comparator<Integer> maxHeapComparator, minHeapComparator;
PriorityQueue<Integer> maxHeap, minHeap;

void addNewNumber(int randomNumber) {
   /* Note: addNewNumber maintains a condition that
    * maxHeap.size() >= minHeap.size() */
   if (maxHeap.size() == minHeap.size()) {
      if ((minHeap.peek() != null) &&
         randomNumber > minHeap.peek()) {
         maxHeap.offer(minHeap.poll());
         minHeap.offer(randomNumber);
      } else {
         maxHeap.offer(randomNumber);
      }
   } else {
      if(randomNumber < maxHeap.peek()) {
         minHeap.offer(maxHeap.poll());
         maxHeap.offer(randomNumber);
```

```java
      }
      else {
         minHeap.offer(randomNumber);
      }
   }
}

double getMedian() {
   /* maxHeap is always at least as big as minHeap. So if maxHeap is empty, then
    * minHeap is also. */
   if (maxHeap.isEmpty()) {
      return 0;
   }
   if (maxHeap.size() == minHeap.size()) {
      return ((double)minHeap.peek()+(double)maxHeap.peek()) / 2;
   } else {
      /* If maxHeap and minHeap are of different sizes, then maxHeap must have one
       * extra element. Return maxHeap's top element.*/
      return maxHeap.peek();
   }
}
```

17.21 Volume of Histogram: Imagine a histogram (bar graph). Design an algorithm to compute the volume of water it could hold if someone poured water across the top. You can assume that each histogram bar has width 1.

EXAMPLE

Input: `{0, 0, 4, 0, 0, 6, 0, 0, 3, 0, 5, 0, 1, 0, 0, 0}`

`(Black bars are the histogram. Gray is water.)`

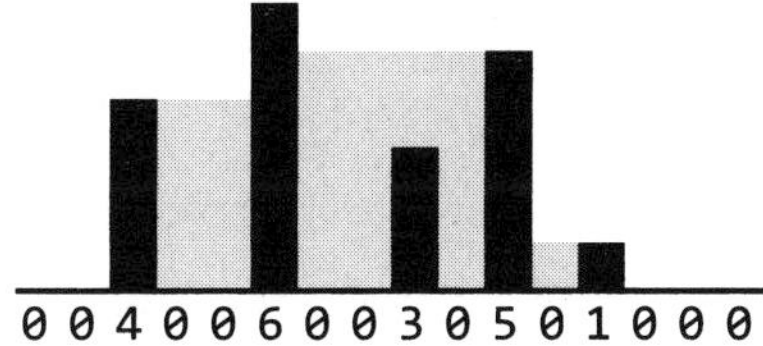

Output: 26

pg 189

SOLUTION

This is a difficult problem, so let's come up with a good example to help us solve it.

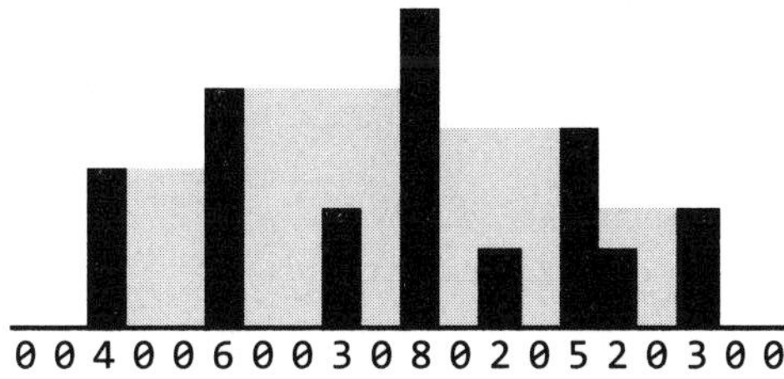

We should study this example to see what we can learn from it. What exactly dictates how big those gray areas are?

Solution #1

Let's look at the tallest bar, which has size 8. What role does that bar play? It plays an important role for being the highest, but it actually wouldn't matter if that bar instead had height 100. It wouldn't affect the volume.

The tallest bar forms a barrier for water on its left and right. But the volume of water is actually controlled by the next highest bar on the left and right.

- **Water on immediate left of tallest bar:** The next tallest bar on the left has height 6. We can fill up the area in between with water, but we have to deduct the height of each histogram between the tallest and next tallest. This gives a volume on the immediate left of: `(6-0) + (6-0) + (6-3) + (6-0) = 21`.
- **Water on immediate right of tallest bar:** The next tallest bar on the right has height 5. We can now compute the volume: `(5-0) + (5-2) + (5-0) = 13`.

This just tells us part of the volume.

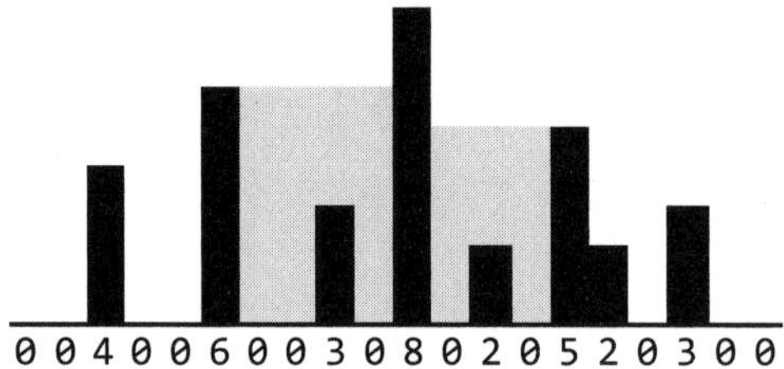

What about the rest?

We have essentially two subgraphs, one on the left and one on the right. To find the volume there, we repeat a very similar process.

1. Find the max. (Actually, this is given to us. The highest on the left subgraph is the right border (6) and the highest on the right subgraph is the left border (5).)
2. Find the second tallest in each subgraph. In the left subgraph, this is 4. In the right subgraph, this is 3.
3. Compute the volume between the tallest and the second tallest.
4. Recurse on the edge of the graph.

The code below implements this algorithm.

```
int computeHistogramVolume(int[] histogram) {
  int start = 0;
  int end = histogram.length - 1;

  int max = findIndexOfMax(histogram, start, end);
  int leftVolume =  subgraphVolume(histogram, start, max, true);
  int rightVolume = subgraphVolume(histogram, max, end, false);

  return leftVolume + rightVolume;
}

/* Compute the volume of a subgraph of the histogram. One max is at either start
 * or end (depending on isLeft). Find second tallest, then compute volume between
 * tallest and second tallest. Then compute volume of subgraph. */
int subgraphVolume(int[] histogram, int start, int end, boolean isLeft) {
  if (start >= end) return 0;
```

```
    int sum = 0;
    if (isLeft) {
      int max = findIndexOfMax(histogram, start, end - 1);
      sum += borderedVolume(histogram, max, end);
      sum += subgraphVolume(histogram, start, max, isLeft);
    } else {
      int max = findIndexOfMax(histogram, start + 1, end);
      sum += borderedVolume(histogram, start, max);
      sum += subgraphVolume(histogram, max, end, isLeft);
    }

    return sum;
}

/* Find tallest bar in histogram between start and end. */
int findIndexOfMax(int[] histogram, int start, int end) {
  int indexOfMax = start;
  for (int i = start + 1; i <= end; i++) {
    if (histogram[i] > histogram[indexOfMax]) {
      indexOfMax = i;
    }
  }
  return indexOfMax;
}

/* Compute volume between start and end. Assumes that tallest bar is at start and
 * second tallest is at end. */
int borderedVolume(int[] histogram, int start, int end) {
  if (start >= end) return 0;

  int min = Math.min(histogram[start], histogram[end]);
  int sum = 0;
  for (int i = start + 1; i < end; i++) {
    sum += min - histogram[i];
  }
  return sum;
}
```

This algorithm takes $O(N^2)$ time in the worst case, where N is the number of bars in the histogram. This is because we have to repeatedly scan the histogram to find the max height.

Solution #2 (Optimized)

To optimize the previous algorithm, let's think about the exact cause of the inefficiency of the prior algorithm. The root cause is the perpetual calls to `findIndexOfMax`. This suggests that it should be our focus for optimizing.

One thing we should notice is that we don't pass in arbitrary ranges into the `findIndexOfMax` function. It's actually always finding the max from one point to an edge (either the right edge or the left edge). Is there a quicker way we could know what the max height is from a given point to each edge?

Yes. We could precompute this information in $O(N)$ time.

In two sweeps through the histogram (one moving right to left and the other moving left to right), we can create a table that tells us, from any index `i`, the location of the max index on the right and the max index on the left.

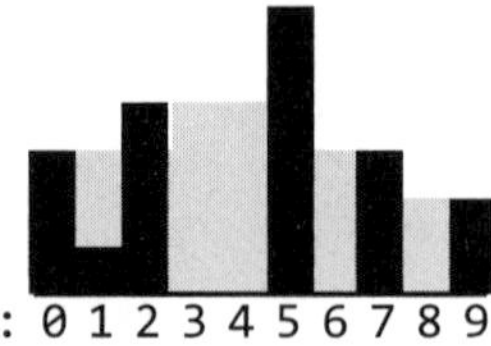

```
          INDEX: 0 1 2 3 4 5 6 7 8 9
         HEIGHT: 3 1 4 0 0 6 0 3 0 2
 INDEX LEFT MAX: 0 0 2 2 2 5 5 5 5 5
INDEX RIGHT MAX: 5 5 5 5 5 5 7 7 9 9
```

The rest of the algorithm precedes essentially the same way.

We've chosen to use a `HistogramData` object to store this extra information, but we could also use a two-dimensional array.

```
int computeHistogramVolume(int[] histogram) {
  int start = 0;
  int end = histogram.length - 1;

  HistogramData[] data = createHistogramData(histogram);

  int max = data[0].getRightMaxIndex(); // Get overall max
  int leftVolume =  subgraphVolume(data, start, max, true);
  int rightVolume = subgraphVolume(data, max, end, false);

  return leftVolume + rightVolume;
}

HistogramData[] createHistogramData(int[] histo) {
  HistogramData[] histogram = new HistogramData[histo.length];
  for (int i = 0; i < histo.length; i++) {
    histogram[i] = new HistogramData(histo[i]);
  }

  /* Set left max index. */
  int maxIndex = 0;
  for (int i = 0; i < histo.length; i++) {
    if (histo[maxIndex] < histo[i]) {
      maxIndex = i;
    }
    histogram[i].setLeftMaxIndex(maxIndex);
  }

  /* Set right max index. */
  maxIndex = histogram.length - 1;
  for (int i = histogram.length - 1; i >= 0; i--) {
    if (histo[maxIndex] < histo[i]) {
      maxIndex = i;
    }
    histogram[i].setRightMaxIndex(maxIndex);
  }

  return histogram;
}

/* Compute the volume of a subgraph of the histogram. One max is at either start
```

```
 * or end (depending on isLeft). Find second tallest, then compute volume between
 * tallest and second tallest. Then compute volume of subgraph. */
int subgraphVolume(HistogramData[] histogram, int start, int end,
                   boolean isLeft) {
  if (start >= end) return 0;
  int sum = 0;
  if (isLeft) {
    int max = histogram[end - 1].getLeftMaxIndex();
    sum += borderedVolume(histogram, max, end);
    sum += subgraphVolume(histogram, start, max, isLeft);
  } else {
    int max = histogram[start + 1].getRightMaxIndex();
    sum += borderedVolume(histogram, start, max);
    sum += subgraphVolume(histogram, max, end, isLeft);
  }

  return sum;
}

/* Compute volume between start and end. Assumes that tallest two bars are at each
 * end. */
int borderedVolume(HistogramData[] data, int start, int end) {
  if (start >= end) return 0;

  int min = Math.min(data[start].getHeight(), data[end].getHeight());
  int sum = 0;
  for (int i = start + 1; i < end; i++) {
    sum += min - data[i].getHeight();
  }
  return sum;
}

public class HistogramData {
  private int height;
  private int leftMaxIndex = -1;
  private int rightMaxIndex = -1;

  public HistogramData(int v) { height = v; }
  public int getHeight() { return height; }
  public int getLeftMaxIndex() { return leftMaxIndex; }
  public void setLeftMaxIndex(int idx) { leftMaxIndex = idx; };
  public int getRightMaxIndex() { return rightMaxIndex; }
  public void setRightMaxIndex(int idx) { rightMaxIndex = idx; };
}
```

This algorithm takes O(N) time. Since we have to look at every bar, we cannot do better than this.

Solution #3 (Optimized & Simplified)

While we can't make the solution faster in terms of big O, we can make it much, much simpler. Let's look at an example again in light of what we've just learned about potential algorithms.

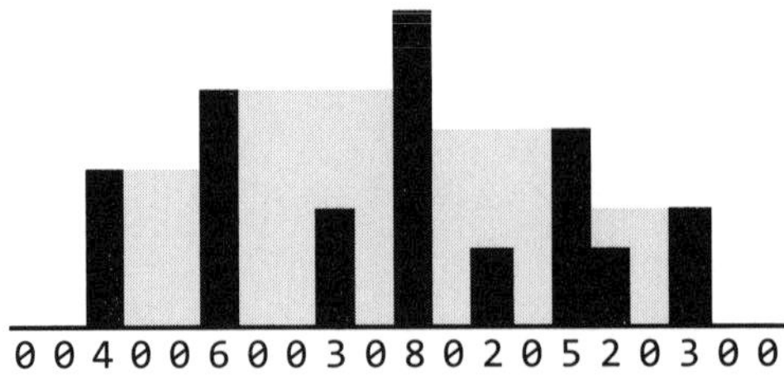

As we've seen, the volume of water in a particular area is determined by the tallest bar to the left and to the right (specifically, by the shorter of the two tallest bars on the left and the tallest bar on the right). For example, water fills in the area between the bar with height 6 and the bar with height 8, up to a height of 6. It's the second tallest, therefore, that determines the height.

The total volume of water is the volume of water above each histogram bar. Can we efficiently compute how much water is above each histogram bar?

Yes. In Solution #2, we were able to precompute the height of the tallest bar on the left and right of each index. The minimums of these will indicate the "water level" at a bar. The difference between the water level and the height of this bar will be the volume of water.

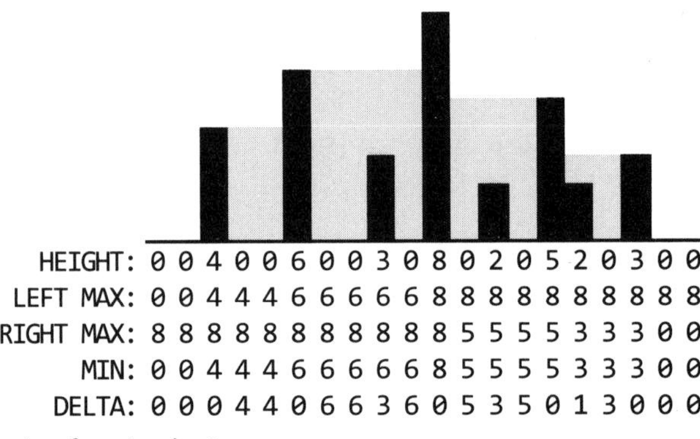

Our algorithm now runs in a few simple steps:

1. Sweep left to right, tracking the max height you've seen and setting left max.
2. Sweep right to left, tracking the max height you've seen and setting right max.
3. Sweep across the histogram, computing the minimum of the left max and right max for each index.
4. Sweep across the histogram, computing the delta between each minimum and the bar. Sum these deltas.

In the actual implementation, we don't need to keep so much data around. Steps 2, 3, and 4 can be merged into the same sweep. First, compute the left maxes in one sweep. Then sweep through in reverse, tracking the right max as you go. At each element, calculate the min of the left and right max and then the delta between that (the "min of maxes") and the bar height. Add this to the sum.

```
/* Go through each bar and compute the volume of water above it.
 * Volume of water at a bar =
 *   height - min(tallest bar on left, tallest bar on right)
 *   [where above equation is positive]
 * Compute the left max in the first sweep, then sweep again to compute the right
 * max, minimum of the bar heights, and the delta. */
int computeHistogramVolume(int[] histo) {
```

```
    /* Get left max */
    int[] leftMaxes = new int[histo.length];
    int leftMax = histo[0];
    for (int i = 0; i < histo.length; i++) {
      leftMax = Math.max(leftMax, histo[i]);
      leftMaxes[i] = leftMax;
    }

    int sum = 0;

    /* Get right max */
    int rightMax = histo[histo.length - 1];
    for (int i = histo.length - 1; i >= 0; i--) {
      rightMax = Math.max(rightMax, histo[i]);
      int secondTallest = Math.min(rightMax, leftMaxes[i]);

      /* If there are taller things on the left and right side, then there is water
       * above this bar. Compute the volume and add to the sum. */
        if (secondTallest > histo[i]) {
          sum += secondTallest - histo[i];
        }
      }

      return sum;
    }
```

Yes, this really is the entire code! It is still O(N) time, but it's a lot simpler to read and write.

17.22 Word Transformer: Given two words of equal length that are in a dictionary, write a method to transform one word into another word by changing only one letter at a time. The new word you get in each step must be in the dictionary.

EXAMPLE

Input: DAMP, LIKE

Output: DAMP -> LAMP -> LIMP -> LIME -> LIKE

pg 189

SOLUTION

Let's start with a naive solution and then work our way to a more optimal solution.

Brute Force

One way of solving this problem is to just transform the words in every possible way (of course checking at each step to ensure each is a valid word), and then see if we can reach the final word.

So, for example, the word bold would be transformed into:

- aold, bold, ..., zold
- bald, bbld, ..., bzld
- boad, bobd, ..., bozd
- bola, bolb, ..., bolz

We will terminate (not pursue this path) if the string is not a valid word or if we've already visited this word.

This is essentially a depth-first search where there is an "edge" between two words if they are only one edit apart. This means that this algorithm will not find the shortest path. It will only find a path.

If we wanted to find the shortest path, we would want to use breadth-first search.

```
LinkedList<String> transform(String start, String stop, String[] words) {
  HashSet<String> dict = setupDictionary(words);
  HashSet<String> visited = new HashSet<String>();
  return transform(visited, start, stop, dict);
}

HashSet<String> setupDictionary(String[] words) {
  HashSet<String> hash = new HashSet<String>();
  for (String word : words) {
    hash.add(word.toLowerCase());
  }
  return hash;
}

LinkedList<String> transform(HashSet<String> visited, String startWord,
                              String stopWord, Set<String> dictionary) {
  if (startWord.equals(stopWord)) {
    LinkedList<String> path = new LinkedList<String>();
    path.add(startWord);
    return path;
  } else if (visited.contains(startWord) || !dictionary.contains(startWord)) {
    return null;
  }

  visited.add(startWord);
  ArrayList<String> words = wordsOneAway(startWord);

  for (String word : words) {
    LinkedList<String> path = transform(visited, word, stopWord, dictionary);
    if (path != null) {
      path.addFirst(startWord);
      return path;
    }
  }

  return null;
}

ArrayList<String> wordsOneAway(String word) {
  ArrayList<String> words = new ArrayList<String>();
  for (int i = 0; i < word.length(); i++) {
    for (char c = 'a'; c <= 'z'; c++) {
      String w = word.substring(0, i) + c + word.substring(i + 1);
      words.add(w);
    }
  }
  return words;
}
```

One major inefficiency in this algorithm is finding all strings that are one edit away. Right now, we're finding the strings that are one edit away and then eliminating the invalid ones.

Ideally, we want to only go to the ones that are valid.

Optimized Solution

To travel to only valid words, we clearly need a way of going from each word to a list of all the valid related words.

What makes two words "related" (one edit away)? They are one edit away if all but one character is the same. For example, `ball` and `bill` are one edit away, because they are both in the form `b_ll`. Therefore, one approach is to group all words that look like `b_ll` together.

We can do this for the whole dictionary by creating a mapping from a "wildcard word" (like `b_ll`) to a list of all words in this form. For example, for a very small dictionary like `{all, ill, ail, ape, ale}` the mapping might look like this:

```
_il -> ail
_le -> ale
_ll -> all, ill
_pe -> ape
a_e -> ape, ale
a_l -> all, ail
i_l -> ill
ai_ -> ail
al_ -> all, ale
ap_ -> ape
il_ -> ill
```

Now, when we want to know the words that are one edit away from a word like `ale`, we look up `_le`, `a_e`, and `al_` in the hash table.

The algorithm is otherwise essentially the same.

```
LinkedList<String> transform(String start, String stop, String[] words) {
  HashMapList<String, String> wildcardToWordList = createWildcardToWordMap(words);
  HashSet<String> visited = new HashSet<String>();
  return transform(visited, start, stop, wildcardToWordList);
}

/* Do a depth-first search from startWord to stopWord, traveling through each word
 * that is one edit away. */
LinkedList<String> transform(HashSet<String> visited, String start, String stop,
                             HashMapList<String, String> wildcardToWordList) {
  if (start.equals(stop)) {
    LinkedList<String> path = new LinkedList<String>();
    path.add(start);
    return path;
  } else if (visited.contains(start)) {
    return null;
  }

  visited.add(start);
  ArrayList<String> words = getValidLinkedWords(start, wildcardToWordList);

  for (String word : words) {
    LinkedList<String> path = transform(visited, word, stop, wildcardToWordList);
    if (path != null) {
      path.addFirst(start);
      return path;
    }
  }

```

```
  return null;
}

/* Insert words in dictionary into mapping from wildcard form -> word. */
HashMapList<String, String> createWildcardToWordMap(String[] words) {
  HashMapList<String, String> wildcardToWords = new HashMapList<String, String>();
  for (String word : words) {
    ArrayList<String> linked = getWildcardRoots(word);
    for (String linkedWord : linked) {
      wildcardToWords.put(linkedWord, word);
    }
  }
  return wildcardToWords;
}

/* Get list of wildcards associated with word. */
ArrayList<String> getWildcardRoots(String w) {
  ArrayList<String> words = new ArrayList<String>();
  for (int i = 0; i < w.length(); i++) {
    String word = w.substring(0, i) + "_" + w.substring(i + 1);
    words.add(word);
  }
  return words;
}

/* Return words that are one edit away. */
ArrayList<String> getValidLinkedWords(String word,
    HashMapList<String, String> wildcardToWords) {
  ArrayList<String> wildcards = getWildcardRoots(word);
  ArrayList<String> linkedWords = new ArrayList<String>();
  for (String wildcard : wildcards) {
    ArrayList<String> words = wildcardToWords.get(wildcard);
    for (String linkedWord : words) {
      if (!linkedWord.equals(word)) {
        linkedWords.add(linkedWord);
      }
    }
  }
  return linkedWords;
}

/* HashMapList<String, String> is a HashMap that maps from Strings to
 * ArrayList<String>. See appendix for implementation. */
```

This will work, but we can still make it faster.

One optimization is to switch from depth-first search to breadth-first search. If there are zero paths or one path, the algorithms are equivalent speeds. However, if there are multiple paths, breadth-first search may run faster.

Breadth-first search finds the shortest path between two nodes, whereas depth-first search finds any path. This means that depth-first search might take a very long, windy path in order to find a connection when, in fact, the nodes were quite close.

Optimal Solution

As noted earlier, we can optimize this using breadth-first search. Is this as fast as we can make it? Not quite.

Imagine that the path between two nodes has length 4. With breadth-first search, we will visit about 15^4 nodes to find them.

Breadth-first search spans out very quickly.

Instead, what if we searched out from the source and destination nodes simultaneously? In this case, the breadth-first searches would collide after each had done about two levels each.

- Nodes travelled to from source: 15^2
- Nodes travelled to from destination: 15^2
- Total nodes: $15^2 + 15^2$

This is much better than the traditional breadth-first search.

We will need to track the path that we've travelled at each node.

To implement this approach, we've used an additional class `BFSData`. `BFSData` helps us keep things a bit clearer, and allows us to keep a similar framework for the two simultaneous breadth-first searches. The alternative is to keep passing around a bunch of separate variables.

```
LinkedList<String> transform(String startWord, String stopWord, String[] words) {
  HashMapList<String, String> wildcardToWordList = getWildcardToWordList(words);

  BFSData sourceData = new BFSData(startWord);
  BFSData destData = new BFSData(stopWord);

  while (!sourceData.isFinished() && !destData.isFinished()) {
    /* Search out from source. */
    String collision = searchLevel(wildcardToWordList, sourceData, destData);
    if (collision != null) {
      return mergePaths(sourceData, destData, collision);
    }

    /* Search out from destination. */
    collision = searchLevel(wildcardToWordList, destData, sourceData);
    if (collision != null) {
      return mergePaths(sourceData, destData, collision);
    }
  }

  return null;
}

/* Search one level and return collision, if any. */
String searchLevel(HashMapList<String, String> wildcardToWordList,
                   BFSData primary, BFSData secondary) {
  /* We only want to search one level at a time. Count how many nodes are
   * currently in the primary's level and only do that many nodes. We'll continue
   * to add nodes to the end. */
  int count = primary.toVisit.size();
  for (int i = 0; i < count; i++) {
    /* Pull out first node. */
    PathNode pathNode = primary.toVisit.poll();
    String word = pathNode.getWord();

    /* Check if it's already been visited. */
    if (secondary.visited.containsKey(word)) {
```

```
            return pathNode.getWord();
         }

         /* Add friends to queue. */
         ArrayList<String> words = getValidLinkedWords(word, wildcardToWordList);
         for (String w : words) {
            if (!primary.visited.containsKey(w)) {
               PathNode next = new PathNode(w, pathNode);
               primary.visited.put(w, next);
               primary.toVisit.add(next);
            }
         }
      }
      return null;
   }

   LinkedList<String> mergePaths(BFSData bfs1, BFSData bfs2, String connection) {
      PathNode end1 = bfs1.visited.get(connection); // end1 -> source
      PathNode end2 = bfs2.visited.get(connection); // end2 -> dest
      LinkedList<String> pathOne = end1.collapse(false); // forward
      LinkedList<String> pathTwo = end2.collapse(true); // reverse
      pathTwo.removeFirst(); // remove connection
      pathOne.addAll(pathTwo); // add second path
      return pathOne;
   }

   /* Methods getWildcardRoots, getWildcardToWordList, and getValidLinkedWords are
    * the same as in the earlier solution. */

   public class BFSData {
      public Queue<PathNode> toVisit = new LinkedList<PathNode>();
      public HashMap<String, PathNode> visited = new HashMap<String, PathNode>();

      public BFSData(String root) {
         PathNode sourcePath = new PathNode(root, null);
         toVisit.add(sourcePath);
         visited.put(root, sourcePath);
      }

      public boolean isFinished() {
         return toVisit.isEmpty();
      }
   }

   public class PathNode {
      private String word = null;
      private PathNode previousNode = null;
      public PathNode(String word, PathNode previous) {
         this.word = word;
         previousNode = previous;
      }

      public String getWord() {
         return word;
      }

```

```
    /* Traverse path and return linked list of nodes. */
    public LinkedList<String> collapse(boolean startsWithRoot) {
       LinkedList<String> path = new LinkedList<String>();
       PathNode node = this;
       while (node != null) {
          if (startsWithRoot) {
             path.addLast(node.word);
          } else {
             path.addFirst(node.word);
          }
          node = node.previousNode;
       }
       return path;
    }
}

/* HashMapList<String, Integer> is a HashMap that maps from Strings to
 * ArrayList<Integer>. See appendix for implementation. */
```

This algorithm's runtime is a bit harder to describe since it depends on what the language looks like, as well as the actual source and destination words. One way of expressing it is that if each word has E words that are one edit away and the source and destination are distance D, the runtime is $O(E^{D/2})$. This is how much work each breadth-first search does.

Of course, this is a lot of code to implement in an interview. It just wouldn't be possible. More realistically, you'd leave out a lot of the details. You might write just the skeleton code of `transform` and `searchLevel`, but leave out the rest.

17.23 Max Black Square: Imagine you have a square matrix, where each cell (pixel) is either black or white. Design an algorithm to find the maximum subsquare such that all four borders are filled with black pixels.

pg 190

SOLUTION

Like many problems, there's an easy way and a hard way to solve this. We'll go through both solutions.

The "Simple" Solution: $O(N^4)$

We know that the biggest possible square has a length of size N, and there is only one possible square of size NxN. We can easily check for that square and return if we find it.

If we do not find a square of size NxN, we can try the next best thing: `(N-1) x (N-1)`. We iterate through all squares of this size and return the first one we find. We then do the same for N-2, N-3, and so on. Since we are searching progressively smaller squares, we know that the first square we find is the biggest.

Our code works as follows:

```
Subsquare findSquare(int[][] matrix) {
   for (int i = matrix.length; i >= 1; i--) {
      Subsquare square = findSquareWithSize(matrix, i);
      if (square != null) return square;
   }
   return null;
}
```

```
Subsquare findSquareWithSize(int[][] matrix, int squareSize) {
   /* On an edge of length N, there are (N - sz + 1) squares of length sz. */
   int count = matrix.length - squareSize + 1;

   /* Iterate through all squares with side length squareSize. */
   for (int row = 0; row < count; row++) {
      for (int col = 0; col < count; col++) {
         if (isSquare(matrix, row, col, squareSize)) {
            return new Subsquare(row, col, squareSize);
         }
      }
   }
   return null;
}

boolean isSquare(int[][] matrix, int row, int col, int size) {
   // Check top and bottom border.
   for (int j = 0; j < size; j++){
      if (matrix[row][col+j] == 1) {
         return false;
      }
      if (matrix[row+size-1][col+j] == 1){
         return false;
      }
   }

   // Check left and right border.
   for (int i = 1; i < size - 1; i++){
      if (matrix[row+i][col] == 1){
         return false;
      }
      if (matrix[row+i][col+size-1] == 1) {
         return false;
      }
   }
   return true;
}
```

Pre-Processing Solution: $O(N^3)$

A large part of the slowness of the "simple" solution above is due to the fact we have to do $O(N)$ work each time we want to check a potential square. By doing some pre-processing, we can cut down the time of `isSquare` to $O(1)$. The time of the whole algorithm is reduced to $O(N^3)$.

If we analyze what `isSquare` does, we realize that all it ever needs to know is if the next `squareSize` items, on the right of as well as below particular cells, are zeros. We can pre-compute this data in a straightforward, iterative fashion.

We iterate from right to left, bottom to top. At each cell, we do the following computation:

```
if A[r][c] is white, zeros right and zeros below are 0
else A[r][c].zerosRight = A[r][c + 1].zerosRight + 1
     A[r][c].zerosBelow = A[r + 1][c].zerosBelow + 1
```

Below is an example of these values for a potential matrix.

(0s right, 0s below)

0,0	1,3	0,0
2,2	1,2	0,0
2,1	1,1	0,0

Original Matrix

W	B	W
B	B	W
B	B	W

Now, instead of iterating through `O(N)` elements, the `isSquare` method just needs to check `zerosRight` and `zerosBelow` for the corners.

Our code for this algorithm is below. Note that `findSquare` and `findSquareWithSize` is equivalent, other than a call to `processMatrix` and working with a new data type thereafter.

```
public class SquareCell {
  public int zerosRight = 0;
  public int zerosBelow = 0;
  /* declaration, getters, setters */
}

Subsquare findSquare(int[][] matrix) {
  SquareCell[][] processed = processSquare(matrix);
  for (int i = matrix.length; i >= 1; i--) {
     Subsquare square = findSquareWithSize(processed, i);
     if (square != null) return square;
  }
  return null;
}

Subsquare findSquareWithSize(SquareCell[][] processed, int size) {
  /* equivalent to first algorithm */
}

boolean isSquare(SquareCell[][] matrix, int row, int col, int sz) {
  SquareCell topLeft = matrix[row][col];
  SquareCell topRight = matrix[row][col + sz - 1];
  SquareCell bottomLeft = matrix[row + sz - 1][col];

  /* Check top, left, right, and bottom edges, respectively. */
  if (topLeft.zerosRight < sz || topLeft.zerosBelow < sz ||
      topRight.zerosBelow < sz || bottomLeft.zerosRight < sz) {
     return false;
  }
  return true;
}

 SquareCell[][] processSquare(int[][] matrix) {
  SquareCell[][] processed =
     new SquareCell[matrix.length][matrix.length];

  for (int r = matrix.length - 1; r >= 0; r--) {
     for (int c = matrix.length - 1; c >= 0; c--) {
        int rightZeros = 0;
        int belowZeros = 0;
```

```
            // only need to process if it's a black cell
            if (matrix[r][c] == 0) {
               rightZeros++;
               belowZeros++;
               // next column over is on same row
               if (c + 1 < matrix.length) {
                  SquareCell previous = processed[r][c + 1];
                  rightZeros += previous.zerosRight;
               }
               if (r + 1 < matrix.length) {
                  SquareCell previous = processed[r + 1][c];
                  belowZeros += previous.zerosBelow;
               }
            }
            processed[r][c] = new SquareCell(rightZeros, belowZeros);
         }
      }
      return processed;
   }
```

17.24 Max Submatrix: Given an NxN matrix of positive and negative integers, write code to find the submatrix with the largest possible sum.

pg 190

SOLUTION

This problem can be approached in a variety of ways. We'll start with the brute force solution and then optimize the solution from there.

Brute Force Solution: $O(N^6)$

Like many "maximizing" problems, this problem has a straightforward brute force solution. This solution simply iterates through all possible submatrices, computes the sum, and finds the largest.

To iterate through all possible submatrices (with no duplicates), we simply need to iterate through all ordered pairs of rows, and then all ordered pairs of columns.

This solution is $O(N^6)$, since we iterate through $O(N^4)$ submatrices and it takes $O(N^2)$ time to compute the area of each.

```
SubMatrix getMaxMatrix(int[][] matrix) {
   int rowCount = matrix.length;
   int columnCount = matrix[0].length;
   SubMatrix best = null;
   for (int row1 = 0; row1 < rowCount; row1++) {
      for (int row2 = row1; row2 < rowCount; row2++) {
         for (int col1 = 0; col1 < columnCount; col1++) {
            for (int col2 = col1; col2 < columnCount; col2++) {
               int sum = sum(matrix, row1, col1, row2, col2);
               if (best == null || best.getSum() < sum) {
                  best = new SubMatrix(row1, col1, row2, col2, sum);
               }
            }
         }
      }
   }
```

```
    return best;
}

int sum(int[][] matrix, int row1, int col1, int row2, int col2) {
    int sum = 0;
    for (int r = row1; r <= row2; r++) {
        for (int c = col1; c <= col2; c++) {
            sum += matrix[r][c];
        }
    }
    return sum;
}

public class SubMatrix {
    private int row1, row2, col1, col2, sum;
    public SubMatrix(int r1, int c1, int r2, int c2, int sm) {
        row1 = r1;
        col1 = c1;
        row2 = r2;
        col2 = c2;
        sum = sm;
    }

    public int getSum() {
        return sum;
    }
}
```

It is good practice to pull the `sum` code into its own function since it's a fairly distinct set of code.

Dynamic Programming Solution: $O(N^4)$

Notice that the earlier solution is made slower by a factor of $O(N^2)$ simply because computing the sum of a matrix is so slow. Can we reduce the time to compute the area? Yes! In fact, we can reduce the time of `computeSum` to `O(1)`.

Consider the following rectangle:

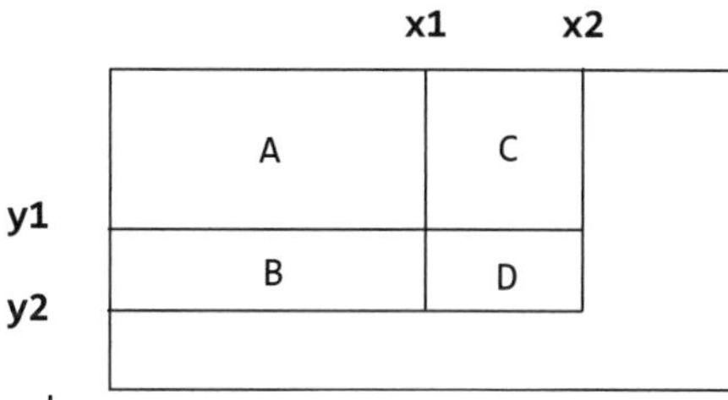

Suppose we knew the following values:

```
ValD = area(point(0, 0) -> point(x2, y2))
ValC = area(point(0, 0) -> point(x2, y1))
ValB = area(point(0, 0) -> point(x1, y2))
ValA = area(point(0, 0) -> point(x1, y1))
```

Each `Val*` starts at the origin and ends at the bottom right corner of a subrectangle.

With these values, we know the following:

```
area(D) = ValD - area(A union C) - area(A union B) + area(A).
```

Or, written another way:

```
area(D) = ValD - ValB - ValC + ValA
```

We can efficiently compute these values for all points in the matrix by using similar logic:

```
Val(x, y) = Val(x-1, y) + Val(y-1, x) - Val(x-1, y-1) + M[x][y]
```

We can precompute all such values and then efficiently find the maximum submatrix.

The following code implements this algorithm.

```
SubMatrix getMaxMatrix(int[][] matrix) {
  SubMatrix best = null;
  int rowCount = matrix.length;
  int columnCount = matrix[0].length;
  int[][] sumThrough = precomputeSums(matrix);

  for (int row1 = 0; row1 < rowCount; row1++) {
    for (int row2 = row1; row2 < rowCount; row2++) {
      for (int col1 = 0; col1 < columnCount; col1++) {
        for (int col2 = col1; col2 < columnCount; col2++) {
          int sum = sum(sumThrough, row1, col1, row2, col2);
          if (best == null || best.getSum() < sum) {
            best = new SubMatrix(row1, col1, row2, col2, sum);
          }
        }
      }
    }
  }
  return best;
}

int[][] precomputeSums(int[][] matrix) {
  int[][] sumThrough = new int[matrix.length][matrix[0].length];
  for (int r = 0; r < matrix.length; r++) {
    for (int c = 0; c < matrix[0].length; c++) {
      int left = c > 0 ? sumThrough[r][c - 1] : 0;
      int top = r > 0 ? sumThrough[r - 1][c] : 0;
      int overlap = r > 0 && c > 0 ? sumThrough[r-1][c-1] : 0;
      sumThrough[r][c] = left + top - overlap + matrix[r][c];
    }
  }
  return sumThrough;
}

int sum(int[][] sumThrough, int r1, int c1, int r2, int c2) {
  int topAndLeft = r1 > 0 && c1 > 0 ? sumThrough[r1-1][c1-1] : 0;
  int left = c1 > 0 ? sumThrough[r2][c1 - 1] : 0;
  int top = r1 > 0 ? sumThrough[r1 - 1][c2] : 0;
  int full = sumThrough[r2][c2];
  return full - left - top + topAndLeft;
}
```

This algorithm takes $O(N^4)$ time, since it goes through each pair of rows and each pair of columns.

Optimized Solution: $O(N^3)$

Believe it or not, an even more optimal solution exists. If we have R rows and C columns, we can solve it in $O(R^2C)$ time.

Recall the solution to the maximum subarray problem: "Given an array of integers, find the subarray with the largest sum." We can find the maximum subarray in `O(N)` time. We will leverage this solution for this problem.

Every submatrix can be represented by a contiguous sequence of rows and a contiguous sequence of columns. If we were to iterate through every contiguous sequence of rows, we would then just need to find, for each of those, the set of columns that gives us the highest sum. That is:

```
maxSum = 0
foreach rowStart in rows
  foreach rowEnd in rows
    /* We have many possible submatrices with rowStart and rowEnd as the top and
     * bottom edges of the matrix. Find the colStart and colEnd edges that give
     * the highest sum. */
    maxSum = max(runningMaxSum, maxSum)
return maxSum
```

Now the question is, how do we efficiently find the "best" `colStart` and `colEnd`?

Picture a submatrix:

rowStart

9	-8	1	3	-2
-3	7	6	-2	4
6	-4	-4	8	-7

12 -5 3 9 -5

rowEnd

Given a `rowStart` and `rowEnd`, we want to find the `colStart` and `colEnd` that give us the highest possible sum. To do this, we can sum up each column and then apply the `maximumSubArray` function explained at the beginning of this problem.

For the earlier example, the maximum subarray is the first through fourth columns. This means that the maximum submatrix is (`rowStart, first column`) through (`rowEnd, fourth column`).

We now have pseudocode that looks like the following.

```
1  maxSum = 0
2  foreach rowStart in rows
3    foreach rowEnd in rows
4      foreach col in columns
5        partialSum[col] = sum of matrix[rowStart, col] through matrix[rowEnd, col]
6      runningMaxSum = maxSubArray(partialSum)
7      maxSum = max(runningMaxSum, maxSum)
8  return maxSum
```

The sum in lines 5 and 6 takes `R*C` time to compute (since it iterates through `rowStart` through `rowEnd`), so this gives us a runtime of $O(R^3C)$. We're not quite done yet.

In lines 5 and 6, we're basically adding up `a[0]...a[i]` from scratch, even though in the previous iteration of the outer for loop, we already added up `a[0]...a[i-1]`. Let's cut out this duplicated effort.

```
maxSum = 0
foreach rowStart in rows
  clear array partialSum
```

```
    foreach rowEnd in rows
      foreach col in columns
        partialSum[col] += matrix[rowEnd, col]
      runningMaxSum = maxSubArray(partialSum)
    maxSum = max(runningMaxSum, maxSum)
  return maxSum
```

Our full code looks like this:

```
SubMatrix getMaxMatrix(int[][] matrix) {
  int rowCount = matrix.length;
  int colCount = matrix[0].length;
  SubMatrix best = null;

  for (int rowStart = 0; rowStart < rowCount; rowStart++) {
    int[] partialSum = new int[colCount];

    for (int rowEnd = rowStart; rowEnd < rowCount; rowEnd++) {
      /* Add values at row rowEnd. */
      for (int i = 0; i < colCount; i++) {
        partialSum[i] += matrix[rowEnd][i];
      }

      Range bestRange = maxSubArray(partialSum, colCount);
      if (best == null || best.getSum() < bestRange.sum) {
        best = new SubMatrix(rowStart, bestRange.start, rowEnd,
                             bestRange.end, bestRange.sum);
      }
    }
  }
  return best;
}

Range maxSubArray(int[] array, int N) {
  Range best = null;
  int start = 0;
  int sum = 0;

  for (int i = 0; i < N; i++) {
    sum += array[i];
    if (best == null || sum > best.sum) {
      best = new Range(start, i, sum);
    }

    /* If running_sum is < 0 no point in trying to continue the series. Reset. */
    if (sum < 0) {
      start = i + 1;
      sum = 0;
    }
  }
  return best;
}

public class Range {
  public int start, end, sum;
  public Range(int start, int end, int sum) {
    this.start = start;
    this.end = end;
```

```
        this.sum = sum;
    }
}
```

This was an extremely complex problem. You would not be expected to figure out this entire problem in an interview without a lot of help from your interviewer.

17.25 Word Rectangle: Given a list of millions of words, design an algorithm to create the largest possible rectangle of letters such that every row forms a word (reading left to right) and every column forms a word (reading top to bottom). The words need not be chosen consecutively from the list, but all rows must be the same length and all columns must be the same height.

pg 190

SOLUTION

Many problems involving a dictionary can be solved by doing some pre-processing. Where can we do pre-processing?

Well, if we're going to create a rectangle of words, we know that each row must be the same length and each column must be the same length. So let's group the words of the dictionary based on their sizes. Let's call this grouping D, where `D[i]` contains the list of words of length `i`.

Next, observe that we're looking for the largest rectangle. What is the largest rectangle that could be formed? It's `length(largest word)`^{2}.

```
int maxRectangle = longestWord * longestWord;
for z = maxRectangle to 1 {
  for each pair of numbers (i, j) where i*j = z {
     /* attempt to make rectangle. return if successful. */
  }
}
```

By iterating from the biggest possible rectangle to the smallest, we ensure that the first valid rectangle we find will be the largest possible one.

Now, for the hard part: `makeRectangle(int l, int h)`. This method attempts to build a rectangle of words which has length `l` and height h.

One way to do this is to iterate through all (ordered) sets of h words and then check if the columns are also valid words. This will work, but it's rather inefficient.

Imagine that we are trying to build a 6x5 rectangle and the first few rows are:

```
there
queen
pizza
.....
```

At this point, we know that the first column starts with `tqp`. We know—or *should* know—that no dictionary word starts with `tqp`. Why do we bother continuing to build a rectangle when we know we'll fail to create a valid one in the end?

This leads us to a more optimal solution. We can build a trie to easily look up if a substring is a prefix of a word in the dictionary. Then, when we build our rectangle, row by row, we check to see if the columns are all valid prefixes. If not, we fail immediately, rather than continue to try to build this rectangle.

The code below implements this algorithm. It is long and complex, so we will go through it step by step.

First, we do some pre-processing to group words by their lengths. We create an array of tries (one for each word length), but hold off on building the tries until we need them.

```
WordGroup[] groupList = WordGroup.createWordGroups(list);
int maxWordLength = groupList.length;
Trie trieList[] = new Trie[maxWordLength];
```

The `maxRectangle` method is the "main" part of our code. It starts with the biggest possible rectangle area (which is `maxWordLength`^{2}) and tries to build a rectangle of that size. If it fails, it subtracts one from the area and attempts this new, smaller size. The first rectangle that can be successfully built is guaranteed to be the biggest.

```
Rectangle maxRectangle() {
   int maxSize = maxWordLength * maxWordLength;
   for (int z = maxSize; z > 0; z--) { // start from biggest area
      for (int i = 1; i <= maxWordLength; i ++ ) {
         if (z % i == 0) {
            int j = z / i;
            if (j <= maxWordLength) {
               /* Create rectangle of length i and height j. Note that i * j = z. */
               Rectangle rectangle = makeRectangle(i, j);
               if (rectangle != null) return rectangle;
            }
         }
      }
   }
   return null;
}
```

The `makeRectangle` method is called by `maxRectangle` and tries to build a rectangle of a specific length and height.

```
Rectangle makeRectangle(int length, int height) {
   if (groupList[length-1] == null || groupList[height-1] == null) {
      return null;
   }

   /* Create trie for word length if we haven't yet */
   if (trieList[height - 1] == null) {
      LinkedList<String> words = groupList[height - 1].getWords();
      trieList[height - 1] = new Trie(words);
   }

   return makePartialRectangle(length, height, new Rectangle(length));
}
```

The `makePartialRectangle` method is where the action happens. It is passed in the intended, final length and height, and a partially formed rectangle. If the rectangle is already of the final height, then we just check to see if the columns form valid, complete words, and return.

Otherwise, we check to see if the columns form valid prefixes. If they do not, then we immediately break since there is no way to build a valid rectangle off of this partial one.

But, if everything is okay so far, and all the columns are valid prefixes of words, then we search through all the words of the right length, append each to the current rectangle, and recursively try to build a rectangle off of `{current rectangle with new word appended}`.

```
Rectangle makePartialRectangle(int l, int h, Rectangle rectangle) {
   if (rectangle.height == h) { // Check if complete rectangle
      if (rectangle.isComplete(l, h, groupList[h - 1])) {
```

```
            return rectangle;
        }
        return null;
    }

    /* Compare columns to trie to see if potentially valid rect */
    if (!rectangle.isPartialOK(l, trieList[h - 1])) {
        return null;
    }

    /* Go through all words of the right length. Add each one to the current partial
     * rectangle, and attempt to build a rectangle recursively. */
    for (int i = 0; i < groupList[l-1].length(); i++) {
        /* Create a new rectangle which is this rect + new word. */
        Rectangle orgPlus = rectangle.append(groupList[l-1].getWord(i));

        /* Try to build a rectangle with this new, partial rect */
        Rectangle rect = makePartialRectangle(l, h, orgPlus);
        if (rect != null) {
            return rect;
        }
    }
    return null;
}
```

The `Rectangle` class represents a partially or fully formed rectangle of words. The method `isPartialOk` can be called to check if the rectangle is, thus far, a valid one (that is, all the columns are prefixes of words). The method `isComplete` serves a similar function, but checks if each of the columns makes a full word.

```
public class Rectangle {
    public int height, length;
    public char[][] matrix;

    /* Construct an "empty" rectangule. Length is fixed, but height varies as we add
     * words. */
    public Rectangle(int l) {
        height = 0;
        length = l;
    }

    /* Construct a rectangular array of letters of the specified length and height,
     * and backed by the specified matrix of letters. (It is assumed that the length
     * and height specified as arguments are consistent with the array argument's
     * dimensions.) */
    public Rectangle(int length, int height, char[][] letters) {
        this.height = letters.length;
        this.length = letters[0].length;
        matrix = letters;
    }

    public char getLetter (int i, int j) { return matrix[i][j]; }
    public String getColumn(int i) { ... }

    /* Check if all columns are valid. All rows are already known to be valid since
     * they were added directly from dictionary. */
    public boolean isComplete(int l, int h, WordGroup groupList) {
        if (height == h) {
```

```
        /* Check if each column is a word in the dictionary. */
        for (int i = 0; i < l; i++) {
          String col = getColumn(i);
          if (!groupList.containsWord(col)) {
            return false;
          }
        }
        return true;
      }
      return false;
    }

    public boolean isPartialOK(int l, Trie trie) {
      if (height == 0) return true;
      for (int i = 0; i < l; i++ ) {
        String col = getColumn(i);
        if (!trie.contains(col)) {
          return false;
        }
      }
      return true;
    }

    /* Create a new Rectangle by taking the rows of the current rectangle and
     * appending s. */
    public Rectangle append(String s) { ... }
  }
```

The `WordGroup` class is a simple container for all words of a specific length. For easy lookup, we store the words in a hash table as well as in an `ArrayList`.

The lists in `WordGroup` are created through a static method called `createWordGroups`.

```
  public class WordGroup {
    private HashMap<String, Boolean> lookup = new HashMap<String, Boolean>();
    private ArrayList<String> group = new ArrayList<String>();
    public boolean containsWord(String s) { return lookup.containsKey(s); }
    public int length() { return group.size(); }
    public String getWord(int i) { return group.get(i); }
    public ArrayList<String> getWords() { return group; }

    public void addWord (String s) {
      group.add(s);
      lookup.put(s, true);
    }

    public static WordGroup[] createWordGroups(String[] list) {
      WordGroup[] groupList;
      int maxWordLength = 0;
      /* Find the length of the longest word */
      for (int i = 0; i < list.length; i++) {
        if (list[i].length() > maxWordLength) {
          maxWordLength = list[i].length();
        }
      }

      /* Group the words in the dictionary into lists of words of same length.
       * groupList[i] will contain a list of words, each of length (i+1). */
```

```
        groupList = new WordGroup[maxWordLength];
        for (int i = 0; i < list.length; i++) {
            /* We do wordLength - 1 instead of just wordLength since this is used as
             * an index and no words are of length 0 */
            int wordLength = list[i].length() - 1;
            if (groupList[wordLength] == null) {
                groupList[wordLength] = new WordGroup();
            }
            groupList[wordLength].addWord(list[i]);
        }
        return groupList;
    }
}
```

The full code for this problem, including the code for `Trie` and `TrieNode`, can be found in the code attachment. Note that in a problem as complex as this, you'd most likely only need to write the pseudocode. Writing the entire code would be nearly impossible in such a short amount of time.

17.26 Sparse Similarity: The similarity of two documents (each with distinct words) is defined to be the size of the intersection divided by the size of the union. For example, if the documents consist of integers, the similarity of `{1, 5, 3}` and `{1, 7, 2, 3}` is `0.4`, because the intersection has size 2 and the union has size 5.

We have a long list of documents (with distinct values and each with an associated ID) where the similarity is believed to be "sparse." That is, any two arbitrarily selected documents are very likely to have similarity 0. Design an algorithm that returns a list of pairs of document IDs and the associated similarity.

Print only the pairs with similarity greater than 0. Empty documents should not be printed at all. For simplicity, you may assume each document is represented as an array of distinct integers.

EXAMPLE

Input:

```
13: {14, 15, 100, 9, 3}
16: {32, 1, 9, 3, 5}
19: {15, 29, 2, 6, 8, 7}
24: {7, 10}
```

Output:

```
ID1, ID2 : SIMILARITY
13, 19   : 0.1
13, 16   : 0.25
19, 24   : 0.14285714285714285
```

pg 190

SOLUTION

This sounds like quite a tricky problem, so let's start off with a brute force algorithm. If nothing else, it will help wrap our heads around the problem.

Remember that each document is an array of distinct "words", and each is just an integer.

Brute Force

A brute force algorithm is as simple as just comparing all arrays to all other arrays. At each comparison, we compute the size of the intersection and size of the union of the two arrays.

Note that we only want to print this pair if the similarity is greater than 0. The union of two arrays can never be zero (unless both arrays are empty, in which case we don't want them printed anyway). Therefore, we are really just printing the similarity if the intersection is greater than 0.

How do we compute the size of the intersection and the union?

The intersection means the number of elements in common. Therefore, we can just iterate through the first array (A) and check if each element is in the second array (B). If it is, increment an `intersection` variable.

To compute the union, we need to be sure that we don't double count elements that are in both. One way to do this is to count up all the elements in A that are *not* in B. Then, add in all the elements in B. This will avoid double counting as the duplicate elements are only counted with B.

Alternatively, we can think about it this way. If we *did* double count elements, it would mean that elements in the intersection (in both A and B) were counted twice. Therefore, the easy fix is to just remove these duplicate elements.

```
union(A, B) = A + B - intersection(A, B)
```

This means that all we really need to do is compute the intersection. We can derive the union, and therefore similarity, from that immediately.

This gives us an `O(AB)` algorithm, just to compare two arrays (or documents).

However, we need to do this for all pairs of D documents. If we assume each document has at most `W` words then the runtime is $O(D^2 W^2)$.

Slightly Better Brute Force

As a quick win, we can optimize the computation for the similarity of two arrays. Specifically, we need to optimize the intersection computation.

We need to know the number of elements in common between the two arrays. We can throw all of A's elements into a hash table. Then we iterate through B, incrementing `intersection` every time we find an element in A.

This takes `O(A + B)` time. If each array has size `W` and we do this for D arrays, then this takes $O(D^2 W)$.

Before implementing this, let's first think about the classes we'll need.

We'll need to return a list of document pairs and their similarities. We'll use a `DocPair` class for this. The exact return type will be a hash table that maps from `DocPair` to a double representing the similarity.

```
public class DocPair {
   public int doc1, doc2;

   public DocPair(int d1, int d2) {
      doc1 = d1;
      doc2 = d2;
   }

   @Override
   public boolean equals(Object o) {
      if (o instanceof DocPair) {
         DocPair p = (DocPair) o;
```

```
      return p.doc1 == doc1 && p.doc2 == doc2;
    }
    return false;
  }

  @Override
  public int hashCode() { return (doc1 * 31) ^ doc2; }
}
```

It will also be useful to have a class that represents the documents.

```
public class Document {
  private ArrayList<Integer> words;
  private int docId;

  public Document(int id, ArrayList<Integer> w) {
    docId = id;
    words = w;
  }

  public ArrayList<Integer> getWords() { return words; }
  public int getId() { return docId; }
  public int size() { return words == null ? 0 : words.size(); }
}
```

Strictly speaking, we don't need any of this. However, readability is important, and it's a lot easier to read `ArrayList<Document>` than `ArrayList<ArrayList<Integer>>`.

Doing this sort of thing not only shows good coding style, it also makes your life in an interview a lot easier. You have to write a lot less. (You probably would not define the entire `Document` class, unless you had extra time or your interviewer asked you to.)

```
HashMap<DocPair, Double> computeSimilarities(ArrayList<Document> documents) {
  HashMap<DocPair, Double> similarities = new HashMap<DocPair, Double>();
  for (int i = 0; i < documents.size(); i++) {
    for (int j = i + 1; j < documents.size(); j++) {
      Document doc1 = documents.get(i);
      Document doc2 = documents.get(j);
      double sim = computeSimilarity(doc1, doc2);
      if (sim > 0) {
        DocPair pair = new DocPair(doc1.getId(), doc2.getId());
        similarities.put(pair, sim);
      }
    }
  }
  return similarities;
}

double computeSimilarity(Document doc1, Document doc2) {
  int intersection = 0;
  HashSet<Integer> set1 = new HashSet<Integer>();
  set1.addAll(doc1.getWords());

  for (int word : doc2.getWords()) {
    if (set1.contains(word)) {
      intersection++;
    }
  }

```

```
28     double union = doc1.size() + doc2.size() - intersection;
29     return intersection / union;
30 }
```

Observe what's happening on line 28. Why did we make `union` a `double`, when it's obviously an `integer`?

We did this to avoid an integer division bug. If we didn't do this, the division would "round" down to an integer. This would mean that the similarity would almost always return 0. Oops!

Slightly Better Brute Force (Alternate)

If the documents were sorted, you could compute the intersection between two documents by walking through them in sorted order, much like you would when doing a sorted merge of two arrays.

This would take `O(A + B)` time. This is the same time as our current algorithm, but less space. Doing this on D documents with W words each would take $O(D^2 W)$ time.

Since we don't know that the arrays are sorted, we could first sort them. This would take `O(D * W log W)` time. The full runtime then is $O(D * W \log W + D^2 W)$.

We cannot necessarily assume that the second part "dominates" the first one, because it doesn't necessarily. It depends on the relative size of D and `log W`. Therefore, we need to keep both terms in our runtime expression.

Optimized (Somewhat)

It is useful to create a larger example to really understand the problem.

```
13: {14, 15, 100, 9, 3}
16: {32, 1, 9, 3, 5}
19: {15, 29, 2, 6, 8, 7}
24: {7, 10, 3}
```

At first, we might try various techniques that allow us to more quickly eliminate potential comparisons. For example, could we compute the min and max values in each array? If we did that, then we'd know that arrays with no overlap in ranges don't need to be compared.

The problem is that this doesn't really fix our runtime issue. Our best runtime thus far is $O(D^2 W)$. With this change, we're still going to be comparing all $O(D^2)$ pairs, but the `O(W)` part might go to `O(1)` sometimes. That $O(D^2)$ part is going to be a really big problem when D gets large.

Therefore, let's focus on reducing that $O(D^2)$ factor. That is the "bottleneck" in our solution. Specifically, this means that, given a document docA, we want to find all documents with some similarity—and we want to do this without "talking" to each document.

What would make a document similar to docA? That is, what characteristics define the documents with similarity > 0?

Suppose docA is `{14, 15, 100, 9, 3}`. For a document to have similarity > 0, it needs to have a 14, a 15, a 100, a 9, or a 3. How can we quickly gather a list of all documents with one of those elements?

The slow (and, really, only way) is to read every single word from every single document to find the documents that contain a 14, a 15, a 100, a 9, or a 3. That will take `O(DW)` time. Not good.

However, note that we're doing this repeatedly. We can reuse the work from one call to the next.

If we build a hash table that maps from a word to all documents that contain that word, we can very quickly know the documents that overlap with docA.

```
1 -> 16
```

```
2 -> 19
3 -> 13, 16, 24
5 -> 16
6 -> 19
7 -> 19, 24
8 -> 19
9 -> 13, 16
...
```

When we want to know all the documents that overlap with docA, we just look up each of docA's items in this hash table. We'll then get a list of all documents with some overlap. Now, all we have to do is compare docA to each of those documents.

If there are P pairs with similarity > 0, and each document has W words, then this will take O(PW) time (plus O(DW) time to create and read this hash table). Since we expect P to be much less than D^2, this is much better than before.

Optimized (Better)

Let's think about our previous algorithm. Is there any way we can make it more optimal?

If we consider the runtime—O(PW + DW)—we probably can't get rid of the O(DW) factor. We have to touch each word at least once, and there are O(DW) words. Therefore, if there's an optimization to be made, it's probably in the O(PW) term.

It would be difficult to eliminate the P part in O(PW) because we have to at least print all P pairs (which takes O(P) time). The best place to focus, then, is on the W part. Is there some way we can do less than O(W) work for each pair of similar documents?

One way to tackle this is to analyze what information the hash table gives us. Consider this list of documents:

```
12: {1, 5, 9}
13: {5, 3, 1, 8}
14: {4, 3, 2}
15: {1, 5, 9, 8}
17: {1, 6}
```

If we look up document 12's elements in a hash table for this document, we'll get:

```
1 -> {12, 13, 15, 17}
5 -> {12, 13, 15}
9 -> {12, 15}
```

This tells us that documents 13, 15, and 17 have some similarity. Under our current algorithm, we would now need to compare document 12 to documents 13, 15, and 17 to see the number of elements document 12 has in common with each (that is, the size of the intersection). The union can be computed from the document sizes and the intersection, as we did before.

Observe, though, that document 13 appeared twice in the hash table, document 15 appeared three times, and document 17 appeared once. We discarded that information. But can we use it instead? What does it indicate that some documents appeared multiple times and others didn't?

Document 13 appeared twice because it has two elements (1 and 5) in common. Document 17 appeared once because it has only one element (1) in common. Document 15 appeared three times because it has three elements (1, 5, and 9) in common. This information can actually directly give us the size of the intersection.

We could go through each document, look up the items in the hash table, and then count how many times each document appears in each item's lists. There's a more direct way to do it.

1. As before, build a hash table for a list of documents.
2. Create a new hash table that maps from a document pair to an integer (which will indicate the size of the intersection).
3. Read the first hash table by iterating through each list of documents.
4. For each list of documents, iterate through the pairs in that list. Increment the intersection count for each pair.

Comparing this runtime to the previous one is a bit tricky. One way we can look at it is to realize that before we were doing `O(W)` work for each similar pair. That's because once we noticed that two documents were similar, we touched every single word in each document. With this algorithm, we're only touching the words that actually overlap. The worst cases are still the same, but for many inputs this algorithm will be faster.

```
HashMap<DocPair, Double>
computeSimilarities(HashMap<Integer, Document> documents) {
  HashMapList<Integer, Integer> wordToDocs = groupWords(documents);
  HashMap<DocPair, Double> similarities = computeIntersections(wordToDocs);
  adjustToSimilarities(documents, similarities);
  return similarities;
}

/* Create hash table from each word to where it appears. */
HashMapList<Integer, Integer> groupWords(HashMap<Integer, Document> documents) {
  HashMapList<Integer, Integer> wordToDocs = new HashMapList<Integer, Integer>();

  for (Document doc : documents.values()) {
    ArrayList<Integer> words = doc.getWords();
    for (int word : words) {
      wordToDocs.put(word, doc.getId());
    }
  }

  return wordToDocs;
}

/* Compute intersections of documents. Iterate through each list of documents and
 * then each pair within that list, incrementing the intersection of each page. */
HashMap<DocPair, Double> computeIntersections(
    HashMapList<Integer, Integer> wordToDocs {
  HashMap<DocPair, Double> similarities = new HashMap<DocPair, Double>();
  Set<Integer> words = wordToDocs.keySet();
  for (int word : words) {
    ArrayList<Integer> docs = wordToDocs.get(word);
    Collections.sort(docs);
    for (int i = 0; i < docs.size(); i++) {
      for (int j = i + 1; j < docs.size(); j++) {
        increment(similarities, docs.get(i), docs.get(j));
      }
    }
  }

  return similarities;
}
```

```

/* Increment the intersection size of each document pair. */
void increment(HashMap<DocPair, Double> similarities, int doc1, int doc2) {
  DocPair pair = new DocPair(doc1, doc2);
  if (!similarities.containsKey(pair)) {
    similarities.put(pair, 1.0);
  } else {
    similarities.put(pair, similarities.get(pair) + 1);
  }
}

/* Adjust the intersection value to become the similarity. */
void adjustToSimilarities(HashMap<Integer, Document> documents,
                          HashMap<DocPair, Double> similarities) {
  for (Entry<DocPair, Double> entry : similarities.entrySet()) {
    DocPair pair = entry.getKey();
    Double intersection = entry.getValue();
    Document doc1 = documents.get(pair.doc1);
    Document doc2 = documents.get(pair.doc2);
    double union = (double) doc1.size() + doc2.size() - intersection;
    entry.setValue(intersection / union);
  }
}

/* HashMapList<Integer, Integer> is a HashMap that maps from Integer to
 * ArrayList<Integer>. See appendix for implementation. */
```

For a set of documents with sparse similarity, this will run much faster than the original naive algorithm, which compares all pairs of documents directly.

Optimized (Alternative)

There's an alternative algorithm that some candidates might come up with. It's slightly slower, but still quite good.

Recall our earlier algorithm that computed the similarity between two documents by sorting them. We can extend this approach to multiple documents.

Imagine we took all of the words, tagged them by their original document, and then sorted them. The prior list of documents would look like this:

$1_{12}, 1_{13}, 1_{15}, 1_{16}, 2_{14}, 3_{13}, 3_{14}, 4_{14}, 5_{12}, 5_{13}, 5_{15}, 6_{16}, 8_{13}, 8_{15}, 9_{12}, 9_{15}$

Now we have essentially the same approach as before. We iterate through this list of elements. For each sequence of identical elements, we increment the intersection counts for the corresponding pair of documents.

We will use an Element class to group together documents and words. When we sort the list, we will sort first on the word but break ties on the document ID.

```
class Element implements Comparable<Element> {
  public int word, document;
  public Element(int w, int d) {
    word = w;
    document = d;
  }

  /* When we sort the words, this function will be used to compare the words. */
  public int compareTo(Element e) {
```

```
      if (word == e.word) {
         return document - e.document;
      }
      return word - e.word;
   }
}

HashMap<DocPair, Double> computeSimilarities(
      HashMap<Integer, Document> documents) {
   ArrayList<Element> elements = sortWords(documents);
   HashMap<DocPair, Double> similarities = computeIntersections(elements);
   adjustToSimilarities(documents, similarities);
   return similarities;
}

/* Throw all words into one list, sorting by the word and then the document. */
ArrayList<Element> sortWords(HashMap<Integer, Document> docs) {
   ArrayList<Element> elements = new ArrayList<Element>();
   for (Document doc : docs.values()) {
      ArrayList<Integer> words = doc.getWords();
      for (int word : words) {
         elements.add(new Element(word, doc.getId()));
      }
   }
   Collections.sort(elements);
   return elements;
}

/* Increment the intersection size of each document pair. */
void increment(HashMap<DocPair, Double> similarities, int doc1, int doc2) {
   DocPair pair = new DocPair(doc1, doc2);
   if (!similarities.containsKey(pair)) {
      similarities.put(pair, 1.0);
   } else {
      similarities.put(pair, similarities.get(pair) + 1);
   }
}

/* Adjust the intersection value to become the similarity. */
HashMap<DocPair, Double> computeIntersections(ArrayList<Element> elements) {
   HashMap<DocPair, Double> similarities = new HashMap<DocPair, Double>();

   for (int i = 0; i < elements.size(); i++) {
      Element left = elements.get(i);
      for (int j = i + 1; j < elements.size(); j++) {
         Element right = elements.get(j);
         if (left.word != right.word) {
            break;
         }
         increment(similarities, left.document, right.document);
      }
   }
   return similarities;
}

/* Adjust the intersection value to become the similarity. *
```

```
void adjustToSimilarities(HashMap<Integer, Document> documents,
                          HashMap<DocPair, Double> similarities) {
  for (Entry<DocPair, Double> entry : similarities.entrySet()) {
    DocPair pair = entry.getKey();
    Double intersection = entry.getValue();
    Document doc1 = documents.get(pair.doc1);
    Document doc2 = documents.get(pair.doc2);
    double union = (double) doc1.size() + doc2.size() - intersection;
    entry.setValue(intersection / union);
  }
}
```

The first step of this algorithm is slower than that of the prior algorithm, since it has to sort rather than just add to a list. The second step is essentially equivalent.

Both will run much faster than the original naive algorithm.

Advanced Topics

XI

This section includes topics that are mostly beyond the scope of interviews but can come up on occasion. Interviewers shouldn't be surprised if you don't know these topics well. Feel free to dive into these topics if you want to. If you're pressed for time, they're low priority.

Advanced Topics

When writing the 6th edition, I had a number of debates about what should and shouldn't be included. Red-black trees? Dijkstra's algorithm? Topological sort?

On one hand, I'd had a number of requests to include these topics. Some people insisted that these topics are asked "all the time" (in which case, they have a very different idea of what this phrase means!). There was clearly a desire—at least from some people—to include them. And learning more can't hurt, right?

On the other hand, I know these topics to be rarely asked. It happens, of course. Interviewers are individuals and might have their own ideas of what is "fair game" or "relevant" for an interview. But it's rare. When it does come up, if you don't know the topic, it's unlikely to be a big red flag.

> Admittedly, as an interviewer, I *have* asked candidates questions where the solution was essentially an application of one of these algorithms. On the rare occasions that a candidate already knew the algorithm, they did not benefit from this knowledge (nor were they hurt by it). I want to evaluate your ability to solve a problem you haven't seen before. So, I'll take into account whether you know the underlying algorithm in advance.

I believe in giving people a fair expectation of the interview, not scaring people into excess studying. I also have no interest in making the book more "advanced" so as to help book sales, at the expense of your time and energy. That's not fair or right to do to you.

(Additionally, I didn't want to give interviewers—who I know to be reading this—the impression that they can or should be covering these more advanced topics. Interviewers: If you ask about these topics, you're testing knowledge of algorithms. You're just going to wind up eliminating a lot of perfectly smart people.)

But there are many borderline "important" topics. They're not often asked, but sometimes they are.

Ultimately, I decided to leave the decision in your hands. After all, you know better than I do how thorough you want to be in your preparation. If you want to do an extra thorough job, read this. If you just love learning data structures and algorithms, read this. If you want to see new ways of approaching problems, read this.

But if you're pressed for time, this studying isn't a super high priority.

▸ Useful Math

Here's some math that can be useful in some questions. There are more formal proofs that you can look up online, but we'll focus here on giving you the intuition behind them. You can think of these as informal proofs.

Sum of Integers 1 through N

What is 1 + 2 + ... + n? Let's figure it out by pairing up low values with high values.

If n is even, we pair 1 with n, 2 with n - 1, and so on. We will have $\frac{n}{2}$ pairs each with sum n + 1.

If n is odd, we pair 0 with n, 1 with n - 1, and so on. We will have $\frac{n+1}{2}$ pairs with sum n.

n is even			
pair #	**a**	**b**	**a + b**
1	1	n	n + 1
2	2	n - 1	n + 1
3	3	n - 2	n + 1
4	4	n - 3	n + 1
...	...	...	...
$\frac{n}{2}$	$\frac{n}{2}$	$\frac{n}{2}+1$	n + 1
total:	$\frac{n}{2}*(n+1)$		

n is odd			
pair #	**a**	**b**	**a + b**
1	0	n	n
2	1	n - 1	n
3	2	n - 2	n
4	3	n - 3	n
...	...	...	...
$\frac{n+1}{2}$	$\frac{n-1}{2}$	$\frac{n+1}{2}$	n
total:	$\frac{n+1}{2} * n$		

In either case, the sum is $\frac{n(n+1)}{2}$.

This reasoning comes up a lot in nested loops. For example, consider the following code:

```
for (int i = 0; i < n; i++) {
   for (int j = i + 1; j < n; j++) {
      System.out.println(i + j);
   }
}
```

On the first iteration of the outer for loop, the inner for loop iterates n - 1 times. On the second iteration of the outer for loop, the inner for loop iterates n-2 times. Next, n - 3, then n - 4, and so on. There are $\frac{n(n-1)}{2}$ total iterations of the inner for loop. Therefore, this code takes $O(n^2)$ time.

Sum of Powers of 2

Consider this sequence: $2^0 + 2^1 + 2^2 + ... + 2^n$. What is its result?

A nice way to see this is by looking at these values in binary.

	Power	Binary	Decimal
	2^0	00001	1
	2^1	00010	2
	2^2	00100	4
	2^3	01000	8
	2^4	10000	16
sum:	2^5-1	11111	32 - 1 = 31

Therefore, the sum of $2^0 + 2^1 + 2^2 + ... + 2^n$ would, in base 2, be a sequence of (n + 1) 1s. This is $2^{n+1} - 1$.

Takeaway: The sum of a sequence of powers of two is roughly equal to the *next* value in the sequence.

Bases of Logs

Suppose we have something in $\log_2$ (log base 2). How do we convert that to $\log_{10}$? That is, what's the relationship between $\log_b k$ and $\log_x k$?

Let's do some math. Assume $c = \log_b k$ and $y = \log_x k$.

```
log_b k = c --> b^c = k          // This is the definition of log.
log_x(b^c) = log_x k             // Take log of both sides of b^c = k.
c log_x b = log_x k              // Rules of logs. You can move out the exponents.
c = log_b k = log_x k / log_x b  // Dividing above expression and substituting c.
```

Therefore, if we want to convert $\log_2 p$ to $\log_{10}$, we just do this:

$$\log_{10} p = \frac{\log_2 p}{\log_2 10}$$

Takeaway: Logs of different bases are only off by a constant factor. For this reason, we largely ignore what the base of a log within a big O expression. It doesn't matter since we drop constants anyway.

Permutations

How many ways are there of rearranging a string of n unique characters? Well, you have n options for what to put in the first characters, then n - 1 options for what to put in the second slot (one option is taken), then n - 2 options for what to put in the third slot, and so on. Therefore, the total number of strings is n!.

$$n! = \underline{n} * \underline{n-1} * \underline{n-2} * \underline{n-3} * \ldots * \underline{1}$$

What if you were forming a k-length string (with all unique characters) from n total unique characters? You can follow similar logic, but you'd just stop your selection/multiplication earlier.

$$\frac{n!}{(n-k)!} = \underline{n} * \underline{n-1} * \underline{n-2} * \underline{n-3} * \ldots * \underline{n-k+1}$$

Combinations

Suppose you have a set of n distinct characters. How many ways are there of selecting k characters into a new set (where order doesn't matter)? That is, how many k-sized subsets are there out of n distinct elements? This is what the expression n-choose-k means, which is often written $\binom{n}{k}$.

Imagine we made a list of all the sets by first writing all k-length substrings and then taking out the duplicates.

From the above *Permutations* section, we'd have $n!/(n-k)!$ k-length substrings.

Since each k-sized subset can be rearranged k! unique ways into a string, each subset will be duplicated k! times in this list of substrings. Therefore, we need to divide by k! to take out these duplicates.

$$\binom{n}{k} = \frac{1}{k!} * \frac{n!}{(n-k)!} = \frac{n!}{k!(n-k)!}$$

Proof by Induction

Induction is a way of proving something to be true. It is closely related to recursion. It takes the following form.

Task: Prove statement P(k) is true for all k >= b.

- Base Case: Prove the statement is true for P(b). This is usually just a matter of plugging in numbers.
- Assumption: Assume the statement is true for P(n).
- Inductive Step: Prove that *if* the statement is true for P(n), then it's true for P(n+1).

This is like dominoes. If the first domino falls, and one domino always knocks over the next one, then all the dominoes must fall.

Let's use this to prove that there are 2^n subsets of an n-element set.

- Definitions: let $S = \{a_1, a_2, a_3, \ldots, a_n\}$ be the n-element set.

- Base case: Prove there are 2^0 subsets of `{}`. This is true, since the only subset of `{}` is `{}`.
- Assume that there are 2^n subsets of $\{a_1, a_2, a_3, \ldots, a_n\}$.
- Prove that there are 2^{n+1} subsets of $\{a_1, a_2, a_3, \ldots, a_{n+1}\}$.

  Consider the subsets of $\{a_1, a_2, a_3, \ldots, a_{n+1}\}$. Exactly half will contain a_{n+1} and half will not.

  The subsets that do not contain a_{n+1} are just the subsets of $\{a_1, a_2, a_3, \ldots, a_n\}$. We assumed there are 2^n of those.

  Since we have the same number of subsets with x as without x, there are 2^n subsets with a_{n+1}.

  Therefore, we have $2^n + 2^n$ subsets, which is 2^{n+1}.

Many recursive algorithms can be proved valid with induction.

Topological Sort

A topological sort of a directed graph is a way of ordering the list of nodes such that if `(a, b)` is an edge in the graph then a will appear before b in the list. If a graph has cycles or is not directed, then there is no topological sort.

There are a number of applications for this. For example, suppose the graph represents parts on an assembly line. The edge (Handle, Door) indicates that you need to assemble the handle before the door. The topological sort would offer a valid ordering for the assembly line.

We can construct a topological sort with the following approach.

1. Identify all nodes with no incoming edges and add those nodes to our topological sort.
   - » We know those nodes are safe to add first since they have nothing that needs to come before them. Might as well get them over with!
   - » We know that such a node must exist if there's no cycle. After all, if we picked an arbitrary node we could just walk edges backwards arbitrarily. We'll either stop at some point (in which case we've found a node with no incoming edges) or we'll return to a prior node (in which case there is a cycle).
2. When we do the above, remove each node's outbound edges from the graph.
   - » Those nodes have already been added to the topological sort, so they're basically irrelevant. We can't violate those edges anymore.
3. Repeat the above, adding nodes with no incoming edges and removing their outbound edges. When all the nodes have been added to the topological sort, then we are done.

More formally, the algorithm is this:

1. Create a queue `order`, which will eventually store the valid topological sort. It is currently empty.
2. Create a queue `processNext`. This queue will store the next nodes to process.
3. Count the number of incoming edges of each node and set a class variable `node.inbound`. Nodes typically only store their outgoing edges. However, you can count the inbound edges by walking through each node n and, for each of its outgoing edges `(n, x)`, incrementing `x.inbound`.
4. Walk through the nodes again and add to `processNext` any node where `x.inbound == 0`.
5. While `processNext` is not empty, do the following:
   - » Remove first node n from `processNext`.

» For each edge `(n, x)`, decrement `x.inbound`. If `x.inbound == 0`, append x to `processNext`.

» Append n to `order`.

6. If `order` contains all the nodes, then it has succeeded. Otherwise, the topological sort has failed due to a cycle.

This algorithm does sometimes come up in interview questions. Your interviewer probably wouldn't expect you to know it offhand. However, it would be reasonable to have you derive it even if you've never seen it before.

▸ Dijkstra's Algorithm

In some graphs, we might want to have edges with weights. If the graph represented cities, each edge might represent a road and its weight might represent the travel time. In this case, we might want to ask, just as your GPS mapping system does, what's the shortest path from your current location to another point p? This is where Dijksta's algorithm comes in.

Dijkstra's algorithm is a way to find the shortest path between two points in a weighted directed graph (which might have cycles). All edges must have positive values.

Rather than just stating what Dijkstra's algorithm is, let's try to derive it. Consider the earlier described graph. We could find the shortest path from `s` to `t` by literally taking all possible routes using actual time. (Oh, and we'll need a machine to clone ourselves.)

1. Start off at `s`.
2. For each of `s`'s outbound edges, clone ourselves and start walking. If the edge `(s, x)` has weight 5, we should actually take 5 minutes to get there.
3. Each time we get to a node, check if anyone's been there before. If so, then just stop. We're automatically not as fast as another path since someone beat us here from `s`. If no one has been here before, then clone ourselves and head out in all possible directions.
4. The first one to get to `t` wins.

This works just fine. But, of course, in the real algorithm we don't want to literally use a timer to find the shortest path.

Imagine that each clone could jump immediately from one node to its adjacent nodes (regardless of the edge weight), but it kept a `time_so_far` log of how long its path would have taken if it did walk at the "true" speed. Additionally, only one person moves at a time, and it's always the one with the lowest `time_so_far`. This is sort of how Dijkstra's algorithm works.

Dijkstra's algorithm finds the minimum weight path from a start node s to *every* node on the graph.

Consider the following graph.

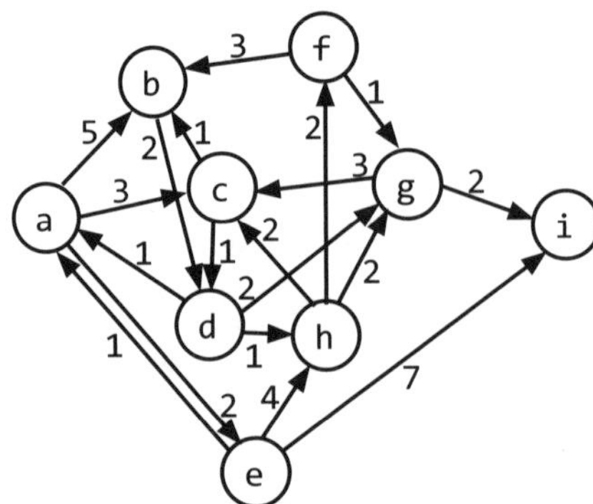

Assume we are trying to find the shortest path from a to `i`. We'll use Dijkstra's algorithm to find the shortest path from a to all other nodes, from which we will clearly have the shortest path from a to `i`.

We first initialize several variables:

- `path_weight[node]`: maps from each node to the total weight of the shortest path. All values are initialized to infinity, except for `path_weight[a]` which is initialized to `0`.
- `previous[node]`: maps from each node to the previous node in the (current) shortest path.
- `remaining`: a priority queue of all nodes in the graph, where each node's priority is defined by its `path_weight`.

Once we've initialized these values, we can start adjusting the values of `path_weight`.

> A (min) **priority queue** is an abstract data type that—at least in this case—supports insertion of an object and key, removing the object with the minimum key, and decreasing a key. (Think of it like a typical queue, except that, instead of removing the oldest item, it removes the item with the lowest or highest priority.) It is an abstract data type because it is defined by its behavior (its operations). Its underlying implementation can vary. You could implement a priority queue with an array or a min (or max) heap (or many other data structures).

We iterate through the nodes in `remaining` (until `remaining` is empty), doing the following:

1. Select the node in `remaining` with the lowest value in `path_weight`. Call this node n.
2. For each adjacent node, compare `path_weight[x]` (which is the weight of the current shortest path from a to x) to `path_weight[n] + edge_weight[(n, x)]`. That is, could we get a path from a to x with lower weight by going through n instead of our current path? If so, update `path_weight` and `previous`.
3. Remove n from `remaining`.

When `remaining` is empty, then `path_weight` stores the weight of the current shortest path from a to each node. We can reconstruct this path by tracing through `previous`.

Let's walk through this on the above graph.

1. The first value of n is a. We look at its adjacent nodes (b, c, and e), update the values of `path_weight` (to 5, 3, and 2) and `previous` (to a) and then remove a from `remaining`.
2. Then, we go to the next smallest node, which is e. We previously updated `path_weight[e]` to be 2. Its adjacent nodes are h and `i`, so we update `path_weight` (to 6 and 9) and `previous` for both of those.

Observe that 6 is `path_weight[e]` (which is 2) + the weight of the edge `(e, h)` (which is 4).

3. The next smallest node is c, which has `path_weight` 3. Its adjacent nodes are b and d. The value of `path_weight[d]` is infinity, so we update it to 4 (which is `path_weight[c] + weight(edge c, d)`. The value of `path_weight[b]` has been previously set to 5. However, since `path_weight[c] + weight(edge c, b)` (which is 3 + 1 = 4) is less than 5, we update `path_weight[b]` to 4 and `previous` to c. This indicates that we would improve the path from a to b by going through c.

We continue doing this until `remaining` is empty. The following diagram shows the changes to the `path_weight` (left) and `previous` (right) at each step. The topmost row shows the current value for n (the node we are removing from `remaining`). We black out a row after it has been removed from `remaining`.

	INITIAL		n = a		n = e		n = c		n = b		n = d		n = h		n = g		n = f		FINAL	
	wt	pr	wt	pr	wt	pr	wt	pr	wt	pr	wt	pr	wt	pr	wt	pr	wt	pr	wt	pr
a	0	-								removed									0	-
b	∞	-	5	a			4	c					removed						4	c
c	∞	-	3	a								removed							3	a
d	∞	-					4	c						removed					4	c
e	∞	-	2	a							removed								2	a
f	∞	-											7	h				removed	7	h
g	∞	-									6	d				removed			6	d
h	∞	-			6	e					5	d			removed				5	d
i	∞	-	∞	-	9	e									8	g			8	g

Once we're done, we can follow this chart backwards, starting at `i` to find the actual path. In this case, the smallest weight path has weight 8 and is a `-> c -> d -> g -> i`.

Priority Queue and Runtime

As mentioned earlier, our algorithm used a priority queue, but this data structure can be implemented in different ways.

The runtime of this algorithm depends heavily on the implementation of the priority queue. Assume you have v vertices and e nodes.

- If you implemented the priority queue with an array, then you would call `remove_min` up to v times. Each operation would take `O(v)` time, so you'd spend $O(v^2)$ time in the `remove_min` calls. Additionally, you would update the values of `path_weight` and `previous` at most once per edge, so that's `O(e)` time doing those updates. Observe that e must be less than of equal to v^2 since you can't have more edges than there are pairs of vertices. Therefore, the total runtime is $O(v^2)$.
- If you implemented the priority queue with a min heap, then the `remove_min` calls will each take `O(log v)` time (as will inserting and updating a key). We will do one `remove_min` call for each vertex, so that's `O(v log v)` (v vertices at `O(log v)` time each). Additionally, on each edge, we might call one update key or insert operation, so that's `O(e log v)`. The total runtime is `O((v + e) log v)`.

Which one is better? Well, that depends. If the graph has a lot of edges, then v^2 will be close to e. In this case, you might be better off with the array implementation, as $O(v^2)$ is better than $O((v + v^2) \log v)$. However, if the graph is sparse, then e is much less than v^2. In this case, the min heap implementation may be better.

Hash Table Collision Resolution

Essentially any hash table can have collisions. There are a number of ways of handling this.

Chaining with Linked Lists

With this approach (which is the most common), the hash table's array maps to a linked list of items. We just add items to this linked list. As long as the number of collisions is fairly small, this will be quite efficient.

In the worst case, lookup is `O(n)`, where `n` is the number of elements in the hash table. This would only happen with either some very strange data or a very poor hash function (or both).

Chaining with Binary Search Trees

Rather than storing collisions in a linked list, we could store collisions in a binary search tree. This will bring the worst-case runtime to `O(log n)`.

In practice, we would rarely take this approach unless we expected an extremely nonuniform distribution.

Open Addressing with Linear Probing

In this approach, when a collision occurs (there is already an item stored at the designated index), we just move on to the next index in the array until we find an open spot. (Or, sometimes, some other fixed distance, like the `index + 5`.)

If the number of collisions is low, this is a very fast and space-efficient solution.

One obvious drawback of this is that the total number of entries in the hash table is limited by the size of the array. This is not the case with chaining.

There's another issue here. Consider a hash table with an underlying array of size 100 where indexes 20 through 29 are filled (and nothing else). What are the odds of the next insertion going to index 30? The odds are 10% because an item mapped to any index between 20 and 30 will wind up at index 30. This causes an issue called *clustering*.

Quadratic Probing and Double Hashing

The distance between probes does not need to be linear. You could, for example, increase the probe distance quadratically. Or, you could use a second hash function to determine the probe distance.

Rabin-Karp Substring Search

The brute force way to search for a substring S in a larger string B takes `O(s(b-s))` time, where `s` is the length of S and `b` is the length of B. We do this by searching through the first `b - s + 1` characters in B and, for each, checking if the next `s` characters match S.

The Rabin-Karp algorithm optimizes this with a little trick: if two strings are the same, they must have the same hash value. (The converse, however, is not true. Two different strings can have the same hash value.)

Therefore, if we efficiently precompute a hash value for each sequence of `s` characters within B, we can find the locations of S in `O(b)` time. We then just need to validate that those locations really do match S.

For example, imagine our hash function was simply the sum of each character (where space = 0, a = 1, b = 2, and so on). If S is `ear` and B = `doe are hearing me`, we'd then just be looking for sequences where the sum is 24 (e + a + r). This happens three times. For each of those locations, we'd check if the string really is `ear`.

char:	d	o	e		a	r	e		h	e	a	r	i	n	g		m	e
code:	4	15	5	0	1	18	5	0	8	5	1	18	9	14	7	0	13	5
sum of next 3:	24	20	6	19	24	23	13	13	14	24	28	41	30	21	20	18		

If we computed these sums by doing `hash('doe')`, then `hash('oe ')`, then `hash('e a')`, and so on, we would still be at `O(s(b-s))` time.

Instead, we compute the hash values by recognizing that `hash('oe ') = hash('doe') - code('d') + code(' ')`. This takes `O(b)` time to compute all the hashes.

You might argue that, still, in the worst case this will take `O(s(b-s))` time since many of the hash values could match. That's absolutely true—for this hash function.

In practice, we would use a better *rolling hash function*, such as the Rabin fingerprint. This essentially treats a string like doe as a base 128 (or however many characters are in our alphabet) number.

```
hash('doe') = code('d') * 128^2 + code('o') * 128^1 + code('e') * 128^0
```

This hash function will allow us to remove the d, shift the o and e, and then add in the space.

```
hash('oe ') = (hash('doe') - code('d') * 128^2) * 128 + code(' ')
```

This will considerably cut down on the number of false matches. Using a good hash function like this will give us expected time complexity of `O(s + b)`, although the worst case is `O(sb)`.

Usage of this algorithm comes up fairly frequently in interviews, so it's useful to know that you can identify substrings in linear time.

AVL Trees

An AVL tree is one of two common ways to implement tree balancing. We will only discuss insertions here, but you can look up deletions separately if you're interested.

Properties

An AVL tree stores in each node the height of the subtrees rooted at this node. Then, for any node, we can check if it is height balanced: that the height of the left subtree and the height of the right subtree differ by no more than one. This prevents situations where the tree gets too lopsided.

```
balance(n) = n.left.height - n.right.height
-1 <= balance(n) <= 1
```

Inserts

When you insert a node, the balance of some nodes might change to -2 or 2. Therefore, when we "unwind" the recursive stack, we check and fix the balance at each node. We do this through a series of rotations.

Rotations can be either left or right rotations. The right rotation is an inverse of the left rotation.

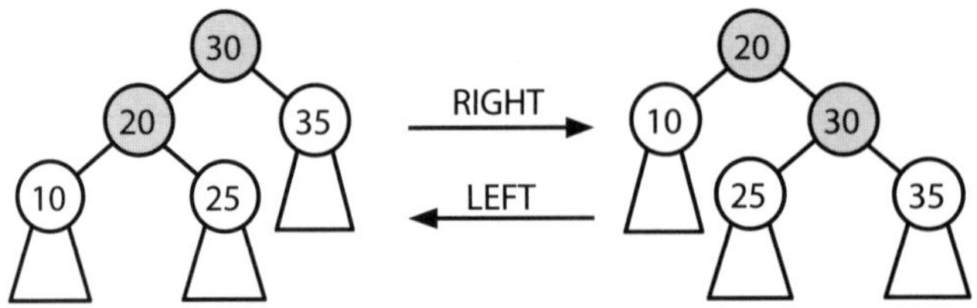

Depending on the balance and where the imbalance occurs, we fix it in a different way.

- *Case 1: Balance is 2.*

  In this case, the left's height is two bigger than the right's height. If the left side is larger, the left subtree's extra nodes must be hanging to the left (as in LEFT LEFT SHAPE) or hanging to the right (as in LEFT RIGHT SHAPE). If it looks like the LEFT RIGHT SHAPE, transform it with the rotations below into the LEFT LEFT SHAPE then into BALANCED. If it looks like the LEFT LEFT SHAPE already, just transform it into BALANCED.

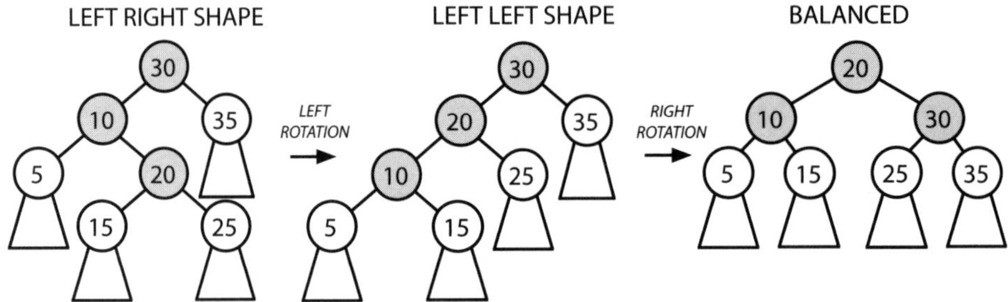

- *Case 2: Balance is -2.*

  This case is the mirror image of the prior case. The tree will look like either the RIGHT LEFT SHAPE or the RIGHT RIGHT SHAPE. Perform the rotations below to transform it into BALANCED.

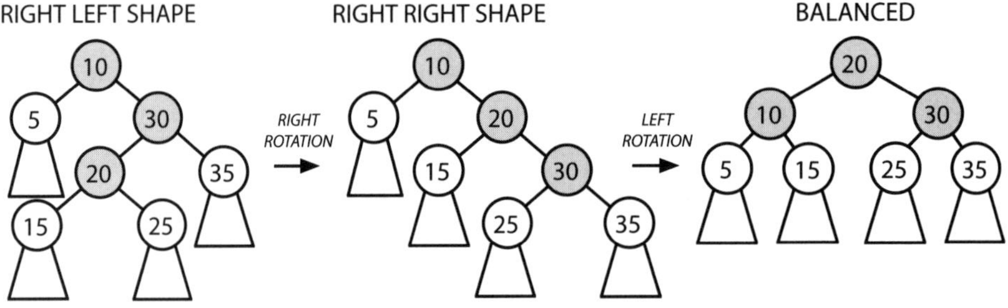

In both cases, "balanced" just means that the `balance` of the tree is between -1 and 1. It does not mean that the `balance` is 0.

We recurse up the tree, fixing any imbalances. If we ever achieve a balance of 0 on a subtree, then we know that we have completed all the balances. This portion of the tree will not cause another, higher subtree to have a balance of -2 or 2. If we were doing this non-recursively, then we could break from the loop.

▸ Red-Black Trees

Red-black trees (a type of self-balancing binary search tree) do not ensure quite as strict balancing, but the balancing is still good enough to ensure `O(log N)` insertions, deletions, and retrievals. They require a bit less memory and can rebalance faster (which means faster insertions and removals), so they are often used in situations where the tree will be modified frequently.

Red-black trees operate by enforcing a quasi-alternating red and black coloring (under certain rules, described below) and then requiring every path from a node to its leaves to have the same number of black nodes. Doing so leads to a reasonably balanced tree.

The tree below is a red-black tree (where the red nodes are indicated with gray):

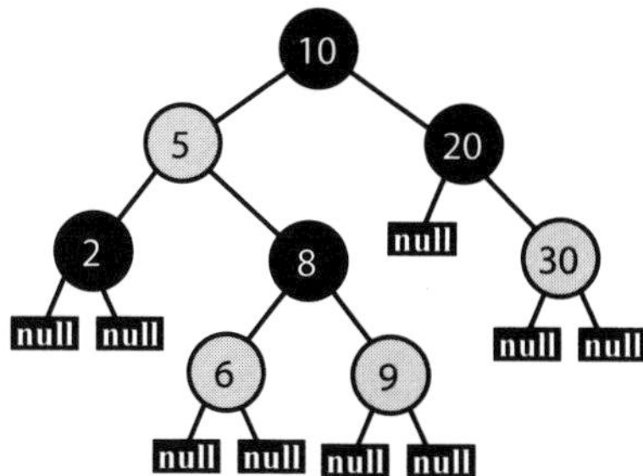

Properties

1. Every node is either red or black.
2. The root is black.
3. The leaves, which are NULL nodes, are considered black.
4. Every red node must have two black children. That is, a red node cannot have red children (although a black node can have black children).
5. Every path from a node to its leaves must have the same number of black children.

Why It Balances

Property #4 means that two red nodes cannot be adjacent in a path (e.g., parent and child). Therefore, no more than half the nodes in a path can be red.

Consider two paths from a node (say, the root) to its leaves. The paths must have the same number of black nodes (property #5), so let's assume that their red node counts are as different as possible: one path contains the minimum number of red nodes and the other one contains the maximum number.

- Path 1 (Min Red): The minimum number of red nodes is zero. Therefore, path 1 has b nodes total.
- Path 2 (Max Red): The maximum number of red nodes is b, since red nodes must have black children and there are b black nodes. Therefore, path 2 has 2b nodes total.

Therefore, even in the most extreme case, the lengths of paths cannot differ by more than a factor of two. That's good enough to ensure an `O(log N)` find and insert runtime.

If we can maintain these properties, we'll have a (sufficiently) balanced tree—good enough to ensure `O(log N)` insert and find, anyway. The question then is how to maintain these properties efficiently. We'll only discuss insertion here, but you can look up deletion on your own.

Insertion

Inserting a new node into a red-black tree starts off with a typical binary search tree insertion.

- New nodes are inserted at a leaf, which means that they replace a black node.
- New nodes are always colored red and are given two black leaf (NULL) nodes.

Once we've done that, we fix any resulting red-black property violations. We have two possible violations:

- Red violations: A red node has a red child (or the root is red).
- Black violations: One path has more blacks than another path.

The node inserted is red. We didn't change the number of black nodes on any path to a leaf, so we know that we won't have a black violation. However, we might have a red violation.

In the special case that where the root is red, we can always just turn it black to satisfy property 2, without violating the other constraints.

Otherwise, if there's a red violation, then this means that we have a red node under another red node. Oops!

Let's call N the current node. P is N's parent. G is N's grandparent. U is N's uncle and P's sibling. We know that:

- N is red and P is red, since we have a red violation.
- G is definitely black, since we didn't *previously* have a red violation.

The unknown parts are:

- U could be either red or black.
- U could be either a left or right child.
- N could be either a left or right child.

By simple combinatorics, that's eight cases to consider. Fortunately some of these cases will be equivalent.

- **Case 1: U is red.**

  It doesn't matter whether U is a left or right child, nor whether P is a left or right child. We can merge four of our eight cases into one.

  If U is red, we can just toggle the colors of P, U, and G. Flip G from black to red. Flip P and U from red to black. We haven't changed the number of black nodes in any path.

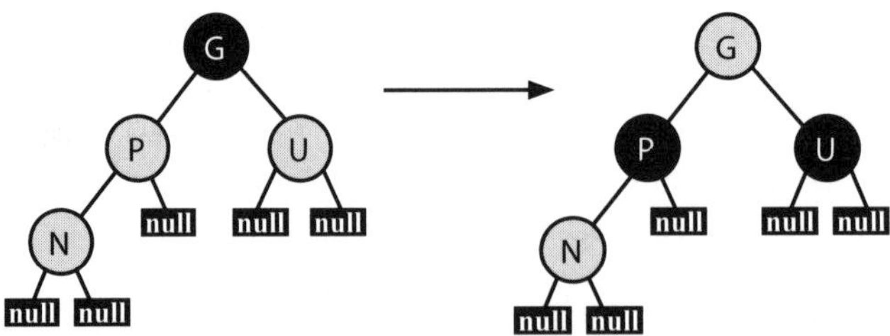

  However, by making G red, we might have created a red violation with G's parent. If so, we recursively apply the full logic to handle a red violation, where this G becomes the new N.

  Note that in the general recursive case, N, P, and U may also have subtrees in place of each black NULL (the leaves shown). In Case 1, these subtrees stay attached to the same parents, as the tree structure remains unchanged.

- **Case 2: U is black.**

  We'll need to consider the configurations (left vs. right child) of N and U. In each case, our goal is to fix up the red violation (red on top of red) without:

  » Messing up the ordering of the binary search tree.

  » Introducing a black violation (more black nodes on one path than another).

  If we can do this, we're good. In each of the cases below, the red violation is fixed with rotations that maintain the node ordering.

  Further, the below rotations maintain the exact number of black nodes in each path through the affected portion of the tree that were in place beforehand. The children of the rotating section are either NULL leaves or subtrees that remain internally unchanged.

  Case A: N and P are both left children.

  We resolve the red violation with the rotation of N, P, and G and the associated recoloring shown below. If you picture the in-order traversal, you can see the rotation maintains the node ordering (a `<= N <= b <= P <= c <= G <=` U). The tree maintains the same, equal number of black nodes in the path down to each subtree a, b, c, and U (which may all be NULL) .

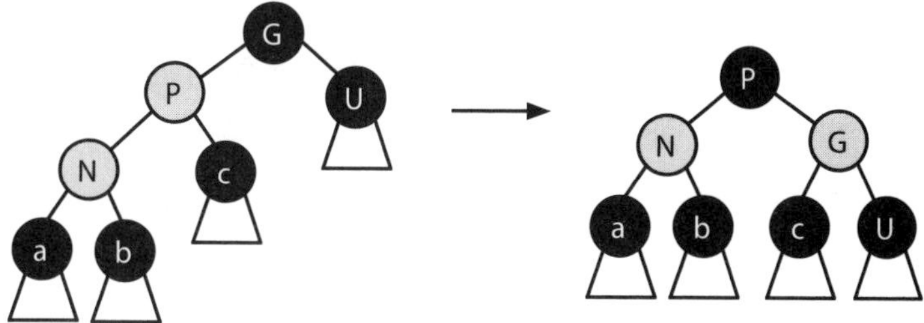

  Case B: P is a left child, and N is a right child.

  The rotations in Case B resolve the red violation and maintain the in-order property: a `<= P <= b <= N <= c <= G <=` U. Again, the count of the black nodes remains constant in each path down to the leaves (or subtrees).

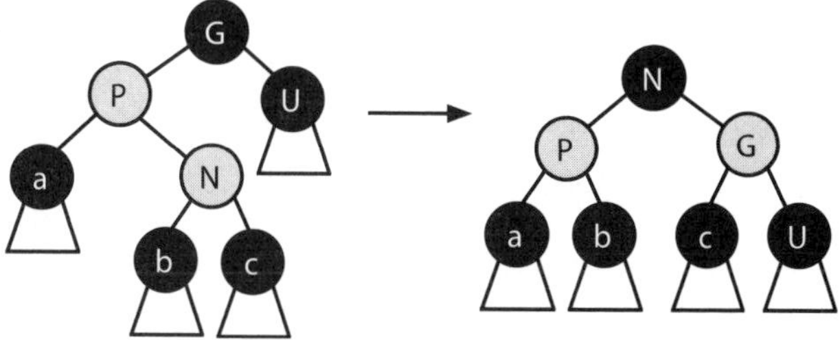

Case C: N and P are both right children.

This is a mirror image of case A.

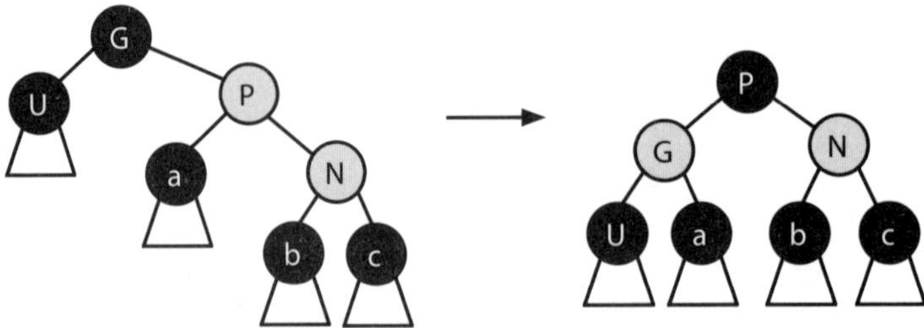

Case D: N is a left child, and P is a right child.

This is a mirror image of case B.

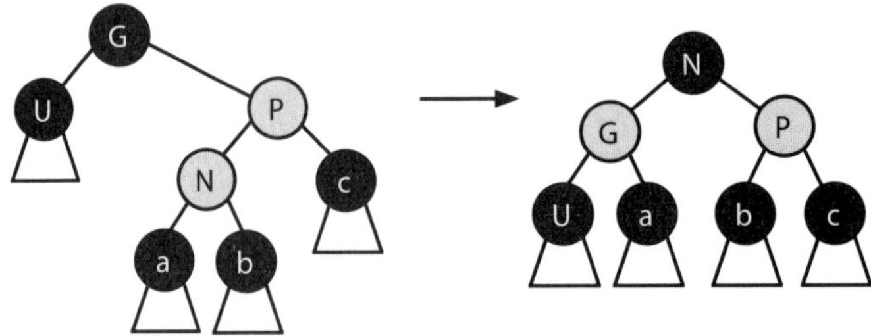

In each of Case 2's subcases, the middle element by value of N, P, and G is rotated to become the root of what was G's subtree, and that element and G swap colors.

That said, do not try to just memorize these cases. Rather, study why they work. How does each one ensure no red violations, no black violations, and no violations of the binary search tree property?

▸ MapReduce

MapReduce is used widely in system design to process large amounts of data. As its name suggests, a MapReduce program requires you to write a Map step and a Reduce step. The rest is handled by the system.

1. The system splits up the data across different machines.
2. Each machine starts running the user-provided `Map` program.
3. The `Map` program takes some data and emits a `<key, value>` pair.
4. The system-provided `Shuffle` process reorganizes the data so that all <key, value> pairs associated with a given key go to the same machine, to be processed by `Reduce`.
5. The user-provided `Reduce` program takes a key and a set of associated values and "reduces" them in some way, emitting a new key and value. The results of this might be fed back into the `Reduce` program for more reducing.

The typical example of using MapReduce—basically the "Hello World" of MapReduce—is counting the frequency of words within a set of documents.

Of course, you could write this as a single function that reads in all the data, counts the number of times each word appears via a hash table, and then outputs the result.

MapReduce allows you to process the document in parallel. The `Map` function reads in a document and emits just each individual word and the count (which is always 1). The `Reduce` function reads in keys (words) and associated values (counts). It emits the sum of the counts. This sum could possibly wind up as input for another call to `Reduce` on the same key (as shown in the diagram).

```
void map(String name, String document):
  for each word w in document:
    emit(w, 1)

void reduce(String word, Iterator partialCounts):
  int sum = 0
  for each count in partialCounts:
    sum += count
  emit(word, sum)
```

The diagram below shows how this might work on this example.

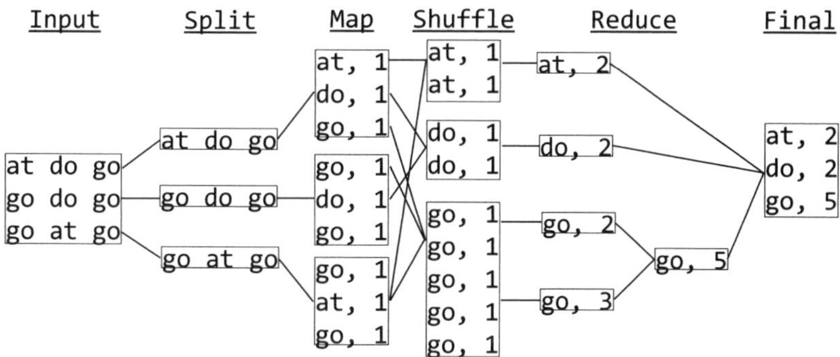

Here's another example: You have a list of data in the form {City, Temperature, Date}. Calculate the average temperature in each city every year. For example {(2012, Philadelphia, 58.2), (2011, Philadelphia, 56.6), (2012, Seattle, 45.1)}.

- **Map**: The Map step outputs a key value pair where the key is `City_Year` and the value is `(Temperature, 1)`. The '1' reflects that this is the average temperature out of one data point. This will be important for the `Reduce` step.
- **Reduce**: The Reduce step will be given a list of temperatures that correspond with a particular city and year. It must use these to compute the average temperature for this input. You cannot simply add up the temperatures and divide by the number of values.

  To see this, imagine we have five data points for a particular city and year: 25, 100, 75, 85, 50. The Reduce step might only get some of this data at once. If you averaged {75, 85} you would get 80. This might end up being input for another Reduce step with 50, and it would be a mistake to just naively average 80 and 50. The 80 has more weight.

  Therefore, our Reduce step instead takes in {(80, 2), (50, 1)}, then sums the *weighted* temperatures. So it does 80 * 2 + 50 * 1 and then divides by (2 + 1) to get an average temperature of 70. It then emits (70, 3).

  Another Reduce step might reduce {(25, 1), (100, 1)} to get (62.5, 2). If we reduce this with (70, 3) we get the final answer: (67, 5). In other words, the average temperature in this city for this year was 67 degrees.

We could do this in other ways, too. We could have just the city as the key, and the value be (Year, Temperature, Count). The Reduce step would do essentially the same thing, but would have to group by Year itself.

In many cases, it's useful to think about what the `Reduce` step should do first, and then design the `Map` step around that. What data does `Reduce` need to have to do its job?

Additional Studying

So, you've mastered this material and you want to learn even more? Okay. Here are some topics to get you started:

- **Bellman-Ford Algorithm**: Finds the shortest paths from a single node in a weighted directed graph with positive and negative edges.
- **Floyd-Warshall Algorithm**: Finds the shortest paths in a weighted graph with positive or negative weight edges (but no negative weight cycles).
- **Minimum Spanning Trees**: In a weighted, connected, undirected graph, a spanning tree is a tree that connects all the vertices. The minimum spanning tree is the spanning tree with minimum weight. There are various algorithms to do this.
- **B-Trees:** A self-balancing search tree (not a binary search tree) that is commonly used on disks or other storage devices. It is similar to a red-black tree, but uses fewer I/O operations.
- **A***: Find the least-cost path between a source node and a goal node (or one of several goal nodes). It extends Dijkstra's algorithm and achieves better performance by using heuristics.
- **Interval Trees**: An extension of a balanced binary search tree, but storing intervals (low -> high ranges) instead of simple values. A hotel could use this to store a list of all reservations and then efficiently detect who is staying at the hotel at a particular time.
- **Graph coloring**: A way of coloring the nodes in a graph such that no two adjacent vertices have the same color. There are various algorithms to do things like determine if a graph can be colored with only K colors.
- **P, NP, and NP-Complete**: P, NP, and NP-Complete refer to classes of problems. P problems are problems that can be quickly solved (where "quickly" means polynomial time). NP problems are those where, given a solution, the solution can be quickly verified. NP-Complete problems are a subset of NP problems that can all be reduced to each other (that is, if you found a solution to one problem, you could tweak the solution to solve other problems in the set in polynomial time).

  It is an open (and very famous) question whether P = NP, but the answer is generally believed to be no.
- **Combinatorics and Probability**: There are various things you can learn about here, such as random variables, expected value, and n-choose-k.
- **Bipartite Graph**: A bipartite graph is a graph where you can divide its nodes into two sets such that every edge stretches across the two sets (that is, there is never an edge between two nodes in the same set). There is an algorithm to check if a graph is a bipartite graph. Note that a bipartite graph is equivalent to a graph that can be colored with two colors.
- **Regular Expressions**: You should know that regular expressions exist and what they can be used for (roughly). You can also learn about how an algorithm to match regular expressions would work. Some of the basic syntax behind regular expressions could be useful as well.

There is of course a great deal more to data structures and algorithms. If you're interested in exploring these topics more deeply, I recommend picking up the hefty *Introduction to Algorithms* ("CLRS" by Cormen, Leiserson, Rivest and Stein) or *The Algorithm Design Manual* (by Steven Skiena).

XII Code Library

Certain patterns came up while implementing the code for this book. We've tried to generally include the full code for a solution with the solution, but in some cases it got quite redundant.

This appendix provides the code for a few of the most useful chunks of code.

The complete compilable solutions can be downloaded from CrackingTheCodingInterview.com.

Code Library

Certain patterns came up while implementing the code for this book. We've tried to generally include the full code for a solution with the solution, but in some cases it got quite redundant.

This appendix provides the code for a few of the most useful chunks of code.

All code for the book can be downloaded from CrackingTheCodingInterview.com.

▸ HashMapList<T, E>

The `HashMapList` class is essentially shorthand for `HashMap<T, ArrayList<E>>`. It allows us to map from an item of type of T to an `ArrayList` of type E.

For example, we might want a data structure that maps from an integer to a list of strings. Ordinarily, we'd have to write something like this:

```
HashMap<Integer, ArrayList<String>> maplist =
  new HashMap<Integer, ArrayList<String>>();
for (String s : strings) {
  int key = computeValue(s);
  if (!maplist.containsKey(key)) {
    maplist.put(key, new ArrayList<String>());
  }
  maplist.get(key).add(s);
}
```

Now, we can just write this:

```
HashMapList<Integer, String> maplist = new HashMapList<Integer, String>();
for (String s : strings) {
  int key = computeValue(s);
  maplist.put(key, s);
}
```

It's not a big change, but it makes our code a bit simpler.

```
public class HashMapList<T, E> {
  private HashMap<T, ArrayList<E>> map = new HashMap<T, ArrayList<E>>();

  /* Insert item into list at key. */
  public void put(T key, E item) {
    if (!map.containsKey(key)) {
      map.put(key, new ArrayList<E>());
    }
    map.get(key).add(item);
```

```
    }

    /* Insert list of items at key. */
    public void put(T key, ArrayList<E> items) {
      map.put(key, items);
    }

    /* Get list of items at key. */
    public ArrayList<E> get(T key) {
      return map.get(key);
    }

    /* Check if hashmaplist contains key. */
    public boolean containsKey(T key) {
      return map.containsKey(key);
    }

    /* Check if list at key contains value. */
    public boolean containsKeyValue(T key, E value) {
      ArrayList<E> list = get(key);
      if (list == null) return false;
      return list.contains(value);
    }

    /* Get the list of keys. */
    public Set<T> keySet() {
      return map.keySet();
    }

    @Override
    public String toString() {
      return map.toString();
    }
}
```

TreeNode (Binary Search Tree)

While it's perfectly fine—even good—to use the built-in binary tree class when possible, it's not always possible. In many questions, we needed access to the internals of the node or tree class (or needed to tweak these) and thus couldn't use the built-in libraries.

The `TreeNode` class supports a variety of functionality, much of which we wouldn't necessarily want for every question/solution. For example, the TreeNode class tracks the parent of the node, even though we often don't use it (or specifically ban using it).

For simplicity, we'd implemented this tree as storing integers for data.

```
public class TreeNode {
  public int data;
  public TreeNode left, right, parent;
  private int size = 0;

  public TreeNode(int d) {
    data = d;
    size = 1;
  }
```

```
    public void insertInOrder(int d) {
       if (d <= data) {
          if (left == null) {
             setLeftChild(new TreeNode(d));
          } else {
             left.insertInOrder(d);
          }
       } else {
          if (right == null) {
             setRightChild(new TreeNode(d));
          } else {
             right.insertInOrder(d);
          }
       }
       size++;
    }

    public int size() {
       return size;
    }

    public TreeNode find(int d) {
       if (d == data) {
          return this;
       } else if (d <= data) {
          return left != null ? left.find(d) : null;
       } else if (d > data) {
          return right != null ? right.find(d) : null;
       }
       return null;
    }

    public void setLeftChild(TreeNode left) {
       this.left = left;
       if (left != null) {
          left.parent = this;
       }
    }

    public void setRightChild(TreeNode right) {
       this.right = right;
       if (right != null) {
          right.parent = this;
       }
    }

}
```

This tree is implemented to be a binary search tree. However, you can use it for other purposes. You would just need to use the `setLeftChild`/`setRightChild` methods, or the `left` and `right` child variables. For this reason, we have kept these methods and variables `public`. We need this sort of access for many problems.

▸ LinkedListNode (Linked List)

Like the TreeNode class, we often needed access to the internals of a linked list in a way that the built-in linked list class wouldn't support. For this reason, we implemented our own class and used it for many problems.

```
public class LinkedListNode {
   public LinkedListNode next, prev, last;
   public int data;
   public LinkedListNode(int d, LinkedListNode n, LinkedListNode p){
      data = d;
      setNext(n);
      setPrevious(p);
   }

   public LinkedListNode(int d) {
      data = d;
   }

   public LinkedListNode() { }

   public void setNext(LinkedListNode n) {
      next = n;
      if (this == last) {
         last = n;
      }
      if (n != null && n.prev != this) {
         n.setPrevious(this);
      }
   }

   public void setPrevious(LinkedListNode p) {
      prev = p;
      if (p != null && p.next != this) {
         p.setNext(this);
      }
   }

   public LinkedListNode clone() {
      LinkedListNode next2 = null;
      if (next != null) {
         next2 = next.clone();
      }
      LinkedListNode head2 = new LinkedListNode(data, next2, null);
      return head2;
   }
}
```

Again, we've kept the methods and variables public because we often needed this access. This would allow the user to "destroy" the linked list, but we actually needed this sort of functionality for our purposes.

▸ Trie & TrieNode

The trie data structure is used in a few problems to make it easier to look up if a word is a prefix of any other words in a dictionary (or list of valid words). This is often used when we're recursively building words so that we can short circuit when the word is not valid.

```java
public class Trie {
  // The root of this trie.
  private TrieNode root;

  /* Takes a list of strings as an argument, and constructs a trie that stores
   * these strings. */
  public Trie(ArrayList<String> list) {
    root = new TrieNode();
    for (String word : list) {
      root.addWord(word);
    }
  }


  /* Takes a list of strings as an argument, and constructs a trie that stores
   * these strings. */
  public Trie(String[] list) {
    root = new TrieNode();
    for (String word : list) {
      root.addWord(word);
    }
  }

  /* Checks whether this trie contains a string with the prefix passed in as
   * argument. */
  public boolean contains(String prefix, boolean exact) {
    TrieNode lastNode = root;
    int i = 0;
    for (i = 0; i < prefix.length(); i++) {
      lastNode = lastNode.getChild(prefix.charAt(i));
      if (lastNode == null) {
        return false;
      }
    }
    return !exact || lastNode.terminates();
  }

  public boolean contains(String prefix) {
    return contains(prefix, false);
  }

  public TrieNode getRoot() {
    return root;
  }
}
```

The Trie class uses the TrieNode class, which is implemented below.

```java
public class TrieNode {
  /* The children of this node in the trie.*/
  private HashMap<Character, TrieNode> children;
  private boolean terminates = false;

  /* The character stored in this node as data.*/
  private char character;

  /* Constructs an empty trie node and initializes the list of its children to an
   * empty hash map. Used only to construct the root node of the trie. */
```

```
    public TrieNode() {
       children = new HashMap<Character, TrieNode>();
    }

    /* Constructs a trie node and stores this character as the node's value.
     * Initializes the list of child nodes of this node to an empty hash map. */
    public TrieNode(char character) {
       this();
       this.character = character;
    }

    /* Returns the character data stored in this node. */
    public char getChar() {
       return character;
    }

    /* Add this word to the trie, and recursively create the child
     * nodes. */
    public void addWord(String word) {
       if (word == null || word.isEmpty()) {
          return;
       }

       char firstChar = word.charAt(0);

       TrieNode child = getChild(firstChar);
       if (child == null) {
          child = new TrieNode(firstChar);
          children.put(firstChar, child);
       }

       if (word.length() > 1) {
          child.addWord(word.substring(1));
       } else {
          child.setTerminates(true);
       }
    }

    /* Find a child node of this node that has the char argument as its data. Return
     * null if no such child node is present in the trie. */
    public TrieNode getChild(char c) {
       return children.get(c);
    }

    /* Returns whether this node represents the end of a complete word. */
    public boolean terminates() {
       return terminates;
    }

    /* Set whether this node is the end of a complete word.*/
    public void setTerminates(boolean t) {
       terminates = t;
    }
}
```

Hints

Interviewers usually don't just hand you a question and expect you to solve it. Rather, they will typically offer guidance when you're stuck, especially on the harder questions. It's impossible to totally simulate the interview experience in a book, but these hints are designed to get you closer.

Try to solve the questions independently when possible. But it's okay to look for some help when you are really struggling. Again, struggling is a normal part of the process.

I've organized the hints somewhat randomly here, such that all the hints for a problem aren't adjacent. This way you won't accidentally see the second hint when you're reading the first hint.

I

Hints for Data Structures

#1. 1.2 Describe what it means for two strings to be permutations of each other. Now, look at that definition you provided. Can you check the strings against that definition?

#2. 3.1 A stack is simply a data structure in which the most recently added elements are removed first. Can you simulate a single stack using an array? Remember that there are many possible solutions, and there are tradeoffs of each.

#3. 2.4 There are many solutions to this problem, most of which are equally optimal in runtime. Some have shorter, cleaner code than others. Can you brainstorm different solutions?

#4. 4.10 If T2 is a subtree of T1, how will its in-order traversal compare to T1's? What about its pre-order and post-order traversal?

#5. 2.6 A palindrome is something which is the same when written forwards and backwards. What if you reversed the linked list?

#6. 4.12 Try simplifying the problem. What if the path had to start at the root?

#7. 2.5 Of course, you could convert the linked lists to integers, compute the sum, and then convert it back to a new linked list. If you did this in an interview, your interviewer would likely accept the answer, and then see if you could do this without converting it to a number and back.

#8. 2.2 What if you knew the linked list size? What is the difference between finding the Kth-to-last element and finding the Xth element?

#9. 2.1 Have you tried a hash table? You should be able to do this in a single pass of the linked list.

#10. 4.8 If each node has a link to its parent, we could leverage the approach from question 2.7 on page 95. However, our interviewer might not let us make this assumption.

#11. 4.10 The in-order traversals won't tell us much. After all, every binary search tree with the same values (regardless of structure) will have the same in-order traversal. This is what in-order traversal means: contents are in-order. (And if it won't work in the specific case of a binary search tree, then it certainly won't work for a general binary tree.) The pre-order traversal, however, is much more indicative.

#12. 3.1 We could simulate three stacks in an array by just allocating the first third of the array to the first stack, the second third to the second stack, and the final third to the third stack. One might actually be much bigger than the others, though. Can we be more flexible with the divisions?

#13. 2.6 Try using a stack.

#14. 4.12 Don't forget that paths could overlap. For example, if you're looking for the sum 6, the paths `1->3->2` and `1->3->2->4->-6->2` are both valid.

#15. 3.5 One way of sorting an array is to iterate through the array and insert each element into a new array in sorted order. Can you do this with a stack?

#16. 4.8 The first common ancestor is the deepest node such that p and q are both descendants. Think about how you might identify this node.

#17. 1.8 If you just cleared the rows and columns as you found 0s, you'd likely wind up clearing the whole matrix. Try finding the cells with zeros first before making any changes to the matrix.

#18. 4.10 You may have concluded that if `T2.preorderTraversal()` is a substring of `T1.preorderTraversal()`, then `T2` is a subtree of `T1`. This is almost true, except that the trees could have duplicate values. Suppose `T1` and `T2` have all duplicate values but different structures. The pre-order traversals will look the same even though `T2` is not a subtree of `T1`. How can you handle situations like this?

#19. 4.2 A minimal binary tree has about the same number of nodes on the left of each node as on the right. Let's focus on just the root for now. How would you ensure that about the same number of nodes are on the left of the root as on the right?

#20. 2.7 You can do this in `O(A+B)` time and `O(1)` additional space. That is, you do not need a hash table (although you could do it with one).

#21. 4.4 Think about the definition of a balanced tree. Can you check that condition for a single node? Can you check it for every node?

#22. 3.6 We could consider keeping a single linked list for dogs and cats, and then iterating through it to find the first dog (or cat). What is the impact of doing this?

#23. 1.5 Start with the easy thing. Can you check each of the conditions separately?

#24. 2.4 Consider that the elements don't have to stay in the same relative order. We only need to ensure that elements less than the pivot must be before elements greater than the pivot. Does that help you come up with more solutions?

#25. 2.2 If you don't know the linked list size, can you compute it? How does this impact the runtime?

#26. 4.7 Build a directed graph representing the dependencies. Each node is a project and an edge exists from A to B if B depends on A (A must be built before B). You can also build it the other way if it's easier for you.

#27. 3.2 Observe that the minimum element doesn't change very often. It only changes when a smaller element is added, or when the smallest element is popped.

#28. 4.8 How would you figure out if p is a descendent of a node n?

#29. 2.6 Assume you have the length of the linked list. Can you implement this recursively?

#30. 2.5 Try recursion. Suppose you have two lists, `A = 1->5->9` (representing 951) and `B = 2->3->6->7` (representing 7632), and a function that operates on the remainder of the lists (`5->9` and `3->6->7`). Could you use this to create the `sum` method? What is the relationship between `sum(1->5->9, 2->3->6->7)` and `sum(5->9, 3->6->7)`?

#31. 4.10 Although the problem seems like it stems from duplicate values, it's really deeper than that. The issue is that the pre-order traversal is the same only because there are null nodes that we skipped over (because they're null). Consider inserting a placeholder value into the pre-order traversal string whenever you reach a null node. Register the null node as a "real" node so that you can distinguish between the different structures.

#32. 3.5 Imagine your secondary stack is sorted. Can you insert elements into it in sorted order? You might need some extra storage. What could you use for extra storage?

#33. 4.4 If you've developed a brute force solution, be careful about its runtime. If you are computing the height of the subtrees for each node, you could have a pretty inefficient algorithm.

#34. 1.9 If a string is a rotation of another, then it's a rotation at a particular point. For example, a rotation of `waterbottle` at character 3 means cutting `waterbottle` at character 3 and putting the right half (`erbottle`) before the left half (`wat`).

#35. 4.5 If you traversed the tree using an in-order traversal and the elements were truly in the right order, does this indicate that the tree is actually in order? What happens for duplicate elements? If duplicate elements are allowed, they must be on a specific side (usually the left).

#36. 4.8 Start with the root. Can you identify if root is the first common ancestor? If it is not, can you identify which side of root the first common ancestor is on?

#37. 4.10 Alternatively, we can handle this problem recursively. Given a specific node within `T1`, can we check to see if its subtree matches `T2`?

#38. 3.1 If you want to allow for flexible divisions, you can shift stacks around. Can you ensure that all available capacity is used?

#39. 4.9 What is the very first value that must be in each array?

#40. 2.1 Without extra space, you'll need $O(N^2)$ time. Try using two pointers, where the second one searches ahead of the first one.

#41. 2.2 Try implementing it recursively. If you could find the (`K-1`)th to last element, can you find the Kth element?

#42. 4.11 Be very careful in this problem to ensure that each node is equally likely and that your solution doesn't slow down the speed of standard binary search tree algorithms (like `insert`, `find`, and `delete`). Also, remember that even if you assume that it's a balanced binary search tree, this doesn't mean that the tree is full/complete/perfect.

#43. 3.5 Keep the secondary stack in sorted order, with the biggest elements on the top. Use the primary stack for additional storage.

#44. 1.1 Try a hash table.

#45. 2.7 Examples will help you. Draw a picture of intersecting linked lists and two equivalent linked lists (by value) that do not intersect.

#46. 4.8 Try a recursive approach. Check if `p` and `q` are descendants of the left subtree and the right subtree. If they are descendants of different subtrees, then the current node is the first common ancestor. If they are descendants of the same subtree, then that subtree holds the first common ancestor. Now, how do you implement this efficiently?

#47. 4.7 Look at this graph. Is there any node you can identify that will definitely be okay to build first?

#48. 4.9 The root is the very first value that must be in every array. What can you say about the order of the values in the left subtree as compared to the values in the right subtree? Do the left subtree values need to be inserted before the right subtree?

#49. 4.4 What if you could modify the binary tree node class to allow a node to store the height of its subtree?

#50. 2.8 There are really two parts to this problem. First, detect if the linked list has a loop. Second, figure out where the loop starts.

#51. 1.7 Try thinking about it layer by layer. Can you rotate a specific layer?

#52. 4.12 If each path had to start at the root, we could traverse all possible paths starting from the root. We can track the sum as we go, incrementing `totalPaths` each time we find a path with our target sum. Now, how do we extend this to paths that can start anywhere? Remember: Just get a brute-force algorithm done. You can optimize later.

#53. 1.3 It's often easiest to modify strings by going from the end of the string to the beginning.

#54. 4.11 This is your own binary search tree class, so you can maintain any information about the tree structure or nodes that you'd like (provided it doesn't have other negative implications, like making `insert` much slower). In fact, there's probably a reason the interview question specified that it was your own class. You probably need to store some additional information in order to implement this efficiently.

#55. 2.7 Focus first on just identifying if there's an intersection.

#56. 3.6 Let's suppose we kept separate lists for dogs and cats. How would we find the oldest animal of any type? Be creative!

#57. 4.5 To be a binary search tree, it's not sufficient that the `left.value <= current.value < right.value` for each node. Every node on the left must be less than the current node, which must be less than all the nodes on the right.

#58. 3.1 Try thinking about the array as circular, such that the end of the array "wraps around" to the start of the array.

#59. 3.2 What if we kept track of extra data at each stack node? What sort of data might make it easier to solve the problem?

#60. 4.7 If you identify a node without any incoming edges, then it can definitely be built. Find this node (there could be multiple) and add it to the build order. Then, what does this mean for its outgoing edges?

#61. 2.6 In the recursive approach (we have the length of the list), the middle is the base case: `isPermutation(middle)` is true. The node `x` to the immediate left of the middle: What can that node do to check if `x->middle->y` forms a palindrome? Now suppose that checks out. What about the previous node `a`? If `x->middle->y` is a palindrome, how can it check that `a->x->middle->y->b` is a palindrome?

#62. 4.11 As a naive "brute force" algorithm, can you use a tree traversal algorithm to implement this algorithm? What is the runtime of this?

#63. 3.6 Think about how you'd do it in real life. You have a list of dogs in chronological order and a list of cats in chronological order. What data would you need to find the oldest animal? How would you maintain this data?

#64. 3.3 You will need to keep track of the size of each substack. When one stack is full, you may need to create a new stack.

#65. 2.7 Observe that two intersecting linked lists will always have the same last node. Once they intersect, all the nodes after that will be equal.

#66. 4.9 The relationship between the left subtree values and the right subtree values is, essentially, anything. The left subtree values could be inserted before the right subtree, or the reverse (right values before left), or any other ordering.

#67. 2.2 You might find it useful to return multiple values. Some languages don't directly support this, but there are workarounds in essentially any language. What are some of those workarounds?

#68. 4.12 To extend this to paths that start anywhere, we can just repeat this process for all nodes.

#69. 2.8 To identify if there's a cycle, try the "runner" approach described on page 93. Have one pointer move faster than the other.

#70. 4.8 In the more naive algorithm, we had one method that indicated if `x` is a descendent of `n`, and another method that would recurse to find the first common ancestor. This is repeatedly searching the same elements in a subtree. We should merge this into one `firstCommonAncestor` function. What return values would give us the information we need?

#71. 2.5 Make sure you have considered linked lists that are not the same length.

#72. 2.3 Picture the list `1->5->9->12`. Removing 9 would make it look like `1->5->12`. You only have access to the 9 node. Can you make it look like the correct answer?

#73. 4.2 You could implement this by finding the "ideal" next element to add and repeatedly calling `insertValue`. This will be a bit inefficient, as you would have to repeatedly traverse the tree. Try recursion instead. Can you divide this problem into subproblems?

#74. 1.8 Can you use `O(N)` additional space instead of $O(N^2)$? What information do you really need from the list of cells that are zero?

#75. 4.11 Alternatively, you could pick a random depth to traverse to and then randomly traverse, stopping when you get to that depth. Think this through, though. Does this work?

#76. 2.7 You can determine if two linked lists intersect by traversing to the end of each and comparing their tails.

#77. 4.12 If you've designed the algorithm as described thus far, you'll have an `O(N log N)` algorithm in a balanced tree. This is because there are N nodes, each of which is at depth `O(log N)` at worst. A node is touched once for each node above it. Therefore, the N nodes will be touched `O(log N)` time. There is an optimization that will give us an `O(N)` algorithm.

#78. 3.2 Consider having each node know the minimum of its "substack" (all the elements beneath it, including itself).

#79. 4.6 Think about how an in-order traversal works and try to "reverse engineer" it.

#80. 4.8 The `firstCommonAncestor` function could return the first common ancestor (if p and q are both contained in the tree), p if p is in the tree and not q, q if q is in the tree and not p, and `null` otherwise.

#81. 3.3 Popping an element at a specific substack will mean that some stacks aren't at full capacity. Is this an issue? There's no right answer, but you should think about how to handle this.

#82. 4.9 Break this down into subproblems. Use recursion. If you had all possible sequences for the left subtree and the right subtree, how could you create all possible sequences for the entire tree?

#83. 2.8 You can use two pointers, one moving twice as fast as the other. If there is a cycle, the two pointers will collide. They will land at the same location at the same time. Where do they land? Why there?

#84. 1.2 There is one solution that is `O(N log N)` time. Another solution uses some space, but is `O(N)` time.

#85. 4.7 Once you decide to build a node, its outgoing edge can be deleted. After you've done this, can you find other nodes that are free and clear to build?

#86. 4.5 If every node on the left must be less than or equal to the current node, then this is really the same thing as saying that the biggest node on the left must be less than or equal to the current node.

#87. 4.12 What work is duplicated in the current brute-force algorithm?

#88. 1.9 We are essentially asking if there's a way of splitting the first string into two parts, x and y, such that the first string is xy and the second string is yx. For example, `x = wat` and `y = erbottle`. The first string is `xy = waterbottle`. The second string is `yx = erbottlewat`.

#89. 4.11 Picking a random depth won't help us much. First, there's more nodes at lower depths than higher depths. Second, even if we re-balanced these probabilities, we could hit a "dead end" where we meant to pick a node at depth 5 but hit a leaf at depth 3. Re-balancing the probabilities is an interesting , though.

#90. 2.8 If you haven't identified the pattern of where the two pointers start, try this: Use the linked list 1->2->3->4->5->6->7->8->9->?, where the ? links to another node. Try making the ? the first node (that is, the 9 points to the 1 such that the entire linked list is a loop). Then make the ? the node 2. Then the node 3. Then the node 4. What is the pattern? Can you explain why this happens?

#91. 4.6 Here's one step of the logic: The successor of a specific node is the leftmost node of the right subtree. What if there is no right subtree, though?

#92. 1.6 Do the easy thing first. Compress the string, then compare the lengths.

#93. 2.7 Now, you need to find where the linked lists intersect. Suppose the linked lists were the same length. How could you do this?

#94. 4.12 Consider each path that starts from the root (there are N such paths) as an array. What our brute-force algorithm is really doing is taking each array and finding all contiguous subsequences that have a particular sum. We're doing this by computing all subarrays and their sums. It might be useful to just focus on this little subproblem. Given an array, how would you find all contiguous subsequences with a particular sum? Again, think about the duplicated work in the brute-force algorithm.

#95. 2.5 Does your algorithm work on linked lists like 9->7->8 and 6->8->5? Double check that.

#96. 4.8 Careful! Does your algorithm handle the case where only one node exists? What will happen? You might need to tweak the return values a bit.

#97. 1.5 What is the relationship between the "insert character" option and the "remove character" option? Do these need to be two separate checks?

#98. 3.4 The major difference between a queue and a stack is the order of elements. A queue removes the oldest item and a stack removes the newest item. How could you remove the oldest item from a stack if you only had access to the newest item?

#99. 4.11 A naive approach that many people come up with is to pick a random number between 1 and 3. If it's 1, return the current node. If it's 2, branch left. If it's 3, branch right. This solution doesn't work. Why not? Is there a way you can adjust it to make it work?

#100. 1.7 Rotating a specific layer would just mean swapping the values in four arrays. If you were asked to swap the values in two arrays, could you do this? Can you then extend it to four arrays?

#101. 2.6 Go back to the previous hint. Remember: There are ways to return multiple values. You can do this with a new class.

#102. 1.8 You probably need some data storage to maintain a list of the rows and columns that need to be zeroed. Can you reduce the additional space usage to `O(1)` by using the matrix itself for data storage?

#103. 4.12 We are looking for subarrays with sum `targetSum`. Observe that we can track in constant time the value of $\texttt{runningSum}_{\texttt{i}}$, where this is the sum from element 0 through element `i`. For a subarray of element `i` through element `j` to have sum `targetSum`, $\texttt{runningSum}_{\texttt{i-1}}$ `+ targetSum` must equal $\texttt{runningSum}_{\texttt{j}}$ (try drawing a picture of an array or a number line). Given that we can track the `runningSum` as we go, how can we quickly look up the number of indices `i` where the previous equation is true?

#104. 1.9 Think about the earlier hint. Then think about what happens when you concatenate `erbottlewat` to itself. You get `erbottlewaterbottlewat`.

#105. 4.4 You don't need to modify the binary tree class to store the height of the subtree. Can your recursive function compute the height of each subtree while also checking if a node is balanced? Try having the function return multiple values.

#106. 1.4 You do not have to—and should not—generate all permutations. This would be very inefficient.

#107. 4.3 Try modifying a graph search algorithm to track the depth from the root.

#108. 4.12 Try using a hash table that maps from a `runningSum` value to the number of elements with this `runningSum`.

#109. 2.5 For the follow-up question: The issue is that when the linked lists aren't the same length, the head of one linked list might represent the 1000's place while the other represents the 10's place. What if you made them the same length? Is there a way to modify the linked list to do that, without changing the value it represents?

#110. 1.6 Be careful that you aren't repeatedly concatenating strings together. This can be very inefficient.

#111. 2.7 If the two linked lists were the same length, you could traverse forward in each until you found an element in common. Now, how do you adjust this for lists of different lengths?

#112. 4.11 The reason that the earlier solution (picking a random number between 1 and 3) doesn't work is that the probabilities for the nodes won't be equal. For example, the root will be returned with probability $\frac{1}{3}$, even if there are 50+ nodes in the tree. Clearly, not all the nodes have probability $\frac{1}{3}$, so these nodes won't have equal probability. We can resolve this one issue by picking a random number between 1 and `size_of_tree` instead. This only resolves the issue for the root, though. What about the rest of the nodes?

#113. 4.5 Rather than validating the current node's value against `leftTree.max` and `rightTree.min`, can we flip around the logic? Validate the left tree's nodes to ensure that they are smaller than `current.value`.

#114. 3.4 We can remove the oldest item from a stack by repeatedly removing the newest item (inserting those into the temporary stack) until we get down to one element. Then, after we've retrieved the newest item, putting all the elements back. The issue with this is that doing several pops in a row will require `O(N)` work each time. Can we optimize for scenarios where we might do several pops in a row?

#115. 4.12 Once you've solidified the algorithm to find all contiguous subarrays in an array with a given sum, try to apply this to a tree. Remember that as you're traversing and modifying the hash table, you may need to "reverse the damage" to the hash table as you traverse back up.

#116. 4.2 Imagine we had a `createMinimalTree` method that returns a minimal tree for a given array (but for some strange reason doesn't operate on the root of the tree). Could you use this to operate on the root of the tree? Could you write the base case for the function? Great! Then that's basically the entire function.

#117. 1.1 Could a bit vector be useful?

#118. 1.3 You might find you need to know the number of spaces. Can you just count them?

#119. 4.11 The issue with the earlier solution is that there could be more nodes on one side of a node than the other. So, we need to weight the probability of going left and right based on the number of nodes on each side. How does this work, exactly? How can we know the number of nodes?

#120. 2.7 Try using the difference between the lengths of the two linked lists.

#121. 1.4 What characteristics would a string that is a permutation of a palindrome have?

#122. 1.2 Could a hash table be useful?

#123. 4.3 A hash table or array that maps from level number to nodes at that level might also be useful.

#124. 4.4 Actually, you can just have a single `checkHeight` function that does both the height computation and the balance check. An integer return value can be used to indicate both.

#125. 4.7 As a totally different approach: Consider doing a depth-first search starting from an arbitrary node. What is the relationship between this depth-first search and a valid build order?

#126. 2.2 Can you do it iteratively? Imagine if you had two pointers pointing to adjacent nodes and they were moving at the same speed through the linked list. When one hits the end of the linked list, where will the other be?

#127. 4.1 Two well-known algorithms can do this. What are the tradeoffs between them?

#128. 4.5 Think about the `checkBST` function as a recursive function that ensures each node is within an allowable `(min, max)` range. At first, this range is infinite. When we traverse to the left, the min is negative infinity and the max is `root.value`. Can you implement this recursive function and properly adjust these ranges as you traverse the tree?

#129. 2.7 If you move a pointer in the longer linked list forward by the difference in lengths, you can then apply a similar approach to the scenario when the linked lists are equal.

#130. 1.5 Can you do all three checks in a single pass?

#131. 1.2 Two strings that are permutations should have the same characters, but in different orders. Can you make the orders the same?

#132. 1.1 Can you solve it in `O(N log N)` time? What might a solution like that look like?

#133. 4.7 Pick an arbitrary node and do a depth-first search on it. Once we get to the end of a path, we know that this node can be the last one built, since no nodes depend on it. What does this mean about the nodes right before it?

#134. 1.4 Have you tried a hash table? You should be able to get this down to `O(N)` time.

#135. 4.3 You should be able to come up with an algorithm involving both depth-first search and breadth-first search.

#136. 1.4 Can you reduce the space usage by using a bit vector?

Hints for Concepts and Algorithms

#137. 5.1 Break this into parts. Focus first on clearing the appropriate bits.

#138. 8.9 Try the Base Case and Build approach.

#139. 6.9 Given a specific door x, on which rounds will it be toggled (open or closed)?

#140. 11.5 What does the interviewer mean by a pen? There are a lot of different types of pens. Make a list of potential questions you would want to ask.

#141. 7.11 This is not as complicated as it sounds. Start by making a list of the key objects in the system, then think about how they interact.

#142. 9.6 First, start with making some assumptions. What do and don't you have to build?

#143. 5.2 To wrap your head around the problem, try thinking about how you'd do it for integers.

#144. 8.6 Try the Base Case and Build approach.

#145. 5.7 Swapping each pair means moving the even bits to the left and the odd bits to the right. Can you break this problem into parts?

#146. 6.10 Solution 1: Start with a simple approach. Can you just divide up the bottles into groups? Remember that you can't re-use a test strip once it is positive, but you can reuse it as long as it's negative.

#147. 5.4 Get Next: Start with a brute force solution for each.

#148. 8.14 Can we just try all possibilities? What would this look like?

#149. 6.5 Play around with the jugs of water, pouring water back and forth, and see if you can measure anything other than 3 quarts or 5 quarts. That's a start.

#150. 8.7 Approach 1: Suppose you had all permutations of `abc`. How can you use that to get all permutations of `abcd`?

#151. 5.5 Reverse engineer this, starting from the outermost layer to the innermost layer.

#152. 8.1 Approach this from the top down. What is the very last hop the child made?

#153. 7.1 Note that a "card deck" is very broad. You might want to think about a reasonable scope to the problem.

#154. 6.7 Observe that each family will have exactly one girl.

#155. 8.13 Will sorting the boxes help in any way?

#156.	6.8	This is really an algorithm problem, and you should approach it as such. Come up with a brute force, compute the worst-case number of drops, then try to optimize that.
#157.	6.4	In what cases will they not collide?
#158.	9.6	We've assumed that the rest of the eCommerce system is already handled, and we just need to deal with the analytics part of sales rank. We can get notified somehow when a purchase occurs.
#159.	5.3	Start with a brute force solution. Can you try all possibilities?
#160.	6.7	Think about writing each family as a sequence of Bs and Gs.
#161.	8.8	You could handle this by just checking to see if there are duplicates before printing them (or adding them to a list). You can do this with a hash table. In what case might this be okay? In what case might it not be a very good solution?
#162.	9.7	Will this application be write-heavy or read-heavy?
#163.	6.10	Solution 1: There is a relatively simple approach that works in 28 days, in the worst case. There are better approaches though.
#164.	11.5	Consider the scenario of a pen for children. What does this mean? What are the different use cases?
#165.	9.8	Scope the problem well. What will and won't you tackle as part of this system?
#166.	8.5	Think about multiplying 8 by 9 as counting the number of cells in a matrix with width 8 and height 9.
#167.	5.2	In a number like `.893` (in base 10), what does each digit signify? What then does each digit in `.10010` signify in base 2?
#168.	8.14	We can think about each possibility as each place where we can put parentheses. This means around each operator, such that the expression is split at the operator. What is the base case?
#169.	5.1	To clear the bits, create a "bit mask" that looks like a series of 1s, then 0s, then 1s.
#170.	8.3	Start with a brute force algorithm.
#171.	6.7	You can attempt this mathematically, although the math is pretty difficult. You might find it easier to estimate it up to families of, say, 6 children. This won't give you a good mathematical proof, but it might point you in the right direction of what the answer might be.
#172.	6.9	In which cases would a door be left open at the end of the process?
#173.	5.2	A number such as `.893` (in base 10) indicates $8 * 10^{-1} + 9 * 10^{-2} + 3 * 10^{-3}$. Translate this system into base 2.
#174.	8.9	Suppose we had all valid ways of writing two pairs of parentheses. How could we use this to get all valid ways of writing three pairs?
#175.	5.4	Get Next: Picture a binary number—something with a bunch of 1s and 0s spread out throughout the number. Suppose you flip a 1 to a 0 and a 0 to a 1. In what case will the number get bigger? In what case will it get smaller?

#176. 9.6 Think about what sort of expectations on freshness and accuracy of data is expected. Does the data always need to be 100% up to date? Is the accuracy of some products more important than others?

#177. 10.2 How do you check if two words are anagrams of each other? Think about what the definition of "anagram" is. Explain it in your own words.

#178. 8.1 If we knew the number of paths to each of the steps before step 100, could we compute the number of steps to 100?

#179. 7.8 Should white pieces and black pieces be the same class? What are the pros and cons of this?

#180. 9.7 Observe that there is a lot of data coming in, but people probably aren't reading the data very frequently.

#181. 6.2 Calculate the probability of winning the first game and winning the second game, then compare them.

#182. 10.2 Two words are anagrams if they contain the same characters but in different orders. How can you put characters in order?

#183. 6.10 Solution 2: Why do we have such a time lag between tests and results? There's a reason the question isn't phrased as just "minimize the number of rounds of testing." The time lag is there for a reason.

#184. 9.8 How evenly do you think traffic is distributed? Do all documents get roughly the same age of traffic? Or is it likely there are some very popular documents?

#185. 8.7 Approach 1: The permutations of `abc` represent all ways of ordering `abc`. Now, we want to create all orderings of `abcd`. Take a specific ordering of `abcd`, such as `bdca`. This `bdca` string represents an ordering of `abc`, too: Remove the d and you get `bca`. Given the string `bca`, can you create all the "related" orderings that include d, too?

#186. 6.1 You can only use the scale once. This means that all, or almost all, of the bottles must be used. They also must be handled in different ways or else you couldn't distinguish between them.

#187. 8.9 We could try generating the solution for three pairs by taking the list of two pairs of parentheses and adding a third pair. We'd have to add the third paren before, around, and after. That is: `()<SOLUTION>`, `(<SOLUTION>)`, `<SOLUTION>()`. Will this work?

#188. 6.7 Logic might be easier than math. Imagine we wrote every birth into a giant string of Bs and Gs. Note that the groupings of families are irrelevant for this problem. What is the probability of the next character added to the string being a B versus a G?

#189. 9.6 Purchases will occur very frequently. You probably want to limit database writes.

#190. 8.8 If you haven't solved 8.7 yet, do that one first.

#191. 6.10 Solution 2: Consider running multiple tests at once.

#192. 7.6 A common trick when solving a jigsaw puzzle is to separate edge and non-edge pieces. How will you represent this in an object-oriented manner?

#193. 10.9 Start with a naive solution. (But hopefully not too naive. You should be able to use the fact that the matrix is sorted.)

#194. 8.13 We can sort the boxes by any dimension in descending order. This will give us a partial order for the boxes, in that boxes later in the array must appear before boxes earlier in the array.

#195. 6.4 The only way they won't collide is if all three are walking in the same direction. What's the probability of all three walking clockwise?

#196. 10.11 Imagine the array were sorted in ascending order. Is there any way you could "fix it" to be sorted into alternating peaks and valleys?

#197. 8.14 The base case is when we have a single value, 1 or 0.

#198. 7.3 Scope the problem first and make a list of your assumptions. It's often okay to make reasonable assumptions, but you need to make them explicit.

#199. 9.7 The system will be write-heavy: Lots of data being imported, but it's rarely being read.

#200. 8.7 Approach 1: Given a string such as `bca`, you can create all permutations of `abcd` that have `{a, b, c}` in the order `bca` by inserting `d` into each possible location: `dbca`, `bdca`, `bcda`, `bcad`. Given all permutations of `abc`, can you then create all permutations of `abcd`?

#201. 6.7 Observe that biology hasn't changed; only the conditions under which a family stops having kids has changed. Each pregnancy has a 50% odds of being a boy and a 50% odds of being a girl.

#202. 5.5 What does it mean if `A & B == 0`?

#203. 8.5 If you wanted to count the cells in an 8x9 matrix, you could count the cells in a 4x9 matrix and then double it.

#204. 8.3 Your brute force algorithm probably ran in `O(N)` time. If you're trying to beat that runtime, what runtime do you think you will get to? What sorts of algorithms have that runtime?

#205. 6.10 Solution 2: Think about trying to figure out the bottle, digit by digit. How can you detect the first digit in the poisoned bottle? What about the second digit? The third digit?

#206. 9.8 How will you handle generating URLs?

#207. 10.6 Think about merge sort versus quick sort. Would one of them work well for this purpose?

#208. 9.6 You also want to limit joins because they can be very expensive.

#209. 8.9 The problem with the solution suggested by the earlier hint is that it might have duplicate values. We could eliminate this by using a hash table.

#210. 11.6 Be careful about your assumptions. Who are the users? Where are they using this? It might seem obvious, but the real answer might be different.

#211. 10.9 We can do a binary search in each row. How long will this take? How can we do better?

#212. 9.7 Think about things like how you're going to get the bank data (will it be pulled or pushed?), what features the system will support, etc.

#213. 7.7 As always, scope the problem. Are "friendships" mutual? Do status messages exist? Do you support group chat?

#214. 8.13 Try to break it down into subproblems.

#215. 5.1 It's easy to create a bit mask of 0s at the beginning or end. But how do you create a bit mask with a bunch of zeroes in the middle? Do it the easy way: Create a bit mask for the left side and then another one for the right side. Then you can merge those.

#216. 7.11 What is the relationship between files and directories?

#217. 8.1 We can compute the number of steps to 100 by the number of steps to 99, 98, and 97. This corresponds to the child hopping 1, 2, or 3 steps at the end. Do we add those or multiply them? That is: Is it `f(100) = f(99) + f(98) + f(97)` *or* `f(100) = f(99) * f(98) * f(97)`?

#218. 6.6 This is a logic problem, not a clever word problem. Use logic/math/algorithms to solve it.

#219. 10.11 Try walking through a sorted array. Can you just swap elements until you have fixed the array?

#220. 11.5 Have you considered both intended uses (writing, etc.) and unintended use? What about safety? You would not want a pen for children to be dangerous.

#221. 6.10 Solution 2: Be very careful about edge cases. What if the third digit in the bottle number matches the first or second digit?

#222. 8.8 Try getting the count of each character. For example, ABCAAC has 3 As, 2 Cs, and 1 B.

#223. 9.6 Don't forget that a product can be listed under multiple categories.

#224. 8.6 You can easily move the smallest disk from one tower to another. It's also pretty easy to move the smallest two disks from one tower to another. Can you move the smallest three disks?

#225. 11.6 In a real interview, you would also want to discuss what sorts of test tools we have available.

#226. 5.3 Flipping a 0 to a 1 can merge two sequences of 1s—but only if the two sequences are separated by only one 0.

#227. 8.5 Think about how you might handle this for odd numbers.

#228. 7.8 What class should maintain the score?

#229. 10.9 If you're considering a particular column, is there a way to quickly eliminate it (in some cases at least)?

#230. 6.10 Solution 2: You can run an additional day of testing to check digit 3 in a different way. But again, be very careful about edge cases here.

#231. 10.11 Note that if you ensure the peaks are in place, the valleys will be, too. Therefore, your iteration to fix the array can skip over every other element.

#232. 9.8 If you generate URLs randomly, do you need to worry about collisions (two documents with the same URL)? If so, how can you handle this?

#233. 6.8 As a first approach, you might try something like binary search. Drop it from the 50th floor, then the 75th, then the 88th, and so on. The problem is that if the first egg breaks at the 50th floor, then you'll need to start dropping the second egg starting from the 1st floor and going up. This could take, at worst, 50 drops (the 50th floor drop, the 1st floor drop, the 2nd floor drop, and up through the 49th floor drop). Can you beat this?

#234. 8.5 If there's duplicated work across different recursive calls, can you cache it?

#235. 10.7 Would a bit vector help?

#236. 9.6 Where would it be appropriate to cache data or queue up tasks?

#237. 8.1 We multiply the values when it's "we do this then this." We add them when it's "we do this or this."

#238. 7.6 Think about how you might record the position of a piece when you find it. Should it be stored by row and location?

#239. 6.2 To calculate the probability of winning the second game, start with calculating the probability of making the first hoop, the second hoop, and not the third hoop.

#240. 8.3 Can you solve the problem in O(log N)?

#241. 6.10 Solution 3: Think about each test strip as being a binary indicator for poisoned vs. non-poisoned.

#242. 5.4 Get Next: If you flip a 1 to a 0 and a 0 to a 1, it will get bigger if the 0->1 bit is more significant than the 1->0 bit. How can you use this to create the next biggest number (with the same number of 1s)?

#243. 8.9 Alternatively, we could think about doing this by moving through the string and adding left and right parens at each step. Will this eliminate duplicates? How do we know if we can add a left or right paren?

#244. 9.6 Depending on what assumptions you made, you might even be able to do without a database at all. What would this mean? Would it be a good idea?

#245. 7.7 This is a good problem to think about the major system components or technologies that would be useful.

#246. 8.5 If you're doing `9*7` (both odd numbers), then you could do `4*7` and `5*7`.

#247. 9.7 Try to reduce unnecessary database queries. If you don't need to permanently store the data in the database, you might not need it in the database at all.

#248. 5.7 Can you create a number that represents just the even bits? Then can you shift the even bits over by one?

#249. 6.10 Solution 3: If each test strip is a binary indicator, can we map , integer keys to a set of 10 binary indicators such that each key has a unique configuration (mapping)?

#250. 8.6 Think about moving the smallest disk from tower `X=0` to tower `Y=2` using tower `Z=1` as a temporary holding spot as having a solution for `f(1, X=0, Y=2, Z=1)`. Moving the smallest two disks is `f(2, X=0, Y=2, Z=1)`. Given that you have a solution for `f(1, X=0, Y=2, Z=1)` and `f(2, X=0, Y=2, Z=1)`, can you solve `f(3, X=0, Y=2, Z=1)`?

#251. 10.9 Since each column is sorted, you know that the value can't be in this column if it's smaller than the min value in this column. What else does this tell you?

#252. 6.1 What happens if you put one pill from each bottle on the scale? What if you put two pills from each bottle on the scale?

#253. 10.11 Do you necessarily need the arrays to be sorted? Can you do it with an unsorted array?

#254. 10.7 To do it with less memory, can you try multiple passes?

#255. 8.8 To get all permutations with 3 As, 2 Cs, and 1 B, you need to first pick a starting character: A, B, or C. If it's an A, then you need all permutations with 2 As, 2 Cs, and 1 B.

#256. 10.5 Try modifying binary search to handle this.

#257. 11.1 There are two mistakes in this code.

#258. 7.4 Does the parking lot have multiple levels? What "features" does it support? Is it paid? What types of vehicles?

#259. 9.5 You may need to make some assumptions (in part because you don't have an interviewer here). That's okay. Make those assumptions explicit.

#260. 8.13 Think about the first decision you have to make. The first decision is which box will be at the bottom.

#261. 5.5 If `A & B == 0`, then it means that A and B never have a 1 at the same spot. Apply this to the equation in the problem.

#262. 8.1 What is the runtime of this method? Think carefully. Can you optimize it?

#263. 10.2 Can you leverage a standard sorting algorithm?

#264. 6.9 Note: If an integer x is divisible by a, and `b = x / a`, then x is also divisible by b. Does this mean that all numbers have an even number of factors?

#265. 8.9 Adding a left or right paren at each step will eliminate duplicates. Each substring will be unique at each step. Therefore, the total string will be unique.

#266. 10.9 If the value x is smaller than the start of the column, then it also can't be in any columns to the right.

#267. 8.7 Approach 1: You can create all permutations of `abcd` by computing all permutations of `abc` and then inserting d into each possible location within those.

#268. 11.6 What are the different features and uses we would want to test?

#269. 5.2 How would you get the first digit in `.893`? If you multiplied by 10, you'd shift the values over to get `8.93`. What happens if you multiply by 2?

#270. 9.2 To find the connection between two nodes, would it be better to do a breadth-first search or depth-first search? Why?

#271. 7.7 How will you know if a user signs offline?

#272. 8.6 Observe that it doesn't really matter which tower is the source, destination, or buffer. You can do `f(3, X=0, Y=2, Z=1)` by first doing `f(2, X=0, Y=1, Z=2)` (moving two disks from tower 0 to tower 1, using tower 2 as a buffer), then moving disk 3 from tower 0 to tower 2, then doing `f(2, X=1, Y=2, Z=0)` (moving two disks from tower 1 to tower 2, using tower 0 as a buffer). How does this process repeat?

#273. 8.4 How can you build all subsets of `{a, b, c}` from the subsets of `{a, b}`?

#274. 9.5 Think about how you could design this for a single machine. Would you want a hash table? How would that work?

#275. 7.1 How, if at all, will you handle aces?

#276. 9.7 As much work as possible should be done asynchronously.

#277. 10.11 Suppose you had a sequence of three elements (`{0, 1, 2}`, in any order. Write out all possible sequences for those elements and how you can fix them to make 1 the peak.

#278. 8.7 Approach 2: If you had all permutations of two-character substrings, could you generate all permutations of three-character substrings?

#279. 10.9 Think about the previous hint in the context of rows.

#280. 8.5 Alternatively, if you're doing 9 * 7, you could do 4*7, double that, and then add 7.

#281. 10.7 Try using one pass to get it down to a range of values, and then a second pass to find a specific value.

#282. 6.6 Suppose there were exactly one blue-eyed person. What would that person see? When would they leave?

#283. 7.6 Which will be the easiest pieces to match first? Can you start with those? Which will be the next easiest, once you've nailed those down?

#284. 6.2 If two events are mutually exclusive (they can never occur simultaneously), you can add their probabilities together. Can you find a set of mutually exclusive events that represent making two out of three hoops?

#285. 9.2 A breadth-first search is probably better. A depth-first search can wind up going on a long path, even though the shortest path is actually very short. Is there a modification to a breadth-first search that might be even faster?

#286. 8.3 Binary search has a runtime of `O(log N)`. Can you apply a form of binary search to the problem?

#287. 7.12 In order to handle collisions, the hash table should be an array of linked lists.

#288. 10.9 What would happen if we tried to keep track of this using an array? What are the pros and cons of this?

#289. 10.8 Can you use a bit vector?

#290. 8.4 Anything that is a subset of `{a, b}` is also a subset of `{a, b, c}`. Which sets are subsets of `{a, b, c}` but not `{a, b}`?

#291. 10.9 Can we use the previous hints to move up, down, left, and right around the rows and columns?

#292. 10.11 Revisit the set of sequences for `{0, 1, 2}` that you just wrote out. Imagine there are elements before the leftmost element. Are you sure that the way you swap the elements won't invalidate the previous part of the array?

#293. 9.5 Can you combine a hash table and a linked list to get the best of both worlds?

#294. 6.8 It's actually better for the first drop to be a bit lower. For example, you could drop at the 10th floor, then the 20th floor, then the 30th floor, and so on. The worst case here will be 19 drops (10, 20, ..., 100, 91, 92, ..., 99). Can you beat that? Try not randomly guessing at different solutions. Rather, think deeper. How is the worst case defined? How does the number of drops of each egg factor into that?

#295. 8.9 We can ensure that this string is valid by counting the number of left and right parens. It is always valid to add a left paren, up until the total number of pairs of parens. We can add a right paren as long as `count(left parens) <= count(right parens)`.

#296. 6.4 You can think about this either as the probability(3 ants walking clockwise) + probability(3 ants walking counter-clockwise). Or, you can think about it as: The first ant picks a direction. What's the probability of the other ants picking the same direction?

#297. 5.2 Think about what happens for values that can't be represented accurately in binary.

#298. 10.3 Can you modify binary search for this purpose?

#299. 11.1 What will happen to the `unsigned int`?

#300. 8.11 Try breaking it down into subproblems. If you were making change, what is the first choice you would make?

#301. 10.10 The problem with using an array is that it will be slow to insert a number. What other data structures could we use?

#302. 5.5 If `(n & (n-1)) == 0`, then this means that n and `n - 1` never have a 1 in the same spot. Why would that happen?

#303. 10.9 Another way to think about this is that if you drew a rectangle around a cell extending to the bottom, right coordinate of the matrix, the cell would be bigger than all the items in this square.

#304. 9.2 Is there any way to search from both the source and destination? For what reason or in what case might this be faster?

#305. 8.14 If your code looks really lengthy, with a lot of if's (for each possible operator, "target" boolean result, and left/right side), think about the relationship between the different parts. Try to simplify your code. It should not need a ton of complicated if-statements. For example, consider expressions of the form <LEFT>OR<RIGHT> versus <LEFT>AND<RIGHT>. Both may need to know the number of ways that the <LEFT> evaluates to true. See what code you can reuse.

#306. 6.9 The number 3 has an even number of factors (1 and 3). The number 12 has an even number of factors (1, 2, 3, 4, 6, 12). What numbers do not? What does this tell you about the doors?

#307. 7.12 Think carefully about what information the linked list node needs to contain.

#308. 8.12 We know that each row must have a queen. Can you try all possibilities?

#309. 8.7 Approach 2: To generate a permutation of `abcd`, you need to pick an initial character. It can be `a`, `b`, `c`, or `d`. You can then permute the remaining characters. How can you use this approach to generate all permutations of the full string?

#310. 10.3 What is the runtime of your algorithm? What will happen if the array has duplicates?

#311. 9.5 How would you scale this to a larger system?

#312. 5.4 Get Next: Can you flip a 0 to a 1 to create the next biggest number?

#313. 11.4 Think about what load testing is designed to test. What are the factors in the load of a webpage? What criteria would be used to judge if a webpage performs satisfactorily under heavy load?

#314. 5.3 Each sequence can be lengthened by merging it with an adjacent sequence (if any) or just flipping the immediate neighboring zero. You just need to find the best choice.

#315. 10.8 Consider implementing your own bit vector class. It's a good exercise and an important part of this problem.

#316. 10.11 You should be able to design an `O(n)` algorithm.

#317. 10.9 A cell will be larger than all the items below it and to the right. It will be smaller than all cells above it and to the left. If we wanted to eliminate the most elements first, which element should we compare the value x to?

#318. 8.6 If you're having trouble with recursion, then try trusting the recursive process more. Once you've figured out how to move the top two disks from tower 0 to tower 2, trust that you have this working. When you need to move three disks, trust that you can move two disks from one tower to another. Now, two disks have been moved. What do you do about the third?

#319. 6.1 Imagine there were just three bottles and one had heavier pills. Suppose you put different numbers of pills from each bottle on the scale (for example, bottle 1 has 5 pills, bottle 2 has 2 pills, and bottle 3 has 9 pills). What would the scale show?

#320. 10.4 Think about how binary search works. What will be the issue with just implementing binary search?

#321. 9.2 Discuss how you might implement these algorithms and this system in the real world. What sort of optimizations might you make?

#322. 8.13 Once we pick the box on the bottom, we need to pick the second box. Then the third box.

#323. 6.2 The probability of making two out of three shots is probability(make shot 1, make shot 2, miss shot 3) + probability(make shot 1, miss shot 2, make shot 3) + probability(miss shot 1, make shot 2, make shot 3) + probability(make shot 1, make shot 2, make shot 3).

#324. 8.11 If you were making change, the first choice you might make is how many quarters you need to use.

#325. 11.2 Think about issues both within the program and outside of the program (the rest of the system).

#326. 9.4 Estimate how much space is needed for this.

#327. 8.14 Look at your recursion. Do you have repeated calls anywhere? Can you memoize it?

#328. 5.7 The value 1010 in binary is 10 in decimal or 0xA in hex. What will a sequence of 101010... be in hex? That is, how do you represent an alternating sequence of 1s and 0s with 1s in the odd places? How do you do this for the reverse (1s in the even spots)?

#329. 11.3 Consider both extreme cases and more general cases.

#330. 10.9 If we compare x to the center element in the matrix, we can eliminate roughly one quarter of the elements in the matrix.

#331. 8.2 For the robot to reach the last cell, it must find a path to the second-to-last cells. For it to find a path to the second-to-last cells, it must find a path to the third-to-last cells.

#332. 10.1 Try moving from the end of the array to the beginning.

#333. 6.8 If we drop Egg 1 at fixed intervals (e.g., every 10 floors), then the worst case is the worst case for Egg 1 + the worst case for Egg 2. The problem with our earlier solutions is that as Egg 1 does more work, Egg 2 doesn't do any less work. Ideally, we'd like to balance this a bit. As Egg 1 does more work (has survived more drops), Egg 2 should have less work to do. What might this mean?

#334. 9.3 Think about how infinite loops might occur.

#335. 8.7 Approach 2: To generate all permutations of `abcd`, pick each character (a, b, c, or d) as a starting character. Permute the remaining characters and prepend the starting character. How do you permute the remaining characters? With a recursive process that follows the same logic.

#336. 5.6 How would you figure out how many bits are different between two numbers?

#337. 10.4 Binary search requires comparing an element to the midpoint. Getting the midpoint requires knowing the length. We don't know the length. Can we find it?

#338. 8.4 Subsets that contain c will be subsets `{a, b, c}` but not `{a, b}`. Can you build these subsets from the subsets of `{a, b}`?

#339. 5.4 Get Next: Flipping a 0 to a 1 will create a bigger number. The farther right the index is the smaller the bigger number is. If we have a number like 1001, we want to flip the rightmost 0 (to create 1011). But if we have a number like 1010, we should not flip the rightmost 1.

#340. 8.3 Given a specific index and value, can you identify if the magic index would be before or after it?

#341. 6.6 Now suppose there were two blue-eyed people. What would they see? What would they know? When would they leave? Remember your answer from the prior hint. Assume they know the answer to the earlier hint.

#342. 10.2 Do you even need to truly "sort"? Or is just reorganizing the list sufficient?

#343. 8.11 Once you've decided to use two quarters to make change for 98 cents, you now need to figure out how many ways to make change for 48 cents using nickels, dimes, and pennies.

#344. 7.5 Think about all the different functionality a system to read books online would have to support. You don't have to do everything, but you should think about making your assumptions explicit.

#345. 11.4 Could you build your own? What might that look like?

#346. 5.5 What is the relationship between how n looks and how `n - 1` looks? Walk through a binary subtraction.

#347. 9.4 Will you need multiple passes? Multiple machines?

#348. 10.4 We can find the length by using an exponential backoff. First check index 2, then 4, then 8, then 16, and so on. What will be the runtime of this algorithm?

#349. 11.6 What can we automate?

#350. 8.12 Each row must have a queen. Start with the last row. There are eight different columns on which you can put a queen. Can you try each of these?

#351. 7.10 Should number cells, blank cells, and bomb cells be separate classes?

#352. 5.3 Try to do it in linear time, a single pass, and `O(1)` space.

#353. 9.3 How would you detect the same page? What does this mean?

#354. 8.4 You can build the remaining subsets by adding `c` to all the subsets of `{a, b}`.

#355. 5.7 Try masks `0xaaaaaaaa` and `0x55555555` to select the even and odd bits. Then try shifting the even and odd bits around to create the right number.

#356. 8.7 Approach 2: You can implement this approach by having the recursive function pass back the list of the strings, and then you prepend the starting character to it. Or, you can push down a prefix to the recursive calls.

#357. 6.8 Try dropping Egg 1 at bigger intervals at the beginning and then at smaller and smaller intervals. The idea is to keep the sum of Egg 1 and Egg 2's drops as constant as possible. For each additional drop that Egg 1 takes, Egg 2 takes one fewer drop. What is the right interval?

#358. 5.4 Get Next: We should flip the rightmost non-trailing 0. The number 1010 would become 1110. Once we've done that, we need to flip a 1 to a 0 to make the number as small as possible, but bigger than the original number (1010). What do we do? How can we shrink the number?

#359. 8.1 Try memoization as a way to optimize an inefficient recursive program.

#360. 8.2 Simplify this problem a bit by first figuring out if there's a path. Then, modify your algorithm to track the path.

#361. 7.10 What is the algorithm to place the bombs around the board?

#362. 11.1 Look at the parameters for `printf`.

#363. 7.2 Before coding, make a list of the objects you need and walk through the common algorithms. Picture the code. Do you have everything you need?

#364. 8.10 Think about this as a graph.

#365. 9.3 How do you define if two pages are the same? Is it the URLs? Is it the content? Both of these can be flawed. Why?

#366. 5.8 First try the naive approach. Can you set a particular "pixel"?

#367. 6.3 Picture a domino laying down on the board. How many black squares does it cover? How many white squares?

#368. 8.13 Once you have a basic recursive algorithm implemented, think about if you can optimize it. Are there any repeated subproblems?

#369. 5.6 Think about what an XOR indicates. If you do a XOR b, where does the result have 1s? Where does it have 0s?

#370. 6.6 Build up from this. What if there were three blue-eyed people? What if there were four blue-eyed people?

#371. 8.12 Break this down into smaller subproblems. The queen at row 8 must be at column 1, 2, 3, 4, 5, 6, 7, or 8. Can you print all ways of placing eight queens where a queen is at row 8 and column 3? You then need to check all the ways of placing a queen on row 7.

#372.	5.5	When you do a binary subtraction, you flip the rightmost 0s to a 1, stopping when you get to a 1 (which is also flipped). Everything (all the 1s and 0s) on the left will stay put.
#373.	8.4	You can also do this by mapping each subset to a binary number. The `ith` bit could represent a "boolean" flag for whether an element is in the set.
#374.	6.8	Let X be the first drop of Egg 1. This means that Egg 2 would do `X - 1` drops if Egg 1 broke. We want to try to keep the sum of Egg 1 and Egg 2's drops as constant as possible. If Egg 1 breaks on the second drop, then we want Egg 2 to do `X - 2` drops. If Egg 1 breaks on the third drop, then we want Egg 2 to do `X - 3` drops. This keeps the sum of Egg 1 and Egg 2 fairly constant. What is X?
#375.	5.4	Get Next: We can shrink the number by moving all the 1s to the right of the flipped bit as far right as possible (removing a 1 in the process).
#376.	10.10	Would it work well to use a binary search tree?
#377.	7.10	To place the bombs randomly on the board: Think about the algorithm to shuffle a deck of cards. Can you apply a similar technique?
#378.	8.13	Alternatively, we can think about the repeated choices as: Does the first box go on the stack? Does the second box go on the stack? And so on.
#379.	6.5	If you fill the 5-quart jug and then use it to fill the 3-quart jug, you'll have two quarts left in the 5-quart jug. You can either keep those two quarts where they are, or you can dump the contents of the smaller jug and pour the two quarts in there.
#380.	8.11	Analyze your algorithm. Is there any repeated work? Can you optimize this?
#381.	5.8	When you're drawing a long line, you'll have entire bytes that will become a sequence of 1s. Can you set this all at once?
#382.	8.10	You can implement this using depth-first search (or breadth-first search). Each adjacent pixel of the "right" color is a connected edge.
#383.	5.5	Picture n and `n-1`. To subtract 1 from n, you flipped the rightmost 1 to a 0 and all the 0s on its right to 1s. If `n & n-1 == 0`, then there are no 1s to the left of the first 1. What does that mean about n?
#384.	5.8	What about the start and end of the line? Do you need to set those pixels individually, or can you set them all at once?
#385.	9.1	Think about this as a real-world application. What are the different factors you would need to consider?
#386.	7.10	How do you count the number of bombs neighboring a cell? Will you iterate through all cells?
#387.	6.1	You should be able to have an equation that tells you the heavy bottle based on the weight.
#388.	8.2	Think again about the efficiency of your algorithm. Can you optimize it?
#389.	7.9	The `rotate()` method should be able to run in `O(1)` time.
#390.	5.4	Get Previous: Once you've solved Get Next, try to invert the logic for Get Previous.
#391.	5.8	Does your code handle the case when `x1` and `x2` are in the same byte?
#392.	10.10	Consider a binary search tree where each node stores some additional data.

#393. 11.6 Have you thought about security and reliability?

#394. 8.11 Try using memoization.

#395. 6.8 I got 14 drops in the worst case. What did you get?

#396. 9.1 There's no one right answer here. Discuss several different technical implementations.

#397. 6.3 How many black squares are there on the board? How many white squares?

#398. 5.5 We know that n must have only one 1 if `n & (n-1) == 0`. What sorts of numbers have only one 1?

#399. 7.10 When you click on a blank cell, what is the algorithm to expand the neighboring cells?

#400. 6.5 Once you've developed a way to solve this problem, think about it more broadly. If you are given a jug of size X and another jug of size Y, can you always use it to measure Z?

#401. 11.3 Is it possible to test everything? How will you prioritize testing?

Hints for Knowledge-Based Questions

#402. 12.9 Focus on the concept firsts, then worry about the exact implementation. How should `SmartPointer` look?

#403. 15.2 A context switch is the time spent switching between two processes. This happens when you bring one process into execution and swap out the existing process.

#404. 13.1 Think about who can access private methods.

#405. 15.1 How do these differ in terms of memory?

#406. 12.11 Recall that a two dimensional array is essentially an array of arrays.

#407. 15.2 Ideally, we would like to record the timestamp when one process "stops" and the timestamp when another process "starts." But how do we know when this swapping will occur?

#408. 14.1 A GROUP BY clause might be useful.

#409. 13.2 When does a finally block get executed? Are there any cases where it won't get executed?

#410. 12.2 Can we do this in place?

#411. 14.2 It might be helpful to break the approach into two pieces. The first piece is to get each building ID and the number of open requests. Then, we can get the building names.

#412. 13.3 Consider that some of these might have different meanings depending on where they are applied.

#413. 12.10 Typically, `malloc` will just give us an arbitrary block of memory. If we can't override this behavior, can we work with it to do what we need?

#414. 15.7 First implement the single-threaded FizzBuzz problem.

#415. 15.2 Try setting up two processes and have them pass a small amount of data back and forth. This will encourage the system to stop one process and bring the other one in.

#416. 13.4 The purpose of these might be somewhat similar, but how does the implementation differ?

#417. 15.5 How can we ensure that `first()` has terminated before calling `second()`?

#418. 12.11 One approach is to call `malloc` for each array. How would we free the memory here?

#419. 15.3 A deadlock can happen when there's a "cycle" in the order of who is waiting for whom. How can we break or prevent this cycle?

#420. 13.5 Think about the underlying data structure.

#421. 12.7 Think about why we use virtual methods.

#422. 15.4 If every thread had to declare upfront what processes it might need, could we detect possible deadlocks in advance?

#423. 12.3 What is the underlying data structure behind each? What are the implications of this?

#424. 13.5 `HashMap` uses an array of linked lists. `TreeMap` uses a red-black tree. `LinkedHashMap` uses doubly-linked buckets. What is the implication of this?

#425. 13.4 Consider the usage of primitive types. How else might they differ in terms of how you can use the types?

#426. 12.11 Can we allocate this instead as a contiguous block of memory?

#427. 12.8 This data structure can be pictured as a binary tree, but it's not necessarily. What if there's a loop in the structure?

#428. 14.7 You probably need a list of students, their courses, and another table building a relationship between students and courses. Note that this is a many-to-many relationship.

#429. 15.6 The keyword `synchronized` ensures that two threads cannot execute synchronized methods on the same instance at the same time.

#430. 13.5 Consider how they might differ in terms of the order of iteration through the keys. Why might you want one option instead of the others?

#431. 14.3 First try to get a list of the IDs (just the IDs) of all the relevant apartments.

#432. 12.10 Imagine we have a sequential set of integers (3, 4, 5, ...). How big does this set need to be to ensure that one of the numbers is divisible by 16?

#433. 15.5 Why would using `boolean` flags to do this be a bad idea?

#434. 15.4 Think about the order of requests as a graph. What does a deadlock look like within this graph?

#435. 13.6 Object reflection allows you to get information about methods and fields in an object. Why might this be useful?

#436. 14.6 Be particularly careful about which relationships are one-to-one vs. one-to-many vs. many-to-many.

#437. 15.3 One idea is to just not let a philosopher hold onto a chopstick if he can't get the other one.

#438. 12.9 Think about tracking the number of references. What will this tell us?

#439. 15.7 Don't try to do anything fancy on the single-threaded problem. Just get something that is simple and easily readable.

#440. 12.10 How will we free the memory?

#441. 15.2 It's okay if your solution isn't totally perfect. That might not be possible. Discuss the tradeoffs of your approach.

#442. 14.7 Think carefully about how you handle ties when selecting the top 10%.

#443. 13.8 A naive approach is to pick a random subset size z and then iterate through the elements, putting it in the set with probability `z/list_size`. Why would this not work?

#444. 14.5 Denormalization means adding redundant data to a table. It's typically used in very large systems. Why might this be useful?

#445. 12.5 A shallow copy copies just the initial data structure. A deep copy does this, and also copies any underlying data. Given this, why might you use one versus the other?

#446. 15.5 Would semaphores be useful here?

#447. 15.7 Outline the structure for the threads without worrying about synchronizing anything.

#448. 13.7 Consider how you'd implement this first without lambda expressions.

#449. 12.1 If we already had the number of lines in the file, how would we do this?

#450. 13.8 Pick the list of all the subsets of an n-element set. For any given item `x`, half of the subsets contain x and half do not.

#451. 14.4 Describe INNER JOINs and OUTER JOINs. OUTER JOINs can have multiple types: left, right, and full.

#452. 12.2 Be careful about the null character.

#453. 12.9 What are all the different methods/operators we might want to override?

#454. 13.5 What would the runtime of the common operations be?

#455. 14.5 Think about the cost of joins on a large system.

#456. 12.6 The keyword `volatile` signals that a variable might be changed from outside of the program, such as by another process. Why might this be necessary?

#457. 13.8 Do not pick the length of the subset in advance. You don't need to. Instead, think about this as picking whether each element will be put into the set.

#458. 15.7 Once you get the structure of each thread done, think about what you need to synchronize.

#459. 12.1 Suppose we didn't have the number of lines in the file. Is there a way we could do this without first counting the number of lines?

#460. 12.7 What would happen if the destructor were not virtual?

#461. 13.7 Break this up into two parts: filtering the countries and then getting a sum.

#462. 12.8 Consider using a hash table.

#463. 12.4 You should discuss vtables here.

#464. 13.7 Can you do this without a `filter` operation?

IV

Hints for Additional Review Problems

#465. 16.12 Consider a recursive or tree-like approach.

#466. 17.1 Walk through binary addition by hand (slowly!) and try to really understand what is happening.

#467. 16.13 Draw a square and a bunch of lines that cut it in half. Where are those lines located?

#468. 17.24 Start with a brute force solution.

#469. 17.14 There are actually several approaches. Brainstorm these. It's okay to start off with a naive approach.

#470. 16.20 Consider recursion.

#471. 16.3 Will all lines intercept? What determines if two lines intercept?

#472. 16.7 Let `k` be `1` if `a > b` and `0` otherwise. If you were given `k`, could you return the max (without a comparison or if-else logic)?

#473. 16.22 The tricky bit is handling an infinite grid. What are your options?

#474. 17.15 Try simplifying this problem: What if you just needed to know the longest word made up of two other words in the list?

#475. 16.10 Solution 1: Can you count the number of people alive in each year?

#476. 17.25 Start by grouping the dictionary by the word lengths, since you know each column has to be the same length and each row has to be the same length.

#477. 17.7 Discuss the naive approach: merging names together when they are synonyms. How would you identify transitive relationships? `A == B`, `A == C`, and `C == D` implies `A == D == B == C`.

#478. 16.13 Any straight line that cuts a square in half goes through the center of the square. How then can you find a line that cuts two squares in half?

#479. 17.17 Start with a brute force solution. What is the runtime?

#480. 16.22 Option #1: Do you actually need an infinite grid? Read the problem again. Do you know the max size of the grid?

#481. 16.16 Would it help to know the longest sorted sequences at the beginning and end?

#482. 17.2 Try approaching this problem recursively.

#483. 17.26 Solution 1: Start with just a simple algorithm comparing all documents to all other documents. How would you compute the similarity of two documents as fast as possible?

#484. 17.5 It doesn't really matter which letter or number it is. You can simplify this problem to just having an array of As and Bs. You would then be looking for the longest subarray with an equal number of As and Bs.

#485. 17.11 Consider first the algorithm for finding the closest distance if you will run the algorithm only once. You should be able to do this in O(N) time, where N is the number of words in the document.

#486. 16.20 Can you recursively try all possibilities?

#487. 17.9 Be clear about what this problem is asking for. It's asking for the kth smallest number in the form $3^a * 5^b * 7^c$.

#488. 16.2 Think about what the best conceivable runtime is for this problem. If your solution matches the best conceivable runtime, then you probably can't do any better.

#489. 16.10 Solution 1: Try using a hash table, or an array that maps from a birth year to how many people are alive in that year.

#490. 16.14 Sometimes, a brute force is a pretty good solution. Can you try all possible lines?

#491. 16.1 Try picturing the two numbers, a and b, on a number line.

#492. 17.7 The core part of the problem is to group names into the various spellings. From there, figuring out the frequencies is relatively easy.

#493. 17.3 If you haven't already, solve 17.2 on page 186.

#494. 17.16 There are recursive and iterative solutions to this problem, but it's probably easier to start with the recursive solution.

#495. 17.13 Try a recursive approach.

#496. 16.3 Infinite lines will almost always intersect—unless they're parallel. Parallel lines might still "intercept"—if they're the same lines. What does this mean for line segments?

#497. 17.26 Solution 1: To compute the similarity of two documents, try reorganizing the data in some way. Sorting? Using another data structure?

#498. 17.15 If we wanted to know just the longest word made up of other words in the list, then we could iterate over all words, from longest to shortest, checking if each could be made up of other words. To check this, we split the string in all possible locations.

#499. 17.25 Can you find a word rectangle of a specific length and width? What if you just tried all options?

#500. 17.11 Adapt your algorithm for one execution of the algorithm for repeated executions. What is the slow part? Can you optimize it?

#501. 16.8 Try thinking about the number in terms of chunks of three digits.

#502. 17.19 Start with the first part: Finding the missing number if only one number is missing.

#503. 17.16 Recursive solution: You have two choices at each appointment (take the appointment or reject the appointment). As a brute force approach, you can recurse through all possibilities. Note, though, that if you take request `i`, your recursive algorithm should skip request `i + 1`.

#504. 16.23 Be very careful that your solution actually returns each value from 0 through 6 with equal probability.

#505. 17.22 Start with a brute force, recursive solution. Just create all words that are one edit away, check if they are in the dictionary, and then attempt that path.

#506. 16.10 Solution 2: What if you sorted the years? What would you sort by?

#507. 17.9 What does a brute force solution to get the kth smallest value for $3^a * 5^b * 7^c$ look like?

#508. 17.12 Try a recursive approach.

#509. 17.26 Solution 1: You should be able to get an `O(A+B)` algorithm to compute the similarity of two documents.

#510. 17.24 The brute force solution requires us to continuously compute the sums of each matrix. Can we optimize this?

#511. 17.7 One thing to try is maintaining a mapping of each name to its "true" spelling. You would also need to map from a true spelling to all the synonyms. Sometimes, you might need to merge two different groups of names. Play around with this algorithm to see if you can get it to work. Then see if you can simplify/optimize it.

#512. 16.7 If k were 1 when `a > b` and 0 otherwise, then you could return `a*k + b*(not k)`. But how do you create k?

#513. 16.10 Solution 2: Do you actually need to match the birth years and death years? Does it matter when a specific person died, or do you just need a list of the years of deaths?

#514. 17.5 Start with a brute force solution.

#515. 17.16 Recursive solution: You can optimize this approach through memoization. What is the runtime of this approach?

#516. 16.3 How can we find the intersection between two lines? If two line segments intercept, then this must be at the same point as their "infinite" extensions. Is this intersection point within both lines?

#517. 17.26 Solution 1: What is the relationship between the intersection and the union? Can you compute one from the other?

#518. 17.20 Recall that the median means the number for which half the numbers are larger and half the numbers are smaller.

#519. 16.14 You can't truly try all possible lines in the world—that's infinite. But you know that a "best" line must intersect at least two points. Can you connect each pair of points? Can you check if each line is indeed the best line?

#520. 16.26 Can we just process the expression from left to right? Why might this fail?

#521. 17.10 Start with a brute force solution. Can you just check each value to see if it's the majority element?

#522. 16.10 Solution 2: Observe that people are "fungible." It doesn't matter who was born and when they died. All you need is a list of birth years and death years. This might make the question of how you sort the list of people easier.

#523. 16.25 First scope the problem. What are the features you would want?

#524. 17.24 Can you do any sort of precomputation to make computing the sum of a submatrix `O(1)`?

#525. 17.16 Recursive solution: The runtime of your memoization approach should be `O(N)`, with `O(N)` space.

#526. 16.3 Think carefully about how to handle the case of line segments that have the same slope and y-intercept.

#527. 16.13 To cut two squares in half, a line must go through the middle of both squares.

#528. 16.14 You should be able to get to an $O(N^2)$ solution.

#529. 17.14 Consider thinking about reorganizing the data in some way or using additional data structures.

#530. 16.17 Picture the array as alternating sequences of positive and negative numbers. Observe that we would never include just part of a positive sequence or part of a negative sequence.

#531. 16.10 Solution 2: Try creating a sorted list of births and a sorted list of deaths. Can you iterate through both, tracking the number of people alive at any one time?

#532. 16.22 Option #2: Think about how an `ArrayList` works. Can you use an `ArrayList` for this?

#533. 17.26 Solution 1: To understand the relationship between the union and the intersection of two sets, consider a Venn diagram (a diagram where one circle overlaps another circle).

#534. 17.22 Once you have a brute force solution, try to find a faster way of getting all valid words that are one edit away. You don't want to create all strings that are one edit away when the vast majority of them are not valid dictionary words.

#535. 16.2 Can you use a hash table to optimize the repeated case?

#536. 17.7 An easier way of taking the above approach is to have each name map to a list of alternate spellings. What should happen when a name in one group is set equal to a name in another group?

#537. 17.11 You could build a lookup table that maps from a word to a list of the locations where each word appears. How then could you find the closest two locations?

#538. 17.24 What if you precomputed the sum of the submatrix starting at the top left corner and continuing to each cell? How long would it take you to compute this? If you did this, could you then get the sum of an arbitrary submatrix in `O(1)` time?

#539. 16.22 Option #2: It's not impossible to use an `ArrayList`, but it would be tedious. Perhaps it would be easier to build your own, but specialized for matrices.

#540. 16.10 Solution 3: Each birth adds one person and each death removes a person. Try writing an example of a list of people (with birth and death years) and then re-formatting this into a list of each year and a +1 for a birth and a -1 for a death.

#541. 17.16 Iterative solution: Take the recursive solution and investigate it more. Can you implement a similar strategy iteratively?

#542. 17.15 Extend the earlier idea to multiple words. Can we just break each word up in all possible ways?

#543. 17.1 You can think about binary addition as iterating through the number, bit by bit, adding two bits, and then carrying over the one if necessary. You could also think about it as grouping the operations. What if you first added each of the bits (without carrying any overflow)? After that, you can handle the overflow.

#544. 16.21 Do some math here or play around with some examples. What does this pair need to look like? What can you say about their values?

#545. 17.20 Note that you have to store all the elements you've seen. Even the smallest of the first 100 elements could become the median. You can't just toss very low or very high elements.

#546. 17.26 Solution 2: It's tempting to try to think of minor optimizations—for example, keeping track of the min and max elements in each array. You could then figure out quickly, in specific cases, if two arrays don't overlap. The problem with that (and other optimizations along these lines) is that you still need to compare all documents to all other documents. It doesn't leverage the fact that the similarity is sparse. Given that we have a lot of documents, we really need to not compare all documents to all other documents (even if that comparison is very fast). All such solutions will be $O(D^2)$, where D is the number of documents. We shouldn't compare all documents to all other documents.

#547. 16.24 Start with a brute force solution. What is the runtime? What is the best conceivable runtime for this problem?

#548. 16.10 Solution 3: What if you created an array of years and how the population changed in each year? Could you then find the year with the highest population?

#549. 17.9 In looking for the kth smallest value of $3^a * 5^b * 7^c$, we know that a, b, and c will be less than or equal to k. Can you generate all such numbers?

#550. 16.17 Observe that if you have a sequence of values which have a negative sum, those will never start or end a sequence. (They could be present in a sequence if they connected two other sequences.)

#551. 17.14 Can you sort the numbers?

#552. 16.16 We can think about the array as divided into three subarrays: `LEFT`, `MIDDLE`, `RIGHT`. `LEFT` and `RIGHT` are both sorted. The `MIDDLE` elements are in an arbitrary order. We need to expand `MIDDLE` until we could sort those elements and then have the entire array sorted.

#553. 17.16 Iterative solution: It's probably easiest to start with the end of the array and work backwards.

#554. 17.26 Solution 2: If we can't compare all documents to all other documents, then we need to dive down and start looking at things at the element level. Consider a naive solution and see if you can extend that to multiple documents.

#555. 17.22 To quickly get the valid words that are one edit away, try to group the words in the dictionary in a useful way. Observe that all words in the form b_ll (such as `bill`, `ball`, `bell`, and `bull`) will be one edit away. However, those aren't the only words that are one edit away from `bill`.

#556. 16.21 When you move a value a from array A to array B, then A's sum decreases by a and B's sum increases by a. What happens when you swap two values? What would be needed to swap two values and get the same sum?

#557. 17.11 If you had a list of the occurrences of each word, then you are really looking for a pair of values within two arrays (one value for each array) with the smallest difference. This could be a fairly similar algorithm to your initial algorithm.

#558. 16.22 Option #2: One approach is to just double the size of the array when the ant wanders to an edge. How will you handle the ant wandering into negative coordinates, though? Arrays can't have negative indices.

#559. 16.13 Given a line (slope and y-intercept), can you find where it intersects another line?

#560. 17.26 Solution 2: One way to think about this is that we need to be able to very quickly pull a list of all documents with some similarity to a specific document. (Again, we should not do this by saying "look at all documents and quickly eliminate the dissimilar documents." That will be at least $O(D^2)$.)

#561. 17.16 Iterative solution: Observe that you would never skip three appointments in a row. Why would you? You would always be able to take the middle booking.

#562. 16.14 Have you tried using a hash table?

#563. 16.21 If you swap two values, a and b, then the sum of A becomes `sumA - a + b` and the sum of B becomes `sumB - b + a`. These sums need to be equal.

#564. 17.24 If you can precompute the sum from the top left corner to each cell, you can use this to compute the sum of an arbitrary submatrix in $O(1)$ time. Picture a particular submatrix. The full, precomputed sum will include this submatrix, an array immediately above it (C), and array to the left (B), and an area to the top and left (A). How can you compute the sum of just D?

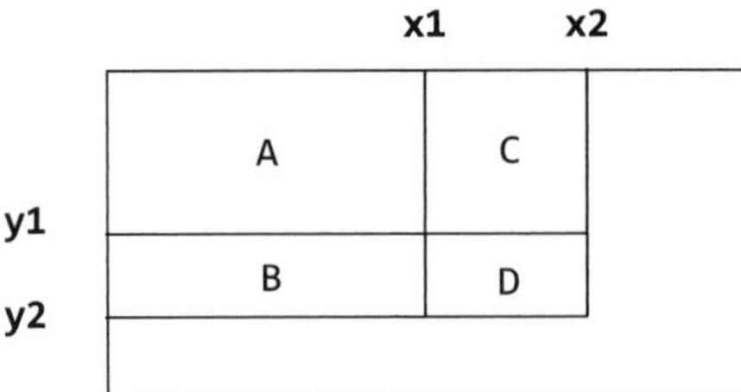

#565. 17.10 Consider the brute force solution. We pick an element and then validate if it's the majority element by counting the number of matching and non-matching elements. Suppose, for the first element, the first few checks reveal seven non-matching elements and three matching elements. Is it necessary to keep checking this element?

#566. 16.17 Start from the beginning of the array. As that subsequence gets larger, it stays as the best subsequence. Once it becomes negative, though, it's useless.

#567. 17.16 Iterative solution: If you take appointment `i`, you will never take appointment `i + 1`, but you will always take appointment `i + 2` or `i + 3`.

#568. 17.26 Solution 2: Building off the earlier hint, we can ask what defines the list of documents with some similarity to a document like {13, 16, 21, 3}. What attributes does that list have? How would we gather all documents like that?

#569. 16.22 Option #2: Observe that nothing in the problem stipulates that the label for the coordinates must remain the same. Can you move the ant and all cells into positive coordinates? In other words, what would happen if, whenever you needed to grow the array in a negative direction, you relabeled all the indices such that they were still positive?

#570. 16.21 You are looking for values a and b where `sumA - a + b = sumB - b + a`. Do the math to work out what this means for a and b's values.

#571. 16.9 Approach these one by one, starting with subtraction. Once you've completed one function, you can use it to implement the others.

#572. 17.6 Start with a brute force solution.

#573. 16.23 Start with a brute force solution. How many times does it call `rand5()` in the worst case?

#574. 17.20 Another way to think about this is: Can you maintain the bottom half of elements and the top half of elements?

#575. 16.10 Solution 3: Be careful with the little details in this problem. Does your algorithm/code handle a person who dies in the same year that they are born? This person should be counted as one person in the population count.

#576. 17.26 Solution 2: The list of documents similar to {13, 16, 21, 3} includes all documents with a 13, 16, 21, and 3. How can we efficiently find this list? Remember that we'll be doing this for many documents, so some precomputing can make sense.

#577. 17.16 Iterative solution: Use an example and work backwards. You can easily find the optimal solution for the subarrays $\{r_n\}$, $\{r_{n-1}, r_n\}$, $\{r_{n-2}, \ldots, r_n\}$. How would you use those to quickly find the optimal solution for $\{r_{n-3}, \ldots, r_n\}$?

#578. 17.2 Suppose you had a method `shuffle` that worked on decks up to `n - 1` elements. Could you use this method to implement a new `shuffle` method that works on decks up to n elements?

#579. 17.22 Create a mapping from a wildcard form (like `b_ll`) to all words in that form. Then, when you want to find all words that are one edit away from `bill`, you can look up `_ill`, `b_ll`, `bi_l`, and `bil_` in the mapping.

#580. 17.24 The sum of just D will be `sum(A&B&C&D) - sum(A&B) - sum(A&C) + sum(A)`.

#581. 17.17 Can you use a trie?

#582. 16.21 If we do the math, we are looking for a pair of values such that `a - b = (sumA - sumB) / 2`. The problem then reduces to looking for a pair of values with a particular difference.

#583. 17.26 Solution 2: Try building a hash table from each word to the documents that contain this word. This will allow us to easily find all documents with some similarity to {13, 16, 21, 3}.

#584. 16.5 How does a zero get into the result of `n!`? What does it mean?

#585. 17.7 If each name maps to a list of its alternate spellings, you might have to update a lot of lists when you set X and Y as synonyms. If X is a synonym of `{A, B, C}`, and Y is a synonym of `{D, E, F}` then you would need to add `{Y, D, E, F}` to A's synonym list, B's synonym list, C's synonym list, and X's synonym list. Ditto for `{Y, D, E, F}`. Can we make this faster?

#586. 17.16 Iterative solution: If you take an appointment, you can't take the next appointment, but you can take anything after that. Therefore, $optimal(r_i, ..., r_n) = max(r_i + optimal(r_{i+2}, ..., r_n), optimal(r_{i+1}, ..., r_n))$. You can solve this iteratively by working backwards.

#587. 16.8 Have you considered negative numbers? Does your solution work for values like 100,030,000?

#588. 17.15 When you get recursive algorithms that are very inefficient, try looking for repeated subproblems.

#589. 17.19 Part 1: If you have to find the missing number in `O(1)` space and `O(N)` time, then you can do a only constant number of passes through the array and can store only a few variables.

#590. 17.9 Look at the list of all values for $3^a * 5^b * 7^c$. Observe that each value in the list will be 3*(some previous value), 5*(some previous value), or 7*(some previous value).

#591. 16.21 A brute force solution is to just look through all pairs of values to find one with the right difference. This will probably look like an outer loop through A with an inner loop through B. For each value, compute the difference and compare it to what we're looking for. Can we be more specific here, though? Given a value in A and a target difference, do we know the exact value of the element within B we're looking for?

#592. 17.14 What about using a heap or tree of some sort?

#593. 16.17 If we tracked the running sum, we should reset it as soon as the subsequence becomes negative. We would never add a negative sequence to the beginning or end of another subsequence.

#594. 17.24 With precomputation, you should be able to get a runtime of $O(N^4)$. Can you make this even faster?

#595. 17.3 Try this recursively. Suppose you had an algorithm to get a subset of size `m` from n - 1 elements. Could you develop an algorithm to get a subset of size `m` from n elements?

#596. 16.24 Can we make this faster with a hash table?

#597. 17.22 Your previous algorithm probably resembles a depth-first search. Can you make this faster?

#598. 16.22 Option #3: Another thing to think about is whether you even need a grid to implement this. What information do you actually need in the problem?

#599. 16.9 Subtraction: Would a negate function (which converts a positive integer to negative) help? Can you implement this using the add operator?

#600. 17.1 Focus on just one of the steps above. If you "forgot" to carry the ones, what would the add operation look like?

#601. 16.21 What the brute force really does is look for a value within B which equals `a - target`. How can you more quickly find this element? What approaches help us quickly find out if an element exists within an array?

#602. 17.26 Solution 2: Once you have a way of easily finding the documents similar to a particular document, you can go through and just compute the similarity to those documents using a simple algorithm. Can you make this faster? Specifically, can you compute the similarity directly from the hash table?

#603. 17.10 The majority element will not necessarily look like the majority element at first. It is possible, for example, to have the majority element appear in the first element of the array and then not appear again for the next eight elements. However, in those cases, the majority element will appear later in the array (in fact, many times later on in the array). It's not necessarily critical to continue checking a specific instance of an element for majority status once it's already looking "unlikely."

#604. 17.7 Instead, X, A, B, and C should map to the same instance of the set `{X, A, B, C}`. Y, D, E, and F should map to the same instance of `{Y, D, E, F}`. When we set X and Y as synonyms, we can then just copy one of the sets into the other (e.g., add `{Y, D, E, F}` to `{X, A, B, C}`). How else do we change the hash table?

#605. 16.21 We can use a hash table here. We can also try sorting. Both help us locate elements more quickly.

#606. 17.16 Iterative solution: If you're careful about what data you really need, you should be able to solve this in `O(n)` time and `O(1)` additional space.

#607. 17.12 Think about it this way: If you had methods called `convertLeft` and `convertRight` (which would convert left and right subtrees to doubly linked lists), could you put those together to convert the whole tree to a doubly linked list?

#608. 17.19 Part 1: What if you added up all the values in the array? Could you then figure out the missing number?

#609. 17.4 How long would it take you to figure out the least significant bit of the missing number?

#610. 17.26 Solution 2: Imagine you are looking up the documents similar to {1, 4, 6} by using a hash table that maps from a word to documents. The same document ID appears multiple times when doing this lookup. What does that indicate?

#611. 17.6 Rather than counting the number of twos in each number, think about digit by digit. That is, count the number of twos in the first digit (for each number), then the number of twos in the second digit (for each number), then the number of twos in the third digit (for each number), and so on.

#612. 16.9 Multiply: it's easy enough to implement `multiply` using add. But how do you handle negative numbers?

#613. 16.17 You can solve this in `O(N)` time and `O(1)` space.

#614. 17.24 Suppose this was just a single array. How could we compute the subarray with the largest sum? See 16.17 for a solution to this.

#615. 16.22 Option #3: All you actually need is some way of looking up if a cell is white or black (and of course the position of the ant). Can you just keep a list of all the white cells?

#616. 17.17 One solution is to insert every suffix of the larger string into the trie. For example, if the word is `dogs`, the suffixes would be `dogs`, `ogs`, `gs`, and `s`. How would this help you solve the problem? What is the runtime here?

#617. 17.22 A breadth-first search will often be faster than a depth-first search—not necessarily in the worst case, but in many cases. Why? Can you do something even faster than this?

#618. 17.5 What if you just started from the beginning, counting the number of As and the number of Bs you've seen so far? (Try making a table of the array and the number of As and Bs thus far.)

#619. 17.10 Note also that the majority element must be the majority element for some subarray and that no subarray can have multiple majority elements.

#620. 17.24 Suppose I just wanted you to find the maximum submatrix starting at row `r1` and ending at row `r2`, how could you most efficiently do this? (See the prior hint.) If I now wanted you find the maximum subarray from `r1` to `(r2+2)`, could you do this efficiently?

#621. 17.9 Since each number is 3, 5, or 7 times a previous value in the list, we could just check all possible values and pick the next one that hasn't been seen yet. This will result in a lot of duplicated work. How can we avoid this?

#622. 17.13 Can you just try all possibilities? What might that look like?

#623. 16.26 Multiplication and division are higher priority operations. In an expression like `3*4 + 5*9/2 + 3`, the multiplication and division parts need to be grouped together.

#624. 17.14 If you picked an arbitrary element, how long would it take you to figure out the rank of this element (the number of elements bigger or smaller than it)?

#625. 17.19 Part 2: We're now looking for two missing numbers, which we will call a and b. The approach from part 1 will tell us the sum of a and b, but it won't actually tell us a and b. What other calculations could we do?

#626. 16.22 Option #3: You could consider keeping a hash set of all the white cells. How will you be able to print the whole grid, though?

#627. 17.1 The adding step alone would convert 1 + 1 -> 0, 1 + 0 -> 1, 0 + 1 -> 1, 0 + 0 -> 0. How do you do this without the + sign?

#628. 17.21 What role does the tallest bar in the histogram play?

#629. 16.25 What data structure would be most useful for the lookups? What data structure would be most useful to know and maintain the order of items?

#630. 16.18 Start with a brute force approach. Can you try all possibilities for a and b?

#631. 16.6 What if you sorted the arrays?

#632. 17.11 Can you just iterate through both arrays with two pointers? You should be able to do it in `O(A+B)` time, where A and B are the sizes of the two arrays.

#633. 17.2 You could build this algorithm recursively by swapping the nth element for any of the elements before it. What would this look like iteratively?

#634. 16.21 What if the sum of A is 11 and the sum of B is 8? Can there be a pair with the right difference? Check that your solution handles this situation appropriately.

#635. 17.26 Solution 3: There's an alternative solution. Consider taking all of the words from all of the documents, throwing them into one giant list, and sorting this list. Assume you could still know which document each word came from. How could you track the similar pairs?

#636. 16.23 Make a table indicating how each possible sequence of calls to `rand5()` would map to the result of `rand7()`. For example, if you were implementing `rand3()` with `(rand2() + rand2()) % 3`, then the table would look like the below. Analyze this table. What can it tell you?

```
1st     2nd     Result
0       0       0
0       1       1
1       0       1
1       1       2
```

#637. 17.8 This problem asks us to find the longest sequence of pairs you can build such that both sides of the pair are constantly increasing. What if you needed only one side of the pair to increase?

#638. 16.15 Try first creating an array with the frequency that each item occurs.

#639. 17.21 Picture the tallest bar, and then the next tallest bar on the left and the next tallest bar on the right. The water will fill the area between those. Can you calculate that area? What do you do about the rest?

#640. 17.6 Is there a faster way of calculating how many twos are in a particular digit across a range of numbers? Observe that roughly $\frac{1}{10}$th of any digit should be a 2—but only roughly. How do you make that more exact?

#641. 17.1 You can do the add step with an XOR.

#642. 16.18 Observe that one of the substrings, either a or b, must start at the beginning of the string. That cuts down the number of possibilities.

#643. 16.24 What if the array were sorted?

#644. 17.18 Start with a brute force solution.

#645. 17.12 Once you have a basic idea for a recursive algorithm, you might get stuck on this: sometimes your recursive algorithm needs to return the start of the linked list, and sometimes it needs to return the end. There are multiple ways of solving this issue. Brainstorm some of them.

#646. 17.14 If you picked an arbitrary element, you would, on average, wind up with an element around the 50th percentile mark (half the elements above it and half the elements below). What if you did this repeatedly?

#647. 16.9 Divide: If you're trying to compute, where $x = a/b$, remember that $a = bx$. Can you find the closest value for x? Remember that this is integer division and x should be an integer.

#648. 17.19 Part 2: There are a lot of different calculations we could try. For example, we could multiply all the numbers, but that will only lead us to the product of a and b.

#649. 17.10 Try this: Given an element, start checking if this is the start of a subarray for which it's the majority element. Once it's become "unlikely" (appears less than half the time), start checking at the next element (the element after the subarray).

#650. 17.21 You can calculate the area between the tallest bar overall and the tallest bar on the left by just iterating through the histogram and subtracting out any bars in between. You can do the same thing with the right side. How do you handle the remainder of the graph?

#651. 17.18 One brute force solution is to take each starting position and move forward until you've found a subsequence which contains all the target characters.

#652. 16.18 Don't forget to handle the possibility that the first character in the `pattern` is b.

#653. 16.20 In the real world, we should know that some prefixes/substrings won't work. For example, consider the number `33835676368`. Although `3383` does correspond to `fftf`, there are no words that start with `fftf`. Is there a way we can short-circuit in cases like this?

#654. 17.7 An alternative approach is to think of this as a graph. How would this work?

#655. 17.13 You can think about the choices the recursive algorithm makes in one of two ways: (1) At each character, should I put a space here? (2) Where should I put the next space? You can solve both of these recursively.

#656. 17.8 If you needed only one side of the pair to increase, then you would just sort all the values on that side. Your longest sequence would in fact be all of the pairs (other than any duplicates, since the longest sequence needs to strictly increase). What does this tell you about the original problem?

#657. 17.21 You can handle the remainder of the graph by just repeating this process: find the tallest bar and the second tallest bar, and subtract out the bars in between.

#658. 17.4 To find the least significant bit of the missing number, note that you know how many `0`s and `1`s to expect. For example, if you see three `0`s and three `1`s in the least significant bit, then the missing number's least significant bit must be a `1`. Think about it: in any sequence of `0`s and `1`s, you'd get a `0`, then a `1`, then a `0`, then a `1`, and so on.

#659. 17.9 Rather than checking all values in the list for the next value (by multiplying each by 3, 5, and 7), think about it this way: when you insert a value `x` into the list, you can "create" the values `3x`, `5x`, and `7x` to be used later.

#660. 17.14 Think about the previous hint some more, particularly in the context of quicksort.

#661. 17.21 How can you make the process of finding the next tallest bar on each side faster?

#662. 16.18 Be careful with how you analyze the runtime. If you iterate through $O(n^2)$ substrings and each one does an $O(n)$ string comparison, then the total runtime is $O(n^3)$.

#663. 17.1 Now focus on the carrying. In what cases will values carry? How do you apply the carry to the number?

#664. 16.26 Consider thinking about it as, when you get to a multiplication or division sign, jumping to a separate "process" to compute the result of this chunk.

#665. 17.8 If you sort the values based on height, then this will tell you the ordering of the final pairs. The longest sequence must be in this relative order (but not necessarily containing all of the pairs). You now just need to find the longest increasing subsequence on weight while keeping the items in the same relative order. This is essentially the same problem as having an array of integers and trying to find the longest sequence you can build (without reordering those items).

#666. 16.16 Consider the three subarrays: `LEFT`, `MIDDLE`, `RIGHT`. Focus on just this question: Can you sort middle such that the entire array becomes sorted? How would you check this?

#667. 16.23 Looking at this table again, note that the number of rows will be 5^k, where k is the max number of calls to `rand5()`. In order to make each value between 0 and 6 have equal probability, $1/7$th of the rows must map to 0, $1/7$th to 1, and so on. Is this possible?

#668. 17.18 Another way of thinking about the brute force is that we take each starting index and find the next instance of each element in the target string. The maximum of all these next instances marks the end of a subsequence which contains all the target characters. What is the runtime of this? How can we make it faster?

#669. 16.6 Think about how you would merge two sorted arrays.

#670. 17.5 When the above tables have equal values for the number of As and Bs, the entire subarray (starting from index 0) has an equal number of As and Bs. How could you use this table to find qualifying subarrays that don't start at index 0?

#671. 17.19 Part 2: Adding the numbers together will tell us the result of `a + b`. Multiplying the numbers together will tell us the result of `a * b`. How can we get the exact values for a and b?

#672. 16.24 If we sorted the array, we could do repeated binary searches for the complement of a number. What if, instead, the array is given to us sorted? Could we then solve the problem in `O(N)` time and `O(1)` space?

#673. 16.19 If you were given the row and column of a water cell, how can you find all connected spaces?

#674. 17.7 We can treat adding X, Y as synonyms as adding an edge between the X node and the Y node. How then do we figure out the groups of synonyms?

#675. 17.21 Can you do precomputation to compute the next tallest bar on each side?

#676. 17.13 Will the recursive algorithm hit the same subproblems repeatedly? Can you optimize with a hash table?

#677. 17.14 What if, when you picked an element, you swapped elements around (as you do in quicksort) so that the elements below it would be located before the elements above it? If you did this repeatedly, could you find the smallest one million numbers?

#678. 16.6 Imagine you had the two arrays sorted and you were walking through them. If the pointer in the first array points to 3 and the pointer in the second array points to 9, what effect will moving the second pointer have on the difference of the pair?

#679. 17.12 To handle whether your recursive algorithm should return the start or the end of the linked list, you could try to pass a parameter down that acts as a flag. This won't work very well, though. The problem is that when you call `convert(current.left)`, you want to get the end of `left`'s linked list. This way you can join the end of the linked list to `current`. But, if `current` is someone else's right subtree, `convert(current)` needs to pass back the start of the linked list (which is actually the start of `current.left`'s linked list). Really, you need both the start and end of the linked list.

#680. 17.18 Consider the previously explained brute force solution. A bottleneck is repeatedly asking for the next instance of a particular character. Is there a way you can optimize this? You should be able to do this in `O(1)` time.

#681. 17.8 Try a recursive approach that just evaluates all possibilities.

#682. 17.4 Once you've identified that the least significant bit is a 0 (or a 1), you can rule out all the numbers without 0 as the least significant bit. How is this problem different from the earlier part?

#683. 17.23 Start with a brute force solution. Can you try the biggest possible square first?

#684. 16.18 Suppose you decide on a specific value for the "a" part of a pattern. How many possibilities are there for b?

#685. 17.9 When you add x to the list of the first k values, you can add 3x, 5x, and 7x to some new list. How do you make this as optimal as possible? Would it make sense to keep multiple queues of values? Do you always need to insert 3x, 5x, and 7x? Or, perhaps sometimes you need to insert only 7x? You want to avoid seeing the same number twice.

#686. 16.19 Try recursion to count the number of water cells.

#687. 16.8 Consider dividing up a number into sequences of three digits.

#688. 17.19 Part 2: We could do both. If we know that `a + b = 87` and `a * b = 962`, then we can solve for a and b: `a = 13` and `b = 74`. But this will also result in having to multiply really large numbers. The product of all the numbers could be larger than 10^{157}. Is there a simpler calculation you can make?

#689. 16.11 Consider building a diving board. What are the choices you make?

#690. 17.18 Can you precompute the next instance of a particular character from each index? Try using a multi-dimensional array.

#691. 17.1 The carry will happen when you are doing 1 + 1. How do you apply the carry to the number?

#692. 17.21 As an alternative solution, think about it from the perspective of each bar. Each bar will have water on top of it. How much water will be on top of each bar?

#693. 16.25 Both a hash table and a doubly linked list would be useful. Can you combine the two?

#694. 17.23 The biggest possible square is NxN. So if you try that square first and it works, then you know that you've found the best square. Otherwise, you can try the next smallest square.

#695. 17.19 Part 2: Almost any "equation" we can come up with will work here (as long as it's not equivalent to a linear sum). It's just a matter of keeping this sum small.

#696. 16.23 It is not possible to divide 5^k evenly by 7. Does this mean that you can't implement `rand7()` with `rand5()`?

#697. 16.26 You can also maintain two stacks, one for the operators and one for the numbers. You push a number onto the stack every time you see it. What about the operators? When do you pop operators from the stack and apply them to the numbers?

#698. 17.8 Another way to think about the problem is this: if you had the longest sequence ending at each element `A[0]` through `A[n-1]`, could you use that to find the longest sequence ending at element `A[n-1]`?

#699. 16.11 Consider a recursive solution.

#700. 17.12 Many people get stuck at this point and aren't sure what to do. Sometimes they need the start of the linked list, and sometimes they need the end. A given node doesn't necessarily know what to return on its `convert` call. Sometimes the simple solution is easiest: always return both. What are some ways you could do this?

#701. 17.19 Part 2: Try a sum of squares of the values.

#702. 16.20 A trie might help us short-circuit. What if you stored the whole list of words in the trie?

#703. 17.7 Each connected subgraph represents a group of synonyms. To find each group, we can do repeated breadth-first (or depth-first) searches.

#704. 17.23 Describe the runtime of the brute force solution.

#705. 16.19 How can you make sure that you're not revisiting the same cells? Think about how breadth-first search or depth-first search on a graph works.

#706. 16.7 When `a > b`, then `a - b > 0`. Can you get the sign bit of `a - b`?

#707. 16.16 In order to be able to sort `MIDDLE` and have the whole array become sorted, you need `MAX(LEFT) <= MIN(MIDDLE and RIGHT)` and `MAX(LEFT and MIDDLE) <= MIN(RIGHT)`.

#708. 17.20 What if you used a heap? Or two heaps?

#709. 16.4 If you were calling `hasWon` multiple times, how might your solution change?

#710. 16.5 Each zero in `n!` corresponds to n being divisible by a factor of 10. What does that mean?

#711. 17.1 You can use an AND operation to compute the carry. What do you do with it?

#712. 17.5 Suppose, in this table, index `i` has `count(A, 0->i) = 3` and `count(B, 0->i) = 7`. This means that there are four more Bs than As. If you find a later spot `j` with the same difference (`count(B, 0->j) - count(A, 0->j)`), then this indicates a subarray with an equal number of As and Bs.

#713. 17.23 Can you do preprocessing to optimize this solution?

#714. 16.11 Once you have a recursive algorithm, think about the runtime. Can you make this faster? How?

#715. 16.1 Let `diff` be the difference between a and b. Can you use `diff` in some way? Then can you get rid of this temporary variable?

#716. 17.19 Part 2: You might need the quadratic formula. It's not a big deal if you don't remember it. Most people won't. Remember that there is such a thing as good enough.

#717. 16.18 Since the value of a determines the value of b (and vice versa) and either a or b must start at the beginning of the value, you should have only `O(n)` possibilities for how to split up the pattern.

#718. 17.12 You could return both the start and end of a linked list in multiple ways. You could return a two-element array. You could define a new data structure to hold the start and end. You could re-use the `BiNode` data structure. If you're working in a language that supports this (like Python), you could just return multiple values. You could solve the problem as a circular linked list, with the start's previous pointer pointing to the end (and then break the circular list in a wrapper method). Explore these solutions. Which one do you like most and why?

#719. 16.23 You can implement `rand7()` with `rand5()`, you just can't do it deterministically (such that you know it will definitely terminate after a certain number of calls). Given this, write a solution that works.

#720. 17.23 You should be able to do this in $O(N^3)$ time, where N is the length of one dimension of the square.

#721. 16.11 Consider memoization to optimize the runtime. Think carefully about what exactly you cache. What is the runtime? The runtime is closely related to the max size of the table.

#722. 16.19 You should have an algorithm that's $O(N^2)$ on an NxN matrix. If your algorithm isn't, consider if you've miscomputed the runtime or if your algorithm is suboptimal.

#723. 17.1 You might need to do the add/carry operation more than once. Adding `carry` to `sum` might cause new values to carry.

#724. 17.18 Once you have the precomputation solution figured out, think about how you can reduce the space complexity. You should be able to get it down to $O(SB)$ time and $O(B)$ space (where B is the size of the larger array and S is the size of the smaller array).

#725. 16.20 We're probably going to run this algorithm many times. If we did more preprocessing, is there a way we could optimize this?

#726. 16.18 You should be able to have an $O(n^2)$ algorithm.

#727. 16.7 Have you considered how to handle integer overflow in `a - b`?

#728. 16.5 Each factor of 10 in `n!` means `n!` is divisible by 5 and 2.

#729. 16.15 For ease and clarity in implementation, you might want to use other methods and classes.

#730. 17.18 Another way to think about it is this: Imagine you had a list of the indices where each item appeared. Could you find the first possible subsequence with all the elements? Could you find the second?

#731. 16.4 If you were designing this for an NxN board, how might your solution change?

#732. 16.5 Can you count the number of factors of 5 and 2? Do you need to count both?

#733. 17.21 Each bar will have water on top of it that matches the minimum of the tallest bar on the left and the tallest bar on the right. That is, `water_on_top[i] = min(tallest_bar(0->i), tallest_bar(i, n))`.

#734. 16.16 Can you expand the middle until the earlier condition is met?

#735. 17.23 When you're checking to see if a particular square is valid (all black borders), you check how many black pixels are above (or below) a coordinate and to the left (or right) of this coordinate. Can you precompute the number of black pixels above and to the left of a given cell?

#736. 16.1 You could also try using XOR.

#737. 17.22 What if you did a breadth-first search starting from both the source word and the destination word?

#738. 17.13 In real life, we would know that some paths will not lead to a word. For example, there are no words that start with `hellothisism`. Can we terminate early when going down a path that we know won't work?

#739. 16.11 There's an alternate, clever (and very fast) solution. You can actually do this in linear time without recursion. How?

#740. 17.18 Consider using a heap.

#741. 17.21 You should be able to solve this in O(N) time and O(N) space.

#742. 17.17 Alternatively, you could insert each of the smaller strings into the trie. How would this help you solve the problem? What is the runtime?

#743. 16.20 With preprocessing, we can actually get the lookup time down to O(1).

#744. 16.5 Have you considered that 25 actually accounts for two factors of 5?

#745. 16.16 You should be able to solve this in O(N) time.

#746. 16.11 Think about it this way. You are picking K planks and there are two different types. All choices with 10 of the first type and 4 of the second type will have the same sum. Can you just iterate through all possible choices?

#747. 17.25 Can you use a trie to terminate early when a rectangle looks invalid?

#748. 17.13 For early termination, try a trie.

XIV

About the Author

Gayle Laakmann McDowell has a strong background in software development with extensive experience on both sides of the hiring table.

She has worked for Microsoft, Apple, and Google as a software engineer. She spent three years at Google, where she was one of the top interviewers and served on the hiring committee. She interviewed hundreds of candidates in the U.S. and abroad, assessed thousands of candidate interview packets for the hiring committee, and reviewed many more resumes.

As a candidate, she interviewed with—and received offers from—twelve tech companies, including Microsoft, Google, Amazon, IBM, and Apple.

Gayle founded CareerCup to enable candidates to perform at their best during these challenging interviews. CareerCup.com offers a database of thousands of interview questions from major companies and a forum for interview advice.

In addition to ***Cracking the Coding Interview***, Gayle has written other two books:

- ***Cracking the Tech Career: Insider Advice on Landing a Job at Google, Microsoft, Apple, or Any Top Tech Company*** provides a broader look at the interview process for major tech companies. It offers insight into how anyone, from college freshmen to marketing professionals, can position themselves for a career at one of these companies.
- ***Cracking the PM Interview: How to Land a Product Manager Job in Technology*** focuses on product management roles at startups and big tech companies. It offers strategies to break into these roles and teaches job seekers how to prepare for PM interviews.

Through her role with CareerCup, she consults with tech companies on their hiring process, leads technical interview training workshops, and coaches engineers at startups for acquisition interviews.

She holds bachelor's degree and master's degrees in computer science from the University of Pennsylvania and an MBA from the Wharton School.

She lives in Palo Alto, California, with her husband, two sons, dog, and computer science books. She still codes daily.

From the Pages of The Three Musketeers

Imagine to yourself a Don Quixote of eighteen; a Don Quixote without his corselet, without his coat of mail, without his cuisses; a Don Quixote clothed in a woolen doublet, the blue collar of which had faded into a nameless shade between lees of wine and a heavenly azure; face long and brown; high cheek bones, a sign of sagacity; the maxillary muscles enormously developed, an infallible sign by which a Gascon may always be detected, even without his cap—and our young man wore a cap set off with a sort of feather; the eye open and intelligent; the nose hooked, but finely chiseled. (page 4)

"All for one, one for all—that is our motto, is it not?" (page 115)

"Oh, nothing but a scratch." (page 241)

Immediately eight swords glittered in the rays of the setting sun, and the combat began with an animosity very natural between men twice enemies. (page 377)

During the evening she despaired of fate and of herself. She did not invoke God, we very well know, but she had faith in the genius of evil—that immense sovereignty which reigns in all the details of human life, and by which, as in the Arabian fable, a single pomegranate seed is sufficient to reconstruct a ruined world. (page 622)